PHONOLOGY AND MORPHOLOGY OF EKEGUSII

EAST AFRICAN
LANGUAGES AND DIALECTS

Volume 12

Editors
Bernd Heine and Wilhelm J.G. Möhlig

Jelle Cammenga

Phonology and Morphology of Ekegusii

A Bantu Language of Kenya

Rüdiger Köppe Verlag · Köln

Die Deutsche Bibliothek – CIP-Einheitsaufnahme
[Ein Titeldatensatz für diese Publikation ist bei Der Deutschen Bibliothek erhältlich.]

ISBN 3-89645-026-3

RÜDIGER KÖPPE VERLAG
Postfach 45 06 43
D - 50881 Köln

www.koeppe.de

Cover: Map of Gusiiland, Kenya

Production: Druckerei Hansen, Bergisch-Gladbach/Germany

Gedruckt auf säurefreiem und alterungsbeständigem Papier.
∞ Printed on acid-free paper which falls within the guidelines of the ANSI to ensure permanence and durability.

To

Nicoline

EDITOR'S PREFACE

Gusii is an East Nyanza Bantu language (Guthrie's classification E.42) spoken by at least one million people. Beyond the level of dialectal variations, it is closely related to other Bantu languages of the region, namely to Kuria, Mfangano and Suba[1]. Although, with respect to the number of speakers, the Gusii language still has a regional importance in Kenya, it is little known.

We owe the first linguistic descriptions of the Gusii grammar to Wilfred Whiteley. In 1956 he published a *Practical Introduction to Gusii,* and in 1960 his work on *The Tense System of Gusii* appeared.

Within the frame of the *Language and Dialect Atlas of Kenya*[2], Wilhelm Möhlig visited the Nyanza Districts several times in the seventies to do research on the Bantu dialects of the area, among others also on Gusii. Most of his phonological and lexical data have not yet been published, but parts of it were used as an empirical base in several of his comparative articles.

In the late eighties, David Lee Schoenbrun collected cultural vocabularies on Gusii and other languages of – as he calls it – *Great Lakes Bantu*[3]. His interest was explicitly historical, and therefore his research did not add very much to the knowledge of the present state and the actual linguistic inventory of Gusii.

The author of this book, Jelle Cammenga, did his field research on the grammar of Gusii in the years 1996 and 1997. His work was done within the Collaborative Research Center 214 on *Identität in Afrika* that the Deutsche Forschungsgemeinschaft sponsored at the University of Bayreuth. He has widened our knowledge on the linguistic inventory and structure of the Gusii language considerably, understanding his grammatical description of Gusii as a direct continuation of Whiteley's pioneer work that, for a long time, had remained the only printed source of the language. He frequently formulates his own findings with reference to Whiteley's statements confirming, correcting or complementing them. In this way, Gusii next to Kuria (E.43) has become one of the best-documented Bantu languages of South West Kenya[4].

---

1 Möhlig, Wilhelm J.G. 2000. Dialektale Nähe unter den Bantusprachen im Nordosten des Victoria Nyanza, in: Rainer Voßen, Angelika Mietzner & Antje Meißner, *"Mehr als nur Worte ..." Afrikanistische Beiträge zum 65. Geburtstag von Franz Rottland.* Köln: Rüdiger Köppe, pp. 439-467.

2 Editors are Bernd Heine and Wilhelm J.G. Möhlig. The first volume appeared in 1980 with Dietrich Reimer in Berlin.

3 Schoenbrun, David Lee 1997. *The Historical Reconstruction of Great Lakes Bantu Cultural Vocabulary. Etymologies and Distributions.* Köln: Rüdiger Köppe.

4 Cammenga, Jelle 1994. *Kuria Phonology and Morphology.* Free University, Amsterdam.

From the Africanist's point of view, there are still three major gaps in the research record of Gusii to be filled: a thorough analysis of the prosodological (tonal) system, a comprehensive dictionary and a scholarly edition of local verbal art.

These studies are somehow urgent, because the language is under heavy pressure of Lwoo, a Nilotic language that is dominant in the whole Nyanza area, and Swahili that is gaining more and more terrain as East African lingua franca particularly among intellectuals. The new socio-linguistic development is to the detriment of Gusii in so far as it is more and more ousted from the public domain and subject to massive linguistic influence from Lwoo and Swahili.

In this perspective, the editors highly welcome the appearance of the author's comprehensive and meticulous description of Gusii as volume 12 of their series on *East African Languages and Dialects*.

Cologne, July 2002

The Editors

TABLE OF CONTENTS

Acknowledgements 13
List of Symbols and Abbreviations 14
Map: Gusiiland 17

Chapter one: Introduction 20
1.1. Gusii and East Nyanza Bantu 20
1.2. Objectives and approach 23
1.3. Brief critique of previous research 24
1.4. Gusii dialectology and linguistic comparison 27
1.5. South Mugirango 28
1.6. Linguistic representation and orthography 32

Chapter two: Gusii phonology 35
2.1. Segments and representation 35
2.1.1. Vowels 35
2.1.2. Consonants, nasals, and glides 51
2.1.3. Prenasals 60
2.1.4. Lexical and postlexical phonology 65
2.1.5. Suprasegmental phonology 66
2.2. The Syllable 71
2.2.1. Syllable structure 71
2.2.2. Syllabification 72
2.3. Lexical phonology 79
2.3.1. Consonantal Voicing Dissimilation 79
2.3.2. Prenasalisation 86
2.3.3. Nasal Homorganisation 87
2.3.4. Defricativisation 88
2.3.5. Nasal Resyllabification 90
2.3.6. Pre-Nasal /i/-Insertion 93
2.3.7. Nasal Velarisation and Palatalisation? 96
2.3.8. Linking Rule 105
2.3.9. x-Trimming 106
2.3.10. Upper Mid Vowel Raising 107
2.3.11. Complex Segment Formation 122
2.3.12. Glide Formation 126
2.3.13. Degliding 130
2.3.14. Mid Vowel Height Spreading 132
2.3.15. /a/-Delinking 148
2.3.16. Intervocalic /a/-Raising 152
2.3.17. /a/-Shortening 153
2.3.18. Constraint on marginal long vowels 155
2.3.19. Pre-Alveolo-Palatal Vowel Lengthening? 156
2.3.20. Rule order 156

2.4. Postlexical phonology 158
2.4.0. Introduction 159
2.4.1. Gliding 161
2.4.1.1. Word-Final Upper Mid Vowel Raising 161
2.4.1.2. Word-Final Complex Segment Formation 163
2.4.1.3. Word-Final Glide Formation 168
2.4.2. Word-Final Lower Mid Vowel Raising 169
2.4.3. Word-Final Vowel Delinking 171
2.4.4. Word-Initial Vowel Spreading 182
2.4.5. Word-Final Intervocalic /a/-Raising 184
2.5. Summary of rules 185

Chapter three: Gusii Morphology 188
3.0. Introduction 188
3.1. Lexical categories 188
3.1.1. Terminology 188
3.1.2. Nouns 191
3.1.3. Adjectives 192
3.1.4. Verbs 193
3.1.5. Adverbs 193
3.1.6. Pronouns 194
3.1.7. Quantifiers and specifiers 195
3.1.8. Numerals 196
3.1.9. Adpositions and associative /-a/ 196
3.1.10. Conjunctions 196
3.2. Morphosyntactic classes and agreement 197
3.2.1. Nouns 198
3.2.1.1. Morphosyntactic classes and prefixes 198
3.2.1.2. The morphosyntactic class system 200
3.2.1.3. Diminutives and augmentatives 204
3.2.1.4. Augmentation and non-augmentation 211
3.2.1.4.1. Personal names 215
3.2.1.4.2. Kinship terms 216
3.2.1.4.3. Cattle terms 220
3.2.1.4.4. Placenames 222
3.2.1.4.5. Postlexical non-augmentation 223
3.2.1.5. Allomorphy of noun class prefixes 226
3.2.1.6. Prefix-stacking 238
3.2.2. Adjectives 240
3.2.3. Verbs 243
3.2.3.0. Preliminaries 243
3.2.3.1. Subject marker 244
3.2.3.2. Relative marker 262
3.2.3.3. Object marker 285
3.2.3.4. Summary of subject markers 293
3.2.4. Adverbs 296
3.2.5. Demonstratives 297

3.2.5.1. Proximate demonstrative: this 298
3.2.5.2. Semi-proximate demonstrative: that 303
3.2.5.3. Non-proximate demonstrative: that (over there) 306
3.2.6. Referential demonstrative and prefix 309
3.2.7. Independent pronouns 309
3.2.8. Interrogative pronouns 315
3.2.9. Possessive pronouns 325
3.2.9.1. Dependent possessive pronouns 325
3.2.9.2. Independent possessive pronouns 332
3.2.10. Adpositions 338
3.2.11. Associative /-a/: the associative construction 339
3.2.12. Quantifiers and specifiers 344
3.2.13. Cardinal numerals and -reeŋga 348
3.2.14. Ordinal numerals 357
3.2.15. Summary 368
3.3. Verbal morphology 370
3.3.1. Basic verbal structure: infinitive and imperatives 370
3.3.2. Extension and extension affixes 372
3.3.2.1. Reflexive prefix /ee-/ 376
3.3.2.2. Resultative suffix /-ak/ 377
3.3.2.3. Stative suffix /-ek/ 378
3.3.2.4. Reversive-intransitive suffix /-ok/ 382
3.3.2.5. Reversive-transitive suffix /-or/ 384
3.3.2.6. Applicative suffix /-er/ 387
3.3.2.7. Reciprocal suffix /-an/ 391
3.3.2.8. Causative suffix /-i/ 392
3.3.2.9. Passive suffix /-u/ 394
3.3.2.10. Semantic specialisation: /-er-an-i-/ 395
3.3.3. Tensed verbal structure and verbal markers 398
3.3.3.1. Focus marker 400
3.3.3.2. Negative markers and Morpholexical /i/-Deletion 400
3.3.3.3. Relative marker 403
3.3.3.4. Subject marker 404
3.3.3.5. Tense markers 404
3.3.3.6. Object marker 405
3.3.3.6.1. Morphology and usage 405
3.3.3.6.2. Relative position in verbal structure 406
3.3.3.6.3. Distinct types of object marker 408
3.3.3.6.4. Relative order of object markers 408
3.3.3.7. Infinitive marker 416
3.3.3.8. Root 417
3.3.3.9. Final vowel 417
3.3.3.10. Locative 417
3.3.4. Morphological fusion 419
3.3.4.1. Perfective /r/-Deletio 419
3.3.4.2. /r/-Deletion (optional) 426
3.3.4.3. Perfective Suffix Vowel Delinking 431
3.3.5. The tense system 434

3.3.6. To be and not to be 497
3.3.6.1. Linking usage: na, -re 497
3.3.6.2. Auxiliary usage: -re, -ß- 501
3.3.6.3. Relative usage: -re, -yi- 505
3.3.6.4. Locative usage: -re 507
3.3.6.5. To be with: -re, -ßuat- 510
3.4. Lexical derivation 512
3.4.1. Primary and secondary derivation 512
3.4.2. Derivation through affixation 513
3.4.2.1. Prefixation: augmentation and non-augmentation 513
3.4.2.2. Suffixation 516
3.4.3. Derivation through reduplication 516
3.4.4. Derivation of nouns 518
3.4.5. Derivation of adjectives 534
3.4.5.1. Non-derived adjectives 534
3.4.5.2. Derived adjectives 534
3.4.5.3. Comparatives and superlatives 539
3.4.5.4. Some adjectives: 'alone, good, many, like, -self' 540
3.4.6. Derivation of verbs 544
3.4.7. Derivation of adverbs 545
3.4.8. Derivation of adpositions 554
3.4.9. Derivation of conjunctions 557
3.5. Other lexical processes 559
3.5.1. Compounding and phrasal lexicalisation 559
3.5.2. Lexical take-over and adaptation 561
3.5.3. Idiomatic expressions 566
3.6. Summary of rules 572

Chapter four: Gusii orthography 573
4.0. Introduction 573
4.1. Different types of representation 573
4.2. The spelling of consonants and glides 574
4.3. The spelling of prenasals 577
4.4. The spelling of vowels 580
4.4.0. Preliminaries 580
4.4.1. Vowel quality 581
4.4.2. Vowel length 585
4.5. The spelling of words 589
4.5.1. Postlexical considerations 589
4.5.2. Lexical considerations 592
4.6. Punctuation 595
4.7. Capitalisation 595
4.8. Summary 596
4.9. Conclusion 598

Appendix one: Test words 600
Appendix two: Informant files 603
Cited references 610

ACKNOWLEDGEMENTS

In one way or another, this study owes much to many, and special thanks are due to the Deutsche Forschungsgemeinschaft for funding the project, the Kenya Government for granting the necessary research permit, and, in their own right, the following individuals.

Professor F. Rottland, for inviting me to the project at Bayreuth and for some preparatory discussion. Ralf Grosserhode, also at Bayreuth, for preparing the map.

Professor G.E. Booij, Department of General Linguistics, Free University of Amsterdam, and Dr G.J. Dimmendaal, Department of African Linguistics, Leyden University, for helpful discussion and suggestions on a number of points.

Professors G.S. Were and B.A. Ogot, of Maseno College, Western Kenya, for hospitality extended to me several times at the College Guesthouse, and for interesting discussions, together with other colleagues, on a variety of topics relating to African languages, cultures, and literature.

Professor J.O. Obura, also of Maseno College, for his valuable help in introducing me to several promising students. Some of these assisted me in lexical research on the Kenyan languages spoken around Lake Victoria/Nyanza and in the research on which the present study is based. Specifically, I should like to thank V.G. Oyaro, B.A., for useful discussion and suggestions, his hospitality, and for introducing me to H. Machuki, B.A., to whom thanks are due also for some discussion and suggestions.

Professor W.J.G. Möhlig, for mediating the publication of the present work, and Mr R. Köppe, the publisher, for his patience.

Very special thanks are due to Mwita and Margaret Gibuni, for their longstanding friendship, hospitality, and helpfulness, not forgetting Desmond, Dennis, and David.

Last, but not least, I should like to thank my informants, both those whom I consulted briefly and whose names are not recorded here, and those whom I consulted much, especially (in alphabetical order) Ernest Maoto, Janet Nyamoita Mokaya, Judith Moraa, Richard Omae Oira, Lilian Nyanchama Onsare, and Shem Mogaka Orioki.

LIST OF SYMBOLS AND ABBREVIATIONS

1-21: These numbers are used to label prefixes, subject markers, and object markers, e.g. px3, sm1, om5. They refer to the Gusii morphosyntactic classes.

Example: /ci-a-et-a/
sm9-t-p-FV

Prefix 15, in combination with final vowel /-a/, marks infinitives and is therefore called the infinitive marker. In addition, the designations 1-3s/p are also used.

Examples: 1-3s: first-third person singular animate class 1
1-3p: first-third person plural animate class 2

==>: morphological derivation
-->: phonological derivation
>: change (phonological or otherwise)
=: morphosyntactic agreement (e.g. 21 = 9, which means that, in the cases discussed in the text, adjectival class 9 may agree morphosyntactically with nominal class 21); also signifies equivalence or identity.

a: augment, augmentative prefix
ap: applicative, applicative suffix (-er)
apx: adjectival prefix
B: beneficiary (object marker)
c: causative, causative suffix (-i)
C: causee (object marker)
f: focus
fv: final vowel, which combines with other prefixes and suffixes to mark finite and non finite forms
I: instrumental (object marker)
npx: numerical prefix
p: passive voice marker (-u or, after a vowel, -γu)
P: patient (object marker)
PB: Proto-Bantu

Note: Traditional transcriptions of cited Proto-Bantu reconstructions have been made to conform to the International Phonetic Alphabet, as follows,

Bantu	IPA
ĩ	i
i	e
e	ɛ
a	a
o	ɔ
u	o
ũ	u

pv: perfective tense suffix (-ir)
px: prefix (also see apx, npx, ppx, rpx, vpx)

Whenever the lexical category of some form is obvious, a simple number (e.g. 1 or 15) is considered sufficient to designate its morphosyntactic class.

ppx: pronominal prefix
R: recipient (object marker)
ref: referent
  s-ref: subject-referent
  o-ref: object-referent
rf: reflexive, reflexive prefix (ee-)
representation, levels of:
  / / underlying phonological representation
  ¦ ¦ any intermediate representation
  [ ] systematic phonetic surface representation
  < > orthographic representation
representation, phonological:
  C = any consonant
  V = any vowel
  N = any nasal
  G = any glide
representation, syllabic:
  σ, N" = syllable
  O = onset
  N = nucleus
  C, N' = coda
rm: relative marker
rpx: relative prefix
sx: suffix
sn: someone (used in some glosses)
sth: something (used in some glosses)
t: marker of tense and/or mood and/or aspect
v.i.: intransitive verb
v.t.: transitive verb
vpx: verbal prefix (subject or object marker)

MAP: GUSIILAND

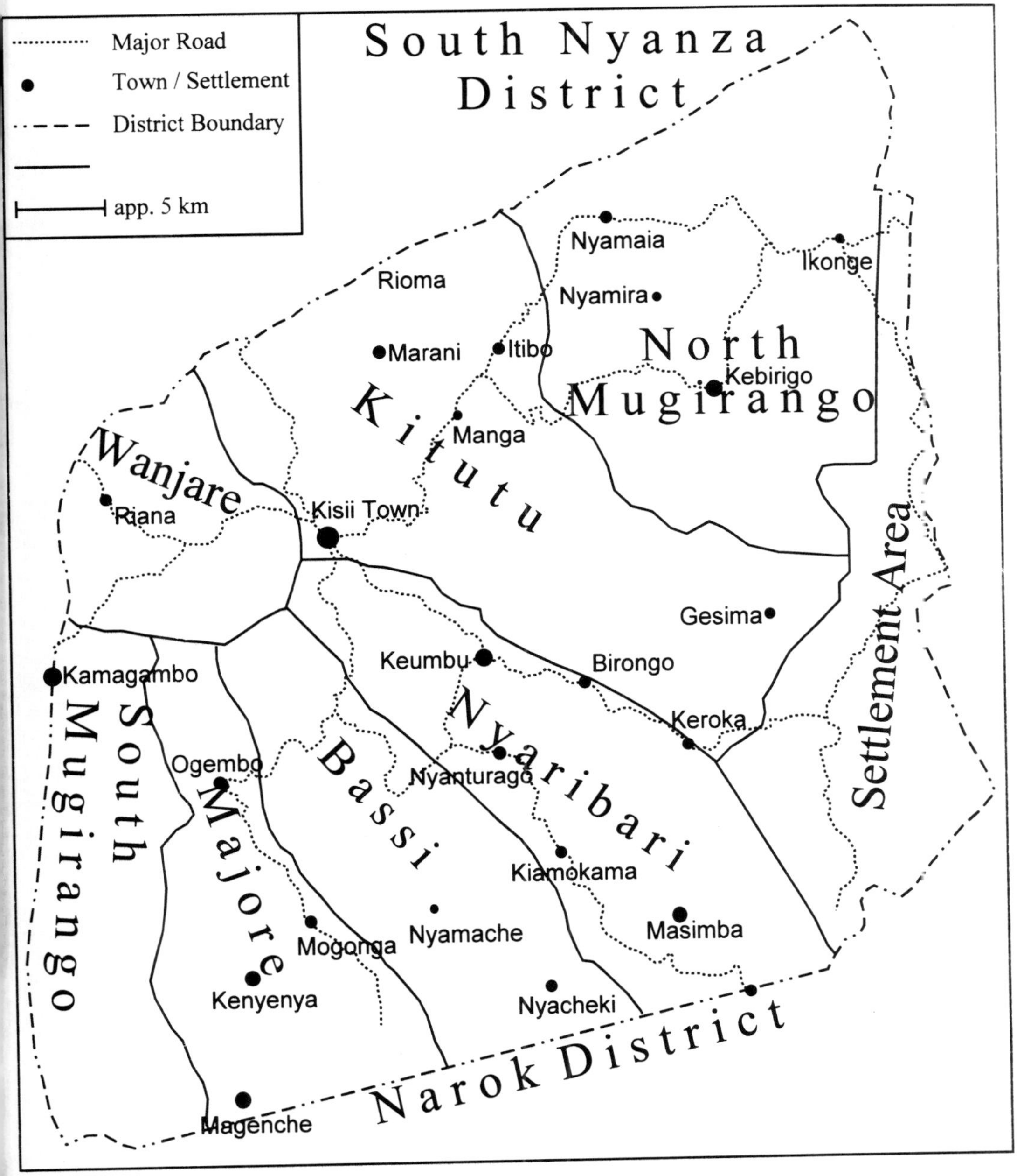

Note: Continuous lines indicate former subtribal or sublocational borders, some of which have changed recently.

GUSII PHONOLOGY AND MORPHOLOGY

CHAPTER ONE

INTRODUCTION[1]

1.1. Gusii and East Nyanza Bantu.

Gusii, the object of this study, is an eastern Bantu language spoken in the northern part of the region between the eastern shore of Lake Victoria, or Lake Nyanza, and the eastern branch of the Great Rift Valley. This region, considered here so as to include the islands along the lakeshore, will be designated conveniently in geographical terms as East Nyanza, so that Gusii may be classified more specifically as an East Nyanza Bantu language. It is labelled E.42 by Guthrie (1971, vol. 2: 45, vol. 3: 13), whose classification will also be quoted with respect to some of the Bantu languages to be mentioned in a moment (he offers a key list in 1971, vol. 3: 11-15).

The language, spoken exclusively in Kenya, is perhaps more commonly known by its English name, viz. Kisii. In the language itself, its proper name is [é̱ke̱γusií] (where underlining indicates [-ATR] quality of the vowels concerned). It is spoken by the [áβaγusií], 'the Gusii (people)' (singular [ó̱mo̱γusií]), in [βoγusii][2] 'Gusiiland' (see map on page 15).

Most of the East Nyanza languages belong to the Bantu family. Some, however, are Nilotic. These are spoken mostly in areas near the Gusii Highlands.

The Bantu languages Logooli (E. 41) and Luyia (E. 32) are spoken farther to the north of Gusii.

Kipsigis, a Nilotic language, is spoken in the region roughly in between these two languages and Gusii, so immediately north, but partly also to the east, of the latter. Maasai, another Nilotic language, is also spoken largely to the east of it, but farther away, nowadays mostly in the Rift Valley and beyond (though some ethnic mixing has taken place in the region on its western escarpment) and partly also to the southeast of it. Luo, another a Nilotic language, is spoken west and southwest of Gusii and extends along the shore of Lake Victoria/Nyanza and inland, down into Tanzania.

Suba is probably best considered as a cluster and mixture of several languages (for discussion see Rottland 1993 and Reh 1994). Its origin and matrix is arguably Bantu, probably to a considerable extent, but it is largely mixed with Nilotic Luo nowadays, the latter being the dominant language of the two in the area where it is spoken. A number of

---

[1] The research on which this study is based was sponsored by the Deutsche Forschungsgemeinschaft (DFG), within the context of a wider research on Identity in Africa (SFB 214), and is part of ongoing research on African languages conducted at the Department of Afrikanistik II of the University of Bayreuth.

[2] Tone unrecorded, as in many surface representations given hereafter.

older speakers can still speak "Suba" with some proficiency, but they are relatively few, and getting fewer still. Moreover, as one of my research assistants confirmed in 1996, there is much code-switching. Depending on the circumstances of conversation, Suba speakers often switch to Luo or even Swahili. Also relevant for the East Nyanza area as a whole, including Suba, is that it may be aptly characterised as a linguistic or dialectal continuum, the details of which, however, require further investigation. "Suba" is spoken to the west and southwest of Gusii, particularly on Mfang'ano Island, more restrictedly on Rusinga Island, but also along the lakeshore, especially in the Gwassi Hills, Kaksingiri, and farther south in Muhururu, extending some way into Tanzania.

Kuria (E. 43), a Bantu language, is spoken to the south of Gusii, extending into Tanzania as far as Musoma, but nowadays not immediately along the lakeshore, unless perhaps in some locations in the region near Musoma. Of all the East Nyanza languages it is probably most closely related to Gusii.

Farther south in Tanzania, partly along the lakeshore, a number of other Bantu languages are spoken, viz. Ngurimi, Ikizu, Shashi, Zanake (E.44), Nata (E.45), and 'Suguti', a collective name for Jita, Kwaya (both classified as E.25), Ruri, and Regi (mentioned in the references enumerated in the next paragraph). Kerewe (E.24), another Bantu language mixed with Luo, is spoken on Kerewe Island and some other islands near the eastern lakeshore.

Beyond a geographical classification, sub-groupings of most of the aforementioned Bantu languages differ, at least to some extent, even in relatively recent publications, such as Heine (1976), Heine and Möhlig (1980), and Hinnebusch, Nurse, and Mould (1981). Since the debate on the classification of Bantu languages continues, the details involving Gusii will not be discussed here. The interested reader is referred to the works quoted in the present section.

From oral traditions of the Gusii themselves and of some of the other East Nyanza ethnic groups, we know that, at least since the eighteenth century, search for land caused much migratory movement in the region, and often involved warfare with neighbouring tribes (see Ochieng' 1974). As a result of this, Gusii underwent diverse linguistic and cultural influences, Bantu and Nilotic, in the course of its history. Evidently, this eventually involved especially the languages mentioned. In any case, for a considerable period of time, right up to the present, in which settlement has largely become fixed, Gusii has been surrounded by them. Potentially, this makes it an interesting language to study, both from a synchronic or comparative, and from an historical point of view. Mutatis mutandis, this also applies to Gusii culture, on the understanding that language and culture tend to be closely interconnected.

However, in order to address comparative and historical linguistic questions interestingly, sufficient description and analysis of the languages to be compared is a prerequisite, preferably based on both historical and synchronic data. Unfortunately, these are lacking to a considerable extent for many East Nyanza Bantu languages. Old written records are lacking. Since much of Africa's history has been approached through comparison of languages recently described, extensively or in part, this is an important circumstance to be reckoned with. Despite attempts, such as Schoenbrun (1990), to provide more context by including non-linguistic sources of potentially valuable historical data, much information remains to be added. Vicious circles in the study of African languages and history, therefore, are something to be guarded against. For East Nyanza, at any rate, it seems early days to propose a comprehensive and detailed account. The reasons that motivate the present study, mentioned in section 1.2, would seem to imply additional support for this statement.

Even synchronic descriptions of East Nyanza Bantu languages are lacking to a considerable extent, especially comprehensive systematic ones, so that, at least for the time being, studies on historical or genetic relations between languages, and accounts of history at large based on this, must often retain a somewhat tentative or piecemeal character. This also bears on historical study of Bantu languages. Since these languages have played a major role in providing data for recent advances in the theory and description of linguistic tone, this state of affairs may have wider theoretical linguistic implications. A call for ongoing thorough, systematic, and comprehensive empirical research on these languages, next to, and together with, theoretical advance seems well-founded therefore.

To the best of my knowledge, only a few of the aforementioned East Nyanza Bantu languages have been described to any extent. At least the following studies may be cited. One is Mekacha (1985), which attempts to study certain regular Nata vowel changes systematically, particularly those involving regular variation in the height of prefix and augment vowels. Next, Whiteley (1955) deals with Kuria verbal morphology and syntax, Aksenova (1977) with its noun classes, Cammenga (1994) with Kuria phonology and morphology as a whole, while Muniko, et al. (1996) provides a lexicon.

In comparison with most other East Nyanza languages, Gusii has been described relatively early, and well, by Whiteley (1956, 1959, 1960). Whiteley (1956) is sometimes referred to in the literature as (1965), presumably because its title-page gives 1965 as the year of publication. The 'Foreword', typewritten by Whiteley himself, gives 1956. Thus it predates both (1959) and (1960) in the order of their completion. Since a distinct progress in descriptive precision and explanatory clarity is noticeable in his work, and the present study makes frequent reference to it, Whiteley (1956, 1965) will hereafter be referred to as (1956).

More recently, certain aspects of Gusii have been scrutinised on the basis of this work. Thus Kingston (1983) discusses the relevance of derived and non-derived tense morphemes for Proto-Bantu reconstruction and comparative study of modern Bantu languages, using aspects of the Gusii tense system for example. Cammenga (forthcoming) examines the nature and extent of Gusii vowel harmony. But apart from titbits in works of general comparative linguistic survey, and unpublished work (heard of in conversations, possibly valuable, but hard to obtain), the aforementioned studies may exhaust the number of segmental descriptions of the East Nyanza Bantu languages. So in addition to fresh descriptions -perhaps beginning with, but not necessarily restricted to, systematic and comprehensive phonologies, morphologies, and dictionaries- there is a need for further extrapolation, amplification, and systematisation of existing descriptions.

This last observation also bears on Gusii. Though Whiteley's work is very valuable as a relatively early source of data, his judgments of their status and his analyses sometimes call for elaboration. Thus Kingston (1983: 55, note 4) observes, for example, that some of his analyses of tense dependency "do not in many cases survive close scrutiny".

The following observations may perhaps be added on Whiteley (1960), arguably his most well-considered work on Gusii. Many phonetic details are given (e.g. 1960: 4-6; also 1956: 3-6), but not all of these are sufficiently exact, so that, if they are to be used for segmental and suprasegmental phonological purposes, they require checking and supplementation. This observation also applies, though to a lesser extent, to their use for morphological purposes, at least where parsing and some cases of allomorphy are concerned. On the whole, the data in question are useful as a starting-point for more elaborate research on Gusii syntax. A systematisation and amplification of Whiteley's work may not only increase our understanding of the language, but also help to prepare the way for more comprehensive and systematic comparison of it with other East Nyanza Bantu languages than has hitherto been possible.

1.2. Objectives and approach.

The primary and main objective of this study is to give a systematic description of Gusii phonology and morphology.

To try and achieve this, first, a critical study of Whiteley's pioneer work (1956, 1959, 1960), taken as a starting-point, was undertaken. Subsequently, it was thoroughly checked during fieldwork. Its considerable descriptive value has already been remarked upon. Especially (1960) compares well with other work on East African Bantu languages produced in the 1950s. Thus, on the whole, his work has proven useful for the purposes of the present study.

A second means to achieve the main objective has been the collection of fresh data. This was carried out in Maseno (western Kenya), roughly from January to April 1996, and in Nairobi, from September to November 1996 and from September to October 1997. Informants consulted, mentioned roughly in chronological order, are: Ernest Mauti Maoto, Richard Omae Oira, Shem Mogaka Orioki, Lilian Nyanchama Onsare, Judith Moraa Onsomu, and Janet Nyamoita Mokaaya, among others.

The following procedure was adopted. Data initially collected with the help of Ernest and Richard were checked against Shem's speech, early 1996. This was processed and, late 1996, checked against Lilian's speech, which also provided the basis for considerably enlarging the body of data incorporated in this study. These were processed and, late 1997, checked against Judith's speech, while Janet went over the tenses. Eventually the three of us rechecked these together.

Though Lilian and Judith come from different locations, their speech has proven to be remarkably uniform. The description and analysis offered in the present study may thus arguably be considered as representative of Gusii as a whole. The only exception, in this respect, at least to some as yet undefined extent, is the speech variety of South Mugirango, for reasons some of which are explained in section 1.4.

It may well be asked whether another study on Gusii, at least on some aspects already pioneered by Whiteley, is warranted. After all, the value of his work has already been admitted. Nonetheless, a reexamination of the language seemed worth the trouble, because of certain shortcomings in earlier work. Accordingly, a second objective of the present study, implied in the main one, has been to try and improve our understanding of Gusii in terms of descriptive accuracy and expliciteness, as well as explanatory systematicness with respect to this earlier work. Thus I have tried to supplement Whiteley's work, whenever this seemed necessary and possible.

A third objective, again more implicit, relates to cross-linguistic study. Gusii is possibly most closely related to Logooli and Kuria, and secondarily to the E. 50 languages. While Kikuyu (E.51) and Kamba (E.55) are mentioned by Whiteley (1960: 1), Embu (E.52) may presumably be included here too, since it appears to be relatively closely connected with Kikuyu. However, the speakers of Gusii I consulted were more inclined to observe on Gusii's similarity to Meru, as did some Meru speakers I consulted. Gusii may also be related more distantly to Luyia at large and some Ugandan languages, as suggested by Whiteley (1960: 1), but the details of this require further research. Of the Kenyan languages mentioned, Kikuyu, Kamba, the Bukusu variety of Luyia, and Kuria have been more or less described. Even though more descriptions and analyses are desirable, a more systematic treatment of Gusii, as attempted here, may faciliate, perhaps even promote, more detailed comparison with these other languages.

A fourth objective, finally, has been to stimulate further study on Gusii itself. To state this, is more than a truism, because much work, both descriptive and practical, remains to be done. For example, despite Whiteley's (1960) sizeable study on the Gusii tense system, which includes a wealth of examples, and his inclusion of a wordlist in (1956: 120-134), there is ample scope for further work on the semantics and the lexicon of the language. Suprasegmentals provide another case in point. For example, tone has only received sketchy treatment so far, and though some of its main elements will be discussed in the next two chapters, the tonal system as a whole will not be treated here either. Nor has Gusii syntax been studied comprehensively so far. And from a practical point of view, there may be room for improvement of Gusii orthography, which may spark off further work on literacy and education (see Chapter 4 for some discussion and suggestions). So there is a need and considerable scope for further research on the language, and relevant suggestions to this effect will be made in the appropriate places. So much for objectives.

This section may be concluded by observing that the approach adopted is a combination of nonlinear and lexical phonology and morphology (see Chapter Two for some clarifying remarks). I have not made use of the more recent Optimality Theory.

1.3. Brief critique of previous research.

In addition to the appreciation for Whiteley's pioneer work on Gusii (1956, 1959, 1960) expressed in the previous section, some of its shortcomings were also noted. Since studies on the language are scarce, the significance of earlier work is relatively great. Any shortcomings must therefore be taken into account by subsequent research, first, because repeating the same mistakes must be avoided, and second, because such a critique may be useful to formulate the more clearly what improvements and additions may be offered. A brief critical appraisal of Whiteley's work will therefore be attempted here.

First, an apparently superficial point of criticism concerns its considerable amount of transcriptional error. This applies also to the more matured part of his work. Even if we restrict our attention to the segmental side of the language, it is not at all exceptional to find ten or more transcriptional errors per page in (1960).

However, this point may only appear to be superficial, for in any empirical science, such as theoretical and descriptive linguistics, data constitute, at least in part, the basis for all subsequent reasoning. Inaccurate transcription, especially when systematic, often leads to analytical and explanatory error. Hence, if this sort of defect is found in a group of languages, it may have repercussions for comparative and historical linguistics. Eventually, it may influence cross-linguistic theorising. Whiteley's account of details of vowel harmony (1960: 3-4), defricativisation (1960: 5), and voicing dissimilation (1960: 6), provides some examples, but others might be added.

This defect somewhat detracts from the usefulness of even his best work, so that anyone wishing to use the material must double-check it systematically. In fact, this was done during the research that underlies the present study. Accordingly, transcriptional errors occurring in examples taken over from Whiteley have been tacitly corrected.

A second shortcoming involves Whiteley's theoretical stance and the methodology that goes with it. Generally, his account is marked by a relative lack of theoretical explicitness. Of course, in an avowed practical introduction, such as (1956), this cannot be marked down as a defect, but with respect to his treatment of the tense system (1960) it can.

In his distributionalist approach to language, the main focus is on linguistic forms and their positional distribution: if morphemes, their distribution in words; and if words, their distribution in sentences. Meaning is largely reduced to a by-product of form and distribution. Accordingly, his aim is "to furnish a formal description of the Gusii tense-system, in the belief that this represents the most economical way of describing the system exhaustively" (1960: 2). In so far as form and distribution must be taken into account, such an approach is viable. However, whether it may be considered sufficient, is debatable.

In the clarification of his classification of one-word tenses, after observing that both shape and meaning may be adopted as a starting-point for classifying tenses, Whiteley (1960: 11-15) argues that the usefulness of choosing one or the other as primary in a classification will depend on the nature of the language under consideration. This seems to beg the question. From a universal point of view, both form and meaning, along with other aspects, play a role and must, on principle and ultimately, be taken into account. Delimitation of a study for certain purposes is another matter. His argumentation is conducted by analogy to Latin, Greek (1960: 11), and Kuria (1960: 12), and is thus ad hoc.

In explaining his own emphasis, he continues (1960: 12), "If, on the other hand, one adopts a classification by shape, this does at least have the merit of accounting for all the relevant tenses without the fear of being misled by labels. Difficulties do arise, however, as soon as one wishes to make use of a schema worked out in one language, for a second, and perhaps closely related, language. While accurate and detailed descriptions of individual languages are both necessary and desirable, it would seem to be equally desirable for the descriptions to be effected in a manner which may make it possible to abstract comparable features from other languages in order to reach a new level of classificatory description".

However, the validity of this methodological statement depends on the comprehensiveness, the adequacy, and the capacity for refinement, of the theory adopted as one's vantage point. In this case, Whiteley's methodology affects both the question whether or not certain data and processes are presented, the manner in which they are or are not presented, and certain accounts that are or are not given. It strongly tends toward analytic listing of certain processes, sometimes to the point of obscuring, rather than clarifying them. Also, Whiteley's formally-based system of tense-labelling does not give much insight beyond differentiating morphologically distinct elements, important though this is. Moreover, semantically motivated tense-labels, if systematically consistent and correct, cannot be misleading. Therefore, his argument based on labelling does not hold.

Next, though a continued supply of descriptions of individual languages is indeed necessary, also for theoretical Bantu and general linguistic theory, the supposition that individual languages can, as it were, decide their own account, seems theoretically naive. Nor can problems encountered in a synchronic description of some language be resolved merely by analogy to other languages, even if related. Whiteley's attempt to account for certain (misconceived) exceptions to consonantal voicing dissimilation and for the intervocalic alternation of alveolo-palatal and velar nasals by analogy to neighbouring Kuria (1960: 6), are cases in point.

A third shortcoming concerns clarity and explicitness in his presentation of data. Since Whiteley does not distinguish between underlying, intermediate, and surface levels of representation (see section 1.6), his examples are often not perspicuous, at least not immediately, to a reader who is not already familiar with Gusii. Furthermore, such lack of distinction causes Whiteley to draw inadequate conclusions in some cases. A minor example is provided by inadequate analysis of some verb roots, due to a lack of sufficient distinction between expansion and extension suffixes.

A fourth shortcoming is that some explanations tend to remain insufficiently consistent and systematic. Different components of the language are not always clearly distinguished in the accounts given in (1956, 1960). Perhaps as a result of this, the system of phonological and morphological rules, as well as their interaction, often receives insufficient attention. The next two chapters provide examples of this.

To conclude, these criticisms are not intended to detract from the value of Whiteley's work, the more so, since the present work does not intend to remedy all of them. However, they do indicate, not only for the present study, but also for future research to be conducted by others, where there is room for improvement. In the course of this study, some such areas will be pointed out.

1.4. Gusii dialectology and linguistic comparison.

What has been observed about the state of our knowledge and understanding of East Nyanza Bantu languages in general, also applies, mutatis mutandis, to Gusii itself. In particular, dialectal variation, whether social or regional, has not been researched much until now. Whiteley recognises the possibility of such variation, but his remarks on the subject do not appear to be the result of systematic geographical linguistic comparison. Perhaps because of this, they are not very detailed and extensive.

However, they are useful, because they provide at least some historical point of reference, due to the time-lap of half a century between his and the present work. Specifically he writes: "On the whole there seems to be little dialectal variation within the language: Luo words have been borrowed, and occur particularly in North and South Mugirango; Swahili words also occur frequently and in the speech of some of the younger generation may form as much as 10% of the vocabulary. Neither Swahili nor English words, however, commonly occur in the areas away from the township of Kisii and the small settlements throughout the Highlands. The grammar differs little from location to location, though some features seem peculiar to one Mission or the other" (1956: 1).

These observations still obtain to a large extent, though some circumstances have changed and are changing. A major change has been the enormous increase of the population, viz. from the 250.000 mentioned by Whiteley (1956: 1) to possibly one or one and a half million today. Such a demographic landslide naturally entails other changes.

Arguably the most fundamental change resulting from it, is that there is not much land anymore to be divided among sons for an inheritance, as was customary and possible in the past. This, in turn, has had far-reaching social and economic implications. Plots of land inherited are becoming smaller and smaller. Accordingly, beyond subsistence farming, yields are becoming less economically viable for many.

Another important factor, especially in conjunction with the previous point, is the lag in road building. Although it is probably easier to reach the Gusii Highlands by main road now than it was in Whiteley's time, within the region itself the road system is still in need of solid construction work in many places. This lag poses problems for transport, both public and agricultural, with (socio-)economic implications.

Further, possibly related to this, but also due to the absence of what many consider tourist attractions, relatively few tourists visit the area. This has economic implications also. But linguistically it probably means that, off the main road, there are many places still where Gusii speech has remained relatively undisturbed. This may be a promising circumstance for historical research.

Nonetheless, due to the introduction of national schools in the 1960s and the influence of modern life generally, there seems to be considerable pressure on the language. Moreover, while, as stated in the quote given above, words were borrowed from Luo,

Swahili, and English in the past, this process has not stopped. Rather, the influence of Swahili and English in particular seems to have increased. Possibly as a result of these factors, the speech of the younger generation seems to be verging away more and more from the 'old' and 'pure' Gusii.

This applies especially to the speech of those who grow up outside the region, but even to some growing up inside of it. None of my informants, for example, most of whom were raised in the area, and who ranged in age between their early twenties and their mid-thirties, knew all the old names of the months. If this fact is representative of the situation as a whole, it would seem that the trend already noted by Whiteley has persisted. It may have become even stronger than it was forty years ago. Also, it may well have caused a greater degree of dialectal variation in modern Gusii, determined by social or generational factors, but it must be left to future research to examine this.

Lexical, and sometimes possibly also phonological, variation in lexical take-overs relating to certain areas of thought, belief, and life, all too briefly illustrated in section 3.5.2, corroborate Whiteley's observation on the contribution of Missions to the extension of Gusii vocabulary. Modern education and modern life generally, already mentioned, are also relevant in this respect. Developments in agriculture, cattle-farming, and technology certainly co-account for the increased lexical influence of English and Swahili. Each of these areas and influences would arguably make for interesting lexical, etymological, and modern anthropological studies.

1.5 South Mugirango.

Though the first clause in the quote from Whiteley given in the preceding section, viz. that "on the whole there seems to be little dialectal variation within the language" is true enough still, its second clause, the qualification that "Luo words have been borrowed, and occur particularly in North and South Mugirango", seems to be true only in part. In view of his meagre substantiation, it may have been only partly true even then. The areas designated as North and South Mugirango are located respectively in the northwest and the southwest of the Gusii Highlands (see map on page 15).

Traditionally, the western part of Gusiiland seems to have been an area in which much migration and intertribal contact took place, especially with the Luo people. However, though both North and South Mugirango border on Luoland, the degree of lexical take-over seems to have been greater in the South. The following observations seem to support this suggestion.

In the first place, it implies that North Mugirango is more like other varieties of Gusii than South Mugirango, supposing, for the moment, that it is sufficiently justified, from a linguistic point of view, to differentiate such varieties. If, for example, the remarkable similarity between the speech of Judith's, who is from North Mugirango, and that of

Lilian's, who comes from Bobaasi[3], is at all representative, it strongly suggests that the implication mentioned is valid. However, comparisons of other idiolects from different areas may have different outcomes. Hence the point, though probable, must first be corroborated more systematically to be ascertained.

Even so, all the Gusii people I consulted have confirmed that South Mugirango is considerably different from all the other real or supposed varieties of the language, viz. Getutu, North Mugirango, Bassi, Wanjare, Majore, and Nyaribaari. They added that the South Mugirango speech variety is probably alone in this respect, at least to the extent that it is different from the rest. They have also pointed out that Getutu is probably the original variety from which the other ones derive, though this requires systematic verification too.

Second, turning to some characteristics of South Mugirango itself, one systematic phonetic difference between it and other speech varieties concerns the pronunciation of the only affricate in the Gusii segment inventory. This segment is regularly rendered as [ç], or prenasalised as [ñç], in the other varieties (this affricate is hereafter represented as [c]). Its place of articulation varied somewhat, in the speech of my informants, between alveolo-palatal and palato-alveolar, though palatal and alveolar pronunciations may possibly occur also in some idiolects (but this requires verification). Further, the combination of focus element /n-/ with class prefix /e-/, followed by a vowel, generally tends to be rendered uniquely as [ndž] in these varieties. In addition, some idiolectal variation may sometimes occur between regular [c] and [dž], and between regular [ñc] and [ndž], as in (1),

(1) /n-ci-re-a/
f-10-be-fv
[ñciria] or [ndžiria]
'10-they are, it is 10-them'

In South Mugirango, however, [dž] regularly replaces the [c] of the other varieties throughout, while [ndž] replaces [ñc], also throughout. For example, the regular pronunciation for [macoγe], the name of one of the areas, is [madžoγe] in South Mugirango. That there may be, in addition to this difference in voicedness, a regular difference in place of articulation of this segment, is suggested by the difference between the (alveolo-)palatal pronunciation of [iñce], at least in Getutu, Baasi, and North Mugirango, as distinct from its alveolo-palatal pronunciation [iñtše] in South Mugirango. However, this point needs to be ascertained more systematically.

Third, there is a regular difference in the pronunciation of the Gusii /t/-segment. In the other varieties, this tends to be a voiceless interdental or a dental-alveolar sound, for the nonce written here as [t̪], as in [t̪aat̪a] 'father'. The speech varieties on which the present study is based have the dental-alveolar sound, which hereafter will be written [t]. It was the opinion of several informants that the interdental quality was characteristic of original

[3] Usually, but incorrectly, written <Bassi>. This clan name presumably derives from /βo-βa-asi/ 'the land of the Asi people'.

Gusii, but that the dental-alveolar quality has been taken over from English or Swahili.

In South Mugirango, on the other hand, the sound regularly has an alveolar quality, viz. [t]. It may have a retroflexed quality as well, at least in some idiolects, but this requires verification.[4] This, and the previous, point of difference is illustrated in the South Mugirango pronunciation of [toraadža] '2s-you have not come', versus [toraaca] elsewhere (where the difference between dental-alveolar and alveolar quality has not been indicated in writing).[5] So much for systematic phonetic differences.

Fourth, South Mugirango is also distinguished from some other varieties of Gusii by lexical and semantic differences. This may be illustrated as in (2),

(2) some lexical differentiation:

		South Mugirango
a. 'machete'	/e-βeeti/ 9-panga [eβeeti] (Baasi)	/o-mo-ɔrɔ/ A-3-panga [ɔmɔɔrɔ] (also NM and G)
b. 'maize'	[e-ke-tuuma] A-7-maize [eγetuuma] (Baasi)	[e-βaandɔ] 9-maize [eβaandɔ] (also NM and G; probably from Luo)
c. 'tray'[6]	[oroteeru] (B, NM, G)	[oroγare]
d. 'ball'	[omopiira] (B, NM, G; prob. from Sw.)	[emboombo]
e. 'salt'	[omooño]	[ecuumbi][7]

---

[4] This was corroborated only by some informants. Possibly, some degree of voicing may also be involved. However, I have not been able to visit the South Mugirango area recently or to consult a speaker born and bred there, in order to check out these points systematically.

[5] From /ti-o-raa-Vc-a/
not-you-tense-come-fv
sm2s

[6] Used for winnowing but also other purposes.

[7] Related to, and possibly derived from, Swahili chumvi 'salt'.

	(B, NM)	(also G)
f. 'donkey'	[eβuunda] (B, NM, G)	[etiγere]
g. '(big) tin'	[omotoriro] (probably B)	[εγɔrɔγɔrɔ]

limited semantico-syntactic differentiation:

h. continuous	[ηkɔγεεnda tore] (G, NM) 'we are going'	[ntoraaγεεndε]
i. be about to	[ή̀gótwééré] (G, NM) 'it is about to rain'	[nééráatwe]
	[eηiti ηgooceere] (NM) 'the animal is about to come'	[eηiti neeraace]

where NM abbreviates North Mugirango, G Getutu, and B Baasi. Possible further varieties of Gusii have not been taken into account in this set of examples.

Several informants affirmed that there are many more lexical differences like (2a-g) between South Mugirango and other varieties of Gusii. However, the sub-grouping of these varieties may fall out differently, depending on the lexical items compared. In any case, there is ample scope for further lexical research on Gusii as a whole, and for a more detailed inquiry into possible dialects. At least, data such as those in (2) suggest that any serious future dialectal research must take the speech of South Mugirango well into account.

Quite possibly, there are tonal or intonational differences between South Mugirango and other varieties of Gusii as well. This was suggested by several informants, but I have not been able to check this systematically.

This and the previous section may be concluded by a summary of the following points. First, my informants, and other people consulted more briefly, suggested that Gusii is changing rapidly, and that those who really know how to speak the 'proper' or 'pure' variety (usually the older people) are becoming fewer.

At the same time, secondly, there are signs of a renewed interest in the language on the part of speakers themselves. This was particularly noticeable among certain students at Maseno University. It seems premature, however, to speak of a concerted effort to tackle language questions consistently, systematically, and communally. Moreover, the resources and definite planning that are necessary for implementing such interests are often lacking. Nonetheless, the revived interest as such is a promising start.

Third, there is evidence of at least some dialectal variation.

Taken together, these factors arguably suggest, first, that the time is ripe for more solid and systematic research on Gusii lexicography, syntax, and dialectology; second, that in some respects a certain urgency may even be involved; and third, that, on the basis of a sufficiently systematic description of at least one variety of Gusii, dialectal research on the language will not only be easier, but may be worth the effort.[8] Perhaps the present research may help to facilitate and to encourage such endeavours.

1.6. Linguistic representation and orthography.

In view of the nature of this study, the following notational conventions (3) will be used to differentiate various levels or types of linguistic representation,

(3) distinct levels of representation

a. / /	underlying phonological representation
b. ¦ ¦	any intermediate phonological representation
c. [ ]	systematic phonetic surface representation
d. < >	orthographic representation

Alternatively, (3b) is often left unmarked.

Generally, the first three types of representation (3a-c) reflect the forms of words considered at rule-related levels that may be differentiated in lexical derivation. Thus they are technical, systematic linguistic distinctions, and as such they differ from type (3d).

These three levels may be defined more specifically, though relatively informally, as follows. First, any underlying representation (3a) may be defined as that representation of a word to which no rule has yet applied. As such, this type of representation is said to underlie, or to constitute the input for, the derivation.

Second, any intermediate representation (3b) may be defined as the representation of a word to which some, but not all, rules have applied. It is intermediate between the underlying (3a) and surface (3b) levels of representation. More than one intermediate

---

[8] This point is supported by the observation that, at least to some degree, most East Nyanza Bantu languages seem to form a speech continuum. This was also mentioned, at a session of the Conference on African Languages and Linguistics (CALL) at Leyden University, September 1996, by Dr C. Kutsch Lojenga, who said that she had come across at least one Kuria speaker who had a five vowel system, whereas the Nyabaasi variety described in my own study (1994) arguably and demonstrably has seven. Also, many Kuria people on the Kenyan side claim to have a close affinity with the Suba people living around and west of Migori. In this respect, East Nyanza as a whole still seems to be largely unbroken ground, linguistically speaking.

levels of representation may occur between the underlying and the surface representations.

Third, any surface representation (3c) may be defined as the representation of a word to which all relevant segmental and suprasegmental phonological, morphological, and phonetic rules have applied. It should be kept in mind, however, that most surface representations given in this study abstract from suprasegmental details of the words concerned. This type of representation is sometimes called the systematic phonetic representation, because it intends to represent the word as it is regularly pronounced by the speakers of a speech community. As such, it is a somewhat idealised representation, since most of the finer non-systematic, possibly idiolectal, phonetic details are left out of consideration.

Fourth, and finally, any orthographic type of representation (3d) often aims to reflect the systematic phonetic level (3c). It may do so more or less adequately, and as such it tends to be less technical and sometimes less systematic. In fact, it often reflects some intermediate representation (see Chapter Four for some discussion) and ends up being determined by a mixture of theoretical considerations and social and cultural conventions. In languages with a long tradition of writing, it may, in addition, be the (often mixed) result of a long historical development. This is what is generally called the spelling of a language.

Occasionally, intermediate representations are used to begin a derivation instead of underlying ones, when the grounds for arguing or ascertaining the underlying representation of the data concerned have been insufficient. This practice avoids unfounded speculation, yet allows us to use certain examples as a starting-point for some derivation that are otherwise not yet or not fully analysable. In some other partial derivations underlying representations are sometimes omitted for the sake of brevity. For the significance of other symbols and abbreviations used in this study, see the List of Symbols and Abbreviations, pp. vi-vii.

The types of representation in (3) are further discussed and clarified, with respect to Gusii, in the next two chapters. To aid the general reader, a conversion table is given in Chapter Four, relating the phonetic symbols used in this study to the orthographic symbols currently used by many Gusii speakers.

CHAPTER TWO

CHAPTER TWO

GUSII PHONOLOGY

Though the present chapter anticipates some aspects of Gusii morphology, it predominantly discusses the segmental phonology of the language.

2.1. Segments and representation.

In addition to the symbols in Chapter One, introduced to differentiate distinct levels of representation, those in (1) will be used to designate elements that play a role within the segmental and non-segmental phonological levels of linguistic representation,

(1) a. in phonological representation

C = any consonant
V = any vowel
N = any nasal
G = any glide

b. in syllabic representation

σ or N" = any syllable node
O = any onset node
N = any nucleus node
C or N' = any coda node

In this section, I will first discuss the representation of vowels (section 2.1.1), of consonants, nasals, and glides (2.1.2), and of prenasals, or prenasalised consonants (2.1.3). In section 2.1.4, I will briefly consider the relevance of the distinction between lexical and postlexical phonology with respect to Gusii. Finally, in section 2.1.5, I will touch on suprasegmental phonology.

2.1.1. Vowels.

Whiteley (1960: 2) lists the following seven basic Gusii vowels (2),

(2) vowel inventory

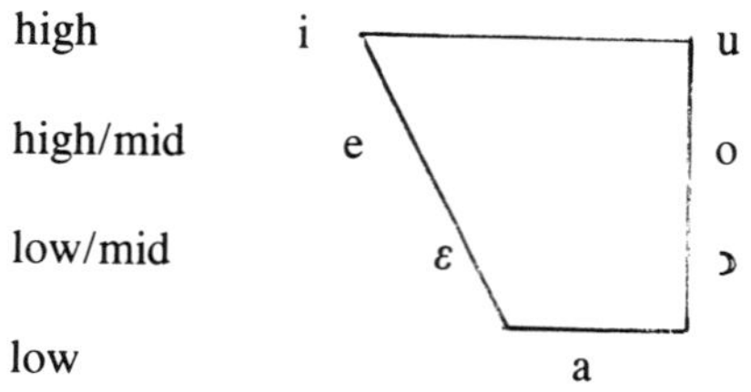

He does not define the phonetic or phonological significance of these symbols exactly (see 1956: 3-4 and 1960: 2-4), but the present research has corroborated the essential adequacy of his inventory. But a few observations are in order.

If inventory (2) is correct, the vowel segments may be differentiated in terms of minimally distinctive phonological features, as in (3),

(3)

	i	e	ɛ	a	ɔ	o	u
high	+	+	-	-	-	+	+
mid	-	+	+	-	+	+	-
back	-	-	-		+	+	+

This characterisation, though necessary, is not exhaustive, but differentiates the vowels presented in (2) sufficiently.[1] It may be noted that /a/ need not be specified for [back]

---

[1] Admittedly, the Gusii vowels may also be characterised in terms of height through a combination of the features [high] and [low],

	i	e	ɛ	a	ɔ	o	u
high	+	+	-	-	-	+	+
low	-	+	+	+	+	+	-

In this case, however, the lower mid vowels, /ɛ/ and /ɔ/, are insufficiently distinguished from low /a/ in terms of height, so that the feature [ATR] would have to be adduced as minimally necessary, in order to differentiate two subsets of vowels for height. This seems awkward. The assumption would be that the mid vowels are [-ATR] and /a/ [+ATR]. However, since some would hold that upper mid vowels are [+ATR], and lower mid [-ATR], this seems doubly awkward.

If the vowels are differentiated in terms of [mid] and [low],

	i	e	ɛ	a	ɔ	o	u
mid	-	+	+	-	-	+	+
low	-	-	+	+	+	+	-

underlyingly. Characterised as [-high, -mid], it is already sufficiently distinguished from the other segments, though phonetically it is [-back].

However, at least from a phonetic point of view, Gusii mid vowels appear to be regularly produced with retracted tongue root. That is, both upper and lower mid vowels appear to be characterised as [-ATR]. According to the present research, therefore, the Gusii vowels could thus be symbolised more accurately, as in (4),

(4)

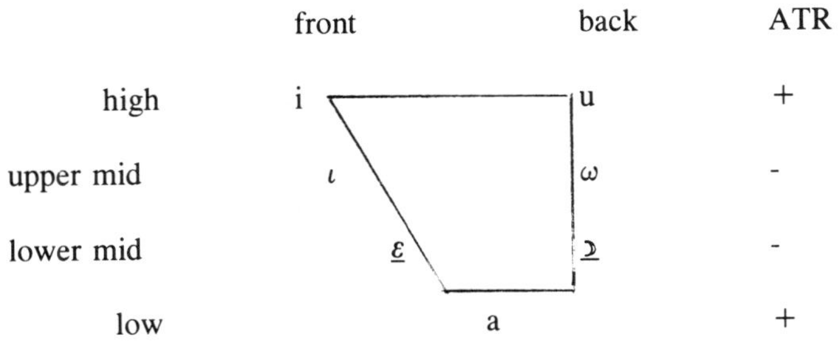

The symbols used to designate the upper mid front and mid vowels in this figure are those of the International Phonetic Alphabet (hereafter abbreviated as IPA). In many Bantu studies, [ɪ] and [ ] are used alternatively for the [-ATR] upper mid front and back vowel respectively, but this is merely a matter of notational convention. Some studies, such as Bendor Samuel (1983: 80), propose to mark tongue root retraction by underlining, so that the Gusii vowel system may be symbolised accordingly as in (5),

(5)

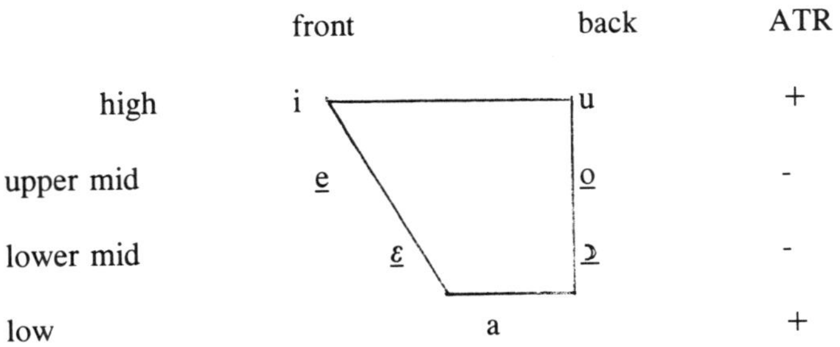

In many of the older Bantu studies the notation used for respresentating a vowel system such as that in (5) would be as in (6),

---

they are sufficiently differentiated in terms of height. But in this case it is more difficult to characterise other processes elegantly, for example the change from /a/ to [e], whenever it occurs between /i/'s. Whichever approach is adopted for Gusii, the representation of some rules will always be awkward. I will return to this in connection with the rules for whose representation it is relevant. Representational problems for height are rendered more elegant by Clements (1991).

(6)

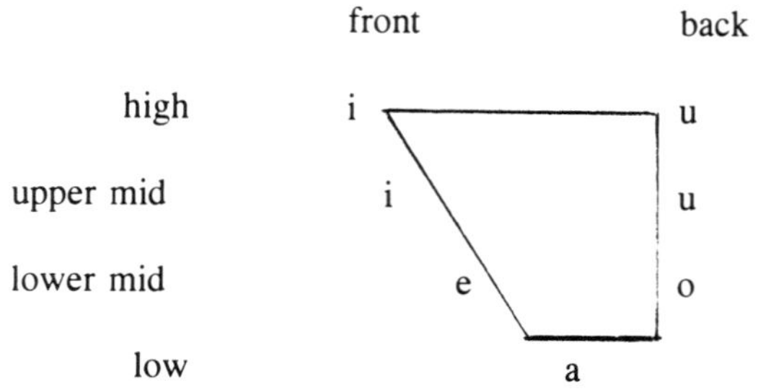

In this case, some theoretical notions, or at least general conceptions of what is a typical Bantu vowel system, may arguably underly this notation. I am referring to the formal similarity between high and upper mid front vowels /i/ and /i/, and between the corresponding back vowels /u/ and /u/. This point will be taken up in a moment. For the present purposes, however, inventory (6) may provisionally be taken as an alternative notation for (5).

Unfortunately, considerable variation in notational convention occurs across descriptive studies. With regard to the feature [ATR], this is probably due to the fact that its significance was discovered relatively late (see especially Stewart 1967). Its value is not usually taken into account in descriptions antedating the late 1960s. Often, other phonological symbols are also left insufficiently defined and their representations may vary too, as is illustrated in the notational variation noted for the upper mid vowels in connection with figures (2, 4-6). In perusing descriptions of Bantu languages, all this must be carefully taken into account.

The important point with respect to Gusii is that the phonetic and phonological significance of the symbols used are to be sufficiently adequate and clear. If it may be supposed that this is the case with respect to the Gusii vowel system, as represented in (5), then for practical reasons I here propose to represent this system henceforth as in (7),

(7)

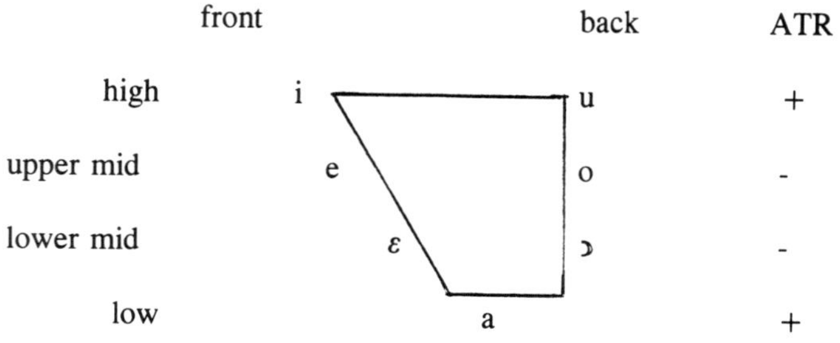

Phonologically it is equivalent to (4-6), notationally it is identical to (2). Thus in the present study [e] does not represent a [+ATR] vowel, as usual, but actually the [-ATR] front vowel [e̲] = [ı] = [ι]. Similarly, [o] represents [-ATR] vowel [o̲], [ω] = [ ]. Occasionally, I shall use underlining to indicate [-ATR] quality for the sake of clarity.

Mid vowels /e/, /o/, /ε/, and /ɔ/ are universally conceived as [+ATR], in contradistinction to [-ATR] /e̲/, /o̲/, /ε̲/, and /ɔ̲/, respectively. Phonetically, the difference between [+ATR] and [-ATR] in such sound pairs regularly entails a difference in vowel height, however slight. Thus, for example, [e̲] tends to be produced phonetically at a somewhat lower segmental height than [e]. Such differences may be represented spatially, as in (8),

(8)

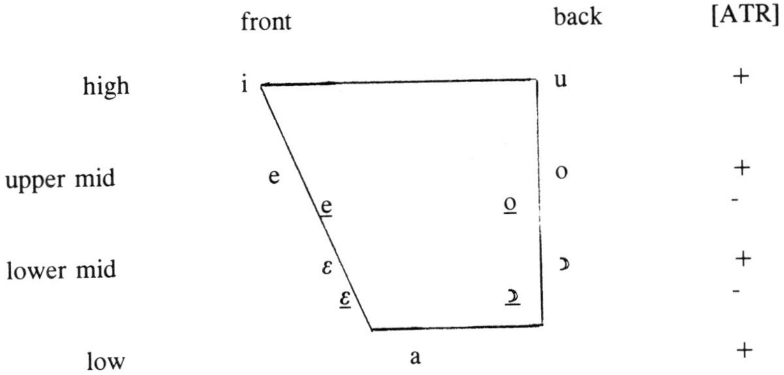

This figure illustrates how close in height the mid vowels really are phonetically. In some languages, in which upper mid [e] and [o] are regularly [+ATR], lower mid [ɛ] and [ɔ] may be [-ATR].

A question with possibly general theoretical or general Bantu linguistic implications is whether upper mid vowels should be represented as /e̲/ (or /e/ in some orthographies) and /o̲/ (or /o/ in some orthographies), thus suggesting a closer phonetic, and perhaps also a closer universal phonological, relationship with IPA /e/ and /o/, or whether they should be represented as /ι/ (or /i/ in some Bantu systems) and /ω/ (or /u/ in some Bantu systems), thus suggesting a closer phonetic, and perhaps also a closer universal phonological, relationship with IPA /i/ and /u/.

It is possible that this notationally complex state of affairs and the late discovery of the importance of the [ATR] feature may have been the combined result of inadeqacies in earlier or even more recent descriptions of Bantu languages, especially those made by listeners whose ears were insufficiently accustomed to the fine distinctions displayed in (8). This supposition might explain errors of transcription found in earlier studies on East Nyanza Bantu languages, involving especially mid vowels. However, I leave possible theoretical aspects of this point to future research and return to Gusii.

If inventory (7) is correct, and both upper and lower mid vowels are to be analysed as [-ATR], the vowel segments may now be characterised as in (9),

(9)

	i	e	ɛ	a	ɔ	o	u
high	+	+	-	-	-	+	+
mid	-	+	+	-	+	+	-
back	-	-	-		+	+	+
ATR	+	-	-	+	-	-	+

However, from a phonological point of view, the feature [ATR] does not appear to be minimally distinctive with respect to Gusii vowels. There does appear to be some variation involving the specification for [ATR] in a number of words, but this seems to be of a purely phonetic nature. I have been unable to discover any systematically conditioned alternations. If this is correct, it would seem, therefore, that the representations in (7) may be maintained together with their interpretation, and that the specified features in (3) may be considered as sufficiently distinctive phonologically.

Next, with regard to length, it may be noted that all of the seven Gusii vowels in inventory (7) may occur distinctively as short and long. In a nonlinear framework, this distinction may be expressed formally by differentiating the following types of representation underlyingly, as in (10),

(10) representation of distinctive length

a. short	b. long	
x	x x	timing tier
|	| /	
o	o	root node
|	|	
/V/	/V/	feature hierachy
[V]	[VV]	phonetic representation

where /V/ represents an underspecified, or any type of, vowel. Within the framework of nonlinear phonology, any of the traditional symbols for vowels, consonants, etc., for example /a/ and /ß/, represents the set of hierachically ordered specified segmental features that combine to characterise the phonological unit concerned. Whenever such a unit is linked to two units on the timing-tier, as in (10b), it is phonetically interpreted as long (written here as [VV], rather than [V:], for the sake of notational simplicity, and therefore without implying any particular theoretical stance).

Specifically, the following hierarchy (11) is tentatively assumed throughout the ensuing discussion,

(11)

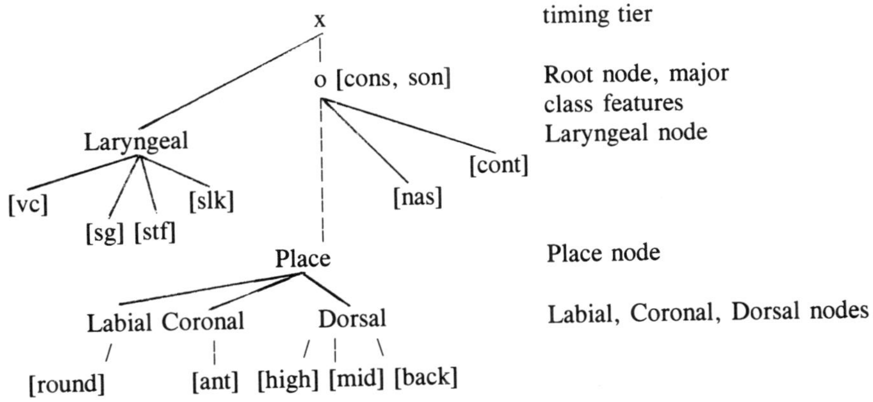

where the various abbreviations used have the following signification: cons(onantal), son(orant), cont(inuant), nas(al), vc = voicedness, slk = slack vocal cords, stf = stiff vocal cords, sg = constricted glottis, and ant(erior). For relevant discussion on the place of certain features see McCarthy (1988: passim) and references cited therein.

Any phonological unit may be characterised in terms of such a hierarchy of specified features distinctively. That is, the unit may be characterised in terms of those specified features that are both necessary and sufficient to distinguish it from the other phonological units in the language. Alternatively, it may be so characterised exhaustively. That is, it may be characterised in terms of all the hierarchically ordered specified features that combine to define it. Because distinctive characterisation is usually sufficient for most purposes, exhaustive characterisations are seldom given, unless to illustrate some specific point.

Whiteley (1960: 3) gives the examples repeated in (12) to substantiate the significant distinction between short and long vowels,

(12) a. -sik- 'respect'
vs. -siik- 'prepare beer'

b. -βas- 'elope'[2]
vs. -βaas- 'to pierce (a skin)'[3]

c. -βer- 'to boil (v.i.)'[4]
vs. -βéér- 'sit, sit down'

d. -tɛm- (= H) 'hit'
vs. -tɛɛm- 'try'

e. -kɔn- 'bewitch'
vs. -kɔɔn- 'to be (noticeably) irritated'[5]

f. -βór- 'to miss'[6]
vs. -βóór- 'say'

g. -kur- 'to scratch (of hens)'[7]
vs. -kuur- 'to shout'[8]

However, these data are insufficient as minimal pair evidence, because due to the additional tonal differences examples (12c,d) do not constitute strict minimal pairs. Even if tone may be neutralised in some tenses, thus yielding true minimal pairs, (12c) must be

---

[2] Thus Whiteley. More specifically, the sense is 'to marry secretly without parental consent', the typical form of illegal marriage in traditional culture, sometimes also today.

[3] In the activity referred to, the animal may be alive, e.g. when blood is drawn; it may be dead, e.g. when a butcher starts skinning it by piercing its skin; or the skin may have been removed already, in which case it may be pierced, for example, in the corners, so that it may be properly stretched and tightened, in order to be dried. Whiteley's translation 'to start skinning a beast' thus seems insufficient at best, if not inaccurate, for [koruusia] 'to remove' is generally used in combination with [riio] 'skin', plural [amao], in order to express this sense, as in [koruusia riio] 'to remove the/a skin'.

[4] Whiteley has 'be boiling'.

[5] Whiteley has 'be annoyed at something'.

[6] Since the sense here is 'not to find'. Whiteley's translation 'lack' seems insufficient.

[7] Whiteley (1960: 3) translates '[to] butt'.

[8] Whiteley has 'cry, scream, ululate'. Contrast with [korera] 'to cry, to shed tears'.

discounted, because /-βeer-/ is a mistransciption, which should be /-βεεr-/ 'to stay (at)'; the word for 'to sit (down)' is [γoikaraansa]. Next, since no tonal analysis is given in (1960), it is not clear whether or not the tones in (12) are distinctive underlyingly, though supposedly they are.

In addition to this, Whiteley presents no further minimal pair evidence. Hence the data in (12) must also be taken, in his account, to establish not only distinctive length, but the seven vowels as such. To substantiate both, supplementary, though still somewhat scanty, evidence is given in (13), where words may be contrasted at a different level of representation in different minimal pairs,

(13) /i/ and /ii/:

[γos**i**ka] 'to respect' vs.
[γos**ii**ka] 'to prepare beer (by mixing flour with water to a paste and letting it stay for three to four days)' vs.
[γos**oo**ka] 'to be shy'

[kor**i**na] 'to refuse (a request)' vs.
[kor**íí**na] 'to climb'

[γos**í**βíá] 'to wash' vs.
[γos**ii**βia] 'to make (sn) drink (by holding a vessel to his mouth)' vs.
[γos**aa**βia] 'to wash (one's hands)'

[γos**i**βa] 'to tie' vs
[γos**ii**βa] 'to take a drink of'

[γosírá] 'to get lost' vs.
[γos**ii**ra] 'to support'

/e/ and /ee/:

[kera] 'all, every' vs.
[keera] 'to the waterfall' (from [ekeera] 'waterfall', pl. [eβiera])

[γoteβa] 'to be barren' vs.
|kot**ee**βa| --> [γot**éé**βá] 'not to forget' (from /ko-ta-eβ-a/)
|kotεεβa| --> [γɔtεεβa] 'to say'

[γos**ee**mia] 'to advise' vs.
[γos**a**mia] 'to grab (by force)'

[γoti**ee**na] 'to play' vs.
[γoti**aa**na] 'to swear, to take an oath'

[korera] 'to cry, to shed tears' vs.
[koreera] 'to cry for'

|korera| --> [korera] 'to cry, to shed tears' vs.
|korεra| --> [kɔrεra] 'to rear, to raise'

[korema] 'to dig' vs.
[koreema] 'to lack, to be without'

|komera| --> [komera] 'to swallow' vs.
|komεra| --> [kɔmεra] 'to come up (from the ground)' (this word is distinct from
[kɔmεra] 'to plant (seed)', which has H on first two vowels)

|kotεεra| --> [γɔtεεra] 'to sing' vs.
|koteera| --> [γoteera] 'to be delayed, to get stuck'

/ε/ and /εε/:

[kɔmεnia] 'to twinkle' vs.
[kɔmεεnia] 'to make (someone) lick'

[γɔtεma] 'to hit' vs.
[γɔtεεma] 'to try'

|kotεma| --> [γɔtεma] 'to hit' vs.
|kotama| --> [γotama] 'to run away'

|kotεεma| --> [γɔtεεma] 'to try' vs.
|kotaama| --> [γotaama] 'not to grow'
(from /ko-ta-am-a/)

[kɔγεsa] 'to harvest' vs.
[kɔγεεsa] 'to add, to stay awake'[9]

[kɔrεra] 'to rear' vs.
[kɔrεεra] 'to be thin on account of' (from applicative verb /ko-rε-er-a/; compare [kɔrεa] 'to be thin')

|komεra| --> [kɔmεra] 'to come up (from the ground)' vs.
|komera| --> [komera] 'to swallow'

---

[9] In the latter sense, the verb is probably a lexical take-over from Swahili kukesha 'to keep watch, to stay awake', for [koñoorwa] 'to be late' was judged by at least one informant to be original Gusii.

¦kosɛka¦ --> [γɔsɛka] 'to laugh' vs.
¦kosɛɛka¦ --> [γɔsɛɛka] 'to stalk (e.g. game) vs.
¦kos**i**ka¦ --> [γosika] 'to respect'

¦komɛña¦ --> [kɔmɛña] 'to live' vs.
¦kom**a**ña¦ --> [komaña] 'to know'

¦koɛɛγa¦ --> [kɔɛɛγa] 'to seduce' vs.
¦ko**ee**γa¦ --> [koeeγa] 'to practice'

/a/ and /aa/:

[koβ**a**sa] 'to marry illegally (s-ref: girl)' vs.
[koβ**aa**sa] 'to pierce'

¦kom**a**ña¦ --> [komaña] 'to know' vs.
¦komɛña¦ --> [kɔmɛña] 'to live'

[γos**a**βia] 'to make (sn) pray' vs.
[γos**áá**βia] 'to assist sn in washing his hands by pouring water' vs.
[γos**ii**βia] 'to make (sn) drink (by holding a vessel to his mouth)'

[γotama] 'to run away' vs.
[γotaama] 'not to grow' (from /ko-ta-am-a/)

[koβ**a**ka] 'to go stale' vs.
[koβ**aa**ka] 'to name, to nickname'

[koβ**a**ra] 'to shine (v.i., s-ref: sun) vs.
[koβ**aa**ra] 'to operate (medically)'

/ɔ/ and /ɔɔ/:

[γɔkɔna] 'to bewitch' vs.
[γɔkɔɔna] 'to dislike, to have no interest'

¦kotɔra¦ --> [γɔtɔra] 'to pluck (esp. leaves of some cash-crop)' vs.
¦kot**oo**ra¦ --> [γotoora] 'to take off (from someone's head)'

¦koγɔɔka¦ --> [kɔγɔɔka] 'to be glad' vs.
¦koγ**oo**ka¦ --> [koγooka] 'to come out (s-ref: milk teeth)'

¦kosona¦ --> [γosona] 'to sew, to stitch' vs.
¦kosɔɔna¦ --> [γɔsɔɔna] 'to lust, to have sexual desire'

¦kos**ɔɔ**ka¦ --> [ɣɔs**ɔɔ**ka] 'to be married (s-ref: girl), to go out (for a short period of time, i.e. out of the house)' vs.
¦kos**oo**ka¦ --> [ɣos**óó**ka] 'to be shy'

/o/ and /oo/:

[koβ**o**ra] 'to miss, not to find' vs.
[koβ**oo**ra] 'to say'

¦kok**oo**ra¦ --> [ɣokoora] 'to finish' vs.
¦kok**ɔ**ra¦ --> [ɣɔk**ɔ**ra] 'to do'

[ɣos**óó**ka] 'to be shy' vs.
[ɣos**ii**ka] 'to prepare (beer)'

¦kot**o**ma¦ --> [ɣot**o**ma] 'to send' vs.
¦kot**oo**ma¦ --> [ɣot**oo**ma] 'not to dry' (from /ko-ta-om-a/) vs.
¦kot**uu**ma¦ --> [ɣot**uu**ma] 'to jump up and down' vs.
¦kot**ɔɔ**ma¦ --> [ɣɔt**ɔɔ**ma] 'not to smear' (from /ko-ta-ɔm-a/)

¦koɣ**oo**ka¦ --> [koɣooka] 'to come out (s-ref: milk teeth)' vs.
¦koɣ**ɔɔ**ka¦ --> [kɔɣ**ɔɔ**ka] 'to be glad'

¦kos**oo**ka¦ --> [ɣos**óó**ka] 'to be shy' vs.
¦kos**ɔɔ**ka¦ --> [ɣɔs**ɔɔ**ka] 'to be married (s-ref: girl), to go out (for a short period of time, i.e. out of the house)'

/u/ and /uu/:

[ɣok**u**ra] 'to scratch, to rake (usual s-ref: hens; o-ref: soil)' vs.
[ɣok**uu**ra] 'to cry (for help), to shout, to scream'

[koβ**u**na] 'to break (v.t.)' vs.
[koβ**i**na] 'to be in labour'

[koβ**u**ca] 'to be plenty' vs.
[koβ**uu**ca] 'to fetch (by scooping, i.e. liquid), to haul up (water)'

[ɣot**uu**ma] 'to jump up and down' vs.
[ɣot**oo**ma] 'not to dry' (from /ko-ta-om-a/)

Though tone (not recorded in most of these examples) is distinct in the members of some word pairs, so that these might be thought not to be strictly minimal, tonal differences are neutralised in at least some of the tenses. Therefore such tenses do provide strictly minimal pairs. Contrast, for example, the infinitival tone patterns of [korina] 'to refuse (a request)' and [koríína] 'to climb' with the forms of their third person plural of the perfective tense, [βaaríníre] and [βaarííníre], where the tonal difference is neutralised.

Similarly, contrast [γosááβia] 'to assist (someone) in washing hands by pouring water' and [γosiiβia] 'to make (someone) drink (by holding a vessel to his mouth)' with [βaasííβirie] and [βaasááβirie]; and again, contrast [γosóóka] 'to be shy' and [γɔsɔɔka] 'to be married, to go out (for a short while)' with [βaasóókire] with [βaasɔɔkire] (where ɔɔ = H).[10]

Anticipating more detailed discussion, it may be observed here that the Gusii infinitive marker, or Bantu class prefix 15, underlyingly postulated as /ko-/, exhibits considerable surface variation due to the cooperation of several rules, specifically Consonantal Voicing Dissimilation (59) (see section 2.3.1) and Mid Vowel Height Spreading (136) (see section 2.3.14), but also other rules. Consonantal Voicing Dissimilation (59) regularly turns /k/ into |γ| under certain conditions, as in /**k**o-sik-a/ --> [γosika] 'to respect'. Mid Vowel Height Spreading (136) regularly lowers upper mid vowels to lower mid, under certain conditions, as in /k**o**-γɛs-a/ --> [kɔγɛsa] 'to harvest'. Both rules have applied in [**γɔ**tɛma] 'to hit', from /**ko**-tɛm-a/. Upper Mid Vowel Raising (108) and Complex Segment Formation (109) may also cooperate to cause surface variation of this and other prefixes (see sections 2.3.10 and 2.3.11).

Whiteley (1960: 3) makes the following observations on combinations or sequences of vowels in Gusii words. First, identical long vowels may succeed each other, and whenever they do, the transition from the one to the other is phonetically marked by a slight pause. In what he would probably have termed surface representations, he indicates this through a period between the vowels concerned, as in (14),

(14) /a-raa-aak-u-e/
3s-t-beat-p-fv
[araa.aakwe]
'he will be beaten (near future)'

However, this surface representation presumably characterises deliberate pronunciation, because it may be, and usually is, shortened to [araaakwe]. In any case, the distinction between [aaaa] and [aaa] is often faintly perceptible phonetically, if at all, especially so in rapid speech.

Second, the same observation is said to hold for any sequence of an identical short and a long vowel, as in [ɛkɛ.ɛɛra] 'a half'. Once again, however, though such distinctions may be motivated morphologically, phonetically the length in such cases is often almost indeterminate. Most sequences of identical vowels, whether long or short, tend to be trimmed down to [VV], though sometimes a slight difference between [VV] and [VVV] may indeed be perceived.

Third, from Whiteley's examples (1960: passim) it may be inferred that successive

---

[10] On the other hand, some infinitival minimal pairs, such as [γɔtɛma] 'to hit' and [γɔtɛɛma] 'to try', may no longer be strictly minimal in certain tenses, e.g. [βaatɛmíre] (ɛ = H) [βaatɛɛmire] (ɛɛ = H). However, since my notes on these forms contain no translation, distinct tenses may be involved here.

identical short vowel symbols are to be interpreted sometimes as one long vowel, sometimes as two short ones. However, without a previous knowledge of the language, this is not immediately clear to the reader, since Whiteley does not differentiate phonological and phonetic transcriptions in his work, nor does he offer transcriptions that make morphological parsing of words explicit.

Fourth, sequences of more than two, and at least three, distinct vowels are said to occur commonly, so that at least one of them may be long. Some examples are given in (15),

(15) a. /n-ci-a-et-a/
f-9they-t-p-fv
[ñciaeta] or [ñcyaeta]
'they passed (today)'

b. /o-ko-ee-ɔrɔk-er-er-i-a/
a-15-rf-show-ap-ap-c-fv
[ɔkɔεεɔrɔkεrεria]
'showing to oneself'

c. /e-βi-a-o/
a-px8-of-sx
[eβiaao]
'8-your (ones), (they are) 8-yours'

d. /a-βa-Nto βa-a-o/
a-2-person 2-of-sx (pron. poss.)
[aβaanto βaao]
'your people'

e. /e-βi-a-ɔ/
a-px8-of-different
--> [eβiaaɔ]
'(they are) 8-different (ones)'

f. /a-βa-Nto a-βa-a-ɔ/
a-2-person 2-of-different
[aβaanto aβaaɔ][11]
'different people'

However, the distinction between underlyingly long vowels, such /ee/ in (15b), and morphologically derived long vowels, such as a + a > [aa] in (15f), or phonologically derived long vowels, as in (15e), is not brought out clearly in Whiteley's work. These cannot be distinguished on the basis of the surface alone, without the necessary morphological and phonological analysis.

---

[11] *[aβaanto βaaɔ].

Several examples may serve to further illustrate this point. Thus, anticipating the discussion of certain rules, in (16),

(16) /βa-a-om-ir-e/
3p-t-dry-pf-fv
[βoomíre]
'they have just become dry'

tense-marker /a/ is delinked and root vowel /o/ spread to the left, resulting in |oom|. Then /a/ of the subject-marker is delinked, and the now long following |oo| is spread leftward, becoming overly long |ooo|. This is trimmed down again by x-Trimming (94). These rules cooperate to derive the long surface vowel in (16). That the underlying representation is indeed the one given, rather than /βa-om-ir-e/, whose surface would also be [βoomire] in virtue of /a/-Delinking (147) and compensatory lengthening of the following /o/, may be verified by comparing the same tense involving another verb, in (17),

(17) /βa-a-rem-ir-e/
3p-t-dig-pf-fv
[βaarémire]
'they have just dug'

Here, the surface output is not *[βaremire], which would have resulted, had the underlying input been /βa-rem-ir-e/.

In the next example (18), which also illustrates vowel length,

(18) /to-a-om-ir-e/
1p-t-dry-pf-fv
[twoomíre]
'we have just become dry'

tense-marker /a/ is again delinked, and root vowel /o/ spread leftward, resulting in |oom|. Upper Mid Vowel Raising (108) then raises the /o/ of the subject-marker to |u|. Complex Segment Formation (109) turns it into |w|, triggering compensatorily lengthening of |oo| to |ooo|, which is trimmed down again to |oo| by x-Trimming (94). The long surface [oo] in (18) is thus derived through cooperation of rules that are partly different from those operative in the derivation of (16-17).

Finally, in (19),

(19) /βa-a-ɔm-ir-e/
3p-t-smear-pf-fv
[βaaɔmíre] (ɔ = H)
'they have just smeared'

no phonological rules are applicable, and the long surface [aa] simply results from juxtaposition of the /a/'s of the subject-marker and the tense-marker, in the course of the derivation, due to the morphological process of prefixation. The fact that [βɔɔmíre] (second ɔ = H) is equally acceptable, suggests that delinking of /a/, which triggers spreading of the next vowel, is optional (see section 2.3.15).[12]

To generalise tentatively, given data such as (15-19), it would seem that, unless certain length-changing rules apply, the underlying length of contiguous vowels is usually retained, so that sequences of short-short, short-long, long-short, and long-long vowels tend to remain unchanged. Because, as mentioned earlier, underlying, intermediate, and surface representations are usually not distinguished by Whiteley, it is impossible to determine the origin and the nature of the length of vowels in many of his examples, unless one is already sufficiently acquainted with Gusii to understand the applicable processes. Therefore, many of his transcriptions involving vowels or vowel sequences require explanation. Though some of this is indeed summarily supplied (1960: 2-4), the present study aims to supplement it.

A fifth remark, finally, is that some of the Gusii vowels appear to have allophones, not indicated in inventory (2). Whiteley (1960: 4) states that "where the stem or radical [root] vowel is /a, u, i/, the vowels of the prefix tend to be realised as neither 'close' nor 'open' but rather intermediate. These variants are, however, in complementary distribution with those cited, are not significant in stems or in radicals, and consequently are not distinguished orthographically (..)". In Bantu linguistics, the term 'stem' is usually defined as the part of any word that follows the prefix domain; that is, the root plus all and any suffixes, including the final vowel. The term 'base' commonly refers to that part of any word that follows the prefix domain, excluding the final vowel or, in some studies, the final syllable. These domains have been differentiated usually for suprasegmental reasons. Whiteley may not have held to the same definitions of these terms, but in any case, the context of the immediately preceding paragraph (1960: 3-4) makes it clear that the phrase "the vowels of the prefix" in the first sentence of this quotation refers to the upper mid vowels /e/ or /o/ of class prefixes 1, 3, 4, 7, 9, 11, 14, or 15. These are involved in mid vowel height spreading.

Unfortunately, Whiteley does not define this additional allophonic variation other than in the quote just given. Nor does he symbolise or exemplify the quality of these allophones. Therefore, on the face of it, his statement is indeterminate. However, the statement just quoted seems to mean that upper mid vowels regularly surface, first, as upper mid, whenever the vowel in the immediately following syllable (i.e. of the root or the stem) is upper mid; second, as lower mid, whenever the vowel in the immediately following syllable of the root or the stem is lower mid; and third, as a vowel in between upper and

[12] Acceptable alternatives for the second person plural are [twa(a)ɔmíre] and [twɔɔmíre] 'we have just smeared' (in each form, root vowel ɔ = H). Also compare the alternatives for another tense, [ńtwá(á)ɔmá] and [ńtwɔɔmá] (each ɔ = H) 'we smeared (earlier today)'. However, for yet another tense, at least one informant gave the judgment [ńtwá(á)ɔmɛtɛ], ?[ńtwɔɔmɛtɛ] (first ɔ = H) 'we smeared (long ago)'. For [ńtwá(á)ɔma] 'we have smeared (recently)', I have recorded no alternative, but this may be due to a lack of systematicness. These data suggest that variation involving the optionality of /a/-Delinking may be due to idiolectal differences or to morphological factors.

lower mid, whenever the vowel in the immediately following syllable of the root or the stem is non-mid, i.e. /i/, /u/, or /a/. For further discussion see section 2.3.14.

2.1.2. Consonants, nasals, and glides.

Turning now to other phonological units of the language, consider Whiteley's inventory of Gusii consonants and glides (1960: 4), repeated in (20),

(20)	Bilababial	Alveolar	Alveolo-Palatal	Velar
VOICELESS:				
Stops	(p)	t		k
Affricates			c	
Fricatives		s		
VOICED:				
Fricatives	b			g
Rolled		r		
Nasal	m	n	ny	ŋ
Semi-vowel	w		y(j)	

The following salient points are in order. First, a comment made by Whiteley himself may be quoted: "'p' occurs in one or two ideophones only, but is increasingly noticeable in the speech of the younger generation who have had contact with Swahili and English" (1960: 4). Unfortunately, the two ideophones are not given. As to the sociolinguistic point about generational speech differences, it is not clear whether these are viewed as systematic or occasional. This will be discussed in a moment.

Second, <c> designates the voiceless alveolo-palatal affricate /cç/.

Third, <b> and <g> are classified as voiced bilabial and velar fricatives, respectively, and thus designate continuant /ß/ and /ɣ/.

Fourth, in most transcriptions <r> usually signifies a rolled alveolar, as in (20), but Whiteley (1956: 4) characterises it as follows, "The 'r' sound is usually that of Swahili, a single tap of the tongue against the teeth ridge. In many contexts, however, it has an 'l'-quality and in yet others a 'd'-quality." This seems to be a somewhat roundabout way of saying that the unit in question is a flapped /r/ (usually, but not in the present study, represented as / /). At least, this is what the present research has established, though it has not corroborated the reported variation with [l], except perhaps in certain lexical take-overs. If this type of phonetic variation occurs at all, perhaps in some idiolects, I have not come across it. However, whenever flapped alveolar /r/ is prenasalised, its allomorph is always [d] in the resulting complex segment [nd], as is observed also by Whiteley (1960: 5). In other words, flapped [r] and [d] are in complementary distribution.

Generally and comparatively, the alveolar liquid tends to be realised as flapped /r/ or as

/l/ in most east African Bantu languages. In some languages, Swahili for example, both /r/ and /l/ occur. A flapped /r/ is found in most East Nyanza Bantu languages. For example, the Nata alveolar liquid is a flapped /r/ (this identification is not based on Mekacha 1985: 17, who gives no phonetic characterisation of this sound, but on an examination of taped Nata data in Prof. F. Rottland's collection, mentioned in the cited references). In Kuria, flapped /r/ may be postulated underlyingly, though rolled [r] also occurs as a derived segment (see Cammenga 1994: 14, 82-90).

Occasionally, a succession of two flapped r's intervened by a mid vowel is realised phonetically as a rolled [r] in rapid Gusii speech. However, this phenomenon appears to be neither as frequent, nor as systematic, as in the Kuria case just mentioned. To account for it, a rule optionally deleting any vowel occurring between two flapped r's could be formulated, to which conditions could be added, if not just any vowel may function as a target, or if the rule is prohibited in some contexts. The resulting succession of flapped r's may then be interpreted phonetically as a rolled [r] (in everyday spelling they may be written <rr>). However, since the process seems to occur relatively infrequently, I consider the point sufficiently dealt with here and do not formulate such a rule.

Fifth, <ny> in inventory (20) designates alveolo-palatal nasal /ñ/. Whiteley's orthography will not be adopted in this case.

Sixth, his inclusion of bilabial semi-vowel <w> presumably means that, had he worked within a nonlinear framework, he would have postulated this sound as occurring underlyingly, that is, as /w/. A similar observation presumably applies to alveolo-palatal semi-vowel /y/. I will return to this.

Seventh, Whiteley writes that "the j of nj may be regarded as a unique variant of y in the context 'n -- y'. The cluster occurs only initially, and expecially as Cl[ass] 4 or 9 prefix, e.g. njaaca 'it came'" (1960: 5). However, this statement is correct only in part. In fact, <nj> strictly derives from the underlying combinations of /n + e-/ or /n + ye-/, where the nasal representes the focus element, /e-/ subject marker 4 or 9, and /ye-/ object marker 4 or 9. Other details of this complex surface segment will be considered in section 2.1.3.

Finally, Whiteley does not substantiate his statements on consonants with the necessary minimal pair evidence.

Taking into account the preceding considerations, the present research warrants a reanalysis of Whiteley's inventory (20), as in (21),

(21)	Bilababial	Alveolar	(Alveolo-) Palatal	Velar
Continuant	/β/ 	 /s/		/γ/
(Flapped Liquid)		/r/		
Obstruent	[b]	/t/ [d]		/k/ [g]
Affricate				/c/ [dž]
Nasal	/m/	/n/	/ñ/	/η/
Glide	[w] [Cw]		/y/ [Cy]	

A specified feature matrix of the Gusii vowels in (7) and the consonants in (21) may be given, as in (22),

(22)	i	e	ε	a	ɔ	o	u	β	γ	[d]	c	ž	s	t	k	m	n	ñ	η	r	w	y
cons	-	-	-	-	-	-	-	+	+	+	+	+	+	+	+	+	+	+	+	+	-	-
syll	+	+	+	+	+	+	+	-	-	-	-	-	-	-	-	-	-	-	-	-	-	-
son	+	+	+	+	+	+	+	-	-	-	-	-	-	-	-	+	+	+	+	+	+	+
high	+	+	-	-	-	+	+	-	+	-	+	+	-	-	+	-	-	+	+	-	+	+
mid	-	+	+	-	+	+	-	+	-	+	-	-	+	+	-	+	+	-	-	+	-	-
back	-	-	-	+	+	+	+	-	+	-	-	-	-	-	+	-	-	-	+	-	+	-
voice	+	+	+	+	+	+	+	+	+	+	-	+	-	-	-	+	+	+	+	+	+	+
nasal	-	-	-	-	-	-	-	-	-	-	-	-	-	-	-	+	+	+	+	-	-	-
cont	+	+	+	+	+	+	+	+	+	-	+	+	+	-	-	-	-	-	-	+	+	+
ant	v	v	v	v	v	v	v	+	-	+	-	-	+	+	-	+	+	-	-	+	+	+
cor	v	v	v	v	v	v	v	-	-	+	-	-	+	+	-	-	+	+	-	+	-	+

where c and ž have been characterised as [-cor], allowing for the possibility that in some idiolects, if not regiolects, they may be [+cor], and where [ž], as a general replacement for [c], is specific to South Mugirango.

A few general and specific observations are in order with respect to the sounds arranged in figure (21). Generally, all of them are produced with egressive air. Whenever there is a distinction between voiced and voiceless for the same place and manner of articulation, the voiceless sound has been placed in the top row, the voiced sound in the bottom row. Strictly phonological units have been enclosed in slashes, derived sounds in phonetic brackets, as elsewhere. Finally, as before, the phonetic significance of the symbols is as defined in recent versions of the International Phonetic Alphabet, unless stated otherwise.

First, since, in contrast with Whiteley's analysis (20), [p] is here interpreted as a borrowed sound, it is excluded from inventory (21). It seems incorrect to consider it as a strictly sociolectal allophone of /β/ differentiating the younger and the older generation. Rather, it is argued here that [p] may be considered more adequately as a relatively restricted variant of /β/, since it occurs exclusively in words taken over from other languages. This is implied also by Whiteley's remark quoted earlier.

Adoption of such words tends to cause their adaptation, in the course of time, to the (phonological, morphological, syllabic, etc.) system of the adopting language. Such adaptation may take place rather quickly in the case of some words, or less quickly in the case of others. This tends to result in a certain amount of surface variation in lexical take-overs, which may thus be viewed, to some extent, as a phonologically relevant lexical subset.

Such phonological adaptation and variation appear to be relatively common in modern Gusii. Apparently, [paapa] is the only form for 'Pope', presumably derived from Church Latin **papa**. With this sense, [βaaβa] is unacceptable. In contrast, *[peendeensia] does not seem to be an acceptable alternative for [βeendeensia], also [βeendeesia], 'penitence', presumably derived from Church Latin **penitentia**. Therefore, this word seems to have adapted more progressively to the Gusii system in the respect under consideration, though it is still irregular in that it does not take a class prefix. Examples such as these suggest that variation in the pronunciation of a lexical take-over is not necessarily associated exclusively with one generation or the other, but rather with the lexical items concerned. Other examples of surface variation will be given in section 3.5.2.

To conclude this point, Whiteley's observation on [p], quoted previously, was made some forty years ago, and it may just be possible that the language has changed in this respect. It would certainly be interesting to find out, through extensive lexicographical research, what might be deduced from a broader lexical data-base, both with regard to surface variation in lexical take-overs generally, and in those involving [p] particularly. With respect to the latter, it is probably more correct to assume that the variation noted by Whiteley was due to causes similar to those operative today, but because he does not elaborate his statement, this assumption must remain a matter of conjecture. The influence of English and Swahili on Gusii, which he states, is nonetheless still in full force. It does not merely affect the pronunciation of certain words, but has changed the lexicon as a whole to a considerable extent and is still doing so.

Second, though /t/ is characterised as an alveolar in (21), it may be rendered as a voiceless interdental obstruent, possibly also as an alveolo-dental or perhaps dental-alveolar obstruent. To establish its exact regiolectal or sociolectal phonetic variation throughout Gusiiland, would require further systematic phonetic research. In section 1.5, a difference in this respect was already noted between South Mugirango and other varieties of Gusii. Several informants maintained that the alveolo-dental or dental-alveolar variety is the 'true' or 'original' Gusii, and that the alveolar variety is a recent innovation due to the influence of Swahili or English. They observed that the interdental variety is still heard relatively more often in the speech of the older generation. Though I have not been able to check this observation systematically, it is not unlikely. The resolution of this phonetic point, and of the question whether it involves the history of the language or merely the current dialectal or idiolectal situation, is left to future areal research.

Third, /c/ represents a voiceless palatal or, probably more often, alveolo-palatal, affricate (elsewhere, but not in the present study, usually represented as /cç/). Apparently, there is some idiolectal variation involving this phonological unit's place of articulation. Some speakers tend toward an alveolo-palatal articulation, others toward a palatal variety.

Moreover, as pointed out in section 1.5, the affricate unit in South Mugirango is regularly pronounced as voiced [dž], so that, for example, proper names, such as Mochooge, Machogu, Machɔɔgɛ, are rendered [modžooγe], [madžoγu], [madžɔɔγɛ], rather than [macooγe], etc. However, the exact nature of this variation, its geographical spread, and its pervasiveness per dialect are not yet clear. Future lexicographical and dialectal research may therefore wish to clarify the limits of this variation, especially since this unit may arguably turn out to be relevant comparatively.

Also previously mentioned in section 1.5, is the fact that the voiced alveolo-palatal affricate [dž], in as far as it occurs in dialects other than South Mugirango, is a uniquely derived allomorphic complex surface segment that only occurs as a prenasal, i.e. [ndž]. In restricted contexts it involves the focus element, /n-/, and subject or object marker 4,9, /e-/ and /ye-/.

Thus, for example, the affricate in neighbouring and related Kuria also involves dialectal variation (see Cammenga 1994: 140, note 3). Both in the Nyabaasi dialect of Kuria and the Bassi dialect of Gusii, which some speakers say are related historically, this sound is an alveolo-palatal affricate. In other varieties of Kuria, the manner of articulation of this phonological unit tends to vary between affricate and continuant pronunciation, and its place of articulation between alveolar, palato-alveolar, alveolo-palatal, and palatal, pronunciation; but no Kuria dialect has more than one sound corresponding to this unit in its phonological system.

Given such differences and similarities between related languages, the affricate may reasonably be expected to have a useful function in any comparative research on at least East Nyanza Bantu languages (involving at least Suba, Gusii, Kuria, Ngoreme, Zita, Kwaya, and Nata) that would be designed to sort out what appears to be a dialectally complex situation and to determine more exactly what are the relationships between these languages. Eventually, such a study may also have practical applications for spellings to be developed or refined. As in Whiteley's work, this phonological unit will be represented hereafter as /c/.

Fourth, allophony involves the voiced continuant segments, viz. bilabial /β/, flapped alveolar liquid /r/, and velar /γ/, occurs, whenever these are prenasalised. Their allophones are [b], [d], and [g] respectively. This variation is discussed in section 2.3.4.

Fifth, /ñ/ represents a palatal or alveolo-palatal nasal (elsewhere, but not in the present study, commonly represented as /ɲ/). There is some degree of phonetic variation in the production of this sound, depending on its context. At least immediately after /i/, its pronunciation tends to be more palatal. Idiolectal differences may occur also, but this requires further research.

Sixth, it may be noted that the high back and front glides, [w] and [y], in the complex segments [Cw] and [Cy], often retain much of the phonetic quality of the high vowels from which they are considered to be derived, viz. /u/ and /i/. Sometimes, however, their pronounciation is very slight or almost imperceptible, especially in [βw] and [ɣw]. Their actual phonetic quality may depend somewhat on the rate and deliberateness of speech.

Further, with respect to the status of these front and back glides, the question is whether or not there are necessary and sufficient reasons for postulating them underlyingly, i.e. as /y/ and /w/. If there are no such reasons, these segments could be considered as derived from underlying high vowels, viz. [y] from /i/ and [w] from /u/. Whiteley (1960: 4-5, 1956: 3-5), as observed, does not distinguish between different levels of representation and, perhaps therefore, does not address this question.

It must be raised nonetheless, at least with respect to the back glide, in view of the following facts. First, on the surface, [w] never seems to occur intervocalically, but only as part of a complex segment, [Cw], called "'w' clusters" by Whiteley (1960: 5). Second, whenever the segment occurs word-initially, it is arguably derived from underlying /o/ or /u/. These facts seem to provide arguments for considering the Gusii back glide strictly as a derived segment.

The case for [y] as a derived segment could be argued by analogy. However, this is not the strongest kind of argument. It is further weakened by the fact that minimal pair evidence supporting the postulation of /y/ as underlyingly present may in fact be adduced, as in (23) below.

Finally, as to the status of complex segments of the type [Cy] and [Cw], an occasional word pair may be found that might suggest, at first sight, that at least some such segments may be established underlyingly; for example, [ɣotwaaŋga] 'to pound, to beat (sth) to pieces', versus [ɣotaaŋga] 'to prevent'. However, a strong argument for considering both [Cy] and [Cw] as derived types of segment, is that vowels following these segments consistently surface as long. This fact may be accounted for by assuming, first, that [Cy] and [Cw] are in fact derived through complex segment formation and, second, that the following vowels are subsequently lengthened compensatorily (also see section 2.3.11).

To summarise, bearing in mind the preceding observations, inventory (21) states that the Gusii phonological system contains at least twelve segments underlyingly, viz. eleven consonants, including an affricate and four nasals, and one front glide.[13] This inventory further indicates that back glide [w] is interpreted, provisionally and asymmetrically, as a derived segment. It also makes clear that complex segments of the type [Cy] and [Cw] are also considered as derived. Though, on the ground of symmetry with respect to the back glide and these complex segments, it might be argued that the front glide is derived from underlying /i/, this would entail ad hoc lexical specification of at least the items in (23),

[13] In contrast, the Kuria consonant inventory includes, in addition, laryngeal /h/. Otherwise, it has the same number of segments as Gusii, though the phonetic details of some of these appear to be slightly different (for discussion see Cammenga 1994: 14 ff, and 140, note 3).

(23) a.
σ
|
/-ii-/

[koiya] 'to dig up, to uproot (in harvesting)'
*[koyia]
(compare [koiywa] 'to be uprooted')

b.
? σ
|
/-ii-/

[koyia] 'to boil (v.i.)', *[koiya]
(contrast [amaace ɳkoiya are] 'the water is boiling'
also contrast the derivative under c)

c.
? σ
|
/-ii-ek-/

[koiyeka] 'to boil, to cook (v.t.)'
*[koyieka] (this is what one would expect in virtue of the underlying representation in b and Glide Formation (109))
e.g. [ɳkoiyeka nde eßiaasi] 'I'm cooking potatoes'

d.
x
|
/-ɳai-/

[koɳaaya] 'to shelter'

To begin with the least problematic form, (23d) may arguably be accounted for as a case of gliding, which takes place after suffixation. However, because even root- or stem-final /i/ may remain unaffected by Glide Formation (114), probably often to preserve morphological identity, gliding cannot be assumed to apply generally in this position. Perhaps even in this example the root-final /i/ must be lexically specified. This would seem to be even more plausible in the case of (23a), in order to prevent [yi] from surfacing.[14] The root for 'to boil (v.i.)' is more problematic, since the position of the surface glide may shift, as shown in (23b-c).

In the language as a whole, these examples seem to be both rare and exceptional. Alternatively, therefore, it is suggested that glides may be postulated underlyingly. Thus instead of the representations in (23a-c), for example, we would get /-iy-/ for (23a) and /-yi-/ for (23b). But given the data, it would still have to be added that in derived forms the allomorph of the latter will be [-iy-]. I leave possible further refinement of this point to

[14] Unfortunately, I have no sentences exemplifying this verb.

future research.

Some evidence substantiating the segmental distinctions made in inventory (21) is given, with distinctive units printed in bold-face, in (24),

(24) /t/: [koßa**t**a] 'to press' vs. [koßaγa] 'to divide'

[koŋaa**t**a] 'to starve' vs.
[koŋaaca] 'to talk ill (or untruthfully) of'

/k/: [koßa**k**a] 'to go stale' vs. [koßata], [koßaγa]

[γosi**k**a] 'to respect' vs. [γosira] 'to get lost'

[γo**k**ira] 'to be quiet' vs. [γosira] 'to get lost'

/c/: [koßa**c**a] 'to evade, to dodge' vs. [koßa**k**a], [koßa**t**a], [koßa**γ**a]
(compare the evidence for /t/ and /k/)

/ß/: [ko**ß**aca] 'to evade', etc. vs.
[koγaca] 'to keep (sth somewhere)'

[ko**ß**ana] 'to prophesy, to foretell' vs.
[koγana] 'to tell a story'

[ko**ß**aaca] 'to hew' vs.
[ko**ŋ**aaca] 'to talk ill (or untruthfully) of'

/γ/: [ko**γ**aca] vs. [ko**ß**aca] (compare the evidence for /ß/)

[koi**γ**ora] 'to open (v.t.)' vs.
[koi**ß**ora] 'to give birth'

[γɔtɛ**γ**a] 'to trap' vs.
[γɔtɛ**k**a] 'to tackle' (e.g. in football)

/s/: [koßa**s**a] 'to be married illegally (s-ref: girl)' vs.
[koßa**t**a], [koßa**γ**a], [koßa**c**a] (compare /t/ etc.)

[γo**s**ira] 'to get lost' vs. [γo**k**ira] 'to be quiet'

/r/: [koßa**r**a] 'to shine (v.i., s-ref: sun), to count' vs.
[koßa**s**a], [koßa**c**a]

[koßoo**r**a] 'to say' vs.
[koßoo**k**a] 'to awake' (from Whiteley 1956: 121)

[koruusia] 'to take (sth) from' vs.
[koβuusia] 'to burrow'

/m/: [korema] 'to cultivate, to hoe' vs.
[korera] 'to cry' (from Whiteley 1965: 123)

[koraama] 'to abuse' vs.
[koraara] 'to sleep'

[γotama] 'to run away' vs.
[γotaβa] 'not to be', from /ko-ta-β-a/

/n/: [koγana] 'to tell (a story)' vs. [koγaña] 'to wait'

[koβina] 'to be in labour' vs. [koβisa] 'to hide'

/ñ/: [koγaña] 'to wait' vs.
[koγana] 'to tell (story)'

[koηaaña] 'to migrate, to change location' vs.
[koηaaya] 'to shelter, to hide behind a shield'

[γɔkɔɔña] 'to help' vs. [γɔkɔɔβa] 'to escort'

[kɔɔηa] 'to give me' (from /ko-V-n-a/, where root-vowel V is underspecified [-high, +mid]) vs.
[kɔɔña] 'help!' (from imperative /kɔɔñ-a/)

/η/: [koηaata] 'to starve' vs. [koβata] 'to press'

[amaηana] 'words' vs. [amaγana] 'hundreds'

[koηaaca] 'to talk ill (or untruthfully) of' vs.
[koβaaca] 'to hew'

/w/: no minimal pair evidence found as yet

/y/: [koiya] 'to dig up' vs.
[koira] 'to take (sth somewhere)'

[koyia] 'to boil(v.i.)' vs. [koria] 'to eat'

[koiyeka] 'to boil, to cook (v.t.)' vs.
[koiγeka] 'to install'

[koηaaya] vs. [koηaaña] 'to change location'

Some of these individual items have been taken from Whiteley's work, but double-checked for the present study. Because tonal differences between members of some pairs are neutralised in certain tenses, the latter provide strictly minimal pairs.

The following conversion table (25) shows how the symbols used to designate the consonants in (21), and in the present study generally, correspond to the spelling currently used by many Gusii people,

(25)

this study	current spelling
[d]	<d>
[dž]	
/β/	<b>
[b]	<b>
/c/	<ch>
/γ/	<g>
[g]	<g>
/k/	<k>
/m/	<m>
/n/	<n>
/ñ/	<ny>
/η/	<ng'>
/r/	<r>
/s/	<s>
/t/	<t>
[w]	<w>
/y/	<y>

Specifically, it indicates that representational differences involve β, c, γ, ñ, and η. The representations of allophones [b], [d], and [g], and of the other symbols t, k, m, n, r, s, w, and y are identical.

Finally, since I have seen no samples of writing containing [dž], I do not know how this segment is usually spelled. In South Mugirango, where it occurs regularly, it may simply be written <ch>, as it will be interpreted automatically as [dž] by speakers. To foreigners, this will have to be explained. If it must be distinguished in this dialect, <z>, <dz>, or <j> might be adopted. If prenasalised, <n> could be attached.

In the other varieties of Gusii, in which prenasal [ndž] seems to occur merely as a unique allomorph, it could be written <nc>; or if a distinction must be made, as <nz>. However, <nc> seems adequate. (Whiteley writes <nj>; see the discussion in section 2.1.3). Whatever letter or letter-combination is used for it in these dialects, its peculiarities will have to be explained to those unfamiliar with the language.

2.1.3. Prenasals.

An inventory of Gusii prenasals, or prenasalised consonants, is given in (26),

(26) Prenasals

	Bilabial	Alveolar	(Alveolo-) Palatal	Velar
Obstruent		[nt]		[ηk]
	[mb]	[nd]		[ηg]
Continuant		[ns]	[ñc]	
				[ndž]
Nasal	[mm]	[nn]	[ññ]	[ηη]

Several remarks are in order with respect to this inventory. First, wherever there are two rows for a class distinguished by place and manner of articulation, the top row contains a prenasalised voiceless consonant and the bottom row the corresponding voiced consonant; for example, prenasalised alveolar obstruents [nt] and [nd].

Second, phonetic bracketing indicates that prenasals are considered as derived complex segments. Their derivation is discussed in section 2.3.2.

Third, as pointed out previously, [ndž] replaces [ñc] regularly in South Mugirango, but occurs as a unique allomorph for the combination n + (y)e (class 4 or 9) in other dialects. Whiteley (1956: 17, 1960: 5) mentions <nj>, but does not define its phonetic significance exactly. Assuming that he employs the phonetic notation proposed by the International Phonetic Association (1949: 10), <j> may signify either a (voiced) palatal frictionless continuant (semi-vowel) or a voiced (alveolo-)palatal fricative. The present research suggests that the second interpretation is the closest approximation, since the unit appears to be a voiced alveolo-palatal affricate. Therefore, in (26) it is represented more exactly as [ndž].

Its uniqueness suggests an historical explanation, at least as a possibility. Interestingly for verbal subject prefix 9, this suggestion seems to derive some support from the shape of the Proto-Bantu pronominal prefix for this class, reconstructed by Meeussen (1967: 97) as /dže-/ (written ji-). But a parallel argument cannot be maintained for pronominal prefix 4, which is reconstructed for Proto-Bantu as /γe-/ (1967: 97).

However, this line of argument may nonetheless suggest a solution. If, synchronically, /Ce-/ may be postulated as the underlying representation of the subject marker for class 4 and 9, where C represents an underspecified voiced alveolo-palatal or palato-alveolar consonant (compare the shape of the object marker /ye-/), then the particular surface shape of [ndž] might be accounted for, in part, by Prenasalisation (61), which would result in |nC|. The final surface segment may then be accounted for by subsequent application of Upper Mid Vowel Raising (108) to the upper mid front vowel /e/, raising it to |i|, which in turn becomes front glide |y| through Complex Segment Formation (109), thus |nCy|. This might co-account for the palatal quality of the resulting complex segment. A relatively informal rule of phonetic interpretation, such as (27),

(27) ¦nCy¦ --> [ndž] / ---]
verbal prefix 4,9

which reads, 'interpret ¦nCy¦ phonetically as [ndž]', might then be formulated to account for the exact surface details. This may be somewhat ad hoc, but then, the resulting complex surface segment is unique in the language.

Fourth, if <nj> is thus correctly interpreted as [ndž], the prenasals in (26) are identical to those mentioned by Whiteley (1960: 4-5), except for [ññ] and [ηη], which occur at least in the first person singular of certain tenses of verbs with a root respectively beginning with /ñ/ and /η/.

Fifth, the voiced prenasalised obstruents [mb], [nd], and [ηg] are considered as respectively derived from the underlying combination of a nasal plus continuant /β/, /r/ and /γ/.

Sixth, any surface combination of a nasal plus a glide, [NG], is considered here not as a prenasalised glide, but, for structural reasons, as a glided nasal (see section 2.3.11).

Seventh, and finally, word-initially the nasal element of prenasalised consonants may surface as syllabic and bear tone.

To conclude this section, the complex segments in (26) are exemplified in (28),

(28) a. prenasalised voiceless obstruents

[nt]:

/ko-mɛNt-a/	/n-to-mañ-et-e/
15-add-fv	f-we-know-t-fv
[kɔmɛɛ**nt**a]	[**nt**omañete]
'to add'	'we know (untimed fact)'

[ηk]:

/e-n-kɔrɔ/	/n-kaan-i-e/
9a-heart	me-refuse-c-fv
[ɛ**ηk**ɔrɔ]	[**ηk**aanie]
'heart'	'make me refuse'

b. prenasalised voiced continuants (which become voiced obstruents)

[mb]:

/n-βa-a-sɔɔm-et-i-e/	/e-n-βεɔ/
f-3p-t-read-pv-c-fv	9a-wind
[**mb**aasɔɔmεtie]	[ε**mb**εɔ]
'they taught (recently)'	'wind, air'

/a-ka-a-n-βuat-i-a/
sm3s-t-t-om1s-follow-c-fv
[akaambwáátia]
'and he followed me (recently)'

[nd]:

/n-rɔɔs-er-i-e/	/n-n-rɔr-e/
me-make-ap-c-fv	f-1s-see-fv
[**nd**ɔɔsεrie]	[nii**nd**ɔrε]
'make for me'	'I will see (soon)'

[ŋg]:

/ko-tuaNγ-a/	/n-γor-er-e/
15-pound-fv	me-buy-ap-fv
[γotwaa**ŋg**a]	[**ŋg**orere]
'to pound (in threshing)	'buy for me'

c. prenasalised voiceless continuants

[ns]:

/e-n-se/	/n-sɔɔm-i-e/
9a-ground	me-read-c-fv
[**ens**é][15]	[**ns**ɔɔmie]
'ground, soil'	'teach me'

[15] Contrast [énsě] 'country, continent, the earth'. Also compare [áse] 'place, area, region'.

[ñc]:

/o-mo-aNc-i/	/n-caβ-e/
a-px1-love-sx	om1s-beat-fv
[omwaa**ñci**]	[(i)**ñcá**β e][16]
'beloved, lover'	'beat me'

d. prenasalised nasals

[mm]:

/n-mo-ruγ-a/	/n-mo-mañ-et-e/
f-2p-cook-fv	f-sm2p-know-t-fv
[**mm**oruγa] or [imoruγa]	[**mm**ómáñeté][17]
'even though/if 2p-you cook'	do 2p-you know?'

/n-mañ-e/
sm1s-know-fv
[mmáñé] (initial m = H)
'that I may know'

(after 1960: 30)

[nn]:

/n-na-a-ruγ-a/	/n-naar-i-a/
f-1s-t-cook-fv	me-accustom-c-fv
[**ńn**áárúγá]	[**nn**aaria]
'I have cooked (earlier today)'	'make me used to'

[16] Contrast with [**ñc**aβe] (ñ and vowels = H) 'I will beat' (hodiernal or near future). The final vowel of these forms is possibly [ε], which would suggest that /a/ may trigger mid vowel height spreading.

[17] An acceptable alternative pronunciation is [ímómáñeté]. In [mmoruγa] and [mmómáñeté], initial /m/ = H, and /a/ in the latter is extra H. Contrast these with /mo-ruγ-a/ --> [moruγa] '2p-you-cook' and /mo-mañ-et-e/ --> [momañete] '2p-you know'.

[ññ]:

/n-ñaar-i-e/	/n-ñɔɔr-e/
me-be able-c-fv	me-find-fv
[ññaarie]	**[ññ**ɔɔrɛ]
'enable me'[18]	'find me'

[ηη]:

/n-ηain-e/
me-cheat-fv
[**ηη**aine]
'cheat me'

e. unique complex surface segment, derived from the underlying combination of a focus nasal with the class 4 or 9 prefix vowel /e-/

[ndž]:

/n-e-a-Vc-a/	|n-e-a-γɛɛnd-a|
f-4/9-t-come-fv	f-4/9-t-walk-fv
[ndžaaca]'[19]	[ndžaaγɛɛnda]
'4-they/9-it came (today)'	'4-they/9-it walked (today)'

/n-e-a-riik-u-a/
f-4/9-t-write-p-fv
[ndžaariikwa]
'4-they were/9-it was written (today)

2.1.4. Lexical and postlexical phonology.

Though Whiteley (1960: 2-6) mentions a number of phonological facts and processes, he hardly works these out into a comprehensive, explicit, and coherent rule-system. Possibly this may be due to his linguistic credo that "Initially (..) the linguist is responsible for collecting and presenting the linguistic facts in as detailed and accurate a manner as possible: only when this has been achieved will there be any chance of his being able to

[18] Compare imperative [ñaara] 'be able', from /ñaar-a/. The infinitive is [koñaara] 'to be able'.

[19] Compare

/n-βi-a-Vc-a/	/n-ci-a-Vc-a/
f-8-t-come-fv	f-10-t-come-fv
[mbiaaca]	[ñciaaca]
'8-they came (today)'	'10-they came (today)'

ask really productive questions" (1960: 67). Presumably, also, the fact that he was a pioneer, the first linguist to attempt a systematic study of Gusii, goes some way toward explaining this general approach. However, it is well known that theoretical insights and their improvement also tend to lead to productive questions, and to more insightful and coherent descriptions of specific languages.

Nonetheless, Whiteley (1960: 3-4) does divide phonological processes involving vowels into "[word-]internal" (lexical), and "[word-]external" (post-lexical) ones. And he further subdivides lexical rules into those operating on "internal, immediate" (contiguous) vowel sequences and those operating on "internal, interrupted" (non-contiguous) vowels. As examples of the former sub-type, he mentions complex segment formation, deletion of the /i/ of negative marker /ti-/, and deletion of /a/ before /e/ or /o/. As an example of the latter sub-type, he mentions what is here called Mid Vowel Height Spreading (136).

However, lexical rules affecting non-contiguous segments may also involve consonants, e.g. Gusii Consonantal Voicing Dissimilation (59).

In the present study, a distinction between lexical and postlexical rules will be maintained that is conceived in terms of more recent and more explicit theory, as developed by Kiparsky (1982, 1985) and others. In this view, it is supposed that lexical rules may operate either cyclically or post-cyclically (see Booij and Rubach 1987).

2.1.5. Suprasegmental phonology.

The time and resources available for the research on which this study is based were insufficient to include a description and analysis of the entire Gusii tone system. Only in the presentation of the tenses has tone been recorded, but even there no systematic account has been attempted. Nor can Whiteley's sketch be considered sufficient, despite several accurate insights. An adequate understanding of this aspect of the language must be left to future, more comprehensive and systematic study.

For these reasons, the discussion of tone will be restricted here to a brief summary of Whiteley's observations on the subject, with a few additions, followed by an outline of the relevant factors that, it may be concluded on the data known so far, must at least be taken into account in a comprehensive study of the subject.

First, Whiteley (1960: 2) notes the occurrence of the following surface tones: high, low, mid, fall, and rise. This statement seems correct, as far as high, low, and mid tone at the surface are concerned. However, if any of these are lexically distinctive, only H and L are. Mid tone is certainly not distinctive and therefore need not be postulated underlyingly in any case. Furthermore, the occurrence of rising tone is restricted mostly to long vowels. Its occurrence on short vowels, which is restricted to word-final position, is extremely rare, and may well be exclusively syntactic or intonational. It is certainly not lexically distinctive. Finally, if falling tone occurs at all, I have not come across any examples.

Second, tone is said to be lexically distinctive, though probably to a limited extent.

Whiteley (1960: 6) lists three pairs of verbal roots that are lexically differentiated by tone. Since neither his, nor this study offers a systematic account of tone, I give the verbal infinitives concerned in full, in (29), rather than his roots alone, so as to provide more of the morphological context,

(29) a. [kɔrɔɔta] (first ɔ = H) 'to check out (sth)'
vs. [kɔrɔɔta] (ɔɔ = H) 'to dream'

b. [koróká] 'to vomit'
vs. [koroka] 'to name'

c. [koβárá] 'to shine (of the sun)'
vs. [koβara] 'to count'

However, the pair in (29a) must be discounted, since the first item is disconfirmed by the present research. Hence only the pairs in (29b-c) remain as evidence. This is slender evidence. Moreover, though these items are indeed differentiated solely by tone, strictly speaking they are not even minimally, but only near-minimally distinctive, for they do not differ from each other by one tonal unit, as required by the criteria for minimal pair-hood, but by two.

This evidence seems too slender a basis to warrant the general claim, made by Whiteley (1960: 7), that verbs having the same CV-pattern may have a different lexical tone or tonal pattern, as in (30),

(30) 1. H on all vowels

a. -CVC-, -CV-, -VC-
b. -CVVC-, CVV-, VVC-
c. -CVCVC-, -VCVC-, -CVCV-

2. L on all vowels

a. -CVC-, -CV-, -VC-
b. -CVVC-, CVV-, VVC-
c. -CVCVC-, -VCVC-, -CVCV(V)-

3. H and L on successive vowels

-VCV(V)C-

4. no mention of tone

-C-
-Z- (i.e. segmentally zero)

where the segmental patterns in (30.1-2) are virtually identical, but may be either H or L throughout.

This analysis is problematic in at least the following respects. First, its claims are insufficiently exemplified, and thus hard to verify on the basis of Whiteley's work. Even if we add the few surface pairs in (31),

(31) a. [kóáá] 'to carry (a child on one's hip or side)'
vs. [koaa] 'to pluck (leaves)'[20]

b. [koáárá] 'to scratch'
vs. [koaara] 'to spread'

c. [ensé] 'ground, soil'
vs. [énsě] 'country, continent, the earth'

d. [γεεtá] 'disturb (imperative)'
vs. [γεεta] 'room for old man in the hut or house'

e. [γótaara] 'to take a walk', from /ko-taar-a/
vs. [γotáárá] 'not to spread', from /ko-ta-ar-a/

f. [γɔtεεra] (εε = H) 'to sing', from /ko-tεεr-a/
vs. [γɔtεεrá] (εε = H) 'not to winnow', from
/ko-ta-εεr-a/
15-not-winnow-fv

g. [γoteera] 'to be/get stuck', from /ko-teer-a/
vs. [γotéérá] 'not to murmur (s-ref: brook, river)', from /ko-ta-er-a/[21]

it may be observed again, first, that these are not strictly minimal, for obvious tonal reasons; second, that they are not strictly lexically distinctive for obvious morphological reasons; and third, that such pairs are relatively few.

Second, it is said that "the tone of all extensions is low" (1960: 8), but this is not substantiated systematically. Hence this still remains to be done (verbal extension is discussed in section 2.3.2).

Third, the only example he adduces (1960: 7) to exemplify tonal pattern (30.3), viz. -γwεnεr- 'be pleasing' (first ε = H, second ε = L), is mistaken on a number of counts. Probably [koβwεεnεra] (εε = H) 'to look smart' is intended, supposedly from /ko-βuεn-er-a/ and related to [koβwεεna] (εε = H) 'to be healed, to recover'. [koγwεnεra] was

---

[20] Not to be confused with /ko-a/ --> [kɔa] 'to give'. This apparently exeptional surface representation occurred in at least one idiolect, which also included [kɔβa] 'to be', from /ko-βa/ or /ko-β-a/. Both [koa] and [koβa] were also found, respectively, in other idiolects.

[21] Besides 'to murmur', [koera] may mean 'to buzz, to drone, to rustle, to swish'. It may also refer to the sound made by an engine.

disconfirmed with the meaning 'be pleasing', and altogether by at least one informant, but judged as an acceptable alternative for 'to recover' by another. However, even if -γwɛnɛr- were confirmed, it still does not exemplify segmental pattern -VCV(V)C- (30.3), but -CVVCVC-, not included in (30). If it were interpreted as /-γwɛn-ɛr-/, it would merely exemplify the segmental (not tonal) patterns (30.1/2c), as well as include extension, which is not otherwise taken into account by Whiteley. Thus it either exemplifies the right tonal pattern with the 'wrong' segmental pattern, or the other way around.

Fourth, tone is not indicated for group (30.4). Nor is it mentioned that the verbs in this group are highly marginal. Thus /-0-/ 'give', unless it may be analysed as /-a-/, is the only segmentally zero verb in the language. Even so, it is more plausibly analysed as /-V-/, where V is an underspecified lower mid vowel (see Appendix One). The second example, /-c-/ 'come' (1960: 7), is more plausibly analysed as /-Vc-/, since it regularly surfaces as [γoocia], from /ko-Vc-a/. The third example /-a-/, 'to chop up [actually: to pluck] vegetables, is not segmentally zero, but consist of a vowel. It and /-á-/ (31a) seem to be the only such verbs in the language.

A fifth point may be added. Whiteley claims that "the tone for all [verbal] prefixes is the same except in the following tenses, where those of Classes 1, 4, and 9 **only** are low, all the rest being high" (1960: 9). He then mentions a number of tenses. However, he does not substantiate his point by working out a paradigm for any of the tenses he mentions and involving the verbal markers for all classes, anywhere in the text. Further, it is not clear, whether he refers to subject markers only, or object and relative markers as well. I am referring to verbal markers 1 (o-, a-, or oyo-), 4 (e- or ye-), and 9 (e- or eye-). Thus his claim still requires verification.

A sixth point is somewhat clearer. It concerns the statement that tone may be "grammatically (..) distinct" (1960: 6). A few tenses, which are segmentally identical, but semantically distinct, are differentiated by their tonal pattern alone. In these cases, the differences in meaning concern the degree of remoteness of the (past or future) time referred to from the moment of speaking, as in (32),

(32) a. [ñcíáéteté] 'they passed (recently)' (ñ = H)
b. [ñcíáetete] 'they passed (long ago)' (ñ = H)

The frequency of occurrence of such tenses, however, seems irrelevant to generalisations on the tonal system as such. No similar semantico-syntactic use of tone occurs elsewhere in the language. Even within the tense system itself, such distinctive use of tone is relatively restricted. Therefore, it must be given its proper, i.e. marginal, place in the tonal system as a whole.

Specifically, Whiteley gives the following account of lexical and grammatical tone. "Such [lexical] examples occur far less frequently than those in which a distinction of tone serves to distinguish formally similar tenses. It is accepted that tenses so distinguished are as much different words as those exemplified above, but there is the additional feature that they are grammatically as well as lexically distinct" (1960: 6). This statement, which considers segmentally identical, but tonally distinct tenses as "different words", seems to confuse lexical with grammatical distinctions somewhat. He then proceeds to give a paragraph on the number and type of tones recognised and distinguished in the text. His terminology is not always clear, however, and levels of representation are not differentiated beyond listing surface representations. Therefore his analysis of the tonal system is not sufficiently clear.

Seventh, and finally, the only non-verbal minimal pair that I was able to find is [énda] 'stomach', plural [cínda], versus [êndá] or [éendá] 'jigger', plural [cíindá].

In fact, to summarise these points, nothing in his account of Gusii tone is accounted for systematically. Nor will I attempt such a treatment of the subject here. Despite Whiteley's valuable pioneering work and the few remarks made here, a comprehensive, systematic description and account of Gusii tone, and of suprasegmental phonology generally, remains a task for future research. Therefore, a brief summary may be given of the factors that must, or may have to, be taken into account as probably or possibly relevant co-determinants of Gusii surface tone in any systematic synchronic account of it.

It would seem that at least the following factors (33) are relevant and must therefore be taken into account,

(33) a. lexical tone (limited)
b. semantico-syntactic tone (tenses, sentence-intonation)
c. postlexical tone (tonal influence across words)
d. syntactic position in the utterance
e. possibly, abstract accent
f. persistent historical properties of some word and persistent properties of lexical take-overs
g. emotive expressiveness and idiolectal differences
h. mood

A few remarks are in order. First, lexical tone (33a) may be defined as tone underlyingly associated with one or more tone-bearers of some lexical item, thereby distinguising it semantically from other items in the lexicon. If near-minimal pairs may be included, a number of words are differentiated by tone at least in their surface representation, as in (31); but even so, their number appears to be limited. It remains to be determined more exactly, if, and to what extent, lexical items are thus differentiated underlyingly. Though nearly all the items thus distinguished, found to date, are verbs, Gusii tone does not appear to be sensitive to distinctions of lexical category, but this requires systematic verification.

Second, a few tenses are systematically differentiated by tone (33b), as exemplified in (32), but this phenomenon is also relatively limited. Similarly, distinct tonal or intonational patterns may differentiate phrases, main- versus sub-clauses (e.g. non-/conditional), and some types of sentences. With regard to sentences, they differentiate at least statements and questions. See the tonal patterns of some tenses used in conditional and interrogative utterances, for example.

Third, postlexically the tonal pattern of some word may be influenced by that of some previous or following word (33c). That is, whenever words are combined into phrases or higher syntactic units, their tonal surface pattern tends to vary at least to some extent, apparently due to changes in arrangement. This suggests that the syntactic position of a word, as well as the distinction between citation forms and their usage in context, is relevant in deriving the tonal surface representation of words (33d).

Related to this, fourth, word-margins, or more generally, utterance margins, i.e. their beginning and end, often seem to have a definite bearing on the tonal surface pattern.

Fifth, relevance of accent, whether abstract or concrete, for the derivation of the tonal surface pattern, is noted here as a possibility (33e). My limited inquiry into the Gusii tonal system has not, as yet, yielded any indication of such accent. Nor is this mentioned as such by Whiteley. But since Gusii does not appear to be a full tone language, the possibility of it being some type of accent-tone language, in which an abstract accent plays a role or in which tone is otherwise predictable, is not an unlikely one. This must be ascertained on the basis of a more comprehensive examination.

Sixth, persistent influence of historical properties of some word, or the persistent influence of properties of lexical items taken over from other languages (33f), is likely to play a role in a comprehensive account of Gusii tone, though probably a subordinate one. If it does, it will probably account for certain tonal subsets or a sub-system of tonal behaviour that cannot be fully accounted for on purely synchronic grounds.

Seventh, emotive expressiveness is a factor that is not expected to play a systematic role in a description of Gusii tone, but is mentioned in so far as it may interfere with the regular systematic tonal pattern. As such, it must be taken into account in future study of the subject. The same can be said of idiolectal tonal surface differences (33g).

Eighth, in some tenses attitudinal differences are apparently expressed through tone (33h). These include the distinction between whether some activity is viewed as real or unreal. However, it has not been possible to ascertain whether this is connected strictly with tonal differences.

Finally, it is far too early to say anything about possible dialectally determined differences in tonal pattern, since too little is known about the language as a whole, not only with regard to its syntax and lexicon, but also with regard to its dialectal variation as such. However, what my informants said on the subject, suggests that South Mugirango is tonally distinct from other dialects at least to some degree, as it is in other respects.

2.2. The Syllable.

2.2.1. Syllable structure.

In terms of Levin's (1985) theory of the syllable, in which codas (N') and syllable-nodes (N") are viewed as projections of the syllable-nucleus (N), typical Gusii syllable structure may be summarised as in (34),

(34)

```
          N"
         /|
        / N'
       /  |
      /   N
     /   / \
   (x)  x  (x)
```

This summary captures the following facts. First, the syllable must contain at least a nucleus. This nucleus may or may not branch, and typically dominates [-cons] segments. If it does branch, it may dominate either two distinct vowels or one long vowel.

Second, the coda, N', which is empty, is considered as a projection of the nucleus, and so is the syllable node, N".

Third, the syllable may or may not contain an onset. This onset may not branch, and typically dominates a [+cons] segment or a glide (which is here interpreted as a high vowel dominated by N"). In the course of the derivation the material dominated by the x that is dominated by the onset may become phonologically complex. Underlyingly extra-syllabic nasals, for example, may come to be dominated by the onset through prenasalisation.

Syllabification is assumed to apply at the level of the prosodic word. Properties of the typical syllable may change in the course of the derivation (see sections 2.2.2 and 2.3.5).

A sample of the kind of segmental material that the Gusii rules of syllabification may encounter in the lexicon is given in (35),

(35)	CVC	/-tɛm-/ 'beat'
	CVVC	/-took-/ 'find'
	V	/o-/ augment class 1, 3
	VV	/ee-/ reflexive prefix
	CV	/-re-/ 'eat'
	CVV	/raa-/ tense prefix
	VC	/-er/ applicative suffix
	VVC	/-aak-/ 'slap, hit'
	VNC	/-aNc-/ 'love, like'
	CHVC	/-tiɔk-/ 'stink, smell'
	CHVNC	/-tuaNγ-/ 'beat, thresh (by beating)'

In segmental representations, H represents any high vowel.

2.2.2. Syllabification.

Initial Gusii syllable structure may be accounted for by the syllable structure assignment rules (hereafter called the SSA-rules, or simply SSA) and condition in (36),

(36) syllable structure assignment rules and condition

x-Placement (37)
N-Placement (41)
Condition on Structure Dependent Rules (43) (CSD)
N-Fusion (45)
N'-Projection (47)
N"-Projection (49)

These will be introduced and briefly discussed in the present section.

First, x-Placement (37),

(37) x-Placement

```
x
¦
o        root-node tier
```

assigns a timing-unit x to every root-node o, as in (38),

(38) a. input: /-βun-/ 'break (v.t.)'

b. x-Placement (37)

```
x x x
| | |
β u n
```

where the symbols /β/, /u/, and /n/ are to be interpreted as summarising at least the hierarchically ordered configuration of specified features necessary and sufficient to characterise the phonological units concerned, and by implication the concomitant fully spelled out configuration of specified features, which are linked to the respective root nodes. Thus (38b) abbreviates (39),

```
(39)  x     x   x
      |     |   |
      o     o   o
      |     |   |
     /β/   /u/ /n/
```

In (38b) the effect of the rule is shown immediately after its being mentioned (this convention will also be used hereafter). Recalling how length is represented underlyingly (10), the effect of x-Placement (37) on a long vowel, as in (40a),

(40) a. input

```
      x
      |
    s i k
```

'to prepare beer' (non-linearly, /-si:k-/)

b. x-Placement (37)

```
    x x x x
    | |/  |
    s i   k
```

automatically produces the correct result, as in (40b).

Next, N-Placement (41),

(41) N-Placement

```
      N
      :
      x
      |
   [-cons]
```

assigns nucleus-status to every feature-matrix containing the feature-specification [-cons], i.e. to every vowel. Its effect on (38b) is shown in (42),

(42) a. input

```
    x x x
    | | |
    β u n
```

b. N-Placement (41)

```
      N
      |
    x x x
    | | |
    β u n
```

To handle representations containing geminate structures, Levin (1985: 89) formulates the following condition on structure dependent rules (hereafter abbreviated as CSD),

(43) Condition of Structure-dependent rules (CSD)

"A structure-dependent phonological rule R will fail to affect the internal feature composition of the form G,

```
  x1 x2
   \ /
[αFeat]
```

unless both x1 and x2 meet the structural description of R and, in the output of R to G, both x1 and x2 meet the structural change of R."

This condition allows N-Placement (41) to apply to, for example, the structure in (40b), as in (44),

(44) a. input

```
x x x x
| |/  |
s i   k
```

b. N-Placement (41), in virtue of CSD (43)

```
  N
  |\
x x x x
| |/  |
s i   k
```

To handle contiguous dissimilar vowels, Levin (1985: 111) proposes the following mechanism,

(45) N-Fusion

```
N     N           N
|     |    -->   / \
x     x         x   x
```

Its effect is to create complex, or branching, nuclei, which is exemplified in (46d),

(46) a. input: /-tiɔk-/ 'stink, smell'

b. x-Placement (37)

```
x x x x
| | | |
t i o k
```

c. N-Placement (41)

```
 N N
 | |
x x x x
| | | |
t i ɔ k
```

d. N-Fusion (45)

```
  N
  |\
x x x x
| | | |
t i ɔ k
```

Next, N'-Projection (47),

(47) N'-Projection

```
N'
:
N
```

projects a coda N' onto a nucleus, as in (48),

(48) a. input: (19b) b. N'-Projection (47)

```
                N'
                |
  N             N
  |             |
x x x         x x x
| | |         | | |
β u n         β u n
```

In virtue of the non-branchingness of the coda, the final /n/ of this root remains as yet unsyllabified.

Finally, the syllable-node is projected onto the coda through (49),

(49) N"-Projection

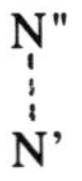

as exemplified in (50),

(50) a. input: (24b)

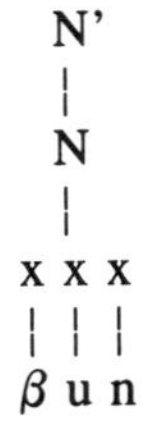

b. N"-Projection (49)

So far, the operation of SSA-rules (36) have been exemplified exclusively on representations of roots or morphemes. If larger units are taken into account, it will be seen that the application of phonological and morphological rules may determine or interact with syllabification. Consider the derivation of the stem in (51),

(51) a. input

/-tuaNγ-/ 'thresh (by beating)'

b. partial morphological derivation

suffixation -tuaNγa

c. syllabification

x-Placement (37)

```
x x x x x x
| | | | | |
t u a N γ a
```

d. Complex Segment Formation (109), Prenasalisation (61), Nasal Homorganisation (62), Defricativisation (65), Linking Rule (90), x-Trimming (94) (all discussed later)

```
x x x x x x
|\ \|  /| |
t u a N γ a
```

e. N-placement (41), CSD, N'-Placement, N"-Placement

```
  N"      N"
  |       |
  N'      N'
 /|      /|
/ N     / N
/ /\   /  |
x x x x x x
|\ \|  /| |
t u a N γ a
```

[twaaŋga] phonetic representation

One of the changes that may take place in the course of the derivation, in the typical structure of the syllable outlined here, is that high vowels may become glides. This is expressed structurally, by their coming to be dominated by an N"-node, instead of a nucleus. Second, nasals may become syllabic word-initially. Since these changes are relatively exceptional, they are appropriately handled by additional rules (see sections 2.3.5, 2.3.11, 2.3.12).

2.3. Lexical phonology.

The lexical rules discussed in this section respectively deal with consonants (section 2.3.1), nasals (sections 2.3.2-4), and vowels and glides (sections 2.3.10-19). The discussion is largely arranged according to the function of these types of segment as a target for the rules involved. Because, in the present approach, vowels and glides are considered to be segmentally identical, they have been grouped together.

Rules involving consonants.

2.3.1. Consonantal Voicing Dissimilation

Consonantal voicing dissimilation rules, which are operative in many Bantu languages, whether identical or similar to the process discussed here, have often been called Dahl's Law in Bantu linguistics, after its discoverer Edmund Dahl. In the general form of this type of dissimilation process, any voiceless target consonant becomes voiced, whenever it is followed by a non-contiguous voiceless trigger consonant, though on the consonant projection it is contiguous. In many East African Bantu languages, however, it takes on a more restricted form. This is also the case in Gusii.

Whiteley (1956: 5) informally describes the process as follows. "Where the first consonant of a noun stem or verb root is voiceless, i.e. k, ch [i.e. /c/], s, t, any k in the prefix will be heard as g" (previously identified as fricative γ). Thus he restricts the applicability of the process to the pre-root domain, in particular to class prefixes. In Whiteley (1960: 5) the process is described in the following more general terms. "Where the voiceless velar stop is followed by a sequence VC, where C is a voiceless sound, it is realised as a voiced velar fricative". Yet, all the examples used there also illustrate its operation exclusively in prefixes.

However, Davy and Nurse, studying multiple applications of consonantal voicing dissimilation in a number of East African Bantu languages, including Gusii, distinguish between its diachronic and synchronic application. Generally, they state that the latter only affects voiceless velar stops and is active only in prefixes in most of the languages they studied (1982: 157-158), except in Gusii, where "we find the alternation [between k and γ] in stem-final syllables as well" (1982: 163). They illustrate this with the examples repeated, with corrections, in (52),

(52) a. /na-a-sɛk-ete/
3s-t-laugh-t
[náásɛγɛtɛ] (first and last ɛ = H)
'he laughed (recently)'

(adapted from 1982: 163)

b. /n-ke-aak-ek-ete/
f-7-beat-sx-t
[ŋkeaaγeγete] or [ŋkiaaγeγete]
'7-it was beatable (long ago)'[22]

c. /a-ko-aak-ete/
3s-om2s-hit-t
[ákoaáγété] or [ákwaáγété]
'he hit you (long ago)'

(adapted from 1982: 180)

In connection with (52c), they add that, according to their findings, the rule tends not to apply in the pre-stem domain, "if the first consonant of the stem [is] itself the product of EABVD [East African Bantu Voicing Dissimilation] application" (1982: 180). Naturally, this must be so, because, since the rule can be triggered only by [-voice] consonants, any effect of the rule, always a [+voice] consonant, cannot function as its trigger on a later cycle.

Further, I have not found the variation they report for Gusii between application and non-application of the rule, at least not within the same style of speech. One must be cautious with stylistic differences, anyway, because highly monitored speech usually involves deliberate corrections, and sometimes even hyper-corrections, as compared to normal, fairly rapid speech. The position of the trigger in the word, whether root-initial or -final (or, stem-initial or -internal), seems to be equally irrelevant in this respect (also see the remarks below on synchronic versus diachronic applications of the rule).

In contrast to Whiteley's view, then, Davy and Nurse's remarks suggest that synchronically the domain of Gusii consonantal voicing dissimilation is not only the pre-stem domain, but the word as a whole. The present research has corroborated this observation. In fact, the rule applies in the pre-root, root-, and post-root domain. This is exemplified in (53),

(53) a. pre-root or pre-stem domain

/ko-tɛɛm-a/ --> [γɔtɛɛma] 'to try'

/ko-tuom-a/ --> [γɔtwooma] 'to knock, to bang'

/ko-it-a/ --> [γoita] or [γwiita] 'to beat (severely, using a stick or a cane)'

/ko-aak-a/ --> [γoaaka] 'to hit'

---

22 Adapted from Davy and Nurse (1982: 163), where /-ak-/ appears to be a mistranscription, given the form of the imperative [aaka] 'beat!' -not *[aka]- and the example under (52c). Contrast with the regular application of the rule in [ŋgekwaaγeka] '7-it was beatable (recently)'.

/ko-aNc-a/ --> [γwaañca] 'to love, to like'

/e-ke-saku/ --> [eγesaku] 'clan'

/e-ke-Nto/ --> [eγeento] 'thing'

/ko-ke-rɔr-a/ --> [γɔkɛrɔra] 'to see 7it'
15-7-see-fv

b. root domain (included in the stem)

/ko-aak-ek-a/ --> [kwaaγeka] 'to be hittable (v.i.)'

/βa-ta-a-simek-et-e/
3p-not-t-plant-pv-fv
[βátáásiméγété]
'they did not plant (recently)'

/na-a-miñɔk-et-e/
3s-t-run-pv-fv
[náámíñɔγɛtɛ] (final ɛ = H)
'he ran (recently)'

c. post-root domain (included in the stem)

/ko-riNγ-ak-ok-a/
15-fold-res-ri-fv
[koriiŋgaγoka]
'to be unfoldable (v.t. or v.i.)'[23]

These examples show that the rule applies throughout the word, regardless of lexical category, lexical sub-domains, and the distinction between finiteness or non-finiteness. It usually does so, whenever it is applicable. Accordingly, this is the analysis proposed here.

It might be argued that a synchronic version of consonantal voicing dissimilation must be distinguished from an historical version of the rule. Thus, in the following examples (54), derived from Proto-Bantu or taken over from contemporary languages (tone being disregarded),

[23] The sense here is not 'to be incapable of being folded', but 'to be capable of being unfolded', i.e. whether of itself or by an external agent.

(54) a. from Proto-Bantu

PB -kɔkɔ 9 'chicken' (Meeussen 1980: 25)
> Gusii /e-n-kɔkɔ/
> historical GVD --> /-γɔkɔ/
==> 9a |e-n-γɔkɔ| --> [εηgɔkɔ] 'hen'

PB -kata 9 'head-pad, head-ring' (Meeussen 1980: 21)
> Gusii /-kata/
> historical GVD /-γata/
==> 9a |e-n-γata| --> [eηgata] 'head-pad, head-ring'

b. from Swahili

Sw. /kisumu/ 'Kisumu (town)'
> Gusii /kesuumu/
> historical GVD /γesuumu/
==> [γesuumu] 'Kisumu (town)'

Sw. /dakika/ 'minute'
> Gusii /-takeka/
> historical GVD /-taγeka/
==> 9 |e-taγeka| --> [etaγeka] 'minute'

c. from English

Eng. /kheik/ 'cake'
> Gusii /-kεεki/
> historical GVD /-γεεki/
==> 9 |e-γεεki| --> [εγεεki] 'cake'[24]

an historical version is supposed to have resulted in certain underlying representations that constitute inputs for any synchronic derivation.

Synchronically, two approaches may be taken, depending on the actual data. On the supposition of a previous historical version of the rule, the synchronic version of the rule may be considered as a cyclic lexical phonological rule, applying to derived environments only. On this view, taking (54c) for an example, if, in some variety of Gusii, only [εγεεki] would occur, the underlying input may be postulated as /-γεεki/; if only [εkεεki] would occur, /-kεεki/ may be postulated. By definition, a cyclic version of the rule could not change either of these underlying representations. If, in some other variety of Gusii, both [εγεεki] and [εkεεki] would occur, this might indicate that the variety concerned has not yet stabilised, at least not in respect of consonantal voicing dissimilation. On the postulate of a cyclic version of the rule, both /-γεεki/ and /-kεεki/ would have to be entered in the lexicon.

---

[24] Judith Moraa pronounced [εkεεki].

Alternatively, the rule might be interpreted as post-cyclic. In a variety with [ɛγɛɛki] only, postulating /-kɛɛki/ and exceptionless application of the rule would then account for the surface representations. In a variety with both [ɛγɛɛki] and [ɛkɛɛki], the roots or stems involved could be lexically specified as variable with respect to the rule, or the rule as optional in this context. In a variety with [ɛkɛɛki] only, which, however, does not seem to occur, a post-cylic interpretation of the rule would be inadequate.

In fact, however, such variation does not extend consistently to whole lexical subsets, not even of lexical take-overs from other languages. The application of the rule rather seems to vary per lexical item. That is, the recent phonological history of different words may take a different course. As just exemplified for several supposed dialects, sometimes such differences may be expressed formally by assigning a different status to some rule, depending on the data, sometimes it is more appropriate to describe such variation in terms of lexical subsets. But usually the rule does apply and exceptions appear to be limited. Idiolectal factors also seem to be relevant, but it is too early to be able to say whether, and which, sociolectal differences play a role, and if so, to what extent.

For lack of both cross-dialectal and extensive lexical research on Gusii, to date, it seems impossible at this point in time to determine which approach to the rule would be most adequate and most economical for the language as a whole. This observation also holds for some other rules. For this reason, and because the rule seems to apply in a larger domain than was observed by Whiteley (1956, 1960), and more regularly than was observed by Davy and Nurse (1982), I propose to conceive of it as a cyclic lexical rule, until data necessitating a different analysis turn up. This is slightly less abstract than a postcyclic interpretation.

This approach has at least the following two advantages. First, underlying representations for words such as those in (54) may be postulated as in (55),

(55)
a. /-γɔkɔ/
b. /-γata/
c. /γesuumu/
d. /-taγeka/
e. /-γɛɛki/

This presupposes a previous historical application of the rule. For any variety of speech in which surface variation occurs, this must be handled, on this approach, by listing different entries in the lexicon for the items concerned. Thus, the entry for (55e) could be something like: /-γɛɛki/ 'cake' (also /-kɛɛki/).

Second, synchronically the rule is supposed to apply yo all derived environments. Thus, though it cannot apply root-internally (i.e. when both a trigger and a target occur within the root), it may, and often does, affect target consonants in the root, in the course of the derivation, due to the presence of a trigger in some suffix.

This cyclic rule is considered to be obligatory in normal, fairly rapid speech, which is the register or style for which the rule is formulated. This analysis is supported as follows. Whiteley claims that "where the voiceless stop is followed by a sequence VVC, VVVC, some anomalies occur" (1960: 6). Thus, supposedly, the rule does not apply regularly in forms such as /ko-aak-a/, of which the output would be [koaaka], rather than [γoaaka] 'to beat' (also compare 1956: 29). However, though the possibility that the distinction between monitored and non-monitored speech is relevant to such variation, may well be granted, the rule regularly does apply in such contexts.

Davy and Nurse (1982: 180), referring to examples such as (52c), report that "in careful speech, EABVD need not be applied to the pre-stem /k/. But this was always accompanied by preservation of the syllable division before the stem-initial vowel: [a.ko.aa.γe.te]". Because their version of the rule (1982: 158), repeated in slightly adapted form in (56),

(56) East African Bantu Voicing Dissimilation (EABVD)

$$\begin{bmatrix} +\text{back} \\ -\text{cor} \\ -\text{voice} \end{bmatrix} \dashrightarrow [+\text{voice}] \;/\; \text{---}\; [-\text{cons}] \;.\; [-\text{voice}]$$

explicitly refers to a syllable boundary (indicated by .), they can argue that the resyllabification in [a.ko.aa.γe.te] "destroys the required conditions for EABVD and it is not clear that rule-failure has occurred at all" (1980: 180).

However, it is argued here that syllable structure and resyllabification are irrelevant to Gusii consonantal voicing dissimilation. Given the appropriateness of the distinction between registers, it is argued that the process may be more plausibly considered as a purely segmental phonological rule that applies regularly in non-monitored speech, as in [akoaaγete]. After the change from |..kete..| into |..γete..|, the structural description of the rule is no longer met in the case of |ko| on a later cycle, since the next non-contiguous consonant (but contiguous on the consonant projection) is now no longer voiceless /k/, but voiced |γ| in the intermediate representation of the root, |aaγ|. Hence it may be concluded that the rule applies quite regularly in this instance.

Furthermore, because the rule is justifiably conceived as a purely phonological rule that is applicable throughout the word, including the root domain, though restricted to derived environments in virtue of its cyclicity, and formulated for a normal rapid style of speech, its formulation need not refer to a syllable boundary.

If, now, the following language-specific redundancy rule may be postulated for continuancy,

(57) $$\begin{bmatrix} +\text{voice} \\ -\text{nas} \end{bmatrix} \dashrightarrow [+\text{cont}]$$

which states that any non-nasal voiced segment is redundantly continuant, this rule correctly involves not only all vowels, but, more relevant to the present context, it also stipulates that all voiced [+cons] segments are redundantly continuant. In virtue of (57), all such segments, in particular /β/, /r/, and /γ/, automatically receive the specification [+cont]. Thus, when /k/ becomes voiced |g| through consonantal voicing dissimilation, it automatically receives the specification [+cont] in virtue of (57), and so becomes [γ].

Given (57), and the fact that /k/ is the only voiceless back consonant in Gusii, consonantal voicing dissimilation might be formulated, in linear fashion, as a feature-changing, as in (58),

(58) Consonantal Voicing Dissimilation

$$[\text{-voice}] \dashrightarrow [\text{+voice}] \;/\; \begin{bmatrix} \text{---} \\ \text{+back} \end{bmatrix} \quad [\text{-voice}] \qquad \text{(consonant projection)}$$

In non-linear fashion it may be formulated as in (59),

(59) Consonantal Voicing Dissimilation (CVD)

```
[+voice]
   :
   :
   o              o
   |              |
[+back]       [-voice]          (consonant projection)
```

Here, non-linkage of the root-nodes to any x on the timing-tier formally expresses the fact that the trigger and the target must be contiguous, not in a strictly temporal sense, but on the consonant projection, as stipulated by the added condition in parenthesis. And since the vocalic tier is thus abstracted from, this formulation allows for any possible number of vowels to intervene between the target and the trigger of the rule. Linking of [+voice] to the target is assumed to delink automatically any specification for this feature by convention. As formulated, the rule applies gratuitously also to [+voice] consonantal targets, but, in virtue of its cyclicity, only to derived environments. Not characterised as optional, it is supposed to apply regularly and generally in non-monitored speech.

This interpretation seems to be supported by the fact that the anomalies previously mentioned by Whiteley and Davy and Nurse either do not occur, or seem to be due to their formulation of the rule or to transcriptional error, or to characterise monitored speech (where different conditions may apply). Given these considerations, there is no need to resolve such supposed exceptions comparatively, as proposed by Whiteley. By comparing Gusii to Kuria, he suggests that "this anomaly may be resolved comparatively. In all examples except the last, the comparable radical in the closely related Kuria has an initial h, thus -hik-, -hit-, -haak-" (1960: 6). However, it is awkward, even on principle, to give any synchronic analysis and description of the system of one language in terms of that of another. The present analysis and the one proposed by Davy and Nurse, therefore, have the advantage over Whiteley's in this respect.

Rules involving nasals.

Some of the phonological rules that have nasals for their targets, in addition involve consonants, some others vowels.

2.3.2. Prenasalisation.

Examples of the various types of Gusii prenasals have already been given in section 2.1.3. The examples in (60) involve the existential or identificatory construction with /n-/ 'it is',

(60) a. some prenasalised consonants

/n-ßaaßa/ --> [mbaaßa] 'it is my grandmother'[25]
/oyo n-taata/ --> [oyo ntaata] 'this is my father'
/o-ria n-taata/ --> [oria ntaata] 'that is my father'
/seito n-caace ña-maiya/ --> [seito ñcaace ña-maiya] 'my home is (the village of) Nyamaiya'
/n-reeru/ --> [ndeeru] 'it is Reeru' (an area in Nyacheki Division)

b. some prenasalised nasals

/o-ria n-maama/ --> [oria mmaama] 'that person over there is my mother'

([nn] accidentally omitted)

/n-ñaγεεŋkε/ --> [ññaγεεŋkε] 'it is Nyageenke Village'
/seito n-ñamiira/ --> [seito ññamiira] 'my home (area) is Nyamira'

|omoo-nto o-ria n-ŋaŋa| --> [omoonto oria ŋŋaŋa] 'that person (over there) is Ng'ang'a[26]'

As pointed out earlier, prenasals are considered here as prenasalised consonants. That is, they are supposed to be derived by a process called prenasalisation, which applies in many Bantu languages, including Gusii. However, it is not formally expressed as such by Whiteley, who, instead, classes prenasalised consonants as "nasal clusters" (1960: 5).

The process may nonetheless be formulated as in (61),

(61) Prenasalisation (PN)

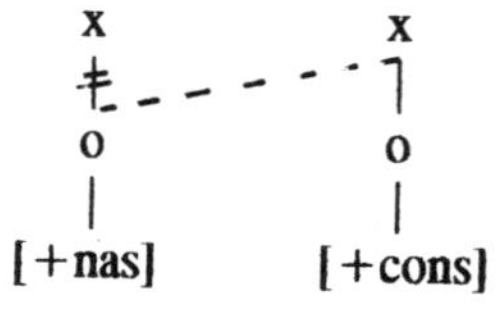

[25] In old Gusii, [ßaaßa] could mean '(my) grandmother, mother'. In modern Gusii, it only means 'grandmother', as distinct from [maama] 'mother', mentioned under (60b).

[26] This is a Taita personal name. There seem to be no Gusii names beginning with velar nasal [ŋ].

This rule states that, whenever a nasal segment is immediately followed by a consonantal segment, in the course of the derivation, the nasal segment is delinked from its x and associated to that of the consonant.

2.3.3. Nasal Homorganisation.

In many languages the nasal element of prenasalised consonants regularly becomes homorganic with those consonants. So too in Gusii. This is discussed in the present section.

Prenasalisation (61) regularly causes the nasal part of a prenasalised consonant to become homorganic with the following consonantal segment. That is, it feeds such homorganisation. Technically, this may be accounted for as spreading of the Place features of the consonantal element to the preceding nasal element, as in (62),

(62) Nasal Homorganisation

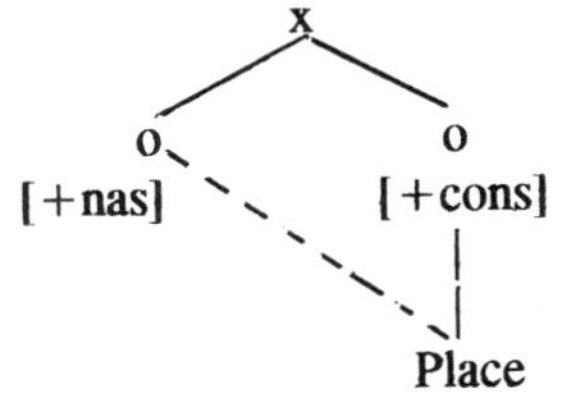

This rule spreads the specified features for Place of any consonantal element leftward to the root node of the preceding nasal element, whenever they are associated to the same x, i.e. whenever they constitute a prenasalised consonant. Its operation is exemplified in the following partial derivation,

(63) input: 9a /e-n-/ + /-γɔkɔ/ 'hen'

Affixation	enγɔkɔ
Prenasalisation (61)	enγɔkɔ
Nasal Homorganisation (62)	eŋγɔkɔ

Since all nasal elements of all prenasalised consonants always become homorganic, or more generally, since all nasal segments immediately followed by a consonantal segment homorganise with the latter, Prenasalisation (61) may arguably be collapsed with Nasal Hormorganisation (62), as in (63),

(64) Prenasalisation-cum-homorganisation

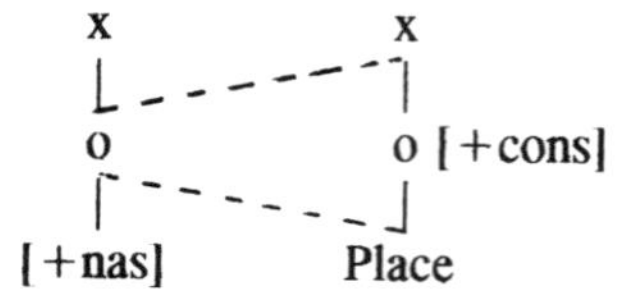

However, Prenasalisation (61) involves rearrangement of entire root nodes with respect to the timing tier, thereby arguably triggering compensatory lengthening of a preceding vowel, while Nasal Homorganisation (62) involves spreading of a specified feature. Moreover, it seems plausible to argue that Prenasalisation (61) actually triggers the Nasal Homorganisation (62), which feeding relation is expressed by the formulation of the latter. So the changes do not seem to be strictly simultaneous and hence their separate formulations are maintained.

2.3.4. Defricativisation.

The regular homorganisation of the nasal element of prenasals is not the only change arguably triggered by prenasalisation. If the consonantal element that is prenasalised is a voiced continuant, it is regularly defricativised, i.e. it becomes non-continuant. This may accounted for as rightward spreading of the [-cont] specification of the nasal to the consonantal element. This is the topic of the present section.

As already observed in sections 2.1.2-3 and 2.3.1, voiced continuants are regularly turned into voiced obstruents, whenever they are prenasalised. This process occurs in many other East African Bantu languages. In Gusii, specifically, /ß/ is turned into [b], /γ/ into [g], and /r/ into [d], under the condition mentioned (also by Whiteley 1960: 5). This may be formulated, as in (65),

(65) Defricativisation

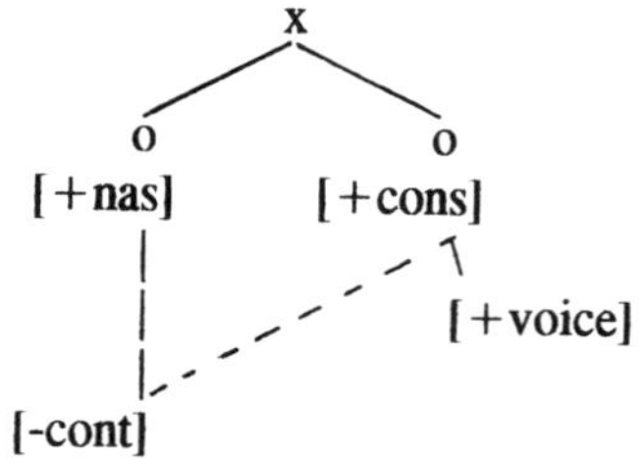

This rule expresses the fact that, whenever some prenasalised consonant is voiced, the specification [-cont] of the preceding nasal element associated with the same x, is spread rightward, thereby rendering the consonantal element non-continuant, in effect a voiced obstruent.

The inclusion of the specification [+voice] in the context of (65) is both necessary and sufficient to define all voiced continuants, hence to exclude all voiceless consonants, as the class of triggers of the rule. This is necessary, because the rule does not apply, whenever the consonantal element is a voiceless continuant, since |ns| always surfaces as [ns], and |nc| as [ñc]. Moreover, /nt/ never surfaces as *[nθ]. Inclusion of [+voice] is also sufficient, because all voiced consonants in Gusii are continuant in virtue of redundancy rule (57) (also compare specified feature matrix (22)).

Being thus restricted, the rule cannot apply generally to prenasalised consonants. Though all and any sequences of a nasal and a consonant are subject to Prenasalisation (61), and all and any nasal elements subject to Nasal Homorganisation (62), including those having voiced continuants for a trigger, only the latter, and no other consonants, may be targets for Defricativisation (65). Therefore, it cannot be collapsed with Prenasalisation (61) or Nasal Homorganisation (62), or with both, into a single rule.

It may be added that /nc/, already excluded by the definition of the trigger class as [+voice], is further excluded, because [c] is an affricate, and its underlying representation may be thus be characterised as in (66),

(66)

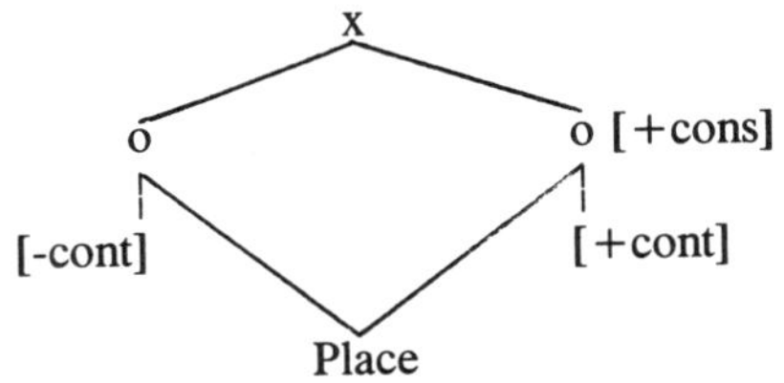

The unique complex surface segment [ndž], which is a voiced prenasalised affricate, is excluded from the structural description of Defricativisation (65) on the same ground. The reason is as follows. Because the definition of the [+cons, +voice] target in the formulation of Defricativisation (65) specifies only one root-node, and any affricate has two, as in (66), [ndž] is excluded from the structural description of the rule. If, on a different definition of affricates, it would come within the scope of this rule after all, presumably spreading of the specification [-cont] of the nasal element would only affect the [-cont] part of affricate [ndž], not its [+cont] part. Thus the correct output would still be produced.

To exemplify the operation of Defricativisation (65), the partial derivation (63) that was broken off in section 2.3.3 may be continued, as in (67),

(67)	intermediate input	eηγɔkɔ
	Defricativisation (65)	eηgɔkɔ

This derivation is still incomplete and other rules are needed to derive the fully correct surface representation, [ɛηgɔkɔ] (disregarding tone), but (67) only serves to show the effect of the rule under discussion.

Finally, from the discussion on the preceding pages it may be concluded that all the Gusii [-cons] segments in inventory (21), may be prenasalised, including nasals themselves.

Perhaps the two glides may also be included here, but complex segments involving these are considered here as glided nasals.

So much for general processes involving prenasals. In sections 2.3.5 and 2.3.6, word-initial behaviour of prenasals will be considered. In some respects, this is different from their behaviour elsewhere in the word.

2.3.5. Nasal Resyllabification.

Prenasals may undergo further modifications. Whenever they occur word-initially, their nasal element may optionally become syllabic and bear tone. This tone may or may not be distinct from that of the next tone-bearer. Such change may occur in word-initial position only. Nor does it seem to be limited to prenasals only. This process is discussed in the present section.

Because the rule is not only optional, but restricted to word-initial position, and perhaps also to monitored speech, it may arguably be conceived as presupposing the operation of the other rules involving nasals discussed so far, and formulated simply as a delinking rule. In turn, it may trigger another rule, which optionally inserts /i/ before such a word-initial syllabic nasal.

Under certain conditions, nasals may be optionally syllabified word-initially. For cases where such a nasal is followed by a consonant, this is exemplified in (68),

(68) a. /n-to-taac-e/
f-1p-fetch-fv
[**n**totaace]
'we will fetch water (from the tap) (today)'

b. /n-mo-taac-e/
f-2p-fetch-fv
[**m**motaace]
'you will fetch water (from the tap) (today)'

c. /n-βa-taac-e/
f-3p-fetch-fv
[**m**bataace][27]
'they will fetch water (from the tap) (today)'

where the syllabic nasals are printed in bold-face. What these examples do not show is that the process is optional, but they do illustrate its word-initial application. It does not

---

[27] This surface representation is not to be confused with [mbátááce] 'they will not come' (m = H), from /m-βa-ta-Vc-e/, which, according to Judith Moraa, is a South Mugirango form equivalent to [mbáre γóóca] (m = H) at least in Getutu, North Mugirango, and Baasi.

apply elsewhere. Moreover, (68b) exemplifies the fact that the following consonant may also be a nasal.

It would seem that, at least in some cases, nasals may also be syllabified before vowels. This is shown in sample derivation (69),

(69)	input	/-eβ-/
	suffixation	-eβe
	prefixation	n-eβ-
	Nasal Resyllabification (71)	**n**eβ-
	Pre-Nasal /i/-Insertion (80)	ineβ-
	Nasal Velarisation	iηeβ-
	tonal rules	
	output	[iηéβ!é] 'forget me!'[28]

The allomorphy due to Pre-Nasal /i/-Insertion (80), also exemplified in (69), is discussed in section 2.3.6.

Before discussing a few other details that may be involved, it would seem that data such as those in (68, 69) may in part be accounted for by (70),

(70) Word-initial Nasal Delinking (optional)

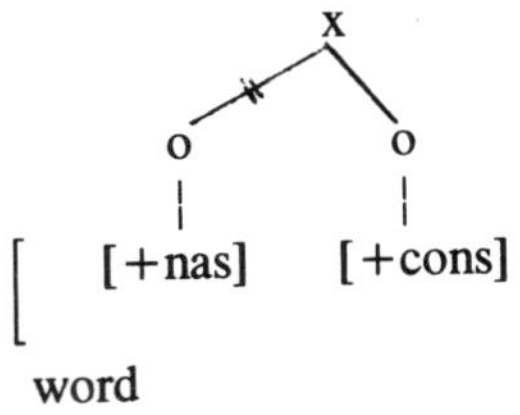

This rule optionally delinks, in word-initial position, the nasal element of a prenasalised consonant from the x to which it is associated.

The resulting word-initial floating nasal, which by convention may not be relinked to the following consonant, is then supposedly resyllabified by (71),

28 Contrast with [niiηeβe] 'I will forget (soon)', presumably from /n-n-eβ-e/. The alternative [niiñeβe] also occurs, but, though acceptable, is considered odd or sub-standard, at least by Judith Moraa.

(71) Nasal Resyllabification (optional)

```
            N
            ¦
            x'
            |
[      [+nas]
word
```

This rule optionally assigns a nucleus to any floating word-initial nasal. The SSA-rules will then automatically assign an N"-node.

Several other observations may be added. The segment following the nasal may be a consonant, including any nasal, or a vowel. Whenever it is a vowel, the application of the rule may be more restricted than when it is a consonant, but this requires further examination. The formulation of the rule may be adjusted accordingly. The details involved in other possible restrictions on the rule also require further looking into.

In the present analysis, word-initial nasals are supposed to prenasalise regularly to a following consonant due to Prenasalisation (61), which triggers Nasal Homorganisation (62) and, if applicable, Defricativisation (65). Then Nasal Delinking (70) and Resyllabification (71) may apply.[29]

As expressed in (70-71), word-initial nasal resyllabification is optional. It may or may not apply. Its application may be style-dependent; that is, it may be a stylistic rule. The rules (70-71) usually apply in monitored and even leisurely normal speech, but their effect is often hardly noticeable in rapid normal or very rapid non-monitored speech. However, examination of the details involved is referred to the future. Generally, syllabicity of nasal elements of word-initial prenasals tends to be absent in rapid, non-monitored speech, where the phonetic output simply tends to be a word-initial prenasalised consonant. Phonetically, the syllabic nasal element of a word-initial prenasal, represented generally as [N̩C], tends to be expressed by the prominence or distinctness that is characteristic of syllabicity.

As exemplified in (68b), finally, nasals may themselves be prenasalised word-initially. Whenever this occurs, the first nasal element may optionally become syllabic through Nasal Delinking (70) and Resyllabification (71). Whiteley's examples (1960: 5) suggest that only [mm] and [nn] are involved in this position, though this is not stated explicitly. However, word-initial [ññ] and [ηη] also occur, as exemplified in (28d).

---

[29] Assuming that there is a distinction between extra-syllabicity due to regular syllabification, and the setting afloat of nasals due to delinking, I take it that Nasal Resyllabification (71) does not need to be ordered with respect to N-Placement (41).

2.3.6. Pre-Nasal /i/-Insertion.

It was explained in section 2.3.5 that the nasal element of word-initial prenasalised consonants may optionally become syllabic. In the present section, another type of allomorphy involving such nasal elements is considered.

Before a word-initial syllabic nasal, an /i/ may be optionally inserted. Accordingly, the resulting surface representations may be [-imC], [inC-], [iñC-], and [iηC-], depending on the specifications for Place of the consonant involved. All types of prenasalised consonant qualify. Compare inventory (26).

However, in some cases at least, a syllabic nasal may be followed word-initially also by a vowel, instead of a consonant. In such cases, the nasal may surface as [iη], though the determinants are arguably morphological, rather than phonological (see section 2.3.7).

Regardless of whether the following segment is a consonant or a vowel, this type of allomorphy, though common, seems to be optional. It may be a stylistic rule, characteristic of more or less monitored speech. However, in certain tenses the /i/ seems to have become lexicalised (see section 3.3.5 for some examples).

The process may be exemplified, as in sample derivation (72),

(72)	input	/-γor-/
	suffixation	-γore
	prefixation	nγore
	Prenasalisation (61)	**n**γore
	Nasal Homorganisation (62)	*η*γore
	Defricativisation (65)	*η*gore
	Nasal Resyllabification (71)	***η***gore
	/i/-Insertion (80)	**i**ηgore
	tonal rules	
	output	[íηgóré] 'I('ll) buy (right now)'

As to whether this allomorphy is free or determined, at least in part, by syntactic category, is not yet clear. Differences in tone may also be relevant. Thus [iηgóré] 'buy me!', originally given by one informant, was judged incorrect by another informant, who generally disallowed /i/-insertion, when the initial nasal was an object marker, and who gave the following judgments, in addition to (72): [ηgóre], *[iηgóre] 'buy me!', and [ηgorére], *[iηgorére] 'buy for me'. Such variation requires further investigation, so that some of what is argued here must necessarily be tentative. The output in (72) is presumably resyllabified as in (73),

```
(73)  N"  N"  N"
      |   /|  /|
      x  x x x x
      | /| | | |
      i ηg ó r!é
```

Next, /n-eβ-e/ --> [iηéβ!é] 'forget me!', *[iñéβ!é], is an example of a form in which a word-initial nasal is followed by a vowel. Presumably, it may be syllabified as in (74),

```
(74)   N" N"  N"
       |  /|  /|
       x x x x x
       | | | | |
       i η é β!é
```

Also compare the following syllabification of an alternative surface representation, characteristic of non-monitored speech, in (75),

```
(75)   N" N"  N"
       |   |  /|
       x   x x x
       |   | | |
       η   é β!é
```

Yet another alternative surface representation for (74) is (76),

```
(76)    N"  N"
        /|  /|
       x x x x
       | | | |
       η é β!é
```

The syllable structure of (74) is identical to that of (73), but distinct from that in (75) and (76), which also differ from each other. Interestingly, while /i/-Insertion (80) applies in the context or word-initial syllabic nasals, once it does apply, it renders these nasals non-word-initial. This, in turn, causes resyllabification.

Given the types of surface variation previously discussed, the approach taken here is to consider the insertion of /i/ as a process that is independent of Nasal Delinking (70) and Resyllabification (71). The following facts also seem to support this analysis.

There is one exception to the tendency of /i/-insertion to apply word-initially only. It involves the verbal focus element, /n(V)-/, but only when this is followed, as in certain tenses, by the homomorphous first person singular subject marker /n(V)-/. In the tenses in which these two elements co-occur, an /i/ regularly precedes the nasal of the subject marker and thus follows the nasal of the focus marker, as exemplified in (77),

(77)

input	/-taar-/ 'walk'	
suffixation	-taare	
prefixation (sm1s)	n-taare	
Prenasalisation (61)	ntaare	
/i/-Insertion (80)	intaare	
prefixation (focus)	na-intaare	
/a/-Delinking (147) & Linking Rule (90)	i	
tonal rules		
output	[nííntáaré]	'I will walk (soon)'

This exception to the general word-initial application of /i/-insertion also holds, whenever the segment following the nasal is a vowel. This is exemplified in (78),

(78)

/n-n-eβ-e/	/n-n-γor-e/	/n-n-aak-e/
f-sm1s-forget-fv	f-sm1s-buy-fv	f-sm1s-beat-fv
[nííŋéβé]	[nííŋgóré]	[nííŋáaké][30]
'I will forget (soon)'	'I will buy (soon)'	'I will hit (soon)'

In contrast with these examples, however, we find that this insertion of /i/ does not apply in focussed tenses in which the nasal of the focus does not immediately precede the nasal of the first person singular. This is exemplified in (79),

(79) /n-βa-n-taar-i-a/
f-3p-om1s-walk-c-fv
[mbáántaariá][31] (m = H), *[mbaintaaria], *[ímbáántaariá]
'they made me walk (today)'

/n-βa-n-γor-a/
f-sm3p-om1s-buy-fv
[mbááŋgorá] (m = H), *[mbáíŋgorá] (m = H), *[ímbááŋgorá]
'they bought me (today)'

There are many other examples similar to these.

Taking all the relevant types of surface variation previously discussed into account, the rule accounting for them may provisionally be formulated as in (80),

---

30 Informant judgments differed as to whether [niiñaake] was an acceptable alternative.

31 Contrast with [mbáantááríá] (m = H) 'they made me walk (long ago)' and [mbáántaarétí] (m = H) 'they made me walk (recently)' (probably should be [mbáántaarété]).

(80) Pre-Nasal /i/-Insertion (optional)

$$\emptyset \dashrightarrow i \;/\; \left[_{\text{word}} \begin{bmatrix} [+\text{nas}] \\ \text{focus} \end{bmatrix} \right. \text{---} \; [+\text{nas}] \; +$$

It inserts an /i/ before any nasal followed by a morpheme boundary, either word-initially, or immediately after a word-initial focus. The morpheme boundary following the [+nas] segment correctly ensures that the rule does not apply, whenever the nasal and some following segment are part of the same morpheme. Thus, given the word-initial facts of Gusii verbal morphology, the rule may apply word-initially either to the nasal of the first person singular subject marker, or to that of the focus element, and word-internally also to the nasal of the former, if, and only if, it is preceded by the nasal of the focus element.

The morpheme boundary + in the context of the rule leaves it open, what type of segment may follow the nasal segment. This allows for the rule to apply, regardless of what the actual following segment is. This is correct, since in fact any type of segment may indeed follow it. However, this element in the context is specifically relevant for subsequent vowels.

Note that, though the surface representations produced by (80) are presumably phonetic alternatives for word-initial syllabic nasals, the rule may be formulated without reference to syllable structure, because it is conceived as a free alternative to, and thus independent of, resyllabification of word-initial nasals.

Finally, if the observation that application of the rule is obligatory in certain tenses only, is correct, this may be expressed formally by marking these as [+(80)].

2.3.7. Nasal Velarisation and Palatalisation?

Whiteley makes the following statement about the alternation between [η] and [ñ] in certain contexts. "Occurring especially in the verbal prefix [i.e. the subject marker] and the infix [i.e. the verbal object marker] of Cl[ass] 1a [i.e. the animate first person singular, here designated 1s] (...), n is realized as η [before ε, ɔ, or u]; as ñ [before i, e, or o]; and as either η or ñ [before a] (quoted from 1960: 6, but also see 1956: 25).

Restricted to surface variation involving the first person singular (subject, object, or relative) marker, this appears to be a statement of phonologically conditioned allomorphy or allophony. The word "especially" is suggestive of broader application, but it remains unexplained. It seems advisable, therefore, to interpret the statement as being of limited application. Thus it may be formulated as in (81),

(81) first person singular nasal variation (Whiteley)

$$n \dashrightarrow \text{a.}\quad \eta\ /\quad \text{---}\quad]_{1s} \left\{ \begin{matrix} \varepsilon, \text{ɔ} \\ u, a \end{matrix} \right\}$$

$$\text{b.}\quad \tilde{n}\ /\quad \text{---}\quad]_{1s} \left\{ \begin{matrix} e, o \\ i, a \end{matrix} \right\}$$

which states that the alveolar nasal of any first person singular marker is realised as velar [η] before lower mid, high back, or low vowels, but as (alveolo-)palatal [ñ] before upper mid, high front, or low vowels. The verbal root /-it-/ 'to kill' is said to be an exception to (81b) (see 1956: 25, 1960: 6), but this is disconfirmed here, as shown hereafter in (86).

The present research takes a different position. Allomorphy of the first person singular verbal (subject or object) marker is indeed involved, and the variation phonologically determined, but the details of the process seem to require a different formulation from that in (81). The nature of the variation and the class of triggers appear to be different, as in (82),

(82) first person singular verbal marker (subject/object) ==>

a. m, n, ñ, η / --- [+cons]
b. η / --- [-cons]

This allomorphy rule states that, whenever the verbal marker is followed by a consonant (82a), its quality is determined by that of the following consonant, through prenasalisation and homorganisation. Underlyingly postulated as /n(V)-/, it may surface not only as [m], [n], [η] or [ñ] (see section 2.1.3 for some examples, also involving the homomorphous verbal focus).

It may be added that the allomorphs in (82) may be subject to various other applicable rules, such as resyllabification and pre-nasal /i/-insertion word-initially (see sections 2 3.5 and 2.3.6), and may exhibit further variation accordingly. Word-initially, alternative surface representations may thus be [im-], [in-], [iñ-], or [iη-], for example, depending on the context and perhaps also the style or rate of speech. The /i/ is accounted for by Pre-Nasal /i/-Insertion (80).

Before a vowel, any vowel, the first person verbal marker regularly surfaces as a velar nasal (82b). But there may be some idiolectal variation here. Some informants held [ñ] to be an acceptable alternative for [η]. However, first, this judgment was not general. Second, it was restricted to certain specific lexical items. Third, informants may have confused the surface representations in question with those that do contain [ñ], but with a different meaning, as (part of) an allomorph for object marker 4 and 9, which are homomorphs, or for object marker 6 /ya-/, as in (83),

(83) before /i/:

a. /na-a-ye-it-e/
f-sm3s-om9-kill-fv
[naayeite] or [naañeite]
'he will kill 9-it (today)'

before /e/:

b. /a-ka-ye-eβ-a/
sm3s-t-om4,9-forget-fv
[akañeeβa], *[akaη(e)eβa]
'(and) he forgot 4-them/9-it (recently)'

c. /o-a-ye-eβ-ir-e/
sm3s-t-om4,9-forget-pv-fv
[oñeeβire], *[oηe(e)βire]
'he has just forgotten 4-them/9-it'

before /a/:

d. /na-a-ya-aak-e/
f-sm3s-om6-beat-fv
[naayaake], [naañaake], *[naaηaake]
'he will beat 6-them' (near future)

e. /o-ya-aak-ir-e/
sm3s-om6-beat-pv-fv
[oyaakire] or [oñaakire]
'he has just beaten 6-them'

Here object marker 4, 9 /ye-/ is allomorphically realised as /ñe-/, and object marker 6 /ya-/ allomorphically as [ña], which suggests that surface alternation involving [η] and [ñ] in verbal markers may not be a purely phonological process of free or contextually determined variation, but may, at least in part, be morphologically or morpholexically determined.

It may be added that the relevant data used in the present study are those of an informant whose linguistic judgments were consistent with (82).

Whenever the verbal focus is immediately followed by the marker of the first person singular (regardless of whether the latter is followed by a consonant or a vowel), the underlying sequence /n(V) + n/ surfaces as [niiN-], where N ranges over any of the four surface nasals. Thus, anticipating several rules, [niiηaaηge] 'I will refuse', underlyingly /n-n-aNγ-e/ and syntactically analysed as f-sm1s-refuse-fv, may presumably be accounted for relatively informally, as in (84),

(84) input /-aNγ-/
suffixation aNγe
phonological rules aaŋge
prefixation naaŋge
allomorphy (82b) ŋaaŋge
Pre-Nasal /i/-Insertion (80) iŋaaŋge
prefixation (focus) naiŋaaŋge
linking convention [niiŋaaŋge]

Some data illustrating nasal velarisation involving the first person singular subject marker, are given in (85),

(85) before /i/:

a. /n-n-irok-e/
f-1s-fear-fv
[niiŋiroke], *[niiñiroke]
'I will be afraid (today)'

(compare [ntoiroke] 'we will be afraid (today)')

b. /n-n-it-e/
f-sm1s-kill-fv
[niiŋite], *[niiñite]
'I will kill (today)'

(compare [ntoite] 'we will kill (today)')

before /e/:

c. /n-n-eβ-e/
f-sm1s-forget-fv
[niiŋeβe], *[niiñeβe]
'I will forget (today)'[32]

before /ε/: accidental gap

---

[32] Compare

/n-to-eβ-e/
f-sm1p-forget-fv
[ntoeβe]
'we will forget (today)'

before /a/:

d. /n-n-aak-e/
f-sm1s-beat-fv
[niiŋaake], *[niiñaake]
'I will beat (later today)'

before /ɔ/:

e. /n-n-ɔm-e/
f-sm1s-plaster-fv
[niiŋɔmɛ], *[niiñɔmɛ]
'I will plaster' (near future)

(contrast with [niŋɔmɛ] in Whiteley 1960: 6)

before /o/: accidental gap

before /u/: accidental gap

Given the same context, the first person singular object marker exhibits the same type of allomorphy. It is exemplified for all contexts in (86),

(86) before /i/:

a. /na-a-n-it-e/
f-sm3s-om1s-kill-fv
[naaŋite], *[naañite]
'he will kill me (today)'

/n-βa-a-n-it-a/
f-sm3p-t-om1s-kill-fv
[mbaaŋita], *[mbaañita]
'they killed me (long ago)'

before /e/:

b. /a-ka-a-n-eβ-a/
sm3s-t-t-om1s-forget-fv
[akaaŋeβa]
'(and) he forgot 1s-me (recently)'

/n-βa-a-n-eβ-a/
3p-om1s-t-forget-fv
[mbaaŋeβa], *[βaañeβa]
'they forgot me (recently)'

/o-a-n-eβ-ir-e/
sm3s-t-om1s-forget-pv-fv
[o(o)ηeβire], *[o(o)ñeβire]
'he has just forgotten 4-them/9-it'

/n-a-a-Vc-e a-n-eβ-e/
f-sm3s-t-come-fv sm3s-om1s-forget-fv
[naace aηeβe] or [naacaaηeβe]
'he will (come and) forget me' (near future)

/a-ko-ci-a ko-n-eβ-a/
sm3s-t-go-fv 15-om1s-forget-fv
[aγocia kooηeβa]
'he is going to forget me (today/soon)'

c. /n-βa-a-n-et-a/
f-sm3p-t-om1s-pass-fv
[mbaaηeta], exceptionally also [mbaañeta]
'they passed me'

before /ε/:

d. /βa-a-n-εr-i-a/
sm3p-t-om1s-finish-c-fv
[βaaηεria]
'they finished me (recently)'

e. /n-βa-a-n-εγ-a/
f-sm3p-t-om1s-seduce-fv
[mbaaηεεγa], *[mbaañεεγa]
'they finished me (recently)'

before /a/:

f. /o-a-n-aak-ir-e/
sm3s-t-om1s-beat-pv-fv
[(o)oηaakire], *[oñaakire]
'he has just beaten me'

/na-a-n-aak-e/
f-sm3s-om1s-beat-fv
[naaηaake], *[naañaake]
'he will beat me' (near future)

g. /na-a-n-aNγ-e/
f-sm3s-om1s-refuse-fv
[naaηaaηge], *[naañaaηge]
'he will refuse me' (near future)

/na-a-n-aNγ-e/
f-sm3s-om1s-refuse-fv
[naaηaaηge], *[naañaaηge]
'he will refuse me' (near future)

before /ɔ/:

h. /n-βa-a-n-ɔrɔk-i-a/
f-sm3p-t-om1s-show-c-fv
[mbaaηɔrɔkia], exceptionally also [mbaañɔrɔkia]
'they showed me (to)'

i. /n-βa-a-n-ɔɔn-i-a/
f-sm3p-t-om1s-sell-c-fv
[mbaaηɔɔnia], *[mbaañɔɔnia]
'they sold me (just now)'

before /o/:

j. /n-βa-a-n-om-i-a/
f-sm3p-t-om1s-dry-c-fv
[mbaaηomia], *[mbaañomia]
'they dried me'

k. /n-βa-a-n-orok-er-a/
f-sm3p-t-om1s-appear-ap-fv
[mbaaηorokera], *[mbaañorokera]
'they appeared to me'

before /u/:

l. /n-βa-a-n-uur-a/
f-sm3p-t-om1s-wrest-fv
[mbaaηuura], *[mbaañuura]
'they wrest from me'

The judgment of the informant whose speech is recorded here was that in all forms [η] was correct and that in the few cases where both [η] and [ñ] were allowed, [η] was still the more acceptable of the two, [ñ] being in fact less correct.

It may be added that, contrary to Whiteley's restrictions summarised in (81), the change from /n/, or, depending on the analysis, /N/, to surface [η] may occur not just before /ε/, /ɔ/, /u/, or /a/, but before any vowel.

Finally, the precise conditions, if any, of the variation between the velar and the palatal nasal that may occur, is not as yet clear to me. In any case, this variation appears to be very limited. At least, there are few words in which it may occur, so there are few such words available for systematic checking. Since, so far I have been unable to discover regularity in it, I tentatively conclude that such variation is probably restricted to a few lexical items, and possibly, perhaps in addition, to some idiolects.

Parenthetically, Whiteley (1960: 9) also lists [ñi-] as a possible alternative surface representation for the first person singular subject marker, but he does not specify any context or exemplify. Nor have I been able to find any examples of this. Thus his listing seems to be an error. The form does however occur as an allomorph for the homomorphous object marker for class 4 and 9, /ye-/. But this allomorphy is not identified as such by Whiteley (1960: 10). The allomorph may occur at least before /e/ and /a/, as in (87),

(87) allomorphy of object marker 4, 9

before /i/:

a. /n-βa-a-ye-it-a/
f-sm3p-t-om4,9-kill-fv
[mbaayeita] or [mbaañeita]
'they killed 9-it (long ago)'[33]

before /e/:

b. /ye-eβ-e/
4/9-forget-fv
[ñieeβe]
'forget 9-it, forget 4-them' (imperative)

compare:

/to-eβ-e/
om1p-forget-fv
[tweeβe]
'forget us'

/βa-eβ-e/
om3p-forget-fv
[βeeβe]
'forget them'

---

[33] 'They killed 4-them (long ago)', though possible in some imaginary setting, such as a fairy tale, is semantically odd in any real situation.

before /a/:

c. /n-βa-a-ye-aNγ-a/
f-sm3s-t-om9-refuse-fv
[mbaayiaaŋga] or [mbaañiaaŋga]
'they refused 9-it/4-them (today/recently)'

The changes exemplified here are ye > yi before /a/, ye > ñe before /e/, and ñe > ñi before /e/ or /a/. Some of these may possibly take place also before other vowels or even any vowel, but this needs to be ascertained. The change from /ye/ to [ñe] does not appear to be a purely phonological process, nor even the variation of a mere nasal, but allomorphy of object marker /ye-/.

Presumably, the processes go something like this. It may be argued that ye + V becomes yi +rough upper mid vowel raising (see section 2.3.10), and that, since [yi], like [wu], is apparently a rare sequence or change in virtue of some version of the Obligatory Contour Principle, as argued by some, in the present case it may cause further tensing of the initial front glide [y] into (alveolo-)palatal nasal [ñ]. But since [ñe] also occurs, it is more plausibly interpreted as a free allomorph of [ye]. In either case, the change from /e/ to [i] may be accounted for by upper mid vowel raising.

Accordingly, the allomorphy of object marker 4,9, may arguably be summarised as in (88),

(88) allomorphy: object marker 4, 9 ==>

[ye] or [ñe] / --- [-cons]

Though optional raising of /e/ to [i] has been substantiated so far only before /e/ and /a/, until disconfirmative data are adduced, I will assume that Upper Mid Vowel Raising (108), as it is formulated hereafter, may apply regularly to either of the allomorphs in (88). The latter will be generalised in section 3.2.3.3.

The following examples (89), finally, illustrate that the various allomorphs for object markers 1s, 4, and 9, also involve different tonal tonal pattern,

(89) a. [mbááŋaaŋgá], *[mbááñaaŋgá]
'they refused me (today/recently)'

b. [mbááñiááŋgá], or [mbááñaáŋgá], or [mbááñiááŋgá]
'they refused 9-it'

(initial [m] = H in all representations)

To conclude, this section has proven to be an anticipation of part of the discussion in Chapter Three. What seemed to be somewhat indeterminate phonological or morphological variation in the quote with which the section began, turns out to be a case of restricted allomorphy. In vowel-initial adjectives, however, a certain degree of what seems to be free variation does occur, involving the intervocalic nasal of class 9a-10a, which may be postulated underlyingly as /n/ or /N/, depending on the degree of abstractness to which one whishes to take the analysis (see 3.2.1.5 for some examples illustrating this variation and its indeterminacy).

2.3.8. Linking Rule.

Before rules involving vowels and glides are considered, it is appropriate at this point to insert a brief discussion of two commonly applicable processes already exemplified in one or two derivations given so far. The first of these is captured in (90),

(90) Linking Rule (LR)

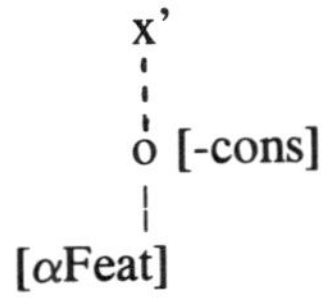

It states that a vocalic root node is spread regularly to any adjacent floating x'. It is assumed to apply regularly in the normal rapid style of speech described in this study. As such, it is triggered by at least Prenasalisation (61), Complex Segment Formation (109), and /a/-Delinking (147), and in these cases may be accounted for as an instance of compensatory lengthening. In slow speech it is assumed to be optional. An alternative formulation is (91),

(91) 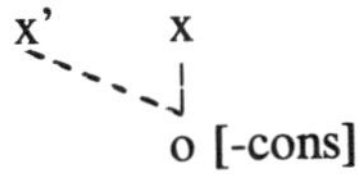

(mirror image)

which associates a vocalic root node to a neighbouring floating x', whether to the left or to the right of it.

The application of Linking Rule (90) is exemplified in the following partial, idealised sample derivations (92),

(92) a. Input Prenasalisation (61) Linking Convention (90)

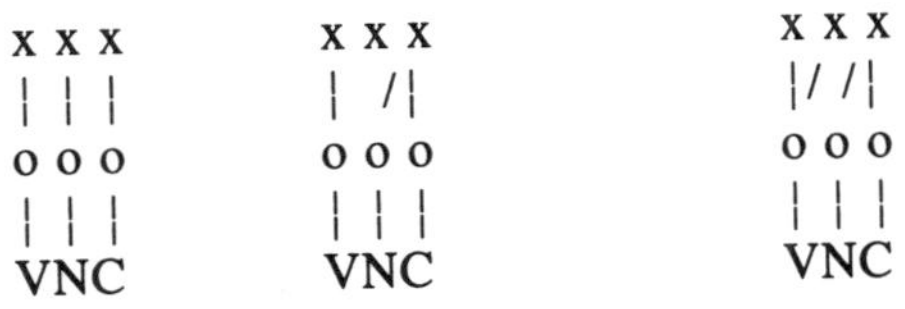

[V N C] [V NC] [VVNC] Phonetic interpretation

```
b.    Input      CSF (109)    Linking Convention (90)

      x x x      x x x        x x x
      | | |      |\  |        |\ \|
      o o o      o o o        o o o
      | | |      | | |        | | |
      CGV        CGV          GGV

      [C G V]    [CG V]       [CGVV]      Phonetic
                                          interpretation
```

Before prenasals and after complex segments containing a post-glide, vowels are often long, as Whiteley (1960: 5) also notes, but does not formulate.

2.3.9. x-Trimming.

When several rules cooperate to produce an overly long vowel, this may usually be trimmed down to a long one, since derived overly long vowels rarely occur. Prenasalisation (61) and Complex Segment Formation (109) provide a case in point. Consider the idealised sample derivation in (93), where the effect of the rule to be proposed is exemplified under (93c),

```
(93)  a. input          b. Prenasalisation (61), CSF (109), LR (90)

      x x x x x          x x x x x
      | | | | |          | | | | |
      o o o o o          o o o o o
      | | | | |          |\ \|/ /|
      CHVN C             CGV  NC

      [GHVNC]            [CGVVVNC] Phonetic interpretation

      c. x-Trimming (94)

      x x x x x
      | | | | |
      o o o o o
      |\ \|  /|
      CGV  NC

      [CGVVNC]                     Phonetic interpretation
```

The rule that reduces the association of the V to three x's under (93b) to two x's under (93c) may be formulated as in (94),

(94) x-Trimming

```
x --> Ø /    x  x ---
             |/
             o
             |
          [αFeat]
```

It stipulates that, whenever some hierarchy of specified feat[ures] is linked to more than two x's on the timing-tier, these will be trimmed down to two.

However, sequences of identical vowels, one of which is long, do seem to occur, so that while the configuration in (95a) seems to be prohibited, the ones in (95b), where V1 and V2 are segmentally identical, seem to be allowed,

```
(95)  a.   *x x x
             \|/
              V

            [V::]                       Phonetic interpretation

      b.   x x x         x x x
           |  \|         |/  |
           V1 V2         V1 V2

           [V::]         [V::]          Phonetic interpretation
```

though, especially in rapid non-monitored speech, even (95b) may be shortened to [V:]. Thus there seems to be some tension between the tendency toward reducing vowels to long ones and the tendency for overly long vowels to surface after all.

A filter similar to (94) was originally formulated for Luganda by Clements (1986), in order to handle overly long vowels. Given the view of phonological reality adopted here, and the fact that overly long consonants do not occur in Gusii, the generalised formulation in (94) may arguably be maintained. The filter is also relevant for the description of neigbouring Kuria (see Cammenga 1994: 50-52). In one form or another it may play a role also in other East Nyanza Bantu languages.

Rules involving vowels and glides.

2.3.10. Upper Mid Vowel Raising.

It was observed in section 2.2 that, though Whiteley (1960: 3-4) seems to postulate both /w/ and /y/ as underlying glides, it is possible to consider at least [w] as a segment derived from underlying high back vowel /u/. In any case, if the glides are considered as derived from underlying vowels, these units may be distinguished from each other in terms of the nonlinear approach adopted here, as in (96),

(96)

	a.		b.		
	N"	N	N"	N	syllabic tier
	|	|	|	|	
	x	x	x	x	timing tier
	|	|	|	|	
	o	o	o	o	root node
	|	|	|	|	
	/i/	/i/	/u/	/u/	symbol summarising hierarchy of specified features
	[y]	[i]	[w]	[u]	phonetic representation

Though Whiteley does not formulate either glide formation or complex segment formation, he does explicitly define some form of gliding in the following, somewhat ad hoc manner: "Where the first member of a sequence (i, o, u) is a component of an affix, it tends to be realised as 'y' or 'w'" (1960: 3). In a footnote on the same page he adds that "There is, however, considerable variation with speed of utterance. Even within a given stem or radical, where the first component of a sequence is 'i', this may be realised as 'y' in very quick speech."

The purport of these statements may be summarised as in (97),

(97) gliding (Whiteley 1960)

a. /i/ --> [y] / ---]$_{\text{affix}}$ [[-cons] $_{\text{morpheme (root, affix?)}}$

b. {/u/, /o/} --> [w] / ---]$_{\text{affix}}$ [[-cons] $_{\text{morpheme (root, affix?)}}$

Whiteley seems to suggest that Gusii glides occur both underlyingly and as derived segments, and that lexical gliding, whether as glide formation proper or as part of complex segment formation, is conceived as a stylistic or style-dependent rule. However, the exact nature and domain of his rule or rules are not made fully and unambiguously clear. At least five points may be noted.

First, though /o/ may be turned immediately into [w], in his account, /e/ is left out of consideration. However, that this upper mid front vowel must be included among the targets of both glide formation and complex segment formation, is supported by evidence such as (98), where discussion of several rules is anticipated,

(98) a. underlying representation:

/e-a-om-ir-e/
sm9-t-dry-pv-fv

derivation:

input	om	
t-suffixation	omir	
	omire	
t-prefixation	aomire	
/a/-Delinking (147) & LR (90)	oomire	
sm-prefixation	eoomire	
UMVR (108)	ioomire	
Glide Formation (114) & x-Trimming (94)	yoomire	
output	[yoomire]	'9-which has dried'

b. underlying representation /e-ke-eηe/ a-px7-short

derivation:

input	-eηe
npx-prefixation	keeηe
UMVR (108)	kieηe
augmentation	ekieηe '7-short'

this may be subsequently changed further into:

CSF (109)	ekyeeηe
Degliding	ekieeηe

c. /e-a-aak-ir-u-e/
rm9-t-hit-pv-p-fv
[yaakirwe]
'9-which has just been hit'

The last three forms in (98b) are acceptable alternative surface representations.

Second, if glide formation and complex segment formation may be distinguished, it turns out that, especially in the case of glide formation proper, /o/ is not always changed into either |u| or |w| word-initially. Thus in (99) [wiika] is disallowed,

(99) /o-ik-a/
3s-arrive-fv
[óika], *[wiika]
'he arrives' (untimed habit)[34]

The allomorph is /ko-/ --> [γw] word-initially (see sections 3.2.3.1 and 3.2.3.2), so that /o-/ is no longer word-initial, hence no longer a target for glide formation. But the /o/ of this allomorph /ko-/ does remain a target for complex segment formation, which regularly applies in these instances.

Third, /e/ is not regularly turned into [i] and [y] in nouns, as shown in (100),

(100) a. /e-usi/
9-thread
[eusi] 'thread'
*[iuusi], *[iusi], *[yusi], or *[yuusi]
plural [ciusi][35]

b. /e-aNγa/
9-cloth
[ea(a)ηga], *[ia(a)ηga], *[ya(a)ηga]
'(piece of) cloth'

---

[34] Compare the full paradigm for this tense,

singular	1 /na-a-ik-a/ -->	[n(a)aika]
	2 /ko-a-ik-a/ -->	[γwa(a)ika]
	3 /o-a-ik-a/ -->	[oika]
plural	1 /to-a-ik-a/ -->	[twa(a)ika]
	2 /mo-a-ik-a/ -->	[mwa(a)ika]
	3 /βa-a-ik-a/ -->	[βa(a)ika]

This is not to be confused with 'I (etc.) used to arrive',

singular	1 /n-ik-a/ -->	[iηiká]
	2 /o-ik-a/ -->	[oiká]
	3 /a-ik-a/ -->	[aiká]
plural	1 /to-ik-a/ -->	[toiká]
	2 /mo-ik-a/ -->	[moiká]
	3 /βa-ik-a/ -->	[βaiká]

[35] This word may have been taken over from Swahili **uzi** 'thread', plural nyuzi.

c. /e-a/
9-of
[ya], *[ea]
'9-of'

This is arguably due to a tendency toward preservation of morphological identity. Word-internally, however, upper mid front vowel /e/ is usually turned into either |i| or |y|, as in (98b), and upper mid back vowel /o/ is usually turned into either |u| or |w|, as in (101),

(101) a. underlying representation /o-mo-eŋe/
a-px1-short

informal derivation:

UMVR (108)	omueŋe '1-short'
CSF (109)	omweŋe
LR (90)	omweeŋe
Degliding	omueeŋe

b. underlying representation /o-mo-omo/
a-px1-dry

informal derivation:

UMVR (108)	omuomo '1-dry'
CSF (109)	omwomo
LR (90)	omwoomo
Degliding	omuoomo

The four representations in each of these derivations are apparently acceptable alternative outputs, at least in different styles of speech.

Fourth, Whiteley does not discuss the nature of the trigger vowel of his rule, as sketched in (97), though the title of his section, "Vowel sequence: Internal, immediate", suggests that the trigger may be any vowel, whether long or short. Nor does he state whether it may be identical to, or must be different from, the preceding target vowel. Thus it is not clear in his account precisely which vowels may, and which may not, function as a trigger of the rule.

Fifth, and finally, perhaps less important in this connection, is that contrasts such as that between [akarúâ] 'he gave a present' and [akarwa] 'he came from' (Whiteley 1960 3), might suggest that glide formation may be influenced by tone, but this is not corroborated here. The example appears to be a mistake. Either [akarúá] or [akarwá] (w = H) may mean both 'he gave a present' and 'he came (from)', and similarly, [áárúá], a different past tense, may mean both 'he gave a present' and 'he came from', though the tonal contrast is retained in the infinitives, [korúá] 'to give a present' versus [korua] 'to come from'. No evidence was found suggesting that gliding may occur in the one, but not in the other, infinitive. Hence the possibility just suggested seems to be unfounded.

In fact, neither Whiteley's nor my own treatment of tone is systematic. For this reason, it is as yet impossible to draw definitive and systematic conclusions about the interaction between the segmental and suprasegmental levels of the language. This requires further study.

To sum up, /i/ or /e/ may be turned into [y], and /u/ or /o/ into [w], under certain conditions. Apparently, a clear-cut distinction must be made between two types of gliding, one due to complex segment formation, the other to glide formation proper, if only because the targets and conditions of these processes are slightly different.

It would seem, however, that the change from /e/ to [y], and from /o/ to [w], is mediate. The data suggest that these upper mid vowels are first raised to high, and that the resulting high vowels constitute the targets for the gliding rules. The latter are discussed in sections 2.3.13 and 2.3.14. The rest of this section concerns raising of upper mid vowels.

Later on, something will be said about the different ordering of raising of upper mid vowels that is possible with respect to mid vowel height spreading, at least in different idiolects. The two rules share the same targets and, in part, their domain. But first we will have to examine the relevant data for upper mid vowel raising. To anticipate, if it is borne in mind that /e/ may not be raised before /i/, and /o/ not before /u/, which excludes these high vowels as triggers in these contexts, the examples given in (102) and (103) illustrate all the remaining cases of upper mid vowel raising before any vowel.

First, consider the data in (102),

(102) raising of /e/ to [i]

before /i/: blocked

/e-me-it-i/	/e-ke-it-i/
a-4-kill-agentive sx	a-7-kill-agentive sx
[emeiti], *[emiiti]	[eγeiti], *[eγiiti]
'big killers' (abusive)	'killer' (abusive term)

before /e/:

/e-ke-eηe/	/e-ke-eβ-i/
a-7-short	a-7-forget-agentive sx
[ekieηe], [ekeeηe]	[ekieβi]
'7-short'	'small forgetful person' (abusive term)

before /ɛ/:

/e-ke-ɛnɛ/	/e-ke-ɛ/
a-7-true	a-7-basket
[ekiɛnɛ], [ɛkɛɛnɛ][36]	[ekiɛ], [ɛkɛɛ]
'truth'	'(small) basket'

/ke-a-ɛɛr-ir-e/
7-t-finish-pv-fv
/ke-ɛɛr-ir-e/ (through /a/-Delinking (147), LR (90), and x-Trimming (94); also see the next example)
[kiɛɛrire]
'7-it has (just) been finished'

before /a/:

/ke-a-ɛɛr-ir-e/	/e-a-ɛɛr-ir-e/
7-t-finish-pv-fv	9-t-finish-pv-fv
[kiaɛɛrire]	[yaɛɛrire][37]
'7-it has (just) been finished'	'9-it has (just) been finished'

before /ɔ/:

/e-me-ɔγɔ/	/e-me-ɔrɔɔrɔ/
a-4-cassava	a-4-soft
[emiɔγɔ], [ɛmɛɔγɔ]	[emiɔrɔɔrɔ], [ɛmɛɔrɔɔrɔ]
'cassavas'	'4-soft (ones)'

before /o/:

/e-me-om-o/	/e-me-oγe/	/e-ke-o/
a-4-dry-sx	a-4-sharp	a-7-sx (indep. pronoun)
[emiomo]	[emioγe]	[ekio]
'4-dry'	'4-sharp'	'7-it, the 7-one'

before /u/:

/ko-ke-ur-a/
15-om7-take(by force)-fv
[γokeura], in rapid speech also [γokiura]
'to take 7-it (by force)'

similarly, /ye-/ > [yi-], or [ñe-] > [ñi-], for om 9

---

36 [ɛkɛɛnɛ] was judged to be more common.

37 [yɛɛrire] was considered unacceptable by some.

To summarise these data, upper mid /e/ may be raised to high [i] before any vowel, except /i/. Though this process applies commonly and frequently, it appears to be optional. When it does apply, it usually triggers gliding and compensatory lengthening of the following vowel through Linking Rule (90), though gliding may be undone again by degliding. These possibilities are not written out for most lexical items in (102), but will be discussed hereafter, when these rules are examined.

As acceptable alternations such as [emi(ɔ)ɔγɔ] or [emy(ɔ)ɔɔγɔ] 'cassavas', on the one hand, and [ɛmɛɔγɔ] 'cassavas' indicate, whenever upper mid vowel raising shares both its domain and targets with mid vowel height spreading, either one or the other may apply, but not both to one and the same form. Accordingly, to take the present example as a representative case, *[ɛmiɔγɔ] and *[emɛɔγɔ] do not occur.

Especially at the beginning of words, upper mid vowel raising may be blocked. Such blocking may be due to a tendency toward preservation of morphological identity, as in (99) and (100). In the case of some lexical items, it may perhaps be due to (a tendency toward) lexicalisation, suggested by the linguistic judgment on [ɛkɛɛnɛ] and ?[ekiɛnɛ].

Some of these points will be taken up again in a moment, but first consider the data in (103),

(103) raising of /o/ to [u]

before /i/:

/o-mo-it-i/
a-1-kill-sx(agentive)
[omoiti]
or [omuiti], [omwiiti] (in rapid speech)
'killer'

before /e/:

/o-mo-et-i/
a-1-pass-sx (agentive)
[omoeti]
or [omueti], [omw(e)eti],
'1-passer-by'

before /ɛ/:

/o-βo-ɛnɛ/	/ko-mo-ɛγɛk-er-er-a/
a-14-true	15-om1-lean-ap-ap-fv
[oβwɛɛnɛ]	[komwɛɛγɛkɛrɛra]
or [ɔβɔɛɛnɛ]	or [kɔmɔɛγɛkɛrɛra]
*[ɔβwɛɛnɛ]	'to lean against 1-him'
'truth'	

/ko-ee-ɔrɔk-i-a/
15-rf-teach-c-fv
[kwεεɔrɔkia]
or [kɔεεɔrɔkia]
'to teach oneself'

before /a/:

|o-mo-ando|
a-3-inheritance
[omuando], [omw(a)ando]
'inheritance'

before /ɔ/:

/ko-ɔm-a/
15-smear-fv
[kuɔɔma]
or [kɔɔma][39]
'to smear'

/ko-ɔk-a/
15-give of light-fv
[γuɔka], [γwɔɔka], *[γɔɔka][38]
'to give off light'

/o-mo-ɔγɔ/
a-3-cassava
[omwɔγɔ], *[εmεɔγɔ]
'cassava'

/o-mo-ɔrɔɔrɔ/
a-3-soft
[omuɔrɔɔrɔ][40], [omwɔɔrɔɔrɔ]
'3-soft (ones)'

/ko-ɔrɔk-i-a/
15-teach-c-fv
[kuɔrɔkia]
or [kwɔɔrɔkia]
but ?[kɔɔrɔkia][41]
'to teach'

/ko-ro-ɔni-a/
15-sell-fv
[koruɔɔnia], [korwɔɔnia]
or [kɔrɔɔnia]
'to sell 11-it'

---

[38] [γɔɔka] means 'to be happy'. There may be a difference in tone, vowel length, or both, between these verbs, or they may be homomorphs, but this was not recorded.

[39] [kɔɔma] is due to Mid Vowel Height Spreading.

[40] [εmεɔrɔɔrɔ] is not recorded, but may be possible.

[41] Different judgments were given on infinitive [kɔɔrɔkia]. However, [omwɔɔrɔkia] and [ɔmɔɔrɔkia] 'teacher' were judged to be acceptable alternatives.

before /o/:

/o-mo-om-o/	/ko-orok-i-a/
a-1,3-dry-sx	15-appear-c-fv
[omwoomo], [omoomo]	[kuorokia], [kwoorokia][42]
'1,3-dry (one)'	'to show'

/o-mo-oγe/
a-1-sharp
[omuoγe], [omwooγe], [omooγe]
'1-sharp witted, bright'[43]

before /u/: blocked

/o-mo-uut-i/
a-1-blow-agentive sx
[omouuti], *[omuuti]
'1-blower'

To summarise these data, /o/ may be raised optionally to [u] before any vowel, except /u/. The observations made on /e/ with respect to the data in (102), are applicable also to /o/ in connection with those in (103), mutatis mutandis. For example, the occurrence of [oβwεεnε], but not *[ɔβwεεnε], and its possible alternative, by mid vowel height spreading, [ɔβɔεεnε], but not *[oβɔεεnε] confirms the remark already made on the mutual exclusiveness of, or the bleeding relation between, upper mid vowel raising and mid vowel height spreading.

If now we take the data in (102) and (103) together, the following conclusions may be drawn. First, upper mid vowels may be raised optionally but quite regularly.

Second, such raising may sometimes be prevented. In some cases this appears to be subject to a tendency toward preservation of morphological identity. It is prevented word-initially in at least some non-deverbal nouns (99, 100) and word-internally sometimes also in verbs.[44] Lexicalisation may possibly account for its non-application in at least some other instances, such as (104),

---

[42] [koorokia] may be possible, but it, and any linguistic judgment on it, is unrecorded.

[43] In other classes, /-oγe/ may mean '(physically) sharp'.

[44] However, in at least one session, both [emiitɔɔŋgɔ] '4-peaceful', from /eme-itɔNγɔ/, and [ekeiγweera] '7-obedient', from /eke-iγweera/, were elicited. These may be deverbal nouns. Should any mistake be involved here, I would expect [emeitɔɔŋgɔ], rather than [ekiiγweera], in these instances.

(104) a. /o-mo-ɔrɔ/
a-3-panga
[ɔmɔ(ɔ)ɔrɔ], *[omuɔrɔ], *[omwɔɔrɔ]
'panga, machete'

contrast with

/o-mo-ɔrɔ/
a-1-lazy
[omuɔrɔ], [omwɔɔrɔ], *[ɔmɔ(ɔ)ɔrɔ]
'1-lazy (person)'

b. |ko-εεnd-a|[45]
15-go-fv
[kɔεεnda]
*[kuεεnda], *[kwεεnda]
'to go'

c. /e-ke-oombe/
a-7-group
[ekeoombe] or [ekioombe]
'group'

Note that while [ekeoombe] seems to be the more common form for [ekioombe] (104c), whereas /e-ke-ara/, for example, regularly surfaces as [ekiaara] or [ekyaara] 'finger', rather than as *[ekeara] or *[ekeaara].

Some apparent exceptions, finally, are plausibly accounted for by their underlying representation. For example, the singular [omooño] 'salt' (*[omuoño], *[omwooño]) has [emeeño] 'salts (i.e. kinds of salt)' (*[emioño], *[emyooño]) for its plural. The particular surface representations and the non-application of upper mid vowel raising (/o/ or /e/ before /o/) suggest that the prefix vowels are lengthened instead.

This calls for a short digression. Such lengthening might be accounted for by postulating a rule lengthening vowels before a palatal or alveolo-palatal nasal. Alternatively, since /oño/ would produce plural */eme-oño/ --> *[emioño], /-Vño/ might be postulated underlyingly, as in (105),

(105)	/o-mo-Vño/	/e-me-Vño/
	a-3-salt	a-4-salt
	[omooño]	[emeeño]
	*[omuoño], *[omwooño] 'salt'	*[emioño], *[emyooño] 'salts'

[45] At least some informants judged this to be an acceptable alternative to |ko-γεεnd-a| --> [kɔγεεnda] 'to go, to walk'. The latter was however considered to be the proper or original Gusii verb. This suggests that [kɔεεnda] may be an adaptation of Swahili [kuenda] 'to go'.

Similar forms do occur, for example [amaañiiηga] 'blood' (no singular), but they appear to be rare. Which account is more plausible, by rule or by underlying representation? Examples such as [omooηina] 'old woman (term of respect)', plural [aβaaηina] 'old women', suggest that a vowel may be lengthened also before a velar nasal, so that the lengthening rule just suggested would be of a broader scope, if we postulate /-ηina/ underlyingly. However, the data in (106),

(106) a. vowel before palatal nasal

[ɔmɔñɛrɛrɛ] '1-slim', *[ɔmɔɔñɛrɛrɛ]

b. vowel before velar nasal

[omoηaañi] '(rat's) hole', *[omooηaañi][46]

[koηwaansa] 'to sacrifice', *[kooηwaansa]
[omoηwaansi] 'sacrificer', *[omooηwaansi]
[ekηwaansɔ] 'sacrifice', *[ekeeηwaansɔ]

[koηaata] 'to starve', *[kooηaata]

indicate that the process is neither regular, nor general before either (alveolo-)palatal or velar nasal. Hence they suggest that their surface representations, as those of the previous examples, are more plausibly accounted for by postulating underlying representations that contain an underspecified vowel, as in (107),

(107) plausible underlying representations

a. /-Vñiiηga/ --> [amaañiiηga]
/-Vño/ --> [omooño] and [emeeño]

but:

/-ñɛrɛrɛ/ --> [ɔmɔñɛrɛrɛ]

b. /-Vηina/ --> [omooηina] and [aβaaηina]

but:

/-ηaañi/ --> [omoηaañi]
¦-ηwaans-¦ --> [koηwaansa]
--> [omoηwaansi]
--> [ekeηwaansɔ]
/-ηaat-/ --> [koηaata]

[46] Compare [eηgoro] 'hole, burrow' (i.e. of any other animal).

The last two examples under (107b) seem to be representative of verbs generally, since I have found no verbs containing a long vowel before a palatal or velar nasal in the root- or stem-initial positions exemplified in (107).

To return to the summary of the main details of upper mid vowel raising, third, because the changes from /e/ to [i] before /i/ and from /o/ to [u] before /u/ are prohibited, the application of the rule must be limited in such a way, that, if the trigger and the target have the same specification for roundness, the trigger may not be higher than the target.

Fourth, in domains where both it and mid vowel height spreading may apply, either one or the other actually applies. Apparently, this may differ per idiolect. Whether it may depend on regiolectal or sociolectal factors, remains to be examined (also see section 2.3.14).

Given the preceding discussion, the rule accounting for the data given may be formulated as in (108),

(108) Upper Mid Vowel Raising (optional) (UMVR)

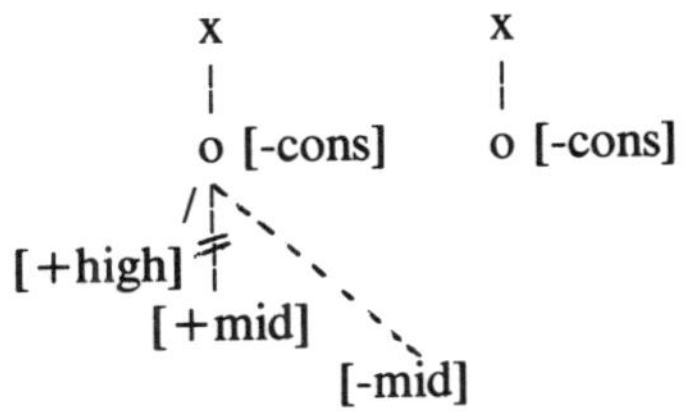

Condition: if target and trigger agree in roundness, the trigger must not be higher than the target

It raises any upper mid target vowel to high, whenever it is immediately followed by another vowel. Technically, this is expressed by assigning [-mid] to the target, thereby delinking [+mid]. The following vowel may be taken as the trigger. The concept of immediate sequence is formally expressed by the linkage of the target and trigger root-nodes to consecutive x's on the timing-tier.

The condition blocks the operation of the rule, whenever the trigger is higher than the target in case both agree in their specification for roundness. That is, target /e/ will not be raised to |i|, if the trigger is /i/, and /o/ will not be raised to |u|, if the trigger is /u/. Thus the outputs *|uu| and *|ii| are correctly prevented.

As pointed out, the rule applies generally and regularly, but may occasionally be limited by tendencies toward preservation of morphological identity and lexicalisation. However, the effect of these may be restricted to some contexts only. As these are further examined, details of the rule (108) may have to be adjusted. To clarify whether or not its application may be connected with distinct lexical categories, classes of morphemes, or even particular morphemes, and to what extent this may be so, are points that may have to be established more systematically. Accordingly, the rule might turn out to be obligatory, but with some classes of lexical items exempted from it. These points are left to future research, but the main outlines of the rule are nonetheless sufficiently clear and empirically substantiated.[47]

---

[47] A few full paradigms, also interesting for other surface variation, may be added here. First, |-iγweeri| 'obedient', may presumably be interpreted as a deverbal adjective derived from /ko-iγu-er-a/ --> |kwiiγweera| 'to obey', which seems to be related to /ko-iγu-a/ --> [koíγwá] or [kwiíγwá] 'to sense, to become aware of through sensory perception, to hear, to smell, to feel, to taste'; in class 4-5, where this adjective, presents a semantic anomaly, |-itɔηg| 'peaceful' is used as an alternative test-word,

1	/omo-iγweeri/	--> [omuiγweeri]	
2	/aβa-iγweeri/	--> [aβaiγweeri]	
3	/o-irok-ir-e/	--> [oirokire] '3-which is feared'	
3	/e-irok-ir-e/	--> [eirokire] '4-which are feared'	
5	/eri-iγweeri/	--> [eriiγweeri] (abusive term)	
6	/ama-iγweeri/	--> [amaiγweeri]	
7	/eke-iγweeri/	--> [ekeiγweeri]	
8	/eβi-iγweeri/	--> [eβiiγweeri]	
9a	/e-n-iγweeri/	--> [eñiγweeri]	
10a	/ci-n-iγweeri/	--> [ciiñiγweeri]	
11	/oro-iγweeri/	--> [oroiγweeri]	
12	/aka-iγweeri/	--> [akaiγweeri]	
14	/oβo-iγweeri/	--> [oβoiγweeri]	
15	/oko-iγweera/	--> [okoiγweera]	'obeying' (verbal noun)
16	/a-itɔNγɔ/	--> [aitɔɔηgɔ]	
21	= 9a		

Next, the paradigm for /-eηe/ 'short',

1	/omo-eηe/	--> [omoeηe]
		--> [omueηe]
		--> [omueeηe]
		--> [omweeηe]
2	/aβa-eηe/	--> [aβeeηe]
3	/omo-eηe/	--> [omueηe]
		--> [omweηe]
		--> [omweeηe]
4	/eme-eηe/	--> [emieηe]
		--> [emyeeηe]
		--> [emieeηe]
5	/eri-eηe/	--> [erieηe]
		--> [eryeeηe]
		--> [erieeηe]
6	/ama-eηe/	--> [ameeηe]
7	/eke-eηe/	--> [ekieηe]
		--> [ekyeeηe]

--> [ekieeηe]
8 /eβi-eηe/ --> [eβieηe]
--> [eβyeeηe]
--> [eβieeηe]
9 /e-n-eηe/ --> [eñeηe]
10 /ci-n-eηe/ --> [ciiñeηe], *[cieηe]
11 /oro-eηe/ --> [orueηe]
--> [erweeηe]
--> [orueeηe]
12 /aka-eηe/ --> [akeeηe]
14 /oβo-eηe/ --> [oβueηe]
--> [oβweeηe]
--> [oβueeηe]
15 /oko-eηe/ --> [okueηe]
--> [okweeηe]
--> [okueeηe]
16 /a-eηe/ --> [aeηe]
21 = 9 or 16

where variation is caused by Upper Mid Vowel Raising, Complex Segment Formation, Compensatory Lengthening, Degliding, and
/a/-Delinking.

Next, the paradigm for /-aNγo/, Prenasalisation --> |-aηgo| 'quick, agile', to which intermediate output Compensatory Vowel Lengthening is applicable,

1	|omo-aηgo|	--> [omuaηgo]
2	|aβa-aηgo|	--> [aβaaηgo
3	|omo-aηgo|	--> [omuaηgo]
4	|eme-aηgo|	--> [emiaηgo]
5	|eri-aηgo|	--> [eriaηgo]
6	|ama-aηgo|	--> [amaaηgo]
7	|eke-aηgo|	--> [ekiaηgo]
8	|eβi-aηgo|	--> [eβiaηgo]
9a	|e-n-aηgo|	--> [eñaηgo]
10a	|ci-n-aηgo|	--> [ciñaηgo]
11	|oro-aηgo|	--> [oruaηgo]
12	|aka-aηgo|	--> [akaaηgo]
14	|oβo-aηgo|	--> [oβuaηgo]
15	|oko-aηgo|	--> [okuaηgo]
16	/a-aηgo/	--> [aaηgo]
21	= 9a	

1 [omoonto omwaaηgo] 'an agile person'
2 [aβaanto aβaaηgo] 'agile persons'
3 [omotwe omwaaηgo] 'a quick[-thinking] head'

2.3.11. Complex Segment Formation.

Given the underlying representation of complex segments that consist of a consonant and a glide, i.e. [Cw] and [Cy] in (7), as a consonant followed by a high vowel, i.e. as /Cu/ and /Ci/ respectively, such complex segments may be considered to be derived through (109),

---

4	[emetwe emiaaŋgo] 'quick[-thinking] heads'
5	[riimwaana riaaŋgo] 'a quick tall child'
6	[amamwaana amaaŋgo] 'quick tall children'
7	[ekeoombe ekiaaŋgo] 'a quick group'
8	[eβioombe eβiaaŋgo] 'quick groups'
9	[ɛmɔɔri eñaaŋgo] 'a quick calf'
	(strictly, [ɛmɔɔri] refers to the stage between a suckling calf and a heifer)
10	[cimɔɔri ciaaŋgo] 'quick calves'
11	[oroñaamboβe oruaaŋgo] 'a quick spider'
12	[akamwaana akaaŋgo] 'a quick small child'
14	[oβomwaana oβwaaŋgo] 'quick small children'
15	[okoɣoro okuaaŋgo] 'a quick leg'
21	[ñaaŋera eaaŋgo] 'quick Blackie'

And finally, the paradigm for /-omo/ 'short',

1 /omo-omo/	--> [omuomo]
2 /aβa-omo/	--> [aβoomo
3 /omo-omo/	--> [omuomo]
4 /eme-omo/	--> [emiomo]
5 /eri-omo/	--> [eriomo]
6 /ama-omo/	--> [amoomo]
7 /eke-omo/	--> [ekiomo]
8 /eβi-omo/	--> [eβiomo]
9a /e-n-omo/	--> [eñomo]
10a /ci-n-omo/	--> [ciiñomo]
11 /oro-omo/	--> [oruomo]
12 /aka-omo/	--> [akoomo]
14 /oβo-omo/	--> [oβuomo]
15 /oko-omo/	--> [okuomo]
16 /a-omo/	--> [aomo]
21 = 9a or 16	

An alternative for 9, 10, and 21 is [-ŋomo].

(109) Complex Segment Formation (CSF)

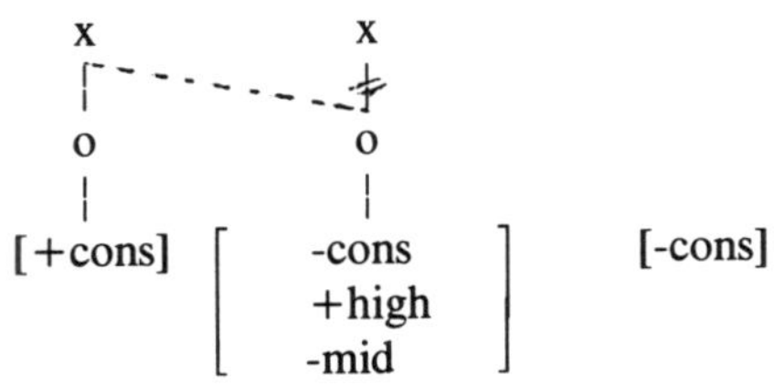

Condition 1: trigger and target may not be identical
Condition 2: the first segment may be front glide y

As formulated, this rule states that, whenever a consonant is immediately followed by a high vowel, the latter, if itself followed by another vowel, is delinked from its x on the timing-tier and spread leftward to the x that dominates the consonantal segment, thereby creating a complex segment. Whenever the high vowel is [+back], the resulting complex segment will be [Cw]; whenever it is [-back], the result will be [Cy].

The condition correctly prevents the changes from /i/ + /i/ to [yi] and from /u/ + /u/ to [wu]. Of these sequences, the former does occur somewhat rarely. Thus object marker /ye/ may be changed into [yi] (though allomorph [ñi] seems to be more common), but presumably [yi] never results from (109). The second sequence, [wu], does not occur in fact.

Whiteley does not make the conditions of this process fully clear, but he does seem to consider it as a widely applicable one, as he states (1960: 5) that any consonant, prenasal, and even front glide /y/ (taken care of by condition 2), may in fact so combine with the back glide, except for the relatively exceptional complex segment <nj> (i.e. [ndž]). According to my own findings, at least the complex segments in (110), involving back glide [w], may be distinguished,

(110)	Bilabial	Alveolar	Alveolo-Palatal	Velar
Obstruent	[βw]			[γw]
		[tw]		[kw]
Fricative		[sw]		
Affricate			[cw]	
Nasal	[mw]	[nw]	[ñw]	[ŋw]
Liquid		[rw]		
Glide			[yw]	

on which the following observations may be made. First, the consonantal parts of [βw] and [γw] are continuant, in contrast to Whiteley's characterisation of them as obstruents, i.e. as [bw] and [gw] respectively (1960: 5). Their continuancy may be very slight sometimes, but it is nonetheless consistent.

Second, because Prenasalisation (61) is characterised as prenasalisation of [+cons] segments, and glides as [-cons] segments dominated by a syllable-node N", any complex segment consisting of a nasal element plus a glide -i.e. [mw], [nw], [ñw], and [ŋw]- cannot properly be handled by Prenasalisation (61). Such complex segments are therefore considered not as prenasalised glides, but as post-glided nasals.

Third, Whiteley's observation that vowels following such segments are regularly long, is correct. It is precisely the length of such vowels that provides an argument for considering the preceding complex segments as derived, rather than as "'w' clusters", as he does (1960: 5). The long vowels may be considered as lengthened compensatorily. However, due to the general constraint on marginal long vowels, word-final vowels are not regularly lengthened (or, alternatively, their lengthening is 'undone'). Thus, for example, the passive voice marker /-u-/, which always occurs in the final syllable, when preceded by a consonant and followed by a vowel, regularly surfaces as [...CwV], rather than as [...CwV:].

Fourth, [ndž] being a unique allomorph derived from /n + e/ or /n + ye/, [džw] probably does not occur by itself. I have been unable to find any surface representations containing the latter. Nor do I expect that any will be found, given the fact that there appear to be no verbal roots beginning with /uV/ (where V is distinct from /u/; see appendix 2). The sequence /n + e + uV/ is not likely to occur, therefore, so that [džw] has not been included in inventory (110).

Finally, Whiteley states that "n + w = mb (rare!)" (1956: 5), i.e. alveolar nasal /n/ followed by back glide /w/ is realised as the bilabial complex segment [mb]. It is characterised as a rare change. However, he does not exemplify. Nor has it been corroborated by the present research. Therefore I suppose that it does not occur, except, perhaps, idiosyncratically.

On the present analysis, then, the segments in (110) may be considered as derived from a consonant followed by /u/ through Complex Segment Formation, regardless of whether the affected sequence occurs in a derived or underived environment. The case of /y/ plus /u/ will be considered in a moment. The segments in (110) are exemplified in (111),

(111) complex segments containing back glide [w]

a. in non-derived environments

/ko-βuat-a/ --> [ko**βw**aata] 'to grasp, to get hold of'
/ko-βuɛn-a/ --> [ko**βw**ɛɛna] 'to recover (from illness)'
/ko-βuɛn-er-a/ --> [ko**βw**ɛɛnɛra] 'to be fit (v.i.)'[48]
/ko-tuar-a/ --> [γo**tw**aara] 'to possess, to have'
/ko-kuan-a/ --> [γo**kw**aana] 'to talk'
/ko-suaγ-a/ --> [γo**sw**aaγa] 'to thresh (by pounding)'

---

[48] /ko-γuɛn-er-a/ --> [ko**γw**ɛɛnɛra] was judged by some, but not all, to be its equivalent.

/ko-cuaγ-a/ --> [γo**cw**aaγa] 'to abandon'
[džw]: data not found and unlikely to be found
/e-muam-u/ --> [e**mw**aamu] '9-black'
/emanueri/ --> [ema**nw**eeri] 'Immanuel'
[ñw]: see under b
/ko-ŋuaNs-a/ --> [ko**ŋw**aansa] 'to sacrifice'[49]
/ko-ŋuan-i-a/ --> [ko**ŋw**aania] 'to whip, to cane'
/ko-ruar-a/ --> [ko**rw**aara] 'to be sick'
[yw]: see under b

b. in derived environments

[γw]:

/ko-aNc-a/	/ko-ko-aNc-a/
15-like-fv	15-om2s-love-fv
[**γw**aañca]	[ko**γw**aañca]
'to like/love'	'to like you'

[mw]:

/mo-a-c-ir-e/
2p-t-come-pv-fv
[**mw**aacire]
'2p-you have come (just now)'

[nw]:

/o-mo-nua/, possibly /o-mo-nu-a/
a-3-mouth
[omo**nw**a]
'mouth'

[ñw]:

/ko-ñu-a/
15-drink-fv
[ko**ñw**a]
'to drink'

[49] More specifically, 'to sacrifice, in order to appease ancestral spirits, by slaughtering an animal'. A synonym is [γɔkɔrɛrana]. Compare [kɔñɛña] 'to slaughter' from /ko-ñɛñ-a/.

[yw]:

/ko-iy-u-a/
15-dig out-p-fv
[koiywa]
'to be dug out'

(compare [koiya] 'to dig out')

It may be added that [yw] was found in derived environments only.

At least the following complex segments containing a front glide (112) also occur on the surface,

(112)

	Bilabial	Alveolar	Alveolo-Palatal	Velar
Obstruent		[ty]		[ky]
Continuant	[βy]	[sy]		[γy]
Affricate			[cy]	
Nasal	[my]	[ny]	[ñy]	
Liquid		[ry]		

However, in the case of /Ci/ the surface [Ci] seems to be more common. I have not been able to establish the occurrence of [ηy] and [wy], so these may not occur.

Exemplification of the segments in inventory (112), finally, constitutes an accidental gap, as I have only collected the examples in (113),

(113) [ñy]:

/ko-γañ-i-a/
15-wait-c-fv
[koγañya], more commonly [koγañia]
'to cause to wait'

(contrast with [koγaña] 'to wait'

/ko-mañ-i-a/
15-know-c-fv
[komañya], more commonly [komañia]
'to cause to know'

2.3.12. Glide Formation.

Whiteley's account of gliding, in which upper mid vowel raising and the actual formation of the glide concerned are not differentiated, is obscured by what seem to be several printing errors. He writes, "(..) where 'o' is followed by 'e, i, a' the sequence tends to be heard as 'we, wi, wa'; and where 'i' is followed by 'e, a, o, u' the sequence tends to be heard as 'wi, wa, we, wu'" (1956: 4). This is neither clear, nor correct. Nor can his more general formulation of gliding, "Where the first member of a sequence (i, o, u) is a component of an affix, it tends to be realized as 'y' or 'w'" (1960: 3), be considered sufficiently adequate.

However, it is correct to say that upper mid vowels may not only be raised by Upper Mid Vowel Raising (108) and be glided subsequently through Complex Segment Formation (109). Under certain conditions, gliding may also occur at the beginning of words, i e. without a consonant preceding the target vowel. This cannot be accounted for by Complex Segment Formation (109), given its structural description, and therefore an additional rule is needed.

Given the characterisation of glides in structural terms (96), glide formation may be formulated in structural terms, as in (114),

(114) Glide Formation (optional)

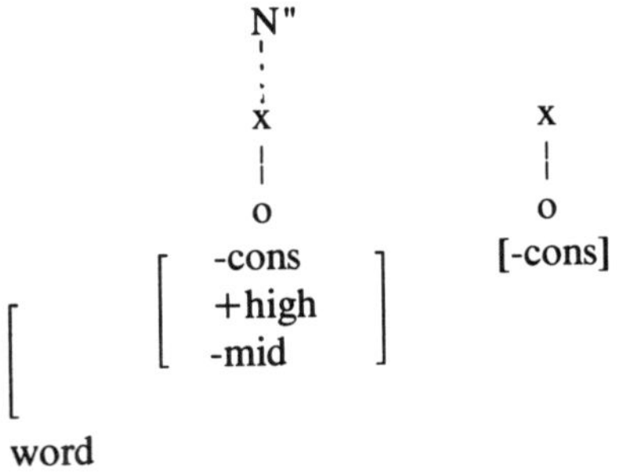

It optionally assigns an N"-node to a word-initial high vowel, which is thereby turned into a glide.

Since the vowel following a word-initial glide may lengthen, an additional rule is needed,

(115) Post-Glide Vowel Lengthening (optional)

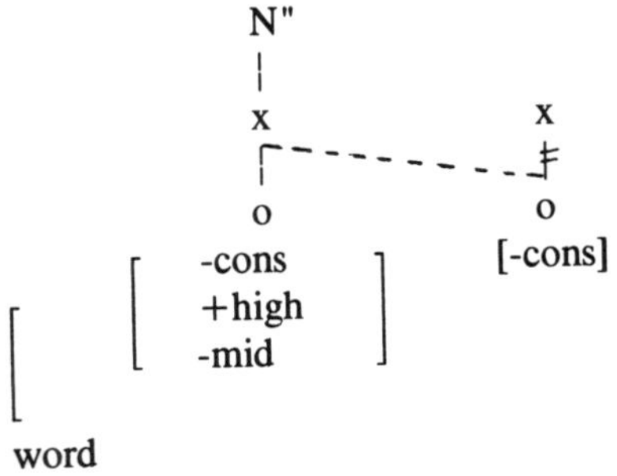

It optionally spreads the node of a vowel to the x of a preceding word-initial glide, thereby lengthening the vowel, having the effect of diphtongisation. From Whiteley's account it is not clear whether a vowel following a word-initial glide always lengthens. Corroborative evidence was hard to obtain due to an abundance of data such as (116a), where such lengthening is explained differently. The rule does however seem to apply regularly in the restricted context of tenses such as (116b),

(116) a.

input	-om-
suffixation	oma
tense-prefixation	aoma
/a/-Delinking (147)	ooma
sm9-prefixation	eooma
UMVR (108)	iooma
Glide Formation (114), PGVL (115), x-Trim (94)	yooma
output	[yooma] '9-which has dried (earlier today)'

b. acceptable alternative surface representations

|e-ak-ir-e|
rm9-hit-pv-fv
[eakire] or [yaakire]
'9-which is hit'

/e-am-a/
sm9-grow-fv
[ea(a)ma] or [yaama]
'9-it grows (always)'

|e-a-γuund-ir-e|
9-t-go bad-pv-fv
[yaaγuundire]
'9-it has reeked (just now)'
(after Whiteley 1960: 47)

In (116a), word-initial /e/ is first raised to |i| through Upper Mid Vowel Raising (108), which in turn is glided to [y]. It should be added that, instead of [yooma], [eooma] and [iooma] are also possible, presumably depending on the style of speech. The limitations on Upper Mid Vowel Raising (108), apparently involving tendencies toward lexicalisation and preservation of morphological identity, also bear on the application of Glide Formation (114), which it feeds.[50]

---

[50] Also compare the linguistic judgments reflected in the following surface representations,

a. doubtful surface representations

|e-eβ-ir-e|
rm9-forget-pv-fv
[eeβire], ?[yeeβire]
'9-which is forgotten'

|e-om-et-e|
rm9-dry-t-fv
[eomete], ?[yoomete]
'9-which has dried (i.e. is dry)'

|e-a-rεεt-ir-u-e|
sm9-t-bring-pv-p-fv
[earεεtirwe], ?[yaarεεtirwe]
'9-it has been brought'

/e-et-a/ --> [eétá], ?[yeétá] '9-it passes (always)'
compare [toétá] '1p-we pass (always)'

/e-eβ-a/ --> [eeβa], ?[yeeβa] '9-it forget (always)'
compare [toeβa] '1p-we forget (always)'

/e-uur-a/ --> [euura], ?[yuura]
'9-it takes (by force) (always)'
compare [touura] '1p-we take (by force) (always)'

/e-aak-a/ --> [eaaka], ?[yaaka]
'9-it hits (always)'
compare [toaaka], [twaaka] '1p-we hit (always)'

b. unacceptable surface representations

|e-it-ir-e|
rm9-kill-pv-fv
[eitire], *[yiitire]
'9-which is killed'

c. overruled by mid vowel height spreading

|e-εr-ir-e|516Xrm9-finish-pv-fv

[εεrire], *[εεrire]
'9-which is finished'

(contrast with
|e-εr-a|
sm9-finish-fv
[yεεra], *[εεra]
'9-it finishes (always)'

/e-εγ-ek-a/
rm9-lean on-sx-fv

Possibly due to preservation of morphological identity, class 9 prefix does not glide regularly in these tenses. [óika], *[wiika] 'he arrives' (untimed habit) has been mentioned in (99). Nominal examples such as [eaaŋga], *[yaaŋga] '9-cloth', have also been discussed (100). Lexicalisation, finally, seems to account for the data in (117),

(117) input |e-ŋiti e-a omoonto|
9-animal 9-of the-person

output [eŋiti ya omoonto] or [eŋiti yoomoonto] 'the animal of the person'
but *[eŋiti eoomoonto]

The conclusion of this section must be somewhat tentative. If all and any vowels would lengthen after any glide, this might be incorporated in the formulation of the gliding rules. But the precise nature and domain of Glide Formation (114) itself may have to be reconsidered. However, some form of lexical (and, as we shall see in section 2.4.1, post-lexical) glide formation clearly does apply, and quite regularly, in normal rapid speech, at least in some idiolects. Possible further details involved may be examined by future research.

2.3.13. Degliding.

The postulation of a degliding rule is motivated by the type of surface variation in (118),

(118) underlying representation: /e-ke-eŋe/ '7-short'

possible acceptable surface representations:

a. [ekieŋe]
b. [ekyeŋe]
c. [ekyeeŋe]
d. [ekieeŋe]

Of these surface representations, (118a) may be accounted for by Upper Mid Vowel Raising (108), (118b) by Complex Segment Formation (109), (118c) by Complex Segment Formation (109) and compensatory lengthening of the following vowel in virtue of the Linking Rule (90), and (118d) either by lengthening of the vowel following the high vowel, or, if we presuppose application of the rules that account for (118a-c), by a rule that deglides the glide previously derived through Complex Segment Formation (109).

The latter process may be formulated as in (119),

[εεγεka], *[yεεγεka]
'9-which is finished'

compare [twεεγεka] 'we are finished'

(119) Degliding (optional)

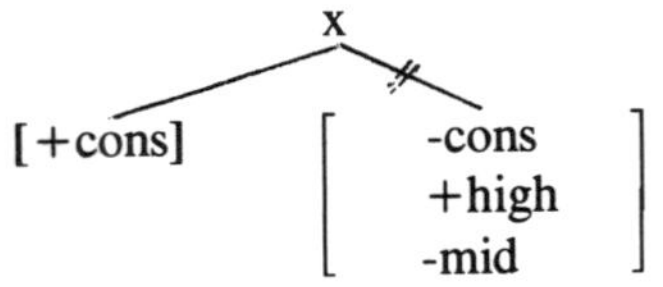

This segmental rule optionally delinks any high vowel segment that is preceded by a consonantal segment with which it forms a complex segment, being associated to the same x on the timing-tier. In effect, it turns [CG] into [CH'] (where H' represents a floating high vowel; by convention, any floating segment does not 'sound').

The following idealised sample derivation (120) exemplifies how the various processes just mentioned cooperate to produce the correct output,

```
(120) a. x-Placement (37)    b. CSF (109), LR (90)

         x x x                  x x x
         | | |                  |\ \|
         CHV                    CHV

         [CHV]                  [CGV:]       phonetic interpret.

      c. Degliding (119)      d. resyllabification

         x  x x                 x x x x
         |   \|                 | |  \|
         CH'V                   CH   V

         [CV:]                  [CHV:]       phonetic interpret.

      e. further syllabification

          N"    N"
          /|     |
         / N     N
        /  |    /|
         x x    x x
         | |     \|
         CH       V

         [CHV:]      phonetic interpretation
```

The input being /CHV/, after x-Placement (37) in (120a), Complex Segment Formation (109) and Linking Rule (90) cooperate to produce the intermediate representation in (120b), to which Degliding (119) optionally applies, resulting in (120c). Resyllabification then takes care of the rest (120d-e), first reassigning an x to the floating H', whether /i/

or /u/, and then adding further suprasegmental syllabic structure. Note that the output in (120e) is bisyllabic.

It could be argued that Degliding (119) is not needed and that the type of surface variation exemplified in (120d) may be accounted for alternatively by a rule that optionally lengthens a vowel following the sequence of a consonant plus a high vowel, regardless of whether or not the high vowel has glided. However, on that interpretation, it would seem that the Gusii data are not done sufficient justice, for at least three reasons.

First, the most relevant fact in this connection is that [ekieŋe] (118a) and [ekyeeŋe] (118c) appear to be common and regular, while [ekyeŋe] (118b) and [ekieeŋe] (118d) seem to be considerably less so, at least in normal non-monitored speech. Complex Segment Formation (109) applies fairly exceptionless in non-monitored, and even in monitored, speech, but may be optional in the latter. Degliding (119) seems to be more characteristic of monitored speech, but more research is needed to make these impressions more precise.

Second, a rule lengthening a vowel after any high vowel would disconnect the data in (118) from Complex Segment Formation (109). Such connection does however seem to be relevant and is therefore is expressed in the name of 'Degliding' for (119).

Third, though such a rule of vowel lengthening after any high vowel would account for both (118c-d), in terms of its effect it would overlap with the Linking Rule (90), which would have to be retained anyway on independent grounds. Degliding (119) does not so overlap. As a formal addition to the phonology, it elegantly reflects the relatively exceptional status of surface representations such as (118d).

Finally, if Degliding (119) and the Linking Rule (90) suffice to account for the data under consideration, both must be characterised as optional rules. If this were not so, [ekyeŋe], for example, would always be changed into [ekyeeŋe] without exception and [ekyeŋe] would be left unaccounted for.

2.3.14. Mid Vowel Height Spreading.

Whiteley's analysis (1960: 3-4) of regular changes in the height of mid vowels may be summarised informally as in (121),

(121) mid vowel variation (Whiteley 1960)

a.	e o	[o e] root	e o
b.	ɛ ɔ	[ɔ ɛ] root	ɛ ɔ
c.	?	[i u a] root	?

In nominal stems of the shape -(V)CV- and verbal radicals of the shape -VC- or -CV-, where V is either upper or lower mid, mid vowels in nominal and verbal prefixes, and in "post-stem positions", are said to vary concomitant with the "stem or radical vowel", as in (121a-b). Those in (121a) are identified as "close", that is, presumably, upper mid, as is borne out also by his transcriptions. Those in (121b) are identified as "open", that is, presumably, lower mid. No further information is added.

At least six points in Whiteley's statement are unclear or seem to be incorrect. First, prefix and suffix vowels are said to be "neither 'close' nor 'open' but rather intermediate" in contexts of the type in (121c). However, since these are said to be in complementary distribution with those in contexts (121a-b), they are "not significant in stems or in radicals", meaning that they are not semantically distinctive. Therefore they are not distinguished orthographically or transcribed phonetically in his study. In addition to this, their quality is nowhere positively defined. Hence these intermediate sounds are represented by a question-mark in (121).

Second, Whiteley's definition of the relevant domain is fuzzy. This is due partly to his terminology generally and partly to his characterisation of the process as such. As far as verbs are concerned, his statement appears to be correct, since he defines a radical (i.e. root) as "the irreducible element of the verb[al]" (1960: 2). However, since a stem is defined as the "non-prefix element in a nominal" (1960: 2), everything that follows the prefix in a nominal is included in this definition. In fact, as far as the triggers of mid vowel variation are concerned, the relevant domain is the root alone, both in nominals and in verbs, and even more broadly, in any lexical category.

Third, contrary to what Whiteley states or seems to imply, the segmental shape of any root, in terms of its CV-structure, appears to be irrelevant for the operation of the process. Thus it may be characterised as a purely phonological rule.

Fourth, though the distinction between (121a) and (121b) is well justified, and correct as far as it goes, the allophones in (121c) do not seem to occur solely if, and only if, /i/,

/u/, or /a/ occur in the root. They also seem to occur, when /e/ and /o/ occur in it, as in (121a).

Fifth, it is left implicit whether the prefixes and suffixes in which the mid vowels occur are immediately adjacent to the root, or may also be non-contiguous. However, his inclusion of the affixes in their entirety, e.g. prefixal ɔCɔ- and suffixal -ɛtɛ, suggests that non-contiguous vowels are indeed included. The examples presented in (1960: passim) confirm this, though it is not made explicit.

Finally, the precise nature of the process is not sufficiently made explicit and accounted for.

To conclude this brief summary, the type of variation in (121) is justly noted and partly exemplified by Whiteley, but it is insufficiently formulated. The rest of this section attempts to remedy this.

In contradistinction to (121), it is suggested that the properties of the process are more adequately summarised, in terms of inventory (5), as in (122a), or, in agreement with the conventions of representation adopted in this study, in terms of inventory (7), as in (122b),

(122) a.	e̱	[i, u	e̱	vs.	ɛ̱	[ɔ̱	ɛ̱
	o̱	e̱, o̱	o̱		ɔ̱	ɛ̱]	ɔ̱
		a]					
		root				root	
b.	e	[i, u	e	vs.	ɛ	[ɔ	ɛ
	o	e, o	o		ɔ	ɛ]	ɔ
		a]					
		root				root	

Some variation involving the specification of the feature [ATR] as such was indeed heard in the field. However, I have not been able to detect any regular phonological variation in terms of it, similar to that involving height, as discussed in the present section. Such [ATR]-variation appears to be merely of a phonetic nature.

Especially at the beginning of words, a difference could be heard between the quality of the augment, i.e. the first vowel in the word, and that of the prefix vowel, i.e. the second vowel in the word. Whenever these vowels had the same tone, they were usually perceived as identical. When the augment was high-toned and the prefix vowel low-toned, the first was often heard as /o/, i.e. as a [+ATR] upper mid vowel, and the second as /o̱/, i.e. as a [-ATR] upper mid vowel. This or similar differences may sometimes be found in older transcriptions, which, however, often do not record tone. For example, compare the East Victoria Nyanza sub-group A 6, comprising two languages, viz. 7, entered as "Ki-guzii (Igi-zii, Ki-siηgiri) or Ki-suba (Kωsωva)", and 7a, entered as Ki-kωria (or Ki-suna, Ki-tende), in Johnston (2/1922: 73ff). However, pending further research, for the present purposes I will not go beyond saying that this variation is phonetic.

Further investigation of this point may be interesting from an East Nyanza cross-linguistic point of view, as well. Variation in the quality of augment and prefix vowels, and sometimes vowels generally, from regiolect to regiolect in different, but related languages, and sometimes in a single language, are noteworthy. Non-sketchy, systematic regional study of this phenomenon may contribute toward further defining the relations between the languages and dialects in the region.

What, then, are the main characteristics of the rule? First, its triggers and targets involve vowels only. Second, these may or may not be contiguous on the timing-tier, but they must be contiguous on the vowel projection in the sense that opaque vowels may not intervene. Third, the trigger is regularly located in the root, so the rule is root-controlled. Fourth, its domain is the entire word. Fifth, it regularly applies, whenever, and as soon as, its structural description is met. Sixth, it operates bidirectionally from the root outward. Seventh, since morphological and structural factors appear to be irrelevant to its operation, it may be interpreted as a purely phonological rule. Finally, for reasons to be discussed in a moment, the rule may be considered as a type of harmony between mid vowels in terms of height, but technically it will be analysed as a form of local height spreading. Thus the term harmony is used somewhat loosely.

Before it is formulated, several examples are presented to illustrate the various details just mentioned. First, consider the examples in (123),

(123) a. /e-ke-tɔNγa/
a-7-basket
[εγεtɔɔŋga]
'(large) basket'[51]

(after Whiteley 1960: 26)

b. /e-ŋɔNβε/
9-cow
[εŋɔɔmbε]
'cow'

(after Whiteley 1960: 30)

c. /o-mo-γεni/
a-1-guest
[ɔmɔγεni]
'stranger, guest'

d. /e-ke-εnε/
a-7-true
[εkεεnε][52]
'the truth' (e.g. of a story)

e. /e-ke-ε/
a-7-basket
[εkεε]
'(specific type of small) basket'

---

[51] Large basket, used for carrying fruits, vegetables, and such like. It is usually carried (by women) on the head, but if by men, on the shoulder.

[52] Presumably from /e-ke-εnε/. Compare its plural /e-βi-εnε/ --> [eβiεnε] (disconfirmed as such by Judith Moraa), and the related adverb [βɔkεεnε] 'truthfully', which is presumably derived from /βo-ke-εnε/ through prefix-stacking. Also compare [ɔβɔkεεnε] '(deep) truth' and [oβwεεnε] '(the) truths'.

These nominals exemplify the effect of the rule on upper mid vowels in prefixes and augments, where such vowels are contiguous, on the vowel projection (and in (123d,e) also on the timing-tier), to the lower mid trigger vowel in the root.

Furthermore, examples such as /o-βo-εnε/ --> [oβwεεnε] 'truth' and /o-mo-εnε/ --> [omwεεnε] 'someone who speaks the truth, a truthful person' (see 123d), suggest that, whenever Upper Mid Vowel Raising (108) and subsequent gliding apply, mid vowel height spreading is prevented. In view of data such as [oβwεεnε], [ɔβɔεεnε], ?[ɔβwεεnε], *[ɔβoεεnε], and *[oβɔεεnε], the reverse is also true. This suggests that UMVR (108) and mid vowel height spreading are mutually exclusive in the same idiolect; perhaps even in the same regiolect, but this requires verification. Pending research on these matters, I will therefore consider forms such as [oβwεεnε] and [ɔβɔεεnε] as regular and acceptable, perhaps depending on the idiolect concerned.

Should forms such as [ɔβwεεnε] and [ɔmwεεnε] occur regularly in some idiolect after all, a different set of data would seem to be involved. High vowels regularly block vowel height spreading, but in such cases they would only seem to do so, if they are full vowels dominated by a nucleus, and not when they are dominated by an onset or syllable node, i.e. when they surface as glides. Still, if this type of variation occurs at all, it seems to be very rare, and restricted to some idiolects only. I will return to the apparent borderline case ?[ɔβwεεnε] in connection with (131) below.

Next, consider the verbal examples in (124),

(124) a. /o-rεNt-ir-e/
3s-bring-t-fv
[ɔrεεntire] ([εε] = H)[53]
'[she] has brought'

(from Whiteley 1960: 17)

b. /o-ko-γεNr-a/
you-t-go-fv
[(kai) ɔkɔγεεnda]
'(where) are you going?'

(from Whiteley 1960: 28)

c. /ta-o-ko-mo-ñɔɔr-a/
not-you2s-t-him-find-fv
[tɔɔkɔmɔñɔɔra] (tɔɔkɔ = H)
'you will not find him (ever)'

(after Whiteley 1960: 22)

In these examples too, all upper mid target vowels in the pre-root domain are contiguous, on the vowel projection, to the lower mid trigger vowel in the root, in the sense that they are uninterrupted by some opaque vowel. All are lowered by one degree to lower mid.

Further, note that various types of prefix are involved in (124). This suggests that

---

[53] The alternative root /-rεεt-/ 'bring' also occurs, but was judged less acceptable by Lilian Nyanchama. It may be an adaptation of a lexical take-over from Swahili, kuleta 'to bring'.

morphological and morpho-syntactic factors are irrelevant to the process. Though no opaque vowel may intervene target vowels and the trigger root-vowel, not all syllables in which targets occur are contiguous to the root. The important point is that all upper mid target vowels must be contiguous to the trigger vowel on the vowel projection in the sense explained.

The following verbal examples (125) show that the process may apply also in the post-root domain,

(125) a. /to-γɛNr-e/
sm1p-go-fv
[tɔγɛɛndɛ]
'let us go'

(after Whiteley 1960: 38)

b. /o-mɛñ-et-e/
sm2s-live-t-fv
[(kai) ɔmɛñɛtɛ]
'(where) do you live?'

(after Whiteley 1960: 50)

c. /n-raa-sɔ-e/
sm1s-t-come-t
[ńdáásɔɛ] (ɔɛ = H)
'will I enter?'

(after Whiteley 1956: 41)

d. /n-ta-a-tɛɛβ-er-i-a/
sm1s-not-t-tell-ap-c-fv
[ntaatɛɛβɛria]
'did I not tell?'[54]

(after Whiteley 1960: 26, who however translates 'should I not tell?)

e. /n-to-βa-tɛɛβ-er-er-i-a/
f-sm1p-om3p-tell-ap-ap-c-fv
[ńtóβátɛɛβɛrɛríá] (ɛrɛr = H)
'we will tell them (with respect to; for)'

f. /ko-rɛ-er-a/
15-thin-ap-fv
[kɔrɛɛra]
'to be thin (for; on account of)'
(compare /ko-rɛ-a/ --> [kɔrɛa]
'to be thin')

Here too, upper mid target vowels are lowered by one degree, regardless of the morphosyntactic nature of the elements in which they occur, under the same conditions as before. Thus the vowels of derivational suffixes, tense markers, subject and object markers are all affected alike, and the harmony is again shown to be purely phonological. Its bidirectionality is exemplified in (125b), and root-control throughout. Root-control is also suggested by examples such as [ataareeŋgeɔ] 'he was not there', presumably from |a-ta-a-reeŋg-e-ɔ|, such that *[ataareeŋgeo] (though this is what Whiteley records, 1960:

[54] Presumably, the applicative and causative suffixes have not retained their original force in this verb, depending on the original meaning of /-tɛɛβ-/. Since current understanding of its etymon may have been lost, it is possible to consider them synchronically as expansion suffixes, i.e. purely formal additions to the root, rather than as productive extension suffixes. This line of reasoning is applicable to many other Gusii words, and also involves other expansion suffixes, some of which may or may not be related to homomorphous extension suffixes. This is an area for further morphological and lexical research.

35, first example) and *[ataarεεŋgεɔ].

Given the correctness of the underlying representations of the relevant affix target vowels as upper mid, as posited in this study, the examples given so far illustrate that the harmony process under discussion is triggered by any lower mid vowel and may affect any upper mid vowel that is contiguous to it on the vowel projection in the sense explained. That this must be due to the presence of a lower mid trigger vowel in the root, becomes clear, when the nominal examples in (123) are contrasted with those in (126),

(126) data

a. /e-usi/	--> [eusi] 'thread', *[εusi]
b. /o-βo-βis-i/	--> [oβoβisi] 'secret', *[ɔβɔβisi]
c. /o-mo-Nto/	--> [omoonto] 'person', *[ɔmɔɔnto]
d. /e-ke-Nto/	--> [eγeento] 'thing', *[εγεεnto]
e. /o-mo-te/	--> [omote] 'tree', *[ɔmɔte]
f. /e-ke-saku/	--> [eγesaku] 'clan', *[εγεsaku]

Here the contiguous nominal root or stem vowels are high (126a-b), upper mid (126c-e), or low (126f), and the rule does not apply. This indicates that it is not triggered by any non-lower mid vowel.

In fact, the non-mid vowels /i/, /u/, or /a/, neither trigger, nor undergo the rule. Their exemption from it is exhibited by the immutability of, for example, /i/ in [ɔmɔγεni] (123c) and [ɔrεεntire] (124a), final /a/ in (124b-c), and the /u/'s in [koñwɔɔmwa] 'to be married (s-ref: girl)', from /ko-ñuɔm-u-a/. In the last example, /u/ is indeed changed to [w], but it is not affected by the process under discussion.

Rather, the non-mid vowels block it. Technically they are said to be opaque with respect to the process. The opaqueness of /i/, especially its blocking effect, is exemplified in (127),

(127) a.
/o-rεNt-ir-e/
sm3s-bring-t-fv
[ɔrεεntire], *[ɔrεεntirε]
'he has brought'

(after Whiteley 1960: 40)

b.
/to-a-sεm-er-et-i-e/
sm-t-trust-sx-t-sx-fv
[twaasεmεrεtie], *[twaasεmεrεtiε]
'we had been expecting'

(after Whiteley 1960: 20)

c.
/mo-n-tεεβ-i-e/
2p-you-me-tell-c-fv
[mɔɔntεεβie]
'2p-tell me'

(after Whiteley 1960: 36)

In these examples, final /e/ is not lowered. The only possible explanation available, is the presence of the preceding /i/. It intervenes the trigger vowel in the root, or the nearest derived lower mid vowel that may function as such, viz. |ɛ| of |-ɛt|, and the potential final target vowel /e/.

When compared with [γɔsɛmɛria] 'to expect', *[γɔsɛma], the underlying representation postulated in (127b) suggests that the root must be /-sɛm-er-i-/, and not /-sɛmɛri-/, for two reasons. First, the morphemes /-er-/ and /-i-/ do not seem to be the applicative and the causative suffix, respectively, for their meanings cannot, apparently, be motivated in this lexical item. In addition to this, second, tense suffix /-et/ may intervene /-er-/ and /-i-/. This would be impossible, if /-sɛmɛri-/ were the underlying representation. Hence /-er-/ and /-i-/ must synchronically be interpreted as expansion suffixes which are homomorphous to the extension suffixes mentioned. However, if postulates of /-sɛm-er-i-/ be generally admitted, the domain of mid vowel height spreading must be defined so as to include elements in the root.

Descriptively, there is no real problem here. Allow underlying representations such as /-sɛm-er-i-/, i.e. parsed roots. Also identify all Gusii expansion suffixes, and define them as a distinct class of morphemes. The morphological data are such that lower mid vowels do not seem to occur outside roots, so that the process remains root-controlled. Then, regardless of whether or not some expansion suffixes are homomorphous with, or even originate from, extension suffixes, mid vowel height spreading may be formulated so as to include relevant upper mid target vowels occurring in this class of morphemes. But, for the time being, some underlying representations must remain indeterminate, for lack of sufficient lexical research on the language.

It may be added here that Whiteley (1960: 40) records the following surface variation (128),

(128)	a.	/o-tɛɛβ-ir-e/ he-say-t-fv [ɔtɛɛβire] 'he has said'	b.	/o-tɛɛβ-ir-e/ he-say-t-fv [ɔtɛɛβirɛ] 'he has said'

In (128a), the harmony of the final vowel is blocked, as expected, due to the intervention of /i/ in the preceding perfective tense-suffix /-ir/, whereas in (128b) the process surprisingly ignores the same intervening /i/, turning final /e/ into [ɛ]. However, the present research disconfirms the surface in (128b), so that it constitutes no exception. Hence the contrast in (128) proves to be spurious.

No other real counter-examples were found in Whiteley's work or during my own fieldwork. Instead, many other examples that corroborate the exposition given here may be found in (1960). Therefore, the opaqueness of /i/ is well-established.

Next, the opaqueness, and especially the blocking effect, of low, hence non-mid, vowel /a/ is exemplified in (129),

(129) a. /o-ka-rɔs-a/
sm2s-t-be tired-fv
[okarɔsa], *[ɔkarɔsa]
'you were tired (far past)'

(after Whiteley 1960: 24)

b. /ti-to-V-ko-na-ko-βa-tεεβ-i-a/
not-we-t-t-t-them-tell-c-fv
[titookoñakoβatεεβia][55], *[titɔɔkɔñakɔβatεεβia]
'we will not be telling them'

(after Whiteley 1960: 36)

These data are fairly straightforward. Initial /o/ in (129a) and any of the /o/'s in (129b) are not lowered, arguably due to the fact that /a/ intervenes the lower mid trigger, i.e. /ɔ/ in (129a) and /εε/ in (129b), and the potential targets.

Finally, given the nature of the relevant data of Gusii morphology that might be brought to bear on the question, the general opaqueness of /u/ with respect to mid vowel height spreading, and especially its blocking effect, is more difficult to establish. First, the data in (130),

(130) /a-tεεβ-et-i-γu-e/
he-tell-t-c-p-fv
[atεεβεtiγwe], *[atεεβεtiγwε]
'he was told (recently/long ago)'

(after Whiteley 1960: 43)

are inadequate, because both /i/ and /u/ intervene lower mid trigger /ε/ and word-final upper mid target /e/ (/γu/ is the allomorph, after a vowel, of passive voice marker /u/). At most, these data allow us to say that /e/ is not lowered, due to intervention of both /i/ and /u/.

Next, consider the data in (131),

[55] In this form, ¦ña¦ may freely alternate with ¦na¦.

(131) a. [ɔβɔεεnε], *[oβɔεεnε], *[ɔβoεεnε]   b. [oβwεεnε], ?[ɔβwεεnε]

c. /e-ñuɔm-o/
9-marry-sx
[eñuɔmɔ], [eñwɔɔmɔ]
'marriage'

d. /ko-ñuɔm-er-i-a/
15-marry-ap-c-fv
[koñuɔmεria], [koñwɔɔmεria][56]
'to marry off' (s-ref: parents, o-ref: girl)

e. /ko-βɔ-an-i-a/
15-tie-r-c-fv
[kɔβɔanania], ?[kɔβwaanania]
'to tie together'
(compare [kɔβɔa] 'to tie')

Here, (131a-b) suggest either that mid vowel height spreading applies throughout, whenever and in as far as it is applicable (131a), or that it may be blocked by a glide, i.e. a high vowel dominated by a syllable node. In (131b), this is back glide [w], i.e. |u| dominated by a syllable node, derived through Upper Mid vowel Raising (108) from underlying /o/. Compare the discussion on (123). Such variation is what one would naturally expect in the case of segments that appear to have charactistics of different types of units, as glides do. It may be significant in this respect that linguistic judgments on ?[ɔβwεεnε] varied somewhat per speaker.

Further, I have neither recorded [εñuɔmɔ] and [εñwɔɔmɔ] as alternatives for (131c), nor [kɔñuɔmεria] and [kɔñwɔɔmεria] as alternatives for (131d). This may be a fieldwork shortcoming, but if correct, these data argue against blocking of harmony by a complex segment containing a glide, at least leftward. Finally, the questioned form in (131e) is odd, but may need to be verified. In any case, all this seems to add to the general picture of indeterminacy.

This last point also pertains to the data in (132),

[56] Compare [koñwɔɔma] 'to marry' (s-ref: man) and [koñwɔɔmwa] 'to be married' (s-ref: girl).

(132) input /a-rɛNt-u-e/
he-bring-p-fv

UMVR (108)
& other rules areɛntue

a. possible derivation:

CSF (109) arɛɛntwe
MVHS (136) - (blocked by |u|)
output [arɛɛntwe]

b. possible alternative derivation:

MVHS (136) arɛɛntwɛ
output [arɛɛntwɛ]

The output may occur in utterances such as [tiγa arɛɛntwɛ] 'let him be brought'. The trouble with the data in (132) is that they are indeterminate. While one informant affirmed both outputs (132), a year later another definitely disconfirmed (132b). Furthermore, the kind of output in (132a) conflicts with the type in (130). Again, such variation is probably due to the somewhat indeterminate nature of glides. Otherwise, no other examples with only /u/ intervening a trigger and a target were found during my fieldwork, to be able to settle the point, nor have I found any in Whiteley (1956, 1959, 1960) and Kingston (1983). Strictly speaking, the blocking effect of /u/ is thus insufficiently supported empirically.[57]

At least three determinants may be involved: idiolect, style of speech, and the status of the high vowel segment as a vowel proper or a glide. The last factor would seem to depend at least on the style of speech, but perhaps also on idiolect. Generally, the opaqueness of high vowel segments with respect to mid vowel height spreading, seems to depend on their position in syllable structure. If they are dominated by a nucleus, i.e. if they are realised as a full vowel in the centre of the syllable, they block it. If they are dominated by the syllable or onset node, they may or may not block it. The analysis of the syllabic structure of the words in which these segments occur, depends on how the word is pronounced, and this, in turn, seems to depend on the style of speech, and perhaps on idiolect.

However, /u/ is clearly opaque in the sense that it is neither a trigger, nor a target of the rule. Moreover, the opaqueness of high front vowel /i/ is well-established. Therefore, it

[57] At least the following Gusii affixes contain non-upper mid vowels underlyingly, so that their vowels block, and do not undergo, the process. Prefixes with underlying /a/ include subject markers 2 /βa-/, 6 /ma-/, 12 /ka-/, negative marker /ta-/, and several tense prefixes. Prefixes with underlying /i/ include 5 /rii-/, 8 /βi-/, 10 /ci-/, 10a /ci-n-/, and negative marker /ti-/. There is at least one suffix with /a/ underlyingly, viz. reciprocal /-an/, at least one with /i/, viz. causative /-i/, and at least one with |u|, viz. passive voice marker /-(γ)u/.

is tentatively concluded, by analogy to all other non-mid vowels, that /u/ is always opaque with respect to mid vowel height spreading, whenever it is syllabic (dominated by an N-node), and mostly also, whenever it is non-syllabic (dominated by an N"-node). The latter point is assumed, until hard evidence to the contrary turns up.

Having established the various details of the rule, it may now be asked how it applies. Does it apply iteratively or across the board? Is it a rule of height harmony proper or a rule of local height spreading? If the theory allows us to formulate it in either fashion, are there compelling empiricial or other grounds for conceiving of it as the one or the other?

To answer such questions, criteria must be established first. Clements (1977) has attempted to give a definition of vowel harmony in terms of the following criteria (133).

(133) a. phonetic motivatedness
b. root control
c. bidirectionality
d. unboundedness
e. non-optionality

These are said to be both necessary and sufficient. However, Anderson, discussing them, concludes that "while Clements' criteria point up important characteristics shared by most vowel harmony systems, they still do not furnish the required basis for a set of necessary and sufficient criteria for differentiating vowel harmony from other types of metaphony" (1980: 13). Nonetheless, if these criteria may be supposed to be correct, the following observations may be made with respect to the process in Gusii.

The various examples given previously tend to support the idea that what has so far been called mid vowel harmony, without argumentation, does indeed meet the criteria in (133). Its trigger definition as [-cons, -high, +mid] sufficiently seems to underpin its phonetic motivatedness. It is root-controlled. It applies bidirectionally. It does so regularly, to the point of being non-optional. If the fact that it applies whenever and as soon as its structural description is met, unless it is blocked by an intervening opaque vowel, sufficiently proves its unboundedness as well, it meets all of the aforementioned criteria.

Significantly, as to the last point, apparent counter-examples found in Whiteley's work, such as [εηgεεco] 'habit, custom' (1956: 116) and [ɔβɔkɔmbe] 'hoe' (1956: 124), turn out to be mistranscriptions. The items just quoted should be [eηeeñco], plural [ciηeeñco], from /-ηeNco/, and [ɔβɔkɔɔmbε], plural [amakɔɔmbε], from /-kɔNβε/. The latter is distinct from [oβokoombe] 'group', plural [amakoombe], from /o-βo-koNβe/. These words are thus consistent with the general pattern and corroborate the present analysis.

Should the criteria in (133) prove insufficient after all, so that additional or different ones would have to be proposed, the Gusii process would have to be re-evaluated accordingly as to its precise nature. But by and large the data seem to be clear. Therefore, if these criteria are both necessary and sufficient for defining vowel harmony proper, the rule may be conclusively characterised as such.

Hence the process may be formulated as in (134),

(134) Mid Vowel Harmony

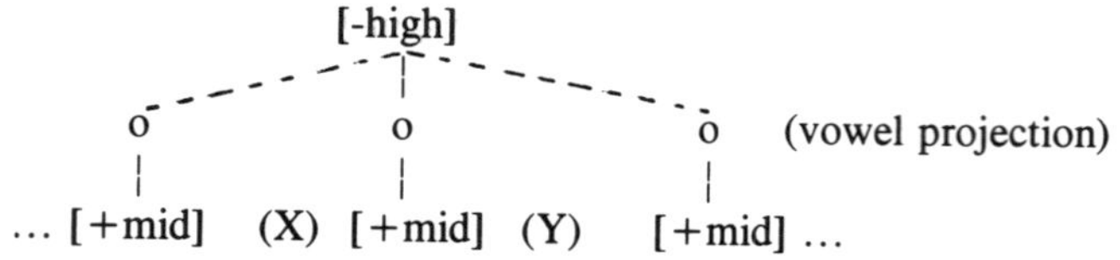

Condition 1: non-mid vowels are opaque
Condition 2: any N"-dominated high vowel segment in X may or may not block the rule

This rule states that the specification [-high] of any [+mid] vowel is spread to all [+mid] vowels in the word that are not interrupted by any [-mid] vowel on the vowel projection. No vowel containing the specified feature [-mid], i.e. /i, u, a/ may intervene (condition 1), while any consonant may.

Condition 2 stipulates that, if the trigger and the target are immediately sequential on the timing-tier, the rule may optionally not apply, as in the prefixes in (131c-d). However, given data such as those in (130-132), this condition is considered as tentative, hence subject to further adjustment, should fresh data so require. Perhaps it may be dropped altogether, if it can be established firmly that the optionality of the rule is dependent on style of speech or idiolect (see section 4.5.1 for some discussion of speech styles).

The process is root-controlled in the sense that the lower mid trigger vowel always occurs in the root. However, since lower mid vowels do not seem to occur outside the root domain underlyingly, this need not be specified in the formulation of the rule. It is inherent in the morphological data.

As the rule is included in the lexical phonological component of the language, its lexical status need not be made explicit in its formulation.

Effectively, the rule lowers all contiguous upper mid target vowels in the word by one degree, thereby making them lower mid. Though the target and the trigger must be contiguous on the vowel projection in the sense explained, they need not be so contiguous on the timing-tier. As formulated, the rule also applies gratuitously to any contiguous lower mid vowels, but, given the postulate of all the relevant affix target vowels as upper mid, they do not in fact occur outside the root. All the same, should they so occur, they would be 'changed into', i.e. remain, lower mid.

The process might be formulated alternatively as a feature-changing rule, as in (135),

(135) $[+\text{high}] \dashrightarrow \begin{bmatrix}\text{-high}\\ +\text{mid}\end{bmatrix} /\ \text{---}\ (X) \begin{bmatrix}\text{-high}\\ +\text{mid}\end{bmatrix}$ (mirror image, vowel-projection)

(where X is not [-cons, -mid])

However, this characterisation does express the necessary changes, especially given the additional conditions also imposed on (134), but it fails to express formally the essential spreading nature, root-controlledness, and pervasiveness of the rule.

Given the fact that lower mid vowels do not seem to occur outside the root underlyingly, a viable alternative to (134) may be to formulate it as a rule of local height spreading. Presupposing the same modifications as for (134), it might thus be formulated as in (136),

(136) Mid Vowel Height Spreading (MVHS)

```
[-high]
 |- - - - - - - -
 o  (X)          o      (mirror image, vowel projection)
 |               |
[+mid]        [+mid]
```

Condition 1: non-mid vowels are opaque
Condition 2: any N"-dominated high vowel segment in X may or may not block the rule

The absence of any x on the timing-tier expresses the fact that the nodes must be contiguous on the vowel projection. Intervening consonantal nodes are thus allowed. Condition 2 ensures that non-mid vowels block and do not undergo the rule. Condition 2 ensures that, if a non-nuclear high vowel (i.e. glide) intervenes the trigger and the target, the rule may or may not apply. The stipulation 'mirror image' ensures its bidirectional application.

If some idiolect or regiolect exhibits consistent application of either (136), or Upper Mid Vowel Raising (108) and subsequent Complex Segment Formation (109), then the formulation in (136) expresses both the necessary changes and the spreading nature of the process for the idiolect or regiolect concerned. The same holds for a particular speech style in some idiolect or regiolect, mutatis mutandis. In these cases, the relevant surface representations may be accounted for by postulating a different order between MVHS (136) and UMVR-cum-CSF. If some idiolect or regiolect may exhibit variation in this respect (though this was denied by my informants), the surface variation might be accounted for by saying that their order is variable. If surface variation may occur in a single word, as in [koñwɔɔmɛria], this suggests that condition 1 added to (136) remains necessary.

If the estimate of the underlying distribution of upper and lower mid vowels in and outside roots underlyingly, given a moment ago, is correct, the root-controlledness of the rule need not be expressed formally, since it is inherent in the morphological data of the language. On this basis, (136) may be preferred over (134), the more so because its formulation is more simple.

The examples in (137) illustrate the operation of Mid Vowel Height Spreading (136) in a particularly clear fashion, for though they are otherwise identical, they contrast in respect of this process,

(137) a. input /o-ko-ee-orok-er-er-i-a/
a-15-rf-appear-ap-ap-c-fv

MVHS (136) (not applicable)
possible output [okoeeorokereria]
or, through UMVR (108)
& CSF (109),
possible output [okweeorokereria]
'making oneself appear to (for or by means of)'

compare:

/ko-orok-a/, [kwooroka] 'to appear'
/ko-orok-i-a/, [kwoorokia] 'to make appear'
/ko-ee-orok-i-a/, [kweeorokia] 'to make oneself appear'

b. input /o-ko-ee-ɔrɔk-er-er-i-a/
a-15-rf-teach-ap-ap-c-fv

MVHS (136) ɔkɔεεɔrɔkεrεr...
possible output [ɔkɔεεɔrɔkεrεria]
or, through UMVR (108)
& CSF (109),
possible output [okwεεɔrɔkεrεria]
'showing for oneself by means of'

Given the distinct roots, /-orok-/ 'appear' and /-ɔrɔk-/ 'teach, show', and Mid Vowel Height Spreading (136), the latter does not apply in (137a), in virtue of its structural description. In (137b), it applies throughout in the first alternative, but rightward only in the second alternative, where, to the left of the trigger, it is overruled by Upper Mid Vowel Raising and Complex Segment Formation (and Linking Rule and x-Trimming, which are not made explicit). Thus the distinct outputs in (137) are readily and correctly accounted for. A similar contrastive pair is given in (138),

(138) a. /ko-ee-mεr-i-a/
15-rf-grow-c-fv
[kɔεεmεria]
also [kwεεmεria]
'to grow of/by itself'
(literally, 'to make oneself/itself grow')

compare:

/ko-mεr-a/, [kɔmεra] 'to grow'
/ko-mεr-i-a/, [kɔmεria] 'to cause to grow'

b. /ko-ee-mer-i-a/
15-rf-swallow-c-fv
[koeemeria]
'to make oneself swallow'

compare:

/ko-mer-a/ --> [komera] 'to swallow'
/ko-mer-i-a/ --> [komeria] 'to cause to swallow'

An inconclusive point concludes this section. Final /e/, in (139), may vary with /ɛ/, or so it seemed on occasion,

(139) a. |n-n-aaŋg-e|
f-sm1s-refuse-fv
[niiŋaaŋge]
'I will refuse'

similarly,

[noaaŋge] '2s-you will refuse',
[naaŋge] 'he will refuse'
etc.

(after Whiteley 1956: 70)

b. |n-n-aak-e|
f-sm1s-beat-fv
[niiŋaakɛ]
'I will beat'
(the rest of the paradigm is similar)

(after Whiteley 1956: 70)

This suggests that /a/, if it occurs in a root, may function as a trigger for Mid Vowel Height Spreading (136). Data such as [neeβa], *[nɛɛβa] 'I will forget', from /na-a-eβ-a/, make clear that it may do so only, when it occurs in the root. However, *[twaaγɛtwɛ], for example, is not allowed instead of [twaaγetwe] 'we were beaten', which suggests that, if /a/ may trigger the rule at all, it does so irregularly. For this reason, and because I am somewhat doubtful about the correctness of my transcriptions in (139), I consider the alternative [ɛ] to be a mistake, and maintain the analysis as previously given.

Should /a/ turn out to be a possible trigger of the process in some variety of Gusii, after all (though, as pointed out, it is not expected to be a regular trigger), (136) could easily be readjusted, as in (140), to accommodate the facts, if need be,

(140) Mid Vowel Height Spreading

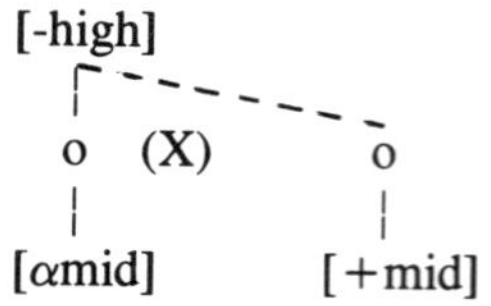

(mirror image, vowel projection)

Condition 1: high vowels are opaque
Condition 2: any N"-dominated high vowel segment in X may or may not block the rule

Because the trigger is defined as [-high, αmid], it now includes both [-high, +mid] segments, i.e. upper mid /e/ and /o/, and [-high, -mid] vowels, i.e. low /a/, given the definition of Gusii vowels in terms of minimally distinctive features, in (9). Otherwise the rule would remain unaffected.

2.3.15. /a/-Delinking.

Whiteley states that "The sequence a-e (short vowel only) is realised as 'ee'; similarly the sequence a-o is realised as 'oo'" (1960: 3). That is, a + e > ee, and a + o > oo.

This seems to be a clear case of delinking-cum-spreading. If his analysis is correct, the rule accounting for the change may therefore be formulated as in (141),

(141) /a/-Delinking (after Whiteley)

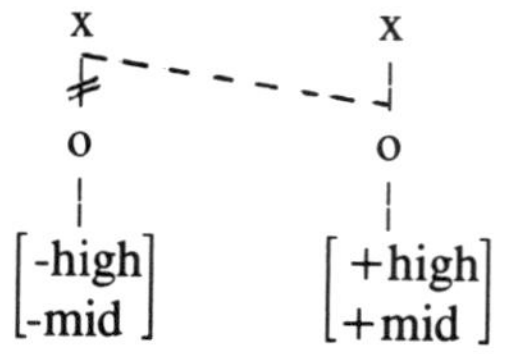

It delinks any [-high, -mid] target vowel, i.e. /a/, whenever this is followed by a [+high, +mid] trigger vowel, i.e. any upper mid vowel, and spreads the root node of the latter to the vacated x of the former. The application of (141) is exemplified in sample derivation (142),

(142)	input	/-oγe/ 'sharp
	prefixation	maoγe
	/a/-Delinking	o
	augmentation	a
	output	[amooγe] '6-sharp'

(singular /e-ri-oγe/ --> [erioγe] '5-sharp')

Two other examples are given in (143),

(143) a. before /o/

/a-ma-omo/
a-6-dry
[amoomo]
'6-dry'

b. before /e/

/o-ka-eβ-a/	/a-ma-eηe/
sm2s-t-forget-fv	a-6-short
[okeeβa]	[amaeηe] or [ameeηe]
'you forgot (recently)'	'6-short'

However, two corrections or improvements may be made. First, as the last example in (143) indicates, the rule is optional. Presumably, [amaomo] and [okaeβa] may occur also, but these alternatives have not been recorded in my notes. Second, the rule may also apply before, or be triggered by, lower mid vowels. Both points are exemplified by the data in (144),

(144) applicability before /ɔ/:

a. |aβa-ɔɔnia| --> [aβaɔɔnia] or [aβɔɔnia] '2-sellers'

b. /a-ma-ɔɔrɔ/ --> [amaɔɔrɔ] or [amɔɔrɔ] '6-lazy'

c.

input	/to-a-ɔm-ir-e/ 1p-t-smear-pf-fv
no rules	[toaɔmire]
or, through UMVR (108), CSF (109), LR (90)	[tw(a)aɔmire]
or, through /a/-Delinking UMVR (108), CSF (109), LR (90)	[twɔɔmire] 'we have just smeared'

(but not *[tɔɔmire], i.e. /o/ of /to/ does not undergo Mid Vowel Height Spreading (136))

d. /e-a-ɔk-ir-e/
sm9-t-give light-pf-fv
[yɔɔkíre], ?[yaɔkíre] (/ɔ/ before /k/ = H)
'9-it has given light (just now)'

but compare:

/e-a-ɔk-ir-e/
sm9-t-give light-pf-fv
[εɔɔkíré] (/ε/ = H)
'has 9-it given light (just now)?'

applicability before /ε/:

e. intermediate input |e-a-εrire|

/a/-delinking - (optionally does not apply)
UMVR (108),
& GF (114), etc. [yaεríre]
'9-it has got finished'
or,
/a/-delinking e-εεrire
UMVR (108),
& GF (114), etc. yεεrire
output [yεεríre]
'9-it has got finished'

/e-a-εr-ir-e/
9-t-finish-pf-fv
[yεεríre], ?[yaεríre] (/ε/ before /r/ = H)
'9-it has got finished'

but compare:

[eaεríré] (/ε/ before /r/ = H)
'has 9-it got finished?'

f. /a-ma-ε/ --> [amaε] or [amεε] '6-big baskets'[58]

In contrast to (144d-e), the rule does not apply regularly in, for example, [amaεnε], *[amεεnε] 'truths (derogatory)', [βaεεra] 'they are finished (always)', and [βaaεεrire] 'they have been finished'. This may be due to a tendency toward preservation of morphological identity, hence distinctness with respect to other similar forms, or to lexicalisation. The data in (144d-e) suggest that some variation in application of the rule may even be tense-related, but this requires more extensive verification.

In any case, given the morphological data of Gusii, contexts such as those in (144) are relatively few (see appendix 1). Therefore, if lexical items are involved, a simple solution would be to exempt these from the rule by marking them as such in the lexicon. Should

[58] To all the items of which 6 /ama-/ is not the regular class prefix, it adds a derogatory connotation to its regular plural meaning.

some contexts definitely have to be excluded, on the results of further research, the rule may be conditioned accordingly. Since the exceptions appear to be marginal, I take it that most relevant targets are adequately handled by interpreting the rule as optional.

Next, data such as those in (146) suggest that the rule does not apply before high vowels,

(145) non-application of /a/-delinking

before /i/:

a. /e-a-ik-ir-e/
sm9-t-arrive-pv-fv
[eaikire] or [ya(a)ikire]
but not *[eiikire] or *[yiikire]
'9-it has (just) arrived'

b. /βa-ik-a/
sm3p-arrive-fv
[βaiká], *[βiiká]
'they arrive (always)'

before /u/:

c. /to-a-ut-ir-e/
sm1p-t-blow-pf-fv
[toautire] or [twaautire]
but not *[touutire] 'we have (just) blown out'

d. /a-ma-usi/
a-6-thread
[amausi], *[amuusi]
'big threads (derogatory)'

Finally, whenever the following trigger vowel is low /a/, the application of the rule is indeterminate. As /a + a/ surfaces as [aa], the output of the rule will always be identical to its input. Thus it may be argued that in that case either the rule does not apply, or that it applies vacuously. The former argument is adopted here, as it permits a simpler formulation of the process.

The data discussed in this section suggest that, in terms of its triggers, the details of the process may be summarised as in (146),

(146) a. /a/ --> 0 / --- {/e, ɛ, o, ɔ/}
b. */a/ --> 0 / --- {/i, u/}
c. (*)/a/ --> 0 / --- /a/

If (146a) be granted only, the specification [+mid] not only necessarily, but sufficiently defines all and any triggers, properly excluding all non-triggers. If /a/ be allowed as a trigger, then the latter must be defined so as to include this low vowel. In terms of matrix (9), the class of triggers would thus have to be defined as "either [+mid] or [-high, -mid]". Since the first analysis of the trigger-class gives much simpler formulation of the rule, it is adopted here. That is, (146c) is decided as */a/ --> 0 / --- /a/, so that /a/ is disallowed as a trigger. Thus the following changes are supposed to be included: a + o

> oo, a + ɔ > ɔɔ, a + e > ee, and a + ε > εε.

Taking all these considerations into account, the formulation in (141), based on Whiteley's analysis, may now be adjusted to (147),

(147) /a/-Delinking (optional)

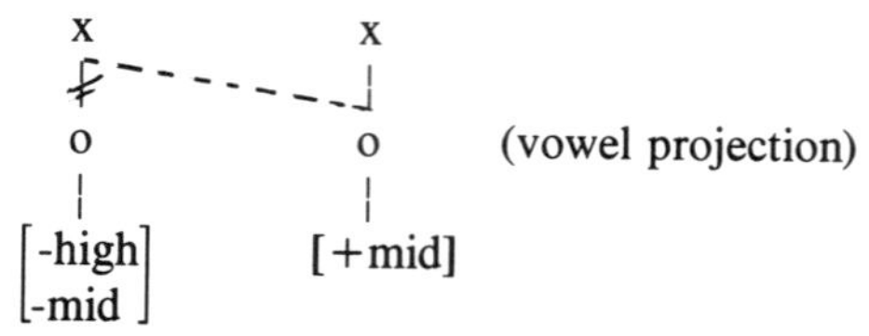

As formulated, (147) states that any [-high, -mid] target vowel, i.e. low /a/, is delinked, whenever it is immediately followed by any mid target vowel, and that the root node of the latter is spread to the vacated x on its left. The stipulation "(vowel projection)" restricts the application of the rule to the vocalic tier, thus defining both the trigger and the target as vowel segments. Their consecutiveness is ensured by linkage of their root nodes to contiguous x's on the timing tier.

Should the trigger regularly turn out to be an upper mid vowel, and only occasionally or very restrictedly a lower mid vowel, the trigger in (147) might be redefined as [αhigh, +mid], and a condition added to the effect that, whenever the trigger is [+high] the rule is obligatory, but whenever it is [-high], it is optional.

2.3.16. Intervocalic /a/-Raising.

The rule discussed in this section optionally raises low target vowel /a/ under certain conditions, and should thus be distinguished from Morpholexical /a/-Raising, discussed in section 3.2.5.2.

Strictly, the designation 'intervocalic', though correct, is too broad, since /a/ may be raised only, whenever it occurs between two high front trigger vowels. That is, trigger /i/ must both precede and succeed target /a/. Such a change from /a/ to [e] occurs more commonly in Eastern Bantu languages. In the present analysis, in terms of (9), it may be formulated as a feature-changing rule. A relatively informal formulation would be (148),

(148) a --> e / i --- i

More formally, it may be expressed, as in (149),

(149) Intervocalic /a/-Raising (optional)

$$\begin{bmatrix}\text{-high}\\ \text{-mid}\end{bmatrix} \text{-->} \begin{bmatrix}\text{+high}\\ \text{+mid}\\ \text{-back}\end{bmatrix} / \begin{bmatrix}\text{-cons}\\ \text{+high}\\ \text{-mid}\\ \text{-back}\end{bmatrix} \text{ --- } \begin{bmatrix}\text{-cons}\\ \text{+high}\\ \text{-mid}\\ \text{-back}\end{bmatrix}$$

That is, /a/ may be changed to /e/, whenever it occurs between /i/ and /i/.[59] The process seems to be a fairly low-level rule and dependent on the style or rate of speech. In most examples in which it is applicable, given elsewhere in this study, it is taken for granted and the change is not made explicit. A postlexical version of the rule also occurs (section 2.4.5). One example, finally, is (150),

(150) /e-ke-Nto ke-a-ito/
a-7-thing 7-of-our
[eγeento γiaito] or [eγeento γieito]
'our thing'

A few more may be found in section 3.2.8.1.

2.3.17. /a/-Shortening.

The context of the rule discussed in this section is similar to, yet slightly different from, that of (149). Compare the data in (151),

(151) a.	/ke-a-ito/	/ke-a-ino/	b.	/ke-a-βɔ/
	7-of-1p	7-of-2p		7-of-them
	[γyaito]	[kyaino]		[kyaaβɔ]
	'7-our'	'7-your'		'7-their'

[59] In terms of the following vowel characterisations,

	i	e	ɛ	a	ɔ	o	u
high	+	+	-	-	-	+	+
low	-	+	+	+	+	+	-

the process could be formulated elegantly as a spreading-cum-delinking rule, as follows

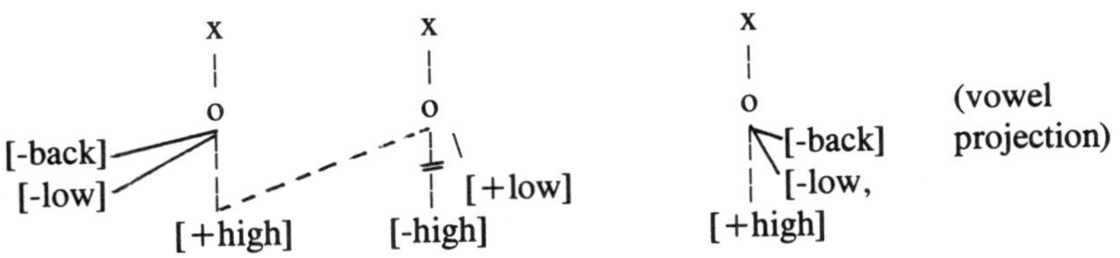

Though Upper Mid Vowel Raising (108) and Complex Segment Formation (109) apply in all of these examples, compensatory lengthening of the /a/ through the Linking Rule (90) applies only in (151b). In (151b), the /a/ may sometimes be so lengthened, but usually it is not.

The same phenomenon may be observed in (152),

(152) a.

/a-βa-ana βa-a-ito/	/a-βa-ana βa-a-ino/
a-2-child 2-of-1p	a-2-child 2-of-2p
[aβaana βaito]	[aβaana βaino]
'our children'	'2p-your children'

b. /a-βa-ana βa-a-βɔ/
a-2-child 2-of-3p
[aβaana βaaβɔ]
'their children'

where the /a/ of the possessive pronoun tends to be short in (152a), but long in (152b). These examples suggest that /aa/ may be shortened optionally to /a/ before /i/.

The output of the partial informal sample derivation in (153), where a rule of /r/-deletion discussed in section 3.3.4.2 is anticipated, corroborates the previous observations,

(153)

input	/na-a-raar-ir-e/
/r/-Deletion	naaraaire
/a/-Shortening	naaraire
other rules	[naaraire]
	'3s-he/she is asleep'

Whiteley (1960: 45) records [naraaire] instead, which may be a mistranscription or an optional alternative.[60]

This optional tendency may be accounted for, as in (154),

(154) /a/-Shortening (optional)

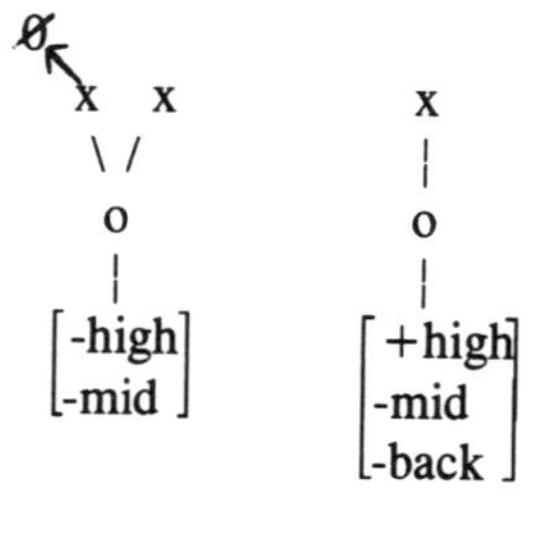

[60] Also compare /n-ta-raa-it-a/, which may apparently be realised as [ntaraaita] or [ntaraita] 'before I beat'. However, I am not certain of this example.

Technically, this rule deletes one of the x's on the timing-tier to which /a/ is associated, thereby shortening it, whenever it is followed by /i/. The x is not just delinked, but deleted. Hence it does not remain afloat, so that no compensatory lengthening of some vowel preceding the /a/ can take place. Since no evidence of such lengthening has been found, deletion is necessary.

Finally, if /n-ta-raa-ut-a/ --> [ntaraauta] or [ntarauta] 'before I blow out' is correct, this alternation suggests that trigger class of (154) may be more extensive. However, I am not certain about this, so the point needs to be verified.

2.3.18. Constraint on marginal long vowels.

Most examples given in this study, if not all, suggest that there is a constraint on word-initial long vowels in Gusii, which may be formulated as in (155),

(155) constraint on word-initial long vowels

```
  *      x  x
          \ /
 [         o
 | [-cons]
 [
 word
```

Barring a few rare exceptions, such as [kwaa] to pluck', there also seems to be a constraint on word-final long vowels. This may be formulated as in (156),

(156) constraint on word-final long vowels

```
  *      x  x
          \ /
           o     ]
    [-cons]      |
                 ]
            word
```

If occasionally there may be exceptions, the constraints formulated in (155) and (156), prohibiting long vowels at word-margins, are at least strong tendencies in the language. If correct, they may be collapsed, as in (157),

(157) constraint on word-marginal long vowels

```
*        x  x
          \ /
[          o
[  [-cons]      (mirror image)
[
word
```

2.3.19. Pre-Alveolo-Palatal Vowel Lengthening?

At first sight, an example such as [omoocokoro] 'grand-child', plural [aβaacokoro], might suggest that vowels are, or may be, lengthened before /c/ or alveolo-palatal segments generally. However, though this does occur in some forms, and though vowels are sometimes lengthened before alveolo-palatal /ñ/ too, this does not appear to be a general process. For example, [γocia] 'to go', [γocaaka] 'to begin', and [omocie] 'village, (large) homestead or settlement' do not regularly surface as *[γoocia], *[γoocaaka], and *[omoocie].

Thus items in which vowels are lengthened before /c/, or an alveolo-palatal segment generally, appear to be exceptions. Therefore, I propose to account for these by postulating an underspecified vowel underlyingly. Both the singular and the plural of the first example in this section may thus be accounted for by /-Vcokoro/. Another example would be [γooca] 'to come', from /ko-Vc-a/, which also has long vowels before /c/ in tenses, e.g. [mbaaceti] 'they did not come recently', from /n-βa-Vc-et-i/[61].

2.3.20. Rule order

In connection with most, if not all, rules discussed so far, considered as part of some particular idiolect, it turned out to be unnecessary to postulate rule order in addition to the rules themselves, on account of their specific nature and formulation. However, it was pointed out that a particular type of surface variation may occur, across idiolects, that may appropriately be accounted for in terms of a postulated difference in the order of the rules involved. Whether this variation may involve dialects (regiolects or sociolects) as well, remains to be researched.

Here the focus of attention is on the variation in rule order that may arguably account for a possible type of surface variation. The rules involved in this variation are, on the one hand, Mid Vowel Height Spreading (136), and on the other hand, Upper Mid Vowel Raising (108), possibly with, in its wake, optional gliding rules, Complex Segment Formation (109) and Glide Formation (114), and lengthening of the vowels following the glided segments.

[61] Not /n-βa-a-Vc-et-i/, as appears from the comparison with [mbaremeti] 'they did not dig (recently)', *[mbaaremeti].

A simple and clear example of the surface variation intended here, is provided by the following data: [ɛkɛɛ], [ekiɛ], [ekyɛ], *[ekyɛɛ], *[ɛkiɛ] '(type of small) basket'[62]. Since the corresponding plural of this word is [eβiɛ], the underlying representation for the singular may be postulated plausibly as /e-ke-ɛ/. Now, first consider the possible derivation in (158),

(158)	input	/-ɛ/
	prefixation	ke-ɛ
	UMVR (108)	kiɛ
	augmentation	ekiɛ
	MVHS (136)	-
	output	[ekiɛ]

After Upper Mid Vowel Raising, Complex Segment Formation might perhaps apply, producing [ekyɛ], but compensatory lengthening of the following vowel is constrained by the constraint on long vowels at word-margins (156). This accounts for *[ekyɛɛ]. The fact that Mid Vowel Height Spreading is not applicable to |ekiɛ| accounts for *[ɛkiɛ].

Next, consider the derivation in (159),

(159)	input	/-ɛ/
	prefixation	keɛ
	MVHS (136)	kɛɛ
	UMVR (108)	-
	augmentation	ekiɛ
	MVHS (136)	ɛkɛɛ
	output	[ɛkɛɛ]

This is a possible derivation, since the output [ɛkɛɛ] is an acceptable alternative for [ekiɛ]. If the two derivations are compared, it will be noted that the difference in output is naturally and elegantly accounted for by postulating a different rule order. In (158) the order is UMVR (108) < MVHS (136), whereas in (159) the order is MVHS (136) < UMVR (108). The fact that Upper Mid Vowel Raising may trigger gliding, and that gliding may trigger compensatory lengthening of a following vowel, is irrelevant to the main issue and thus left out of consideration here.

It must be added, however, that by all accounts such a change may not occur intra-idiolectally. It follows, therefore, that Mid Vowel Height Spreading (136) must be ordered before Upper Mid Vowel Raising (108) in some idiolect, but Upper Mid Vowel Raising before Mid Vowel Height Spreading in some other dialect, as the case may be. Should both alternatives be possible in a single idiolect, this might be accounted for by optionality of the rules or by assuming that their order is variable.

The same type of surface variation, similarly accountable, is also exemplified in (160),

---

[62] The equivalent of this word in related neighbouring Kuria is /e-ke-hɛ/, [ekɛhɛ], plural [iβihɛ] (in both, fv = H).

(160) a.	input	/-ɔm-/ 'smear'
	suffixation	ɔma
	prefixation	koɔma
	MVHS (136)	ɔ
	UMVR (108)	-
	output	[kɔɔma] 'to smear'
b.	input	/-ɔm-/ 'smear'
	suffixation	ɔma
	prefixation	koɔma
	UMVR (108)	u
	MVHS (136)	-
	CSF (109)	kw
	LR (90)	ɔɔ
	output	[kwɔɔma] 'to smear'

Another example is provided by the equivalent verbal nouns [ɔkɔɛra] and [okwɛɛra] 'finishing'.

In contrast, since *[ekiɛnɛ] was rejected, by the informants whom I consulted on this, as an acceptable alternative for [ɛkɛɛnɛ] 'truth', from /e-ke-ɛnɛ/, plural [iβiɛnɛ], this may be accounted for in several ways. For one, the surface representation judged acceptable, if characteristic of Gusii in general, may have become lexicalised. Another possibility is that [ɛkɛɛnɛ] is characteristic of some idiolects, i.e. the ones of my informants and those they are familiar with. But contrast [omwɛɛnɛ], [ɔmɔɛɛnɛ] '1-truthful, truthful person'. Finally, |eme-ɔγɔ|, [emyɔɔγɔ], *[ɛmɛɔɔγɔ] 'cassavas' seems to provide a similar case of lexicalisation. In idiolects which contain only a few exceptions to the general rule, the lexical items concerned could be marked in the lexicon as exempted from its application.

This concludes the discussion of Gusii lexical phonology.

2.4. Postlexical phonology.

In this section, certain phonological rules are discussed that apply at the postlexical level. As such, they are distinct from the lexical rules discussed in section 2.3. Apart from what is involved in their application at this level, and a few other minor differences in the case of some of these rules, most of them resemble their lexical counterpart quite closely.

A point of terminology is that, though all the rules discussed in this section are understood to be postlexical rules, they are not explicitly so termed. Instead, the fact that their triggers and targets belong to distinct contiguous words is intimated their names by the terms 'word-initial' and 'word-final'. Their postlexical nature is of course technically expressed in their formulation.

A final note on representation is that any word-final vowel is represented in the text as V), and any word-initial one as (V. A postlexical sequence of /a/ and /o/, for example, will be thus be represented as a)(o.

2.4.0. Introduction.

After a few general introductory remarks, Whiteley's treatment of postlexical rules will be briefly considered here. Those that have been corroborated by the present research will be discussed more specifically in subsections 2.4.1-5.

To begin with, generally postlexical phonological rules appear to involve vowels only. The reason for this is simple. All Gusii words begin and end with a vowel, so that consonants do not occur at word-margins. The augment of some words may be deleted, so that these may constitute an exception in this respect, but even here no postlexical consonantal rules are applicable. Consequently, there are no postlexical rules involving consonants.

Next, if all seven Gusii vowels would occur both at the beginning and at the end of words, then logically there would be 49 possible contexts. In actual fact, however, /u/ never occurs word-initially, and /i/ very rarely so. This reduces the number of actual contexts to at least 35. It may be added that, for a number of rules, vowel length would probably be immaterial. But in any case, vowels tend to be short at word-margins in virtue of constraint (157).

Whiteley's treatment of postlexical vowel change, which he terms change of "external vowel sequences" (1960: 4), involves five statements. Four of these concern statements of actual change or statements of non-change. One relates to the nature of the speech that he uses as a basis for characterising the postlexical processes. His treatment is fairly informal, and none of these are explicitly or fully formulated. Three of his statements are touched on here. The other two are discussed in the following sections.

Whiteley's first statement amounts to saying that consecutive identical vowels do not undergo any change postlexically (1960: 4). This may be expressed as in (161),

(161) postlexical non-change (after Whiteley)

$$V_i\,]_{word}\,[_{word}\,V_i \;\; \text{-->} \;\; V_i\,]_{word}\,[_{word}\,V_i$$

Only four examples are given, exemplifying sequences of /a/'s, /o/'s, /i/'s, and /e/'s.

However, though this constraint does capture a generally observable surface tendency, in most cases it is not needed. Whenever the configuration in (161) occurs, any delinking-cum-spreading rule may apply, producing a surface representation identical to the underlying input. The few rules for which this account is inadequate may be conditioned so as to achieve the necessary effect. At least Upper Mid Vowel Raising (108) provides a case in point. This alternative approach would seem to render (161) unnecessary.

It is further supported by a more general principle. The present approach operates on the assumption that, if all changes that may and do occur are sufficiently handled, there is no need for any additional formal statement on non-change, for the simple reason that what is not formulated will not take effect. Rules are needed to account for regulated processes that may or must occur, not for those that may or do not occur.

In fact, the tendency toward non-change of consecutive identical vowels may well be conceived as the combined general empirical effect of all and any applicable postlexical rules. Hence it need not be formulated. Thus beyond a necessary and sufficient system of such rules, (161) is superfluous and need not be incorporated in a formal treatment of the language. Of course, it may be mentioned as the combined general empirical effect of the operation of the rules.

A second process is stated by Whiteley, somewhat imprecisely, as follows. "Sequences of dissimilar vowels in which both are mid-front or mid-back vowels tend to be realised as long, with the quality of the first member of the sequence" (1960: 4). Only one example is given, viz. |εηɔɔmbε eye| --> [εηɔɔmbεεye] 'this cow', and it is added that "this realisation is not represented in the following pages."

However, the quote states more than is illustrated by the example. Moreover, it overlaps with at least one other of Whiteley's statements. Strictly, it involves postlexical sequences of non-identical mid vowels that agree in backness or roundness. In addition to the exemplified sequence ε)(e, this includes the sequences e)(ε, ɔ)(o, and o)(ɔ, but these are not exemplified.

Presumably, the change expressed may be characterised as delinking of a word-initial mid vowel and concomitant rightward spreading of a preceding word-final mid vowel, provided the trigger and the target agree in roundness. But all this is not explicitly stated. In any case, if this interpretation is correct, the process may be formulated, in somewhat abbreviated form, as in (162),

(162) delinking-cum-rightward spreading (after Whiteley)

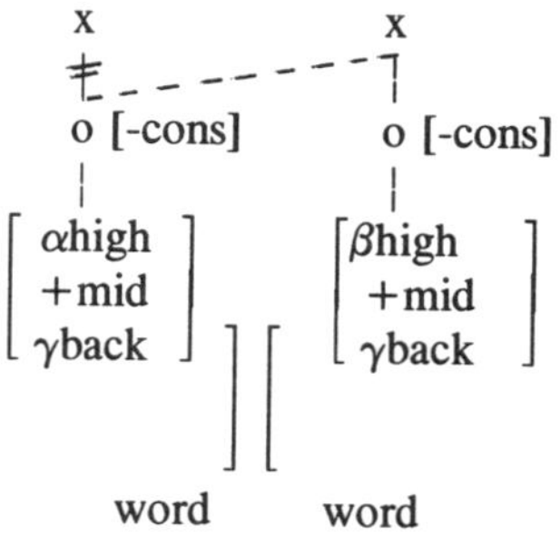

In actual fact, however, this change does not seem to occur; or at least, it was disconfirmed by the research on which the present study is based. Rather, the reverse appears to be the case. In the contexts covered by the statement just quoted, it is the final vowel of the first word that is delinked, and the first vowel of the following word that may or may not be spread leftward, i.e. lengthened. Thus the regular output of the example just given is [εηɔɔmbeeye].

This process is also noted by Whiteley (1960: 4), but in the present study it is taken as the effect of the cooperation of two rules. These will be discussed in sections 2.4.3 and 2.4.4.

Third, having made his four statements on rules, Whiteley adds that "such realisations occur in normal 'quick' speech, at which most of the examples were recorded. They tend not to occur in the slower varieties" (1960: 4). Two observations are in order here.

First, since his comment is made immediately after the examples that illustrate delinking of a word-final vowel and leftward spreading of a following word-initial vowel, it is not clear whether it is intended as qualifying this particular process alone or all of the processes he has just mentioned. If the phrase "most of the examples" refers to the examples recorded throughout his study (1960), then the comment may be taken as qualifying all the processes. If it refers to his immediately preceding examples only, it presumably qualifies only the supposed delinking of a word-final vowel and leftward spreading of the following word-initial vowel.

In this respect, then, his account is indeterminate. Thus it is unclear to any reader who has no prior knowledge of Gusii, and who is not in a position to verify his statements. Hence it is necessary to confirm here that the quoted comment applies to all of his examples, hence to all of his rules.

Second, the pronunciation characterised in the previous quote as being typical of a "normal 'quick'" rate of speech identified as Whiteley's data-base, is distinguished from that of a "slower" rate of speech. Though this distinction is not further specified, the comment does seem to imply that postlexical processes are taken as style-dependent. By and large, the research on which the present study is based confirms this supposition. The ensuing discussion will bear this out.

To conclude this section, it has already been suggested that not all the processes noted by Whiteley have been confirmed by the present research. Nor have all the corroborated ones necessarily been confirmed in all their details. Some of this has already been discussed. Other details will be elaborated in the following sections.

2.4.1. Gliding.

Postlexically, gliding may be considered as the result of the cooperation of several rules, viz. Word-Final Upper Mid Vowel Raising (section 2.4.1.1), Complex Segment Formation (section 2.4.1.2), and Glide Formation (section 2.4.1.3).

2.4.1.1. Word-Final Upper Mid Vowel Raising.

The data involved in postlexical raising of word-final upper mid vowels differ considerably from those involved in the lexical version of the rule. At least four points may be noted.

First, the sequences e)(u and o)(u do not occur, simply because /u/ does not occur word-initially.

Second, e) is not regularly raised before (i, so that this change must also be excluded from the postlexical version of the rule. At the lexical level, this was done by stipulating that if the target and trigger agree in roundness, the trigger must not be higher than the target. At the postlexical level, where the data are different, it is sufficient to stipulate that the trigger and the target must be dissimilar in roundness.

Third, in the sequence o)(i, which is exempt from Word-Final Vowel Delinking (184), /o/ may be optionally raised to [u]. In all other postlexical contexts, word-final upper mid vowels followed by a word-initial vowel are affected by Word-Final Vowel Delinking (184). The sequence o)(i is rare, since few words begin with /i/.

Finally, because both of these rules are optional, raising of upper mid vowels word-finally must be defined so as to handle those relevant sequences that are optionally passed over by the delinking rule, even if the latter would be ordered before the raising rule.

If these considerations are correct, the process may be formulated as in (163),

(163) Word-Final Upper Mid Vowel Raising (optional) (WUMVR)

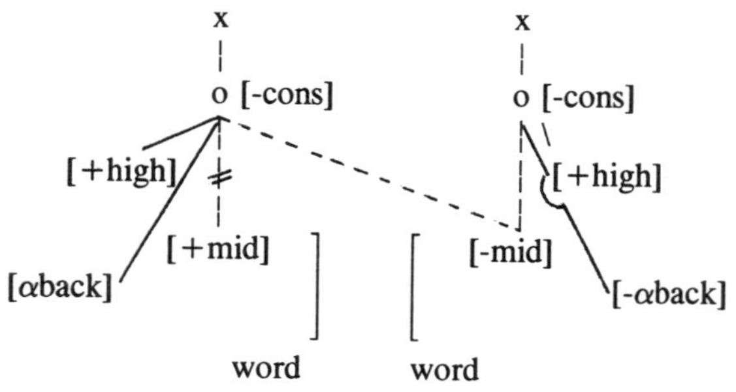

This rule raises any word-final upper mid target vowel to high, whenever it is followed by a word-initial high trigger vowel, provided that the target and the trigger differ in their specification for the feature [back]. Technically, (163) spreads the specification [-mid] of the trigger to the target, delinking the latter's specification [+mid] in the process. This formulation strictly includes both e)(u and o)(i, but since, as we have just seen, e)(u does not occur in fact, o)(i is the only sequence actually handled by the rule.

The definition of the target as [αback] and of the trigger as [-αback], correctly blocks the operation of the rule, whenever they agree in their specification for the feature [back]. That is, target /e/ will not be raised to |i|, if the trigger is /i/, whenever this sequence occurs. And /o/ would not be raised to |u|, if the trigger, had it occurred word-initially, would be /u/.

The operation of (163) is exemplified in (164), where Word-Initial Vowel Spreading (186) is anticipated,

(164)	input	omoko iγoro
		?fig tree on-top-of
	WUMVR (163)	omoko**u**iγoro
	WCSF (168)	omok**w**iγoro
	WIVS (186)	omokw**ii**γoro
	Degliding (119)	omok**u**iiγoro
		'on top of the fig-tree'

Since all of the rules adduced in (164) are optional, most of the intermediate outputs, especially the last two, may also serve as acceptable alternative surface outputs. In fact, all of the rules may optionally not apply, so that [omoko iγoro] is an acceptable output also. Apparently, [omok**o**iiγoro] is possible too, but this is not handled by any of the rules discussed: no raising of the word-final /o/ obtains, and yet word-initial /i/ is lengthened. This may be accounted for as a hybrid situation. However, *[omokiiγoro], which would result from delinking of word-final /o/ and spreading of word-initial /i/, is unacceptable. Future research may wish to explore, if, and to what extent, stylistic factors may co-determine this surface variation.

To conclude this section, raising of upper mid vowels word-finally turns out to be a process that is not only optional, but of more limited application than its lexical counterpart. Given the data discussed, it appears to be somewhat ad hoc.

2.4.1.2. Word-Final Complex Segment Formation.

With respect to postlexical gliding, Whiteley (1960: 4) observes, first, that word-final /i/ and /u/ "tend to be realised as" glides. This formulation indicates that he takes the process as a tendency, rather than a regular exceptionless rule. Moreover, as a process that is considered to be characteristic of normal quick speech, it is probably viewed as style-dependent.

As such, however, it seems to apply fairly regularly, though with a certain amount of variation. By contrast, in a slow, deliberate, or monitored style of speech, in which words are pronounced almost one by one, the process does not seem to apply at all. Since even in normal rapid speech some variation is evident, I suggest that the rule may be characterised as optional.

Second, and more specifically, Whiteley says that the sequence i)(V is regularly turned into [yV], and u)(V into [wV]. As stated, this implies that the second, word-initial vowel is not lengthened, whether compensatorily or otherwise. However, such lengthening does occur quite frequently, even though it does not necessarily do so always. For this reason, and also because such lengthening seems to apply optionally after Word-Final Vowel Delinking (184), discussed in section 2.4.3, it is here considered as a separate, optional rule, which may be fed by gliding or Word-Final Vowel Delinking (184). Technically it involves leftward spreading of a word-initial vowel, which is discussed in section 2.4.4.

Third, postlexical gliding is said to apply optionally in the case of i)(a, and never in the case of u)(o. However, these statements are disconfirmed by the present research. Though the process must be defined as optional, it is exceptionless as far as its potential triggers or contexts are concerned. That is, it may apply before any vowel.

Fourth, there is one exception, however, which Whiteley sought to exclude by stipulating that sequences of identical vowels may not undergo change postlexically. Thus, i)(i may not be turned into [yi] or [yii]. His stipulation may be taken as a language-specific constraint. Alternatively, the problem may perhaps be handled by invoking some version of the Obligatory Contour Principle. Intended as a universal principle, it states that "at the melodic level, adjacent elements are prohibited" (McCarthy 1986: 208). The status and exact form of this principle is still debated, however. Another solution might be to exclude the sequence i)(i from the structural description of postlexical gliding.

Fifth, Whiteley does not make clear that the word-final glided high vowel glides to a preceding consonant, though this does occur. Thus postlexical gliding turns out to be an instance of the formation of complex segments involving post-glides. That is, the postlexical version of the rule closely resembles the lexical version, except for a few details and the fact that the trigger vowel belongs to the next word.

Going by Whiteley's brief description only, it would be difficult to formulate the process, other than as a low-level phonetic phenomenon. Phonologically, it would be something like (165),

(165) postlexical gliding (after Whiteley 1960: 4)

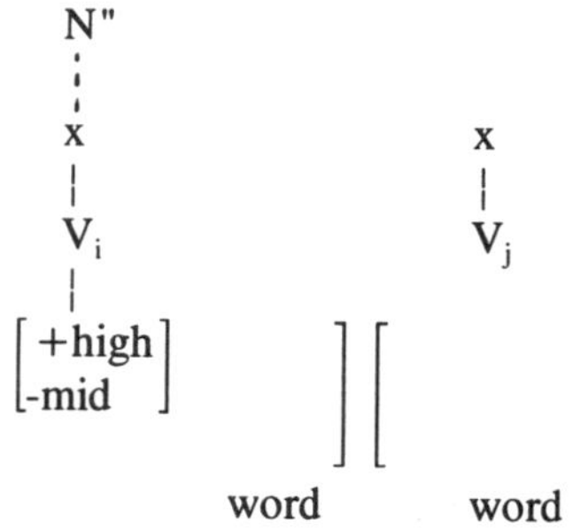

Condition 1: optional, iff V_i = /i/ and V_j = /a/
Condition 2: blocked, iff V_i = /u/ and V_j = /o/

This version needs to be adjusted, but before this is done, it may be observed, finally, that Whiteley (1960: 4) does not exemplify the process. This still remains to be done and this is a good place to do it. Accordingly, first consider the data in (166), which exemplify postlexical gliding in the context i)(V,

(166) i)(i

in this context, the rule may not apply:

¦ekeβusi iγoro¦[63]
the-cat on-top-of
[ekeβusiiγoro], *[ekeβusy(i)iγoro]
'on top of the cat'

i)(e

¦ekeβusi ekiɔɔrɔ¦
the-cat lazy
[ekeβusiekiɔɔrɔ¦]
or [ekeβusyekiɔɔrɔ¦]
or rapidly, [ekeβusyeekyɔɔrɔ¦]
'the lazy cat'

i)(ε

¦ekeβusi εkεnεnε¦
the-cat big
[ekeβusiεkεnεnε]
or [ekeβusyεkεnεnε]
or [ekeβusyεεkεnεnε]
'the big cat'

i)(a

¦aβaremi aβakoro¦
farmers old
[aβaremiaβakoro]
or [aβaremyaβakoro]
or [aβaremyaaβakoro]
'old farmers'

i)(ɔ

¦omoremi ɔmɔkε¦
farmer small
[omoremiɔmɔkε]
[omoremyɔmɔkε]
[omoremyɔɔmɔkε]
'(a/the) small farmer'

---

[63] Instead of [ekeβusi], [eke(e)mβusi] also occurs, without any difference in meaning.

i)(o

¦omoremi omokoro¦
farmer old
[omoremiomokoro]
or [omoremyomokoro]
or [omoremyoomokoro]
'(the/an) old farmer'

* i)(u

Next, consider the data in (167), which exemplify postlexical gliding involving the sequence u)(V,

(167) u)(i

¦eγetaaβu iγoro¦
book on top
[eγetaaβuiγoro]
or [eγetaaβwiγoro]
or [eγetaaβwiiγoro] 'on top of a book'

u)(e

¦eγetaaβu eγekoro¦
book old
[eγetaaβueγekoro]
or [eγetaaβweγekoro]
or [eγetaaβweeγekoro] 'an old book'

u)(ε

¦eγetaaβu εkεnεnε¦
book big
[eγetaaβuεkεnεnε]
or [eγetaaβwεkεnεnε]
or [eγetaaβwεεkεnεnε] 'a big book'

u)(a

¦oroteeru aβwaate¦[64]
basket he-was-holding
[oroteeruaβwaate]
or [oroteerwaβwaate]
or [oroteerwaaβwaate] 'a basket he was holding'

---

[64] Or, possibly, [aβwaatε].

u)(ɔ

|oroteeru ɔrɔnɛnɛ|
basket big
[oroteeruɔrɔnɛnɛ]
or [oroteerwɔrɔnɛnɛ]
or [oroteerwɔɔrɔnɛnɛ] 'a big basket'

u)(o

|oroteeru oroγima|
basket whole
[oroteeruoroγima]
or [oroteerworoγima]
or [oroteerwooroγima] 'a whole basket'

u)(u

this context does not occur in fact, since word-initial /u/ does not occur

In this presentation and elsewhere, the order i, e, ɛ, a, ɔ, o, u is maintained for the triggers, in accordance with the chart of Gusii vowels (7), taken counter-clockwise. The surface representations of each example are arranged so as to demonstrate, successively, non-application of gliding, its application, and the application of both gliding and Word-Initial Vowel Spreading (186).

Given data such as those in (166-167), the rule may now be formulated definitively, as in (168),

(168) Word-Final Complex Segment Formation (optional) (WCSF)

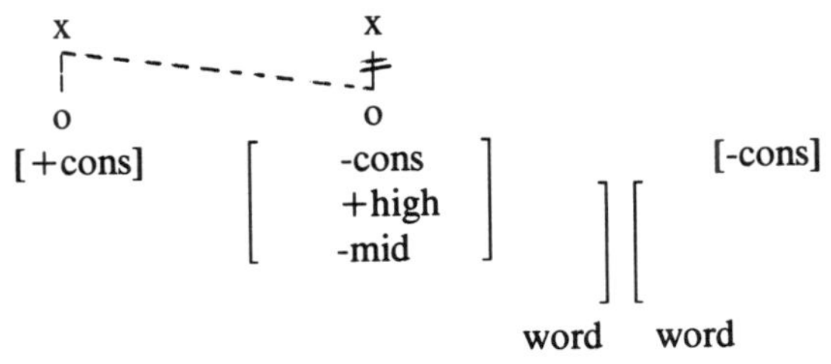

Condition: trigger and target may not be identical

This rule states that, whenever a consonant is immediately followed by a word-final high vowel, the latter, if itself followed by another, word-initial vowel, is delinked from its x on the timing-tier and spread leftward to the x dominating the consonant, thereby creating a complex segment. Whenever the high vowel is [+back], the resulting complex segment will be [Cw]; whenever it is [-back], the result will be [Cy]. The condition correctly prevents the change from i)(i into [yi]; and similarly, should it occur, from u)(u into

[wu].

This rule and its lexical counterpart differ only in two minor respects. First, the lexical version regularly applies in normal rapid speech, whereas the postlexical version is characterised as optional for the same style of speech. Second, the formulation in (168) ensures that the rule may apply only, whenever it is followed by a word-initial vowel. This correctly implies that complex segments formed by these rules never occur in word-final syllables of citation forms, where no word, and hence no word-initial vowel, follows.

2.4.1.3. Glide Formation.

It may be added that glide formation proper may also occur postlexically, as in /ηηai o-mɛñ-et-e/ --> [ηηayɔɔmɛñɛtɛ] 'where do you live?' This may be formulated as in (169),

(169) Word-Final Glide Formation (optional) (WGF)

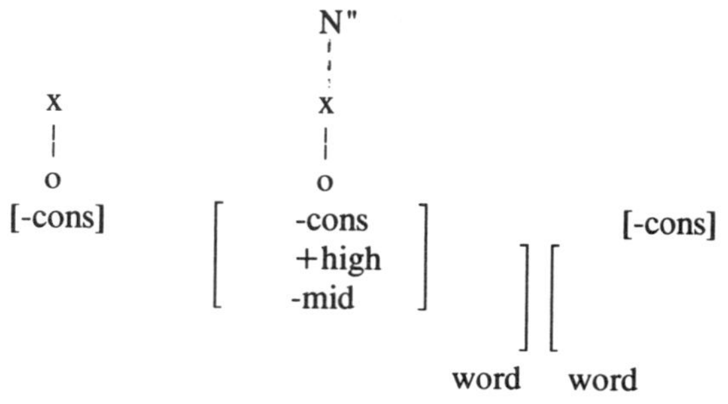

Condition: trigger and target may not be identical

It optionally assigns an N"-node to a word-final high vowel, whenever it is preceded by another vowel and followed by yet another word-initial vowel. Since this overrules regular syllabification, it is assumed that the N-node on the word-final high vowel is automatically delinked by the process.

However, this leaves possible lengthening of the following word-initial vowel as yet unaccounted for. This may be accounted for, as in (170),

(170) Word-initial Post-Glide Vowel Lengthening (optional)

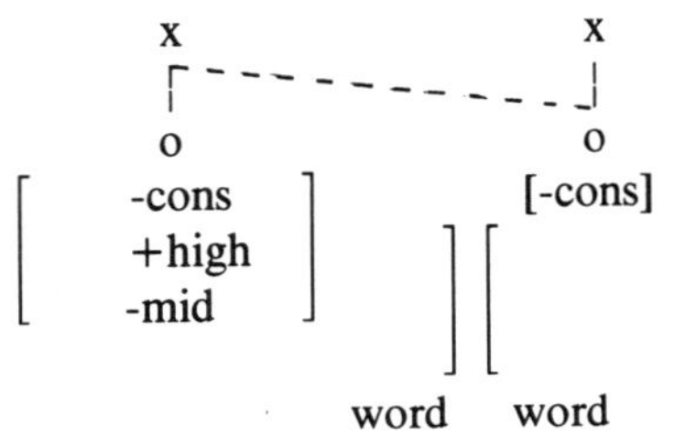

Condition: trigger and target may not be identical

It optionally spreads a word-initial vowel to a preceding word-final high vowel. Optionality is assumed, since it is as yet uncertain, whether or not the word-initial vowels involved lengthen regularly.

To conclude, even though Word-Initial Vowel Spreading (186), Word-Final Glide Formation (169), and Word-Final Glide Formation (170) may be low level phonetic rules, they indicate that some version of both Complex Segment Formation and Glide Formation (and compensatory lengthening of the following vowel) are needed postlexically, for the one cannot be adduced to account sufficiently for the output of the other, and vice versa. Their output is obviously the same, viz. a glide.

2.4.2. Word-Final Lower Mid Vowel Raising.

In order to formulate the rule discussed in this section, first consider the changes exemplified in (171),

(171) a. word-final ε becomes e before word-initial i

> |εηɔɔmbε iγoro|
> cow on-top-of
> [εηɔɔmbεiγoro] or [εηɔɔmbeiγoro]
> 'on top of the cow'
>
> |amatɔɔkε iγoro|
> [amatɔɔkεiγoro] or [amatɔɔkeiγoro]
> 'on top of the bananas'

b. word-final ɔ becomes o before word-initial i

|ekeβusi ekiɔɔrɔ iγoro|
cat lazy on-top-of
[ekeβusiekiɔɔrɔiγoro] or [ekeβusiekyɔɔroiγoro]
'op top of the lazy cat'

|ɔmɔtεγɔ iγoro|
[ɔmɔtεγɔiγoro] or [ɔmɔtεγoiγoro]
'on top of the trap'

The outputs in (171) exemplify the fact that a word-final lower mid vowel may be raised by one degree, whenever the following word-initial trigger vowel is [+high, -mid]. Since /u/ does not occur word-initially, the trigger can only be /i/. If representative, these data suggest that such raising may occur, regardless of whether or not the target and the trigger agree in their specification for the feature [back], as in (171a) and (171b) respectively. The possible alternative outputs in (171) further suggest that the process is optional.

In contrast, raising of word-final upper mid vowels in the same context seems to be restricted to triggers and targets that disagree in their specification for the feature [back] (see section 2.4.1.1). For example, compare the derivation of |omote iγoro|, in (172),

(172)	input	|omote iγoro|
	WUMVR (163)	-
	output	[omoteiγoro], *[omotiiγoro]
		'on top of the tree'

with the derivation of |eγeento iγoro|, in (173),

(173) a.	input	|eγeento iγoro|	
	WUMVR (163)	[eγeentuiγoro]	
	WCSF (168)	[eγeentwiγoro]	
	Postlexical CL	[eγeentwiiγoro]	
	output	[eγeentwiiγoro]	
		'on top of the thing'	
b.	input	|eγeento iγoro|	
	WUMVR (163)	-	(optional)
	WCSF (168)	-	
	Postlexical CL	-	
	output	[eγeentoiγoro]	
		'on top of the thing'	

It may be observed that Word-Final Upper Mid Vowel Raising (163) may or may not apply in (173), but not at all in (172).

It may be noted further that the asterisked form in (172) is also prohibited as an output of

Word-Final Vowel Delinking (184) (see section 2.4.3). Since high back vowel /u/ does not occur word-initially, contexts involving it, though theoretically included in the formulation of these rules, do not occur in fact. From data such as those in (171-173), it follows that Word-Final Upper Mid Vowel Raising (163) may not be subsumed under Word-Final Lower Mid Vowel Raising, but needs to be formulated as a separate rule.

This section may be concluded by formulating the rule under discussion, as in (174),

(174) Word-Final Lower Mid Vowel Raising (optional)

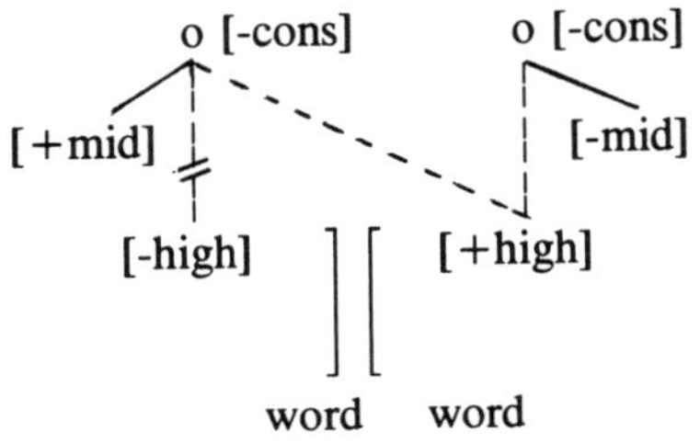

This rule states that, whenever a word-final lower mid vowel ([-high, +mid]) is followed by a word-initial high vowel ([+high, -mid]), postlexically the specification [+high] of the latter is spread leftward to the former. The [-high] of the word-final lower mid vowel is delinked in the process or by convention and in effect becomes [+high, +mid], that is upper mid.

2.4.3. Word-Final Vowel Delinking.

Whiteley observes that postlexical sequences of dissimilar vowels, V_i)(V_j, other than those handled by the processes discussed in section 2.4.1, "tend to be realised as V_j" (1960: 4).

Before we look at some examples and formulate the rule, a few comments are in order. First, though Whiteley, in his brief observation on postlexical delinking of word-initial vowels (discussed and discarded in section 2.4.0), does mention subsequent rightward spreading of the preceding word-final vowel, he does not do so in his presentation of the process discussed here. That is, he conceives of word-final vowel delinking as occurring without any lengthening of the following word-initial vowel, whether compensatorily or otherwise. The way in which he represents the change, as in <omwan(a) omoke> 'small child', confirms this interpretation. In actual fact, this example is more regularly pronounced as [omwaanɔɔmɔkɛ], though [omwaanɔmɔkɛ] does indeed occur also.

Second, the words "tend to be realised as" characterise this process as a tendency, rather than as an exceptionless change. Since this nature of the rule appears to be associated again with the rate of speech, which cannot easily be defined cross-linguistically or even cross-idiolectally, it is concomitantly problematic to pinpoint the factors that determine the application of the rule, other than was done in connection with gliding (see section 2.4.1). However, such difficulties notwithstanding, word-final vowel delinking applies regularly and widely in 'normal quick' speech, of which it is indeed characteristic (and so does subsequent Word-Initial Vowel Spreading (186); see section 2.4.4). By characterising the rule as optional, any problems of its application are resolved, including its association with some specific style or rate of speech, whether or not such association may differ per dialect or idiolect.

Third, Whiteley (1960: 4) exemplifies the process as something that occurs regularly in the contexts a)(o, e)(o, o)(e, o)(a, a)(e, and e)(a; and as something that occurs optionally in the context u)(o. Recall that this sequence was exempted by him from postlexical gliding. He does not exemplify the process for the contexts V)(i, V)(ε, V)(ɔ, ɔ)(V, ε)(V, i)(V, and u)(e. The context *V)(u does not occur, because u does not occur word-initially. Nonetheless, all the possible contexts are indeed actual contexts. That is, the structural description of the rule includes any type of vowel that may occur word-initially for its trigger or context; and it applies regularly, whenever its structural description is met.

Fourth, and finally, consecutive identical vowels need not be exempted from postlexical word-final vowel delinking by some special condition, constraint, or convention. Whenever the rule applies to such sequences, followed by Word-Initial Vowel Spreading (186), the output simply happens to be identical to the input. This is sometimes called 'vacuous' or 'gratuitous' rule application, but it should be borne in mind that this terminology only applies to the effect of the rules in question, not to their application as such. Such, at least, is the case here.

Provisionally summing up part of the preceding observations, the process as described by Whiteley (1960: 4) might be formulated as in (175),

(175) word-final vowel delinking (optional) (after Whiteley)

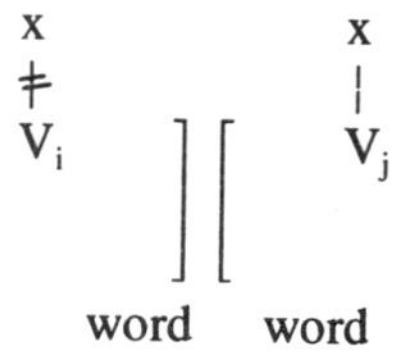

However, this formulation is too general, for the rule does not apply, whenever V_i is /i/ or /u/, i.e. [+high, -mid]. The formulation will be adjusted in a moment, therefore, but it is pertinent first to look at some examples.

To begin with, the sequence i)(V is shown to be exempted from the application of the rule, in (176),

(176) i)(i

¦ekeβusi iγoro¦
cat on-top-of
*[ekeβusyiiγoro], [ekeβusiiγoro]
'on top of the cat'

i)(e

¦ekeβusi ekiɔɔrɔ¦
cat lazy
*[ekeβuseekiɔɔrɔ¦]
'lazy cat'

i)(ε

¦ekeβusi εkεnεnε¦
cat big
*[ekeβusεεkεnεnε]
'big cat'

i)(a

¦aβaremi aβakoro¦
farmers old
*[aβaremaaβakoro]
'old farmers'

¦tari amataambe¦
[tari amataambe]
*[taraamataambe]
'6-they are not long'

i)(ɔ

¦omoremi ɔmɔkε¦
farmer small
*[omoremɔɔmɔkε]
'a small farmer'

i)(o

¦omoremi omokoro¦
farmer old
*[omoremoomokoro]
'old farmer'

i)(u: this context does not occur, since word-initial /u/ does not occur

Instead of the prohibited outputs, the acceptable ones are [ekeβusiekiɔɔrɔ] or [ekeβusyeekiɔɔrɔ], and so on. Note that word-final /i/ in these examples may be affected by gliding, except in the context i)(i.

The data in (177) exemplify non-application of word-final vowel delinking in context u)(V,

(177) u)(i

¦eγetaaβu iγoro¦
book on top
*[eγetaaβiiγoro]
'on top of a book'

u)(e

¦eγetaaβu eγekoro¦
book old
*[eγetaaβeeγekoro]
'an old book'

u)(ε

¦eγetaaβu εkεnεnε¦
book big
*[eγetaaβεεkεnεnε]
'a big book'

u)(a

¦oroteeru aβwaatε¦
basket he-was-holding
*[oroteeraaβwaatε]
'he was holding a basket'

u)(ɔ

¦oroteeru ɔrɔnεnε¦
basket big
*[oroteerɔɔrɔnεnε]
'a big basket'

u)(o

|oroteeru oroγima|
basket whole
*[oroteerooroγima]
'a whole basket'

|omokuuηgu oyo|
*[omokuuηgooyo]
'this woman'
(from Whiteley 1956: 5)

u)(u

this context does not occur, since word-initial /u/ does not occur

However, word-final /u/ may undergo postlexical gliding in these contexts, due to Word-Final Complex Segment Formation (168).

Next, though the sequence V)(i is relatively rare in fact, the data in (178) may nonetheless be adduced to exemplify the non-application of word-final vowel delinking,

(178) e)(i

|moaruete iγoro|
[mwaarueteiγoro]
but *[mwaaruetiiγoro]
'2p-you cam from up (there)'

ε)(i

|εηɔɔmbε iγoro|
[εηɔɔmbεiγoro]
or, through Word-Final Lower Mid Vowel Raising,
[εηɔɔmbeiγoro]
but *[εηɔɔmbiiγoro]
'on top of the cow'

a)(i

|γɔtεεra isikɔ|
[γɔtεεraisikɔ]
but *[γɔtεεriisikɔ]
'to sing outside'

ɔ)(i

|ekeβusi ekeɔɔrɔ iγoro|
cat lazy on-top-of
[ekeβusi ekyɔɔrɔiγoro]
or, through Word-Final Lower Mid Vowel Raising, [ekeβusi ekyɔɔroiγoro]
but *[ekeβusi ekyɔɔriiγoro]
'op top of the lazy cat'

o)(i

|omoko iγoro|
[omokoiγoro]
or, through Word-Final Upper Mid Vowel Raising (163), followed by Word-Final Complex Segment Formation (168) and optional Word-Initial Vowel Spreading (186),
[omokw(i)iγoro]
and Degliding (119),
[omokoiiγoro]
but *[omokiiγoro]
'on top of the fig-tree'

u)(i

|eγetaaβu iγoro|
[eγetaaβu iγoro]
or, through Word-Final Glide Formation and optional Compensatory Lengthening,
[eγetaaβw(i)iγoro]
but *[eγetaaβiiγoro]

Fourth, and finally, context V)(u is excluded not only in virtue of the condition of the rule, but also because /u/ does not occur word-initially. This may be symbolised as *(u. Thus the data in (176-177) exemplify the non-application of word-final vowel delinking.

In contrast, the data in (179-183) exemplify the application of the rule in various contexts. First, those in (179) do so for context e)(V,

(179) e)(e

¦orute eβite¦
[orut(e)eβite]
'(may) you draw sticks'

e)(ε

¦oγore εηɔɔmbε¦
[oγor(ε)εηɔɔmbε]
'(may) you buy a cow'

e)(a

¦otome aβaanto¦
[otom(a)aβaanto]
'(may) you send people'

¦amaace aya¦
[amaacaaya]
'this water'
(from Whiteley 1956: 5)

e)(ɔ

¦omote ɔmɔnεnε¦
[omoteɔmɔnεnε]
?[omotɔɔmɔnεnε]
'a big tree'

e)(o

¦otome omoonto¦
[otom(o)omoonto]
'(may) you send the person'

¦omoiseke omuya¦
[omoisek(o)omuya]
'a good girl/lady'
(from 1956: 5)

¦ase oβwaaηgo¦
in quickness
[asooβwaaηgo]
'quickly'

Next, the data in (180) exemplify the application of word-final vowel delinking in context ε)(V,

(180) ε)(e

|εηɔɔmbε eye|
[εηɔɔmbeeye]
'this cow'

ε)(ε

|εηɔɔmbε εyεεmɔ|
[εηɔɔmbεεyεεmɔ] (due to vacuous application)
'one cow'

ε)(a

|εηɔɔmbε aaγete|
[εηɔɔmbaaγete]
'the cow (that) he beat'

ε)(ɔ

|εηɔɔmbε ɔγɔtεγa|
[εηɔɔmbɔɔγɔtεγa]
'the cow (that) you are trapping'

ε)(o

|εηɔɔmbε oγoaaka|
[εηɔɔmbooγwaaka]
'the cow (that) you are beating'

The following data (181) exemplify the application of word-final vowel delinking in context a)(V,

(181) a)(e

|γoaaka eγeento|
[γoaakeeγeento]
'to hit something'

|erieta erimɔ|
[erieteerimɔ]
'one name, a single word' (from whiteley 1956: 5)

a)(ε

|γoaaka εkεε|
[γoaakεεkεε]
'to hit a basket'

a)(a

¦γoaaka aβaanto¦
[γoaakaaβaanto]
'to beat people'

a)(ɔ

¦γoaaka ɔmɔtεγɔ¦
[γoaakɔɔmɔtεγɔ]
'to hit a trap'

¦omwaana ɔmɔkε¦
[omwaanɔɔmɔkε]
'a small child/baby' (from Whiteley 1956: 5)

a)(o

¦γoaaka omoonto¦
[γoaakoomoonto]
'to beat a person'

The data in (182) exemplify its application in context ɔ)(V,

(182) ɔ)(e

¦ekeβusi ekiɔɔrɔ ekeiγa¦
cat lazy it-here
[ekeβusi ekyɔɔreekeiγa]
'the lazy cat is here'

ɔ)(ε

¦ekeβusi ekeɔɔrɔ εkεnεnε¦
cat lazy big
[ekeβusi ekyɔɔrεεkεnεnε]
'the big lazy cat'

ɔ)(a

|amatɛɛrɔ amaya|
songs good
[amatɛɛraamaya]
'good songs'[65]

|amatimɔ amataambe|
[amatimaamataambe|]
'long spears' (from Whiteley 1956: 5)

ɔ)(ɔ

|ɔmɔkɔ ɔnɛ|
in-law my
[ɔmɔkɔɔnɛ] (due to vacuous application)
'my in-law'

ɔ)(o

|ɔγɔtɛɛrɔ okuya|
[ɔγɔtɛɛrookuya]
'a good song'

The data in (183) exemplify the (optional) application of word-final vowel delinking in the context o)(V,

(183) o)(e

|eγeento eγekoro|
[eγeenteeγekoro]
'an old thing'

|emeyio emeeŋge|
[emeyi(e)emeeŋge]
'many knives' (from Whiteley 1956: 5)

o)(ɛ

|eγeento ɛkɛnɛnɛ|
[eγeentɛɛkɛnɛnɛ]
'a big thing'

---

[65] Judith Moraa judged |amatɛɛra| to be a possible alternative. Of course, the output of this is [amatɛɛraamaya]. She added that the output of |amatɛɛrɔ amaya| should be [amatɛɛrɔamaya]. At least in this example, or this context, then, the word-final vowel appears not to be delinked in her speech. In that of Lilian Nyanchama it did.

o)(a

|aβaanto aβanεnε|
[aβaantaaβanεnε]
'big persons'

o)(ɔ

|omoonto ɔmɔnεnε|
[omoontɔɔmɔnεnε]
'a big person'

o)(o

|omoonto omokoro|
[omoontoomokoro]
'an old person'

In all of the data in (179-183), optional non-application of word-final vowel delinking is exemplified in the intermediate representations. Optional subsequent Word-Initial Vowel Spreading (186) of the word-initial trigger vowel of this rule, through leftward Word-Initial Vowel Spreading (186) (see section 2.4.4), is indicated by parenthesis of the vowels concerned in the surface representations. It should be kept in mind that, whenever word-final vowel delinking applies, in its wake compensatory lengthening through Word-Initial Vowel Spreading (186) applies more often than not.

The process may be formulated as in (184),

(184) Word-Final Vowel Delinking (optional) (WVD)

x ... x
≠ ... |
o] [o
[-cons]] [[-cons]
word ... word

Condition: trigger or target may not be [+high, -mid]

It states that, whenever any two vowels are juxtaposed postlexically, the first of these is delinked. Furthermore, the condition states, first, that /i/ and /u/ may not be a target of the rule; that is, if either of them occurs word-finally, the rule does not apply. Second, it states that no target vowel is affected by the rule, whenever /i/ or /u/ occur as the word-initial trigger or context vowel (recall that /u/ does not in fact occur in this position anyway).

Several comments may be made. First, ordering Word-Final Vowel Delinking (184) after gliding would not solve the first problem of excluding /i/ and /u/ as possible targets. and ordering it after Word-final Upper Mid Vowel Raising (163) would not solve the second problem of excluding them as possible triggers. These problems could not be resolved, not even if the relative order of the rules mentioned could be accounted for by the Elsewhere Condition. The reason for this is that all of these rules are optional. Therefore, they may optionally not apply, hence Word-Final Vowel Delinking (184) may encounter the contexts i), u), (i, and *(u, and this necessitates the condition.

Second, given the formulation of the rule and its condition, in (184), it is unnecessary, as in Whiteley's account, to specify that its target and trigger must be dissimilar. Whenever the two vowels are identical, the rule simply applies 'vacuously', as explained. The exceptions, i)(i and *u)(u, are already handled by the condition.

Finally, it has been mentioned already that the rule itself does not handle, but usually feeds, spreading of the word-initial trigger vowel. This is formulated as a separated rule, discussed in the next section.

2.4.4. Word-Initial Vowel Spreading.

Several of the postlexical rules discussed so far, feed the optional process to be discussed here, viz. spreading of a word-initial vowel. In the nature of the case, being a postlexical rule, it can only spread the vowel leftward. The process may be taken as a case of compensatory lengthening.

Consider the examples in (185),

(185) a)(i

/o-mo-ana o-iγoro/
a-1-child 1-up
|omwaana oiγoro|
[omwaano(o)iγoro]
'an upper class child'
(lit. 'a child of up/high')

a)(e

/o-ko-γoro ko-a e-ηiti/
a-15-leg 15-of 9-animal
|okoγoro kwa eηiti|
[okoγoro kweeηiti]
'the leg of the animal'

a)(ε

/rii-γuNcara ri-a e-ηɔNβε/
5-horn 5-of 9-cow
¦riiγuuñcara ria εηɔɔmbε¦
[riiγuuñcara riεεηɔɔmbε]
'the horn of the cow'

a)(a

/o-mo-ana βo-a a-βa-kuNγu/
a-1-child 1-of a-2-woman
¦omwaana βwa aβakuuηgu¦
[omwaana βwaaβakuuηgu]
'the child of the women'
(where the sense is obviously not progenitive)

/a-βa-ana βa-a a-βa-kuNγu/
a-2-child 2-of a-2-woman
¦aβaana βaa aβakuuηgu¦
[aβaana βaaβakuuηgu]
'the children of the women'

a)(ɔ

/rii-kori ri-a o-mo-ñεnε/
5-path 5-of a-1-owner
¦riikori ria ɔmɔñεnε¦
[riikori riɔɔmɔñεnε]
'the path of the owner'

a)(o

/o-mo-ana βo-a o-mo-kuNγu/
a-1-child 1-of a-1-woman
¦omwaana βwa omokuuηgu¦
[omwaana βwoomokuuηgu]
'the child of the woman'

*a)(u: this context does not occur

It will be clear from these data that the process may involve any type of word-initial vowel, whenever it is preceded by word-final /a/. The process may also apply, whenever the word-final vowel is /e/, /ε/, /ɔ/, or /o/, as exemplified in (179-183). However, it may not apply, when the word-final or word-initial vowel is a high vowel, i.e. /i/ or /u/, as exemplified previously in (176, 177).

Given such data, the rule may be formulated as in (186),

(186) Word-Initial Vowel Spreading (optional) (WIVS)

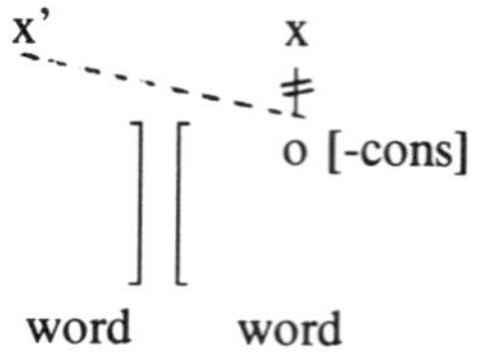

Condition: trigger or target may not be [+high, -mid]

It links any word-initial vowel to any word-final floating x', and it may apply optionally after at least Complex Segment Formation and Word-Final Vowel Delinking (184), except when, as the condition stipulates, either the trigger or the target is an /i/ or a /u/.

The following sample derivations (187) provide two more examples,

(187)	a.	input	/a-se a-kε/,	
		WVD (184)	ø	
		WIVS (186)	a	
		output	[asaakε] 'a small place'	
	b.	input	¦omo-ana βoa omokuNγu¦	
		CSF (109)	w	
		LR (90)	-	blocked word-finally
		WVD (184)	ø	
		WIVS (186)	o	
		other rules		
		output	[omwaana βwoomokuŋgu] 'a child of the woman'	

As with all the other rules, it is assumed, with Whiteley (1960: 4), that the process is characteristic of normal rapid non-monitored speech. Should the language be reinvestigated in terms of stylistics, it seems not improbable that various rules will turn out to be characteristic of different styles or rates of speech.

A final observation is that the combined effect of Word-Final Vowel Delinking (184) and Word-Initial Vowel Spreading (186) is that of liaison.

2.4.5. Word-Final Intervocalic /a/-Raising.

The example in (188) illustrates the possible postlexical change from /a/ to [e].

(188) /ko-ci-a isikɔ/
15-go-fv outside
a. [ɣocia isikɔ] (no rules)
b. [ɣociisikɔ] (WVD (184) and WIVS (186)
c. [ɣocieisikɔ]
'to go outside'

The three alternative outputs (188a-c) are all possible, but the change exemplified in (188c) has not yet been accounted for. It may be expressed, relatively informally, as in (189),

(189) Word-Final Intervocalic /a/-Raising (optional)

$$a \rightarrow e / \ i \ \text{---} \ i \ \Big]_{\text{word}} \Big[_{\text{word}}$$

This rule states that a word-final low target vowel /a/, whenever it is both preceded and, at the beginning of the following word, succeeded by high front vowel /i/, may optionally be turned into upper mid front vowel /e/.

A lexical version of the rule was discussed in section 2.3.16.

2.5. Summary of rules.

Most of the rules discussed in Chapter Two are lexical phonological rules. Some of them deal with syllabification. A few, anticipating the next chapter, concern allomorphy. For quick and easy reference, these several classes of rules are enumerated here.

Allomorphy rules discussed are those in (190),

(190) a. unique allomorphy rule (27)
b. first person singular verbal marker (SM, OM) (82)
c. object marker 4, 9 (88)

Syllable structure assignment rules and a condition discussed are those in (191),

(191) a. x-Placement (37)
b. N-Placement (41)
c. Condition on Structure Dependent Rules (43)
d. N-Fusion (45)
e. N'-Projection (47)
f. N"-Projection (49)
g. Nasal Resyllabification (optional) (71)

Lexical phonological rules and some constraints or tendencies are summarised in (192),

(192) a. Continuancy Redundancy Rule (57)
b. Consonantal Voicing Dissimilation (59)
c. Prenasalisation (61)
d. Nasal Homorganisation (62)
e. Defricativisation (65)
f. Word-initial Nasal Delinking (optional) (70)
g. Pre-Nasal /i/-Insertion (optional) (80)
h. Linking Rule (optional) (90)
i. x-Trimming (94)
j. Upper Mid Vowel Raising (optional) (108)
k. Complex Segment Formation (109)
l. Glide Formation (optional) (114)
m. Post-Glide Vowel Lengthening (optional) (115)
n. Degliding (optional) (119)
o. Mid Vowel Height Spreading (136)
p. /a/-Delinking (optional) (147)
q. Intervocalic /a/-Raising (optional) (149)
r. /a/-Shortening (optional) (154)
s. Constraint on word-marginal long vowels (157)

Finally, the postlexical rules in (193), all conceived as optional, such that their optionality probably depends on the rate or style of speech, have also been discussed,

(193) a. Word-Final Upper Mid Vowel Raising (163)
b. Word-Final Glide Formation (169)
c. Word-initial Post-Glide Vowel Lengthening (optional) (170)
d. Word-Final Lower Mid Vowel Raising (174)
e. Word-Final Vowel Delinking (184)
f. Word-Initial Vowel Spreading (186)
g. Word-Final Intervocalic /a/-Raising (189)

So much for the lexical and postlexical phonology of the language. Its morphology will be discussed in Chapter Three. Interaction between Gusii phonology and morphology, has been assumed throughout this study. Occasionally it was exemplified by derivations in this chapter, as it will be in the next.

CHAPTER THREE

CHAPTER THREE

GUSII MORPHOLOGY

3.0. Introduction.

The present chapter deals with Gusii lexical morphology. More particularly, I discuss the lexical categories of the language (3.1); its morphosyntactic classes and the agreement that exists between heads and modifiers in terms of these classes (3.2); its verbal morphology (3.3), including the tense system (3.3.5); and some processes of lexical derivation (3.4). Section 3.5, finally, touches on ways of expanding the lexicon other than by lexical derivation and presents a few common idiomatic expressions.

Some of these aspects of Gusii morphology interact with its phonology, some with its syntax, and some arguably with both. Though Gusii syntax will not be considered here at any length, such types of interaction will be noted in their appropriate places, in as far as this is possible within the limits of the present study.

3.1. Lexical categories.

In the present section, I will briefly consider a few points of terminology involving the major lexical categories (3.1.1) and then discuss their characteristics from a morphological, syntactic, and/or semantic viewpoint. It deals successively with nouns (section 3.1.2), adjectives (3.1.3), verbs (3.1.4), adverbs (3.1.5), pronouns (3.1.6), specifiers and quantifiers, including determiners (3.1.7), numerals (3.1.8), and finally, adpositions (3.1.9). In section 3.2, these categories will be reconsidered in terms of their morphosyntactic classes and agreement.

3.1.1. Terminology.

Since characteristics used to differentiate lexical categories cross-linguistically have not been universally identical for each category, and since their definitions are therefore not necessarily univocal universally, it may not be inappropriate to begin a discussion of Gusii lexical categories and their defining characteristics with a few remarks on terminology.

Taking into account certain characteristics of Bantu languages in general, Whiteley (1960: 2) differentiates the following lexical categories and domains with respect to Gusii. Lexical categories or 'classes' distinguished are verbs, nominals, and invariable words. Lexical domains or 'elements' distinguished are the root and the stem. These will be considered briefly in this order.

As to his subdivision of lexical categories it may be observed first that, though the Gusii tense system is the subject of Whiteley (1960), no formal definition is given of the lexical category of verbs. His study nonetheless touches on most of the aspects of the verbal system (1960: 6-10). To the extent that it does, it describes, if only by implication, and thereby delimits, what the Gusii verb is and what it is not.

Second, nominals are subdivided further into "short-series" and "long-series" nominals. Short-series nominals are defined as "commonly associated with a relatively limited series of prefixes (..) which are commonly identified in terms of the singular/plural dichotomy" (1960: 2). They are also referred to as nouns. Long-series nominals are defined as "associated with a relatively longer series of prefixes, a full series [of prefixes] in many cases" (1960: 2). This sub-class is said to include adjectives, demonstratives, and possessives.

Third, the lexical category of invariable words is defined as including those words "which are never associated with simple verbal or nominal prefixes, and which are outside the system of agreement or control" (1960: 2).

As may be seen from these definitions, Whiteley differentiates short- and long-series nominals on strictly formal grounds. But he immediately modifies this subdivision by observing, on the definition of short-series nominals, or nouns proper, that "the term - 'relatively' is important, however, since many stems may be associated with several such pairs of prefixes" (1960: 2). He then proceeds to give an example. As far as prefixation and strictly formal criteria are concerned, this qualification implies that nouns and adjectives, demonstratives, and possessives are perhaps more similiar than his distinction suggests. But since it is not further specified to what degree, his subdivision into short- and long-series nominals remains somewhat fuzzy.

In addition to this, there are other criteria, not strictly morphological, that may be brought to bear on the distinction between Gusii nouns and adjectives. For example, like nouns proper, many adjectives may function as heads. For this reason I will not adopt his terminology, but continue to use the terms 'noun' and 'adjective', to be defined in a moment.

Furthermore, the term 'nominal' will sometimes be used as a collective term to designate both nouns, and adjectives used as a noun. Thus it refers to the behaviour typical of nouns, or to the position in a sentence or phrase typically taken by nouns. Demonstratives and possessives, and, for that matter, any other pronouns, are thus excluded from the class of Gusii nominals. Hence my use of the term differs from Whiteley's.

Pronouns also may be used as heads and thus behave like nouns. But the extent of this behaviour, especially from a combined morphosyntactic and semantic point of view, is considerably less than that of adjectives. These tend to behave much like nouns, morphosyntactically and semantically, whenever they function as heads. Pronouns do so only to a lesser extent.

Finally, the categories of numerals and adverbs are also differentiated by Whiteley (1956), but not defined.

Two observations may be added to this brief consideration of terminology involving lexical categories. First, as we have just seen, Whiteley (1960) proposes some new terminology in this connection. Yet, his earlier position seems to be more relevant. It is expressed as follows. "(...) Care has been taken to avoid the use of new obscure grammatical terms. This is not from a conviction that traditional terms are more accurate or more suitable for such a language, but rather from the belief that the majority of those wishing to learn African languages have so hazy an idea about grammatical terms in general that any but the simplest inspire both confusion and fear" (1956: 2). If this remark still holds true, even if in modified form, it rather argues against introducing new terms, whether or not in an ad hoc manner. Therefore I have continued to use conventional terms, the more so since it has been my aim, as much as possible, to make the present study accessible also to the general reader. The definitions of some of the terms have however been adjusted to suit Gusii.

Second, another argument against traditional terminology for lexical categories, still heard sometimes, is that African languages have been forced into western or ancient grammatical terminology, and thereby distorted. Undoubtedly, some aspects of some languages have occasionally been represented wrongly or insufficiently in some descriptions. But the argument can easily be overstated, especially when overly generalised.

The rather sobering fact, on the contrary, is that many African languages have still been insufficiently studied and described so far. To be sure, questions of terminology are important, viewed from the perspectives of both Bantu and general linguistics. But the real issue here is one of proper definition. The study of language is, and will continue to be, at least in part, an empirical discipline. So theory must remain in close touch with the relevant linguistic data. There must be a necessary and sufficient fit between them.

For quite a number of reasons, not discussed here, there is still a great need for more, and more accurate, descriptions of specific Bantu languages, at least in East Africa. The point here is that, as their number will increase, definitions descriptively more adequate than some of the current ones may be developed, if necessary, but Bantu and general linguistics must also be taken into account, at the same time, for real and lasting progress to be made. For the time being, I will continue to use traditional terminology and attempt to define the various lexical categories in a way that is both necessary and sufficient for Gusii and for the present purposes.

In addition to the aforementioned lexical categories, Whiteley also identifies at least two lexical domains. The first of these is the verbal root. It is defined as the irreducible element of the verb, variously called "radical", "root", or "core" (1960: 2). In contrast, I will omit the terms "radical" and "core" and restrict myself to the use of the term 'root'. It is defined slightly differently as the irreducible semantic and morphological core of any word. This includes any verb.

The second domain distinguished is the stem. Whiteley (1960: 2) defines it as the non-prefix element of the nominal. Again in contrast, here it is used to designate that part of any word, including any nominal, that follows the prefix domain.

In addition, third, the term 'base' will be used in this study to designate that part of a word that comprises its stem minus the final syllable or vowel. Future suprasegmental research on Gusii must settle the indeterminacy of the phrase 'syllable or vowel' in this definition by a more systematic examination of the tonal and other suprasegmental facts of the language.

It may be clear that prefixes play an important role in this account. A brief note on abbreviations may therefore be in order here. The general abbreviation used for prefix is 'px'. Depending on the type of word or lexical category to which prefixes may be attached, several types of prefix may be differentiated. These and their abbreviations may be designated as follows: nominal prefix (npx), referential prefix (rpx), and pronominal prefix (ppx).

Whiteley (1960: 8-9) uses the term "the verbal prefix" for the subject prefix or marker of the verb. Strictly, however, there are various types of verbal prefix. This phrase may therefore conceivably be used more appropriately as a general term to designate any type of verbal prefix. Instead of his phrase, I will here use the term "subject marker" (sm) to designate the specific prefix concerned. Several types of verbal object prefixes or markers (om) also occur. These prefixes will be considered paradigmatically, in the rest of this chapter, in their appropriate places.

In morphological or syntactic analyses, the abbreviations just introduced may designate the prefix proper or the augmented prefix. For example, nominal prefix /omo-/ may be designated npx, or, if its class is to be indicated, npx1 or npx3. But when it is necessary to differentiate the augment and the prefix proper, the latter may be designated by the relevant abbreviation and the augment separately by the letter "a". Thus, /o-mo-/ may be labelled "a-npx", or, if its class is to be indicated, class 1 for example, "a-npx1".

3.1.2. Nouns.

A preliminary general remark is that, in the present discussion of the phonology and morphology of the lexical categories, it is assumed throughout that more research on the semantics and the (phrasal and sentential) syntax of the language is needed, in order to be able to elaborate and further refine at least some of what will be said here.

Gusii nouns enter into a system of pairs of prefixes that mark the semantico-syntactic categories of singular and plural. Of each pair, one prefix marks the singular of the word to which it is prefixed, while the other prefix marks the corresponding plural. For example, nominal prefix class 1 /omo-/ regularly corresponds with nominal class 2 prefix /aβa-/. So the plural of [ómoγááka] 'old man (term of respect)' is [áβaγááka].

Traditionally, these prefixes have usually been called concord or agreement prefixes. The classes of words marked by the singular-plural combinations of these prefixes have usually been termed concord classes. However, I prefer to use the term 'morphosyntactic' classes or agreement, for three reasons.

First, many, if not all, of the lexical classes marked by these prefixes originally seem to have had a semantic motivation. This is still the case with class 1-2, which refers to persons or animate beings. This semantic motivation now seems to have been lost for most of the other classes, though traces of it may still be found or reconstructed. The prefixes nonetheless continue to mark these lexical classes morphosyntactically.

Second, it may be argued that there is more than a semantic aspect to the distinction of singular and plural. Besides their designation of the semantic notions of singularity and plurality (Gusii has no form for a dual plural), they also function as syntactic categories. As such, they determine the agreement between a verb and the heads (usually nominals) syntactically bound by it in the sentence, or vice versa, and also the concord between heads and their modifiers. Both types of agreement are marked by the same set of prefixes. The shapes of these prefixes are morphologically identical, or at least very similar, for the various lexical categories. Hence the phrase 'morphosyntactic agreement' is used to designate either of these two types of agreement, and 'morphosyntactic classes' is used to refer to the singular-plural classes which are thus marked by the prefix combinations involved.

Finally, in the sentence, nouns typically function as a subject, object, verbal complement, prepositional object, or nominal predicate. In the phrase, they typically function as heads. Semantically, they typically function as substantives, naming persons, animals, places, things, or ideas. At least these properties characterise the Gusii noun, together with the system of morphosyntactic agreement just mentioned.

3.1.3. Adjectives.

As pointed out in section 3.1.1, adjectives may behave like nouns morphologically, syntactically, and semantically. For this reason, they are sometimes classed together as nominals. But there are some differences between them as well. Here these will be discussed in general. In due course, they will be considered in some detail.

A first, semantic point is that in Gusii, as in many other languages, adjectives typically designate attributes.

Possibly because of this, second, syntactically they are typically used attributively. That is, they typically function as modifiers. As such, they regularly follow their head. So in this respect adjectives differ from nouns, which typically function as heads.

Third, however, when, from a semantic point of view, they are used substantivally in their nominal usage, adjectives may also function as heads. As such, they may perform the same syntactic functions as nouns, viz. that of subject, object, verbal complement, prepositional object, or nominal predicate.

Fourth, morphologically, adjectives behave almost exactly like nouns, except in the following two respects. First, a partial difference concerns the behaviour of nouns and adjectives with respect to prefixation in morphosyntactic classes 9-10 and 9a-10a. Consonant-initial noun stems take either /e-/ and /ci-/ (9-10), or /e-n-/ and /ci-n-/ (9a-10a). Compare 9 [ekaβira] 'tribe', plural 10 [cikaβira] with 9a [embaata] 'duck', plural 10a [cimbaata]. The prefixation of the word for 'cow' appears to be irregular, since its singular is [εŋɔɔmbε], presumably from /e-ŋɔɔmbε/, but its plural [ciɔɔmbε]. This indeterminacy may in fact relate to the variation between 9-10 and 9a-10a as such, which is found more generally. Vowel-initial noun stems take 9-10, as in [eaŋga] 'cloth' and [eusi] 'thread'. I have found no such nouns proper that take 9a-10a. All adjectives, however, take /e-n-/ and /ci-n-/ (9a-10a) only, regardless of whether their stem begins with a vowel or a consonant. This includes vowel-initial adjectives used as a noun. See section 3.2.1.5 for some examples.

Second, the prefix for the relatively marginal class 21 is distinct for nouns and adjectives. Nouns invariably take /ña-/ but adjectives either /e-/ or /a-/. The distinction for adjectives may possibly involve a difference in meaning (see section 3.2.2 for some examples).

To sum up, adjectives typically, but not exclusively, function as modifiers. The may function as heads. Nouns typically and exclusively function as heads. Apart from this major difference in syntactic function, and from the aforementioned other details, adjectives largely behave like nouns.

3.1.4. Verbs.

The verb is traditionally defined as the part of speech that is used to predicate, of which the typical function in the sentence is that of predication. This basic definition also holds for Gusii.

Semantically, the Gusii verb typically expresses some physical activity, a state of affairs, including relations, a mental activity, or a state of mind.

Most verbs are lexical verbs. Some, however, are auxiliary or linking verbs. These are discussed in sections 3.3.5 and 3.3.6.

From a combined semantic and syntactic viewpoint, the Gusii verb is typically the part of speech that expresses tense, mood, and aspect, except in infinitive and imperative forms. The infinitive, for example, is marked morphologically by word-initial prefix 15 /ko-/, hence also called the infinitive marker, and final suffix vowel /-a/. However, other semantic or syntactic categories may also be encoded on the verb. The resulting type of agglutinative verbal morphology is actually characteristic of many Bantu languages. These and other verbal properties are discussed more fully in sections 3.2.3 and 3.3.

3.1.5. Adverbs.

The adverb is traditionally defined as the part of speech that modifies or qualifies another word (an adjective, a verb, or another adverb) or word-group (phrase, clause, or sentence), and that usually expresses a perceived relation of place, time, circumstance, manner, cause, degree, or an intellectual judgment as such, e.g. a reason, or a judgment of probability, possibility, or certainty. Given the correctness of this general definition, the following additional observations may be made on Gusii adverbs in particular.

First, Whiteley (1956: 43-44 and 1960: passim) does not offer examples of adverbs that qualify adjectives or other adverbs, nor have I come across such examples during fieldwork. Some adverbs, however, may qualify word-groups, even up to the level of the sentence. Nonetheless, the typical function of the Gusii adverb is to qualify or modify verbs. Even [koβua] 'more than', which literally means 'to surpass, to conquer' and is used in comparisons[1], really qualifies a verb, though usually it occurs immediately next to a word-group or even a single nominal.

Second, though the types of single-word adverb that commonly occur across languages, such as the equivalents of "well", 'always', 'everywhere'[2], etc., seems relatively small in Gusii, this lexical sub-category does not seem to be a closed one. Adverbs may be, and often are, derived from other lexical categories.

Third, adverbs are regularly non-augmented, and sometimes also non-prefixed. This will be discussed in subsection 3.4.7.

Fourth, to a limited extent adverbs may undergo reduplication. This will be discussed in subsection 3.4.3.

Finally, at least the following semantically different types of adverb occur in the language,

(1) a. adverbs of time or duration
b. adverbs of place or direction
c. adverbs of manner
d. adverbs of attitude
e. adverbs of reason

However, other types, such as adverbs of circumstance, result, or cause, probably also occur, to be ascertained by more extensive semantic lexical research. The types differentiated in (1) will be exemplified in section 3.4.7.

3.1.6. Pronouns.

The pronoun is traditionally defined as the part of speech that is used instead of (Latin: 'pro') a noun, in order to designate, without naming, a person, animal, thing, idea, etc., that is already known from the linguistic context or the non-linguistic co-text, or that forms the subject of inquiry.

Syntactically, Gusii pronouns may function as modifiers or adjectives. In this dependent or attributive usage they regularly follow their heads.

Furthermore, in any complete grammatical utterance, containing at least a subject and a verb, pronominal reference is encoded on the verb. Such encoding is obligatory.

---

[1] This way of expressing comparison is characteristic of many Bantu languages, certainly those in East Africa.

[2] Etymologically, however, 'always' and 'everywhere' are composed of two different words, respectively from 'all ways' and 'every where'.

However, in addition to this, it may also be expressed through a distinct lexical item, such that both means of expression may be used together in the sentence.

At least the following types of pronoun may be differentiated: demonstrative pronouns (3.2.5), referential demonstrative (3.2.6), independent pronouns (section 3.2.7), interrogative pronouns (3.2.8), and possessive pronouns (3.2.9).

Pronominal reference encoded on the verb is expressed through subject and object markers. Subject markers may be non-relative (section 3.2.3.1) or relative (3.2.3.2).

3.1.7. Quantifiers and specifiers.

Broadly speaking, quantifiers are words that express measure, extent, or quantity. Logically, they define the extent of the application of a term or a proposition. More specifically, a quantifier is a logical term related to linguistic expressions that, in contrast with expressions that name or refer, gives information about the quantity of referents about which a subject or predicate refers, i.e. about which a sentence makes a predication.

Viewed from a strictly logical viewpoint, there are only four quantifiers universally, viz. the concepts 'all', 'no', 'some', and 'some-not'. These may be variously expressed in some language. In English one may say, for example, 'all people', but also 'everybody'. These logical concepts may also be variously expressed across different languages. A somewhat imperfect example is the following one. In English, one may say, for example, '(at) all times', 'always', 'every day'. Logically, these have the same import, but linguistically or pragmatically a difference may be implied. The equivalent Swahili expression is 'kila siku', i.e. 'every day', but, as pointed out, the example is imperfect, for 'sikuzote', literally 'all days', and other expressions also occur.

A specifier may be defined as a word or a word-group that expresses the concept of specificity, distinctness, or definiteness. Some English examples are 'both', 'either', and 'other'. There is arguably some overlap with quantifiers, particularly when actual species are talked about. In the case of specifiers, the idea of definiteness seems uppermost. Semantically, they are therefore more or less related to quantifiers.

Determiners are also words that express the concept of indefiniteness or definiteness, or some degree in between. Though sometimes proposed as a distinct class of words, they appear to be a sub-class of, or simply another term for, specifiers. For example, the English definite and indefinite articles, 'the', 'a', 'an', are sometimes called determiners, but may well be considered as a sub-class of specifiers or even quantifiers, as the case may be. With respect to Gusii, 'specifier' and 'determiner' may be used interchangeably. This will therefore be their usage in the present study.

The concept of definitiness or indefiniteness need not always be expressed in the same way across languages. Nor is it necessarily expressed by means of separate lexical items. It may also be expressed through bound morphemes. In some Bantu languages, for example, the distinction may be expressed through the presence or absence of an augment. In others, and sometimes in addition to (non-)augmentation, the distinction may be expressed through the absence or presence of a subject or object marker encoded on the verb.

Syntactically, Gusii quantifiers and specifiers behave like pronouns or adjectives. They are discussed more fully in section 3.2.12.

3.1.8. Numerals.

A numeral may be defined as any word or phrase that expresses or denotes the concept of number. Gusii numerals and the system in which they occur are discussed in sections 3.2.13 and 3.2.14.

3.1.9. Adpositions and associative /-a/.

Adpositions are words or phrases that occur next to other words, whether immediately preceding them, in which case they are called prepositions, or immediately following them, in which case they are called postpositions. As all words in all languages precede and follow other words, this definition is evidently insufficient to distinguish them from other sorts of words. More specifically, then, adpositions are words or phrases that govern a noun or a pronoun and that express the latter's relation to another word.

Accordingly, a preposition is traditionally defined as a part of speech that precedes and syntactically governs a noun or a pronoun, expressing the latter's relation to another word. The definition of a postposition is identical, except that it follows the word it so governs. These definitions hold true also for Gusii.

The kinds of relation that may be expressed by monomorphemic prepositions may also be expressed, in Gusii, by prepositional phrases. There appear to be no postpositional phrases. For further discussion of adpositions and prepositional phrases, see sections 3.2.10 and 3.4.8.

In addition to this, some relations usually expressed through adpositions or prepositional phrases may also be encoded on the Gusii verb by means of extension suffixes. This phenomenon is discussed in section 3.3.2, especially subsection 3.3.2.6.

Finally, at this point mention may be made of the associative construction, as it is often called in Bantu linguistics. It too expresses typically prepositional meanings. It involves what is usually called the 'associative' element /-a/, or alternatively also 'connective' or 'linking' /-a/. It is so called, because the meanings it expresses are identical, or at least very similar, to those expressed by the English preposition 'of'. Associative /-a/ and the construction in which it is used are discussed more fully in section 3.2.11.

3.1.10. Conjunctions.

Conjunctions are commonly defined as uninflected words used to connect clauses or sentences (by relation of coordination or subordination), or, at a lower syntactic level, to co- or subordinate words or phrases in a clause. This definition is applicable also to Gusii. As such, conjunctions are sometimes designated as function words, i.e. as expressing a syntactic relation. However, the state of affairs described thereby, as conceived in the mind, is of course implied.

Some conjunctions appear to take a class-prefix, especially when they are derived from another lexical category, sometimes by zero-derivation, though their etymology and morphological make-up may be unclear synchronically. An example of zero derivation appears to be [ɛkɛrɔ] 'when', which is also a noun meaning 'time', referring to a particular occasion (Whiteley 1956: 133). Most of them, if at all prefixed, do not appear to be augmented. An example is [γose] 'or'. Some conjunctions are non-parsible monomorphemic words. An example of this is /na/ 'and'.

All of them, as conjunctions, are morphologically invariable: they do not participate in the system of morphosyntactic agreement. Hence also, they are not discussed in section 3.2, which deals specifically with this aspect of the language. For a brief discussion of the derivation of some conjunctions, however, see section 3.4.9. This concludes the introduction of Gusii lexical categories.

3.2. Morphosyntactic classes and agreement.

This section deals with the morphosyntactic classes that are characteristic of the language. Thus it discusses the various phonological, morphological, syntactic, and semantic aspects of the prefixes that mark these classes, if not the semantic properties of the classes themselves. Since the shape of some of these prefixes varies somewhat per lexical category, this variation will be taken into account as well. Finally, since the various lexical categories discussed in section 3.1 agree with each other morphosyntactically in terms of these classes, whenever they function as parts of speech in a phrase, clause, or sentence, this agreement will also be considered.

The lexical categories introduced in section 3.1 will be reconsidered in the following order: nouns (section 3.2.1), adjectives (3.2.2), verbs (3.2.3), adverbs (3.2.4), various pronouns (3.2.7 through 3.2.9), adpositions (3.2.10), including the associative construction involving associative element /-a/ (3.2.11), quantifiers and specifiers (3.2.12), and numerals (3.2.13 and 3.2.14). A summary of the prefixes that mark the morphosyntactic classes for the various lexical categories will be given in section 3.2.15.

Since, as pointed out in section 3.1.10, conjunctions are few and invariable, they are therefore not reconsidered in the present section. Invariability, as understood here, means that a word is morphologically invariable. As such, it does not enter into the system of morphosyntactic affixation. Hence it does not participate in the morphosyntactic class system and agreement. Next to conjunctions, most, if not all, adverbs and adpositions are invariable too, and so are some adjectives.

It may be added that the verb is considered here only in so far as it participates in morphosyntactic agreement. Since it does this through its non-relative or relative subject marker, and secondarily also through its object markers, it is these verbal elements that will be discussed in section 3.2.3. Other aspects of verbal syntax and morphology will be taken up in section 3.3.

Similarly, and more generally, lexical derivation is not considered here, but will be discussed in section 3.4.

3.2.1. Nouns.

3.2.1.1. Morphosyntactic classes and prefixes.

As pointed out in section 3.1.1, Gusii nouns may be said to enter into morphosyntactic classes marked by prefixes indicating their singular and their corresponding plural. Whiteley's presentation of this nominal prefix system (1956: passim) is repeated here in (2),

(2) nominal class prefix system (Whiteley 1956)

1	omo-
2	aβa-
3	omo-
4	eme-
5	rii-
6	ama-
7	eke-
8	eβi-
9	e-
9a	en-
10	ci-
10a	cin-
11	oro-
12	aka-
14	oβo-
15	oko-
16	a-

However, the present research has revealed that this system is slightly more complex, as in (3),

(3) Gusii noun prefixes

1	omo-
1a	mo-
1b	Ø
2	aβa-
3	omo-
4	eme-
5	eri-
6	ama-
7	eke-
8	eβi-
9	e-
9a	e-n-
10	ci-
10a	ci-n-
11	oro-
12	aka-
14	oβo-
15	oko-
16	a-
21	ña-

This arrangement is such that, for classes 1-10a, the unevenly numbered prefixes regularly indicate the singular of the nouns to which they are attached, while the evenly numbered ones immediately following them indicate the corresponding plural. The numbers 11-21 do not express such correspondence between singular and plural.

Postponing a discussion of the sometimes considerable surface variation possible in the case of at least some prefixes, the morphosyntactic prefix system in (3), may be exemplified, for the moment sufficiently, by the words in (4),

(4) 1 ¦omo-rem-i¦ --> [omoremi] 'farmer'
1b /Ø-taata/ --> [taata] 'father'
2 ¦aβa-rem-i¦ --> [aβaremi] 'farmers'
2b /aβa-taata/ --> [aβataata] 'fathers'
3 ¦omo-te¦ --> [omote] 'tree'
4 ¦eme-te¦ --> [emete] 'trees'
5 ¦eri-eta¦ 'name'
¦rii-tɔɔkɛ¦ --> [riitɔɔkɛ] 'banana'
6 ¦ama-tɔɔkɛ¦ --> [amatɔɔkɛ] 'bananas'
7 ¦eke-saku¦ --> [eγesaku] 'clan'
8 ¦eβi-saku¦ --> [eβisaku] 'clans'
9 /e-kaβira/ --> [ekaβira] 'tribe'[3]
9a ¦e-n-raaγera¦ --> [endaaγera] 'food'

---

3 Possibly a lexical take-over from Swahili **kabila** 'tribe'.

10	¦ci-kaβira¦	--> [cikaβira] 'tribes'
10a	¦ci-n-raaγera¦	--> [cindaaγera] 'foods'
11	¦oro-ko¦	--> [oroko] 'firewood'
12	¦aka-ana¦	--> [akaana] 'small honeycomb'
14	¦oβo-koombe¦	--> [oβokoombe] 'hoe'
15	¦oko-γoro¦	--> [okoγoro] 'leg, foot'
16	/a-se/	--> [âsé][4] 'place'
21	/ña-miira/	--> [ñamiira] 'Nyamira' (a placename)

If Whiteley's presentation in (2) and the one in (3) are compared, the following observations may be made, together with a few non-comparative ones. First, though 1a /mo-/ is added to the paradigm in (3), it is essentially a non-augmented lexical allomorph of 1 /omo-/; it is discussed as such by Whiteley. Second, 1b /0-/ and 21 /ña-/ are added. Third, a different form has been entered for class 5. Fourth, Whiteley's apparent restriction of prefix 9a to adjectives (1956: 17) is inadequate. Fifth, though singular prefix 9a regularly corresponds with plural prefix 10a, the latter may also correspond with singular prefix 11 /oro-/. Sixth, and finally, Whiteley's restriction of prefix 16 to one word, viz. [ase] 'place' (1956: 38), is correct only in so far as nouns are concerned. These differences will be elaborated hereafter.

3.2.1.2. The morphosyntactic class system.

Several observations may be made on the morphology, the semantics, and the syntax of the prefixes in (3), including as yet undiscussed possible combinations of some of them to form singular-plural correspondences. I will take up the latter first and touch on the former afterwards.

As pointed out in section 3.2.1.1, combinations of unevenly and evenly numbered prefixes 1-10a in (3) represent morphosyntactic singular-plural classes. However, several other combinations also occur. Whiteley (1956: passim) gives the following ones,

(5)	1 omo-,	2 aβa-
	3 omo-,	4 eme-
	5 ri-,	6 ama-
	7 eke-,	8 eβi-
	9 e-,	10 ci-
	11 oro-,	10a cin-
	12 aka-,	8 eβi-
	14 oβo-,	6 ama-
	15 oko-,	6 ama-

This survey may however be extended, as in (6), where possibly special status of some class is indicated and where tentative semantic characterisations are added, partly derived

[4] Also pronounced [áasé], where lengthening of the initial vowel may be due to interaction between the tonal and the segmental tier.

from Whiteley (1956),

(6) Gusii singular-plural correspondences

1 omo-	2 aβa-	personal, spiritual, animate beings, kinship terms, i.e. God, angels, devils, the spirits of ancestors, and human beings currently alive
1b Ø-	2 aβa-	kinship terms
3 omo-	4 eme-	socioculturally relevant objects, events, or periods; trees; parts of the body; other
5 eri-	6 ama-	various types of common nouns, e.g. natural or cultural objects and locations, tools, parts of the body, fruits
5 eri-	6 ama-	augmentative, ± pejorative
7 eke-	8 eβi-	inanimate, mostly cultural objects; some parts of the body; some animals; some shrubs or plants; language names
7 eke-	8 eβi-	diminutive, ± pejorative, usually +
7 ke-		no plural: adverbs, placenames
9 e-	10 ci-	many names of animals; socially or culturally relevant entities (places, objects, events); some concepts
9a e-n-	10a ci-n-	same as 9-10
11 oro-	10a ci-n-	sociocultural and some natural objects
12 aka-	8 eβi-	diminutive
12 aka-	14 oβo-	diminutive, non-pejorative
14 oβo-	6 ama-	some body parts; culturally relevant entitites (objects, places, events, actitivities); some crop names
14 oβo-		no plural: concepts
14 βo-		no plural: adverbs, placenames
15 oko-	6 ama-	three body parts; abstract nouns mostly referring to activities or events conceived abstracly (usually without plural)
15 ko-		infinitive marker (together with word-final suffix /-a/), expressing activities or events
16 a-	[ase]	'place' only, no plural
21 ña-		no regular plural: proper names, of persons, individual heads of cattle, and places

These correspondences or morphosyntactic classes may be exemplified, as in (7),

(7)	1	[omoonto] 'person'
		[omwaana] 'child'
	2	[aβaanto] 'persons'
		[aβaana] 'children'
	1b	[βaaβa] 'mother'
		[maaγokoro] 'grandmother'
		[sookoro] 'grandfather'

2 [aβaβaaβa] 'mothers'
[aβamaaγokoro] 'grandmothers'
[aβasookoro] 'grandfathers'

3 [omotwe] 'head'
4 [emetwe] 'heads'

5 [riiγɔkɔ] 'foodrest (in cooking-pan)'
[riaana] 'honeycomb'
6 [amaγɔkɔ] 'foodrests (in cooking-pan)'
[amaana] 'honeycombs'

7 [ekeηwaansɔ] 'sacrifice'
8 [eβiηwaansɔ] 'sacrifices'

7 [γεtεεmbε] 'Kisii town' (no plural)[5]

9 [eusi] 'thread'
10 [ciusi] 'threads'

9a |e-n-βaata| --> [embaata] 'duck'[6]
|e-n-raaγera| --> [endaaγera] 'food'
10a |ci-n-βaata| --> [cimbaata] 'ducks'
|ci-n-raaγera| --> [cindaaγera] 'foods'[7]

11 |oro-ko| --> [oroko] 'firewood'
10a |ci-n-ko| --> [ci(i)ηko] '(pieces of) firewood'

12 |aka-ana| --> [akaana] 'small honeycomb
8 |eβi-ana| --> [eβiaana] 'small honeycombs'[8]

12 [akamoonto] 'a small person'
14 [oβomoonto] 'small persons'

---

[5] [εγεtεεmbε] is the name for a tree or plant, but I have been unable to elicit the English equivalent for it.

[6] Evidence for this postulate is derived from a comparison with its diminutive forms, singular [akaambaata] 'small duck', plural [eβimbaata] 'small ducks' and the unacceptability of the alternatives *[akaβaata] and *[eβiβaata].

[7] Contrast with verbal noun [okoraaγera] 'eating' and the unacceptability of *[okondaaγera].

[8] Apparently, these forms may mean 'small child' and 'small children' at least in some idiolects. The (more) regular forms are however derived through prefix-stacking, viz. [akamwaana] 'small child' and [eβimwaana] 'small children'.

14 [oβota] 'bow'
6 [amata] 'bows'

14 [oβosaaca] 'manhood, manliness'
(abstract noun, no plural)

14 [βosooηgo] 'Kisii town' (no plural)

15 [ɔkɔβɔkɔ] 'arm'
[okoγoro] 'leg'
[oγoto] 'ear'
[okoruγa] 'cooking'
(and numerous similar verbal nouns)
6 [amaβɔkɔ] 'arms'
[amaγoro] 'legs'
[amato] 'ears'

16 [ase] 'place' (no plural)

21 [ñaaηera][9] 'Blackie' (cattle proper name, no plural)
[ñaγεεηkε] 'Nyageenke village' (no plural)

In the description of many Bantu languages, a subclass 1a-1b is sometimes distinguished of which the singular and the plural are respectively marked by prefixes /mo-/ and /βa-/. Strictly speaking, however, these non-augmented prefixes, hence this class, may be considered as instances of lexically determined allomorphy, or else, as a pragmatically determined case of postlexical augment deletion, and thus, in either case, as a species of class 1-2. For example, 1a [momura] 'brother', plural 2a [βamura], is a kinship term, often used in address, as in [momura omiinto] 'my brother' (|o-miinto| means 'of our place/home'). It derives from [omomura] '(circumcised) young man' and thus refers to a brother belonging to that social age-group.

Subclass 2b, not postulated here, seems to come under the same heading, but class 1b must be postulated, at least on morphological grounds, since zero prefixation is exceptional.

Generally, the semantic motivation of class 1-2 still appears to be somewhat stronger synchronically than that of the other classes, as the characterisations in (6) indeed suggest. Also, the diminutive or augmentative meanings expressed with or without pejorative connotation by some classes, are relatively clear-cut (see section 3.2.1.3). The meanings of some classes nonetheless seem to be more easily definable than those of others. Though a comprehensive semantic characterisation of morphosyntactic classes would require more extensive lexical and semantic research than may be attempted here, by and large the broad semantic characterisations given in (6) appear to be correct as far

[9] Derived from /ña-/ and /e-ηera/ 'buffalo'. The reference is to the greyish black colour of the East African buffalo.

as they go.

3.2.1.3. Diminutives and augmentatives.

The following singular-plural combinations of morphosyntactic class prefixes may serve to mark diminutive and augmentative classes (8),

(8) a. diminutive classes

singular	plural
7 eke-	8 eβi-
12 aka-	8 eβi-
12 aka-	14 oβo-

b. augmentative class

singular	plural
5 eri-	6 ama-

These are to be interpreted as follows. Whenever a word properly belonging to some other class is transferred to any of the classes in (8a), at least the idea of diminution is necessarily added to its basic meaning. Whenever some such word is transferred to the class in (8b), at least the idea of augmentation is added to its basic meaning.

As indicated in the summary of morphosyntactic classes marked by combinations of corresponding singular and plural prefixes (6), 7 eke-, 8 eβi-, 14 oβo-, 5 eri-, and 6 ama-function as regular class prefixes, in addition to marking diminutive or augmentative class. This underlines the fact that it is the particular combination of singular and corresponding plural prefix that constitutes some class and determines its meaning. Prefix 12 /aka-/ is the one exception, since it expresses diminutive meaning only. This double function of prefixes 5, 6, 7, 8, 12, and 14 entails that words belonging a class marked by any of them cannot be 'transferred' to the class to which it already belongs regularly, in order to express diminution or augmentation.

Occasionally, diminution or augmentation is impossible, when the result would be homomorphy or morphological confusion. For example, from [omoremi] 'farmer', it is possible to derive the diminutive [ekemoremi] 'small farmer', plural [eβimoremi], but [ekeremi], plural [eβiremi], is unacceptable, presumably since it already means 'hoe'. Again, [akamoremi] 'small farmer', and presumably also plural [oβomoremi], are possible too, though one informant judged *[oβomoremi], but [oβoremi] is unacceptable with the meaning 'small farmers', presumably because it already means 'famine', probably from "(time of) small harvests". However, augmentative [riiremi] 'big farmer' was judged to be possible, next to [riimoremi], but the judgment for its plural was [amaremi], *[amamoremi]. This lexical and semantic aspect of the language remains to be examined more comprehensively.

In both diminution and augmentation through class transference there may be the added element of pejorative connotation. Whenever a word so transferred is considered to be used appropriately with respect to the designated referent, it may, but need not, imply a negative attitude towards the latter on the part of the speaker. This applies at least in the case of 12 /aka-/. The use of [akaana] 'small child', for example, may be considered appropriate, and thus non-pejorative, or inappropriate, and thus pejorative. But when the use of a word so transferred is considered inappropriate with respect to the designated referent, it implies a negative attitude or even deliberate abusiveness towards the latter on the part of the speaker. For example, [akamoonto] 'a small person', if applied to an adult, is more likely to have a pejorative connotation. The meaning of 12 aka-, and the morphosyntactic class marked by it, may thus be defined as [diminutive, ± pejorative].

This account may be applicable also to the other prefixes and classes, including the augmentative, of which the meaning would then be definable as [augmentative, ± pejorative]. As a matter of fact, however, my informants differed somewhat in their judgment on the status of the pejorative connotation of such diminutives and augmentatives, specifically as to its being possible, usual, or necessary. By and large, it seems to be not only a possible, but a usual, if not necessary, part of the meaning of a word thus transferred, also when prefixes other than 12 aka- are used. The augmentative meaning of a word prefixed, through prefix-stacking, by both 5 eri- or rii- and 7 ke-, and in the plural by both 6 ama- and 7 ke-, is always abusive. Whether this is so in other cases of prefix-stacking, requires verification.

This point may be concluded as follows. Until evidence to the contrary turns up, it will be assumed that most, if not all, diminutives and augmentatives which are derived through class transference usually have a pejorative connotation. It is recognised, moreover, that this will depend on the degree to which their use is considered appropriate or inappropriate with respect to the referent. An example of a [± pejorative] augmentative is given under (10b) below. However, the present point admittedly requires further research.

Non-pejorative diminution or augmentation is regularly expressed through modification by an appropriate adjective, such as /kɛ-/ 'small' and /-nɛnɛ/ 'big, tall'. The possibility of further, adverbial qualification of such an adjective remains to be examined.

Furthermore, by combining transference to diminutive or augmentative class with adjectival modification, various degrees of pejorativeness may be expressed. Moreover, an adverb may be added to further qualify such an adjective, in order to express an extreme degree.

Diminution through class transference, with pejorative connotation (including the logical impossibility, for this purpose, of 'transferring' a word to its own regular class), non-pejorative diminution through adjectival modification, and the expression of degrees of pejorativeness through a combination of these two means, with or without an added adverb, are all exemplified in (9),

(9) diminution

a. non-pejorative

/o-mo-Nto o-mo-kɛ/	/a-ßa-Nto a-ßa-kɛ/
a-1-person a-1-small	a-2-person a-2-small
[omoonto ɔmɔkɛ]	[aßaanto aßakɛ]
'a small person'	'small persons'

b. pejorative or non-pejorative, in increasing degrees

|aka-mo-Nto|
a-12-1-person
[akamoonto]
'a small person (±pejorative)'

Note: the plural [oßomoonto] 'small persons' is usually pejorative.

|aka-mo-Nto aka-kɛ|
a-12-1-person a-12-small
[akamoonto aγakɛ]
'a very small person (±pejorative)'

|aka-mo-Nto aka-kɛ mɔnɔ|
a-12-1-person a-12-small very
[akamoonto aγakɛ mɔnɔ]
'a very, very small person (±pejorative)'

c. pejorative in increasing degrees:

|e-ke-mo-Nto|	|e-ßi-mo-Nto|
a-7-1-person	a-7-1-person
[ekemoonto]	[eßimoonto]
'small person (pejorative)'	'small persons (pejorative)'

|e-ke-mo-Nto e-ke-kɛ|
a-7-1-person a-7-small
[ekemoonto ɛγɛkɛ]
'a very small person (pejorative)'
plural [eßimoonto eßikɛ]

|e-ke-mo-Nto e-ke-kɛ mɔnɔ|
a-7-1-person a-7-small very
[ekemoonto ɛγɛkɛ mɔnɔ]
'a very, very small person (pejorative)'
plural [eßimoonto eßikɛ mɔnɔ]

The same aspects are exemplified for augmentation, in (10),

(10) augmentation

a. non-pejorative

|omo-Nto omo-nɛnɛ| |a-β a-Nto aβa-nɛnɛ|
a-1-person a-1-big a-1-person a-1-big
[omoonto ɔmɔnɛnɛ] [aβaanto aβanɛnɛ]
'a big person' 'big persons'

b. non-pejorative or, more usually, pejorative

|rii-mo-Nto|
5-1-person
[riimoonto]
'a big person (±pejorative)'

plural [amamoonto][10]

c. abusive

|rii-ke-mo-Nto|
5-7-1-person
[riikemoonto]
'a big person (abusive)'

plural [amakemoonto]

d. pejorative (more than a and b)

|rii-mo-Nto rii-nɛnɛ|
5-1-person 5-big
[riimoonto riinɛnɛ]
'a very big person (pejorative)'

plural [amamoonto amanɛnɛ]

Similarly, compare the examples for other morphosyntactic classes in (11), where potential pejorative connotation is taken for granted, unless noted otherwise,

---

10 Stacking of the augmentative prefixes is obligatory in this example, for *[rioonto] and *[amoonto] are unacceptable.

(11) 1b basic: [βaaβa] 'mother'

diminutive: [akaβaaβa] 'small mother'
[oβoβaaβa] 'small mothers'

augmentative:

[riiβaaβa] 'big mother', *[riimoβaaβa]
[amaβaaβa] 'big mothers', *[amamoβaaβa]

3-4 basic: [omotwe] 'head', [emetwe] 'heads'

diminutive:

|a-ka-mo-tue|
a-12-3-head
[akamotwe]
'a small head'

or [aγatwe], [eγetwe], [ekemotwe] 'small head'
plural [oβotwe], [oβomotwe], [eβitwe], [eβimotwe] 'small heads'

compare:

[omotwe ɔmɔkɛ] 'a small head (non-pejorative)'
[emetwe ɛmɛkɛ] 'small heads (non-pejorative)'

augmentative:

[riitwe], [riimotwe] 'big head'
[amatwe], [amamotwe] 'big heads'

5-6 regular or augmentative class

basic:

[riitɔɔkɛ] 'banana'
[amatɔɔkɛ] 'bananas'

diminutive:

singular [aγatɔɔkɛ], [ɛγɛtɔɔkɛ] 'small banana'
plural [ɔβɔtɔɔkɛ] or [eβitɔɔkɛ] 'small bananas'

augmentative:

[riitɔɔkɛ riinɛnɛ] 'big banana'
*[riitɔɔkɛ] 'big banana' (regular basic singular)

[amatɔɔkɛ amanɛnɛ] 'big bananas'
*[amatɔɔkɛ] 'big bananas' (regular basic plural)

pejorative:

[riitɔɔkɛ riiβe] 'bad banana', *[riiγɔtɔɔkɛ]

pejorative augmentative:

[riitɔɔkɛ riiβe riinɛnɛ] 'a big bad banana, a bad big banana'
[riitɔɔkɛ riinɛnɛ riiβe] 'a big bad banana, a bad big banana'[11]

7-8 regular or diminutive class

basic:

singular	[eγetaaβu] 'book'
plural	[eβitaaβu] 'books'

diminutive:

singular	[aγataaβu], [akaγetaaβu] 'small book'
plural	[oβotaaβu], [oβoγetaaβu], [oβoβitaaβu] 'small books'

augmentative:

singular	[riitaaβu], [riiγetaaβu], [riiβitaaβu] 'big book'
plural	[amataaβu], [amaγetaaβu], [amaβitaaβu] 'big books'

9-10 basic:

singular	[ɛcɔɔka] 'chalk'
plural	[cicɔɔka] 'chalks, pieces of chalk'

---

[11] Whiteley states (the form of his statement is slightly adapted here) that "where two or more dependent items follow a noun, that which immediately follows is most important to the sense of the speaker, thus

Gusii 'cow this black' = English '**this** black cow'
Gusii 'cow black this' = English 'this **black** cow'

Where a noun is associated with two or more adjectives, the first is followed by 'naende'; if it is followed simply by 'na' it is assumed that two separate things or persons are under discussion" (1956: 7). This statement conflicts with the judgment reflected in the data given here in the text. It was said by informants that difference in emphasis would be expressed through loudness, intonation, or a combination of both. Word order in phrases is evidently a subject for further syntactic research.

diminutive:

singular [aγacɔɔka] 'small chalk'
plural [ɔβɔcɔɔka], [eβicɔɔka] 'small chalks'

augmentative:

singular [riicɔɔka] 'big chalk'
plural [amacɔɔka] 'big chalks'

9a-10a [embaata] 'duck'

[akaambaata], [ekeembaata] 'small duck'
[oβoombaata], [eβiimbaata] 'small ducks'

[riimbaata] 'big duck'
[amaambaata] 'big ducks'

11-10a [oroteeru] 'tray'
[ciinteeru] 'trays'

[aγateeru] 'small tray'
[oβoteeru] 'small trays'

[riiteeru] 'big tray'
[amateeru] 'big trays'

12 diminutive class only

14 regular basic singular with a corresponding plural, abstract singular noun without a plural, or a diminutive plural,

basic:

singular [oβokoombe] 'hoe'
plural [amakoombe] 'hoes'

diminutive:

singular [aγakoombe] 'small hoe'
plural [ciiŋkoombe] 'small hoes'

augmentative:

singular [riikoombe] 'big hoe'
plural [amakoombe amanɛnɛ] 'big hoes'

(*[amakoombe], because it is already the regular plural of the basic word)

15 [okoγoro] 'leg'
[amaγoro] 'legs'

[akaγoro], [ekeγoro] 'small leg'
[oβoγoro], [eβiγoro] 'small legs'

16 /a-se a-kε/
16-place 16-small
[asaakε]
'small place'

*[aγase], *[eγese], *[oβose], *[eβise]

/a-se a-nεnε/
16-place 16-big
[asaanεnε]
'big place'

21 [ñaηera εkε] 'small Blackie (cow)' (non-pejorative)
[ñaηera εnεnε] 'big Blackie (cow)' (non-pejorative)

In the nature of the case, formation of diminutives and augmentatives through class transfer is possible only with nominals designating countable referents, hence not with mass nouns, e.g. words meaning 'water', 'air', 'sand'.

Prefix 14 /oβo-/ may function both as a diminutive plural prefix to correspond with diminutive singular 12 /aka-/, and as a regular singular corresponding with plural 6 /ama-/. It may also be prefixed to a noun expressing an abstract concept, in which case the noun may not be transferred to a diminutive or augmentative class. While diminutive singular 12 /aka-/ may be without pejorative connotation, it remains to be examined whether this holds for its regular diminutive plural marked by 14 /oβo-/ as well.

Prefix-stacking, as exemplified in (10-11), regularly occurs, is well understood, but considered grammatically less correct than straightforward diminutives and augmentatives, except where it is necessary to avoid homomorphy. There appear to be some restrictions on which prefixes may be stacked on which, but this requires further examination also.

Generally, details of the semantics and syntax of diminutives and augmentatives require more attention than they have received here.

3.2.1.4. Augmentation and non-augmentation.

If augmentation may be considered as the basic or regular state of affairs, then non-augmentation taking the form of augment-deletion may be characterised as the special case. On the opposite view, augmentation would be the special case.

Generally, both syntactic and semantic factors determine whether or not a word may take an augmented or non-augmented prefix, both at the lexical and the postlexical level. Also, derivation is supposed to start with the root, and to branch out rightward and then leftward by affixation. In suffixation, for example, extension suffixes are affixed first, the final vowel last; and in prefixation, the prefix is affixed first, and the augment afterwards.

In Gusii, a distinction must be made between lexical and postlexical non-augmentation. Lexical non-augmentation, as far as nominals are concerned, involves especially various types of proper names. But it also involves the other lexical categories, since verbal infinitives, adverbs, quantifiers, specifiers, numerals, prepositions, and conjunctions are regularly non-augmented. Since prefixation of pronouns and demonstratives is somewhat mixed or irregular, compared with other lexical categories, they are relatively indeterminate in this respect.

It may be said that the regulation of the presence versus the absence of the augment is determined lexically, by lexical category membership or lexically determined allomorphy, and postlexically, through allomorphy determined by syntactic or syntactic and semantic factors. With respect to nouns, lexical category membership determines that nominal prefixes in morphosyntactic classes 1-8 and 11-15 may or may not be augmented, whereas the other prefixes, 1b /0-/, 9(a) /e-(n)-/, 10(a) /ci-(n)-/, 16 /a-/, and 21 /ña-/, are never augmented. Generally, (non-)augmentation may and does vary per lexical category per morphosyntactic class (see the overview of the prefixes that mark them, section 3.2.15).

Generally too, lexically determined allomorphy in the form of non-augmentation involves not only the lexical sub-category of proper names as distinct from other nouns, but also most other lexical categories as distinct from nominals. In the case of proper names, this seems to be determined semantically. The criterion seems to be specificness or definiteness. For proper names designate individuals or collective entities considered individually, and thus are thus specific by definition or in the nature of things. They are regularly non-augmented. This includes not only Gusii personal names (3.2.1.4.1), but also kinship terms (3.2.1.4.2), cattle names or terms (3.2.1.4.3), and placenames (3.2.1.4.4).

Given this kind of lexical non-augmentation, postlexical non-augmentation is supposedly determined by the syntactic position or function of a lexical category in an utterance (phrase, clause, sentence, discourse). Though it may perhaps involve any lexical item on principle, it especially involves lexical items that are regularly augmented. That is, nouns other than proper names, and nominals, any word that may be used as a noun, such as adjectives, verbs, and some pronouns.

For nominals, augmentation appears to be the regular state of affairs at the lexical level, and non-augmentation the special case of lexical allomorphy that is characteristic of some lexical categories or sub-categories. This means that whenever a non-augmented lexical item is related to another, augmented one, whether in the same or in some other lexical category, the relationship between them may be conceived of in one of two ways. One is augment deletion, the other is lexically determined prohibition of augmentation, i.e. derivational non-augmentation.

For example, [βotaambe] 'usually, always' is an adverb of time or manner that is morphologically and semantically related to [oβotaambe] 'length' (compare [γotaamba] 'to be long'). One account of this relationship would be to argue that the adverb is derived from the noun through augment deletion. The other account would be to argue that both lexical items derive from /-taNβ-/ (or /-tanβ-/, /-taamb-/) through affixation, and that the adverb is not augmented in virtue of a lexical allomorphy rule or constraint. It might be argued in favour of deletion that this would account for the shape of the adverbial prefix, since, for example, [omotaambe] 'long person' also occurs. In favour of the alternative account, it might simply be argued that /βo-/ may be used to derive adverbs, and that [βotaambe] is one of them. Technically, this would be the most economic solution. However, I leave it to more comprehensive lexical, semantic, and syntactic research on the language, to decide which account of lexical augmentation is most appropriate.

The borderline between lexical and postlexical augmentation may sometimes be fuzzy. For example, [momura] 'brother', may be considered as a case of lexical non-augmentation, derived from [omomura] '(uncircumcised) boy or young man', because it is a kinship term or has a definite meaning. But it could arguably be a case of postlexically determined non-augmentation which has grammaticalised, because it is often used to address the blood-relation in question.

Several remarks may be added on the underlying representations of noun and nominal prefixes, in (12),

(12) Gusii prefixes

	nouns	nominals
1	omo-	omo-
1b	Ø-	
2	aβa-	aβa-
3	omo-	omo-
4	eme-	eme-
5	eri-	eri-
6	ama-	ama-
7	eke-	eke-
8	eβi-	eβi-
9	e-	
9a	e-n-	e-n-
10	ci-	eci-
10a	ci-n-	eci-n-
11	oro-	oro-
12	aka-	aka-
14	oβo-	oβo-
15	oko-	oko-
16	a-	a-
21	ña-	9 or 16

Class 1a /mo-/, plural 2a /βa-/, is often listed as a separate morphosyntactic class in many descriptions of Bantu languages, but, as argued, it is here considered as the non-augmented lexical allomorph of 1-2 for nouns. Allomorphy of other prefixes will be discussed in due course.

In most instances, the 'full' Gusii prefix properly consists of an augmented prefix, i.e. the classical Bantu combination of an augment vowel, /V-/, also called pre-prefix or initial vowel, with a prefix proper, usually consisting of a consonant plus a vowel, /CV-/. The underlying representation for such a full prefix is thus /V-CV-/. At least, this general statement covers nominal prefixes classes 1-8 and 10-15.

The term 'prefix' will accordingly be used hereafter to refer to a prefix proper or more loosely to an augmented prefix. When this may conceivably cause misunderstanding, its usage will be restricted to the prefix proper, while 'augmented prefix' will then be used for an augmented prefix.

Lexically, prefix 5 is regularly augmented eri- in nominals of which the stem begins with a vowel, but non-augmented rii- in nominals of which the stem begins with a consonant. This appears to be a case of phonologically determined allomorphy.

Prefixes 9 /e-/ and 16 /a-/ consist of a vowel only, which may not be augmented.

The distinction between 9 e- / 10 ci- and 9a e-n- / 10a ci-n- will be taken up in a moment.

So far, the focus of attention has been on augmentation versus non-augmentation, lexically or postlexically determined. The regulation of the shape or quality of the augment may now be considered briefly. The question is, how the shape of the augments in (12) may be accounted for.

To answer this question sufficiently, at least the following facts must be taken into account. It may be said, first, that all CV-shaped prefixes are augmentable, except for noun prefixes 10 /ci-/, 10a /ci-n-/, 21 /ña-/, and allomorphically for 5, just discussed. Second, except in the case of 5 /eri-/, 8 /eβi-/, and 10 /eci-/, the augment is a copy of the prefix vowel. These data, hence the shape of the augment in nominal prefixes, may be accounted for relatively informally by the following rule,

(13) nominal prefix-augmentation

> copy the vowel of prefix CV- to the left of input, such that any non-low output vowel must be [+mid]

This formulation includes all relevant prefixes and augments, but properly excludes augmentation of all V-shaped prefixes. It ensures moreover that the [+high, -mid] or high front prefix vowel of 5 /ri-/, 8 /βi-/, and 10(a) /ci-n-/ is lowered to a [+high, +mid] or upper mid front augment vowel /e/.

Prefix 10a is here subsumed under 10, on the assumption that the nasal in it may be considered as an element regularly added to the basic prefix 10 /ci-/. Hence, also, its postulate as 10a /ci-n-/, rather than 10a /cin-/. Should this analysis turn out to be inadequate, then CV in (13) might be expanded to CV(n)-, in order to include 10a.

The rule must be prevented from applying incorrectly to noun prefix 21. Two approaches are possible. Either the rule may be conditioned so as not to apply to it, or the prefix may be marked in the lexicon as [-(13)]. Either approach correctly marks this prefix as relatively exceptional. So much for augmentation and augments at this point.

Lexically determined non-augmentation of nominals, proper names in particular, is further discussed and exemplified in sections 3.2.1.4.1-4. In as far as it involves other lexical categories, it is discussed in the relevant sections in 3.4 that deal with the derivation of these categories. Postlexical non-augmentation is further discussed in section 3.2.1.4.5.

3.2.1.4.1. Personal names.

Personal names, a sub-class of proper names, are regularly non-augmented, whether or not they are used to address someone directly. At least prefixes 1 /mo-/, 6 /ma-/, 14 /ʒo-/, and 21 /ña-/ are used in personal names.

Sometimes the prefix proper is omitted and only the augment is used. For example in [orioki] 'Orioki', which may derive from /e-rioki/ --> [erioki] 'smoke', the word-initial /o-/ is presumably the augment of class 1, or possibly a lexicalised occurrence of the relative subject marker (section 3.3.3.3).

Originally, Gusii personal names were often associated with the circumstances surrounding a person's birth. In the course of time, these names came to be established and were passed on simply by inheritance. Some examples are given in (14),

(14) a. /ma-koori/
6-path
[makoori]
'Makoori'

(male personal name, compare [riikoori] 'path', plural [amakoori])

b. /ña-n-cera/
21-9a-path
[ñaañcera]
'Nyanchera'

(female personal name, compare [eñcera] 'path', plural [ciñcera])

c. /mo-raa/
1-tree
[moraa]
'Moraa'

(compare [omoraa] 'fig tree'; or [koraa] 'to lead')

d. ¦mo-γaaka¦
1-old man
[moγaaka]
'Mogaaka'

(male personal name, compare [omoγaaka] 'old man')

e. /βo-caβ-er-i/
14-adorn-ap-sx
[βocaβeri]
'Bochaberi'

(female proper name, compare [γocaβera] 'to adorn, to decorate')

The etymology of these words is arguably as indicated. The first three examples probably reflect the circumstances of birth of the persons originally so named. They may have been born in the open air: those named [makoori] and [ñaañcera] near or on a path, and those named [moraa] near or under a fig tree. If the latter was associated with [koraa] 'to lead', it may have expressed the wish on the part of the parents that their child would become a leader. Finally, [moγaaka] may have originally been a name expressing respect, while [βocaβeri] may either have been given upon observed beauty or a wish of future beauty. For lack of further lexical and etymological research, however, these suppositions must, for the time being, remain conjectural.

3.2.1.4.2. Kinship terms.

Kinship terms, too, regularly have no augment. It will be obvious that they are regularly used to address a relative. The morphology of some of them requires further research. Some of them are interesting, from a comparative and historical point of view, in that they may have been taken over from Nilo-Saharan; for example [maamɛ] '(my) maternal uncle'.[12]

Pending further research, a sample of them is presented in (15), where some of the representations postulated underlyingly are necessarily tentative,

---

[12] Presumably from /maa-mɛ/. This point was suggested to me by G.J. Dimmendaal, Leyden University, who mentioned that [mamɛ], or derivatives from it, occurs in many Nilo-Saharan languages. e.g. [mamai] in Teso and [amai] in Turkana.

(15)	/ña-o-ko-ro-mɛ/ [ñɔkɔrɔmɛ] '(your) maternal uncle'	/ŋina-ro-mɛ/ [ŋinarɔmɛ] '(his/her) maternal uncle'
	/0-taata/ [taata][13] 'father'	/0-taata mo-kɛ/ father 1-small [taatamɔkɛ] '(my) paternal uncle' (literally, 'my little father')
	/is-ɔ/ [isɔ] '(your) father' (i.e. of the addressee)	/is-ɔ mo-kɛ/ your-father 1-little [isɔ mɔkɛ] '(your) paternal uncle' (i.e. of the addressee; literally, 'your little father')
	/is-ɛ/ [isɛ] '(his/her) father'	/is-ɛ mo-kɛ/ his-father 1-little [isɛ mɔkɛ] '(his/her) paternal uncle' (literally, his/her little father')

/maa-kɔ mo-kɛ/
mother-?-1-little
[maakɔ mɔkɛ]
'my (maternal or paternal) aunt'
(literally, 'my little mother')

/ñɔ-ko mo-kɛ/
your-mother 1-little
[ñɔkɔ mɔkɛ]
'your (maternal or paternal) aunt'
(literally, 'your little mother')

/ŋina mo-kɛ/
his-mother 1-little
[ŋina mɔkɛ]
'his/her (maternal or paternal) aunt'
(literally, 'his/her little mother')

---

[13] Used in direct address, but also in reference. The general plural [aβataata] 'fathers' occurs, but in the nature of things 'my fathers' is impossible.

/o-mo-kɔ/
a-1-in-law
[ɔmɔkɔ]
'in-law'
(esp. sister, brother, or cousin of wife or husband, plural /a-βa-kɔ/ --> [aβakɔ] 'in-laws')

/mo-kɔ o-yo-a-nɛ/	/mo-kɔ o-yo-a-o/
1-in-law rpx1-of-my	1-in-law rpx1-your
[mɔkɔ(ɔ)yɔɔnɛ]	[mɔkoyoo]
'(my) in-law'	'(your) in-law'
(term of address)	(term of address)

/mo-kɔ o-yo-a-yɛ/
1-in-law rpx1-of-his
[mɔkɔ(ɔ)yɔɔyɛ]
'(his/her) in-law'
(term of address; augmented, when the reference is to a third person)

/ka-maa-ti/
[kamaati]
'sister (of husband)' (term used by wife)
'wife (of brother)' (term used by sister)

/mo-ka a-nɛ/
1-wife-of-my
[mokaanɛ]
'my wife' (term of address or reference)
plural [aβakaanɛ] 'my wives'[14]

/mo-ka a-o/	/mo-ka a-yɛ/
1-wife of-your	1-wife of-his
[mokaao]	[mokaayɛ]
'your wife'	'his wife'

plurals corresponding to the previous three forms are:

/a-βa-kuuŋgu βa-a-nɛ/
a-2-wife 2-of-my
[aβakuuŋgu βaanɛ] 'my wives'
(similarly, [βaao] 'your', [βaayɛ] 'his', [βaito] 'our', [βaino] 'your (pl)', [βaaβɔ] 'their')

[seemo] 'brother-in-law'
(term used by a husband to address his wife's sister's husband)

[14] Possible in a polygamous society, used for young wives.

/o-yo-Nre/
rpx1-other
[oyoonde]
'(the) other one' (term of mutual address, used by mothers of wives of one polygamous husband)

/maa-a-ko-koro/
6-of-15-old
[maaγokoro]
'grandmother'
(literally, 'old mother')
plural [aβamaaγokoro]

/maa ko-βiar-a/ mother to-give birth-fv [maakoβiaara] '(my) mother-in-law'	/taata βiar-a/ father give-birth-fv [taata βiaara] '(my) father-in-law'
[ñɔkɔ βiaara] '(your) mother-in-law'	[isɔ βiaara] '(your) father-in-law'
[ηina βiaara] '(his) mother-in-law'	[isε βiaara] '(his) father-in-law'

/ko-rεr-a/
15-raise-fv
[kɔrεra]
'parent'
(term of mutual address used by the parents of a husband and wife; [kɔrεra] is a verb meaning 'to raise, to bring up, children')

Some alternative, generally used words for 'wife' are those in (16),

(16) /o-mo-kuNγu/
a-1-wife
[omokuuηgu]
'wife'
(plural [aβakuuηgu])

/o-mo-ruγ-i
a-1-cook-agent
[omoruγi]
'wife'
(literally, 'cook', cooking being an important responsibility of wives in traditional, as in modern, culture; plural [aβaruγi] 'wives')

/o-mo-Vηena o-nɛ/
a-1-old woman 1-my
[omooηena ɔnɛ] 'my old woman'
(respectful term of address of a wife, used by husband)

Some alternative, generally used words for 'husband' are (17),

(17)	/o-mo-saaca o-nɛ/ a-1-man 1-my [omosaacɔ ɔnɛ] 'my husband'	/o-mo-γaaka o-nɛ/ a-1-old man 1-my [omoγaakɔ ɔnɛ] 'my old man'

A few common terms relating to the sexes, some of which have already been mentioned, are enumerated in (18), finally, in terms of their respective socio-cultural connection,

(18) a. terms of respect

(uncircumcised)	[omomura] 'boy'
(circumcised)	[omosaaca] '(young) man'
(aged)	[omoγaaka] 'old man'
(uncircumcised)	[omoiseke] '(little) girl'
(circumcised)	[omokuuηgu] '(young) woman'
(aged)	[omooηena] 'old woman'

b. terms of abuse (to be avoided in general usage)

[omoisia] '(uncircumcised) boy'
[eγesaγane] '(uncircumcised) girl'

3.2.1.4.3. Cattle terms.

Cattle names or terms are also regularly non-augmented. I use the disjunction advisedly, because I have not been able to study cattle-keeping and cattle-terminology sufficiently, in order to establish whether, besides proper names, technical terms are also involved. Some examples are given in (19),

(19) a. /ña-a-ηera/
21-of-buffalo
[ñaaηera]
'Blackie'

(proper name for a cow with characteristics, specifically the colour, of a buffalo, East African water-buffaloes being greyish black)

b. /ña-sero/
21-?
[ñasero]

(proper name for a cow with a hide patterned like that of a Frisian; etymology unknown)

c. ? | ña-o-usi |
one-with-black
[ñousi]
'Blackie'

(possibly taken over from Swahili **ñeusi** 'black'; underlying representation unclear; proper name vor a black cow or, possibly, steer)

d. /ña-mo-tik-a/
21-1-?-fv
[ñamotika]

(proper name for a grey cow)

e. /ke-βuusɛ/
7-clay
[keβuusɛ]

(proper name for a greyish white cow, i.e. a cow with the colour of [ekeβuusɛ], pl. eβi-, which is a type of greyish white clay found in Gusiiland that takes on a whitish appearance, when it is mixed with water and smeared on a wall (an application used in building houses)

f. /ña-mo-γuumɔ/
21-1-?
[ñamoγuumɔ]

(proper name or technical term for a hornless cow or a cow with cut horns; one informant said [ñamoγuumu]; etymology unclear)

g. /ña-i-βu/
21-?5-ashes
[ñaiβu]

(proper name for an ash-coloured cow; compare [riiβu] 'ashes'; plural probably [amariiβu])

h. [ñaansanako]

(proper name for a red-spotted cow)

i. [mɔkɔñɔɔrɛ]

(proper name for a lame cow, a bandy-legged cow, or a cow with knocked legs (with the feet pointing sideways; etymology unclear)

These terms are applied to individual heads of cattle, whether as proper names, or possibly as technical terms, to identify them. Information on their syntax is conflicting. Some said these words may not be modified by adjectives, thus *[ñaaŋera ɛnɛnɛ] 'big Blackie', others considered this possible. This requires further examination. A relative phrase appears to be possible. An example is [ñamoɣuumɔ eri emwaamu] 'Nyamoguumo (or, the hornless cow) which is black' (in /e-ri/ '9-which-is', class 9 corresponds with a head belonging to class 21).

3.2.1.4.4. Placenames.

Placenames arguably constitute another borderline case between lexical or postlexical non-augmentation. They may be lexically non-augmented, since logically they are a species of proper names, or postlexically, since they are often used adverbially and this usage may have become grammaticalised (as a lexical category, adverbs are regularly non-augmented). They are used adverbially in phrases such as "in Nairobi" and "to(ward) Nairobi". But whenever placenames are not used as adverbials, as in sentences of the types "Nairobi is a big place", where the placename is a subject, and "he saw Nairobi in the distance", where it is an object, they are still unaugmented. In short, placenames are always non-augmented.

Morphologically, placenames may be marked at least by the prefixes 7 /ke-/, 5 /ri-/, 14 /ßo-/, and 21 /ña-/.

Semantically, it seems that many, if not most, placenames were or are originally associated with local geographical or other features associated with the place named; for example, with events that once took place there, with persons who lived there or founded it, or with natural aspects of it. Some examples are (20),

(20) a. |ßo-sooŋgo| --> [ßosooŋgo] 'Kisii town'

b. |ke-tɛɛmbɛ| --> [ɣɛtɛɛmbɛ] 'Kisii town'

c. |ña-ɣɛɛŋkɛ| --> [ñaɣɛɛŋkɛ] 'Nyageenke village'

d. |ri-a-kwɔrɔ|
[riakwɔ(ɔ)rɔ]
'Riakworo (village)'

e. /ke-tarɛ/
[ɣetarɛ]
'Getare (village)'

f. |ßo-ɣɛr-ɛ|
[ßɔɣɛrɛ]
'Luoland'

g. |ßo-tɛɛndɛ|
[ßɔtɛ nd]
'Kurialand'

h. |βo-maasai| [βomaasai] 'Maasailand'

i. /βo-siγiisi/ [βosiγiisi] 'Kipsigisland'

Of these, (20a) literally means 'place of white people'. It may derive from Swahili **mzungu** 'white person', and probably dates from colonial times, when Kisii town developed into an administrative centre. The etymology of (20b) is not clear, but may possibly be ascertained by consulting older speakers. It was said that [ɔmɔtɛɛmbɛ] is a (possibly extinct) type of tree that originally may have been common in the area. Next, [riakwɔɪɔ] literally means '(at the) place of, or associated with, [ɛkwɔrɔ]', an extinct species of bird; the name suggests that this bird was extant in large quantities, at the time of name-giving, in or around the place so named. (20e) is plausibly derived, from [eγetarɛ] 'bare rock', and thus literally means '(at the) place of bare rock'. Perhaps [βoγɛrɛ] derives from /ko-γɛr-a/ --> [kɔγɛra] 'to measure a quantity', since trade with the Luo's dates back a long time (another meaning of this verb, 'to cause to happen', seems to be irrelevant). Finally, (20h) presumably derives from Swahili or Maa **maasai**. Another Gusii name for Maasailand is [βomaañi].

The examples in (20f-i) suggest that 14 /βo-/ is typically used for districts or larger areas, though not exclusively so, as is evidenced by (20a).

Placenames may be modified. Morphosyntactic agreement for class 21 /ña-/ may apparently be expressed through classes 9 and 16. An example for class 9 is [ñaγɛɛŋkɛ eri ɛnɛnɛ] '(the) Nyageenke which is big'. Possible co-occurrence restrictions on such agreement (9 or 16) have not been examined. Placenames may also be modified by adjectives.

3.2.1.4.5. Postlexical non-augmentation.

As previously pointed out, post-lexical non-augmentation appears to be determined by syntactic function. Thus regularly augmented lexical items may drop the augment, at least when they are used as a vocative, i.e. to address someone, as a verbal or prepositional complement, as an adverb, and when they are focussed. Some of these uses may be combined, as in a focussed adverb.

The following common words are often used adverbially to indicate location or direction, as in (21),

(21) a. [omoγoondo] '(vegetable-)garden, (farming-)field, shamba'[15]

==> [mmoγoondo]

(a) 'in the garden'
(b) 'to, toward, the garden, into the garden'

e.g. |n-mo-γoondo a-re]
f-1-shamba 3s-be
[mmoγoondo are]
'he/she is in the **shamba**'
literally, '(it is) the shamba (where) he is'

[mmoγoondo aγocia]
'he/she is going to the shamba'

b. [eñoomba] 'house'

==> [ñoomba] 'in the house, into the house'

e.g. |n-ko-γεεnda a-re ñoomba|
f-15-walk-fv 3s-be into-the-house
[ŋkɔγεεndaare ñoomba]
'he is walking into the house'

compare:

|n-ko-γεεnda a-re ko-ci-a ñoomba|
f-15-walk-fv 3s-be 15-go-fv the-house
[ŋkɔγεεndaare γocia ñoomba]
'he is walking to the house (in order to enter it)',
'he is walking into the house'

[ŋkɔγεεndaare γocia ase ñoomba]
'he is walking toward the house (not to enter it)'

c. [orooce] 'river'[16]

==> [rooce]
'in the river, to/toward the river, into the river'

---

[15] The word 'shamba' comes from Swahili, but has been taken over by East African English.

[16] The derivation from /oro-rooce/ to [orooce] 'river' (plural /cin-rooce/ --> [ciindooce] 'rivers') is unusual to the point of being apparently unique. Therefore I will propose no rule to account for it.

e.g. |n-ro-Vce a-ko-ci-a|
f-11-river 3s-15-go-fv
[ndooce aγocia]
'he is going to the **river**'
(lit. '(it is) to the river he is going')

[γoocia are rooce]
'he is going to the river'

|ro-Vce ime a-re|
11-river in 3s-be
[rooce imaare]
'he is in the river'

|ndooce iγoro are|
[ndoociγoraare]
'he is on the **river**'

d. [orosaana] 'forest'

==> [rosaana]
'in, into, to(ward) the forest'

|iγɔ a-ko-taar-a ko-ci-a ro-saana ime|
gramm. 3s-t-walk-fv 15-go-fv 11-forest in
[iγɔ aγotaara γocia rosaana ime]
'he is walking into the forest'

|iγɔ a-ko-taar-a ko-ci-a a-se ro-saana|
gramm. 3s-t-walk-fv 15-go-fv 16-place 11-forest
[iγɔ aγotaara γocia ase rosaana]
'he is walking towards the forest'[17]

Such adverbial usage is common also in Eastern and Southern Nilotic.[18]

---

[17] In

|orosaana ime are|
forest in he-is
[orosaana ime are]
'he is in the forest'

the augment is not deleted, probably due to placement of the adverb at the beginning of the utterance. Gusii topicalisation seems to be a promising subject for further research.

[18] This was pointed out to me by G.J. Dimmendaal.

Location or direction may be expressed through adpositions as well, sometimes without augment deletion, as in (22),

(22) a. [ekanisa] 'church' (from Swahili: kanisa)

[γocia kanisa ime]
(going) to church in(side)
'into the church'

[ekanisa ime are]
church inside he-is
'he is in(side) (the) church'

|e-kanisa n-ko-ci-a|
9-church 1s-t-go to-fv
[ekanisa ηgocia]
'I am going to church'

/n-ko-sɔ-a βa-re e-kanisa/
f-15-enter-fv 3p-are 9-church
[ηgɔsɔa βare ekanisa]
'they are entering the church'

/n-ko-γεNr-a βa-re e-kanisa/
f-15-go-fv 3p-are 9-church
[ηkɔγεnda βare ekanisa]
'they are going to church'

/βa-a-ci-ir-e ci-kanisa/
3p-t-go-pv-fv 10-church
[βaacire cikanisa]
'they have gone to the churches'

b. [esukuuru] 'school' (from the English)
[γocia esukuuru] 'to school'
[esukuuru ime] 'in school'
[γocia esukuuru ime] 'into the school'

Usually, however, the augment is dropped in this syntactic function. Failure of augment deletion may be restricted to lexical subsets. This is suggested by the fact that both [ekanisa] and [esukuuru] are recent lexical take-overs. But I leave this to future research.

3.2.1.5. Allomorphy of noun class prefixes.

Noun or nominal class prefixes exhibit a certain amount of allomorphy. It is due to the operation and cooperation of a number of lexical and postlexical rules, as well as to morphological rules discussed in this and the previous chapter. It seems appropriate at his point to summarise the surface variation that may result.

Generally, first, all augmented prefixes may be non-augmented, whether at the lexical or the postlexical level, whenever the appropriate semantic or syntactic conditions are present, as discussed in the immediately preceding sections.

Still generally, second, the prefix vowels are subject to the lexical phonological rules discussed in Chapter Two, whenever these are applicable to them.

This second point may be exemplified again here. For example, class prefix vowel /a/ may be delinked through /a/-Delinking and the vowel following it raised compensatorily, as in /a-βa-eηe/ --> [aβeeηe] '2-short (ones)'.

Upper mid prefix vowels may be raised through Upper Mid Vowel Raising. This may involve the vowel of the prefix proper in 1,3 /omo-/, 4 /eme-/, 7 /eke-/, 11 /oro-/, 14 /oβo-/, and 14 /oko-/. The upper mid vowels thus raised to high, and also underlyingly high vowels, as in 8 /eβi-/ and 10 /(e)ci-/, may be turned into a glide by Complex Segment Formation or Glide Formation. The following vowel of the stem is often lengthened compensatorily. Consider for example the surface variation of prefixes 1, 3 /omo-/ and 4 /eme-/, in (23),

(23) a. unchanged: omo-, eme-

[omoiti] '1-killer', [omouuti] '1-blower'
[emeiti] '4-killers', [emeuuti] '4-blowers'[19]

b. omu- or omw-, emi- or emy-

[omwaansu] 'sugar cane'
[omuomo], [omwoomo] '1/3-dry'
[omwɔɔrɔɔrɔ] '3-soft'

[emyaansu] '(sticks of) sugar cane'
[emiomo] '4-dry'
[emiɔɔrɔɔrɔ], [emyɔɔrɔɔrɔ] '4-soft'

Degliding is taken into account also in (24),

(24)	input	omoeηe
	Upper Mid Vowel Raising	omueηe
	Complex Segment Formation	omweηe
	Compensatory Lengthening	omweeηe
	Degliding	omueeηe

---

[19] These two surface representations are semantically odd in real life, but are possible in a fairy-tale, in which trees, for example, are personified.

These forms have deliberately not been marked for level of representation, since each of them may be an acceptable final output, the applicable rules indicated being optional (see Chapter Two). In presentations of examples given hereafter, the operation of most of such rules will be taken for granted and only one surface representation will usually be given.

Upper mid prefix vowels may be affected by Mid Vowel Height Spreading, as in [ɔmɔñɛnɛ] '1/3-big' and [ɛmɛñɛnɛ] '4-big'.

Voiceless velar obstruent /k/, in 7 /eke-/, 12 /aka-/, and 15 /oko-/ is subject to Consonantal Voicing Dissimilation. Its application, whether in cooperation with the aforementioned rules or separately, co-accounts for the possible surface variation in these prefixes. For example, /eke-/ may exhibit the following types of surface surface variation,

(25) a. no change: [eke-]

|eke-ŋwaanso| --> [ekeŋwaanso] 'sacrifice

b. through Upper Mid Vowel Raising: [eki-]

|eke-eŋe| --> [ekieŋe] '7-short'

c. through Upper Mid Vowel Raising and Complex Segment Formation (and compensatory lengthening of the following vowel): [eki-]

|eke-eŋe| --> [ekyeeŋe] '7-short'

c. through Consonantal Vowel Dissimilation: [eγe-]

|eke-saku| --> [eγesaku] 'clan'

d. through Upper Mid Vowel Raising and Consonantal Vowel Dissimilation in cooperation: [eγi-]

|eke-aito| --> [eγiaito] '7-ours'

e. through Mid Vowel Height Spreading: [ɛkɛ-]

|eke-ɛ| --> [ɛkɛɛ] 'basket'

f. through Mid Vowel Height Spreading and Consonantal Vowel Dissimilation: [ɛγɛ-]

|eke-tɔɔŋga| --> [ɛγɛtɔɔŋga] 'basket'

Other combinations are also possible and non-augmentation may cause additional surface variation.

A third general point is that the surface variation of some prefixes may be due to allomorphy or lexical rules. Some of these may be phonologically induced, but by triggers other than those discussed in Chapter Two. Several prefixes are involved here.

Thus, three types of allomorpy involve prefix 5. The first type seems to be phonologically determined and may be formulated as in,

(26) allomorphy: nominal prefix 5 ==>

a. eri- / --- [-cons] [
stem

b. rii- / --- [+cons] [
stem

This allomorphy rule states that prefix 5 is realised as eri- before any vowel, but as rii- before any consonant. /ri-/ is merely the non-augmented allomorph of /eri-/, and as such its occurrence is governed by the usual applicable lexical and postlexical rules, though judgments among informants varied somewhat as to when which rule was applicable. Because the behaviour of nouns and adjectives is identical in this respect, the discussion of adjectives is thus anticipated.

To facilitate generalisation over this instance of allomorphy across lexical categories, /eri-/ has been selected as the underlying representation of prefix 5 in the present study. Since this allomorph is prefixed to words with a vowel-initial stem, and since such words appear to be fewer, and thus occur less frequently, than those with a consonant-initial stem, it tends to occur less frequently in fact.

This allomorphy of prefix 5 is exemplified in (27),

(27)	a.	input	/-eŋe/ (adj)
		Prefixation ==>	|ri-eŋe|
		Augmentation ==>	|e-rieŋe|
		other rules	
		ouput	[erieeŋe] '5-short'
		Similarly,	
		/rii-kɛ/ -->	[riikɛ] '5-small' (adj)
	b.	Input:	/-tɔɔkɛ/ 'banana' (class 5)
		Prefixation (b) ==>	|rii-tɔɔkɛ|
		Augmentation (26)	does not apply
		Output	[riitɔɔkɛ] 'banana'
		Similarly,	

/rii-nɛnɛ/ --> [rii-nɛnɛ] 'big' (adj)

Some more examples are those in (28),

(28) a. before a vowel

¦(i)ηηa riria rieηe¦
give-me 5-that(one) 5-short
[(i)ηηa riria rieηe] or [...erieηe]
'give me that short one'

compare

[erieηe ηkoria] or [rieηe ηkoria]
'I am eating a/the 5-short one'

and

[riimoonto (e)riɔɔrɔ] 'a big lazy person (abusive)'

similarly,

[(e)riaηgo] '5-quick'
[(e)riɛɛnɛ] '5-true'
[(e)riaaηgo] '5-quick'
[(e)riaaɔ] '5-different'
[(e)riaao] '5-your'
[(e)riɔnsi] '5-all'
[(e)riooka] '5-only'
[(e)rioomo] 'dry'
[(e)riooγe] '5-sharp'
[(e)riɔɔrɔ] '5-lazy'

b. before a consonant

[riiγusu] '5-light (of weight)'
(*[eriγusu], similarly the following examples)
[riiβariiri] '5-red'
[riikoro] '5-old'
[riiγɔtu] '5-old'
[riiraβu] '5-white'

A second type of allomorphy involving prefix 5 seems to be lexically determined, since it is restricted to the small and possibly closed set of words in (29),

(29) a. [erieta] 'name, word'
plural [amarieta]
(PB -jét- 'call'; Meeussen 1980: 12, 36)

b. [erieme] '(animal) conception, pregnancy'[20]
plural [amarieme]
(PB -jémi 5 'pregnancy')

c. [eriɔγɔ] 'medicine'
plural [amariɔγɔ]

d. [erioγi] 'voice, sound, noise'
plural /a-ma-rioγi/, [amarioγi]
(PB -joi 'voice, word'; Meeussen 1980: 29, 54)

e. [erioki] 'smoke'
plural [amarioki] '(plumes of) smoke'
(PB -jɔki 3 (ɔ is H) 'smoke'; Meeussen 1980: 25, 51)

f. [eriikɔ] 'hearth, fireplace'
plural [amariikɔ]
(PB -jíkɔ 5 'hearth'; Meeussen 1980: 9, 42)

g. [eriansa] 'space (between the teeth; i.e. left by a tooth or teeth come out or taken out)'
plural [amariansa]

Perhaps [erioβa] 'sun' (PB -jóba 5 'sun'; Meeussen 1980: 27, 52) may be added to this set, but since it has no plural, it cannot illustrate the point about to be discussed.

The prima facie problem is that the words in (29) appear to be indeterminate as to their morphosyntactic class membership. To take [erieme] (29b) for example, given its plural [amarieme], the question is how to analyse the word. At least two analyses are possible.

One approach is to postulate the stem /-eme/ underlyingly. Accordingly, the singular must be interpreted as /e-ri-eme/, which would be quite regular, from a synchronic point of view, given the general allomorphy rule in (26). Concomitantly, the corresponding plural must then be interpreted as a case of prefix-stacking, viz. /a-ma-ri-eme/. On this interpretation, this particular Gusii word would thus retain the class number of its postulated Proto-Bantu source.

[20] A common expression is [neetaγete erieme] '9-it is in heat', which literally means 'it wants pregnancy', from

/na-e-tak-et-e/
f-sm9-want-pv-fv

Another approach would be to postulate a change from Proto-Bantu -jémi to Gusii /-rieme/. Accordingly, the singular must be interpreted as belonging to class 9: |e-rieme|. This interpretation would imply that, in the relevant set of words (29), a class 9 singular is exceptionally combined with a class 6 plural, viz. |ama-rieme|. That is, something like the following allomorphic sub-rule (30) would have to be formulated,

(30) Allomorphy: nominal prefix 5 ==>

a. e- / --- [lexical subset

b. ri- / --- elsewhere

where 'lexical subset' refers to the set of words in (29).

However, this additional formalism would seem to be rather costly from the viewpoint of descriptive economy, for it must be remembered that the relevant words are very few. Hence, this sub-rule would be rather ad hoc. Moreover, in terms of the regular singular-plural combinations in (6), this approach would have to be considered highly irregular synchronically. For these reasons, I adopt the first analysis, interpreting the plural as a case of prefix-stacking. Thus the words in (29) are analysed synchronically as in (31),

(31)
a. /e-ri-eta/, plural /a-ma-ri-eta/
b. /e-ri-eme/, plural /a-ma-ri-eme/
c. /e-ri-ɔγɔ/, plural /a-ma-ri-ɔγɔ/
d. /e-ri-oγi/, plural /a-ma-ri-oγi/
e. /e-ri-oki/, plural /a-ma-ri-oki/
f. /e-ri-ikɔ/, plural /a-ma-ri-ikɔ/
g. /e-ri-ansa/, plural /a-ma-ri-ansa/

Again, /e-ri-oβa/ 'sun' may perhaps be added to the list.

Though prefix-stacking is relatively exceptional too, it occurs more widely than the combination of a singular prefix 9 /e-/ with a plural prefix 6 /ama-/. Accordingly, the relevant words (29) may be entered in the lexicon with an ad hoc specification of their exceptional plural: 6 /ama-/ + 5 /ri-/.

On this analysis, [riiriɔɔña] 'feather', plural [amariɔɔña] (Whiteley 1960: 31), which might superficially be taken as an apparent exception to the pattern in (31), is readily accounted for by postulating /-riɔɔña/ underlyingly. Given this representation, and allomorphy rule (30), its singular and plural surface representations, as well as the non-occurrence of *[eriɔɔña] for its singular, are regularly accounted for. Similarly, [eriisɔ] 'eye', plural [amaisɔ] (PB -jícɔ 5 'eye'; Meeussen 1980: 9, 39), is accounted for by postulating /-isɔ/; and [eriinɔ] 'tooth', plural [amainɔ] (PB -jínɔ 'tooth'; Meeussen 1980: 7, 53), is accounted for by postulating /-inɔ/. Given allomorphy rule (30), the surface representations of these words follow automatically.

A third type of allomorphy involving nominal prefix 5 is associated with an interrogative construction, expressed by the element /ki/ 'which (in particular)?'. Further research must determine whether it is best considered as a separate word that cliticises to the item that is being questioned, /ki/, or as a suffix or postclitic, /-ki/. Consider the examples in (32),

(32) /i-tɔɔkɛ ki/ --> [itɔɔkɛki] 'which banana?'
(otherwise this is regularly [riitɔɔkɛ])

/i-kɛ ki/ --> [ikɛki][21] 'which 5-small (one)?'

/i-nɛnɛ ki/ --> [inɛnɛki] 'which 5-big (one)?'

These and similar ones may be accounted for by the following rule (33),

(33) Allomorphy: prefix 5 ==> i- / --- $[\quad]_{\text{nominal}}$ ki[22]

In this context, the augment of other prefixes is regularly deleted, as exemplified for /-eηe ki/ 'which short (one)?', in (34),

(34)	1	[mweeηeki]
	2	[βeeηeki]
	3	[mweeηeki]
	4	[mieeηeki]
	5	[ieηeki]
	6	[meeηeki]
	7	[kieeηeki]
	8	[βieeηeki]
	9	[yeeηeki]
	10	[cieeηeki]
	11	[rweeηeki]
	12	[keeηeki]
	14	[βweeηeki]
	15	[kweeηeki]
	16	[aeηeki]
	21	= 9 or 16

---

[21] Non-application of Consonantal Voicing Dissimilation (see 2.3.1) in [ikɛki] (*[iγɛki]) may be taken as evidence for considering /ki/ as a separate word. But this is somewhat inconclusive, because, if it may be conceived of as a clitic, non-application of the rule may be caused by a tendency to preserve the morphological identity of the root /-kɛ/.

[22] More detailed research is necessary to determine whether or not ki is actually suffixed to the nominal.

So much for the three types allomorphy involving nominal prefix 5.

Another instance of the third general point on surface variation of some prefixes due to allomorphy or lexical rules, involves the distinction between class 9 /e-/ and 10 /ci-/ versus 9a /e-n-/ and 10a /ci-n-/. Whiteley correctly notes that adjectives only take prefixes 9a /e-n-/ and 10a /ci-n-/, regardless of whether their stem begins with a vowel or a consonant, except when they begin with a nasal (1956: 17), as in (35),

(35) a. adjectives beginning with a vowel

/en-ansu/	-->	[eŋansu], ?[eñansu][23] '9a-sweet'
/en-ŋgo/	-->	*[eŋaŋgo], [eñaŋgo][24] '9a-quick'
/en-ɛnɛ/	-->	[ɛŋɛnɛ] or [ɛñɛnɛ] '9a-true'
/en-eŋe/	-->	[eñeŋe][25] '9a-short'
/en-omo/	-->	[eŋomo] or [eñomo] '9a-dry'
/en-ɔrɔ/	-->	[ɛŋɔrɔ] or [ɛñɔrɔ] '9a-lazy', *[ɛɔrɔ]
/en-uuti/	-->	[eŋuuti], ?[eñuuti] '9-one that blows'
/en-uuri/	-->	[eŋuuri], *[eñuuri] '9-one that takes (by force)'
/en-it-i/	-->	[eŋiti], ?[eñiti] '9-one that kills'

b. adjectives beginning with a consonant

/ɛ-ŋɔɔmbɛ e-n-koro/
9-cow 9a-old
[ɛŋɔɔmbɛ eŋkoro]
'an old cow'
(compare [omoonto omokoro] 'an old person')

/en-γima/	-->	[Eßuku eŋgima] 'a full/whole Bible'
/cin-γima/	-->	[Cißuku ciŋgima] 'full/whole Bibles'
/en-raßu/	-->	[endaßu] '9-white'

c.

/e-nɛnɛ/	-->	[ɛnɛnɛ] '9-big'
/e-ñɛnɛ/	-->	[ɛñɛnɛ] '9-by itself'
/e-muamu/	-->	[emwaamu] '9-black'

The nasal element of resulting prenasals is subject to the applicable nasal rules discussed in Chapter Two, as in (35b). Resulting intervocalic nasals may palatalise or velarise somewhat freely in adjectives, as in (35a), but the details of this variation in adjectives

[23] Judith Moraa judged that [eñansu] goes with, for example, [eñama] 'animal', and as such is acceptable, but that this form is generally less acceptable than [eŋansu].

[24] At least one informant also allowed for [eaŋgo].

[25] Judith Moraa judged *[eŋeŋe] to be incorrect, though, she said, it does occur.

require further research, since there seem to be no clear and consistent determinants one way or the other (see section 2.3.7 for such variation in verbal markers and Whiteley's claims thereon).

Prefixation of the adjective /-ia/ 'good' may be mentioned here in connection with class 9a-10a, as in (36),

(36) /e-n-γi-ya/ --> [eeηgiya] '9a-good'
/ci-n-γi-ya/ --> [ciingiya] '10a-good'

In this particular case, the additional element /-γi-/ is interpreted as part of the adjectival stem, rather than as another allomorph of the prefix, by reason of contrast with, for example, [omuya] '1-good', and because this adjective is exceptional in other respects too. Its full paradigm is given in (518) later on.

The distinction between 9-10 and 9a-10a is not discussed by Whiteley with respect to nouns. Consider the common examples in (37),

(37) a. /e-ciiro/ --> [eciiro][26] 'market

also compare

[eciiro ime] 'in the market'
[γocia ciiro] 'to the market, into the market'
[γocia ase ciiro] 'toward the market'

b. /e-n-cera/ --> [eñcera] 'road'

also compare

[ñcera] 'in/on the road', 'to the road'
[ñcera iγoro] 'on (top of/the sufrace of) the road'
[γocia ñcera] 'onto/into the road'
[γocia ase ñcera] 'toward the road'

These seem to indicate that some nouns take prefixes 9-10, while other nouns take 9a-10a. The question is whether the nasal in example (37b) is part of the prefix or part of the stem. The following deverbal or at least verb-related nouns (38) provide evidence for suggesting that the distinction between 9-10 and 9a-10a is sufficiently well-founded,

(38)	a.	/ko-raaγ-er-a/	/e-n-raaγ-er-a/
		15-eat-ap-fv	9a-eat-ap-fv
		[koraaγera]	[endaaγera]
		'to eat (a meal)'	'food'

[26] Presumably taken over from Luo **ciro** 'market'.

b. /ko-βusur-a/ /e-n-βusur-o/
15-sow-fv 9a-sow-fv
[koβusura] [embusuro]
'to sow'[27] 'seed'

c. /ko-sɔɔk-a/ /e-n-sɔɔk-ɔ/
15-well-fv 9-a-well-sx
[γɔsɔɔka] [εnsɔɔkɔ]
'to well up' 'well'

In all of these cases the root clearly does not begin with a nasal, but with a consonant.

Similarly, the words in (39), taken from Whiteley (1956: 24), have class 11 singulars with corresponding class 10a plurals,

(39)

singular	plural	
[oroteeru]	[ciinteeru]	'winnowing tray'
[oroβaγɔ]	[ciimbaγɔ]	'fence'
[oroβeβe]	[ciimbeβe]	'boundary'
[ɔrɔγεεndɔ]	[ciiŋgεεndɔ]	'journey'
[orooce]	[ciindooce]	'river'
[oroko]	[ciiŋko]	'(piece of) firewood'
[orosaana]	[ciinsaana]	'wood(land)'

Thus they corroborate the distinction between 9-10 and 9a-10a.
At first sight, the examples in (40), may seem to be counter-examples,

(40) a. singular: /e-n-γɔkɔ/, [εŋgɔkɔ] 'hen'
plural: /ci-n-γɔkɔ/, [ciŋgɔkɔ] 'hens'
diminutive: /a-ka-n-γɔkɔ/, [akaŋgɔkɔ] 'small hen'
plural: /o-βo-n-γɔkɔ/, [ɔβɔŋgɔkɔ] 'small hens'

b. singular: /e-n-βaata/ --> [embaata] 'duck'
plural: /ci-n-βaata/ --> [cimbaata] 'ducks'
diminutive: /a-ka-n-βaata/ --> [akambaata] 'small duck'[28]

---

[27] That is, by scattering seed.

[28] The surface respresentations of this word provide an interesting contrast with their equivalent in neighbouring Kuria. Compare,

singular: /e-N-βaata/ --> [eembaata] 'duck'
plural: /ci-N-βaata/ --> [ciimbaata] 'ducks'
diminutive: /a-ka-βaata/ --> [akaβaata] 'small duck'

In the surface representation of the Kuria diminutive, the nasal is absent. This has been plural: /o-βo-n-βaata/ --> [oβombaata] 'small ducks'

[embura], [cimbura] 'rain'
[ɛŋgɔri], [ciŋgɔri] 'rope'
[eñcara], [ciñcara] (a) 'hunger, famine', (b) nail
[embori], [cimbori] 'goat'

If taken by themselves, they might suggest that here the nasal is part of the stem, since it occurs both in the basic and in the diminutive forms, the more so, because there are other class 9-10 words that have a nasal neither in their basic, nor in their diminutive form. as in (41),

(41) a. singular: /e-usi/ --> [eusi][29] 'thread'
plural: /ci-usi/ --> [ciusi] 'threads'
diminutive: [aγausi] 'small thread'
plural: [oβousi] 'small threads'

b. singular: /e-kaβira/ --> [ekaβira][30] 'tribe'
plural: /ci-kaβira/ --> [cikaβira] 'tribes'
diminutive: [aγakaβira] 'small tribe'
plural: [oβokaβira] 'small tribes'

c. singular: /e-ñama/ --> [eñama] 'meat'
plural: /ci-ñama/ --> [ciñama] 'meats'
diminutive: [akañama] 'small (piece of) meat'
plural: [oβoñama] 'small (pieces of) meat'

However, if the various types of evidence are taken together, this does not seem to constitute sufficient counter-evidence. It is argued here that words in class 9a-10a regularly retain the nasal part of the prefix in their derived forms, at least in their diminutive and augmentative form. The formation of such derived forms may thus be considered as an instance of prefix-stacking (see section 3.2.1.6). If this account is sufficiently plausible, the plausibility of these composite prefixes, and hence the distinction between morphosyntactic sub-classes 9-10 and 9a-10a, is established. So much for lexically or otherwise determined allomorphy.

A fourth, specific point concerns the morphosyntactic classes that are used in many Bantu languages to express location or other spatial concepts and relations. Whiteley (1956: 37-

taken as a basis for arguing that, in Kuria, the nasal belongs to the prefix, and that concomitantly the postulate of morphosyntactic sub-class 9a-10a, as distinct from 9-10, is well-justified for that language (for further, adjectival evidence supporting this postulate, see Cammenga 1994: 160-161).

[29] Possibly a lexical take-over from Swahili **nyusi** 'thread'.

[30] Possibly a lexical take-over from Swahili **kabila** 'tribe'.

39) correctly notes that, unlike other Bantu languages, Gusii has no nominal and adjectival prefixes for classes 16-18, which usually signify 'place', or some aspect of, or relation to, place. The one exception is a word signifying 'place', which takes class prefix 16 /a-/, viz. /a-se/ --> [ase], sometimes pronounced [aase]. However, in concord with this word, a homomorphic verbal and possessive prefix /a-/ does occur regularly. It is morphologically identical to the verbal subject prefix for the third person singular.

A fifth and final point, also specific, involves nominal prefix 21 /ña-/. It is not discussed as such by Whiteley. For Proto-Bantu, it is postulated by Welmers (1974), but not by Meeussen (1967). In Gusii, it occurs to a limited extent in that it may be prefixed only to a number of nouns, largely restricted to placenames, cattle terms, and kinship terms. No corresponding distinct verbal subject- or object marker and adjectival prefixes occur. To mark agreement with it, prefixes 9(a) /e-(n-)/ or 16 /a-/ are regularly used instead, depending on the nature and meaning of the head. For example, when the proper name [ñaaηera] 'Blackie' is modified or agreed with morphosyntactically, a class 9 prefix or marker will be used, but for a placename such as [ñaγεεηkε] 'Nyageenke (village)' prefix 16 will be used.[31]

3.2.1.6. Prefix-stacking.

The term prefix-stacking designates the combined affixation of several prefixes to one stem in a certain order.

As suggested in section 3.2.1.5, the formation of diminutives and augmentatives may regularly involve prefix-stacking in the case of class 9a-10a words. Another example is given in (42),

(42) /e-n-βeece/
9a-warthog
[embeece]
'warthog'

diminutive:

¦e-ke-n-βeece¦	or	¦a-ka-n-βeece¦
a-7-9a-warthog		a-12-9a-warthog
[ekeembeece]		[akaambeece]
'small warthog'		'small warthog'

[31] G.J. Dimmendaal has pointed out to me that /ña-/ is an old genitive marker for class 9.

diminutive plural:

¦e-βi-n-βeece¦	or	¦o-βo-n-βeece¦
a-8-9a-warthog		a-14-9a-warthog
[eβiimbeece]		[oβoombeece]
'small warthogs'		'small warthogs'

This may be contrasted with, for example, (43),

(43)	/e-βica/	/ci-βica/
	9-picture	10-picture
	[eβica]	[ciβica]
	'picture'	'pictures'

diminutive:

¦eke-βica¦ 'small picture', pl. ¦eβi-βica¦
¦aka-βica¦ 'small picture', pl. ¦oβo-βica¦

augmentative:

¦rii-βica¦ 'large picture', pl. ¦ama-βica¦

However, the examples in (44) suggest that at least some class 1-2 words may also involve prefix-stacking,

(44)	a.	basic word	diminutive	diminutive plural
		/o-mo-ana/	/a-ka-mo-ana/	/o-βo-mo-ana/
		a-1-child	a-12-1-child	a-14-1-child
		[omwaana]	[akamwaana]	[oβomwaana]
		'child'	or [ekemwaana]	or [eβimwaana]
			also [akaana]	also [eβiana]
			or [ekiana]	'small children'
			'small child'	
	b.	basic word	augmentative	augmentative plural
		/o-mo-Nto/	/rii-mo-Nto/	/a-ma-mo-Nto/
		a-a-person	5-1-person	a-6-1-person
		[omoonto]	[riimoonto]	[amamoonto]
		'person'	'big person'	'big persons'

It must be added, however, that, at least in the case of the diminutive for (44a), prefix-stacking may be motivated, in addition, by the necessity of, or at least a tendency to preservation of morphological identity. Contrast this with (45),

(45)

basic word	diminutive	diminutive plural
/e-ri-ana/	/a-ka-ana/	/o-βo-ana/
a-5-honeycomb	a-12-honeycomb	a-14-honeycomb
[eriana]	[akaana]	[oβwaana]
'honeycomb'	or [ekiana]	or [eβiana]
	'small honeycomb'	'small honeycombs'

Informant judgments differed on the acceptability of [akaana], [ekiana], and [eβiana] as diminutives meaning 'small child(ren)'.

Further, the examples in (46) suggest that at least some nouns in class 3-4 also regularly involve prefix-stacking,

(46)

basic word	diminutive	diminutive plural
/o-mo-te/	/a-ka-mo-te/	/o-βo-mo-te/
a-3-tree	a-12-3-tree	a-14-3-tree
[omote]	[akamote]	[oβomote]
'tree'	'small tree'	'small trees'
or	/e-ke-mo-te/	/o-βo-mo-te/
	a-12-3-tree	a-14-3-tree
	[ekemote]	[oβomote]
	'small tree'	'small trees'
	augmentative	augmentative plural
	/rii-mo-te/	/a-ma-mo-te/
	5-3-tree	a-7-3-tree
	[riimote]	[amamote]
	'big tree'	'big trees'

However, here too, preservation of morphological distinctness may be involved. Compare the derived forms [aγate], plural [oβote], or [eγete], plural [eβite], 'stick', and [riite] 'big stick', plural [amate].

Precisely when prefix-stacking may or must occur, and when not, or in what types of words, and which other prefixes may possibly be stacked onto each other, are questions that require further research.

3.2.2. Adjectives.

Like nouns, adjectives enter into the Gusii morphosyntactic class system. Morphologically speaking, the prefixes used to mark them closely resemble those of the nouns, as is evident in (47),

(47) adjectival prefixes

1	/omo-/
2	/aβa-/
3	/omo-/
4	/eme-/
5	/eri-/
6	/ama-/
7	/eke-/
8	/eβi-/
9	/e-/
9a	/e-n-/
10	/ci-/
10a	/ci-n-/
11	/oro-/
12	/aka-/
14	/oβo-/
15	/oko-/
16	/a-/
21	= 9 /e-/
	or 16 /a-/

The noun phrases in (48), consisting of a noun followed by a adjectival modifier, /-nɛnɛ/ 'big, tall, important', exemplify both the system of adjectival prefixation and morpho-syntactic agreement,

(48) 1 [omoonto ɔmɔnɛnɛ] 'the big person'
2 [aβaanto aβanɛnɛ] 'the big persons'

3 [omote ɔmɔnɛnɛ] 'the big tree'
4 [emete ɛmɛnɛnɛ] 'the big trees

5 [riitɔɔkɛ riinɛnɛ] 'the big banana'
(compare [riimwaana (e)riaaŋgo] 'a quick big child')
6 [amatɔɔkɛ amanɛnɛ] 'the big banana'

7 [eγeento ɛkɛnɛnɛ] 'the big thing'
8 [eβiinto eβinɛnɛ] 'the big things'

9 [eŋiti ɛnɛnɛ] 'the big snake'
(compare [eŋiti eaŋgo] 'the quick snake')

10 [ciŋiti cinɛnɛ] 'the big snakes'
(compare [ciŋiti ciaŋgo] 'the quick snakes')

9a [eŋiti eñaŋgo] 'the quick snake'
10a [ciŋiti ciñaŋgo] 'the quick snakes'

11 [oroko ɔrɔnɛnɛ] 'the big (piece of) firewood'
12 [akaana akanɛnɛ] 'the large honeycomb'
14 [oβokima ɔβɔnɛnɛ] 'the big (lump of) ugali'
15 [ɔkɔβɔkɔ ɔkɔnɛnɛ] 'the big arm'
16 [ase anɛnɛ] 'the big place'
21 = 9 [ñaγɛɛŋkɛ anɛnɛ] 'the big Nyageenke'
or 16 [ñaaŋera ɛnɛnɛ] 'big Blackie'

At least four comments may be made. First, informant judgments on the details of agreement for class 21 differed. Thus Lilian insisted that morphosyntactic agreement of 9 with 21 is regularly used to refer to a place, while agreement of 16 with 21 is used to refer to an area. Judith rejected *[ñaγɛɛŋkɛ ɛnɛnɛ] with the meaning 'the big (village of) Nyageenke', but judged the following utterances acceptable,

(49) a. noun phrases

[ñaγɛɛŋkɛ ɛnɛnɛ]
or [ñaγɛɛŋkɛ nɛɛnɛnɛ]
'Nyageenke is big'

[ñaγɛɛŋkɛ naanɛnɛ] 'Nyageenke is a big area (or place, conceived as an extensive area)'

[Nairobi ɛnɛnɛ] 'Nairobi town is big', 'Nairobi is a big town'

[Nairobi naanɛnɛ] 'Nairobi is a big place' (i.e. is spread out over an extensive area, covers an extensive area)

b. comparative construction

[Nairobi nɛɛnɛnɛ koβua Kisumu]
Nairobi is-big to-surpass Kisumu
'Nairobi is (a) bigger (place) than Kisumu'

Second, most of the representations in (48) may also have an indefinite meaning. For example, [omoonto ɔmɔnɛnɛ] may mean 'a big person'. Which meaning they bear, will depend on the context in which they are used. In exemplification, the possibility of such alternative indefinite meanings is usually taken for granted.

Third, prefix 21 is an exception in this respect, presumably for the semantic reason that, to borrow a term from logic, it is always prefixed to words that designate singulars. It may be added, incidentally, that indefiniteness may be expressed lexically as well, e.g. through [γete] 'some (unspecified)'.

Fourth, and finally, possibly a distinction between theme and rheme function may determine augmentation and non-augmentation of adjectives, respectively. Theme function adds, or is supposed to add, new information. For example, in [riimwaana riire eriaŋgo] 'this child is quick', the quickness of the child talked about is, at least supposedly, new information. In contrast, rheme function (also called rhema) designates supposedly known information. For example, in [riana riaŋgo] 'a/the quick child', the child talked about is known to be quick or supposed to be quick always. No new information is supposed to be added.

At least one informant[32] suggested that this was also the kind of distinction expressed by 9 versus 9a. For example, in [eŋiti eaŋgo] 'a/the quick animal (or, snake)', where the adjective takes prefix 9, the information is supposed to be new, i.e. to have theme status. By contrast, in [eŋiti eñaŋgo] 'a/the quick animal (or, snake)', where the adjective takes prefix 9a, the quickness is supposedly known or understood, i.e. to have rheme status. However, since she judged the corresponding plurals, [ciŋiti ciñaŋgo][33] and [ciŋiti ciaŋgo] to be equivalent in meaning and usage, this suggestion is inconclusive and requires further systematic checking.

In this section, adjectives have mainly been considered in connection with their participation or non-participation in the morphosyntactic class system and agreement. Their derivation will be discussed in section 3.4.5.

3.2.3. Verbs.

3.2.3.0. Preliminaries.

Morphosyntactic agreement in the verb is expressed primarily through a prefix that marks the subject. Hence this is called the subject marker. It is grammatically obligatory.

Agreement may be expressed secondarily through a prefix that marks an object, called the object marker. It is grammatically optional. Its usage is based on the meaning that a speaker wishes to express and the way in which he wishes to express it.

Subject markers may be further subdivided into non-relative and relative subject markers. Without further qualification, the term **subject marker** will usually designate a non-relative subject marker (abbreviation: sm; see section 3.2.3.1). But it may be used also to designate both types collectively. The term **relative marker** strictly designates any relative subject marker (abbreviation: rm; see section 3.2.3.2).

Each type of subject marker may designate either an agent or a patient subject. An agent may be defined generally as that which acts, and a patient as that which is acted upon. Thus it is possible to speak of agent and patient (non-)relative subject markers. This semantico-syntactic distinction, as such, does not seem to determine the choice of allomorphs. But the distribution of some morphemes of the first and second person singular may possibly differ according to whether they mark an agent or a patient subject. This point relates to some features of the subject marker sub-system that I have not been

[32] Judith Moraa.

[33] In this example, *[ciŋaŋgo].

able to clarify completely and therefore it requires further examination.

The object marker (general abbreviation: om) may be further subdivided into four distinct types. These are discussed in sections 3.2.3.3 and 3.3.3.6.

3.2.3.1. Subject marker.

The non-relative subject marker designates the grammatical subject of the activity expressed by the verb. In active tenses the grammatical subject designated by this marker regularly performs the role of agent. But in passive tenses it regularly performs the role of patient, being logically the object of the activity expressed by the verb. An English example of this would be 'the ball' in the sentence 'the ball was kicked by John'.

This subject marker has the underlying representations in (50) for the various morphosyntactic classes,

(50) non-relative subject marker (sm)

a.	1	a-	'he, she' (= 3s under b)
	2	βa-	'they' (= 3p under b)
	3	o-	'it'
	4	e-	'they'
	5	ri-	etc.
	6	a-	
	7	ke-	
	8	βi-	
	9	e-	
	10	ci-	
	11	ro-	
	12	ka-	
	14	βo-	
	15	ko-	
	16	a-	
	21	= 16 a-	

b. Class of personal or animate referents

singular	plural
1 n(a)- 'I'	1 to- 'we'
2 o- 'you'	2 mo- 'you'
3 a- 'he, she' (= class 1 under a)	3 βa- 'they' (= class 2 under a)[34]

[34] The morphology of class 1 is somewhat complex, especially the allomorphy of the second and third person singular subject markers. Whiteley (1956: 10, 100-102) lists the various allomorphs involved, but specifies neither their contexts, nor their triggers.

His treatment is more specific in (1960: 9), where he identifies some contexts in which the different allomorphs occur, using the term 'verbal prefix' to include both the relative and the non-relative subject marker. But these are otherwise insufficiently differentiated, so that much is left implicit in his account.

His position on class 1 subject markers, made more explicit and systematic, is repeated here in summary fashion,

class 1 singular subject markers (Whiteley 1960: 9)

1 n-, η-, ñi-

2 a. ko- / --- a [tense

o- / elsewhere?

b. βw- / --- [e, o root

3 a. a-, o- (oyo)

b. βw- / --- [e, o root

Several remarks are in order. First, /ñi-/ is disconfirmed as such by the present research.

Second, Whiteley correctly identifies the context for second person singular /ko-/ as "(..) any tense numbered '2'"; that is, any tense where tense marker /a/ immediately follows the subject marker. That allomorph second person singular /o-/ occurs elsewhere, is not indicated by him, but deduced here. His statement, that second person singular βw- (from /βo-/, though this is not stated) occurs in tenses B1a and C1a only, is incorrect, nor is it anywhere exemplified.

Third, concerning the alternation for the third person singular (3a) he says, "In tenses which may be translated by a relative both a- and o- occur. The latter occurs where a preceding [noun] controls the verbal prefix, the former where it does not. See tenses A2/1, Px2/1, A2/2, Px2/2, A5, Px9, B9, Qx2/3, C1/1, C2/1, C2/2, C2/3, D2/1, D2/2. Sx2/1, Sx2/2" (1960: 9).

However, this statement is cryptic for the following reasons. For one, the term 'control' is not explained, the reference is indiscriminately to different types of tense, some of which, moreover, contain a-, while others contain o-, so that the distinctive criteria for

In order to accommodate Bantu linguistic practice, the markers for class 1 and 2 have been entered under (50a), and for the sake of paradigmatic integrity and ease of reference they have been repeated under (50b). This practice will be continued hereafter.

The subject markers in (50) are exemplified in (51),

(51)	a.	1	/a-/	(see under b)
		2	/βa-/	(see under b)
		3	[okaγwá]	'3-it fell (recently)'
		4	[ekaγwá]	'4-they fell (recently)'
		5	[rikaγwá]	etc.
		6	[akaγwá]	
		7	[γekaγwá]	
		8	[βikaγwá]	
		9	[ekaγwá]	
		10	[cikaγwá]	

---

these two allomorphs are neither necessarily, nor sufficiently defined. However, elsewhere, in a note on the general relative tense, Whiteley offers the following explanation: "It seems to be true that the o- in the 3rd Person occurs where the relative is the subject of the verb, i.e. the man who does ... The a-prefix seems to occur where the relative is the object of the verb, and also after 'iγɔ' and 'ɛkɛrɔ' (...) This will also be found to be true of other relative tenses" (1956: 59). This is nearer the mark, but as quoted it is still insufficient.

Furthermore, it is not made clear, in (1960), whether third person singular oyo- is an alternative for o-, a-, or both. Nor are its conditions of occurrence otherwise explained. My own findings are that oyo-, as a relative subject marker, is connected with o-. In (1956: 68) it is said that "where the relative is the object rather than the subject of the verb, the form [of the relative marker, J.C.] is slightly different; here the relative follows the object and is the same shape as the demonstrative (1) but with a different tone" (where "demonstrative (1)" is the proximate demonstrative discussed in section 3.2.5.1.)

The first part of this quote seems to be correct, if "object" means patient and "subject" means agent. Its second part seems to be incorrect or irrelevant, for the relative always follows its head. From his spelling in an example such as |omoonto ɔyɔkɔra emeremo eye| 'the man who did this job' (1956: 68), his meaning seems to be that, as a subject, the relative is part of the tense form; whereas examples such as |amarɛ aya twaarɔra| 'the clouds which we saw' and |amarɛ aria twaarɔra| 'those clouds which we saw' seem to indicate that, as an object, the relative marker is a separate morpheme segmentally identical with, but tonally distinct from, the proximate demonstrative (oyo, aya). Unfortunately, my own final notes were insufficiently clear to be able to confirm or disconfirm this point as far as tone is concerned.

Fourth, and finally, the details given for allomorph third person singular βw are insufficient, and the added remark that it occurs in tense C2/1 only (1960: 9), is incorrect. These points will be taken up again in sections 3.2.3.1-2.

11	[rokaγwá]
12	[γakaγwá]
14	[βokaγwá]
15	[γokaγwá]
16	[akaγwá]
21	= 9 or 16

b. Class of personal or animate referents

singular	plural
1 [ŋkaγwá] 'I fell'	1 [tokaγwá] 'we fell'
2 [okaγwá] 'you fell'	2 [mokaγwá] 'you fell'
3 [akaγwá] 'he/she/it fell' (= 1 under a)	3 [βakaγwá] 'they fell' (= 2 under a)[35]

Phonologically determined surface variation of these subject markers may be accounted for by phonological rules discussed in Chapter Two. Since 1-3s and their relative counterparts treated in section 3.2.3.2 exhibit, in addition, a certain amount of allomorphy not so accountable, more attention must be given to the morphology of these three items, especially 2-3s. Later on, some remarks will be added on the use of the subject marker.

The underlying representation for subject marker first person singular is postulated as /n(a)-/. This sums up the following allomorphy rule,

(52) allomorphy: subject marker 1s ==>

a. na- / --- [-cons]
b. n- / --- [+cons]

Together with other applicable rules, it accounts for all the relevant surface representations. It is supposed that the /a/ of /na-/ is regularly delinked before a vowel by /a/-Delinking (see section 2.3.15). In a few tenses, /na-/ and /n-/ may occur in free variation before consonants (see section 3.3.5), which is why /na-/ is postulated instead of /nV-/. The same account applies to the identical object marker 1s (see section 3.2.5.3). Phonologically determined allomorphs of /n-/ (52b) are [(i)m-], [(i)n-], [(i)ñ-], and [(i)ŋ-].

Subject marker second person singular varies morphologically according to whether the designated subject is non-relative or relative, and agent or patient. Here the non-relative agent and patient subject marker is considered (its relative counterpart is discussed in 3.2.3.2). Its allomorphy may be accounted for by the following rule,

[35] Surface [w] is also high, whether phonologically because its underlying /u/ is high, or phonetically in anticipation of the high final vowel. The effect of Consonantal Voicing Dissimilation shows in subject markers 7, 12, and 15.

(53) allomorphy: non-relative subject marker third person singular ==>

a. o-/ --- [root or stem[36]

b. βo-/ --- [{e, ε, a, ɔ, o} root or stem

c. ko-/ --- [a tense marker

This rule states, first, that allomorph /o-/ of non-relative subject marker second person singular regularly occurs before a root-initial vowel or consonant (53a). If the root begins with a high vowel, /i/ or /u/, this allomorph is obligatory. If the root begins with another vowel (e, ε, a, ɔ, or o), both /o-/ and /βo-/ (53b) are possible.

Informant judgements differed somewhat on which allomorphs were allowed before non-high vowels /e, ε, a, ɔ, o/. Some allowed for both /βo-/ and /o-/ in this context, some allowed for /βo-/ only. All said that the latter was more common. Hence the provisional formulation of the rule in (53), where the structural description of (53b) is included in the more general one of (53a). Thus there is some overlap.

In idiolects in which /o-/ may occur before consonants and high vowels only, the two allomorphs are exactly in complementary distribution (this point may require further research). A possible explanation for this variation between idiolects is that the language may be in the process of changing the distribution of the allomorphs. The following examples show that the distinction between agent and patient has no bearing on the allomorphy of non-relative subject marker second person singular.

---

[36] Nearly all examples to be given include in fact the context immediately preceding a root. But the following example shows that, at least in some cases, the context may be broader than the root,

pattern: /sm-ko-rem-a/
sm-t-dig-fv
'I dig'

sg	1	[ŋkorema]	pl	1	[tokorema]
	2	[okorema]		2	[mokorema]
	3	[akorema]		3	[βakorema]

It is supposed that this may hold for other allomorphs too, especially since subject marker allomorphy mainly seems to be determined phonologically; but whether and to what extent this supposition is correct, remains to be checked.

The obligatory occurrence of second person singular allomorph /o-/ before a root-initial consonant, /i/, or /u/ is exemplified in (54),

(54) non-relative subject marker second person singular

allomorph /o-/ before a root vowel or consonant

test-pattern: sm-verb-suffixes
2s-root-t

[orema] 'you (always) dig', *[βorema]
[outa] 'you (always) blow', *[βouta]
[oiká] 'you (always) arrive', *[βoika]

[oremire] 'you are dug', *[βoremire]
[outire] 'you are blown', *[βoutire]
[oirire] 'you are taken', *[βoirire]

The occurrence of its allomorphs before non-high vowels (a-b) is exemplified in (55),

(55) non-relative subject marker second person singular

allomorphs /βo-/ and /o-/ before a non-high vowel

test-pattern: sm-verb-suffixes
2s-root-tense

a. agent

[βweeβa] or [oeβa] '2s-you (always) forget' (*[weeβa])
[βwεεγa] or [ɔε(ε)γa] '2s-you (always) seduce'
[βwaañca] or [oa(a)ñca] '2s-you (always) love'
[βwɔɔkia] '2s-you light (always)' (accounted for by Complex Segment Formation) or [βɔɔkia] '2s-you light (always)' (accounted for by Mid vowel Height Spreading)[37]
[βwoomia] or [oomia] '2s-you (always) dry'

---

[37] *[ɔɔkia], presumably due to tendency toward preservation of morphological identity, for [ɔɔkia] means 'he (always) lights'.

b. patient

[βweeβire] or [oeβire] '2s-you are forgotten'
[βwεεγire] or [ɔεεγire] '2s-you are seduced'
[βwaañcire] or [oaañcire] '2s-you are loved'
[βwɔɔkire] '2s-you are lit', *[ɔ(ɔ)kire] (this means 'he is lit' and would, therefore, cause confusion)
[βwoomirie] or [oomirie] '2s-you are dried'
([oomirie] or [aomirie] also means '3s-he is dried')

Rule (53) also states that before tense marker /a/ the regular allomorph for non-relative subject marker second person singular is /ko-/, as in (56),

(56) non-relative subject marker second person singular

a. agent

allomorph /ko-/ before tense marker /a/

test-pattern: sm-a-verb-suffixes
2s-t-root-tense

/ko-a-eβ-a/, [kweeβa] '2s-you forgot (earlier today)'
/ko-a-εγ-a/, [kwaεγa] or [kwεεγa] '2s-you seduced (earlier today)'
/ko-a-anc-a/, [γwaañca] '2s-you loved (earlier today)'
/ko-a-ɔk-i-a/, [γwɔɔkia] '2s-you lit (earlier today)
/ko-a-om-i-a/, [kwoomia] '2s-you dried (earlier today)'

a. patient

/ko-a-eβ-ir-e/, [kweeβire] '2s-you were forgotten'
/ko-a-εγ-ir-e/, [kwεεγire] '2s-you were seduced'
/ko-a-anc-ir-e/, [γwaañcire] '2s-you were loved'
/ko-a-ɔk-ir-i-e/, [γɔɔkirie] '2s-you were lit'
/ko-a-om-ir-e/, [kwoomire] '2s-you were dried'

[γwautire] '2s-you were blown'
[γwaitire] '2s-you were hit'
[kwaaremire] '2s-you were dug'

Next, the allomorphy of the non-relative subject marker third person singular may be formulated as in (57),

(57) allomorphy: non-relative subject marker third person singular ==>

a. agent/patient

a-/ --- [root or stem

b. agent

o-/ --- a [tense marker

c. patient

a-/ --- a [tense marker

The non-relative agent/patient subject marker third person singular (57a) is exemplified in (58),

(58) non-relative agent/patient subject marker third person singular

allomorph /a-/ before any root vowel or consonant

test-pattern: sm-verb-suffixes
3s-root-tense/extension

a. agent

[aeßa] or [eeßa] '3s-he (always) forgets'
[aɛ(ɛ)γa] or [ɛɛγa] '3s-he (always) seduces'
[aañca] '3s-he (always) loves'
[ɔɔkia][38] '3s-he (always) lights'
[aomia] or [oomia] '3s-he (always) dries'
[auta] '3s-he (always) blows' (*[uuta])
[aika] '3s-he (always) arrives' (*[iika])
[arema] '3s-he (always) digs'

[38] In monitored speech probably also [aɔkia].

b. patient

[aeβire] or [eeβire] '3s-he is/was forgotten'[39]
[aεγire] or [εγire] '3s-he is seduced'
[aañcire] '3s-he is loved'
[aɔkire] or [ɔkire][40] '3s-he is lit'
[aomirie] or [oomirie] '3s-he is dried'[41]
[autire] '3s-he is blown' (*[uutire])
[airire] '3s-he is taken' (*[iirire])
[aremire] '3s-he (always) digs'

Whether the subject is an agent or a patient, has no bearing on the morphology of its marker, but surface variation may be due to the operation of phonological rules.

The non-relative agent subject marker third person singular (57b) is exemplified in (59),

(59) non-relative agent subject marker third person singular

allomorph /o-/ before tense marker /a/

test-pattern: sm-a-verb-suffixes
3s-a-root-tense/extension

/o-a-eβ-a/ --> [o(e)eβa] '3s-he forgot (earlier today)'
[ɔ(ε)εγa] '3s-he seduced (earlier today)'
[oaañca] '3s-he loved (earlier today)'
/o-a-ɔk-i-a/ --> [ɔɔkia][42] '3s-he lit (earlier today)'
[oomia] '3s-he dried (earlier today)'
[outa] '3s-he blew (earlier today)' (*[βwauta], *[βwuuta])
[óika][43] '3s-he arrived (earlier today)' (*[βwaika], *[βwiika])
[orema] '3s-he dug (earlier today)'

---

[39] The difference in meaning corresponds with a difference in tone, thus [ééβiré] '3s-he is forgotten (today)' and [éeβíré] '3s-he was forgotten (recently)'. Similarly in the following examples, where the difference is not indicated.

[40] Derived through /a/-Delinking, compensatory spreading of /ɔ/, and word-initial vowel shortening.

[41] [oomirie], from |o-om-irie| also means '2s-you are dried'.

[42] Compare homomorphous [ɔɔkia] 'he (always) lights', derived from /a-ɔk-i-a/, through /a/-Delinking and compensatory lengthening (possibly with a different tone pattern).

[43] Contrast with [oiká] 'he (always) digs'.

Two remarks must be added here. First, tense marker /a/ is regularly deleted in this context, at least when it is immediately followed by a root-initial consonant or high vowel, as in the last three examples in (59). Moreover, since a form such as [ɔγεεndire] may mean both '3s-he has just gone' and '3-it has just gone', it seems that this deletion also applies in the case of the subject marker for class 3.[44] It may be accounted for by

---

[44] Compare the full paradigms below,

a. testframe

/sm-a-γεNr-ir-e/
sm-t-walk-pv-fv
'sm has/have just gone'

animate singular

1	/na-a-γεNr-ir-e/ 'I have gone (just now)'	-->	[naaγεεndire]	
2	/ko-a-γεNr-ir-e/	-->	[kwaaγεεndire]	
3	/o-a-γεNr-ir-e/	-->	[ɔγεεndire]	(= class 1)

animate plural

1	/to-a-γεNr-ir-e/	-->	[twaaγεεndire]	
2	/mo-a-γεNr-ir-e/	-->	[mwaaγεεndire]	
3	/βa-a-γεNr-ir-e/	-->	[βaaγεεndire]	(= class 2)

other classes

3	/o-a-γεNr-ir-e/	-->	[ɔγεεndire]
4	/e-a-γεNr-ir-e/	-->	[yaaγεεndire]
5	/ri-a-γεNr-ir-e/	-->	[riaaγεεndire]
6	/a-a-γεNr-ir-e/	-->	[aγεεndire]
7	/ke-a-γεNr-ir-e/	-->	[kiaγεεndire]
8	/βi-a-γεNr-ir-e/	-->	[βiaγεεndire]
9	/e-a-γεNr-ir-e/	-->	[yaaγεεndire]
10	/ci-a-γεNr-ir-e/	-->	[ciaγεεndire]
11	/ro-a-γεNr-ir-e/	-->	[roaγεεndire]
12	/ka-a-γεNr-ir-e/	-->	[kaaγεεndire]
14	/βo-a-γεNr-ir-e/	-->	[βwaaγεεndire]
15	/ko-a-γεNr-ir-e/	-->	[kwaaγεεndire]
16	/a-a-γεNr-ir-e/	-->	[aγεεndire]
21	= 9 or 16		

the following somewhat ad hoc, but necessary rule (60),

---

b. testframe

/sm-a-Vc-ir-e/
sm-t-come-pv-fv
¦sm-acire¦

(from /ko-Vc-a/ --> [γooca] 'to come', distinct from /ko-ci-a/ --> [γocia] 'to go)

animate singular

1	/na-a-ci-ir-e/	-->	[naacire] 'I have just come'
2	/ko-a-ci-ir-e/	-->	[γwaacire]
3	/o-a-ci-ir-e/	-->	[ocire] (= class 1)

animate plural

1	/to-a-ci-ir-e/	-->	[twaacire]
2	/mo-a-ci-ir-e/	-->	[mwaacire]
3	/βa-a-ci-ir-e/	-->	[βaacire] (= class 2)

other classes

3	/o-a-ci-ir-e/	-->	[ocire]
4	/e-a-ci-ir-e/	-->	[yaacire]
5	/ri-a-ci-ir-e/	-->	[ryaacire]
6	/a-a-ci-ir-e/	-->	[acire]
7	/ke-a-ci-ir-e/	-->	[γyaacire]
8	/βi-a-ci-ir-e/	-->	[βyaacire]
9	/e-a-ci-ir-e/	-->	[yaacire]
10	/ci-a-ci-ir-e/	-->	[cyaacire]
11	/ro-a-ci-ir-e/	-->	[rwaacire]
12	/ka-a-ci-ir-e/	-->	[γaacire]
14	/βo-a-ci-ir-e/	-->	[βwaacire]
15	/ko-a-ci-ir-e/	-->	[γwaacire]
16	/a-a-ci-ir-e/	-->	[acire]
21	= 9 or 16		

It is assumed that the surface representations of subject markers 6 and 16 are accounted for by the constraint on word-marginal long vowels.

(60) Tense /a/-Deletion

$$a \dashrightarrow \emptyset \,/\, [_{\text{sm1/3}}\ o\ \ [_{\text{tense}}\ \text{---}\ \ [_{\text{root}}\{C, i, u\}$$

The rule also applies, whenever it is preceded by the relative subject marker third person singular in this context (see section 3.2.3.2).

In the present case, the structural description of the rule may possibly include the examples in (59), where the initial root vowel is non-high, but this is somewhat indeterminate. If only [oeβa] and [ɔεγa] are possible, (60) certainly applies here too; but if [oeeβa] and [ɔεεγa] are possible in addition, (60) is optional in this context. That is, it may optionally not apply and give way to /a/-Delinking and compensatory lengthening of the following vowel.

The remaining data are indeterminate, because, even if (60) does optionally not apply, [oaañca] would be derived from /o-a-aNc-a/ by prenasalisation, compensatory lengthening of the preceding vowel, /a/-Delinking and compensatory lengthening of the following vowel, and x-Trimming. Similarly, [ɔɔkia] would derive from /o-a-ɔk-i-a/, and [oomia] from /o-a-om-i-a/, through /a/-Delinking and compensatory lengthening of the following vowel, followed by Mid Vowel Height Spreading and x-Trimming.

If (60) applies obligatorily in these contexts, the results would be the same, except for [oeβa] and [ɔεγa]. By analogy to the case for the relative marker third person singular, pending compelling counter-evidence, the analysis in (57) and the formulation in (60) are argued here.

A second remark on allomorph /o-/ for non-relative agent subject marker third person singular before tense marker /a/, is that at least one informant allowed for /βo-/ as a possible alternative in this context, if, and only if, the following root vowel were /e, o, a/, as in (61),

(61) possible allomorph for non-relative subject marker third person singular

/βo-/ before both tense marker /a/ and a non-high root vowel

test-pattern: sm-a-verb-suffixes
3s-a-root-tense/extension

[βweeβa] '3s-he forgot (earlier today)'
[βwaañca] '3s-he loved (earlier today)'
[βwoomia] '3s-he dried (earlier today)'
*[βwɔɔkia] '3s-he lit (earlier today)'
(but [βwɔɔkia] 'sm2s-you (always) light')
?[βwεεγa] '3s-he seduced (earlier today)' (not checked)

However, since not all informants agreed on the allomorphy in (61), and since some of its details may have been overlooked (e.g. the allomorphs in the test-words may have been confused by the informants with their relative counterparts), it will be entered in the final summary in section 3.2.3.4, but subject to further research.

The non-relative patient third person singular subject marker (57c) is exemplified, somewhat sparsely, in (62),

(62) non-relative patient subject marker third person singular

allomorph /a-/ before tense marker /a/

/a-a-ɔβɔ-et-u-e/, [ɔɔβɔɛtwɛ] '3s-he was feared'
/a-a-irok-et-u-e/, [airoγetwe] '3s-he was feared'
/a-a-sik-et-u-e/, [aasiγetwe] '3s-he was respected'

Next, a few additional general remarks on the use of the non-relative subject marker are in order. First, it serves to mark grammatical agreement with a preceding subject head in the same sentence. This function seems to be purely syntactic and, as pointed out, is obligatory. Thus, if a head is present in the sentence, the subject marker need not be translated.

Second, it may similarly agree with a subject that is either mentioned previously in the (written or spoken) text, but not in the sentence in which it occurs, or with a subject that is merely known or understood from the co-text. Whenever the finite form in which it occurs is thus used independently, the subject marker may usually be translated as 'it' for any singular, and as 'they' for any plural.

Third, whenever two or more subjects are designated in the same sentence by nouns belonging to distinct morphosyntactic classes, there are several possibilities. First, the subjects, each with the appropriate agreement, may be mentioned explicitly, with the predicate repeated, as in (63),

(63) ¦aβaa-nto ññoomba βare na eβi-roγo ññoomba βi-re¦
2-person f-in-the-house 2-be and 8-chair f-in-the-house 8-be
[aβaanto ññoomba βare na eβiroγo ññoomba βire]
'the persons and the chairs are in the house'

[amatɔɔkɛ arɛɛtirwe na cimɛɛsa ciarɛɛtirwe
the-bananas have-been-brought and the-tables have-been-brought
'the bananas and the tables have been brought'

Alternatively, second, [βɔiγɔ] 'also' or a similar expression may be used instead of the repetition of the predicate, as in (64),

(64) [amatɔɔkɛ arɛɛtirwe na cimɛɛsa βɔiγɔ]
the-bananas have-been-brought and the-tables also
'the bananas and the tables have been brought'

|aβaa-nto βa-aikire na ecii-ηiti βɔiγɔ|
2-person 2-have-arrived and 10-animal also
the-people have-arrived and the-animals also
[aβaanto βaikire na eciηiti βɔiγɔ]
'the people and the animals have arrived'

|cii-ηiti ci-aikire na aβaa-nto βɔiγɔ|
10-animal 10-have-arrived and 2-person also
the-animals have-arrived and the-people also
[ciηiti ciaikire na aβaanto βɔiγɔ]
'the animals and the people have arrived'

|ci-ɔɔmbɛ ci-aikire amɔ na eβi-roγo|
10-cow 10-have-arrived together with 8-chair
the-cows have-arrived together with the-chairs
[cyɔɔmbɛ ciaikire amɔ na eβiroγo]
'the cows and the chairs have arrived'

|aβaa-nto ñoomba βa-re na eβi-roγo βɔiγɔ|
2-person in-the-house 2-be and 8-chair also
the-persons in-the-house are and the-chairs also
[aβaanto ñoomba βare na eβiroγo βɔiγɔ]
'the persons and the chairs are in the house'

In these examples, the composite subject is split up. Its second part is postposed, and connected with the rest of the sentence through the coordinating conjunction 'na'. The second part almost seems to be added as a kind of afterthought.

One informant suggested that some subject marker might agree with two or more heads belonging to different morphosyntactic classes, but this was disconfirmed by others, who said that examples such as those in (65) are unacceptable,

(65) *[aβaanto na eβiroγo ñoomba βire]
*[aβaanto na eβiroγo ñoomba βare]
'the people and the chairs were in the house'

*|ci-mɛɛsa na eβi-roγo βi-arɛɛtirwe|
10-table and 8-chair 8-have-been-brought
*[cimɛɛsa na eβiroγo βiarɛɛtirwe]
'the tables and the chairs have been brought'

*|ci-ɔɔmbɛ na eβi-roγo βi-aikire|
10-cow and 8-chair 8-have-arrived
*[cyɔɔmbɛ na eβiroγo βiaikire]
'the cows and the chairs have arrived'

This point of second and third person singular allomorphy may be concluded with the following observations. First, the allomorphs of the second and third person singular non-relative subject markers, whether agent or patient, may be summarised as in (66),

(66) non-relative agent/patient singular subject markers 2-3s

contexts:

	a. / --- [root/stem	b. / --- $\begin{bmatrix} \text{-cons} \\ \alpha\text{high} \\ \beta\text{mid} \end{bmatrix}$ [root	c. /--- a [tense

(not both α = + and β = -)

markers:

	a.	b.	c.
2s	o-	βo-	ko-
3s	a-		agent o- (βo-?) patient a-[45]

---

[45] Compare the following paradigms, some of which are complete, for the class of animate referents,

1. non-relative subject markers: agent

a. before a (non-root) consonant

pattern: /sm-ko-rem-a/
sm-t-dig-fv
'I dig'

sg	1	[ηkorema]	pl	1	[tokorema]
	2	[**o**korema]		2	[mokorema]
	3	[**a**korema]		3	[βakorema]

b. before tense vowel /a/

pattern: /sm-a-rem-ir-e/
sm-t-dig-pv-fv
'I have dug'

sg	1	[naaremire]	pl	1	[tokoremire]
	2	[**kw**aaremire]		2	[mokoremire]
	3	[**o**koremire]		3	[βakoremire]

Context (66b), with its condition in parenthesis, gives formal expression to the fact that the trigger vowel following the allomorph may not be high, i.e. [+high, -mid]; in other words, it must be /e, ɛ, a, ɔ, o/.

Second, an informant whose speech was quite consistent judged that composite subjects consisting of words from different classes may not combine with a single subject marker encoded on a verb. Instead, either distinct verb forms must be used to agree with each separate class, or [βɔiγɔ] must be used.

Third, Whiteley's suggestion (1956: 14) that class 8 subject marker may be used generally to agree with heads belonging to different classes, is disconfirmed by the

---

c. before another (root) vowel

2s /βo-ɔβɔ-et-e/, [βwɔɔβɔɛtɛ] '2s-you fear'
/o-irok-et-e/, [oiroγete] '2s-you fear'

3s /a-ɔβɔ-et-e/, [(ɔ)ɔβɔɛtɛ] '3s-he fears'
/a-irok-et-e/, [airoγete] '3s-he fears'

2. non-relative subject marker: patient

a. before a consonant

		active tense	passive tense
pattern:		/sm-rem-ir-e/ sm-dig-pv-fv 'am/is/are dug'	/sm-ta-a-sik-et-u-e/ who-not-t-root-t-p-fv 'was/were not respected'
sg	1	[ndemire]	[ntaasiγetwe]
	2	[oremire]	[otaasiγetwe]
	3	[aremire]	[ataasiγetwe]
pl	1	[toremire]	[totaasiγetwe]
	2	[moremire]	[motaasiγetwe]
	3	[βaremire]	[βataasiγetwe]

b. before tense marker /a/

/ko-a-ɔβɔ-et-u-e/, [kwɔɔβɔɛtwɛ] '2s-you were feared'
/ko-a-irok-et-u-e/, [kwairoγetwe] '2s-you were feared'
/ko-a-sik-et-u-e/, [γwaasiγetwe] '2s-you were respected'

/a-a-ɔβɔ-et-u-e/, [ɔɔβɔɛtwɛ] '3s-he was feared'
/a-a-irok-et-u-e/, [airoγetwe] '3s-he was feared'
/a-a-sik-et-u-e/, [aasiγetwe] '3s-he was respected'

present research.

Fourth, and finally, when subjects belong to the same class, they may form a composite subject with which one subject marker of the same class may agree.

Anticipating the discussion of the relative marker in section 3.2.3.1, this may be an appropriate place to account for the allomorphy of subject and relative marker 4, 9 /e-/. Given the applicable context, it may be raised to /i/, which regularly glides to /y/, as in (67) (after Whiteley 1960: 3),

(67) a.

input	/e-a-om-a/
	9-t-be dry-fv
/a/-Delinking and Linking Rule	e-ooma
Upper Mid Vowel Raising	iooma
Glide Formation	y
output	[yooma]

'4-they/9-it has dried' (i.e. '9-it is dry')
'4-which have/9-which has dried (i.e. 'is dry')

e.g. /e-aηga e-a-om-a/
npx9-cloth rm9-t-dry-fv
[eaηga yooma]
'the cloth (which) has dried'[46]

b.

input	/e-aNc-ir-e/
	9-love-pv-fv
Upper Mid Vowel Raising and other rules	iaañcire
Glide Formation	y
output	[yaañcire]
	'4-they are/9-it is loved'
	'4-which are/9-which is loved'

[46] Compare the plurals

/ci-aηga n-ci-a-om-a/
npx10-cloth f-sm10-t-dry-fv
[ciaηga ñciooma]
'the clothes have dried'

/ci-aηga ci-a-om-a/
npx10-cloth rm10-t-dry-fv
[ciaηga ciooma]
'the clothes which have dried'

c. /e-a-Vc-ir-e/
sm4/9-t-come-pv-fv
[yaacíre]
'9-it/4-they have come (now)'[47]

A unique allomorph, finally, which was first mentioned in section 2.1.3, is prenasalised [ndž], further exemplified in (68),

(68) /n-e-a-et-a/
f-4/9-t-pass-fv
[ndžaeta]
'4-they/9-it passed (recently/long ago)'[48]

/e-aŋga n-e-a-om-a/
npx9-cloth f-sm9-t-dry-fv
[eaŋga ndžooma]
'the cloth has dried'

/iγɔ ń-e-om-a/
[iγɔ ńdžóóma]
'have 4-they/has 9-it dried?'[50]

[eaŋga eria ¦ ndžooma]
'that cloth ¦ has dried'[49]

/n-e-aŋga-ki e-a-om-a/
f-9-cloth-which 9-t-dry-fv
[ndžaaŋgaki yooma]
'which is the cloth ¦ that has dried?'

Since this change may apparently involve both the subject marker and the nominal prefix (as in the last example), this allomorphy may be accounted as in (69),

---

[47] Compare

/βa-a-Vc-ir-e/
sm3p-t-come-pv-fv
[βaacíre]
'3p-they have come (now)'

[48] Compare /n-to-a-et-a/ --> [ntwaeta] 'we passed (recently or long ago)'.

[49] Compare

[eaŋga ¦ eria yooma ¦ neeye]
'the cloth ¦ which has dried ¦ is this one'

[eaŋga ¦ yooma ¦ neeye]
'the cloth ¦ which has dried ¦ is this one'

[50] Compare [niiγɔ yooma] '9-it has dried', where the focus or identificatory /na-/ is attached to [iγɔ].

(69) allomorphy prefix 4, 9

e --> dž/ [+nas] --- [-cons]
4,9

It changes 4, 9 /e-/, whether it is a verbal or a nominal prefix, into [dž], whenever it is preceded by a nasal and followed by a vowel. Though (69) appears to be somewhat ad hoc, nonetheless it is thus quite general.

3.2.3.2. Relative marker.

Syntactic functions, especially subject and object heads, may be relativised in Gusii. When this occurs, morphosyntactic agreement is maintained and regularly expressed by a relative subject marker encoded on the verb, here simply called the relative marker.

Generally, the syntactic function of the antecedent of the relative subject marker, whether subject or object, seems to be irrelevant for its allomorphy. Nor, strictly, does its own function, whether as agent or patient of activity of the verb on which it is encoded, have any bearing on this (except, perhaps, on the distribution of certain allomorphs; I will return to this in a moment). Generally, allomorphy rather seems to be due to the distinction between non-relativity and relativity, and to certain differences in morphological or phonological context.

Except for class 1, and perhaps class 16, the relative marker is identical in shape to the corresponding non-relative subject marker for all morphosyntactic classes, as in (70),

(70) relative subject marker (rm)

1	/o-/	(= 3s)
2	/βa-/	(= 3p)
3	/o-/	
4	/e-/	
5	/ri-/	
6	/a-/	
7	/ke-/	
8	/βi-/	
9	/e-/	
10	/ci-/	
11	/ro-/	
12	/ka-/	
14	/βo-/	
15	/ko-/	
16	/a-/	
21	= 16	

To anticipate the discussion of the present section, it may be observed at once that in certain contexts one allomorph for class 1 and 3 /o-/ is /βo-/. To anticipate the discussion of later sections, it may be added that the relative marker may be used also with other lexical categories, in order to express morphosyntactic agreement. Since it is so used especially with pronouns, it will then be called pronominal prefix (abbreviation: ppx). In such usage, its morphology is virtually they same as in (70), but with some few additions, as in (71),

(71) pronominal prefix (ppx)

1	o-/βo-
2	βa-
3	o-/βo-
4	e-
5	ri-
6	a- (associative: ya-)
7	ke-
8	βi-
9	e-
10	ci-
11	ro-
12	ka-
14	βo-
15	ko-
16	a-
21	= 9 or 16

Allomorphs 1,3 /βo-/ and 6 /ya-/ may occur before a vowel, such that /βo-/ may do so generally (discussed for the relative marker in the rest of this section), but /ya-/ only with associative /-a/ (see sections 3.2.5.1 and 3.2.11). The term 'pronominal prefix' is thus proposed as a general term for the prefixes in (70, 71). But in as far as they are used as a verbal marker, they will be called 'relative marker'.

My analysis of the relative subject marker first person singular has been insufficiently researched and is therefore tentative, but presumably either the non-relative subject marker /n(a)-/, or relative marker /o-/ may be used for this purpose. Consider (72),

(72) singular

1	[iñce ŋɔɔβɔire] '(it is) I who am feared'
2	[ayɛ βwɔɔβɔire] '(it is) you who are feared'
3	[ɛrɛ βwɔɔβɔire] '(it is) he who is feared'

plural

1	[intwe twɔɔβɔire] '(it is) we who are feared'
2	[inwe mwɔɔβɔire] '(it is) you who are feared'
3	[βaraβwɔ βɔɔβɔire] '(it is) they who are feared'

Supposedly, [ŋɔɔβɔire] derives from /n-na-ɔβɔ-ir-e/[51]. As in the case of classes 3-21, the markers for the plural are identical to the non-relative subject markers. Anticipating later discussion, in the following paradigm (73) /oyo/ is added in the singular and /aβo/[52] in the plural,

(73) singular

1 [iñce oyo (ɔ)ɔβɔire]
or, through liaison, [iñce oyɔɔβɔire][53]
'(it is) I who am feared'
or 'I (am) the-one who-is-feared' (also below)

2 [ayɛ oyo (ɔ)ɔβɔire]
or, through liaison, [ayɛ oyɔɔβɔire]
'(it is) you who are feared'

3 [ɛrɛ oyo (ɔ)ɔβɔire]
or, through liaison, [ɛrɛ ɔyɔɔβɔire]
'(it is) he who is feared'

plural

1 [intwe aβo twɔɔβɔire] '(it is) we who are feared'
2 [inwe aβo mwɔɔβɔire] '(it is) you who are feared'
3 [βaraβwɔ aβo βɔɔβɔire] '(it is) they who are feared'

---

[51] This paradigm may be mixed, possibly because the data were collected, before the subject markers were sufficiently understood. Compare the following non-relative subject markers,

/n-ɔβɔ-ir-e/, [ŋɔβɔire] 'I am feared'
/βo-ɔβɔ-ir-e/, [βwɔɔβɔire] 'you are feared'
/a-ɔβɔ-ir-e/, [ɔɔβɔire] 'he is feared'
(plural: twɔɔ, mwɔɔ, βɔɔ)

or focussed,

/n-n-ɔβɔ-ir-e/, [ŋŋɔβɔire] 'I am feared (thematic)'
/n-n-ɔβɔ-et-e/, [ŋŋɔβɔɛtɛ] 'I fear (thematic)'

[52] I have not been able to establish definitively whether the surface representation of this form was [aβo], [aβu], or [aβɔ]. In fact there seemed to be idiolectal variation. Judith Moraa, for example, discounted [aβo] and [aβuɔ], but others wavered between [aβo] and [aβu] or [aβo] and [aβɔ].

[53] This form is supposed, but requires verification.

As we will see in a moment, the markers for the second and the third person singular are the regular ones for the relative subject marker. Possibly because /oyo/ precedes the tense-form, the first person singular seems to follow suit. If this is correct, it seems that the relative marker for class 1 in (70) and, given the appropriate context (not checked for 1s), its allomorph /βo-/, may also to be used with the first person singular, or at least with its independent pronoun [iñce].

The same type of alternation recurs in the relative verb form, noted also in (1956: 67) with slightly different details, exemplified in (74),

(74) $\left\{\begin{matrix} \text{sm} \\ \text{rm} \end{matrix}\right\}$ - ko - root - a

singular

1 [iñce ηkwɔɔβɔa] '(it is) I who fear'
n-ko-ɔβɔ-a

[iñce oyo ηkɔɔβɔa] or [...ɔyɔɔkɔɔβɔa]
'(it-is)-I who fear'

2 [ayε ɔkɔɔβɔa] or [ayɔɔkɔɔβɔa]
'(it-is)-you who-fear'

[ayε oyo ɔkɔɔβɔa] or [ayɔɔyɔɔkɔɔβɔa]
'(it-is)-you who fear'

3 [εrε ɔkɔɔβɔa] or [εrɔɔkɔɔβɔa]
'(it-is)-he who-fears'

[εrε oyo ɔkɔɔβɔa] or [εrɔɔyɔɔkɔɔβɔa]
'(it-is)-he who fears'[54]

---

[54] The structure of the corresponding plural appears to be slightly different, viz. sm=rm - V - ko - root - a, witness the following data,

1 [intwe tɔɔkɔɔβɔa]
'(it-is)-we who-fear'
[intwe aβu tɔɔkɔɔβɔa]
'(it-is)-we who fear'

2 [inwe mɔɔkɔɔβɔa]
'(it-is)-you who-fear'
[inwe aβu mɔɔkɔɔβɔa]
'(it-is)-you who-fear'

So much for the relative marker for the first person singular. Next, the second and third person singular will be considered.

The allomorphs and their contexts for relative subject marker second person singular may

---

3 [βaraβwɔ βaakɔɔβɔa]
'(it-is)-they who-fear'
[βaraβwɔ aβu βaakɔɔβɔa]
'(it-is)-they who fear'

It will be recalled that the non-relative and relative subject markers 1-3 plural are identical. The underspecified vowel, V, must be postulated, apparently, in order to account for these surface representations. The following paradigm confirms this account,

1 [iñce ηkɔγεεnda]
'(it-is)-I who-go'
[iñce oyo ɔkɔγεεnda]
'(it-is)-I who go'

2 [ayε ɔkɔγεεnda]
'(it-is)-you who-go'
[ayε oyo ɔkɔγεεnda]
'(it-is)-you who go'

3 [εrε ɔkɔγεεnda]
'(it-is)-he who-goes'
[εrε oyo ɔkɔγεεnda]
'(it-is)-he who goes'

plural

1 [intwe tɔɔkɔγεεnda]
'(it-is)-we who-go'
[intwe aβu tɔɔkɔγεεnda]
'(it-is)-we who go'

2 [inwe mɔɔkɔγεεnda]
'(it-is)-you who-go'
[inwe aβu mɔɔkɔγεεnda]
'(it-is)-you who go'

3 [βaraβwɔ βaakɔγεεnda]
'(it-is)-they who-go'
[βaraβwɔ aβu βaakɔγεεnda]
'(it-is)-they who go'

I have not checked this construction for classes 3-21.

be accounted for as in (75),

(75) allomorphy: relative agent subject marker second person singular ==>

a. o-/ --- $\left[\begin{Bmatrix} C \\ i, u \end{Bmatrix}\right.$
root/stem

b. βo-/ --- [{e, ε, a, ɔ, o}
root

c. ko-/ --- [a
tense marker

First, (75a) is exemplified in (76),

(76) relative agent subject marker second person singular

allomorph /o-/ before a root-initial consonant or high vowel

test-pattern: rm-verb-suffixes
2s-root-tense

[naayε oremete]
'it is 2s-you (who) have dug (recently)'

[naayε ɔrεmεtε]
'it is 2s-you (who) are brave'

[naayε outete]
'it is 2s-you who have blown (recently)'

[naayε oiγete]
'it is 2s-you who arrived (recently)'

Allomorph /βo-/ does not seem to occur in this context.

Second, (75b) is exemplified in (77),

(77) relative agent subject marker second person singular

allomorph /βo-/ before a root-initial non-high vowel

test-pattern: rm-verb-t-(i)-fv
2s-root-past-(c)-t

[naayε βwɔɔγεtie]
'it is 2s-you (who) have lit (recently)'

[naayε βwεεγεtε]
'it is 2s-you (who) have seduced (recently)'

[naayε βwaañcete]
'it is 2s-you (who) have loved (recently)'

[naayε βweeβete]
'it is 2s-you (who) have forgotten (recently)'

[naayε βwoometie]
'it is 2s-you (who) have dried (recently)'

Allomorph /o-/ does not seem to occur in this context.

Third, (75c) is exemplified in (78),

(78) relative agent subject marker second person singular

allomorph /ko-/ before tense marker /a/

test-pattern: rm-a-verb-fv
2s-t-root-t

[ayε (oyo) kwaarema] '2s-you who dug (earlier today)'
[ayε (oyo) γwɔɔkia] '2s-you who lit (earlier today)'
[ayε (oyo) kwεεγa] '2s-you who seduced (earlier today)'
[ayε (oyo) γwaañca] '2s-you who loved (earlier today)'
[ayε (oyo) kweeβa] '2s-you who forgot (earlier today)'
[ayε (oyo) kwoomia] '2s-you who dried (earlier today)'
[ayε (oyo) γwauta] '2s-you who blew (earlier today)'
[ayε (oyo) γwaika] '2s-you who arrived (earlier today)'

Neither /o-/, nor /βo-/ seem to occur in this context. If this is correct, it may be concluded that the three allomorphs for the agent relative subject marker third person singular are in complementary distribution.

The allomorphs for the relative patient subject marker second person singular are identical to those of its agent counterpart, but their distribution appears to be somewhat different, as in (79),

(79) allomorphy: relative patient subject marker second person singular ==>

a. o-/ --- [root/stem

b. βo-/ --- [{e, ε, a, ɔ, o} root/stem

c. ko-/ --- [a tense marker

This rule states in effect that either /o-/ or /βo-/ may occur before root vowels /e/, /ε/, /a/, /ɔ/, and /o/, that only /o-/ may occur before a root-initial consonant or a high vowel, and that only /ko-/ may occur before tense marker /a/. In other words, /o-/ may occur anywhere immediately preceding a root. Thus its distribution is slightly wider than that of its non-relative counterpart.

First, (79a) is exemplified in (80),

(80) relative patient subject marker second person singular

allomorph /o-/

a. before a root-initial consonant or high vowel

test-pattern: rm-verb-suffixes
2s-root-tense/extension

[naayε outire] 'it is you 2s-who are blown' (*[βoutire])
[naayε oitire] 'it is you 2s-who are hit' (*[βoitire])
[naayε oremire] 'it is you 2s-who are dug' (*[βoremire])

b. before a root-initial non-high vowel

test-pattern: rm-verb-suffixes
2s-root-tense/extension

[naayε oeβire] 'it is you 2s-who are forgotten'
[naayε ɔεγire] 'it is you 2s-who are seduced'
[naayε oaañcire] 'it is you 2s-who are loved'
[naayε ɔɔmire] 'it is you 2s-who are smeared'
[naayε oomirie] 'it is you 2s-who are dried'

Second, (79b) is exemplified in (81),

(81) relative patient subject marker second person singular

/βo-/ before a root-initial non-high vowel

test-pattern: rm-verb-suffixes
2s-root-tense/extension

[naayɛ βweeβire] 'it is you 2s-who are forgotten'
[naayɛ βwɛɛγire] 'it is you 2s-who are seduced'
[naayɛ βwaañcire] 'it is you 2s-who are loved'
[naayɛ βwɔɔmire] 'it is you 2s-who are smeared'
[naayɛ βwoomirie] 'it is you 2s-who are dried'[55]

Third, (79c) is exemplified in (82),

(82) relative patient subject marker second person singular

allomorph /ko-/ before tense marker /a/

test-pattern: rm-a-verb-suffixes
2s-t-root-t/passive

[naayɛ γwaɔkiiγwe] 'it is you 2s-who have been lit'
[naayɛ kwaɛγirwe][56] 'it is you 2s-who have been seduced'
[naayɛ γwaakirwe] 'it is you 2s-who have been hit'
[naayɛ kwaeβirwe][57] 'it is you 2s-who have been forgotten'
[naayɛ kwaomiiγwe][58] 'it is you 2s-who have been dried'
[naayɛ γwautirwe] 'it is you 2s-who have been blown'
[naayɛ γwaitirwe] 'it is you 2s-who have been hit'
[naayɛ kwaaremirwe] 'it is you 2s-who have been dug'

To conclude this part of the present section, the allomorphs for the agent and patient relative subject marker second person singular are identical, viz. /o-/, /βo-/, and /ko-/.

---

[55] By the wind, for example.

[56] Or, after the application of /a/-Delinking and compensatory lengthening of the following vowel, [kwɛɛγirwe].

[57] Or, in virtue of /a/-Delinking and other rules, [kweeβirwe].

[58] Or [kwoomiiγwe]. These surface representations derive from

/ko-a-om-ir-i-γu-e/
rm2s-t-dry-pv-c-p-fv

The distribution of /βo-/ and /ko-/ in either use is also identical. But the distribution of /o-/, immediately preceding the root, seems to be unrestricted in its use as agent marker, but restricted in its use as patient marker, where only a consonant or a high vowel may follow it.

The relative subject marker for the third person singular, i.e. class 1, has only two allomorphs, viz. /o-/ and /βo-/. Here too, there is a slight difference in the distribution of /o-/ in its use as an agent marker, as opposed to its use as a patient marker. The distribution of its allomorphs, when it is used as an agent, may be expressed as in (83),

(83) allomorphy: relative agent subject marker third person singular ==>

a. o-/ --- [(a) [{C, i, u}
tense root/stem

b. βo-/ --- [(a) [{e, ε, a, ɔ, o}
tense root/stem

That is, /o-/ occurs, whenever, with or without intervening tense marker /a/, it is followed by a root-initial consonant or high vowel, but /βo-/ occurs, whenever, with or without intervening tense marker /a/, it is followed by a root-initial non-high vowel.

First, allomorph /o-/ in its several contexts is exemplified in (84),

(84) relative agent subject marker third person singular

allomorph /o-/ followed by a root-initial consonant or high vowel, possibly with intervening tense marker /a/

a. test-pattern: rm-verb-suffixes
3s-root-tense/extension

[nεεrε oremete]
'it is he (3s-who) has dug (recently)'

[nεεrε ɔrεmεtε]
'it is he (3s-who) is brave'

[nεεrε outete]
'it is he 3s-who has blown (recently)'

[nεεrε oiγete]
'it is he 3s-who arrived (recently)'

b. test-pattern: rm-a-verb-suffixes
3s-t-root-tense/extension

[ɛrɛ (oyo) outa] 'he 3s-who blew (earlier today)'
[ɛrɛ (oyo) oika] 'he 3s-who arrived (earlier today)'
[ɛrɛ (oyo) orema] 'he 3s-who dug (earlier today)'

In the context without intervening /a/, no phonological rules apply and the derivation is straightforward. When tense marker /a/ intervenes, it is deleted in this context. This may be accounted for by (85),

(85) Tense /a/-Deletion

a --> Ø/ [o [--- [{i,u,C}
rm3s tense root/stem

which is virtually identical with (60) previously discussed, so that these two rules may be collapsed into one, as in (86),

(86) Tense /a/-Deletion

a --> Ø/ [o [--- [{i,u,C}
3s tense root/stem

Since third person singular, without further qualification, simply designates the third person singular subject marker, it may be interpreted here so as to include both the non-relative and the relative subject marker. Together, allomorphy (83a) and (86) account for the fact that, for example, an underlying representation such as /o-a-ut-a/ will surface as [outa].

Second, (83b) is exemplified in (87),

(87) relative agent subject marker third person singular

allomorph /βo-/ before any non-high vowel, possibly with intervening tense marker /a/

a. test-pattern: rm-verb-suffixes
3s-root-tense/extension

[nɛɛrɛ βwɔɔγɛtie]
'it is he (3s-who) has lit (recently)'

[nɛɛrɛ βwɛɛγɛtɛ]
'it is he (3s-who) has seduced (recently)'

[nεεrε βwaañcete]
'it is he (3s-who) has loved (recently)'

[nεεrε βweeβete]
'it is he (3s-who) has forgotten (recently)'

[nεεrε βwoometie]
'it is he (3s-who) has dried (recently)'

b. test-pattern: rm-a-verb-suffixes
3s-t-root-tense/extension

[εrε (oyo) βwɔɔkia] 'he 3s-who lit (earlier today)'
[εrε (oyo) βwεεγa] 'he 3s-who seduced (earlier today)'
[εrε (oyo) βwaañca] 'he 3s-who loved (earlier today)'
[εrε (oyo) βweeβa] 'he 3s-who forgot (earlier today)'
[εrε (oyo) βwoomia] 'he 3s-who dried (earlier today)'

In the context without intervening /a/, phonological rules such as Upper Mid Vowel Raising (βo > βu), Complex Segment Formation (βu > βw), and compensatory lengthening of the following vowel (βwV > βwVV) may regularly apply. When tense marker /a/ does intervene, /a/-Delinking may apply and trigger compensatory lengthening of the following vowel.

To conclude this part of the discussion, the allomorphs for the relative agent subject marker third person singular may be said to be in complementary distribution.

The allomorphs for the relative patient subject marker are identical to those for its relative agent counterpart, viz. /o-/ and /βo-/, and their distribution is almost identical too, as in (88),

(88) allomorphy: relative patient subject marker third person singular ==>

a. o-/ --- [(a) [
tense root/stem

b. βo-/ --- [(a) [{e, ε, a, ɔ, o}[59]
tense root/stem

That is, /o-/ occurs, whenever, with or without intervening tense marker /a/, it is followed by any root-initial segment, but /βo-/ occurs, whenever, with or without intervening tense marker /a/, it is followed by a root-initial non-high vowel.

[59] Judith Moraa judged /o-/ to be possible, but /βo-/ to be more acceptable or correct, before /e/, /ε/, /a/, /ɔ/, and /o/.

First, (88a) is exemplified in (89),

(89) relative patient subject marker third person singular

allomorph /o-/ before a root-initial consonant or vowel, possibly with intervening tense marker /a/

a. test-pattern: rm-verb-suffixes
3s-root-tense/extension

[nεεrε oremire] 'it is he 3s-who is dug' (*[βoremire])
[nεεrε outire] 'it is he 3s-who is blown' (*[βoutire])
[nεεrε oitire] 'it is he 3s-who is hit' (*[βoitire])
[nεεrε oeβire] 'it is he 3s-who is forgotten'
[nεεrε ɔεγire] 'it is he 3s-who is seduced'
[nεεrε oaañcire] 'it is he 3s-who is loved'
[nεεrε ɔɔmire] 'it is he 3s-who is smeared'
[nεεrε oomirie] 'it is he 3s-who is dried'

b. test-pattern: rm-a-verb-suffixes
3s-t-root-tense/extension

[nεεrε oremirwe] 'it is he 3s-who has been dug'
(*[βoaremirwe], *[βoremirwe])
[nεεrε outirwe] 'it is he 3s-who has been blown'
(*[βoautirwe], *[βoutirwe])
[nεεrε oitirwe] 'it is he 3s-who has been hit'
(*[βoaitirwe], *[βoitirwe])
[nεεrε oeeβirwe][60] 'it is he 3s-who has been forgotten'
[nεεrε ɔε(ε)γirwe][61] 'it is he 3s-who has been seduced'
[nεεrε oaakirwe] 'it is he 3s-who has been hit'
[nεεrε ɔɔkiiγwe] 'it is he 3s-who has been lit'
[nεεrε oomiiγwe][62] 'it is he 3s-who has been dried'

---

[60] In monitored speech presumably also [oaeβirwe].

[61] Note that, if the relative patient subject marker third person singular were /a-/, hence the underlying representation of the present tense form /a-a-εγ-ir-u-e/, /a/-Delinking, compensatory lengthening, and x-Trimming would cooperate to derive [εεγirwe]. Thus morphological distinctness, and along with it some semantic clues, would be lost. Therefore, preservation of morphological identity may account, at least in part, for the allomorphy found for the third person singular. Also note that the shape of the allomorph is that of class 1 prefix vowel or augment, viz. /o/.

[62] From /o-a-om-ir-i-γu-e/
rm3s-t-dry-pv-c-p-fv

Second, (88b) is exemplified in (90),

(90) relative patient subject marker third person singular

allomorph /βo-/ before a root-initial non-high vowel, possibly with intervening tense marker /a/

a. test-pattern: rm-verb-suffixes
3s-root-tense/extension

[nεεrε βweeβire] 'it is he 3s-who is forgotten'
[nεεrε βwεεγire] 'it is he 3s-who is seduced'
[nεεrε βwaañcire] 'it is he 3s-who is loved'
[nεεrε βwɔɔmire] 'it is he 3s-who is smeared'
[nεεrε βwoomirie] 'it is he 3s-who is dried'[63]

b. test-pattern: rm-a-verb-suffixes
3s-t-root-tense/extension

[nεεrε βwaeβirwe][64] 'it is he 3s-who has been forgotten'
[nεεrε βwεεγirwe][65] 'it is he 3s-who has been seduced'
[nεεrε βwaakirwe] 'it is he 3s-who has been hit'
[nεεrε βwɔɔkiiγwe] 'it is he 3s-who has been lit'[66]
[nεεrε βwaomiiγwe][67] 'it is he 3s-who has been dried'

Thus the allomorphs of the patient relative marker third person singular are identical to those of its agent counterpart, the distribution of /βo-/ is the same in either case, but that of patient /o-/ appears to be wider than that of its agent counterpart.

---

[63] By the wind, for example.

[64] Or, in virtue of /a/-Delinking etc., [βweeβirwe].

[65] Or, after the application of /a/-Delinking and compensatory lengthening of the following vowel, [βwεεγirwe].

[66] From

/βo-a-ɔk-ir-i-γu-e/
rm3s-t-light-pv-c-p-fv

[67] Or [βwoomiiγwe]. These surface representations derive from

/βo-a-om-ir-i-γu-e/
rm3s-t-dry-pv-c-p-fv

(91) relative agent and patient singular subject markers 2-3s

contexts:

	a. / --- [{C,i,u} root/stem	b. / --- [-cons, αhigh, βmid] [root/stem (not both α = + and β = -)	c. / --- [a tense
markers:			
2s	o-	βo- or o-	ko-
3s	o-	βo-	

The 2s patient allomorph /o-/ may precede any root-initial segment, its agent counterpart only a consonant or a high vowel; that is, the /o-/ under (91b) may be patient only. In the case of either agent or patient third person singular, tense marker /a/ may intervene the allomorph and the root-initial segment in contexts a and b.[68]

---

[68] Some more examples are

1. relative marker: agent

a. before a consonant

pattern: /rm-sik-et-e/
who-respect-t-fv
'who respect'

sg	1	(iñce) [nsiγete]
	2	(ayε) [**osi**γete]
	3	(εrε) [**osi**γete]
pl	1	(intwe) [tosiγete]
	2	(inwe) [mosiγete]
	3	(βaraβuo) [βasiγete]

b. before tense vowel /a/

pattern: /rm-a-ku-et-e/
who-t-fall-t-fv
'who fell'

Whiteley's treatment of relative markers in (1960: 9) is insufficient, in that it mentions, but does not account for, the morphemes about to be discussed. His account in (1956: 56, 68) is clear semantically, but only in part morphologically. With respect to "the general relative" of 'to be' he says that "Two forms occur: 1. 'The man who...; The basket which...' Formed from the auxiliary [i.e. -re] (...) with special prefixes in Class 1 (2nd.

---

sg	1	(iñce) [naaγweete]
	2	(ayε) [**kw**aaγweete]
	3	(εrε) [**o**γweete]
pl	1	(intwe) [twaaγweete]
	2	(inwe) [mwaaγweete]
	3	(βaraβuo) [βaaγweete]

2. relative marker: patient

a. before a consonant

		active tense	passive tense
pattern:		/rm-sik-ir-e/ who-root-pv-fv 'who is/are respected'	/rm-ta-a-sik-et-u-e/ who-not-t-root-t-p-fv 'who was/were not respected'
sg	1	(iñce) [nsikire]	[ntaasiγetwe]
	2	(ayε) [**o**sikire]	[**o**taasiγetwe]
	3	(εrε) [**o**sikire]	[**o**taasiγetwe]
pl	1	(intwe) [twaasikire]	[totaasiγetwe]
	2	(inwe) [mwaasikire]	[motaasiγetwe]
	3	(βaraβuo) [βaasikire]	[βataasiγetwe]

b. before a vowel

pattern:		/rm-aNc-ir-e/ who-love-pv-fv 'who is/are respected'
sg	1	(iñce) [naañcire]
	2	(ayε) [**βw**aañcire]
	3	(εrε) [**βw**aañcire]
pl	1	(intwe) [twaañcire]
	2	(inwe) [mwaañcire]
	3	(βaraβuo) [βaañcire]

(or /-anc-/; either underlying representation is turned into |-aañc-|)

and 3rd. Person) only: Cl. 1/2 nde, kware, ore, tore, more, bare; Cl. 3/4 ore/ere; Cl. 5/6 rire/are; etc. [meaning the relative markers previously discussed] 2. 'The particular man who...; the particular thing which...' As 1, but with initial vowel. Note the inter-vocalic 'y' in classes 1,3,4,6, and 9: Cl. 1/2 oyore/abare; Cl. 3/4 oyore/eyere; Cl. 5/6 erire/ayare; Cl. 7/8 ekere/ebire; Cl. 9/10 eyere/echire; Cl. 11 orore; Cl. 12 akare; Cl 14 obore; Cl. 15 okore, Cl. 16 aare" (1960: 56; his spelling is retained).

Apart from the fact that the paradigm for the singulars in the first type of relative seems to mix tenses with and without tense marker /a/, the basic distinction between the two types of relatives is semantically correct. The first type is the one previously discussed in this section. The second type is correctly defined semantically as "particular". The markers are identical to the proximate demonstrative discussed in section 3.2.5.1 and also by Whiteley (1956: 15-16).

He suggests that this demonstrative or its homomorph may also be used as a relative subject marker, instead of the regular relative markers. However, this does not seem to be correct, except, possibly, in the case of classes 1 and 3, in some tenses. Generally, the relative marker is retained and, depending on the meaning to be expressed, the relevant demonstrative may be added, as in (92),

(92) a. non-relative

[omoonto oyo aγεεnda] 'this man used to go'

b. non-particular relative

[omoonto ɔγεεnda] 'a/the man who went'

c. proximate demonstrative or particular relative

[omoonto oyo ɔγεεnda]

'this man who went' (physically near)
'the (aforementioned) man who went'

Similarly, another supposedly representative example, <rigena eriagwa> (1956: 68), turned out to be [riiγena eri riaaγwa] 'the stone which fell'. Also compare [ciηiti ciria ciaciete] 'the (those) animals that went (recently)' and [ciηiti eci cire aiγa] 'the animals that are here'. In view of examples such as these, perhaps the simplest account is to say that the proximate demonstrative may mean either 'this', where the referent is physically present and near, or 'the particular one, the aforementioned one', where the referent may not be present, but has been recently mentioned, and is certainly known or understood.[69] Thus it seems appropriate to talk of the proximate or referential demonstrative.

---

[69] The distinction between (92b) and (92c) may possibly correspond respectively with the difference between rheme and theme, but this supposition requires systematic verification.

It may be added that the non-proximate demonstrative may also be used in this way, but with the different sense of either 'that' (i.e. visibly over there) in its demonstrative use, or 'the one, that one' (physically absent, but mentioned a while ago and certainly known or understood) in what will here be termed its referential use. A similar usage of the semi-proximate demonstrative is exemplified below.

The proximate demonstrative or its homomorph may also be used as a prefix proper. This is here termed the referential prefix (abbreviation: rpx). It may be so used at least with some parts of speech other than the verb. But perhaps it may be so used to a limited extent also with verbs (I will return to this in a moment).

First, consider the paradigm of this demonstrative-cum-prefix in (93),

(93) proximate/referential demonstrative and referential prefix

1	/oyo(-)/
2	/aβa(-)/
3	/oyo(-)/
4	/eye(-)/
5	/eri(-)/
6	/aya(-)/
7	/eke(-)/
8	/eβi(-)/
9	/eye(-)/
10	/eci(-)/
11	/oro(-)/
12	/aka(-)/
14	/oβo(-)/
15	/oko(-)/
16	/aya(-)/
21	= 9 or 16

Its (optional) usage as a referential demonstrative in combination with the relative marker, in order to express particular meaning, is exemplified in (94), together with the referential usage of the non-proximate demonstrative,

(94) a. pattern: /rm-a-ku-et-e/
rm-t-fall-t-fv
'which fell (recently)'

1	(oyo, oria) [oγweete]
2	(aβa, βaria) [βaaγweete]
3	(oyo, oria) [oγweete]
4	(eye, eria) [yaaγweete]
5	(eri, riria) [riaγweete]
6	(aya, aria) [a(a)γweete]
7	(eke, keria) [kiaγweete]
8	(eβi, βiria) [βiaγweete]

9 (eye, eria) [yaaγweete]
10 (eci, ciria) [ciaγweete]
11 (oro, roria) [rwaγweete]
12 (aka, karia) [kaaγweete]
14 (oβo, βoria) [βwaγweete]
15 (oko, koria) [kwaγweete]
16 (aa, aria) [aγweete][70]
21 = 9 or 16

b. pattern: /rm-sik-ir-e/
rm-respect-pv-fv
'which was respected (recently)'

1 (oyo, oria) [osikire]
2 (aβa, βaria) [βasikire]
3 (oyo, oria) [osikire]
4 (eye, eria) [esikire]
5 (eri, riria) [risikire]
6 (aya, aria) [asikire]
7 (eke, keria) [kesikire]
8 (eβi, βiria) [βisikire]
9 (eye, eria) [esikire]
10 (eci, ciria) [cisikire]
11 (oro, roria) [rosikire]
12 (aka, karia) [γasikire]
14 (oβo, βoria) [βosikire]
15 (oko, koria) [γosikire]
16 (aa, aria) [asikire]
21 = 9 or 16

c. pattern: /rm-aNc-ir-e/
rm-love-pv-fv
'which was loved (recently)'

1 (oyo, oria) [βwaañcire]
2 (aβa, βaria) [βaañcire]
3 (oyo, oria) [βwaañcire]
4 (eye, eria) [yaañcire]
5 (eri, riria) [riaañcire]
6 (aya, aria) [aañcire]
7 (eke, keria) [γiaañcire]
8 (eβi, βiria) [βiaañcire]
9 (eye, eria) [yaañcire]
10 (eci, ciria) [ciaañcire]
11 (oro, roria) [rwaañcire]

---

[70] Also [ase (aiγa) aγweete] 'the place here which fell'.

12 (aka, karia) [γaaañcire]
14 (oβo, βoria) [βwaañcire]
15 (oko, koria) [γwaañcire]
16 (aa, aria) [aañcire]
21 = 9 or 16

The referential proximate demonstrative may be linked to the following tense-form through liaison, accounted for by the rules discussed in section 2.4. Thus the example previously given, [omoonto oyo ɔγεεnda] 'this man who went, the (aforementioned) man who went' may be rendered as [omoonto oyɔ ɔγεεnda].

Such liaison may have led Whiteley to misinterpret the morphological details of the particular relative. It may also account for his mistaken interpretation of the distinction between agent and patient relatives. When he supposes that "where the relative is the object rather than the subject of the verb (..), the relative follows the object and is the same as demonstrative (1) but with a different tone: amare aya twarora 'the clouds which we saw'" (1956: 68). However, the meaning here may just be, as before, a particular relative.[71]

Nonetheless, it is just possible that the referential prefix may be used as a relative marker, but in classes 1 and 3 only, and perhaps in some tenses only. Relativisation with indefinite meaning is regularly expressed without proximate or non-proximate demonstrative, and its counterpart with definite meaning regularly with either of these, as in (94). But instead of, for example, ¦o-mo-onto oyo o-a-γεεnd-et-e¦ --> [omoonto oyo ɔγεεndετε] or [..oyɔ ɔγεεndετε], the alternatives in (95) were also found,

---

[71] This point may require further examination. Examples such as [ntwaarɔra amaγena aya] 'we saw these stones' and [amaγena aya twaarɔra] 'the (particular) stones (that) we saw' (relative marker left implicit) do exhibit a tonal difference, but this involves the examples as a whole. And there is a tonal and semantic difference between the following examples,

[éáηgá ¦ eriá yoomá]
'the cloth ¦ that has dried'
(where the cloth is absent)

[éáηgá ¦ ériá yóomá]
'the/that cloth ¦ that has dried'
(where the cloth is present)

but this, if correct, appears to be of a different nature. I have not been able to corroborate Whiteley's suggested tonal difference corresponding to the object or subject function of the relative marker. However, since neither he, nor I give a systematic account of Gusii tone, it seems inadvisable to speculate on this point in the present state of our knowledge of the language.

(95) 1 |o-mo-onto oyo o-yo-a-γɛɛnd-et-e|
a-1-man dem-1 a-rm1-t-walk-t-fv
[omoonto oyo ɔyɔɔγɛɛndɛtɛ]
'the/this man who walked (long ago)'

3 |o-yo o-yo-a-γɛɛnd-et-e| --> [oyo ɔyɔɔγɛɛndɛtɛ]

The forms for the other morphosyntactic classes in the same paradigm (not exemplified) are as in (94a). There is as yet no independent rule that accounts for the delinking of tense marker /a/ and the spreading of the /o/ of /yo/. Unless these examples may be accounted for by postulating underlying representations such as /o-yo-o../, they are somewhat idiosyncratic. But a possible alternative account may be to argue that the /o/ of /yo/ is delinked, just like the regular relative marker /o/, whenever it is followed by tense marker /a/, such that the former is lenghtened compensatorily and stays that way since it occurs word-internally, whereas word-initial /o/ is either trimmed down again in virtue of the constraint on marginal long vowels, after being so lengthened, or not lengthened at all in virtue of the same constraint (depending on how one views the nature of the latter).

Tentatively adopting the allomorphy approach in such tenses, I observe that the same type of restricted allomorpy seems to be possible in definite relativisation involving the semi-proximate demonstrative (i.e. as demonstrative, not as a relative marker). Compare the forms for classes 1 and 3 in paradigm (96),

(96) 1 |omoonto o-yo-o o-a-γɛɛnd-et-e|
a-1-man 1-that rm1-t-walk-t-fv
[omoonto oyuo ɔγɛɛndɛtɛ]
'that person who went'

2 |aβaanto a-βa-o βa-a-γɛɛnd-et-e|
a-2-man 2-those rm2-t-walk-t-fv
[aβaanto aβuo βaaγɛɛndɛtɛ]
'those people who went'

3 |o-yo-o a-γɛɛnd-et-e| --> [oyuo ɔγɛɛndɛtɛ]
4 |e-ye-o e-a-γɛɛnd-et-e| --> [eyio yaaγɛɛndɛtɛ]
5 |e-ri-o ri-a-γɛɛnd-et-e| --> [erio riaγɛɛndɛtɛ]
6 |a-ya-o a-a-γɛɛnd-et-e| --> [ayuo aγɛɛndɛtɛ]
7 |e-ke-o ke-a-γɛɛnd-et-e| --> [ekio kiaγɛɛndɛtɛ]
8 |e-βi-o βi-a-γɛɛnd-et-e| --> [eβio βiaγɛɛndɛtɛ]
9 |e-ye-o e-a-γɛɛnd-et-e| --> [eyio yaaγɛɛndɛtɛ]
10 |e-ci-o ci-a-γɛɛnd-et-e| --> [ecio ciaγɛɛndɛtɛ]
11 |o-ro-o ro-a-γɛɛnd-et-e| --> [orwo rwaγɛɛndɛtɛ]
12 |a-ka-o ka-a-γɛɛnd-et-e| --> [akuo kaaγɛɛndɛtɛ]
14 |o-βo-o βo-a-γɛɛnd-et-e| --> [oβwo βwaγɛɛndɛtɛ]
15 |o-ko-o ko-a-γɛɛnd-et-e| --> [okwo kwaγɛɛndɛtɛ]
16 |a-ya-o a-γɛɛnd-et-e| --> [ayuo aγɛɛndɛtɛ]
21 = 9 or 16

with their apparently acceptable alternatives in paradigm (97),

(97)
1 [omoonto oyuo ɔyɔγεεndεtε] 'that person who went'
2 [aβaanto aβuo aβaaγεεndεtε] 'those people who went'
3 |o-yo-o o-yo-o-a-γεεnd-et-e| --> [oyuo ɔyɔγεεndεtε]
4 |e-ye-o e-ye-a-γεεnd-et-e| --> [eyio eyaaγεεndεtε]
5 |e-ri-o e-ri-a-γεεnd-et-e| --> [erio eriaγεεndεtε]
6 |a-ya-o a-ya-a-γεεnd-et-e| --> [ayuo ayaaγεεndεtε]
7 |e-ke-o e-ke-a-γεεnd-et-e| --> [ekio ekiaaγεεndεtε]
8 |e-βi-o e-βi-a-γεεnd-et-e| --> [eβio eβiaaγεεndεtε]
9 |e-ye-o e-ye-a-γεεnd-et-e| --> [eyio eyaaγεεndεtε]
10 |e-ci-o e-ci-a-γεεnd-et-e| --> [ecio eciaaγεεndεtε]
11 |o-ro-o o-ro-a-γεεnd-et-e| --> [orwo orwaaγεεndεtε]
12 |a-ka-o a-ka-a-γεεnd-et-e| --> [akuo akaaγεεndεtε]
14 |o-βo-o o-βo-a-γεεnd-et-e| --> [oβwo oβwaaγεεndεtε]
15 |o-ko-o o-ko-a-γεεnd-et-e| --> [okwo okwaaγεεndεtε]
16 |a-ya-o a-ya-a-γεεnd-et-e| --> [ayuo ayaaγεεndεtε]
21 = 9 or 16

A final remark on relativisation is that allomorphy of the relative marker is not at all determined by the syntactic function of its antecedent, which may be a subject, an object, or a complement in the sentence. Consider (98),

(98) a. agentive relative marker

/na-a-ro-oc-e o-mo-Nto o-a-ak-et-e/
sm1-t-see-pv-fv a-1-person 1-t-kick-past-fv
[naarooce omoonto oaaγεtε]
'I saw the man who kicked (recently)'[72]

/o-mo-Nto o-a-ak-et-e n-a-a-ro-oc-u-e/
a-1-man 1rel-t-kick-past-fv f-3s-t-see-pv-p-fv
[omoonto oaaγete naaroocwe na iñce]
'the man who kicked was seen with me'
(not 'by me')

/o-mo-Nto o-a-ak-et-e na-a-a-mo-ro-oc-u-e/
a-1-man 1rel-t-kick-past-fv f-3s-t-him-see-pv-p-fv
[omoonto oaaγete naamorooce]
the-person who-kicked I-saw-him
'I saw the man who kicked'

[72] -rooce is an exceptional perfective, from |korɔra| 'to see'.

/o-mo-Nto βo-a-ak-et-e n-a-a-ro-oc-u-e/
a-1-man 1rel-t-kick-past-fv f-3s-t-see-pv-p-fv
[omoonto βoaaγete naaroocwe]
the-person who-kicked he-was-seen
'the man who kicked was seen'

or (no difference)

/o-mo-Nto o-yo o-a-ak-et-e n-a-a-ro-oc-ii-γu-e
a-1-man a-1rel-t-kick-past-fv f-3s-t-see-pv-c-pas-fv
na n-ce/
by f-me
[omoonto oyo oaaγete naaroociiγwe na iñce]
'the man who kicked was seen by me'

b. patient relative marker

/n-na-a-ro-oc-e o-mo-Nto o-yo o-a-ak-et-u-e/
f-sm1-t-see-pv-fv a-1-person this 1-t-kick-past-p-fv
[nnaarooce omoonto oyooaaγetwe]
'I saw the man who was kicked'
(here */o-a-ak-et-u-e/ --> *[oaaγetwe] was given at first with some hesitation and then rejected)

/n-na-a-ro-oc-e o-mo-Nto o-yo-a-ak-et-u-e
f-sm1-t-see-pv-fv a-1-person a-1rel-t-kick-past-p-fv
na a-βa-r-a-βa-ɔ/
by a-2-demonstrative
[nnaarooce omoonto oyoaaγetwe na aβarabuɔ]
'I saw the man who was kicked by them'

/o-mo-Nto o-yo-o-a-ak-et-u-e
a-1-man a-1rel-1-t-kick-past-p-fv
n-a-a-ro-oc-ii-γu-e na n-ce/
f-3s-t-see-pv-c-pas-fv by f-me
[omoonto oyooaaγetwe naarooci iγwe na iñce]
'the man who kicked was seen with me'

(with the same sense: /o-a-ak-et-u-e/ --> [oaaγetwe])

To summarise, relativisation is regularly expressed through a relative subject marker encoded on the verb. This may be made particular through the additional referential use of the proximate or non-proximate demonstratives. The various relative constructions distinguished by Whiteley (1956: 56-57, 67-68) are essentially variations on this theme. Finally, as one or two examples already given indicate, relativity may also be left implicit (as in English; contrast 'the man I saw' with 'the man whom I saw').[73]

3.2.3.3. Object marker.

The verbal object marker (om), the morphology and use of which is discussed here, takes the following underlying forms for the various morphosyntactic classes,

(99) verbal object marker

a.	1	/mo-/ (= 3s under b)
	2	/βa-/ (= 3p under b)
	3	/yo-/
	4	/ye-/
	5	/ri-/
	6	/ya-/
	7	/ke-/
	8	/βi-/
	9	/ye-/
	10	/ci-/
	11	/ro-/
	12	/ka-/
	14	/βo-/
	15	/ko-/
	16	/ya-/
	21	= 16

[73] Another example is

omoonto oria | | twaita
a/the man | (whom) | we saw
'a/the man whom we beat' (the man is absent).

The following one was also recorded

[omoonto oyo |oria| twaita]
the man |whom| we saw
'the man whom we beat' (the man is present and visible)

This seems odd, as it combines the referential use of both the proximate and the non-proximate demonstrative. If correct, it suggests that the latter is indeed used as a relative pronoun proper. But since my data are insufficient on this point, I must leave this to future research. I have also accidentally omitted to check restrictive versus non-restrictive relativity.

b. Class of personal or animate referents

singular	1 /n(V)-/ 'me' 2 /ko-/ 'you' 3 /mo-/ 'him, her, it' (= 1 under a)
plural	1 /to-/ 'us' 2 /βa-/ 'you' 3 /βa-/ 'them' (= 2 under a)

This agrees with Whiteley's presentation (1956: 25, 1960: 10), except in the case of class 16, for which he gives /a-/. His entry /ya-/ for class 4 in (1960: 10) appears to be an error, but he corrrectly gives /ye-/ in (1956: 25).

As pointed out, the verbal object marker is optional. It seems to depend on the choice of meaning one wishes to express and the way in which one wishes to express it. In addition to the direct object, there are other types of object. Several of these may be simultaneously encoded on some verb form. Though they are morphologically identical to the markers in (99), each of them performs a different semantic role. They are discussed in section 3.3.3.6. The rest of this section is devoted to the markers in (99) and their allomorphy.

When the object markers are followed by a consonant, which is followed in turn by a non-lower mid vowel, their underlying representations in (99) regularly appear on the surface. In other contexts, applicable phonological rules discussed in Chapter Two and some additional ones, regularly cause surface variation. Some of this is exemplified in (100),

(100) verbal object markers exemplified

1. infinitival test-pattern: /ko-om-it-a/
15-om-beat-fv

a. class 1-21

1	/ko-mo-it-a/ 15-him-beat-fv	-->	[komoita] 'to beat 1-him'
2	/ko-βa-it-a/ 15-them-beat-fv	-->	[koβaita] 'to beat 2-them'
3	/ko-yo-it-a/ 15-it-beat-a	-->	[koyoita], [koñoita] 'to beat 3-it'
4	/ko-ye-it-a/ 15-them-beat-fv	-->	[koyeita], [koñeita] 'to beat 4-them'
5	/ko-ri-it-a/	-->	[koriita] 'etc.'
6	/ko-ya-it-a/	-->	[koyaita], [koñaita]
7	/ko-ke-it-a/	-->	[koγeita]
8	/ko-βi-it-a/	-->	[koβiita]
9	/ko-ye-it-a/	-->	[koyeita], [koñeita]

10	/ko-ci-it-a/	-->	[γociita]
11	/ko-ro-it-a/	-->	[koroita]
12	/ko-ka-it-a/	-->	[koγaita]
14	/ko-βo-it-a/	-->	[koβoita]
15	/ko-ko-it-a/	-->	[koγoita]
16	/ko-ya-it-a/	-->	[koyaita], [koñaita]
21	= 9 or 16		

b. Class of personal or animate referents

singular

1	/ko-n-it-a/ -->	[kooηita] 'to beat me'
2	/ko-ko-it-a/ -->	[koγoita] 'to beat you'
3	/ko-mo-it-a/ -->	[komoita] 'to beat him/her/it'

plural

1	/ko-to-it-a/ -->	[γotoita] 'to beat us'
2	/ko-βa-it-a/ -->	[koβaita] 'to beat you'
3	/ko-βa-it-a/ -->	[koβaita] 'to beat them'

2. infinitival test-pattern: /ko-om-ur-a/
15-om-snatch[74]-fv

1	/ko-mo-ur-a/ 15-him-beat-fv	-->	[komoura] 'to snatch 1-him'
2	/ko-βa-ur-a/ 15-them-beat-fv	-->	[koβaura] 'to snatch 2-them'
3	/ko-yo-ur-a/ 15-it-beat-fv	-->	[koyoura], [koñoura] 'to snatch 3-it'
	and, leaving out syntactic and semantic details,		
4	/ko-ye-ur-a/	-->	[koyeura], [koñeura]
5	/ko-ri-ur-a/	-->	[koriura]
6	/ko-ya-ur-a/	-->	[koyaura], [koñaura]
7	/ko-ke-ur-a/	-->	[koγeura]
8	/ko-βi-ur-a/	-->	[koβiura]
9	/ko-ye-ur-a/	-->	[koyeura], [koñeura]
10	/ko-ci-ur-a/	-->	[γociura]
11	/ko-ro-ur-a/	-->	[koroura]
12	/ko-ka-ur-a/	-->	[γokaura]
14	/ko-βo-ur-a/	-->	[koβoura]
15	/ko-ko-ur-a/	-->	[γokoura]
16	/ko-ya-ur-a/	-->	[koyaura], [koñaura]
21	= 9 or 16		

---

[74] The full sense is 'to snatch from, to take (by force)'.

First, allomorphy of object markers 7, 12, 15 and infinitival marker 10 in (100.1) is accounted for by Consonantal Voicing Dissimilation (see section 2.3.1).

Second, in both paradigms, apparently free variation which may occur between [yV] and [ñV] is also indicated. In any object marker of the shape /yV-/, front-glide /y/ may alternate with palatal nasal /ñ/. This may be accounted for as in (101),

(101) allomorphy: free morphological variation (optional)

y --> ñ / [---
object marker

Since verbal morphosyntax is such that this variation always occurs intervocalically, and no other possible determinants of the change were discovered, the preceding vowel need not be specified in the context of this rule. This involves object markers 3 /yo-/, 6 /ya-/, 9 /ye-/, and 16 /ya-/.

Because, in addition, other phonological rules discussed in Chapter Two, such as Upper Mid Vowel Raising (see 2.3.10), Complex Segment Formation (2.3.11), and Mid Vowel Height Spreading (2.3.14), may apply, the allomorphs [yo or ño, yu or ñu, yw or ñw, yɔ or ñɔ] may occur for object marker class 3, and [ye or ñe, yi or ñi, or ñy, yɛ or ñɛ] may be found for object marker class 9.

Moreover, Complex Segment Formation may trigger compensatory lengthening of the following vowel, and the /a/ of 6, 16 /ya/ or /ña/ may undergo /a/-Delinking and likewise trigger compensatory lengthening of the following vowel. These types of variation are also found in the imperatives in (102), where the object markers in question occur word-initially,

(102) object marker allomorphy

[yoire], [ñoire] 'take 3-it'
[yeire], [ñeire] 'take 4-them'
[yaire], [ñaire] 'take 6-them'
[yeire], [ñeire] 'take 9-it'

[ñweeβe] 'forget 3-it'
[ñieeβe] 'forget 4-them'
[yaeβe], [ñaeeβe], [ñeeβe] 'forget 6-them'
[ñeeβe] 'forget 9-it'

[ñwɛγɛkɛ] 'hit 3-it'
[yɛɛγɛkɛ], [ñɛɛγɛkɛ] 'hit 4-them'
[yaɛγɛkɛ], [ñaɛγɛkɛ] 'hit 6-them'
[ñɛɛγɛkɛ], *[yɛɛγɛkɛ] 'hit 9-it'

[ñwaake] 'hit 3-it'
[ñiaake] 'hit 4-them'
[yaaake] 'hit 6-them'
[ñiaake] 'hit 9-it'

[ñwɔɔnie] 'sell 3-it'
[yɛɔnie] 'sell 4-them' (presumably also [ñɛɔnie])
[yaɔnie] 'sell 6-them'
[ñɛɔnie] 'sell 9-it' (possibly also [ñeɔnie], where Mid vowel Height Spreading has not applied)

[ñworokie], ?[yworokie] 'make 3-it appear'
[ñiorokie], ?[yeorokie] 'make 4-them appear'
[yaorokie], ?[ñaorokie] 'make 6-them appear'
[ñiorokie], [yiorokie], [yiorokie] 'make 9-it appear'

[ywomie], [ñwomie] 'dry 3-it'
[yeomie], [ñiomie] 'dry 4-them'
[yaomie], [ñaomie] 'dry 6-them'
[yeomie], [ñiomie] 'dry 9-it'

[youte], [ñoute] 'blow 3-it out'[75]
[yeute], [ñeute], *[ñiute] 'blow 4-them out'
[yaute], [ñaute] 'blow 6-them out'
[yeute], [ñeute] 'blow 9-it out'[76]

Prenasalisation and compensatory lengthening of the preceding vowel is exemplified in /βa-n-tɛm-a/ --> [βaantɛma] 'they beat me (untimed past)'.

Next, a derivation such as /ko-n-it-a/ --> [kooŋita] 'to beat me' in (100.1.b.1s) shows not only that the underlying alveolar or underspecified nasal is turned into a velar one at the surface, but also that the vowel of the infinitive marker before this first person singular object marker is lengthened. Though this kind of lengthening does occur, its condition and the extent to which it may occur are as yet insufficiently clear, despite Whiteley's summary remarks on it (1960: 6; also see section 2.3.7). The same observation applies to the change of the underlying alveolar or underspecified nasal to a velar or, as in /βa-ka-n-eβ-a/ [βakaañeβa] 'they forgot me (long ago)', a palatal surface nasal. It would seem that the process may plausibly be considered as a fairly low-level rule of phonetic implementation.

The types of allomorphy or phonologically determined surface variation equally occur in tenses, as in (103),

---

[75] Or 'blow on 3-it'; thus also in the following examples.

[76] Judith Moraa judged allomorphs of the shape [ñV] more correct than [yV], but thought both acceptable and grammatical.

(103) test-pattern: /sm-a-om-eβ-ir-e/
sm-t-om-forget-pv-fv
'sm has/have forgotten om'

a. 1 /βa-a-mo-eβ-ir-e/ --> [βaamweeβire]
15-t-him-forget-fv
'they have forgotten 1-him'

2 /βa-βa-eβ-ir-e/ --> [βaβeeβire]
15-them-forget-fv
'they have forgotten 2-them'

3 /βa-a-yo-eβ-ir-e/ --> [βañweeβire]
15-t-it-forget-fv
'they have forgotten 3-it'

4 /βa-a-ye-eβ-ir-e/ --> [βañieβire]
15-t-them-forget-fv
'they have forgotten 4-them'

similarly,

5 /βa-a-ri-eβ-ir-e/ --> [βaarieβire]
6 /βa-a-ya-eβ-ir-e/ --> [βaañeeβire][77]

7 /βa-a-ke-eβ-ir-e/ --> [βaakieβire]
8 /βa-a-βi-eβ-ir-e/ --> [βaaβieβire]

9 /βa-a-ye-eβ-ir-e/ --> [βaañieβire]
10 /βa-a-ci-eβ-ir-e/ --> [βaacieβire][78]

11 /βa-a-ro-eβ-ir-e/ --> [βaarweeβire]
12 /βa-a-ka-eβ-ir-e/ --> [βaakeeβire]
14 /βa-a-βo-eβ-ir-e/ --> [βaaβweeβire]
15 /βa-a-ko-eβ-ir-e/ --> [βaakweeβire]
16 /βa-a-ya-eβ-ir-e/ --> [βaayeeβire][79]
21 = 9 or 16

---

[77] Contrast with 6 /βa-a-ya-**iβ**-ir-e/ --> [βaañaiβire] 'they have stolen 6-them'.

[78] or [..cyee..], [..cee..].

[79] Judith Moraa claimed that, if non-specific, [ya] would be used, but if specific, [ña] would be used. This seems doubtful and requires further examination.

b. Class of personal or animate referents

singular

1 /βa-ka-n-eβ-a/	-->	[βakaañeβa] 'they forgot me (long ago)'
2 /βa-ka-ko-eβ-a/	-->	[βaγakweeβa] 'they forgot you'
3 /βa-ka-mo-eβ-a/	-->	[βakamweeβa] 'they forgot him/her'

plural

1 /βa-ka-to-eβ-a/	-->	[βakatweeβa] 'they forgot us'
2 /βa-ka-βa-eβ-a/	-->	[βakaβeeβa] 'they forgot you'
3 /βa-ka-βa-eβ-a/	-->	[βakaβeeβa] 'they forgot them'

Various types of surface variation, e.g. Mid Vowel Height Spreading, are also exemplified in (104),

(104) infinitival test-pattern:

/ko-om-ɛγɛk-er-a/
15-om-support-ap-fv
'to lean against, to support'

1 /ko-mo-ɛγɛkɛr-a/
15-him-lean against-fv
[kɔmɔɛγɛkɛra]
'to lean against 1-him'

2 /ko-βa-ɛγɛkɛr-a/
15-them-lean against-fv
[koβaɛγɛkɛra] or [kɔβɛɛγɛkɛra]
'to lean against 2-them'

3 /ko-yo-ɛγɛkɛr-a/
15-it-lean against-fv
[kɔyɔɛγɛkɛra] or [koywɛ(ɛ)γɛkɛra]
'to lean against 3-it'

4	/ko-ye-ɛγɛkɛr-a/	-->	[kɔyɛɛγɛkɛra] or [koyiɛγɛkɛra]
5	/ko-ri-ɛγɛkɛr-a/	-->	[koriɛγɛkɛra]
6	/ko-ya-ɛγɛkɛr-a/	-->	[koyaɛγɛkɛra] or [kɔyɛɛγɛkɛra] (or ñ for y in either case)
7	/ko-ke-ɛγɛkɛr-a/	-->	[γɔkɛɛγɛkɛra] or [γokiɛγɛkɛra]
8	/ko-βi-ɛγɛkɛr-a/	-->	[koβiɛγɛkɛra]
9	/ko-ye-ɛγɛkɛr-a/	-->	[kɔyɛɛγɛkɛra] or [koñiɛγɛkɛra]
10	/ko-ci-ɛγɛkɛr-a/	-->	[γociɛγɛkɛra]
11	/ko-ro-ɛγɛkɛr-a/	-->	[kɔrɔɛγɛkɛra] or [korwɛɛγɛkɛra]
12	/ko-ka-ɛγɛkɛr-a/	-->	[γokaɛγɛkɛra] or [γokɛɛγɛkɛra]

14 /ko-βo-εγεkεr-a/ --> [kɔβɔεγεkεra] or [koβwεεγεkεra]
15 /ko-ko-εγεkεr-a/ --> [γɔkɔεγεkεra] or [γokwεεγεkεra]
16 /ko-ya-εγεkεr-a/ --> [koyaεγεkεra] or [kɔyεεγεkεra]
21 = 9 or 16

These examples are evidence for a relatively free variation in the order of Upper Mid Vowel Raising, and subsequent Complex Segement Formation and compensatory lengthening of the next vowel, on the one hand, and Mid Vowel Height Spreading, on the other hand, in Judith's speech, who commented moreover that this type of variation depends on the speaker or may differ per utterance in the speech of one and the same speaker.

This tension between Mid Vowel Height Spreading versus Upper Mid Vowel Raising and other rules triggered off by it, is further exemplified, with other rules, in (105),

(105) infinitival test-pattern

|ko-om-ɔti-a|
15-om-warm-fv
'to warm om'

1 /ko-mo-ɔt-i-a/
15-him-warm-c-fv
[kɔmɔɔtia] or [komwɔɔtia]
'to warm 1-him'

2 /ko-βa-ɔt-i-a/
15-them-warm-c-fv
[kɔβɔɔtia]
'to warm 2-them'

similarly, for 'it' and 'them',

3 /ko-yo-ɔt-i-a/ --> [kɔyɔɔtia], [koñwɔɔtia]
4 /ko-ye-ɔt-i-a/ --> [koyeɔtia], [koyiɔtia], [koñiɔɔtia]
5 /ko-ri-ɔt-i-a/ --> [koriɔtia]
6 /ko-ya-ɔt-i-a/ --> [koyaɔtia], [koñaɔtia], [koñɔɔtia]
7 /ko-ke-ɔt-i-a/ --> [koγeɔtia], [koγiɔtia]
8 /ko-βi-ɔt-i-a/ --> [koβiɔtia]
9 /ko-ye-ɔt-i-a/ --> [koyeɔtia], [koyiɔtia], [koñiɔtia]
10 /ko-ci-ɔt-i-a/ --> [γociɔtia], [γoc(y)ɔɔtia]
11 /ko-ro-ɔt-i-a/ --> [koruɔtia]
12 /ko-ka-ɔt-i-a/ --> [kɔγɔɔtia]
14 /ko-βo-ɔt-i-a/ --> [koβuɔtia]
15 /ko-ko-ɔt-i-a/ --> [koγuɔtia]
16 /ko-ya-ɔt-i-a/ --> [kɔyɔɔtia], [kɔñɔɔtia]
21 = 9 or 16

Here /a/-Delinking does apply, together with the Linking Rule, in 2, 12, and 16 (a + ɔ > ɔɔ), but not in 6. Neither Mid Vowel Height Spreading, nor Upper Mid Vowel Raising apply in 4 and 7. However, the former does apply in 1 and 3 (o + ɔ > ɔɔ), and the latter in 9, 11, 14, and 15 (e + ɔ > iɔ and o + ɔ > uɔ). This paradigm not only exemplifies that surface variation may be considerable, but also that certain types of rule-application are optional. Generally, a tension is often noticeable between, on the one hand, the tendency of certain rules to apply and, on the other hand, a tendency toward preservation of morphological identity.

Other aspects of the verbal object marker, such as its relative position in verbal structure, the differentiation of various types of object marker, and the relative order of these sub-types in verbal structure, will be discussed in subsections 3.2.3.3.1-3.

3.2.3.4. Summary of subject markers.

It may be useful to summarise the results of the discussion of the subject markers in sections 3.2.3.1-2 in one place, as in (106), where "non-high" strictly designates non-high vowels only,

(106) second and third person singular subject markers

second person singular (agent/patient):

a. non-relative[80]

	context	allomorph
(1)	--- a [tense	ko-
(2)	--- [non-high root/stem	*β*o-
(3)	--- [root/stem	o-

[80] The following alternative arrangement for agent and patient second person singular subject marker visually expresses the difference in distribution of its allomorph /o-/ in its non-relative and relative usage more immediately,

	context	a. non-relative	b. relative
(1)	--- a [tense	ko-	ko-
(2)	--- [non-high root/stem	*β*o-	*β*o-
(3)	--- [root/stem	o-	
(4)	--- [{C,i,u} root/stem		o-

b. relative

	context	allomorph
(1)	--- a [tense	ko-
(2)	--- [non-high root/stem	βo-
(3)	--- [{C,i,u} root/stem	o-

third person singular:

c. non-relative

	context	allomorph	
(1)	--- a [tense	o- a-	(agent; also βo-?[81]) (patient)
(2)	--- [root/stem	a-	(agent/patient)

[81] In context

/--- [a [non-high
tense root

d. relative

	context	allomorph	
(1)	--- (a)[$_{tense}$ [$_{root/stem}$ non-high	βo-	(agent/patient)
(2)	--- (a)[$_{tense}$ [$_{root/stem}$ {C,i,u}	o-	(agent)
(3)	--- (a)[$_{tense}$ [$_{root/stem}$	o-	(patient)

If these data and their analysis are correct, the allomorphy of 2-3s subject markers may be summarised as follows.

Before tense vowel /a/, second person singular is always /ko-/ in any usage (106a.1, b.1). Immediately before a root or stem, its allomorphy seems to be phonologically determined and distributed differently according to non-relative or relative usage. If non-relative, its allomorphs are in partial complementary distribution, viz. /βo-/ before non-high root vowels only (106a.2) and /o-/ anywhere (106a.3). If relative, its allomorphs are in strict complementary distribution: /βo-/ before non-high vowels only (106b.2) and /o-/ elsewhere (106b.3).

The allomorphy of subject marker third person singular is as follows. If non-relative, before tense marker /a/, it is /o-/, if an agent (more restrictedly possibly also /βo-/), and /a-/, if a patient (106c.1); but elsewhere /a-/, whether agent or patient (106c.2). If relative, agent or patient, third person singular is /βo-/ before a root-initial non-high vowel, with or without intervening tense marker /a-/ (106d.1). If agent, its allomorph /o-/ occurs elsewhere in the same context, in complementary distribution (106d.2). If patient, it may occur anywhere in the same context, in partial complementary distribution (106d.3).[82]

3.2.4. Adverbs.

Whiteley lists about a pageful of adverbs (1956: 43-44, 120). He differentiates adverbs of time, place, and manner (1956: 43). In addition, he notes that, "in contrast with the other

---

[82] Since some of the details of this sub-system became clear after I left the field, hence without opportunity for further checking and collection of additional data, I suspect that this analysis, though more explicitly argued and more fully exemplified than Whiteley's exposition of it, is susceptible to further refinement, especially with respect to the analysis of the third person singular marker.

parts of speech (..), adverbs have neither suffixes nor prefixes, they are invariable", and that many adverbs "are formed simply by the omission of an initial vowel" (1956: 43).

At least three comments may be made. As stated, the claim that adverbs have neither prefixes nor suffixes, is incorrect or at least insufficient. Many of them are in fact derived through affixation, such as the adverbs of place in (107),

(107) /a-iγ-a/ --> [aiγa] 'here' (literally, '16-this' or 'this place')

/a-a/ --> [aa] 'here, this place'

/a-γa-o/ --> [aγuo], [aγwo] 'there' (i.e. away from the speaker, but near the addressee; literally, '16-that', or 'that place')

/a-ri-a/ --> [aria] (a) 'over there' (i.e. away from both speaker and addressee, but visible to both of them; literally '16-that (over there)', or 'that place over there'); (b) 'aforementioned' (invisible, but known or understood)

/a-rɔ-rɔ/ --> [arɔrɔ] '(over) there (far away from both speaker and addressee, and out of their sight)'

(This form is mostly used in reported speech to refer to some place mentioned earlier)

Though some adverbs, such as [rεεrɔ] 'today' and [βɔɔnɔ] 'now', may be unanalysable, most of those listed by Whiteley (1956: 120) may in fact be parsed.

Adverbs are indeed regularly non-augmented, and many adverbs are moreover morphologically and semantically related to words belonging to another lexical category. Hence, at least these might be considered as derived from other lexical categories through augment-deletion. In fact, this would account for the shape of the prefix of most adverbs.

Finally, also, adverbs are invariable, but this is to be understood in the sense that they do not participate in the morphysyntactic class and agreement system of the language.

For some more details, see section 3.4.7.

3.2.5. Demonstratives.

In Gusii, deixis is expressed by at least three demonstrative words. These may be used both independently as pronouns, and dependently or attributively as adjectives, so that they might be termed either demonstrative pronouns, or demonstrative adjectives. But regardless of these distinctions, they may be, and are, simply called demonstratives.

Whiteley's discussion of their forms is succinct, but good as far as it goes (1956: 15-16, 85), and therefore taken as a starting-point and more fully worked out here. At least three types of demonstrative may differentiated. These are the proximate demonstrative discussed in section 3.2.5.1, the semi-proximate demonstrative discussed in section 3.2.5.2, and the non-proximate demonstrative discussed in section 3.2.5.3.

3.2.5.1. Proximate demonstrative: this.

The demonstrative discussed here, Whiteley's "demonstrative 1" (1956: 15), is morphologically identical to the referential prefix mentioned in section 3.2.3.2.

Syntactically, it may be used attributively or adjectivally, but also independently or pronominally. In either usage, it may have demonstrative or so-called referential meaning and will here be called demonstrative.

If used attributively with demonstrative meaning, it expresses physical proximity to the speaker, and may thus be translated 'this/these'. Hence it is termed the proximate demonstrative. Of course, if the speaker and his addressee(s) are in close proximity, the referent will also be near to the latter; but though this may accidentally be the case in fact, it is not a necessary part of the meaning.

If used attributively with referential meaning, it designates a known or understood referent which need not be physically present, and may therefore be translated 'the/a (particular or aforementioned)'.

If used independently or pronominally, it may also have demonstrative or referential meaning. These meanings are essentially identical to those in its attributive usage. If demonstrative, it may therefore be translated 'this (one)', plural 'these (ones)'; if referential, it may be translated 'the (aforementioned or particular) one(s)'.

For all classes, the demonstrative is regularly augmented, such that it takes the form [eye] for class 9, [eci] for class 10, and [aya] for class 16. The paradigm, anticipated in section 3.2.3.2, may be repeated for the demonstrative usage, as in (108),

(108) proximate or referential demonstrative

1	/o-yo/	-->	[oyo]
2	/a-βa/	-->	[aβa]
3	/o-yo/	-->	[oyo]
4	/e-ye/	-->	[eye]
5	/e-ri/	-->	[eri]
6	/a-ya/	-->	[aya]
7	/e-ke/	-->	[eke]
8	/e-βi/	-->	[eβi]
9	/e-ye/	-->	[eye]
10	/e-ci/	-->	[eci]
11	/o-ro/	-->	[oro]
12	/a-ka/	-->	[aka]
14	/o-βo/	-->	[oβo]
15	/o-ko/	-->	[oko]
16	/a-ya/	-->	[aya]
	/a-a/	-->	[aa]
	/a-iγa/	-->	[aiγa]
21	= 9 or 16		

Its independent use is exemplified in (109)

(109) singular: 'this one only/alone'
plural: 'these ones only/alone'

1	/o-yo βo-eka/	-->	[oyo βweeka]
2	/a-βa βa-oka/	-->	[aβa βooka]
3	/o-yo βo-oka/	-->	[oyo βwooka]
4	/e-ye e-oka/	-->	[eye yooka]
5	/e-ri ri-oka/	-->	[eri ryooka]
6	/a-ya a-oka/	-->	[aya ooka] or [ayooka]
7	/e-ke ke-oka/	-->	[eke γyooka]
8	/e-βi βi-oka/	-->	[eβi βyooka]
9	/e-ye e-oka/	-->	[eye yooka]
10	/e-ci ci-oka/	-->	[eci cyooka]
11	/o-ro ro-oka/	-->	[oro rwooka]
12	/a-ka ka-oka/	-->	[aka γyooka]
14	/o-βo βo-oka/	-->	[oβo βwooka]
15	/o-ko ko-oka/	-->	[oko γwooka]
16	/a-ya a-oka/	-->	[aya ooka] or [ayooka]
	/n-se a-a/	-->	[(i)nsaa] 'down here'
21	= 9 or 16		

For class 16, the phrase [ase aiγa ooka], in rapid speech [asaiγooka], 'this place only', also occurs. The word /a-iγ-a/ --> [aiγa], used attributively here, means 'this place, here'. Compare [ase aya] 'this place'. Whiteley gives /-iγa/ as the 'more emphatic' form for class 16 (1956: 15), as in (110),

(110) 1	/o-yo-iγa/	-->	[oyoiγa]	'this here'
2	/a-βa-iγa/	-->	[aβaiγa]	'these here'
3	/o-yo-iγa/	-->	[oyoiγa]	etc.
4	/e-ye-iγa/	-->	[eyeiγa]	
5	/e-ri-iγa/	-->	[eriiγa]	
6	/a-ya-iγa/	-->	[ayaiγa]	
7	/e-ke-iγa/	-->	[ekeiγa]	
8	/e-βi-iγa/	-->	[eβiiγa]	
9	/e-ye-iγa/	-->	[eyeiγa]	
10	/e-ci-iγa/	-->	[eciiγa]	
11	/o-ro-iγa/	-->	[oroiγa]	
12	/a-ka-iγa/	-->	[akaiγa]	
14	/o-βo-iγa/	-->	[oβoiγa]	
15	/o-ko-iγa/	-->	[okoiγa]	
16	/a-ya-iγa/	-->	[ayaiγa]	
	/a-iγa/	-->	[aiγa]	
21	= 9 or 16			

Used attributively, the demonstrative, like other modifiers, regularly follows its head, as in [omoonto oyo] 'this person' and [aβaanto aβa] 'these persons'. However, special emphasis may be expressed by a change in this regular word-order, as in (111),

(111) a. [aiγa ñaγεεnkε] 'this Nyageenke' (i.e. as distinct from another place bearing the same name)

contrast with:

[ñaγεεnkε aa][83] 'this Nyageenke'
[ñaγεεnkε aiγa] 'here in Nyageenke'

b. |e-ye N ña-a-ηera|
9-this is 21-of-black cow
[eye ññaaηera]
'this is Nyang'era'
(i.e. black cow, used as proper name)

contrast with:

[ñaaηera eye] 'this Nyang'era', as in
|ña-a-ηera e-ye ta-e-re ko-ri-a βo-ñaansi βo-omo|
21-of-black cow 9-this neg-9-be 15-eat-fv 14-grass 14-dry
[ñaaηera eye terikoria βoñaansi βwoomo]
'this Nyang'era does not eat dry grass'

The independent referential usage of this demonstrative, in an identificatory or emphatic

[83] This example is not certain.

construction, which means '(it is) this (one)' or 'and this one' in the singular, and '(it is) these (ones)' or 'and these ones' in the plural, is exemplified in (112),

(112)	1	/na o-yo/	-->	[nooyo]
	2	/na a-βa/	-->	[naaβa]
	3	/na o-yo/	-->	[nooyo]
	4	/na e-ye/	-->	[neeye]
	5	/na e-ri/	-->	[neeri]
	6	/na a-ya/	-->	[naaya]
	7	/na e-ke/	-->	[neeke]
	8	/na e-βi/	-->	[neeβi]
	9	/na e-ye/	-->	[neeye]
	10	/na e-ci/	-->	[neeci]
	11	/na o-ro/	-->	[nooro]
	12	/na a-ka/	-->	[naaka]
	14	/na o-βo/	-->	[nooβo]
	15	/na o-ko/	-->	[nooko]
	16	/na a-a/	-->	[naa] 'it is here'
		/na a-ya/	-->	[naaya] 'it is 16-this one'[84]
		/na a-iγa/	-->	[naaiγa] 'it is here'
	21	= 9 or 16		

An additional, idiomatic point is that /oyo na oyo/, [oyo nooyo] 'this and that one' is distinct from /oyȯ na ɛrɛ/, [oyo nɛɛrɛ] 'this is the 1-one' (literally, '1-this is he/him').

The discussion of the semi-proximate demonstrative may be anticipated by observing that the demonstratives may be combined in various constructions, such as the associative construction. Its relevant structure, /head of head/, and, in this case, its prefixation are as in (113),

(113) associative construction

[referential demonstrative]	[/ppx-a/]	[semi-proximate demonstrative]
'the-one'	'of'	'that-one'
head		head (prepositional object)

This is exemplified in (114),

[84] At least one informant disconfirmed this alternative.

(114) a. singular: 'the one/this of 1/3-that (one)'
plural: 'the ones/these of 1/3-that (one)'[85]

1	/o-yo βo-a o-yi-o/	-->	[oyo βwooyio]
2	/a-βa βa-a o-yi-o/	-->	[aβa βooоyio]
3	/o-yo βo-a o-yi-o/	-->	[oyo βwooyio]
4	/e-ye e-a o-yi-o/	-->	[eye yooyio]
5	/e-ri ri-a o-yi-o/	-->	[eri riooyio]
6	/a-ya ya-a o-yi-o/	-->	[aya yooyio]
7	/e-ke ke-a o-yi-o/	-->	[eke kiooyio]
8	/e-βi βi-a o-yi-o/	-->	[eβi βiooyio]
9	/e-ye e-a o-yi-o/	-->	[eye yooyio]
10	/e-ci ci-a o-yi-o/	-->	[eci ciooyio]
11	/o-ro ro-a o-yi-o/	-->	[oro rwooyio]
12	/a-ka ka-a o-yi-o/	-->	[aka kooyio]
14	/o-βo βo-a o-yi-o/	-->	[oβo βwooyio]
15	/o-ko ko-a o-yi-o/	-->	[oko kwooyio]
16	/a-ya ya-a o-yi-o/	-->	[aya yooyio]
21	= 9 or 16		

b. singular: 'the one/this of 12-that (one)'
plural: 'the ones/these of 12-that (one)'

1	/o-yo βo-a a-ka-o/	-->	[oyo βwaakuo]
2	/a-βa βa-a a-ka-o/	-->	[aβa βaakuo]
3	/o-yo βo-a a-ka-o/	-->	[oyo βwaakuo]
4	/e-ye e-a a-ka-o/	-->	[eye yaakuo]
5	/e-ri ri-a a-ka-o/	-->	[eri riaakuo]
6	/a-ya ya-a a-ka-o/	-->	[aya yaakuo]
7	/e-ke ke-a a-ka-o/	-->	[eke γiaakuo]
8	/e-βi βi-a a-ka-o/	-->	[eβi βiaakuo]
9	/e-ye e-a a-ka-o/	-->	[eye yaakuo]
10	/e-ci ci-a a-ka-o/	-->	[eci ciaakuo]
11	/o-ro ro-a a-ka-o/	-->	[oro ruaakuo]
12	/a-ka ka-a a-ka-o/	-->	[aka γaakuo]
14	/o-βo βo-a a-ka-o/	-->	[oβo βwaakuo]
15	/o-ko ko-a a-ka-o/	-->	[oko γwaakuo]
16	/a-ya a-a a-ka-o/	-->	[ayaakuo]
21	= 9 or 16		

Note that the form of pronominal prefix 16 is /ya-/ in (114a), but /a-/ in (114b). The

[85] Semi-proximate [oyio] may belong to class 1 or 3.

determinants of this and similar allomorphy are not clear.[86]

3.2.5.2. Semi-proximate demonstrative: that.

The demonstrative discussed in this section is called semi-proximate demonstrative, in contradistinction to the proximate demonstrative discussed in section 3.2.5.1 and to the non-proximate demonstrative discussed in section 3.2.5.3. It is identical to Whiteley's "demonstrative 3" (1956: 15).

It expresses distance from the speaker(s), but not from the addressee(s), i.e. nearness to the latter. If used attributively or adjectivally, it may be translated 'that', plural 'those'. If used independently or pronominally, it may be translated 'that (one)', plural 'those (ones)'. Like the proximate demonstrative, it may also have referential meaning in the sense of 'known or understood, but not seen' and possibly 'the aforementioned' (the latter is also noted in 1956: 15).

Syntactically, it may be used attributively, and as such it regularly follows its head, as in [omoonto oyio] 'that person' or [aβaanto aβuo] 'those persons'. However, a unique allomorph for class 21, to be discussed in a moment, may precede its head, as in [aγuo ñaγεεηkε] 'that Nyageenke'. However, since this demonstrative may also be used independently, the latter example may be conceived of as the apposition of two heads, viz. 'that place' and 'Nyageenke'.

Morphologically, this demonstrative may be formed in one of two ways. One allomorph is composed of the referential prefix (93) (homomorphous with the proximate demonstrative) to which suffix /-o/ is attached, as in (115),

(115) semi-proximate demonstrative ==> /rpx/ + /-o/

---

86 It remains to be ascertained whether the associative contruction may take the form /demonstrative-a-demonstrative/. If this is a possible alternative, the derivation of, for example, class 9, might then be as follows,

input	/e-ye-a-a-ka-o/
Morpholexical /a/-Raising	e-ye-a-a-kuo
Upper Mid Vowel Raising	e-yiaaka-o
Complex Segment Formation	e-yyaakuo
Compensatory Lengthening	e-yyaaakuo
Obligatory Contour Principle	e-yaaakuo
x-Trimming	e-yaakuo
output	[eyaakuo]

I recorded this derivation among my notes, but it escaped the final and definitive round of checking. If this supposition is correct, the alternative for class 16 under (114b) might in fact be /a-ya-a-a-ka-o/ underlyingly. This remains to be checked.

Consider its paradigm in (116),

(116) semi-proximate demonstrative: that.

1	/o-yo-o/	-->	[oyuo]
2	/a-βa-o/	-->	[aβuo]
3	/o-yo-o/	-->	[oyuo]
4	/e-ye-o/	-->	[eyio]
5	/e-ri-o/	-->	[erio]
6	/a-ya-o/	-->	[ayuo]
7	/e-ke-o/	-->	[ekio]
8	/e-βi-o/	-->	[eβio]
9	/e-ye-o/	-->	[eyio]
10	/e-ci-o/	-->	[ecio]
11	/o-ro-o/	-->	[oruo]
12	/a-ka-o/	-->	[akuo]
14	/o-βo-o/	-->	[oβuo]
15	/o-ko-o/	-->	[okuo]
16	/a-ya-o/	-->	[ayuo]
21	= 9 or 16		

An acceptable, and apparently unique, allomorph for class 16 is /a-γa-o/ --> [aγuo].

The change from /a/ to [u] may be accounted for, relatively informally, by (117),

(117) Morpholexical /a/-Raising

$$/a/ \dashrightarrow [u] \;/\; \text{---}\; o \;\Big]_{\left\{\begin{array}{l}\text{semi-proximate demonstrative}\\ \text{independent pronoun}\end{array}\right\}}$$

It simply states that /a/ is changed into [u], whenever it is followed by word-final /o/ in semi-proximate demonstratives and independent pronouns.[87]

[87] As also observed elsewhere, it seems that the final vowel of the independent pronoun may vary idiolectally. If correct, this somewhat ad hoc, but necessary rule may be adjusted by redefining the trigger so as to range over, for example, /o/ and /ɔ/, as the case may be, as follows,

Morpholexical /a/-Raising

$$/a/ \dashrightarrow [u] \;/\; \text{---}\; \begin{bmatrix}\text{-cons}\\ \text{+mid}\\ \text{+back}\end{bmatrix} \Big]_{\text{semi-proximate demonstrative independent pronoun}}$$

At least for the subset of classes 1, 3, 4, 6, 9, and possibly for 16[88], i.e. in all instances where the pronominal prefix has the shape /V-/, the CV-segment following it may be either [yu] or [yi], while the forms for the other classes exhibit no allomorphy. That is, classes 1, 3, 4, and perhaps 16, may also take the exceptional shape [oyio], and classes 4 and 9 the exceptional shape [oyuo]. However, it seems that [oyio] for at least 1, 3, 6 is in fact more common than [oyuo]. This may be formulated in a somewhat ad hoc manner, as in (118),

(118) allomorphy: semi-proximate demonstrative ==>

a. ppx $\left\{\begin{matrix} \text{yi} \\ \text{yu} \end{matrix}\right\}$ o]
classes 1, 3, 4, 6, 9, 16

b. rpx-o]
elsewhere

This, in as far as it yields allomorphy different from that in (116), is exemplified in (119),

(119) semi-proximate demonstrative allomorphy

1	/o-yi-o/	-->	[oyio]
3	/o-yi-o/	-->	[oyio]
4	/e-yu-o/	-->	[eyuo]
6	/a-yi-o/	-->	[ayio]
9	/e-yu-o/	-->	[eyuo]
16	/a-yi-o/	-->	[ayio]
21	= 9 or 16		

The independent usage of semi-proximate demonstrative is further exemplified in (120),

Similarly, should the rule turn out to be applicable also in other lexical categories, it may be further readjusted.

[88] Informant judgments were not unanimous on this.

(120)	1	/o-yo-o βo-eka/	-->	[oyuo βweeka]
	2	/a-βa-o βa-oka/	-->	[aβuɔ βooka]
	3	/o-yo-o βo-oka/	-->	[oyuo βwooka]
	4	/e-yi-o e-oka/	-->	[eyio yooka]
	5	/e-ri-o ri-oka/	-->	[erio ryooka]
	6	/a-yi-o a-oka/	-->	[ayio ooka]
	7	/e-ke-o ke-oka/	-->	[ekio γyooka]
	8	/e-βi-o βi-oka/	-->	[eβio βyooka]
	9	/e-yi-o e-oka/	-->	[eyio yooka]
	10	/e-ci-o ci-oka/	-->	[ecio cyooka]
	11	/o-ro-o ro-oka/	-->	[orwo rwooka]
	12	/a-ka-o ka-oka/	-->	[akwo γooka]
	14	/o-βo-o βo-oka/	-->	[oβwo βwooka]
	15	/o-ko-o ko-oka/	-->	[okwo γwooka]
	16	/a-γa-o a-oka/	-->	[aγuo ooka]
	21	= 9 or 16		

where each singular means 'that (one) only/alone' and each plural 'those (ones) only/alone', i.e. away from the speaker(s), but near the addressee(s).

A final example involves the identificatory or emphatic construction, meaning '(it is) that (one)' in the singular and '(it is) those (ones)' in the plural, as in (121),

(121)	1	/na o-yi-o/	-->	[nooyio]
	2	/na a-βa-o/	-->	[naaβuo]
	3	/na o-yi-o/	-->	[nooyio]
	4	/na e-yi-o/	-->	[neeyio]
	5	/na e-ri-o/	-->	[neerio]
	6	/na a-yi-o/	-->	[naayio]
	7	/na e-ke-o/	-->	[neekio]
	8	/na e-βi-o/	-->	[neeβio]
	9	/na e-yi-o/	-->	[neeyio]
	10	/na e-ci-o/	-->	[neecio]
	11	/na o-ro-o/	-->	[nooruo]
	12	/na a-ka-o/	-->	[naakuo]
	14	/na o-βo-o/	-->	[nooβuo]
	15	/na o-ko-o/	-->	[nookuo]
	16	/na a-γa-o/	-->	[naaγuo]
		/na a-ya-o/	-->	[naayuo]
		/na a-yi-o/	-->	[naayio]
	21	= 9 or 16		

Not all possible allomorphy is actually exemplified in this paradigm.

3.2.5.3. Non-proximate demonstrative: that (over there).

The non-proximate demonstrative expresses distance from both the speaker(s) and the addressee(s) (Whiteley's "demonstrative 2", 1956: 15). It may be used attributively or adjectivally, and also independently or pronominally. If used attibutively, it may be translated 'that/those (over there)'. If used independently, it may be translated 'that (one) (over there), those (ones) (over there)'.

Morphologically, it is composed of a pronominal prefix and the demonstrative stem. Its underlying representation may well be postulated as /ppx-ri-a/.[89] Consider its paradigm in (122)

(122) singular: 'that (one) (over there)'
plural: 'those (ones) (over there)'

1	/o-ri-a/	-->	[oria]
2	/βa-ri-a/	-->	[βaria]
3	/o-ri-a/	-->	[oria]
4	/e-ri-a/	-->	[eria]
5	/ri-ri-a/	-->	[riria]
6	/a-ri-a/	-->	[aria]
7	/ke-ri-a/	-->	[keria]
8	/βi-ri-a/	-->	[βiria]
9	/e-ri-a/	-->	[eria]
10	/ci-ri-a/	-->	[ciria]
11	/ro-ri-a/	-->	[roria]
12	/ka-ri-a/	-->	[karia]
14	/βo-ri-a/	-->	[βoria]
15	/ko-ri-a/	-->	[koria]
16	/a-ri-a/	-->	[aria]
21	= 9 or 16		

Termed non-proximate demonstrative, it is distinct from both the proximate demonstrative discussed in section 3.2.5.1, and the semi-proximate demonstrative discussed in section 3.2.5.2, since it designates something or someone that is spatially or temporally, and at least conceptually, at a relatively great distance from both the speaker(s) and the addressee(s), expressed by '(over there)' in its gloss.

It is exemplified in (123)

[89] A possible alternative might be /ppx-re-a/, from which |ppx-ria| may be derived through Upper Mid Vowel Raising.

(123) singular: 'that (over there) only/alone'
plural: 'those (over there) only/alone'

1	/o-ri-a βo-eka/	-->	[oria βweeka]
2	/βa-ri-a βa-oka/	-->	[βaria βooka]
3	/o-ri-a βo-oka/	-->	[oria βwooka]
4	/e-ri-a e-oka/	-->	[eria yooka]
5	/ri-ri-a ri-oka/	-->	[riria ryooka]
6	/a-ri-a a-oka/	-->	[aria ooka] or [aryooka]
7	/ke-e-a ke-oka/	-->	[keria γyooka]
8	/βi-ri-a βi-oka/	-->	[βiria βyooka]
9	/e-ri-a e-oka/	-->	[eria yooka]
10	/ci-ri-a ci-oka/	-->	[ciria cyooka]
11	/ro-ri-a ro-oka/	-->	[roria rwooka]
12	/ka-ri-a ka-oka/	-->	[karia γooka]
14	/βo-ri-a βo-oka/	-->	[βoria βwooka]
15	/ko-ri-a ko-oka/	-->	[koria γwooka]
16	/a-ri-a a-oka/	-->	[aria ooka] or [aryooka]
21	= 9 or 16		

Syntactically, this demonstrative regularly follows its head, whenever it is used attributively, as in [omoonto oria] 'that person' or [aβaanto βaria] 'those persons', except when it forms a phrase with class 21 heads. In that case, the order may be reversed, as in [aria ñamira] 'that is Nyamira', 'there (visibly) is Nyamira' (as distinct from another place of the same name). Contrast [ñamira aria] 'there in Nyamira' (as usable in a story). Compare [ñamira eria] 'thát Nyamira' (where Nyamira is visibly there; presumably as opposed to some other place of the same name). [eria ñamira] 'that is Nyamira (invisible)'. This change in order may be possible only for class 16, for while [ekeroγo keria] 'that chair', for example, is possible, *[keria ekeroγo] 'that is a chair' is not.

In the identificatory construction, using /na/ before vowels and /n/ before consonants, the representations of this demonstrative are those in (124),

(124)	1	/na o-ri-a/	-->	[nooria]
	2	/n βa-ri-a/	-->	[mbaria]
	3	/na o-ri-a/	-->	[nooria]
	4	/na e-ri-a/	-->	[neeria]
	5	/n ri-ri-a/	-->	[ndiria]
	6	/na a-ri-a/	-->	[naaria]
	7	/n ke-ri-a/	-->	[ηkeria]
	8	/n βi-ri-a/	-->	[mbiria]
	9	/na e-ri-a/	-->	[neeria]
	10	/n ci-ri-a/	-->	[ñciria]
	11	/n ro-ri-a/	-->	[ndoria]
	12	/n ka-ri-a/	-->	[ηkaria]
	14	/n βo-ri-a/	-->	[mboria]
	15	/n ko-ri-a/	-->	[ηkoria]
	16	/na a-ri-a/	-->	[naaria]
	21	= 9 or 16		

Adverbs of place derived from the demonstrative discussed here are briefly considered in section 3.4.7.

A concluding remark is that the proximate, semi-, and non-proximate demonstratives discussed in this and the previous two sections (e.g. 1 oyo-, oyio, and oria), and forms of the independent pronoun discussed in section 3.2.7, may, and often do, express distance in space or time, when they are used in conjunction, in order to differentiate distinct referents, as in (125),

(125) [eri] 'this (5-one)'
[erio] 'that (5-one)'
[eria] 'that (5-one over there)'
[rirɔriɔ] 'that (5-one), the (particular) 5-one'

[oyo] 'this (1/3-one)'
[oyio] 'that (1/3-one)'
[oria] 'that (1/3-one over there)'
[εrε] 'the (particular) 1-one

3.2.6 Referential demonstrative and prefix.

The term 'referential' is used in connection with a prefix (93) and a homomorphous pronoun or demonstrative (93, 108). Combinations of the prefix are mentioned in (115), (161), (172), (203), (252), (465), and section 3.2.13, those of the demonstrative in (112) and (113). To these places the reader is referred.

3.2.7. Independent pronouns.

Independent pronouns may be used either as a subject or as an object. Since both subject and object, if present, are regularly encoded on the verb, independent pronouns, if used in addition, regularly express some form of emphasis. They may be used appositively in the same sentence, or they may be used independently as an isolated utterance.

To begin with, the singular and plural independent personal pronouns for the class of animate referents and the underlying representations postulated to account for them, are given in (126),

(126) independent personal pronouns (subject or object)

singular

1 /n-ce/	--> [iñce]	'I, me'
2 /a-yε/	--> [ayε]	'you'
3 /e-rε/	--> [εrε]	'he/him, she/her'

plural

1 /n-to-e/	--> [intwe]	'we, us'
2 /n-o-e/	--> [inwe]	'you'
3 /β a-ra-β a-o/	--> [βaraβuo]	'they, them'[90]

For independent personal pronoun third person plural (subject or object), alternative /a-βa-ɔ/ --> [aβuɔ] may also occur. The surface representations in (126) are accounted for by rules discussed in Chapter Two.[91]

The meaning of the independent pronouns is clear, though it must be borne in mind that they can function both as subject and object. The sense of the non-personal independent

---

[90] Not */βa-ɔ/ --> [βuɔ]. Focussed, [mbaraβuo], but not */n-βa-ɔ/ --> [mbuɔ]. There appears to be free variation between final [o] and [ɔ].

[91] The underlying representations of the independent pronouns may tentatively be argued as follows. First, 1s /n-/ seems plausible enough by analogy to the identical verbal subject and object marker 1s. But /a-/ seems unusual for second person singular. Though /e-/ may seem unusual for third person singular, it does occur elsewhere in association with class 1. For example, /-e-ka/ 'only, alone' and /-e-nsi/ 'all, whole' combine exclusively with prefix 1, instead of /-o-ka/ and /-o-nsi/. Elsewhere, as to the plurals, the underlying pronominal element of 1p may be postulated as /to-/ by analogy to the identical verbal subject and object marker 1p, discussed in sections 3.2.3.1-3. The initial /n-/ may be plausibly interpreted as a focus element. Final segment /-e/ may be associated with the animate class. The postulate of /n-to-e/ thus seems plausible. By analogy, 2p /n-o-e/ may be postulated as follows: focus /n-/, pronominal segment /o/ (also occurs in subject marker /mo-/), and final segment /-e/ as in 1p. Since Nasal Palatalisation and Nasal Velarisation are not applicable here, the form [inwe] seems to be exceptional, and may thus simply be postulated as /inwe/ underlyingly. Finally, the underlying representation for 3p seems straightforward.

pronoun in the other classes may be glossed as 'it' (subject or object) for the singular, and 'they' (subject) or 'them' (object) for the plural.

Morphologically, these pronouns are composed of a pronominal prefix and a pronominal stem, as in (127),

(127) independent pronouns

singular: 'it, the one' (class 1: 'he, she, him, her')
plural: 'them, the ones'

1	/e-rɛ/ -->	[ɛrɛ]	(= 3s)
2	/a-βa-ɔ/ -->	[aβuɔ]	(= 3p)
3	/o-rɔ/ -->	[ɔrɔ]	
4	/e-rɔ/ -->	[ɛrɔ]	
5	/e-ri-ɔ/ -->	[eriɔ]	
6	/a-r-ɔ/ -->	[arɔ]	
7	/e-ke-ɔ/ -->	[ekiɔ]	
8	/e-βi-ɔ/ -->	[eβiɔ]	
9	/e-rɔ/ -->	[ɛrɔ]	
10	/e-ci-ɔ/ -->	[eciɔ]	
11	/o-ro-ɔ/ -->	[oruɔ]	
12	/a-ka-ɔ/ -->	[akuɔ]	
14	/o-βo-ɔ/ -->	[oβuɔ]	
15	/o-ko-ɔ/ -->	[okuɔ]	
16	/a-rɔ/ -->	[arɔ]	
21	= 9 or 16		

However, the pronominal prefix does not conform strictly to its regular paradigm here, for the regular shape of prefix 1 /o-/ is here replaced by the relatively exceptional /e-/, and moreover, all the CV-shaped prefixes are augmented. This may be expressed as in (128),

(128) prefixation: independent pronoun ==>

a. e- / class 1
b. ppx / elsewhere

condition: all CV-prefixes are augmented[92]

The stem of the independent pronoun also exhibits allomorphy. It may be expressed as in (129),

---

[92] Informant judgments did not agree on the final vowel of classes 2-21. It would seem that [o] may alternate with [ɔ] after VCV-prefixes only, but I do not know, whether this variation is idiolectal or due to some other factor.

(129) allomorphy: independent pronoun ==>

a.	-r-ɛ /	class 1
b.	-r-ɔ /	classes 3, 4, 6, 9, 16, 21
c.	-ɔ /	elsewhere

This rule specifies that underlyingly the independent pronoun takes the shape /-rɛ/ in class 1, /-rɔ/ in classes 3, 4, 6, 9, 16, and 21, and /-ɔ/ elsewhere.[93] The combined effect of

---

[93] An alternative, ad hoc approach might be to postulate the following paradigm for a mixed prefix,

mixed prefix (mpx)

1	/o-/	(semi-proximate demonstrative)
	/e-/	(independent pronoun)
2	/aβa-/	
3	/o-/	
4	/e-/	
5	/eri-/	
6	/a-/	
7	/eke-/	
8	/eβi-/	
9	/e-/	
10	/eci-/	
11	/oro-/	
12	/aka-/	
14	/oβo-/	
15	/oko-/	
16	/a-/	(independent pronoun)
	/aya-/ or /aγa-/	(semi-proximate demonstrative)
21	= 9 or 16	

In terms of this paradigm, the independent pronoun might then be said to take the mixed prefix. The allomorphy of the semi-proximate demonstrative might be similarly accounted for, as follows,

allomorphy: semi-proximate demonstrative ==>

a. -yi-o / V ---]mpx

b. -o / VCV ---]mpx

these two rules is that whenever the pronominal prefix is a vowel, the stem takes the shape r-V (1 -ɛ, elsewhere -ɔ); but whenever the prefix consists of an augmented CV-shape, the stem will be -ɔ.

The independent pronouns may be used in the Identificatory construction, as in (130)

(130) singular: 'it is it/the one' (1: 'it is s/he, him')
plural: 'it is them/the ones'

1	/na e-rɛ/	-->	[nɛɛrɛ]
2	/na βa-ɔ/	-->	[na βuɔ]
3	/na o-rɔ/	-->	[nɔɔrɔ]
4	/na e-rɔ/	-->	[nɛɛrɔ]
5	/na ri-ɔ/	-->	[na riɔ]
6	/na a-r-ɔ/	-->	[naarɔ]
7	/na ke-ɔ/	-->	[na kiɔ]
8	/na βi-ɔ/	-->	[na βiɔ]
9	/na e-rɔ/	-->	[nɛɛrɔ]
10	/na ci-ɔ/	-->	[na ciɔ]
11	/na ro-ɔ/	-->	[na ruɔ]
12	/na ka-ɔ/	-->	[na kuɔ]
14	/na βo-ɔ/	-->	[na βuɔ]
15	/na ko-ɔ/	-->	[na kuɔ]
16	/na a-ɔ/	-->	[naaɔ]
21	= 9 or 16		

The CV-prefixes in (130) may also be augmented, as in /na a-βa-ɔ/ --> [naaβuɔ]. Besides allomorphy rule (129), several other rules co-account for the surface representations in (130), namely Word-Final Vowel Delinking in 1-3s, 1-2p, 3, 4, 6, 9, and 16, Mid Vowel Height Spreading in 1, 3, 4, and 9, Morpholexical /a/-Raising in 12, Upper Mid Vowel Raising in 7, 11, 14, and 15.

The representations in (130), especially those for classes 5, 6, 8, and 10-15, over and against the rest, suggest that the underlying representation of the identificatory element may be postulated as /na/ 'it is'. This presumably cliticises to the pronoun through liaison. Thus the identificatory phrase takes the general shape of /na + independent pronoun/ underlyingly, as further exemplified in the following sentence (131),

---

which states that, whenever the mixed prefix is V-shaped, the underlying representation of the demonstrative is /-yi-o/, and that, whenever the prefix is VCV-shaped, the demonstrative is stem /-o/ (see section 3.2.5.2). However, in order to avoid a proliferation of prefix paradigms, needed merely to account for some idiosyncracies in some lexical categories, I will not adopt this alternative approach.

(131) /a-ma-tɔɔkɛ a-ya na a-rɔ n-tak-et-e/
a-6-banana 6-these are 6-ones 1s-want-t-fv
[amatɔɔkaaya naarɔ ntaγete]
'these bananas are the ones I want'

For some of the items in (130) there are alternatives, as in (132),

(132) the (particular) one

a. non-focussed

(1	/e-rɛ/	-->	[ɛrɛ])
2	/βa-ra-βa-o/	-->	[βaraβuo]
(3	/o-rɔ/	-->	[ɔrɔ])
(4	/e-rɔ/	-->	[ɛrɔ])
5	/ri-rɔ-riɔ/	-->	[rirɔriɔ]
6	/a-rɔ-rɔ/	-->	[arɔrɔ]
7	/ke-rɔ-ke-ɔ/	-->	[kɛrɔkiɔ]
8	/βi-rɔ-βi-ɔ/	-->	[βirɔβiɔ]
(9	/e-rɔ/	-->	[ɛrɔ])
10	/ci-rɔ-ci-ɔ/	-->	[cirɔciɔ]
11	/ro-rɔ-ro-ɔ/	-->	[rɔrɔrwɔ]
12	/ka-rɔ-ka-ɔ/	-->	[karɔkwɔ]
14	/βo-rɔ-βo-ɔ/	-->	[βɔrɔβwɔ]
15	/ko-rɔ-ko-ɔ/	-->	[kɔrɔkwɔ]
16	/a-rɔ-rɔ/	-->	[arɔrɔ]
21	= 9 or 16		

b. focussed

1	/na e-rɛ/ --> [nɛɛrɛ]	
2	/n βa-ra-βa-o/ -->	[mbaraβuo]
3	/na o-rɔ/ -->	[nɔɔrɔ]
4	/na e-rɔ/ -->	[nɛɛrɔ]
5	/n ri-rɔ-riɔ/ -->	[ndirɔriɔ]
6	/na a-rɔ-rɔ/ -->	[naarɔrɔ]
7	/n ke-rɔ-ke-ɔ/ -->	[ηkɛrɔkiɔ]
8	/n βi-rɔ-βi-ɔ/ -->	[mbirɔβiɔ]
9	/na e-rɔ/ -->	[nɛɛrɔ]
10	/n ci-rɔ-ci-ɔ/ -->	[ñcirɔciɔ]
11	/n ro-rɔ-ro-ɔ/ -->	[ndɔrɔrwɔ]
12	/n ka-rɔ-ka-ɔ/ -->	[ηkarɔkwɔ]
14	/n βo-rɔ-βo-ɔ/ -->	[mbɔrɔβwɔ]
15	/n ko-rɔ-ko-ɔ/ -->	[ηkɔrɔkwɔ]
16	/na a-rɔ-rɔ/ -->	[naarɔrɔ]
21	= 9 or 16	

Independent pronouns may be combined with /-oka, -eka/ 'alone, by itself/themselves', as in (133),

(133) singular: 'it only/alone'
plural: 'them only/alone'

1	/e-rɛ βo-eka/	-->	[ɛrɛ βweeka]
2	/a-βa-o βa-oka/	-->	[aβuo βooka]
3	/o-rɔ βo-oka/	-->	[ɔrɔ βwooka] 'it'
4	/e-rɔ e-oka/	-->	[ɛrɔ yooka] 'they, them'
5	/ri-rɔ-ri-ɔ ri-oka/	-->	[rirɔriɔ ryooka] etc.
6	/a-r-ɔ a-oka/	-->	[arɔ ooka] or [arooka]
7	/ke-rɔ-ke-ɔ ke-oka/	-->	[kɛrɔkiɔ γyooka]
8	/βi-rɔ-βi-ɔ βi-oka/	-->	[βirɔβiɔ βyooka]
9	/e-rɔ e-oka/	-->	[ɛrɔ yooka]
10	/ci-rɔ-ci-ɔ ci-oka/	-->	[cirɔciɔ cyooka]
11	/ro-rɔ-ro-ɔ ro-oka/	-->	[rɔrɔrwɔ rwooka]
12	/ka-ra-ka-ɔ ka-oka/	-->	[karakwɔ γooka]
14	/βo-rɔ-βo-ɔ βo-oka/	-->	[βɔrɔβwɔ βwooka]
15	/ko-rɔ-ko-ɔ ko-oka/	-->	[kɔrɔkwɔ γwooka]
16	/a-rɔ a-oka/	-->	[arɔ ooka] or [arooka]
21	= 9 or 16		

The identificatory use of the subject or object independent personal pronoun for the class of inanimate referents is exemplified in (134),

(134) singular

1 /na n-ce/ --> |na iñce| --> [niiñce] 'it is I/me'
2 /na a-yɛ/ --> [naayɛ] 'it is you'
3 /na e-rɛ/ --> [nɛɛrɛ] 'it is he/she, him/her'

plural

1 /na n-to-e/ --> [na intwe| --> [niintwe] 'it is we/us'
2 /na n-o-e/ --> |na inwe| --> [niinwe] 'it is you'
3 /na βa-ɔ/ --> [naβuɔ] 'it is they/them'

Instead of 3p [naβuɔ], /n βa-ra-βa-o/ --> [mbaraβuo] is also used.

Next to the independent pronouns discussed in this section, it was pointed out in sections 3.2.5.1-3 that the proximate demonstrative pronouns may also be used independently, with either obviously demonstrative, or referential meaning.

3.2.8. Interrogative pronouns.

Interrogative 'who/which (specifically)?', inquiring after one or more definite individuals out of a number, may be expressed either through non-augmentation plus /ki/, or through an interrogative pronoun the structure of which will be discussed in a moment.

First, consider the non-focussed forms, with rhematic meaning, in (135),

(135)	1	/mo-Nto ki/ =->	[moontoki] 'which person?'
	2	/βa-Nto ki/ =->	[βaantoki] 'which persons?'
	3	/mo-te ki/ =->	[moteki] 'which tree?'
	4	/me-te ki/ =->	[meteki] 'which trees?'
	5	/i-tɔɔkɛ ki/ =->	[itɔɔkɛki] 'which banana'?
	6	/ma-tɔɔkɛ ki/ =->	[matɔɔkɛki] 'which bananas'?
	7	/ke-Nto ki/ =->	[γeentoki] 'which thing?'
	8	/βi-Nto ki/ =->	[βiintoki] 'which things?'
	9	/ηiti ki/ =->	[ηitiki] 'which animal?'
	10	/ciηiti ki/ =->	[ciηitiki] 'which animals?'
	9a	/n-ko ki/ =->	[ηkoki] 'which firewood?'
	10a	/ci-n-ko ki/ =->	[ciηko ki] 'which (pieces of) firewood?'[94]
	11	/ro-ko ki/ =->	[rokoki] 'which piece of firewood?'
	12	/ka-ana ki/ =->	[kaanaki] 'which small honeycomb?'
	14	/βo-kima ki/ =->	[βokimaki] 'which ugali?'
	15	/ko-γoro ki/ =->	[koγoroki] 'which leg?'
	16	/a-se ki/ =->	[aseki] 'which place?'
	21	/ña-γɛNkɛ ki/ =->	[ñaγɛɛηkɛki] 'which Nyageenke?'

[94] Not *[ηko ki], presumably because this would be identical with the singular and so lead to morphological indistinctness. However, data such as the following ones also occur,

[eraaηgi] 'colour'
[ciraaηgi] 'colours'

[ndaaηgi ki] 'which colour?'
[ciraaηgi cirici] 'which colours?'
but *[ciraaηgi ki] 'which colours?'

and

[eñoomba] 'house'
[ciñoomba] 'houses'

[ñoomba ki] 'which house?'
[ciñoomba cirici] 'which houses?'
but *[ciñoomba ki] 'which houses?'

It is not clear why these plurals are prohibited. If this phenomenon is not restricted to some idiolects, it remains to be investigated, which types of class 10(a) lexical items are subject to such restrictions.

Data such as [rokoki], *[roγoki] 'which piece of firewood?', where the /k/ of /ko/ is not turned into [γ] triggered by the /k/ of /ki/ in virtue of Consonantal Voicing Dissimilation, suggest that at least in some idiolects /ki/ is not a clitic or a dependent morpheme.

Next, consider the focussed forms in (136),

(136) '(it is) which ..?'

1	[mmoonto ki] 'which person?'
2	[mbaanto ki] 'which persons?'
3	[mmote ki] 'which tree?'
4	[mmete ki] 'which trees?'
5	?[itɔɔkɛ ki] 'which banana'?[95]
6	[mmatɔɔkɛ ki] 'which bananas'?
7	[ŋgeento ki] 'which thing?'
8	[mbiinto ki] 'which things?'
9	[ŋŋiti ki] 'which animal?'
10	[ñciŋiti cirici] 'which animals?'
9a	[ŋko ki] 'which (piece of) firewood?'
10a	[ciiŋko cirici] 'which (pieces of) firewood?'
11	[ndoko ki] 'which arm?'
12	[ŋkaana ki] 'which small honeycomb?'
14	[mbokima ki] 'which ugali?'
15	[ŋkoγoro ki] 'which leg?'
16	/a-se ki/ =-> [aseki] 'which place?'
21	/ña-γɛNkɛ ki/ =-> [ñaγɛɛŋkɛki] 'which Nyageenke?'
	or [ñaγɛɛŋkɛ ereri] 'which Nyageenke?'
	?[ñaaŋeraki], but, more acceptably, [ñaaŋera ereri] 'which Blackie?'

Their meaning is thematic. Supportive evidence for the analysis of class 1 is provided by the acceptablility of, for example, [na moontoki] 'with what person?', which would derive from /na mo-Nto ki/, and the unacceptability of *[noomoontoki] 'with what person?', which would have been the regular surface representation derived from */na o-mo-Nto ki/.

As anticipated by the plurals for 10 and 10a, the type of question under discussion may also be expressed by means of an interrogative pronoun, as in (137),

[95] There is an accidental gap in my data here. Presumably this will be [niitɔɔkɛ ki].

(137) interrogative pronoun

'which (one) (in particular)?'

1	/o-r-o-r-i/	-->	[orori]
2	/βa-r-a-β-i/	-->	[βaraβi
3	/o-r-o-r-i/	-->	[orori]
4	/e-r-e-r-i/	-->	[ereri]
5	/ri-r-i-r-i/	-->	[ririri]
6	/a-r-a-r-i/	-->	[arari]
7	/ke-r-e-k-i/	-->	[kereki]
8	/βi-r-i-β-i/	-->	[βiriβi]
9	/e-r-e-r-i/	-->	[ereri]
10	/ci-r-i-c-i/	-->	[cirici]
11	/ro-r-o-r-i/	-->	[rorori]
12	/ka-r-a-k-i/	-->	[karaki]
14	/βo-r-o-β-i/	-->	[βoroβi]
15	/ko-r-o-k-i/	-->	[koroki]
16	/a-r-a-r-i/	-->	[arari]
21	= 9 or 16		

It may also be used independently or pronominally, as in the following type of interrogative existential or identificatory construction (138),

(138) '(it is) which one?'

1	/na o-r-o-r-i/	-->	[noorori]
2	/n βa-r-a-β-i/	-->	[mbaraβi
3	/na o-r-o-r-i/	-->	[noorori]
4	/na e-r-e-r-i/	-->	[neereri]
5	/n ri-r-i-r-i/	-->	[ndiriri]
6	/na a-r-a-r-i/	-->	[naarari]
7	/n ke-r-e-k-i/	-->	[ηkereki]
8	/n βi-r-i-β-i/	-->	[mbiriβi]
9	/na e-r-e-r-i/	-->	[neereri]
10	/n ci-r-i-c-i/	-->	[ñcirici]
11	/n ro-r-o-r-i/	-->	[ndorori]
12	/n ka-r-a-k-i/	-->	[ηkaraki]
14	/n βo-r-o-β-i/	-->	[mboroβi]
15	/n ko-r-o-k-i/	-->	[ηkoroki]
16	/na a-r-a-r-i/	-->	[naarari]
21	= 9 or 16[96]		

[96] One informant judged 9 [arai] acceptable, but [arari] unacceptable; similarly, 21 [erei] and *[ereri]. However, given the analogy of the rest of this sub-system, the corresponding focussed forms of the interrogative pronoun discussed below, and the fact that a form of /r/-Deletion is applicable here, I have entered 16 and 21 as in the text.

These are exemplified in (139),

(139) 'this/these ... is which?'

1	[omoonto oyo noorori] 'person'
2	[aβaanto aβa mbaraβi] 'persons'
3	[omote oyo noorori] 'tree'
4	[omote eye neereri] 'trees'
5	[riita eri ndiriri] 'saliva'
6	[amata aya naarari] 'saliva'
7	[eγeento eke ηkereki] 'thing'
8	[eβiinto eβi mbiriβi] 'things'
9	[eηiti eye neereri] 'snake'
10	[ciηiti eci ñcirici] 'snakes'
11	[oroko oro ndorori] 'firewood'
12	[akaana aka ηkaraki] 'child'
14	[oβokoombe oβo mboroβi] 'hoe'
15	[okoγoro oko ηkoroki] 'leg'
16	[ase aya naarari] 'place'
21	= 9 or 16

The attributive use of this form of the interrogative pronoun is exemplified, for some classes, in (140),

(140) [omoonto orori] 'which person?'
[aβaanto βaraβi] 'which persons?'
[omote orori] 'which tree?'
[emete ereri] 'which trees?'
[riitɔɔkε ririri] 'which banana?'
[amatɔɔkε arari] 'which bananas?'
etc.

When used attributively or adjectivally, it regularly follows its head.

Morphologically, the interrogative pronoun is composed of a pronominal prefix and the relevant pronominal stem: ppx-stem. The variety in (137) suggests that its surface representations are derived from two distinct underlying representations. These may be accounted for by the following rule (141),

(141) allomorphy: interrogative pronoun ==>

a. -r-V-r-i / 1, 3, 4, 6, 9, 16
b. -r-V-C-i / elsewhere

(where V = ppx-vowel and C = ppx-consonant)

Since the form of the pronominal stem thus appears to vary according to the shape of the prefix which is attached to it, this may be expressed, as in (142),

(142) interrogative pronoun (alternative formulation) = = >

a. $$\text{-r-}\underset{\alpha}{\text{V}}\text{-r-i} \;/\; \underset{\alpha}{\text{V}} \quad \text{---} \; \Big]_{\text{ppx}}$$

b. $$\text{-r-}\underset{\alpha}{\text{V}}\text{-}\underset{\beta}{\text{C}}\text{-i} \;/\; \underset{\beta}{\text{C}}\underset{\alpha}{\text{V}} \quad \text{---} \; \Big]_{\text{ppx}}$$

This formulation states that if the pronominal prefix consists of a vowel, as for classes 1, 3, 4, 6, 9, 16, the underlying representation of the interrogative pronoun is /-r-V-r-i/, such that the vowel is a copy of the pronominal prefix vowel (142a). If the pronominal prefix is shaped /CV-/, the underlying representation of the interrogative pronoun is /-r-V-C-i/, the underspecified vowel and consonant being copies of the vowel and consonant of the pronominal prefix (142b).[97]

Interrogative pronoun 16 may be used in expressions inquiring after a particular place, but another common way to do this is to use /ppx-rai/ 'wherabouts?', as in (143),

---

[97] Some informants considered the following type of surface variation possible,

'which (one)?'

1 /o-r-o-r-i/	-->	[orori], [oroi], [orwi]
3 /o-r-o-r-i/	-->	[orori], [oroi], [orwi]
4 /e-r-e-r-i/	-->	[ereri], [erei]
6 /a-r-a-r-i/	-->	[arari], [arai]
9 /e-r-e-r-i/	-->	[ereri], [erei]
11 /ro-r-o-r-i/	-->	[rorori], [roroi], [rorwi]
16 /a-r-a-r-i/	-->	[arari], [arai]
21 = 9 or 16		

However, since others did not, this alternation needs to be checked more widely both with other idiolects and other lexical items and categories that meet the conditions of the change; a fortiori, since this particular paradigm may have been constructed by analogy to that of /-rai/, discussed immediately hereafter, and since the alternation cannot be accounted for by independently established rules of /r/-Deletion (see sections 3.3.4.1 and 3.3.4.2).

(143) 1 [orai]
2 [βarai]
3 [orai]
4 [erai]
5 [rirai]
6 [arai]
7 [kerai]
8 [βirai]
9 [erai]
10 [cirai]
11 [rorai]
12 [karai]
14 [βorai]
15 [korai]
17 [arai]
21 [ñaaηera erai]
[Nairobi erai]

It should be noted further that, in asking 'where?', different elements of an utterance may be questioned, as in (144),

(144) a. ¦eme-te n-e-a-reeηge a-iγa¦
4-tree f-4-t-be 16-here
[emete ndžareeηge aiγa]
'the trees were here (earlier today)'

Question:

¦a-rai¦
16-place
[arai]
'where?' (literally, 'which place?')

b. ¦e-ye na eme-te e-rai¦
4-these F 4-tree 4-wherabouts
[eye neemete erai]
'these trees, where are they?'
(literally, 'these are trees, whereabouts?')

c. [ηηai ere emete eye], or
[ηkai ere emete eye]
'(it-is)-where 4-are 4-trees 4-these
'where are these trees?'

The difference between (144b) and (144c) appears to be one in emphasis, such that (144b) stresses the trees, but (144c) stresses the place.

Alternatively, compare (145)

(145) 'where is/are …?'

1	[kai are]
2	[kai βare]
3	[kai ore]
4	[kai ore]
5	[kai rire]
6	[kai are]
7	[kai kere]
8	[kai βire]
9	[kai ere]
10	[kai cire]
11	[kai rore]
12	[kai kare]
14	[kai βore]
15	[kai kore]
17	[kai are]
21	ñaaŋera: [kai ere]
	Nairobi: [kai ere][98]

A generalised form of asking 'What?' is [iŋki], which may be used, without antecedent, in response to some remark or question that was not sufficiently heard or understood, as in the following possible exchange,

(146) a. speaker A

/tiγ-a n-ko-tεεβ-i-e e-ke-Nto γete/
allow sm1s-om2-tell-c-fv a-7-thing some
[tiγa ŋgɔtεεβie eγeento γete]
'let me tell you something (in particular)'[99]

b. speaker B

rhematic question	or	thematic question
/in-ki/		/na in-ki/
f-what		it-is f-what
[iŋki]		[iŋki]
'What?'		'What?'

By contrast, the response to (146a) may not be any of (147),

---

[98] Throughout this paradigm, [kai] is pronounced as a diphthong.

[99] [γete] 'some (particular)'. Contrast with [tiγa ŋgɔtεεβie omoγano] 'let me tell you a story'.

(147) a. [eγeento iηki]
a-thing what?
'what is some/a thing?'

b. |eγeento na iηki|
a-thing it-is f-what?
'what thing?' (emphatic)

c. |γeento ki|
thing what?
'what thing (in particular)?' (emphatic)

d. |eγeento na ki|
a-thing and what?
'something and what?'

compare

[niiηki εηɔɔmbε] 'what is a cow?'
[εηɔɔmbε niiηki] 'a cow is what?'

(difference in emphasis only)

In turn, these are not to be confused with [γeentoki] 'which thing (in particular)?', which however is not used as a response to (146), either.

A general form of asking 'Who?' is [iηo], which arguably derives from /n-ηo/. At least some of its usage is exemplified in (148),

(148) [niiηo oreeηge aa] 'who was here?'
[niiηo oreeηge aiγa] 'who was here?'
[niiηo oreeηge iγaa] 'who was here?'

Also compare (149),

(149) a. input — /oyio na n-ηo/
1-this is f-who

Prenasalisation,
Nasal Allomorphy — oyio na iηηo

Cliticisation,
Word-final Vowel Delinking,
Word-initial Vowel Spreading — niiηηo
Obligatory Contour Principle — niixηo
Compensatory Lengthening — niiiηo
x-Trimming — niiηo
output — [oyio niiηo] or ?[niηo] 'who is that?'
(compare [niiηo oyo] 'who is this?')

b. input | eke na n-ki
7-this is f-what

Prenasalisation,
Nasal Allomorphy | eke na iŋki

Cliticisation,
Word-final Vowel Delinking,
Word-initial Vowel Spreading | niiŋki
output | [eke niiŋki] '7-this is what?'

compare [niiŋki eke] 'what is 7-this?'

c. input | oyio na n-ki
3-this one is f-what

Prenasalisation,
Nasal Allomorphy | oyio na iŋki

Cliticisation,
Word-final Vowel Delinking,
Word-initial Vowel Spreading | niiŋki
output | [oyio niiŋki] '3-that is what?'

compare [oyio noorori] 'that is 3-what?'
[oria niŋo] '1-that is who?'

(after Whiteley 1956: 37)

Or more briefly, (150),

(150) a. |n-βaanto ki| --> [mbaantoki] 'which, what people?'

|n-maγena ki| --> [mmaγenaki] 'which, what stones?'

b. /n na ki/
it-is with what
[nnaki]
'how are things?', 'how are you?'[100]

(from Whiteley 1956: 37)

/ki/ 'which (in particular)?', see the discussion of prefix 5 in section 3.2.1.5.

---

[100] At the end of this expression, adverbs may be added such as [rɛɛrɔ] 'today' or [βɔɔnɔ] 'now, at the moment', thus [nnaki βɔɔnɔ] 'how are you now?', [nnaki rɛɛrɔ] 'how are you today?'. These expressions are informal ways of greeting among young people, especially friends or agemates.

Finally compare (151),

(151) [(i)ndiriri rieŋe]
it-is-5which-one 5-short
'which one is short?'

(compare, for class 1, [noorori omweeŋe] 'who is short?')

[rieŋe ndiriri]
5-short it-is-5which-one
'which short one?'

So much for several types of interrogative pronouns and their exemplification.

3.2.9. Possessive pronouns.

Before the possessive pronouns are presented, a few general introductory remarks are in order. First, morphologically it is necessary to distinguish between dependent and independent usage of such pronouns. These usages consistently involve distinct underlying representations of the prefixes for at least some of the morphosyntactic classes.

Second, at least within the dependent usage of possessive personal pronouns, another type of allomorphy involves the part of the stem that is prefixed to the basic pronominal element which it also contains.

Third, semantically, though the possessive pronouns may and do express possession or a possessive relationship, they may also express other types of genitival relationship.

Fourth, it is the pronominal prefix (ppx) that is used with possessive pronouns to express morphosyntactic agreement.

Fifth, their combination with identificatory /na/ will also be discussed.

Sixth, not all possible surface variation is fully spelled out in the examples given below. Much of it is taken for granted.

Finally, reconsideration of the possessive pronouns here is warranted, since Whiteley (1956: 20-21) mistranscribes some of them.

3.2.9.1. Dependent possessive pronouns.

To begin with, the underlying representations in (152) are the basic pronominal elements (abbreviation: pro) that make up the stems of possessive personal pronouns,

(152) possessive personal pronominal stem-elements

singular

1	/-nɛ/	'my'
2	/-o/	'your' (sometimes /-γo/)
3	/-yɛ/	'his, her'

plural

1	/-ito/	'our'
2	/-ino/	'your'
3	/-βɔ/	'their'

The term 'personal' strictly refers to the class of animate referents here. But, though necessary, these minimal elements are not sufficient to derive the full representation of the possessive pronominal stem. They must be preceded by /o/ for classes 1 and 3, and by the associative element /a/ elsewhere, as expressed in (153),

(153) allomorphy: possessive personal pronominal stem ==>

a.	-o-pro /	1, 3
b.	-a-pro /	elsewhere

For classes 2-21 we thus get the underlying representations in (154),

(154) possessive personal pronoun stems 2-21

singular

1	/-a-nɛ/	'my'
2	/-a-o/	'your' (sometimes /-a-γo/
3	/-a-yɛ/	'his, her'

plural

1	/-a-ito/	'our'
2	/-a-ino/	'your'
3	/-a-βɔ/	'their'

It is to these stems, that the pronominal prefix is attached, in order to derive the full representations of the possessive personal pronouns as they are used attributively.

Given the preceding statement of allomorphy, prefixation of the attributively used possessive personal pronoun may simply be formulated as in (155),

(155) prefixation: attributive possessive personal pronoun

0 ==> ppx/ ---- [stem

If classes 1 and 7 may be used for example, the preceding observations may be exemplified as in (156),

(156) attributive possessive personal pronouns

a.	singular	1 /o-nɛ/	-->	[ɔnɛ] '1-my'
		2 /o-o/	-->	[oo] '1-your'
		3 /o-yɛ/	-->	[ɔyɛ] '1-his/her'
	plural	1 /o-ito/	-->	[oito] '1-our'
		2 /o-ino/	-->	[oino] '1-your'
		3 /o-βɔ/	-->	[ɔβɔ] '1-their'
b.	singular	1 /ke-a-nɛ/	-->	[kyaanɛ] '7-my'
		2 /ke-a-o/	-->	[kyaao] '7-your'
		3 /ke-a-yɛ/	-->	[kyaayɔ] '7-his, her'
	plural	1 /ke-a-ito/	-->	[γyaito] '7-our'
		2 /ke-a-ino/	-->	[kyaino] '7-your'
		3 /ke-a-βɔ/	-->	[kyaaβɔ] '7-their'

where [kyV] may alternate with [kiV], in virtue of Complex Segment Formation (see section 2.3.12), and where the surface representation 1p may also be [γyeito] and 2p [kyeino], in virtue of Intervocalic /a/-Raising (see section 2.3.17). Some more surface allomorphy is exemplified in (157),

(157) a. /o-mo-ana o-nɛ/
a-1-child ppx1-my
[omwaana ɔnɛ], [omwaanɔɔnɛ]
'my child'

/o-mo-ana o-o/
a-1-child ppx1-your (2s)
[omwaana oo], [omwaanoo]
'your child'

/o-mo-ana o-yɛ/
a-1-child ppx1-his/her
[omwaana ɔyɛ], [omwaanɔɔyɛ]
'his/her child'

/o-mo-ana o-ito/
a-1-child ppx1-our
[omwaana oito], [omwaan(o)oito]
'our child'

/o-mo-ana o-ino/
a-1-child ppx1-your (2p)
[omwaana oino], [omwaan(o)oino]
'your child'

/o-mo-ana o-βɔ/
a-1-child ppx1-their
[omwaana ɔβɔ], [omwaanɔɔβɔ]
'their child'

b. (In each of the following examples, only one surface representation is given, Complex Segment Formation and Degliding being taken for granted.)

/e-ke-Nto ke-a-nɛ/
a-7-thing ppx7-of-my
[eγeento kianɛ]
'my thing'

/e-ke-Nto ke-a-o/
a-7-thing ppx7-of-your (2s)
[eγeento kiao]
'your thing'

/e-ke-Nto ke-a-yɛ/
a-7-thing ppx7-of-his/her
[eγeento kiayɛ]
'his/her thing'

/e-ke-Nto ke-a-ito/
a-7-thing ppx7-of-our
[eγeento γiaito]
'our thing'

/e-ke-Nto ke-a-ino/
a-7-thing ppx7-of-your (2p)
[eγeento kiaino]
'your thing'

/e-ke-Nto ke-a-βɔ/
a-7-thing ppx7-of-their
[eγeento kyaaβɔ]
'their thing'

The alternative surface representations under (157a) represent monitored and non-monitored speech, respectively.

The full range of the attributively used possessive personal pronouns is exemplified in (158),

(158) a. possessive personal pronouns singular

		first person 'my'	second person 'your'	third person 'his/her'
1	/o-mo-ana/ [omwaana] 'my, etc. child'	/o-nɛ/ [ɔnɛ]	/o-o/ [oo]	/o-yɛ/ [ɔyɛ]
2	/a-βa-ana/ [aβaana] 'children'	/βa-a-nɛ/ [βaanɛ]	/βa-a-o/ [βaao]	/βa-a-yɛ/ [βaayɛ]
3	/o-mo-te/ [omote] 'tree'	/o-nɛ/ [ɔnɛ]	/o-o/ [oo]	/o-yɛ/ [ɔyɛ]
4	/e-me-te/ [emete] 'trees'	/e-a-nɛ/ [yaanɛ]	/e-a-o/ [yaao]	/e-a-yɛ/ [yaayɛ]
5	/rii-γena/ [riiγena] 'stone'	/ri-a-nɛ/ [rianɛ]	/ri-a-o/ [riao]	/ri-a-yɛ/ [riayɛ]
6	/ama-γena/ [amaγena] 'stones'	/a-a-nɛ/ [aanɛ]	/a-a-o/ [aao]	/a-a-yɛ/ [aayɛ]
7	/e-ke-Nto/ /eγento/ 'thing'	/ke-a-nɛ/ [kianɛ] [kyaanɔ]	/ke-a-o/ [kiao] [kyaao]	/ke-a-yɛ/ [kiayɛ] [kyaayɛ]
8	/e-βi-Nto/ /eβiinto/ 'things'	/βi-a-nɛ/ [βianɛ] [βyaanɛ], etc.	/βi-a-o/ [βiao] [	/βi-a-yɛ/ βiayɛ]
9	/e-kaβira/ [ekaβira] 'tribe'	/e-a-nɛ/ [yaanɛ]	/e-a-o/ [yaao]	/e-a-yɛ/ [yaayɛ]

10	/ci-kaβira/ [cikaβira] 'tribes'	/ci-a-nε/ [cianε] [cyaanε], etc.	/ci-a-o/ [ciao]	/ci-a-yε/ [ciayε]
11	/o-ro-ko/ [oroko] 'firewood'	/ro-a-nε/ [rwaanε]	/ro-a-o/ [rwaao]	/ro-a-yε/ [rwaayε]
12	/a-ka-ana/ [akaana] 'small honeycomb'	/ka-a-nε/ [kaanε]	/ka-a-o/ [kaao]	/ka-a-yε/ [kaayε]
14	/o-βo-kima/ [oβokima] 'ugali'	/βo-a-nε/ [βwaanε]	/βo-a-o/ [βwaao]	/βo-a-yε/ [βwaayε]
15	/o-ko-γoro/ [okoγoro] 'leg'	/ko-a-nε/ [kwaanε]	/ko-a-o/ [kwaao]	/ko-a-yε/ [kwaayε]
16	/a-se/ [ase] 'place'	/a-a-nε/ [(a)anε]	/a-a-o/ [(a)ao]	/a-a-yε/ [(a)ayε]
21	/ña-γεNkε/ [ñaγεεηkε]	= 9 or 16 no difference in meaning) '(the village of) Nyageenke'		

b. possessive personal pronouns plural

		first person	second person	third person
		'our'	'your'	'their'
1	/o-mo-ana/ [omwaana] 'our, etc. child'	/o-ito/ [oito]	/o-ino/ [oino]	/o-βɔ/ [ɔβɔ]
2	/a-βa-ana/ [aβaana] 'children'	/βa-a-ito/ [βaito]	/βa-a-ino/ [βaino]	/βa-a-βɔ/ [βaaβɔ]
3	/o-mo-te/ [omote] 'tree'	/o-ito/ [oito]	/o-ino/ [oino]	/o-βɔ/ [ɔβɔ]
4	/e-me-te/ [emete] 'trees'	/e-a-ito/ [yaito]	/e-a-ino/ [yaino]	/e-a-βɔ/ [yaaβɔ]

5	/rii-γena/ [riiγena] 'stone'	/ri-a-ito/ [riaito]	/ri-a-ino/ [riaino]	/ri-a-βɔ/ [riaaβɔ]
6	/ama-γena/ [amaγena] 'stones'	/a-a-ito/ [aito]	/a-a-ino/ [aino]	/a-a-βɔ/ [aaβɔ]
7	/e-ke-Nto/ /eγeento/ 'thing'	/ke-a-ito/ [γiaito]	/ke-a-ino/ [kiaino]	/ke-a-βɔ/ [kiaaβɔ]
8	/e-βi-Nto/ /eβiinto/ 'things'	/βi-a-ito/ [βiaito]	/βi-a-ino/ [βiaino]	/βi-a-βɔ/ [βiaaβɔ]
9	/e-kaβira/ [ekaβira] 'tribe'	/e-a-ito/ [yaito]	/e-a-ino/ [yaino]	/e-a-βɔ/ [yaaβɔ]
10	/ci-kaβira/ [cikaβira] 'tribes'	/ci-a-ito/ [ciaito] [cyaito], etc.	/ci-a-ino/ [ciaino]	/ci-a-βɔ/ [ciaaβɔ]
11	/o-ro-ko/ [oroko] 'firewood'	/ro-a-ito/ [rwaito]	/ro-a-ino/ [rwaino]	/ro-a-βɔ/ [rwaaβɔ]
12	/a-ka-ana/ [akaana] 'small honeycomb'	/ka-a-ito/ [γaito]	/ka-a-ino/ [kaino]	/ka-a-βɔ/ [kaaβɔ]
14	/o-βo-kima/ [oβokima] 'ugali'	/βo-a-ito/ [βwaito]	/βo-a-ino/ [βwaino]	/βo-a-βɔ/ [βwaaβɔ]
15	/o-ko-γoro/ [okoγoro] 'leg'	/ko-a-ito/ [γwaito]	/ko-a-ino/ [kwaino]	/ko-a-βɔ/ [kwaaβɔ]
16	/a-se/ [ase] 'place'	/a-a-ito/ [aito]	/a-a-ino/ [aino]	/a-a-βɔ/ [(a)aβɔ]
21	/ña-γεNkε/ [ñaγεεηkε] '(the village of) Nyageenke'	= 9 or 16		

Three comments may be made. First, the optional change from |iai| to [iei], observable in several examples, has already been discussed in section 2.3.16.

Second, there is some surface variation between a long and a short vowel in the sequence |aai| versus |ai|, whether initially, as in [aino] or [aaino] and [aanɛ] or [anɛ] in class 16, or medially, as in [βaito] or [βaaito] and [βaino] or [βaaino] in class 2. In some forms, this variation is due to a different underlying representation, as in /a-nɛ/ versus /a-a-nɛ/. Where this account is not available, it may be interpreted as a fairly low-level optional rule of phonetic variation.

Third, [CiV(:)] alternates fairly freely with [CyV(:)], and [CwV(:)] with [CuV(:)].

Non-personal possessive pronouns are not used attributively, presumably because possession is associated with animate beings or persons. For example, if the topic of a conversation is some tree and its parts, and reference must be made to those parts, an expression equivalent to the phrase 'the parts of it' will be used in Gusii, instead of 'its parts'. Nor are non-personal possessive pronouns used much independently. Sentences such 'it is theirs' or 'they are theirs' seem to be semantically odd in Gusii, whenever the referents of 'theirs' are non-personal. The same holds true for the singular in the sentences 'it is its' and 'they are its', which are of course odd in English too. Again, the Gusii expression will be the equivalent to 'ppx-of-me/it (etc)', as in (159),

(159) example: 'mine, its', etc. (literally '7-it of 1-21')

1	[kiaayɛ]
2	[kiaaβɔ]
3	[kiɔɔrɔ]
4	[kiɔɛrɔ]
5	[kiarirɔriɔ]
6	[kiayarɔriɔ] or [kiañarɔriɔ]
7	[γiakɛrɔkiɔ]
8	[kiaβirɔβiɔ]
9	[kiɔɛrɔ]
10	[γacirɔciɔ]
11	[kiarɔrɔrwɔ]
12	[γiakarɔkwɔ]
14	[kiaβɔrɔβwɔ]
15	[γiakɔrɔkwɔ]
16	[kiaarɔrɔ]
21	= 9 or 16

3.2.9.2. Independent possessive pronouns.

In this section, the independent use of personal and non-personal possessive pronouns will be discussed, beginning with the personal ones (mine, 1s-yours, his, hers, its, ours, 2p-yours, theirs).

Consider the representative paradigm in (160), where the possessive personal pronoun for the first person singular is used for example,

(160) independent possessive personal pronouns

1	/o-yo-o-nɛ/	-->	[ɔyɔɔnɛ]	'1-mine'
2	/a-βa-a-nɛ/	-->	[aβaanɛ]	'2-mine'
3	/o-yo-o-nɛ/	-->	[ɔyɔɔnɛ]	'etc.'
4	/e-ye-a-nɛ/	-->	[eyaanɛ]	
5	/e-ri-a-nɛ/	-->	[erianɛ]	
6	/a-ya-a-nɛ/	-->	[ayaanɛ]	
7	/e-ke-a-nɛ/	-->	[ekianɛ]	
8	/e-βi-a-nɛ/	-->	[eβianɛ]	
9	/e-ye-a-nɛ/	-->	[eyaanɛ]	
10	/e-ci-a-nɛ/	-->	[ecianɛ]	
11	/o-ro-a-nɛ/	-->	[oruanɛ]	
12	/a-ka-a-nɛ/	-->	[akaanɛ]	
14	/o-βo-a-nɛ/	-->	[oβuanɛ]	
15	/o-ko-a-nɛ/	-->	[okuanɛ]	
16	/a-ya-a-nɛ/	-->	[ayaanɛ]	
21	= 9 or 16			

As usual, the possible optional application of various rules, such as Complex Segment Formation, Compensatory Lengthening, and Degliding, have not been exemplified, but taken for granted. From these examples, it will be clear that the underlying representation of the pronominal stem in its independent use exhibits the same type of allomorphy as when used attributively (see section 3.2.9.1). Its prefixation is different, however. Whenever the possessive personal pronoun is used independently, the referential prefix is attached to its stem, in order to derive the full representation of the pronoun, as in (161),

(161) prefixation: independent possessive personal pronoun ==>

a. rpx-o-pro /	classes 1 and 3
b. rpx-a-pro /	elsewhere

The independent possessive personal pronouns may be used in identificatory statements. Since they always begin with a vowel, identificatory allomorph /na/ is used. In the following paradigm (162), the independent possessive personal pronoun of the first person singular is used again for example,

(162) independent possessive personal pronoun 1s

identificatory construction

1	/na o-yo-o-nε/ -->	[nɔɔyɔɔnε] '(it is) 1-mine'
2	/na a-βa-a-nε/ -->	[naaβaanε] '(it is) 2-mine'
3	/na o-yo-o-nε/ -->	[nɔɔyɔɔnε] 'etc.'
4	/na e-ye-a-nε/ -->	[neeyaanε]
5	/na e-ri-a-nε/ -->	[neerianε]
6	/na a-ya-a-nε/ -->	[naayaanε]
7	/na e-ke-a-nε/ -->	[neekianε]
8	/na e-βi-a-nε/ -->	[neeβianε]
9	/na e-ye-a-nε/ -->	[neeyaanε]
10	/na e-ci-a-nε/ -->	[neecianε]
11	/na o-ro-a-nε/ -->	[nooruanε]
12	/na a-ka-a-nε/ -->	[naakaanε]
14	/na o-βo-a-nε/ -->	[nooβuanε]
15	/na o-ko-a-nε/ -->	[nookuanε]
16	/na a-ya-a-nε/ -->	[naayaanε]
21	= 9 or 16	

Given the underlying representations postulated in (162), the corresponding surface representations are regularly accounted for by postlexical Word-final Vowel Delinking and Word-initial Vowel Spreading. Other surface features are accounted for by Upper Mid Vowel Raising and Mid Vowel Height Spreading (see Chapter Two). Again other lexical phonological rules account for further possible surface variation not exemplified here. This concludes the discussion of attributively and independently used possessive personal pronouns.

I will now turn to non-personal possessive pronouns. In Gusii, these involve classes 3-21, though words normally belonging to class 1-2 may be transferred to other classes, particularly the augmentative and diminutive. The Gusii expressions normally used in these cases are equivalent to the English phrase 'it (is) of them', 'they (are) of it', etc., as in (163),

(163) [it {they / them}] [-a] [it / them]

subject, object — 'of' — prepositional object

In expressions such as these, depending on the meaning required, the referential pronoun (e.g. eβi- '8-they', '8-them', identical to the proximate demonstrative) or the non-proximate demonstrative (e.g. βiria '8-those') may be used to mark the subject or object. Again depending on the meaning required, the independent pronoun or the semi-proximate demonstrative may be used as a prepositional object (see the discussion of the associative construction in 3.2.11).

If we take the independent pronoun for example, as in (164),

(164)	1	/e-rɛ/	-->	[ɛrɛ] 'him, her'
	2	/a-βa-ɔ/	-->	[aβuɔ] 'they,them'
	3	/o-rɔ/	-->	[ɔrɔ] 'it'
	4	/e-rɔ/	-->	[ɛrɔ] 'they, them'
	5	/ri-rɔ-ri-ɔ/	-->	[rirɔriɔ] etc.
	6	/a-r-ɔ/	-->	[arɔ]
	7	/ke-rɔ-ke-ɔ/	-->	[kɛrɔkiɔ]
	8	/βi-rɔ-βi-ɔ/	-->	[βirɔβiɔ]
	9	/e-rɔ/	-->	[ɛrɔ]
	10	/ci-rɔ-ci-ɔ/	-->	[cirɔciɔ]
	11	/ro-rɔ-ro-ɔ/	-->	[rɔrɔrwɔ]
	12	/ka-ra-ka-ɔ/	-->	[karakwɔ]
	14	/βo-rɔ-βo-ɔ/	-->	[βɔrɔβwɔ]
	15	/ko-rɔ-ko-ɔ/	-->	[kɔrɔkwɔ]
	16	/a-rɔ-rɔ/	-->	[arɔrɔ]
	21	= 9 or 16		

the independently used non-personal possessive pronoun may be analysed, in a somewhat simplified manner, as in (165),

(165) non-personal possessive pronoun ==>

[[rpx-a] (of) [independent pronoun stem]]

'of it/them'

The minimal representation here consists of /-a + independent pronoun/. Whenever this pronoun is used attributively, the pronominal prefix will be attached to it, instead of the referential prefix. In either case, the class of the prefix agrees with that of the antecedent subject or object.

The independent use of the non-personal possessive pronoun in the identificatory construction is exemplified in (166), where class 8 is taken for example and where classes 1-2 are added for good measure,

(166) [/na/] is/are [[eβi] 8-rpx [a] of [independent pronoun] stem]

'8-they are his/hers/its/theirs'

1 /na eβi-a-a-yɛ/	-->	[neeβiaayɛ]
2 /na eβi-a-a-βɔ/	-->	[neeβiaaβɔ]
3 /na eβi-a-o-rɔ/	-->	[neeβiɔɔrɔ]
4 /na eβi-a-e-rɔ/	-->	[neeβiɛɛrɔ]
5 /na eβi-a-ri-rɔ-ri-ɔ/	-->	[neeβiarirɔriɔ]
6 /na eβi-a-a-r-ɔ/	-->	[neeβiaarɔ]
7 /na eβi-a-ke-rɔ-ke-ɔ/	-->	[neeβiakɛrɔkiɔ]
8 /na eβi-a-βi-rɔ-βi-ɔ/	-->	[neeβiaβirɔβiɔ]
9 /na eβi-a-e-rɔ/	-->	[neeβiɛɛrɔ]
10 /na eβi-a-ci-rɔ-ci-ɔ/	-->	[neeβiacirɔciɔ]
11 /na eβi-a-ro-rɔ-ro-ɔ/	-->	[neeβiarɔrɔruɔ]
12 /na eβi-a-ka-rɔ-ka-ɔ/	-->	[neeβiakarɔkuɔ]
14 /na eβi-a-βo-rɔ-βo-ɔ/	-->	[neeβiaβɔrɔβuɔ]
15 /na eβi-a-ko-rɔ-ko-ɔ/	-->	[neeβiakɔrɔkuɔ]
16 /na eβi-a-a-rɔ-rɔ/	-->	[neeβiarɔrɔ]
21 = 9 or 16		

Whenever the possessor is animate, i.e. a person or an animal, this construction is semantically acceptable, but whenever the possessor is inanimate, the construction is semantically odd.

Next, with the non-proximate demonstrative for a subject or object, the non-personal possessive pronoun used independently in the identificatory or existential construction is further exemplified in (167), where class 1-2 has again been included,

(167) 1 /βi-ri-a βi-a-a-yɛ/
ppx8-those (over there)2 ppx8-of-of-possessive
[βiria βiaayɛ]
'8-those (over there) of his/hers'

2 /βi-ri-a βi-a-a-βɔ/
ppx8-those (over there) ppx8-of-of-possessive
[βiria βiaaβɔ]
'8-those (over there) of theirs'

3 /βi-ri-a βi-a o-rɔ/
ppx8-those (over there) ppx8-of 3-independent pro
[βiria βiɔɔrɔ]
'8-those (over there) of 3-it'

4 /βi-ri-a βi-a e-rɔ/
ppx8-those (over there) ppx8-of 4-independent pro
[βiria βiɛɛrɔ]
'8-those (over there) 8-of 4-them'

similarly:

5 /βi-ri-a βi-a ri-rɔ-ri-ɔ/ --> [βiria βiarirɔriɔ]
6 /βi-ri-a βi-a a-r-ɔ/ --> [βiria βiaarɔ]
7 /βi-ri-a βi-a ke-rɔ-ke-ɔ/ --> [βiria βiakɛrɔkiɔ]
8 /βi-ri-a βi-a βi-rɔ-βi-ɔ/ --> [βiria βiaβirɔβiɔ]
9 /βi-ri-a βi-a e-rɔ/ --> [βiria βiɛɛrɔ]
10 /βi-ri-a βi-a ci-rɔ-ci-ɔ/ --> [βiria βiacirɔciɔ]
11 /βi-ri-a βi-a ro-rɔ-ro-ɔ/ --> [βiria βiarɔrɔrwɔ]
12 /βi-ri-a βi-a ka-rɔ-ka-ɔ/ --> [βiria βiakarɔkwɔ]
14 /βi-ri-a βi-a βo-rɔ-βo-ɔ/ --> [βiria βiaβɔrɔβwɔ]
15 /βi-ri-a βi-a ko-rɔ-ko-ɔ/ --> [βiria βiakɔrɔkwɔ]
16 /βi-ri-a βi-a a-rɔ-rɔ/ --> [βiria βiaarɔrɔ][101]
21 = 9 or 16

In (168), the non-proximate demonstrative is used as an example both as a head, and as a prepositional object used to express the genitival relationship,

(168) '8-those (over there) 8-of ppx-those (over there)'

1 /βi-ri-a βi-a o-ri-a/ --> [βiria βiooria]
2 /βi-ri-a βi-a βa-ri-a/ --> [βiria βiaβaria]
3 /βi-ri-a βi-a o-ri-a/ --> [βiria βiooria]
4 /βi-ri-a βi-a e-ri-a/ --> [βiria βieeria]
5 /βi-ri-a βi-a ri-ri-a/ --> [βiria βiariria]
6 /βi-ri-a βi-a a-ri-a/ --> [βiria βiaaria]
7 /βi-ri-a βi-a ke-ri-a/ --> [βiria βiakeria]
8 /βi-ri-a βi-a βi-ri-a/ --> [βiria βiaβiria]
9 /βi-ri-a βi-a e-ri-a/ --> [βiria βieeria]
10 /βi-ri-a βi-a ci-ri-a/ --> [βiria βiaciria]
11 /βi-ri-a βi-a ro-ri-a/ --> [βiria βiaroria]
12 /βi-ri-a βi-a ka-ri-a/ --> [βiria βiakaria]
14 /βi-ri-a βi-a βo-ri-a/ --> [βiria βiaβoria]
15 /βi-ri-a βi-a ko-ri-a/ --> [βiria βiakoria][102]
16 /βi-ri-a βi-a a-ri-a/ --> [βiria βiaaria]
21 = 9 or 16

---

101 16 [βiria βiɔɔrɔrɔ] was also reported with the same meaning, presumably derived from /βi-ri-a βi-a o-rɔ-rɔ/, but an error of judgment may be involved here.

102 This phrase is homomorphous with [βiria βiakoria] 'those edible 7-ones', from /βi-ri-a βi-a ko-ri-a/, '7-those things 7-of 15-eat-fv', literally 'those things to eat'.

To conclude this discussion, in the following paradigm (169) the non-proximate demonstrative is used for the subject or object, and the semi-proximate demonstrative (116) for the prepositional object expressing the genitival relationship,

(169) '8-those (over there) 8-of ppx-that'

1 /βi-ri-a βi-a o-yi-o/	-->	[βiria βiooyio]
2 /βi-ri-a βi-a a-βa-o/	-->	[βiria βiaaβwo]
3 /βi-ri-a βi-a o-yi-o/	-->	[βiria βiooyio]
4 /βi-ri-a βi-a e-yi-o/	-->	[βiria βieeyio]
5 /βi-ri-a βi-a e-ri-o/	-->	[βiria βieerio]
6 /βi-ri-a βi-a a-yi-o/	-->	[βiria βiaayio]
7 /βi-ri-a βi-a e-ke-o/	-->	[βiria βieekio]
8 /βi-ri-a βi-a e-βi-o/	-->	[βiria βieeβio]
9 /βi-ri-a βi-a e-ye-o/	-->	[βiria βieeyio]
10 /βi-ri-a βi-a e-ci-o/	-->	[βiria βieecio]
11 /βi-ri-a βi-a o-ro-o/	-->	[βiria βioorwo]
12 /βi-ri-a βi-a a-ka-o/	-->	[βiria βiaakwo]
14 /βi-ri-a βi-a o-βo-o/	-->	[βiria βiooβwo]
15 /βi-ri-a βi-a o-ko-o/	-->	[βiria βiaakwo]
16 /βi-ri-a βi-a a-γa-o/	-->	[βiria βiaaγwo]
21 = 9 or 16		

3.2.10. Adpositions.

In Gusii, there are prepositions proper, words placed before other words of which they express some sort of relation, but also a few postpositions, which similarly express some sort of relation but are placed after the words they qualify. An example of the latter is [ime] in [ñoomba ime] 'in/inside the house'. The term 'adposition' is used to generalise over these two sub-classes.

This possibility of post-nominal position of such words in Gusii is an exception, relatively speaking, for East African Bantu languages and suggests the possibility of a Nilo-Saharan substratum in the language.

Semantically, the definition 'some sort of relation' is admittedly somewhat vague, but nonetheless applicable. This includes the notions of location or direction. For example, [ñoomba ime] may mean, in addition, 'the room inside' or 'the inner room'. Which sense it bears, will depend on the context. Some other adpositions may also denote location or direction. Which meaning is applicable, again depends on the linguistic or non-linguistic context.

Morphologically, adpositions are regularly invariant. That is, they do not participate in the Gusii system of morphosyntactic agreement. This holds not only for monomorphemic prepositions, such as /na/ 'with', but also for morphologically composite prepositions. There are no composite postpositions.

Composite prepositions may contain elements that normally do participate in the morphosyntactic agreement system, but not as part of the prepositional phrase to which they belong. As such, they may have become lexicalised, as in (170),

(170) /kati e-a or ya-a/
middle 9-of or 16-of
[γati ya]
'in between, in the middle of'[103]

In the following examples (171) there is no preposition-internal agreement either,

(171) a.	/a-rɛ ko-ru-a/	b. /a-ηe na/
	16-far coming-from	16-near with
	[arɛ korwa]	[aηe na]
	'far from'	'near to'

The underlying representations, /a-rɛ/ and /aηe/ are, moreover, conjectural.

On the whole, the class of adpositions is relatively small. Many, if not most, prepositional relationships, which in many other languages tend to be expressed through prepositions (e.g. 'in', 'on', 'to', 'for', and 'with' in English), are expressed through verbal extension suffixes in Gusii, notably the applicative suffix /-er/ discussed in section 3.3.2.6.

Some additional discussion on adpositions, especially their derivation, is offered in section 3.4.8.

3.2.11. Associative /-a/: the associative construction.

The element discussed in this section is called 'associative' /-a/ for syntactic and semantic reasons. Syntactically, it connects two nominals in what might be termed an associative or genitival (though not necessarily possessive) construction. Semantically, it expresses some sort of association between the referents. The concept expressed by it may usually be translated by the word 'of' and roughly corresponds to the range of meanings or relations expressed by this English preposition. Hence the word 'of' is used to label associative /-a/ in syntactic representations.

---

[103] One informant also gave the following example,

/a-ri-a ya-a/
16-(that place)-over-there 16-of
[aria ya]
'far from'

but this was disconfirmed by another one.

This element basically takes the pronominal prefix, but with a difference. Consider its paradigm in (172),

(172)	1	/βo-a/	-->	[βwa]
	2	/βa-a/	-->	[βaa]
	3	/βo-a/	-->	[βwa]
	4	/e-a/	-->	[ya]
	5	/ri-a/	-->	[ria]
	6	/ya-a/	-->	[yaa]
	7	/ke-a/	-->	[kia]
	8	/βi-a/	-->	[βia]
	9	/e-a/	-->	[ya]
	10	/ci-a/	-->	[cia]
	11	/ro-a/	-->	[rwa]
	12	/ka-a/	-->	[kaa]
	14	/βo-a/	-->	[βwa]
	15	/ko-a/	-->	[kwa]
	16	/a-a/	-->	[aa]
	21	= 9 or 16		

Prefix 1/3 is the regular allomorph of the pronominal prefix before a vowel. Prefix 6 is allomorph /ya-/, instead of the regular /a-/. It may be exceptional as far as the form of the pronominal prefix is concerned, but its shape is identical to referential prefix /aya-/ and object marker /ya-/. Class 16 may surface as [ya] too, possibly deriving from /ya-a/, but more plausibly from /e-a/ (that is, the informants who gave this allomorph confused 16 with 21; or perhaps, agreement for place, other than for the word /a-se/ 'place' itself, is somewhat ambivalent). These considerations apart, associative /-a/ regularly takes the pronominal prefix (71).

It may be added, first, that the long final vowel of 2, 6, and 12 (and 16, if it derives from /ya-a/) is usually shortened. Second, the final vowel, whether long or short, generally tends to be delinked postlexically, causing spreading of the initial vowel of the following word. The combined effect is that of liaison.

Morphosyntactically, the pronominal prefix agrees with the class of the word preceding the associative, i.e. its head. Semantically, however, this head expresses the referent that stands in a genitival relationship to the referent referred to by the word following the associative element.

The resulting phrase is the following genitival or associative construction (173),

(173) associative construction

$$\left[\begin{bmatrix} \text{px-head} \\ \alpha \end{bmatrix} \quad \begin{bmatrix} \text{ppx-a} \\ \alpha \end{bmatrix} \quad \begin{bmatrix} \text{px-word} \end{bmatrix} \quad \right]$$

Here, px denotes any type of prefix (determined by the type of head, but usually a nominal prefix), and α denotes identity of morphosyntactic class. This construction is exemplified in (174),

(174) 1 /o-mo-ana βo-a o-mo-kuNγu/
a-1-child 1-of a-1-(married) woman
[omwaana βwoomokuuŋgu]
'the child of the woman'

2 /a-βa-ana βa-a o-mo-saaca/
a-2-child 2-of a-1-(married) man
[aβaana βoomosaaca]
'the children of the man'

3 /o-mo-te βo-a o-mo-saaca/
a-3-tree 3-of a-1-man
[omote βwoomosaaca]
'the tree of the man'

4 /e-me-te e-a o-mo-saaca/
a-4-tree 4-of a-1-man
[emete yoomosaaca]
'the trees of the man'

/e-me-te e-a a-βa-saaca/
a-4-tree 4-of a-2-man
[emete yaaβasaaca]
'the trees of the men'

5 /rii-tɔɔkɛ ri-a o-mo-ana/
5-banana 5-of a-1-child
[riitɔɔkɛ ryoomwaana]
'the banana of the child'

6 /a-ma-tɔɔkɛ ya-a o-mo-ana/
a-6-banana 6-of a-1-child
[amatɔɔkɛ yoomwaana]
'the bananas of the child'

7 /e-ke-saku ke-a o-mo-saaca/
a-7-clan 7-of a-1-man
[eγesaku kioomosaaca]
'the clan of the man'

8 /e-βi-saku βi-a o-mo-saaca/
a-8-clan 8-of a-1-man
[eβisaku βioomosaaca]
'the clans of the man'[104]

9 /e-ηiti e-a o-mo-saaca/
9-animal 9-of a-1-man
[eηiti yoomosaaca]
'the animal of the man'

10 /ciηiti ci-a o-mo-saaca/
10-animal 10-of a-1-man
[ciηiti cioomosaaca]
'the animals of the man'

11 /o-ro-ko ro-a o-mo-saaca/
a-11-firewood 11-of a-1-man
[oroko rwoomosaaca]
'the firewood of the man'

12 /a-ka-ana ka-a o-mo-kuNγu/
a-12-honeycomb 12-of a-1-woman
[akaana koomokuuηgu]
'the small honeycomb'

14 /o-βo-kima βo-a o-mo-kuNγu/
a-14-ugali 14-of a-1-woman
[oβokima βwoomokuuηgu]
'the ugali of the woman'

15 /o-ko-γoro ko-a o-mo-saaca/
a-15-leg 15-of a-1-man
[okoγoro kwoomosaaca]
'the leg of the man'

16 /a-se a-a o-mo-saaca/
16-place 16-of a-1-man
[ase oomosaaca]
'the place of the man'

21 = 16 [ñamira anɛnɛ yoomosaaca]
'the big Nyamira of the man'

As previously pointed out, the final vowel of the associative element is regularly linked to

[104] Since a person is normally a member of one clan only, this example is culturally odd.

the following word, in virtue of Word-final Vowel Delinking and Word-initial Vowel Spreading (see sections 2.4.3 and 2.4.4). At a normal rate of speech, for example, [eβisaku βia omosaaca] will tend to be rendered [eβisaku βioomosaaca]. In rapid speech, the final vowel may moreover be shortened, [eβisaku βiomosaaca].

As usual, all possible surface variation has not been given in (174). Using the items for class 4 for example, the following sample derivation may suffice to show that several rules may in fact combine to derive the surface representations in (175),

(175)	Input	e-me-te e-a o-mo-saaca	
	UMVR	i	
	Glide Formation	y	
	Compensatory Lengthening	-	(blocked word-finally)
	Word-final Vowel Delinking	~~a~~	
	Word-initial Vowel Spreading	o	
	Output	[emete yoomosaaca]	
	Input	e-me-te e-a a-βa-saaca	
	UMVR	i	
	Glide Formation	y	
	Compensatory Lengthening	-	(blocked word-finally)
	Word-final Vowel Delinking	~~a~~	
	Word-initial Vowel Spreading	a	
	Output	[emete yaaβasaaca]	

Finally, the derivation of the associative construction for class 16 is sketched in (176),

(176)	Input	|ase aa omosaaca|
	Word-final VV-Shortening	~~a~~
	Word-final Vowel Delinking	~~a~~
	Word-initial Vowel Spreading	o
	Output	[ase oomosaaca]

It illustrates that the constraint on word-final long vowels obtains. We have seen that it prohibits certain phonological rules, such as Compensatory Lengthening, from applying word-finally. As a phonological convention, presumably, it does not prevent morphological rules, such as prefixation. Hence it must be interpreted either as a corrective principle, or as a language-specific constraint that, in cases such as the one under discussion, motivates some rule (here for the nonce termed Word-final VV-Shortening) delinking one of the x's to which the long [aa] of associative element for 16 is linked.[105]

---

[105] Presumably because of the effects due to liaison, the type of output involving associative element /ppx-a/ tends to pose problems of orthography even for Gusii speakers themselves. Nor is Whiteley's enumeration of its shapes for classes 1-10 sufficient (1956: 21). See Chapter Four for some discussion of orthographical problems.

3.2.12. Quantifiers and specifiers.

In this section I will briefly discuss the specifiers and quantifiers in (177),

(177) a. /-Nre/ 'other' (i.e. other than what one has, but not of a different sort)
b. /-o-Nsi, -e-Nsi/ 'all, whole'
c. /-Nre -o-Nsi, -Nre -e-Nsi/ 'any whatever'
d. /-o-ka, e-ka/ 'alone, by oneself'
e. /kera/ 'each, every, all'
f. /γete/ 'some (particular)'

These words take the pronominal prefix. Whiteley's observation that they take 'verbal prefixes' is not sufficiently definite (1956: 21). However, (177e,f) are invariant. The allomorphy of (177b-d) will be discussed presently.

Syntactically, the words in (177) behave like adjectives in at least two respects. They may be used both independently, i.e. as nominals, and attributively; and when used attributively as modifiers, they regularly follow their heads. The exception is [kera], which, like its presumable Swahili cognate **kila** 'every, all', precedes its head.

Next, [kera] and [γete] are said to be invariant. This means that they are morphologically invariable, and that, as such, they do not enter into the system of morphosyntactic affixation, classes, and agreement.

From a semantic point of view, some roots may be considered to have a more typically adjectival meaning than others. A case in point might be /-o-ka, e-ka/ 'alone, by oneself' (for its paradigm, see section 3.4.5.4). It would seem, however, that all adjectival roots or stems may be used as nouns, so that there is no compelling semantic reason for listing some of them specifically as adjectives in the lexicon. Designating them as a nominal may be sufficient.

Several other details may now be discussed. Consider the underlying and corresponding surface representations of /ppx-Nre/ 'other' (177a) for all morphosyntactic classes, in (178),

(178)	1	/o-Nre/	-->	[onde]
	2	/βa-Nre/	-->	[βaande]
	3	/o-Nre/	-->	[onde]
	4	/e-Nre/	-->	[ende]
	5	/ri-Nre/	-->	[riinde]
	6	/a-Nre/	-->	[ande]
	7	/ke-Nre/	-->	[keende]
	8	/βi-Nre/	-->	[βiinde]
	9	/e-Nre/	-->	[ende]
	10	/ci-Nre/	-->	[ciinde]
	11	/ro-Nre/	-->	[roonde]
	12	/ka-Nre/	-->	[kaande]
	14	/βo-Nre/	-->	[βoonde]
	15	/ko-Nre/	-->	[koonde]
	16	/a-Nre/	-->	[ande]
	21	= 9 or 16		

Word-initial vowels, involving prefixes 1, 3, 4, 6, 9, 16, are regularly shortened. Otherwise this paradigm is regular.

Next, the paradigm for /-o-Nsi, -e-Nsi/ 'all, whole' (177b) is given in (179),

(179) 'all, whole'

1	/βo-e-Nsi/	-->	[βweensi]
2	/βa-ɔ-Nsi/	-->	[βɔɔnsi]
3	/βo-ɔ-Nsi/	-->	[βwɔɔnsi]
4	/e-ɔ-Nsi/	-->	[yɔɔnsi]
5	/ri-ɔ-Nsi/	-->	[riɔɔnsi]
6	/a-ɔ-Nsi/	-->	[ɔɔnsi]
7	/ke-ɔ-Nsi/	-->	[γiɔɔnsi]
8	/βi-ɔ-Nsi/	-->	[βiɔɔnsi]
9	/e-ɔ-Nsi/	-->	[yɔɔnsi]
10	/ci-ɔ-Nsi/	-->	[ciɔɔnsi]
11	/ro-ɔ-Nsi/	-->	[rwɔɔnsi][106]
12	/ka-ɔ-Nsi/	-->	[γɔɔnsi]
14	/βo-ɔ-Nsi/	-->	[βwɔɔnsi]
15	/ko-ɔ-Nsi/	-->	[γwɔɔnsi]
16	/a-ɔ-Nsi/	-->	[ɔɔnsi]
21	= 9 or 16[107]		

---

106 Judith Moraa also judged 11 [rweensi] and 14 [βweensi] to be correct.

107 At least the following phonological rules co-account for the surface representations in this paradigm. Upper Mid Vowel Raising in 1, 3, 4, 7, 11, 14, 15, Complex Segment Formation in 1, 3, 11, 14, 15, Prenasalisation and related nasal rules in all classes, /a/-Deletion in 2, 6, 12, 16, Compensatory Lengthening in all classes, but

In addition to these representations, the class of animate referents may include representations for the first and second persons plural, as in (180),

(180) 1s [iñce βweensi] 'all of me'
2s [ayε βweensi] 'all of you'
3s [εrε βweensi] 'all of him/her'

1p [intwe tweensi] 'all of us, we all'
2p [inwe mweensi] 'all of you, you all'
3p [βaraβuo βɔɔnsi] 'all of them'

The allomorphy for class 1, including 1-3s and 1-2p, may thus be accounted for as in (181),

(181) allomorphy: /-V-Nsi/ ==>

a. -e-Nsi / 1-3s, 1-2p
b. -ɔ-Nsi / elsewhere

This rule regulates the quality of the vowel that is a part of the morphologically composite stem of this specifier, stating that the relevant vocalic element is /e-/ in class 1 (1-3s) and 1-2p, but /ɔ-/ in morphosyntactic classes 2-21.[108]

Though /-e-/ is relatively exceptional, it also occurs as an allomorph for the regular pronominal prefix 1 /o-/ of the third person singular of the independent personal pronoun (i.e. /e-rε/ --> [εrε] 'he, him, she, her', see section 3.2.7). Thus in this case it is again associated with class 1.
This same type of allomorphy also involves the stem /-o-ka, e-ka/ 'alone, by oneself' (177d).

Two specifiers just discussed may be combined to form the composite specifier /ppx-Nre ppx-V-Nsi/ 'any whatever' (177c). Its two pronominal prefixes, being coreferential, are identical, but exhibit the usual allomorphy as in [**o**nde **β**weensi]. The paradigm of this specifier, presenting surface representations only, is given in (182),

---

optionally word-initially, as in 6 and 16, and Consonantal Voicing Dissimilation. Since Complex Segment Formation, Compensatory Lengthening, and Degliding are optional, [ryɔɔnsi] and [riɔnsi], for example, may also occur next to [riɔɔnsi]. Not all possible surface representations are spelled out for each class.

[108] Compare the peculiar form [ɔnsepi], probably a hybrid form (-pi appears to be taken over from Swahili), as in [ɔnsepi ñamiira niiγɔ are aγaya] 'Nyamira as a whole is a good place', of which [kera ase ñamiira niiγɔ are aγaya] is a semantic equivalent.

(182) 'any whatever'

1	[onde βweensi]
2	[βaande βɔɔnsi]
3	[onde βwɔɔnsi]
4	[ende yɔɔnsi]
5	[riinde riɔɔnsi]
6	[ande ɔɔnsi] or [aandɔɔnsi]
7	[keende γiɔɔnsi]
8	[βiinde βiɔɔnsi]
9	[ende yɔɔnsi]
10	[ciinde ciɔɔnsi]
11	[roonde rwɔɔnsi]
12	[kaande γɔɔnsi]
14	[βoonde βwɔɔnsi]
15	[koonde γwɔɔnsi]
16	[ande ɔɔnsi] or [aandɔɔnsi]
21	= 9

Word-initial vowels may apparently be long here.

Next, since quantifier (177f) consistently appears as invariant on the surface, its underlying representation is postulated here as /γete/ 'some'. Future research may wish to settle the question, whether or not it derives from /ke-te/. Like most other modifiers, it regularly follows the head it modifies, as exemplified in (183), though it may also precede it.

(183) |oyo na omo-Nto γete omo-nεnε|
1-this be 1-person some 1-big
[oyo noomoonto γete ɔmɔnεnε] or [omoonto γetɔɔmɔnεnε]
'this is some big person' (emphatic)

since [γete] may refer either to the preceding or to the following word, this sentence may mean more specifically, either 'this is some particular big person' or 'this is quite a big person'

contrast with:

|oyo na omo-Nto o-mo-nεnε/
1-this be 1-person 1-big
[oyo noomoonto ɔmɔnεnε] or [noomoontɔɔmɔnεnε]
'this is a big person'

Finally, /-aaɔ/ 'other, different' (i.e. of a different sort), though it might be taken as a specifier on account of its meaning 'other', is more plausibly considered as a nominal. A semantic reason for suggesting this, is that its gloss does not mean 'another specimen of the same kind' but 'of a diferent sort'. A morphosyntactic reason is that it regularly takes the nominal prefix. Consider its paradigm in (184), where a homomorph, /-ŋaaɔ/ is also spelled out,

(184) /-aaɔ/ 'other, different (kind)'

1	[omwaaɔ]	[omoŋaaɔ]
2	[aβaaɔ]	[aβaŋaaɔ]
3	[omwaaɔ]	[omoŋaaɔ]
4	[emiaaɔ]	[emeŋaaɔ]
5	[eriaaɔ]	[riiŋaaɔ], *[eriŋaaɔ]
6	[amaaɔ]	[amaŋaaɔ]
7	[ekiaaɔ]	[ekeŋaaɔ]
8	[eβiaaɔ]	[eβiŋaaɔ]
9	[eŋaaɔ]	[eŋaaɔ]
10	[ciŋaaɔ]	[ciŋaaɔ]
11	[orwaaɔ]	[oroŋaaɔ]
12	[akaaɔ]	[akaŋaaɔ]
14	[oβwaaɔ]	[oβoŋaaɔ]
15	[okwaaɔ]	[okoŋaaɔ]
16	[aaaɔ]	[aŋaaɔ]

So much for quantifiers and specifiers.

3.2.13. Cardinal numerals and -reeŋga.

A numeral may be defined as any word or phrase that denotes or expresses the concept of number (thus in section 3.1.8). This includes any specific number concept. The definition holds for Gusii.

The traditional linguistic distinction between cardinal and ordinal numerals also holds for Gusii. Cardinal numerals are words or phrases that refer to primitive numbers, e.g. one, two, three, twenty, one hundred and twelve, or one thousand. They are discussed in the present section. Ordinal numerals will be defined and discussed in section 3.2.14.

Prefixation of cardinal numerals may vary. This depends partly on the particular numeral involved, partly on their usage. First, the numeral /-mɔ/ 'one' regularly takes the referential prefix.

Second, all other numerals take the pronominal prefix, but with a difference. Since in the nature of the case all of them designate a number higher than one, only plural prefixes are ever used. Moreover, instead of the regular pronominal prefix /ci-/, numerals take the unique allomorph /i-/ for class 10. Though it is not necessary to set up a distinct prefix paradigm merely to account for this difference, the pronominal prefix might nonetheless be called counting prefix (abbreviation: cpx) in this usage, as long as it is borne in mind that the allomorph for class 10 is /i-/.[109]

Third, and finally, in counting this is the very prefix that is used with any numeral.

Since /-mɔ/ may be used both as a numeral, meaning 'one', and as an adjective, meaning 'at one, belonging together', in the sense of 'belonging to the same class' or 'at one place', it may be used with both singular and plural refential prefixes, as in (185),

[109] The paradigm would be as follows,

Numeral prefix

1	o-/βo-
2	βa-
3	o-/βo-
4	e-
5	ri-
6	a-
7	ke
8	βi-
9	e-
10	i-
11	ro-
12	ka-
14	βo-
15	ko-
16	a-
21	= 9 or 16

(185) singular: 'one'
plural: '(belonging) together'

1	/o-yo-o-mɔ/	-->	[ɔyɔɔmɔ]
	a-rpx-1-one		
2	/a-βa-a-mɔ/	-->	[aβaamɔ]
3	/o-yo-o-mɔ/	-->	[ɔyɔɔmɔ]
4	/e-ye-e-mɔ/	-->	[ɛyɛɛmɔ]
5	/e-ri-mɔ/	-->	[erimɔ]
6	/a-ya-a-mɔ/	-->	[ayaamɔ]
7	/e-ke-mɔ/	-->	[ɛkɛmɔ]
8	/e-βi-mɔ/	-->	[eβimɔ]
9	/e-ye-e-mɔ/	-->	[ɛyɛɛmɔ]
10	/e-ci-mɔ/	-->	[ecimɔ]
11	/o-ro-mɔ/	-->	[ɔrɔmɔ]
12	/a-ka-mɔ/	-->	[akamɔ]
14	/o-βo-mɔ/	-->	[ɔβɔmɔ]
15	/o-ko-mɔ/	-->	[ɔkɔmɔ]
16	/a-ya-mɔ/	-->	[ayamɔ]
	/a-mɔ/	-->	[aamɔ]
21	= 9 or 16		

Postlexical (non-)augmentation may apply. In addition to phonological variation in (185), which may be accounted for by various rules discussed in Chapter Two, there is some morphological variation. This may be accounted for by (186),

(186) allomorphy ==>

a. V-mɔ / 1-4, 9, 16
b. -mɔ / elsewhere

(where V = copy of the augment or prefix vowel)

Since 21 may be equivalent to either 9 or 16, it is implied in (186a). As indicated, pronominal prefix /a-/ may be an alternative for 16, also long. One would have expected referential prefix 16 to be long too, thus [ayaamɔ], but in fact only [ayamɔ] was given in the field. These points may need further inquiry.

The different meanings of /-mɔ/ are exemplified in (187),

(187) a. |cim-bori eci-mɔ]
10a-goat 10-one
[cimbori ecimɔ]
'goats belonging to one class'

b. |eβi-saβɔ[110] βi-ɔnsi a-mɔ|
6-branch 6-all 16-one
[eβisaβɔ βiɔnsi amɔ]
'all the branches together'

c. [omoonto ɔyɔɔmɔ] 'one person'
versus [aβaanto aβaamɔ] 'persons of one family' (literally, 'belonging together')

d. [emete εyεεmɔ] 'trees belonging together, trees of the same species'.

The plural pronominal prefixes used with cardinal numerals are exemplified in (188),

(188) /-βere/ 'two'

2	/βa-βere/	--> [βaβere]
4	/e-βere/	--> [eβere]
6	/a-βere/	--> [aβere]
8	/βi-βere/	--> [βiβere]
10	/i-βere/	--> [iβere]
14	/βo-βere/	--> [βoβere] (augmentative)
16	/a-ra-ka-βere/	--> [arakaβere]

/-taanɔ/ 'five'

2	/βa-taanɔ/	--> [βataanɔ]
4	/e-taanɔ/	--> [etaanɔ]
6	/a-taanɔ/	--> [ataanɔ]
8	/βi-taanɔ/	--> [βitaanɔ]
10	/i-taanɔ/	--> [isaanɔ]
14	/βo-taanɔ/	--> [βotaanɔ] (augmentative)

/-tato/ 'three'

2	/βa-tato/	--> [βatato]
4	/e-tato/	--> [etato]
6	/a-tato/	--> [atato]
8	/βi-tato/	--> [βitato]
10	/i-tato/	--> [isato]
14	/βo-tato/	--> [βotato] (augmentative)

[110] Or [eβisaβo].

The form for class 16 is relatively exceptional. Anticipating the discussion of ordinals in the next section, the following semantic variation involving class 16 may be noted here,

(189) [ase arakaβere] 'two places' (cardinal numeral)
[ase ayakaβere] 'the second place' (ordinal numeral)
[ase aakaβere] 'the second place' (ordinal numeral, used by itself as a monophrasal sentence)

The change from /t/ to |s| is found in /-tato/ and /-taanɔ/. Compare /βi-tato/ --> [βitato] '8-three' with /i-tato/ --> [isato] '10-three'. However, it only occurs in class 10, as in (188). These exceptional allomorphs may be entered in the lexicon, as in (190),

(190) /-taanɔ/ 'five'; 10 /-saanɔ/
/-tato/ 'three'; 10 /-sato/

Using the head [eβiinto] '7-things' for example, numerals 2-10 take the following forms,

(191)	2	[βiβere]
	3	[βitato]
	4	[βinɛ]
	5	[βitaanɔ]
	6	[βitaanɔ kɛmɔ]
	7	[βitaanɔ βiβere]
	8	[βitaanɔ βitato]
	9	[kiaanda]
	10	[ikomi]

Note the use of the singular, [kɛmɔ], here morphosyntactic class 7, in the expression for numeral six.

The interrogative specifier /-reNγa/ --> [-reeηga] 'how many?' also takes the pronominal-cum-numeral prefix. Whiteley's statement that this interrogative adjective takes a verbal prefix, seems incorrect (1956: 21). Naturally, since it questions a plural number of referents, it only occurs with plural prefixes, as in (192),

(192)	2	/βa-reNγa/	-->	[βareeηga]
	4	/e-reNγa/	-->	[ereeηga]
	6	/a-reNγa/	-->	[areeηga]
	8	/βi-reNγa/	-->	[βireeηga]
	10	/i-reNγa/	-->	[ireeηga]
	14	/βo-reNγa/	-->	[βoreeηga]

The use of class 10 may be generalised, even when this word is used attributively, as in [riitɔɔkɛ ireeηga ɔkɔɔnia] 'you are selling the banana for how much?', or in the ethically improper, but linguistically correct example [ireeηga ɔkɔɔnia omwaana] 'for how much are you selling the baby?'.

Having discussed the morphosyntactic prefixes and agreement of cardinal numerals, it remains to consider the numbering system as such. Only a brief outline of it will be given here, beginning with a few general introductory remarks.

First, apart from prefixation, the cardinal numerals for 1-5 and 9, 10, 100, and 1000 are monomorphemic, but all other numerals are morphologically composite. For example, the numeral for 6, |i-saanɔ na e-mɔ|, literally means 'five and one'. Due to phonological liaison, it is normally pronounced as [isaanɛɛmɔ] in non-monitored speech.

Second, in counting, the augmented numeral prefix 9, /e-ye-/, or merely its vowel or augment /e-/, is used with /-mɔ/ 'one'. Numeral prefix 10 /i-/ is used with numerals 2-8. Numeral 9 /kianda/ 'nine' is always invariant, even when it is used attributively with non-numerals of any morphosyntactic class, as in [ciñoomba kiaanda] 'nine houses' or [aβaanto kiaanda] 'nine persons'. Whenever numerals are used attributively in composite cardinals, however, they agree morphosyntactically with the class of the head they modify, as in (193),

(193) |e-me-rɔɔŋgɔ e-taanɔ|
npx4-tenfold cpx4-five
[ɛmɛrɔɔŋgɔ etaanɔ] or [ɛmɛrɔɔŋgeetaanɔ]
literally, 'five tenfolds'
'fifty'

|e-riβu e-ye-mɔ|
9-thousand a-9-one
[eriβu ɛyɛɛmɔ] or [eriβwɛɛyɛmɔ]
'one thousand'

|ci-riβu i-komi|
10-thousand 10-ten
[ciriβu ikomi] or [ciriβw(i)ikomi]
'ten thousand'

Third, multiples of 10, from 20 to 90, are formed by means of the word [ɛmɛrɔɔŋgɔ] 'tenfolds', singular /omo-rɔɔŋgɔ/ --> [ɔmɔrɔɔŋgɔ]. Thus, for example, [ɛmɛrɔɔŋgɔ eβere], literally translated, means 'two tenfolds', i.e. 'twenty'. This type of expression is somewhat similar to the traditional way of counting in English, in expressions such as 'threescore and ten' for 70, and 'fourscore' for 80, where **score** evidently means 'twenty-fold'.

Fourth, the change from /t/ to [s] in numerals 3 and 5 has already been noted, but a change involving numeral 4 has not yet been mentioned. Apparently, the form of the word is /-ñɛ/, whenever it occurs in class 10, but /-nɛ/, whenever it occurs in any of the other classes. For examples, see the forms of the numerals for 4 and 40 in (194).

The rest of the Gusii numeral system, as used in counting, consistently derives from the representations and principles in (194), using class 10 for the numbers 2-8 and 10,

(194) cardinal numerals

1	/e-ye-e-mɔ/	-->	[ɛyɛɛmɔ]
2	/i-βere/ 10-two	-->	[iβere]
	similarly:		
3	/i-tato/	-->	[isato]
4	/i-ñɛ/	-->	[iñɛ]
5	/i-taanɔ/	-->	[isaanɔ]
6	/i-taanɔ na e-mɔ/ 10-five and 9-one	-->	[isaanɔ nɛɛmɔ] 'five and one'
	or /i-taanɔ e-mɔ/	-->	[isaanɔ ɛɛmɔ] 'five one' or [isaanɛɛmɔ]
7	/i-taanɔ na i-βere/ 10-five and 10-two	-->	[isaanɔ na iβere] 'five and one'
	/i-taanɔ i-βere/ 10-five 10-two	-->	[isaanɔ iβere]
	hybrid form: [isaanaiβere]		
8	/i-taanɔ na i-tato/ 10-five and 10-three	-->	[isaanɔ na isato] 'five and three'
	or		
	/i-taanɔ i-tato/ 10-five 10-three	-->	[isaanɔ isato]
	or		
	hybrid form: [isaanaisato]		

(the alternative expressions for 6, 7, 8 may recur in composite numbers containing these, such as 26, 27, 28, etc.)

9	/kianda/	-->	[kianda][111]
10	/i-komi/	-->	[ikomi]

[111] This may also be pronounced as [kiaanda] or [kyaanda], depending on the style of speech.

11 /i-komi na e-ye-mɔ/ --> [ikominεεyεεmɔ]
cpx10-ten and rpx9-one

or

/i-komi na e-mɔ/ --> [ikominεεmɔ]
cpx10-ten and cpx9-one

similarly:

12 ¦ikomi na iβere¦
13 ¦ikomi na isato¦
14 ¦ikomi na iñε¦

15 ¦ikomi na isaanɔ¦
16 ¦ikomi na isaanɔ εmɔ¦ or [isaanεεmɔ¦
17 ¦ikomi na isaanɔ iβere¦
18 ¦ikomi na isaanɔ isato¦
19 ¦ikomi na kianda¦

20 /e-me-rɔNγɔ e-βere/ --> [εmεrɔɔηgɔ eβere]
npx4-tenfold 4-two

21 /e-me-rɔNγɔ e-βere na e-ye-mɔ/
npx4-tenfold 4-two and rpx4/9-one
[εmεrɔɔηgɔ eβere nεεyεmɔ]

22 /e-me-rɔNγɔ e-βere na i-βere/
npx4-tenfold 4-two and rpx10-one
[εmεrɔɔηgɔ eβere na iβere]

similarly:

23 [εmεrɔɔηgɔ eβere na isato]
24 [εmεrɔɔηgɔ eβere na iñε]
25 [εmεrɔɔηgɔ eβere na isaanɔ]
26 [εmεrɔɔηgɔ eβere na isaanɔ nεεmɔ]
27 [εmεrɔɔηgɔ eβere na isaanɔ na iβere]
28 [εmεrɔɔηgɔ eβere na isaanɔ na isato]
29 [εmεrɔɔηgɔ eβere na kianda]

30 ¦e-me-rɔɔηgɔ e-tato¦ --> [εmεrɔɔηgɔ etato]
npx4-tenfold 4-three

similarly:

40 ¦εmεrɔɔngɔ εnε¦
50 ¦εmεrɔɔngɔ etaanɔ¦

60 |e-me-rɔɔngɔ e-taanɔ na o-mɔ|
npx4-tenfold cpx4-five and ppx3-one
five and one (i.e. six) tenfolds
[ɛmɛrɔɔngɔ etaanɔ nɔɔmɔ][112]

similarly:

70 |ɛmɛrɔɔngɔ etaanɔ na eβere|[113]
80 |ɛmɛrɔɔngɔ etaanɔ na etato|[114]
90 |ɛmɛrɔɔngɔ kianda|

100 /e-mia/ --> [emia] 'a hundred'
9-hundred

or

/e-mia e-ye-mɔ/ --> [emia ɛyɛɛmɔ][115] 'one hundred'
9-hundred rpx9-one

110 |e-mia ɛyɛ-ɛmɔ na i-komi|
9-hundred rpx9-one and 10-ten

or

|e-mia na i-komi|
9-hundred and 10-ten

etc.

199 |emia ɛyɛɛmɔ na ɛmɛrɔɔηgɔ kianda na kianda|
hundred one and tenfolds nine and nine

---

112 An alternative surface representation recorded here is [ɛmɛrɔɔηgɔ etaanɔɔmɔ], from /eme-rɔɔηgɔ etaanɔ o-mɔ/, where the final element, /o-mɔ/ 'one', refers to class 1. The prefix of any numeral participating in the system of morphosyntactic agreement and functioning as a final element in composite numerals such as this, will agree with the class of its syntactic head.

113 Also |ɛmɛrɔɔngɔ etaanɔ neeβere|, |ɛmɛrɔɔngɔ etaanɔ eβere|, or [ɛmɛrɔɔngɔ etaaneeβere].

114 Also [ɛmɛrɔɔngɔ etaanɔ neetato], [ɛmɛrɔɔngɔ etaanɔ etato], or [ɛmɛrɔɔngɔ etaaneetato].

115 Also [emiɛɛyɛɛmɔ]. By itself, [emia] means 'a hundred'. [emia ɛyɛɛmɔ] more emphatically means '**one** hundred'.

200 /ci-mia i-βere/ --> [cimia iβere]
10-hundred 10-two

1000 /e-riβu e-ye-mɔ/ --> [eriβu ɛyɛɛmɔ]
cpx9-thousand rpx9-one

10.000 /ci-riβu i-komi/ --> [ciriβu ikomi]
cpx10-thousand rpx10-ten

100.000 /ci-riβu e-mia e-ye-mɔ/
10-thousand 9-hundred a-9-one
[ciriβu emia ɛyɛɛmɔ]

1.000.000 [emiiriooni]

Presumably, 1000 [eriβu] is a lexical take-over, with some phonological adaptation, from Swahili **elfu**, and similarly, the word for 100.000, [emiiriɔn], is taken over from English **million**. The reader may wish to deduce the rest of the system for himself.

More surface variation is possible than has been recorded here. Future investigation may wish to detail this.

3.2.14. Ordinal numerals.

Ordinal numerals may be defined as words or phrases that express numbers with reference to their position in a series, e.g. first, second, twentieth, one hundred and thirteenth, a thousandth.

Most Gusii ordinal numerals are derived from the cardinal numerals. Since these have already been discussed in section 3.2.15, only the barest outline need be given here of the ordinal numeral system. I will first consider their underlying representations, using classes 1 and 7 for examples, and then their morphosyntactic agreement, distinguishing between their attributive and independent usage.

To begin with, consider the representations of ordinals in (195),

(195) 1st /o-mo-taaŋ-an-i/
npx7-lead-rc-fv
[omotaaŋani][116]

/e-ke-taaŋ-an-i/
npx7-lead-rc-fv
[eγetaaŋani]

---

[116] The full paradigm is

1	[omotaaŋani]
2	[aβataaŋani]
3	[omotaaŋani]
4	[emetaaŋani]
5	[riitaaŋani]
6	[amataaŋani]
7	[eγetaaŋani]
8	[eβitaaŋani]
9	[entaaŋani]
10	[cintaaŋani]
11	[orotaaŋani]
12	[aγataaŋani]
14	[oβotaaŋani]
15	[oγotaaŋani]
16	[ataaŋani]
21	= 9 or 16

2nd /(oyo-)o-ka-βere/
rpx1-ppx1-ppx12-two
[(oyo)okaβere][117]
'the second (one)'

/e-ke-a-ka-βere/
rpx7-of[118]-ppx12-two
[eγiaakaβere]
'the second U

/o-yo-o-ka-tato/ --> [oyooγatato]

/e-ke-a-ka-tato/ --> [ekiaaγatato]
4th /o-yo-o-ka-nε/ --> [oyookanε]
/e-ke-a-ka-nε/ --> [eγiaakanε]
5th /o-yo-o-ka-taanɔ/ --> [oyooγataanɔ]
/e-ke-a-ka-taanɔ/ --> [ekiaaγataanɔ]

6th /o-yo-o-ka-taanɔ na ri-mɔ/
rpx1-ppx1-ppx12-five and ppx5-one
[oyooγataanɔ na rimɔ]
or [oyooγataanɔ na ɔmɔ] > [..nɔɔmɔ]

---

[117] The full paradigm is

1	[okaβere]
2	[βaakaβere]
3	[okaβere]
4	[yaakaβere]
5	[riaakaβere]
6	[akaβere]
7	[γiaakaβere]
8	[βiaakaβere]
9	[yaakaβere]
10	[ciaakaβere]
11	[rwaakaβere]
12	[γaakaβere]
14	[βwaakaβere]
15	[γwaakaβere]
16	[akaβere]
21	= 9 or 16

[118] Strictly, /a-ka/ may be analysed as referential prefix 12, i.e. an augment and a prefix proper, but it seems more plausible to interprete these elements as a sequence of the associative element plus pronominal prefix 12.

/e-ke-a-ka-taanɔ na ri-mɔ/
rpx7-of-ppx12-five and ppx5-one
[ekiaγataanɔ na rimɔ]
or [..na kεmɔ]

(it is grammatically more correct to have the numbers agree morphosyntactically, but increasingly the alternative [rimɔ], though less correct, is becoming the standard, especially in the speech of the younger generation)

7th /o-yo-o-ka-taanɔ (na) ka-βere/
rpx1-ppx1-ppx12-five (and) 12-two
[oyooγataanɔ (na) kaβere]
'the seventh (one)'

/e-ke-a-ka-taanɔ (na) ka-βere/
rpx7-of-ppx12-five (and) 12-two
[ekiaγataanɔ (na) kaβere]
'the seventh (one)'

8th /o-yo-o-ka-taanɔ na ka-tato/
rpx1-ppx1-ppx12-five and 12-three
[oyooγataanɔ (na) γatato]

/e-ke-a-ka-taanɔ (na) ka-tato/
rpx7-of-ppx12-five (and) 12-three
[ekiaγataanɔ (na) γatato]

9th /o-yo-o-kianda/
rpx1-ppx1-nine
[oyookiaanda]

/e-ke-a-kianda/
rpx7-of-nine
[eγiakiaanda]

10th /o-yo-o-i-komi/
rpx1-ppx1-cpx10-ten
[oyoikomi][119]

/e-ke-a-i-komi/
rpx7-of-cpx10-ten
[eγiaikomi]

[119] |oo| is shortened before /i/, thus |oyooikomi| --> [oyoikomi].

11th |eγiaikomi na kεmɔ|
7-tenth and 7-one
[eγiaikomi na kεmɔ]

similarly:

12th [eγiaikomi na kaβere]
13th [eγiaikomi na γatato]
14th [eγiaikomi na kanε]
15th [eγiaikomi na γataanɔ]
16th [eγiaikomi na γataanɔ kεmɔ][120]
17th [eγiaikomi na γataanɔ kaβere]
18th [eγiaikomi na γataanɔ γatato]
19th [eγiaikomi na γataanɔ kianda]

20th /oyo βwa eme-rɔɔŋgɔ e-βere/
rpx1 1-of 4-tenfold 4-two
'1-the-one 1-of two tenfolds'
[oyo βwεεmεrɔɔŋgɔ eβere]
or [oyo βwεεmεrɔɔŋge(e)βere]
'1-twentieth'

similarly:

30th [oyo βwεεmεrɔɔŋgɔ etato]
40th [oyo βwεεmεrɔɔŋgɔ εnε]
50th [oyo βwεεmεrɔɔŋgɔ etaanɔ]
60th [oyo βwεεmεrɔɔŋgɔ etaanɔ (na) ɔmɔ]
70th [oyo βwεεmεrɔɔŋgɔ etaanɔ (na) eβere]
80th [oyo βwεεmεrɔɔŋgɔ etaanɔ (na) etato]
90th [oyo βwεεmεrɔɔŋgɔ kianda]

similarly, 10th-90th with class 7:

10th [eγiaikomi]
20th [ekiaεmεrɔɔŋgɔ eβere]
30th [ekiaεmεrɔɔŋgɔ etato]
40th [ekiaεmεrɔɔŋgɔ εnε]
50th [ekiaεmεrɔɔŋgɔ etaanɔ]
60th [ekiaεmεrɔɔŋgɔ etaanɔ (na) kεmɔ] (or ɔmɔ)
70th [ekiaεmεrɔɔŋgɔ etaanɔ (na) βiβere] (or eβere)
80th [ekiaεmεrɔɔŋgɔ etaanɔ (na) βitato] (or etato)

[120] Or [...rimɔ], especially with the younger generation.

90th [ekia εmεrɔ ɔŋgɔ kianda])[121]

100th /o-yo βo-a e-mia e-ye-e-mɔ/
rpx1 1-of 9-hundred rpx9-ppx9-one
1-the-one 1-of one hundred
[oyoβweemia εyεεmɔ]
'1-one hundredth'

/e-ke-a e-mia e-ye-e-mɔ/
rpx7 9-hundred rpx9-ppx9-one
7-(the-one)-of one hundred
[ekia emia εyεεmɔ] or [ekieemiεεyεεmɔ]
'7-hundredth'

200th /o-yo βo-a ci-mia i-βere/
rpx1 1-of 10-hundred 10-two
1-(the-one) 1-of two hundred
[oyoβweecimia iβere]
'1-two hundredth'

/e-ke-a e-ci-mia i-βere/
rpx7-of rpx10-hundred 10-two
7-(the-one)-of two hundred
|ekia ecimia iβere|
[eγieecimiiβere]
'7-two hundredth'

It is clear from this array that the word meaning 'first' is constructed differently from the remainder of the system. It may arguably be considered as a deverbal adjective meaning '(the) leading (one)', since it is derived from /ko-taaŋ-an-a/ --> [γotaaŋana] 'to lead'. Further, its prefixation for classes 1 and 3 may be accounted for as, in (196)

(196) ordinal numerals: prefixation ==>

a. rpx-ppx- / class 1, 3
α α

b. rpx-a- / elsewhere

the rest of the system may be said to be constructed, in a somewhat ad hoc manner, as in (197),

---

121 Note that [oyo] and [ekia] mean 'the one' and, as such, are optional; in counting, [oyo βw(a)] and [ekia] are omitted.

(197) ordinal numeral system

a. 2nd-5th

$rpx_{\alpha}\text{-}\left\{\begin{matrix} a \\ ppx \end{matrix}\right\}_{\alpha}\text{-ka-cardinal}$

b. 6th-8th

6th $rpx_{\alpha}\text{-}\left\{\begin{matrix} a \\ ppx \end{matrix}\right\}_{\alpha}\text{-ka-taanɔ}$ ri-mɔ $\left[\begin{matrix} \\ \text{ka-}\beta\text{ere} \\ \gamma\text{a-tato} \end{matrix}\right]$

7th

8th

ppx-numeral

(where /ri-/ = ppx 5 and /ka-/ = ppx 12)

c. 9th-10th

$rpx_{\alpha}\text{-}\left\{\begin{matrix} a \\ ppx \end{matrix}\right\}_{\alpha}\text{-cardinal}$

d. 11th

$rpx_{\alpha}\text{-}\left\{\begin{matrix} a \\ ppx \end{matrix}\right\}_{\alpha}\text{-ikomi na ppx-mɔ}$

e. 12th-19th

$rpx_{\alpha}\text{-}\left\{\begin{matrix} a \\ ppx \end{matrix}\right\}_{\alpha}\text{ -ikomi na ka-cardinal}$

f. 20th-50th

$rpx_{\alpha}\text{-}\left\{\begin{matrix} a \\ ppx\text{-}a \end{matrix}\right\}_{\alpha}\text{-εmεrɔɔŋgɔ ppx4-cardinal}$

g. 60th-80th

$rpx_{\alpha}\text{-}\left\{\begin{matrix} a \\ ppx\text{-}a \end{matrix}\right\}_{\alpha}\text{-εmεrɔɔŋgɔ etaanɔ na ppx- mɔ}$ α $\begin{matrix} \beta\text{ere} \\ \text{tato} \end{matrix}$

(where ppx affixed to -βere and -tato is the plural of rpx)

h. 90th

rpx-{ a }-ɛmɛrɔɔŋgɔ kianda
α {ppx1-a}
α

i. 100th, etc

rpx-{ a }-cpx-mia ppx-cardinal
α {ppx1-a} ß ß
α

(where α and ß indicate class identity)

Additions to tenfolds and hundredfolds are made through /na/ + cardinal, as in (198),

(198) 42nd /eke-a e-me-rɔɔŋgɔ e-nɛ na kaßere|
rpx7-of npx4-tenfold cpx4-four and ppx12-two
|ekia ɛmɛrɔɔŋgɔ ɛnɛ na kaßere|
7-of four tenfolds and two
'forty-second'

When ordinals are used attributively, their morphosyntactic agreement is expressed through the pronominal prefix. If we bear in mind the representational variation in (199),

(199) agreement of ordinals used attributively

a. ppx-ka-cardinal / classes 1, 3, 16
b. ppx-a-ka-cardinal / elsewhere

the simplest underlying representation of ordinals is summed up in ppx-(a)-ka-cardinal, as in (200)

(200) a. ppx-ka-ßere '(the) second'
b. ppx-a-ka-ßere '(the) second'

Compare the examples in (201),

(201) 1 /o-mo-Nto o-ka-βere/
[omoonto okaβere]
'the second person'

2 /a-βa-Nto βa-a-ka-βere/[122]
[aβaanto βaakaβere]
'the second people'

3 /o-mo-te o-ka-βere/
[omote okaβere]
'the second tree'

4 /e-me-te e-a-ka-βere/
[emete yaakaβere]
'the second trees'

5 /rii-tɔɔkɛ ri-a-ka-βere/
[riitɔɔkɛ riakaβere]
'the second banana'

6 /a-ma-tɔɔkɛ a-ka-βere/
[amatɔɔkɛ akaβere]
'the second bananas'

7 /e-ke-Nto ke-a-ka-βere/
[eγeento γiakaβere]
'the second thing'

8 /e-βi-Nto βi-a-ka-βere/
[eβiinto βiakaβere]
'the second things'

9 /e-ηiti e-a-ka-βere/
[eηiti yaakaβere]
'the second animal'

10 /ci-ηiti ci-a-ka-βere/
[ciηiti ciakaβere]
'the second animals'

---

122 /a-βa-Nto βa-a-ka-βere/ is postulated on the basis of Lilian's and Judith's speech. Another informant insisted on [βakaβere], which would necessitate /βa-ka-βere/. The difference may be idiolectal. Of course, [βaakaβere] is what one would expect by analogy to the rest of the sub-system displayed here, since it involves CV-prefixes.

11 /o-ro-ko ro-a-ka-βere/
[oroko ruakaβere]
'the second (piece of) firewood'

12 /a-ka-ana ka-a-ka-βere/
[akaana γaakaβere]
'the second little child'

14 /o-βo-kima βo-a-ka-βere/
[oβokima βwaakaβere]
'the second (portion of) ugali'

15 /o-ko-βɔkɔ ko-a-ka-βere/
[ɔkɔβɔkɔ γwaakaβere]
'the second arm'

16 /a-se a-ka-βere/
[ase akaβere]
'the second place'

21 = 9 or 16

Postlexical surface variation, such as [ciηiti ciakaβere], [ciaakaβere], [cyaakaβere], [cyakaβere], and [c(a)akaβere], may occur, depending on deliberateness and rate of speech.

Also compare the paradigm for 'fourth', in (202),

(202) 1 [omoonto okanɛ]
2 [aβaanto βaakanɛ]
3 [omote okanɛ]
4 [emete yaakanɛ]
5 [riitɔɔkɛ riakanɛ]
6 [amatɔɔkɛ akanɛ]
7 [eγeento γiakanɛ]
8 [eβiinto βiakanɛ]
9 [eηiti yaakanɛ]
10 [ciηiti ciakanɛ]
11 [oroko roakanɛ][123]
12 [aγaanto γaakanɛ]
14 [oβokima βwaakanɛ]
15 [oγokoro γwaakanɛ]
16 [ase akanɛ]
21 = 9 or 16

[123] The usual surface variation is possible in this paradigm; thus also, for example, [ruakanɛ], [ruaakanɛ], [rwaakanɛ].

Finally, independently used ordinals take an augmented prefix. The underlying representation of simple numerals consistently seems to be rpx-a-ka-cardinal throughout the paradigm (recall that the referential prefix is augmented). This is exemplified in (203), where rpx-a-ka-βere 'the second one(s)' is used as an example,

(203)	1	/o-yo-o-ka-βere/	-->	[oyookaβere] 'the second 1-one'
	2	/a-βa-a-ka-βere/	-->	[aβaakaβere] 'the second 2-ones'
	3	/o-yo-o-ka-βere/	-->	[oyookaβere]
	4	/e-ye-a-ka-βere/	-->	[eyaakaβere]
	5	/e-ri-a-ka-βere/	-->	[eriakaβere]
	6	/a-ya-a-ka-βere/	-->	[ayaakaβere]
	7	/e-ke-a-ka-βere/	-->	[eγiakaβere]
	8	/e-βi-a-ka-βere/	-->	[eβiakaβere]
	9	/e-ye-a-ka-βere/	-->	[eyaakaβere]
	10	/e-ci-a-ka-βere/	-->	[eciakaβere]
	11	/o-ro-a-ka-βere/	-->	[orwa(a)kaβere]
	12	/a-ka-a-ka-βere/	-->	[aγaakaβere]
	14	/o-βo-a-ka-βere/	-->	[oβwa(a)kaβere]
	15	/o-ko-a-ka-βere/	-->	[oγwa(a)kaβere]
	16	/a-a-ka-βere/	-->	[aakaβere] or
		/a-ya-a-ka-βere/	-->	[ayaakaβere]
	21	= 9 or 16		

Also compare (204),

(204) 'the fourth one(s)'

1	[oyookanε]
2	[aβaakanε]
3	[oyookanε]
4	[eyaakanε]
5	[eria(a)kanε]
6	[ayaakanε]
7	[eγiaakanε]
8	[eβiaakanε]
9	[eyaakanε]
10	[eciaakanε]
11	[orwaakanε]
12	[aγaakanε]
14	[oβwaakanε]
15	[oγwaakanε]
16	[aakanε] or [ayaakanε]
21	= 9 or 16

As indicated in several places in this section, there may be a few gaps in the account of the numerals. Future research may wish to fill these in.

3.2.15. Summary.

A summary of the morphosyntactic class prefixes discussed previously is given in (205),

(205)

	nominal prefix (npx)	referential prefix (ppx)	pronominal prefix (rpx)	
1	o-mo-	o-yo-	o-/βo-	
(1a	mo-)			
(1b	0-)			
2	a-βa-	a-βa-	βa-	
3	o-mo-	o-yo-	o-/βo	
4	e-me-	e-ye-	e-	
5	e-ri-	e-ri-	ri-	
6	a-ma-	a-ya-	a-	(associative: ya-)
7	e-ke-	e-ke-	ke-	
8	e-βi-	e-βi-	βi-	
9	e-	e-ye	e-	
9a	e-n-			
10	ci-	e-ci-	ci-	
10a	ci-n-			
11	o-ro-	o-ro-	ro-	
12	a-ka-	a-ka-	ka-	
14	o-βo-	o-βo-	βo-	
15	o-ko-	o-ko-	ko-	
16	a-	a-ya-	a-	
21	ña-/9,16	9,16	9,16	

verbal prefixes:

	subject marker (sm)	relative marker (rm)	object marker (om)
1	a-	o-/βo-	mo-
2	βa-	βa-	βa-
3	o-	o-/βo-	yo-
4	e-	e-	ye-
5	ri-	ri-	ri-
6	a-	a-	ya-
7	ke-	ke-	ke-
8	βi-	βi-	βi-
9	e-	e-	ye-
10	ci-	ci-	ci-
11	ro-	ro-	ro-
12	ka-	ka-	ka-
14	βo-	βo-	βo-
15	ko-	ko-	ko-
16	a-	a-	ya-
21	= 9/16	9/16	6/16

animate

1s n(a)-	n(a)-, o-/βo-	n(a)-
2s o-/βo-, ko-	o-/βo-, ko-	ko-
3s a-, o-	o-, βo-	mo-
1p to-	to-	to-
2p mo-	βa-	βa-
3p βa-	βa-	βa-

(where class 1 = 3s and class 2 = 3p)

This survey only takes the regular underlying representation of the prefixes into account. Postlexical non-augmentation has thus been left out of consideration. Lexical non-augmentation has been indicated only for nominal prefix 1a and 1b (the segmentally zero prefix for the latter naturally excludes the augment). The allomorphs for nominal prefix 5, viz. /rii-/ and /ri-/, and for pronominal prefix 1, viz. /βo-/, are accounted for by rule. In most types of augmented class prefix, the augment is a copy of the class prefix proper, but when the prefix vowel is high, its augment, otherwise identical, is upper mid.

Apart from allomorphy and allophony, several similarities and contrasts between the paradigms may be noted in survey (205), and some observations may be added.

First, CV-prefixes 1-3p, 2, 5, 7, 8, 10-15 are identical for all paradigms. Second, nominal and referential prefixes are similar, except that where the former have /m/, the latter have /y/; where the former are /V/, the latter are /VyV/ (9 and 16, where V is identical); and where the former has /ci-/, the latter has /eci-/. Third, except for class 1 /mo-/, the verbal object marker is identical to the referential prefix. Fourth, the pronominal prefix is identical with the subject marker, except for class 1 and pronominal allomorph 3 /βo-/. Fifth, the pronominal prefix is identical with the relative marker, but for pronominal allomorph 6 /ya-/. By implication, sixth, the subject marker is identical with the relative marker, except for class 1 and relative allomorph 3 /βo-/.

Several observations may be added. First, when used with numerals, pronominal prefix allomorph 10 /i-/ replaces /ci-/. Second, pronominal prefix allomorph 6 /ya-/ only occurs with associative /-a/. Third, when used with the independent pronoun, all pronominal CV-prefixes are augmented. Fourth, /y/ of object markers may freely vary with /ñ/ intervocalically. Fifth, for details of the allomorphy of pronominal prefix and relative marker 1 and 3, and of 1-3s, the reader is referred to sections 3.2.3.1 and 3.2.3.2.

With regard to the usage of the prefixes in survey (205), the following concluding remarks may be made. First, the nominal prefixes are generally used with nouns and adjectives.

Second, the referential prefix has several uses. It may be used with the independent possessive personal pronoun, the non-personal possessive pronoun, the semi-proximate demonstrative, numeral /-mɔ/ 'one' and other numerals. It, or the homomorph of this prefix, the proximate demonstrative, may be used, independently or attributively, as a separate morpheme meaning 'this' or 'the one, the aforementioned one'. Finally, the referential prefix may be used as a relative marker with /-re/ 'to be' and possibly also with other verbs, though as such it is usually followed by the regular relative marker and may be restricted to classes 1 and 3, so that its second and third use are hard to distinguish (this point requires further research).

The pronominal prefix may be used as relative marker, with associative /-a/ (where 6 = ya-), arguably with semi-proximate demonstrative allomorph /-yi-/ (classes 1, 3, 4, 6, 9, and possibly 16), with the non-proximate demonstrative, the independent pronoun (where 1 = e-), the interrogative pronoun, the attributive possessive personal pronoun, quantifiers and specifiers, and cardinal and ordinal numerals (where 10 = i-).

3.3. Verbal morphology.

In this section, I will consider, respectively, non-tensed basic verbal structure as exemplified in the infinitive and some imperatives (3.3.1), the possible extension of this basic structure by various affixes (3.3.2), the structure and elements of tensed verb forms (3.3.3), morphological fusion involving some of these affixes (3.3.4), the system of tenses (3.3.5), and several forms of the Gusii equivalent for 'to be' (3.3.6).

3.3.1. Basic verbal structure: infinitive and imperative.

A discussion of verbal morphology may conveniently begin with at least some indication of what is meant by verbal structure. The term designates the formal and functional arrangement of positions in verb forms onto which semantic and syntactic categories, such as focus, negation, subject, object, tense (including mood and aspect), reflexivity, applicativeness, reciprocity, causation, and voice may be encoded. The positions where these categories may be marked are sometimes called their structural slots.

The actual verbal elements or morphemes used to express the categories in these slots will also be considered in this and the following sections (see especially section 3.3.3)

The discussion may well begin with a consideration of the basic structure of the infinitive. It consists at least of class prefix 15, which functions as the infinitive marker (labelled 15), a verbal root, which is the morphological and semantic core of the verb, and a final vowel (fv). These elements always co-occur in this order, as in (206),

(206) plain infinitive

/ko-ruɣ-a/
15-cook-fv
[koruɣa]
'to cook'

The infinitive may occur, with or without a focus element, as a verbal complement in certain complex tenses. Such a focus is prefixed to the infinitive marker, as in (207),

(207) focussed infinitive

/n-ko-ruγ-a/
f-15-root-fv
[ηkoruγa]
'cooking'

Here, as elsewhere, 'f' is used to label this focus element. The main difference between focussed, as opposed to non-focussed tenses, seems to be that between theme and rhema. In some other, especially complex, tenses, where there appears to be no such distinction, the focus seems to have become grammaticalised (see section 3.3.5 for some examples).

The infinitive may also be used as a verbal noun. In this usage it is regularly augmented, as in (208),

(208) augmented infinitive, used as a verbal noun

/o-ko-ruγ-a/
a-15-root-fv
[okoruγa]
'cooking'

Here, as elsewhere, syntactic label 'a' designates the augment.

The non-augmented infinitive may also be used independently as a verbal noun. Compare the examples in (209),

(209) a. [koruγa] 'to cook'

e.g. [koruγa mbuya] 'to cook is good'
[mbuya koruγa] 'it is good to cook'

b. [okoruγa] '(the activity of) cooking'

e.g. [okoruγa nookuya] 'cooking is good'
(presumably from /na okuya/)

In this use it may be focussed too. For example, [ηkoruγa] may have thematic or identificatory meaning, viz. 'indeed, to cook' or 'it is to cook'.

While the infinitive marker, the root, and the final vowel are minimally necessary elements, and must therefore be present in the infinitive, the concept of negation may also be endoded on it through the addition of negative prefix /ta-/. Whenever this element occurs in the infinitive, it occurs between the infinitive marker and the root, as in (210),

(210) negative infinitive

/ko-ta-ruγ-a/
15-not-cook-fv
[γotaruγa]
'not to cook'

Since this negative prefix may also occur in tenses, where tense prefixes may occur between it and the root, it will be discussed again in section 3.3.3.2, together with another negative prefix, /ti-/, which occurs in tensed forms only.

3.3.2. Extension and extension affixes.

Generalising over both tensed and non-tensed forms, minimal verbal structure may be said to consist of the root and a final vowel. At least these two elements must be present. However, this minimal structure may be extended further through affixation.

Such extension involves one prefix, and seven or, if the passive voice marker may be included as such, eight suffixes. In the infinitive, such affixes immediately precede or follow the root. In tenses, certain tense-suffixes may occur between the root and some of the extension suffixes, or between some of the extension suffixes.

Next to extension suffixes, there are also expansion suffixes. These two types are differentiated as follows. Expansion affixes are those affixes that merely add to the root formally without changing its meaning, whereas extension suffixes add to the root both morphologically and semantically, extending both the form and the meaning of the root. This distinction will not be pursued in detail here, in that expansion suffixes will not be researched and discussed any further.

If, for the moment, we disregard actual combinations of extension affixes in specific verb forms, their occurrence and relative order may be summarised generally as in (211),

(211) number and arrangement of extension affixes

1		2	3 4	5	(5)	6	(6)	7	8	9
ee-	root	-ak	-ok -or	-ek	(-ek)	-er	(-er)	-an	-i	-u

Here, and in other figures, morphemes placed in one column are considered to be mutually exclusive. That is, either one, or the other of the column members, but not both at the same time, may occur in any one verb form. Thus /-ok/ and /-or/ may not co-occur.

A tentative basic semantic characterisation of these affixes is given in (212), together with their abbreviatory labels,

(212) /ee-/ reflexive prefix (rf)
/-ak/ resultative intransitive suffix (rs)
/-ek/ stative suffix (st)
/-ok/ reversive-intransitive suffix (ri)
/-or/ reversive-transitive suffix (rt)
/-er/ applicative suffix (ap)
/-an/ reciprocal suffix (rc)
/-i/ causative suffix (c)
/-u/ passive suffix (p)

This semantic characterisation is said to be basic, since at least some affixes may have a variety of meanings, even though these are usually more or less related to the basic one. Some of this variety will be considered in connection with examples to be given in a moment. The characterisation in (212) is also considered tentative, in the sense that it assumes the necessity of more extensive lexical and semantic research on this aspect of the language.

The words in (213) suggest that at least one more extension suffix may be added to the list in (212), viz. /-ar/,

(213)	/ko-riNγ-a/	/ko-riNγ-ar-a/
	15-fold-fv	15-fold-?-fv
	[koriiŋga]	*[koriiŋgara]
	'to fold (v.t.)'	'to fold (v.t.)'

However, as indicated by the question mark, its meaning is not exactly clear. Besides, similarly related word pairs appear to be rare. The word pairs in (214), for example, do not seem to be related,

(214) a. /ko-tiγ-a/
15-stop-fv
[γotiγa]
'to stop (v.t.)' (usually, o-ref: some activity)

/ko-tiγar-a/
15-stop-sx-fv
[γotiγara]
'to remain (behind) (v.i.)'

b. /ko-tu-a/
15-pick-fv
[γotwa]
'to pick, to pluck (fruit, vegetables)'

/ko-tuar-a/
15-pick-sx-fv
[γotwaara]
'to have, to possess'

c. /ko-ru-a/
15-give-fv
[korwa]
'to give (present, donation)'

/ko-ruar-a/
15-be sick-sx-fv
[korwaara]
'to be/become sick'

Their underlying representations are thus more plausibly postulated as /-tiγar-/, /-tuar-/, and /-ruar-/, rather than /-tiγ-ar-/, /-tu-ar-/, and /-ru-ar-/. On the basis of these few words, then, /ar/ cannot be established as an extension suffix. Moreover, there appear to be relatively few other verbs containing /-ar-/, if at all, since my informants could not supply any more. In view of such indeterminacy, this segment is more plausibly interpreted as an expansion suffix, than as an extension suffix. For the same reasons, it may not be possible to define its sense.

This state of affairs reflects the one postulated for Proto-Bantu, of which it is said that "the extension -ad- appears partly as an expansion, partly as a suffix with ill-defined meaning" (Meeussen 1967: 90).

Whenever the meanings of the affixes in (212) retains their full force, several general observations obtain. First, whichever of the affixes co-occur in any one verb form, they always occur in the order given in (211). That is, their relative order tends to be fixed.

Whiteley (1960: 8) does record at least one example, viz. <sangerererekan> 'be assembled together', in which the relative order of /-ek/ and /-er/ seems to have been reversed, but it is possible that /-er/ has lost its original semantic force here, and may therefore be considered as an expansion suffix. Since some expansion suffixes are homomorphous with some extension suffixes, this interpretation may account for many examples in which the extension suffix order seems to be reversed, but where in fact one or more homomorphous expansion suffixes are followed by one or more extension suffixes.

Second, the co-occurrence of extension affixes appears to be determined, at least in part, by logical and semantic factors. Thus, for example, reflexive prefix /ee-/ 'self' is evidently incompatible with reciprocal suffix /-an/ 'each other'.

Third, with respect to any infinitive, the arrangement in (212) must be interpreted to mean that the infinitive marker must, and negative prefix /ta-/ may, precede /ee-/, while final vowel /-a/ must follow the penultimate extension suffix, by definition.

Fourth, /-ek/ and /-er/ may be reduplicated in some verb forms, though not usually at the same time. This possibility is indicated, in (212), by their addition in parenthesis.

Fifth, the underlying representation of the passive voice marker is postulated as /-u/. As such, it occurs after consonants. Its allomorph, /-γu-/, occurs after vowels. The passive voice marker is included here as an extension suffix, since it behaves much like other extension suffixes. However, from a syntactic point of view, it might perhaps be classed differently (see section 3.3.2.9 for some discussion). It may be added that active voice is not marked morphologically.

Sixth, all upper mid affix vowels are subject to Mid Vowel Height Spreading (see section 2.3.14), whenever its structural description is met.

Seventh, and finally, if the passive voice marker may be included, at least four distinct types of extension suffix may co-occur in a single verb form.

A random, non-exhaustive sample of possible combinations, as exemplified in the infinitive /ko-kɔr-a/, is given in (215), where it is also shown that, for logical and semantic reasons, not all verbs may take all possible combinations of affixes,

(215)	underlying representation	surface representation
basic e.g. [γɔkɔra] 'to do'	-a	-a
reflexive e.g. [γwεεkɔra] 'to do oneself'	ee-	ee-
resultative *[γɔkɔraka]	-ak	-aka
reversive-intransitive *[γɔkɔrɔka]	-ok-a	-oka
reversive-transitive *[γɔkɔrɔra] (but [γɔkɔrɔra] 'to cough')	-or-a	-ora
stative e.g. [γɔkɔrεka] (a) 'to be done', (b) 'to be doable'	ek-a	-eka
stative e.g. [γɔkɔrεγεka] 'to be (latently) doable'	ek-ek-a	-eγeka (reduplicated)
applicative e.g. [γɔkɔrεra] 'to do for'	-er-a	-era
applicative e.g. [γɔkɔrεrεra] 'to do for'	-er-er-a	-er-er-a (reduplicated)
applicative-passive	-er-u-a	-erwa

applicative-causative	-er-i-a	-eria
applicative-causative-passive	-er-i-γu-a	-eriγwa
applicative-reciprocal e.g. [γɔkɔrɛrana] 'to do for each other'	-er-an-a	-erana
applicative-reciprocal-causative e.g. [γɔkɔrɛrania] 'to do simultaneously'	-er-an-i-a	-erania
applicative-reciprocal-causative-passive	-er-an-i-γu-a	-eraniγwa
reciprocal *[γɔkɔrana]	-an-a	-ana
reciprocal-passive	-an-u-a	-anwa
reciprocal-causative	-an-i-a	-ania
reciprocal-causative-passive	-an-i-γu-a	-aniγwa
causative e.g. [γɔkɔria] 'to cause to do'	-i-a	-ia
passive e.g. [γɔkɔrwa] 'to be done'	-u-a	-wa
causative-passive e.g. [γɔkɔriγwa] 'to be caused to do'	-i-γu-a	-iγwa

Not all possibilities have been listed in this array and not all listed possibilities have been exemplified. The affixes introduced here will be elaborated on in sections 3.3.2.1-10.

3.3.2.1. Reflexive prefix /ee-/.

To the best of my knowledge, reflexive prefix /ee-/ is not treated of in Whiteley (1956), though it is mentioned briefly as a pre-root extension in (1960: 8). As the term suggests, this prefix basically expresses reflexive meaning. It may be added that reflexivity implies non-transitivity.

This extension affix may be represented underlyingly as in (216a),

(216) reflexive prefix

a. Underlying representation   b. Derived

```
   x              x  x
   |              \ /
   e-              e-
```

Derivation of (216b) from (216a) will be in virtue of x-Assignment (see section 2.2.2).

Some verbs containing this prefix are exemplified in (217),

(217) a. /ko-ee-it-a/
15-rf-beat-fv
[γweéítá]
'to beat oneself, to kill oneself'

b. |ko-iraneria|
15-answer
[koíráneria]
'to answer, to reply (in speaking or writing)'

|ko-ee-iraneria|
15-rf-answer
[koeeiraneria]
'to answer oneself'

c. /ko-ee-sɔɔm-i-a/
15-rf-read-c-fv
[γɔεεsɔɔmia]
'to teach oneself'
(literally, 'to cause oneself to read')

d. /ko-ee-tεεr-i-a/
15-rf-sing-c-fv
[γɔεεtεεria]
'to make oneself sing'

It is arguably a moot point whether /ee-/ must be considered as an extension suffix proper, or as a special instance of the object marker. See section 3.3.3.6.2 for some discussion of this.

3.3.2.2. Resultative-intransitive suffix /-ak/.

Extension suffix /-ak/ is not mentioned as such by Whiteley (1956, 1960). It is termed resultative, because it seems to express a resulting state or condition; and intransitive, because it changes the transitive meaning of a root into an intransitive one. The syntactic label used to designate it in representations is rs. It is exemplified in (218),

(218) /ko-riNγ-a/
15-fold-fv
[koriiηga]
'to fold (v.t.)'

/ko-riNγ-ak-a/
15-fold-rs-fv
[koriiηgaka]
'to be folded (v.i.)'
(i.e. to be in a condition or state of foldedness)

e.g. |ri-a-riiηg-ak-ir-e|
5-t-fold-rs-t-fv
[riariiηgakire]
'5-it has just got folded (v.i.; i.e. got into a state of being folded)'

e.g. |ri-riiηg-ak-et-e|
rpx5-fold-rs-t-fv
[eririiηgaγete]
'5-it has (hence: is) folded (v.i.)'

e.g. /rii-sakara n-ko-riNγ-ak-a ri-re/
5-paper f-15-fold-rs-fv 5-be
[riisakara ηkoriiηgaka rire]
'the paper is folding (v.i.)'

3.3.2.3. Stative suffix /-ek/.

Extension suffix /-ek/ (label: st) basically expresses stative meaning. However, this characterisarion may be insufficient. It may be reduplicated. If non-reduplicated, it seems to express an actual state of affairs considered intransitively, glossed as 'to be (actually) [verb]ed'. If reduplicated, it seems to express a potential state of affairs considered intransitively, rendered as 'to be (potentially) [verb]ed'. Its precise meaning requires closer examination, but capacity to undergo the activity expressed by the verb or to effect the potential expressed by it, definitely seems to be intended. This is not passivity as expressed by the passive marker. Though Whiteley does not sufficiently define its sense, his paraphrase, "(..) the form is (..) common for the translation of such English adjectives as end in -able" (1956: 75), is thus surely to the point.

This extension suffix is exemplified in (219),

(219) a. /ko-βun-a/
15-break-fv
[koβuna]
'to break (v.t.)'

/ko-βun-ek-a/
15-break-st-fv
[koβuneka]
'to break (v.i.)'

/ko-βun-ek-ek-a/
15-break-st-st-fv
[koβuneγeka]
'to be breakable (v.i.)'

e.g. [εγεkɔɔmbε kiaβunekire] 'the cup is broken',
[εγεkɔɔmbε kiaβuneka] 'the cup is breakable, the cup breaks' (present perfect expresses a resulting state: 'has broken', hence 'is broken');
[εγεkɔɔmbε ŋkoβuneka kire] 'the cup is breaking'

b. /-rɔr-/ 'see'

/ko-rɔr-a/
15-see-fv
[kɔrɔra]
'to see (v.t.)'

/ko-rɔr-ek-a/
15-see-st-fv
[kɔrɔrεka]
'to be (actually) seen (v.i.)'
(i.e. it can be, and is, seen)

e.g. [omoriiko ɔkɔrɔrεka] 'the handwriting is (actually, clearly) visible' (i.e. legible);
[omoonto naarɔrεka] 'that person was seen'

/ko-rɔr-ek-ek-a/
15-see-st-st-fv
[kɔrɔrεγεka]
'to be (potentially) visible'

also:

/ko-rɔr-ek-an-a/
15-see-st-rc-fv
[kɔrɔrɛkana]
'to be (actually) seen mutually'

e.g. [ŋkɔrɔrɛkana ere] '9-it is (actually) visible';
[eγaari nɛɛrɔrɛkanete] 'the car is (actually) visible'

infrequently used, but possible, is:

/ko-rɔr-ek-ek-an-a/
15-see-st-st-rc-fv
[kɔrɔrɛγɛkana]
'to be (potentially) visible to each other' (i.e. the persons involved may see each other, but this is not actually the case)

c. /ko-riNγ-a/
15-fold-fv
[koriiŋga]
'to fold (v.t.)'

/ko-riNγ-ek-a/
15-fold-st-fv
[koriiŋgeka]
'to be folded (v.i.)'
'to be (actually, easily, readily) foldable (v.i.)'
(or 'to be ready for being folded')

e.g. /ti-e-ko-riNγ-ek-a/
not-9-t-fold-st-fv
[tekoriiŋgeka]
'it-9 is unfoldable, it-9 cannot be folded'

e.g. /rii-sakara n-ko-riNγ-ek-a ri-re/
5-paper f-15-fold-st-fv 5-be
[riisaka ŋkoriiŋgeka rire]
'the paper is (being) folded (v.i.)'
'the paper is foldable'

/ko-riNγ-ek-ek-a/
15-fold-st-st-fv
[koriiŋgeγeka]
'to be (potentially, latently) foldable (v.i.)'
(though this is not actually or readily the case)

where [kɔrɔrɛkana] shows that further extension of stative verbs is possible.

Somewhat detailed discussion of /-ek/ with one informant[124] suggested that it regularly expresses an actual capacity, such that the subject, in and of itself, may undergo the activity expressed by the verb. For example, if something is breakable, then of course it can be broken by an external agent, but this suffix expresses intransitive capacity. If this is correct, it makes the meaning of the root intransitive. But apparently the suffix may also be used by some in the following sense. When reduplicated, i.e. /-ek-ek/, it expresses a potential, or at least not yet actualised, state or capacity. In English, either of these meanings may be translated by words ending in -able or -ible. The informant suggested that this usage is due to insufficient grammatical understanding of some.

These shades of meaning are made more explicit in the following examples (220),

(220) a. /ko-aak-a/ --> [γwaaka] 'to hit'
/ko-aak-u-a/ --> [γwaakwa] 'to be hit' (passive transitive)
/ko-aak-ek-a/ --> [koaaγeka], 'to be hit', 'to be (actually) hittable'
e.g. [omoonto oria akwaaγeka] 'that person can be hit'
/ko-aak-ek-ek-a/ --> [koaakeγeka] 'to be (potentially) hittable'
e.g. [aγwaakeγeka] 'he may be hit'

b. /ko-ñu-a/ --> [koñwa] 'to drink'
/ko-ñu-ek-a/ --> [koñueka] 'to be drunk', 'to be (actually) drinkable'
/ko-ñu-ek-ek-a/ --> [koñueγeka] 'to be (potentially) drinkable'

c. /ko-miñɔk-a/ --> [komiñɔka] 'to run (v.t.)'
e.g. [aβaana ηkomiñɔka βare] 'the kids are running'
/ko-miñɔk-ek-a/ --> [komiñɔγεka] 'to be (actually) runable', [ase aria ηkomiñɔγεka are] 'that place is runnable' (i.e. it is possible to hold a race there, for example)
/ko-miñɔk-ek-ek-a/ --> [komiñɔkεγεka] 'to be (potentially) runnable', e.g. [ase aria ηkomiñɔkεγεka are] 'that place is (potentially or latently) runnable' (i.e. it may be used as a racecourse, for example, but not readily so: it will first have to be made fit for that purpose)

d. /ko-raβ-a/ --> [koraβa] 'to clean'
/ko-raβ-ek-a/ --> [koraβeka] 'to be clean', 'to be (actually) cleanable
e.g. [ekoraβeka] '9-it is cleanable, it may be cleaned'
/ko-raβ-ek-ek-a/ --> [koraβeγeka] 'to be (potentially) cleanable'

e. /ko-ri-a/ --> [koria] 'to eat'
/ko-ri-ek-a/ --> [korieka] 'to be (actually) edible'
/ko-ri-ek-ek-a/ --> [korieγeka] 'to be (potentially) edible'
(e.g. when something is in the fridge)

---

[124] Lilian Nyanchama.

f. /ko-βuat-a/ --> [koβwaata] 'to hold, to seize'
/ko-βuat-ek-a/ --> [koβwaateka] 'to be held, to be (actually) holdable'
/ko-βuat-ek-ek-a/ --> [koβwaateγeka] 'to be (potentially) holdable'

Possibly, there may be a co-occurrence restriction on stative suffix /-ek/ and causative suffix /-i/.

Meeussen (1967: 92) posits /-ek-/ for Proto-Bantu, calling it the neuter suffix. His example, converted into the system of transcription used here, is /-βɔn-ek-/, which is turned into |-βɔn-ɛk-| 'to be in sight' through vowel harmony, which he discusses under morphophonology (Meeussen 1967: 84). If his reconstruction is correct, it may be observed that the Gusii reflect of this extension suffix seems to have retained both the basic sense of, and is morphologically identical to, its proto-form.

3.3.2.4. Reversive-intransitive suffix /-ok/.

The extension suffix /-ok/ reverses the meaning of the root into its semantic opposite and, in addition, depending on the type of verb thus changed, makes it intransitive. Generally, much lexical work is still to be done on the verbal system, in order to differentiate semantically distinct verb types by defining their necessary and sufficient properties. With respect to the suffix under discussion, consider (221),

(221) a. /ko-riNγ-a/
15-fold-fv
[koriiŋga]
'to fold (v.t.)'

e.g. [naariiŋga riisakara] 'he has just folded the paper'

/ko-riNγ-ok-a/
15-fold-ri-fv
[koriiŋgoka]
'to unfold (v.i.)'

e.g [ŋiariiŋgoka] 'it has (just) unfolded'

/ti-e-ko-riNγ-ok-a/
not-9-t-fold-ri-fv
[tekoriiŋgoka]
'it does not unfold'[125]

[125] The connotation may be either 'it cannot unfold', or 'it is unfoldable'.

b. /ko-βuat-a/
15-fold-fv
[koβwaata]
'to hold, to seize (v.t.)'

/ko-βuat-ok-a/
15-fold-ri-fv
[koβwaatoka]
'to stop holding (of own's accord) (v.i.)'

e.g. [naaβwaatoka εγεkɔɔmbε] 'he stopped holding the cup (just now)'

(compare [koβwaatoria] 'to cause someone to stop holding', e.g. [naambwaatoria] 'he stopped me from holding, he made me not to hold')

That the semantic opposite is not exactly the same as a negation of the original meaning, becomes clear when we compare (221a) with the words in (222),

(222) /ko-ta-riNγ-a/
15-not-fold-fv
[γotariiηga]
'not to fold (v.t.)'

/ko-ta-riNγ-ok-a/
15-not-fold-ri-fv
[γotariiηgoka]
'not to unfold (v.i.)'

This extension suffix is not discussed as such in Whiteley (1956). However, it is briefly mentioned, together with /-ek/, in (1960: 7-8) as "extension 2", but without exemplification or semantic definition. This suggests that Whiteley may have considered these suffixes as having the same meaning. Though one has non-reversive, and the other reversive meaning, the semantic distinction between them may indeed be subtle. It is easily missed, therefore, in back-translation.

Though reduplication of the reversive-intransitive suffix, i.e. /-ok-ok/, does seem to be possible, it was considered odd by at least one informant[126], and in any case, it does not seem to occur frequently. Its combination with the stative suffix, i.e. /-ok-ek/, appears to be more common. Consider the examples in (223),

(223) /ko-cɔɔm-a/
15-fix-fv
[γɔcɔɔma]
'to fix (a handle)' (e.g. of a hoe or an axe)

/ko-cɔɔm-ok-a/
15-fix-ri-fv
[γɔcɔɔmɔka]
'to come unfixed/unstuck/loose (v.i.)'

126 Lilian Nyanchama.

/ko-cɔɔm-ʊk-ek-a/
15-fix-ri-st-fv
[γɔcɔɔmɔγεka]
' to be capable of becoming unstuck (v.i.)'[127]

compare:

/ko-cɔɔm-ek-ek-a/
15-fix-st-st-fv
[γɔcɔɔmεγεka]
'to be (potentially) fixable (v.i.)'

and

/ko-cɔɔm-ek-a/
15-fix-st-fv
[γɔcɔɔmεka]
'to be fixed'
'to be (actually) fixable (v.i.)'

and also (224),

(224) /ko-βuat-ok-a/
15-fold-ri-fv
[koβwaatoka]
'to stop holding' ('to unseize') (v.i.)

/ko-βuat-ok-ek-a/
15-fold-ri-ap-fv
[koβwaatoγeka]
'to be capable of being unheld (unseized)'
'to be easy to let go of'

([koβwaatoγoka] has the same meaning)

3.3.2.5. Reversive-transitive suffix /-or/.

Extension suffix /-or/ is designated 'reversive-transitive', first, because it turns the

[127] Systematically possible, but unfamiliar, and perhaps non-existent, is

?/ko-cɔɔm-ok-ok-a/
15-fix-ri-ri-fv
[γɔcɔɔmɔγɔka]
'to be un-fixable (v.i.)'
(i.e. to be capable of becoming unstuck)

meaning of the verb into its semantic opposite. Whiteley's discussion of it is restricted to the observation that it 'occurs in relatively few verbs, and in meaning is the opposite of the simple form' (1956: 77).

Second, it makes the verb meaning transitive. Any intransitive meaning is thereby obviously converted into a transitive one, while an originally transitive meaning remains what it is.[128]

Depending on the tense involved, there may be an added element of inchoation, in which case the sense is 'to become the opposite of, or to come to do the opposite of, what is expressed by the verb'. However, this is not exemplified and its details require further investigation.

Compare the forms in (225),

(225) a. /ko-aNc-a/
15-love-fv
[γwaañca]
'to love, to like'

?/ko-aNc-or-a/
15-love-rt-fv
[γwaañcora]
'to come to dislike, to come to hate; to dislike'

b. /ko-riNγ-a/
15-fold-fv
[koriiηga]
'to fold (v.t.)'

/ko-riNγ-or-a/
15-fold-rt-fv
[koriiηgora]
'to unfold (v.t.)'

e.g. [ηkoriinηgora nde amaraaηgeti]
'I'm unfolding the blankets'

/ti-o-ko-riNγ-or-a/
not-2s-t-fold-rt-fv
[tokoriiηgora]
'you cannot unfold (v.t.)'

---

128 There is a gap in my data in that this change from intransitive to transitive is not exemplified.

/ti-o-ri ko-riNγ-or-a/
not-2s-be 15-fold-rt-fv
[tori koriiηgora]
'you are not unfolding (v.t.)'

similarly:

c. /ko-kun-a/ --> [γokuna] 'to touch'
/ko-kun-or-a/ --> [γokunora] 'to open (v.t.)'
(compare /ko-kun-ek-a/ --> [γokuneka] 'to close (with a lid; v.t.)'

d. /ko-miin-a/ 'to plait, to twist, to twirl (hair)'
/ko-miin-or-a/ --> [komiinora] 'to unplait, to untwirl (v.t.)'

e. [γotiica] 'to stop up (v.t.)' (e.g. a hole)
[γotiicora] 'to unstop (v.t.)'

The meaning here is not negation of the verbal meaning as such, but reversal into its opposite. This becomes clear, if we compare the infinitives in (225b) with those in (226),

(226) /ko-ta-riNγ-a/	/ko-ta-riNγ-or-a/
15-not-fold-fv	15-not-fold-rt-fv
[γotariiηga]	[γotariiηgora]
'not to fold (v.t.)'	'not to unfold (v.t.)'

Data such as those in (227) suggest that a homomorphous expansion suffix /-or/ also occurs,

(227) [koeeβutora] 'to cut oneself'
[koβutora] 'to cut'
*[koβuta]

However, [koβuta] does occur, but with the meaning 'to visit, to stay with', and thus involves a distinct root. Arguably the minimal underlying representation accounting for the acceptable forms in (227) may be postulated as /-βutor-/, rather than /-βut-or-/.

Finally, data such as those in (228) show that sometimes various derived verbs may occur, whereas what is arguably their common source, which in this case would be the basic verb *[γosima], does not occur synchronically,

(228) [γosimora] 'to pull out (v.t.)'
[γosimoreka] 'to be out-pullable (v.i.)'
(potential patient role expressed intransitively)'
[γosimoka] 'to come out (v.i.)'
[γosimoγeka] 'to be capable of coming out (v.i.)'[129]
(potential agent role is expressed intransitively)

3.3.2.6. Applicative suffix /-er/.

Presumably because its various meanings are such as are typically expressed by means of prepositions in English, Whiteley (1956: 54) calls /-er/ the 'prepositional' suffix, and any verb derived through it a prepositional verb. However, such an approach by analogy seems insufficient, since it presupposes a knowledge of English on the part of the reader. Moreover, it provides no semantic definition.

Generally, the applicative suffix may be said to express the concept of connection or application, such that, within this general designation, it may carry various shades of meaning.

First, it expresses the concept of application or applicative relation. If the meaning of the verb on which it is encoded is generally positive or constructive, the meaning of this suffix is beneficiary and may be translated 'for, for the benefit of', or 'on behalf of'. If the meaning of the verb is in some sense negative or detrimental, the meaning expressed by the suffix may be translated 'to the detriment of, at the expense of', or by some equivalent expression. The positive meaning is exemplified in (229),

(229) /ko-sɛk-er-a/
15-laugh-ap-fv
[γɔsɛkɛra]
'to laugh at, to smile at'
(i.e. with the intention of getting a positive response)

/ko-tɛɛr-er-a/
15-sing-ap-fv
[γɔtɛɛrɛra]
(1) 'to sing for/to' (beneficiary)
(2) 'to sing at' (location)

Examples of the negative sense were reported, but are not recorded and constitute an accidental gap in my data.

Second, the suffix may have the instrumental sense 'by means of' or 'with the help of', as in (230),

---

[129] Not to be confused with [γosimeka] 'to plant' and [γosimeγeka] 'to be (actually or potentially) plantable'.

(230) [koriina] 'to climb'
[koriinera] 'to climb with/by means of'

Third, it may have locative meaning, as in (231),

(231) /ko-riNγ-ok-er-a/
15-fold-ri-ap-fv
[koriiηgokera]
'to be unfolded at (v.i.)'

/ko-riNγ-ak-er-a/
15-fold-rs-ap-fv
[koriiηgakera]
'to lie folded at/in/on' (intransitive result)

/ko-riNγ-ek-er-a/
15-fold-st-ap-fv
[koriiηgekera]
(a) 'to be/lie folded at/in/on'
(b) 'to be foldable at'

As this suffix may express different meanings, at least some verbs derived by this extension suffix may bear several of these meanings, as in (232),

(232) a. /ko-riNγ-er-a/
15-fold-ap-fv
[koriiηgera]
(1) 'to fold with, by means of' (instrumental sense)
(2) 'to fold for' (beneficiary sense)
(3) 'to fold at,in' (locative sense)

b. /ko-riNγ-or-er-a/
15-fold-rt-ap-fv
[koriiηgorera]
(1) 'to unfold at' (locative sense)
(2) 'to unfold for' (beneficiary sense)
(3) 'to unfold by means of (instrumental sense)

c. /ko-sɛk-a/
15-laugh-fv
[γɔsɛka]
'to laugh'

/ko-sɛk-er-a/
15-laugh-ap-fv
[γɔsɛkɛra]
(1) 'to laugh at, to look at laughingly'
(2) 'to laugh in' (e.g. the hall)

d. /ko-βuat-er-a/
[koβwaatera]
'to hold by means of' or 'to hold for'

e. /ko-βutor-er-a/
[koβutorera]
'to cut with' or 'to cut for'

f. /ko-kuan-er-a/
[γokwaanera]
'to talk with/by means of (e.g. by using a loudspeaker)', 'to talk for/on behalf of'

g. /ko-sɔɔm-er-a/
[γɔsɔɔmɛra]
'to read for (the benefit of)',
'to read by means of' (e.g. using spectacles),
'to read with (the help of)' (e.g. a lamp),
'to read in' (i.e. some place)

Furthermore, this suffix may be reduplicated, in which case two of the senses differentiated may be expressed simultaneously in a single verb, as in (233),

(233) a. /ko-riNγ-er-er-a/
15-fold-ap-ap-fv
[koriiŋgerera]
'to fold for at' (beneficiary and locative sense)[130]

b. /ko-sɛk-er-er-a/
15-laugh-ap-ap-fv
[γɔsɛkɛrɛra]
'to laugh at in connection with'[131]

/ko-sɛk-er-er-an-a/
15-laugh-ap-ap-rc-fv
[γɔsɛkɛrɛrana]
'to laugh at each other in connection with' (or 'for', 'on account of')

---

130 This form was questioned by Lilian Nyanchama.

131 Also translated 'to laugh at the expense of' by one informant. If correct, this would suggest that reduplication has changed the positive meaning of [γɔsɛkɛra] 'to smile at' into a pejorative one. Such a change was not found to be generally involved by reduplication.

c. /ko-βuat-er-a/
15-hold-ap-fv
[koβwaatera]
'to hold for, to hold on behalf of'
'to hold at/in'
'to hold by means/with the help of'

/ko-βuat-er-er-a/
15-hold-ap-ap-fv
[koβwaaterera]
'to hold on to (sth) for support'

d. [γotiɔka] 'to smell, to give forth (strong) scent' (v.i.)
[γotiɔkεra] 'to smell, to give forth scent to' (applicative v.i.)
[γotiɔkεrεra] 'to smell' (v.t.)

e.g. [tiɔkεrεrεra riimutu ria riuγa eri]
smell the-scent 5-of flower 5-this
'smell the scent of this flower'

e.g. ¦ri-oγa η-goo-n-tiɔk-εr-a ri-re¦
5-flower f-15-om1s-smell-ap-fv 5-is
[rioγa ηgoontiɔkεra rire]
'the scent of the flower is impressing itself upon me'
(literally, 'the flower is smelling to/for me')

Apparently, this suffix may involve semantic specialisation even when it occurs only once in a single form. Compare the examples in (234),

(234)	/ko-aNc-a/	/ko-aNc-er-a/
	15-love-fv	15-love-ap-fv
	[γwaañca]	[γwaañcera]
	'to love, to like'	'to allow, to permit'

Whenever the suffix is reduplicated, and two distinct senses of the suffix are not expressed, semantic specialisation may also occur, as in (235),

(235) /ko-aNc-er-er-a/
15-love-ap-ap-fv
[γwaañcerera]
'to favour (someone) (with)'
(literally, 'to show love to someone by means of')[132]

e.g. ¦niγɔ a-ko-anc-er-er-a John koβua a-βa-aNre¦
thus 3s-t-love-ap-ap-fv John above a-2-other
[niγɔ aγwaañcerera John koβua aβaande]
'(it is that) he favours John more than others'

A reduplicated applicative suffix may also express intensity. Thus in (236),

(236) a. [koeeorokeria] 'to make (sth) appear to oneself'
b. [koeeorokereria] 'to make appear to oneself (intensively, repeatedly)'

the multiply extended verb in (236a) includes one occurrence of the applicative suffix, which clearly comes out in the gloss, while reduplication of the applicative suffix adds intensity to the same meaning.

It seems plausible to suggest, finally, that such types of semantic specialisation may historically lead or contribute to the neutralisation of extension affixes in at least some words, that is, to a change from their status as an extension affix to that of an expansion affix.

3.3.2.7. Reciprocal suffix /-an/.

As the term designates, the suffix /-an/ usually expresses reciprocity, that is, mutual relation or action (see Whiteley 1956: 77), as exemplified in (237),

(237) a. /-rɔr-/ 'see'

==> /ko-rɔr-an-a/ ==> /ko-rɔr-ek-an-a/
15-see-rc-fv 15-see-st-rc-fv
[kɔrɔrana] [kɔrɔrεkana]
'to see each other' 'to be visible (to)'

b. [kɔγεεnda] 'to go'
*[kɔγεεndana]
==> [kɔγεεndεrana] 'to go simultaneously, to go with each other'
==> [kɔγεεndεrania] 'to go for a while/forever'

It may also express collectivity or distributedness, possibly, but not necessarily, implying some sort of mutuality. This is suggested by the meaning of (238),

[132] This explanation is uncertain.

(238) /ko-βun-ek-an-a/
15-break-st-rc-fv
[koβunekana]
'to be broken (in several pieces) (v.i.)'

where it seems to have lost its original sense and the verb seems to have taken on a collective or distributive meaning.

Finally, semantic specialisation is exemplified in (239b), and semantic change presumably involved in a change of the regular order of the extension suffixes in (239c, d) implies a change in meaning.

(239) a. /ko-sɔɔm-a/
15-learn/read-fv
[γɔsɔɔma]
'to learn, to read'

b. /ko-sɔɔm-an-a/
15-learn-rc-fv
[γɔsɔɔmana]
'to study each other's character'
(literally, 'to read each other')

c. /ko-sɔɔm-er-an-a/
15-read-ap-rc-fv
[γɔsɔɔmɛrana]
'to read for each other'

d. /ko-sɔɔm-an-er-a/
15-read-rc-ap-fv
[γɔsɔɔmanera]
'to read on behalf of each other'

The precise details of the change in the regular suffix order, as also the phenomenon of semantic specialisation generally, require further investigation.

3.3.2.8. Causative suffix /-i/.

The sense of causative suffix /-i/ has been characterised correctly as 'generally associated with causing someone else to do something' (1956: 65). This is its causative meaning proper, as in [kɔγɛɛndia] 'to cause to go, to drive, to operate', in contrast with [kɔγɛɛnda] 'to go'.

It is also said to make an intransitive meaning transitive, but as far as Whiteley's examples go, this is really a restatement of the first meaning. Thus, [γoicora] 'to be full (v.i.)' may be turned into [γoicoria] 'to fill (v.t.)', but this is the same as 'to cause to be(come) full'. Similarly, /ko-βook-a/ 'to rise (v.i.)' may be turned into /ko-βook-i-a/ --

> [koβookia] 'to raise, to wake up (v.t.)'[133], but this is really 'to cause to rise'. In short, causation logically implies transitiveness.

Sometimes it is possible to speak of semantic specialisation, as in the pair [γɔsɔɔma] 'to read' and [γɔsɔɔmia]. The latter literally means 'to cause to read', but is more commonly used with the meaning 'to educate'.

The suffix is further said to express intensive meaning, though less commonly so. However, apart from the fact that the term 'intensive' is left undefined, only two tenses of one verb are cited for example. Their meanings are not given and the example is in fact mistaken. For [βaaγεεndirie] means 'they have driven (earlier today)' and [βaaγεεndεtie] 'they drove (recently)'. Hence they are derived from [kɔγεεndia], and do not express some "intensive" meaning of the basic verb [kɔγεεnda] 'to go', as suggested by Whiteley (1956: 65).

Finally, it is correctly observed that 'there are a number of verbs in common use which behave as causative but which are not associated with causative meanings, e.g. [kɔrɔɔsia] 'to repair, to fix', [γocia] 'to go (to)', [γɔtεεβia] 'to tell', and [koriisia] 'to herd cattle'. In short, in items such as these, the causative extension suffix is arguably absent. It remains to be investigated whether this /-i/ is the causative suffix become lexicalised, a homomorphous expansion suffix, or part of an unanalysable root.

Thus, for example, pre-final /-i/ is evidently part of the root of the items in (240),

(240)	/ko-sinini-a/	/ko-riri-a/
	15-tiny-fv	15-foolish-fv
	[γosininia]	[koriria]
	'to be tiny'	'to be foolish'

Not only does [omoriri] 'foolish person, fool' also occur, but the following causative verbs (241) may be derived from those in (240),

(241)	/ko-sinini-i-a/	/ko-riri-i-a/
	15-tiny-c-fv	15-foolish-c-fv
	[γosininiia]	[koririia]
	'to make very small'	'to make foolish'

To conclude this section, causative suffix /-i/ has causative meaning only, but may involve semantic specialisation.

---

133 Another meaning is 'to plough'. [korema], usually translated 'to dig, to cultivate' refers to the initial working of the land, or first ploughing, during which scrubs and stones are removed, while [koβookia] refers to the second ploughing, i.e. the more immediate preparation of the land for planting and sowing.

3.3.2.9. Passive suffix /-u/.

Whiteley (1956: 76) argues that, because passive suffix /-u/ is one out of a number of extension affixes, it cannot be considered as a marker of the passive voice proper, as in Latin. Either it must be considered as an extension suffix, so his argument goes, or the other extension suffixes must be considered as expressing voice. However, this is an argument based on form only. Moreover, logically it does not follow.

The category of voice may involve several sub-distinctions. Classical Greek, for example, had an active, a passive, and a middle voice. By contrast, in Gusii only active and passive are differentiated, such that the active voice is unmarked and the passive voice is marked by the suffix /-u/. From the fact that the means of expressing the passive voice is the same as that for most extensions of the verb meaning, viz. by suffixation, grammatical or semantic identity of /-u/ and other suffixes does not necessarily follow.

Significantly, as Whiteley (1956: 76) also notes, the passive suffix /-u/ may modify all and any verbs, and combine with all and any of the extension suffixes, provided no logical or semantic anomaly results. Thus there are relatively more semantic restrictions on the other extension suffixes. This suggests a basic semantic distinction between them and the passive voice marker. But morphosyntactically they are quite similar. Therefore, and for the sake of convenience, the passive voice marker is treated here together with extension suffixes.

Semantically, as its designation implies, it makes the active verb meaning passive.

Allomorphy of the passive voice marker may be accounted for as in (242),

(242) allomorphy: passive voice marker ==>

a. -u / [+cons] ---
b. -γu/ [-cons] ---

This allomorphy rule stipulates that after a consonant the form of the passive voice marker is /-u/, regularly turned into [w] through Complex Segment Formation, whereas after a vowel its form is /-γu/, which regularly surfaces as [γw], as in (243),

(243)	/ko-sɔɔm-u-a/	/ko-sɔɔm-i-γu-a/
	15-read-p-fv	15-read-c-p-fv
	[γɔsɔɔmwa]	[γɔsɔɔmiγwa]
	'to be read'	'to be taught'

(compare [γɔsɔɔmia] 'to cause to read, to teach')

At least one verb, the root of which ends in /-u/, drops final vowel /a/ in the passive infinitive, as in (244),

(244) irregular passive infinitive: no final vowel -a

basic ==> /ko-βu-a/ --> [koβua] 'to win, to conquer'
passive ==> /ko-βu-u/ --> [koβuu] 'to be conquered, to lose', *[koβuua]

A few other such verbs take suffix /-e/ followed by passive allomorph /-γu/, as in (245),

(245) irregular passive infinitive: -e-γu-

/ko-ñu-a/ --> [koñwa] 'to drink'
/ko-ñu-e-γu-a/ --> [koñweeγwa] 'to be drunk', *[koñuu]

/ko-ru-a/ --> [korwa] 'to give, to offer'
/ko-ru-e-γu-a/ --> [korweeγwa] 'to be given', *[koruu]

also compare [kɔa] 'to give' with [kɔεεγwa] 'to be given' (see appendix 1)

It may be added that [koγua] 'to fall', being intransitive, cannot be turned into a transitive passive. The irregular forms in (244, 245) appear to be rare.

3.3.2.10. Semantic specialisation: /-er-an-i-/.

When two or more extension affixes co-occur, they may retain their original sense. In that case, each affix contributes its meaning to the whole meaning of the verb simply by extending, or adding to, the basic meaning of the root. Examples of this have already been given in preceding sections. Some may be repeated or added in (246),

(246) /ko-riNγ-ok-ek-a/
15-fold-ri-st-fv
[koriiŋgoγeka]
'to be unfoldable (v.i)' (i.e. of itself)

/ko-riNγ-or-ek-a/
15-fold-rt-st-fv
[koriiŋgoreka]
'to be unfoldable (v.t.)' (i.e. by an external agent)

/ko-riNγ-ak-ek-a/
15-fold-rs-st-fv
[koriiŋgaγeka]
'to be foldable (v.i.)' (i.e. of itself)

/ko-riNγ-ak-ek-i-a/
15-fold-rs-st-c-fv
[koriiŋgaγekia]
'to be foldable (v.t.)' (i.e. by an external agent)

/ko-riNγ-ak-ok-a/
15-fold-rs-ri-fv
[koriiηgaγoka]
'to be unfoldable (v.i.)'
(the sense here is not 'to be incapable of being folded', but 'to be capable of being unfolded of itself')

e.g. /rii-sakara ri-ko-riNγ-ak-ok-a/
5-paper 5-t-fold-rs-ri-fv
[riisakara rikoriiηgaγoka]
'the unfoldable paper' (v.i.)
(i.e. it can become unfolded of itself)

However, it is not unusual for multiply-extended verbs to exhibit semantic specialisation. This may occur, when two or more affixes combine to extend some verb, and at least one of them loses its original sense. In that case, lexicalisation may take place. For example, in (247) the reflexive prefix and the reversive-transitive suffix have retained their original meaning, while the reciprocal and causative suffixes seem to have lost it,

(247) /rii-ko-ee-riNγ-an-i-a/
5-t-rf-fold-rc-c-fv
[riikweeriiηgania]
'it-5 is folding (v.i.) (i.e. itself or of itself)'

|rii-sakara η-ko-ee-riiηg-an-i-a ri-re]
5-paper f-15-rf-fold-fv-rc-c-fv 5-be
[riisakara ηkweeriiηgania rire]
'the (piece of) paper is folding itself'

/a-ko-ee-riNγ-an-i-a/
3s-t-rf-fold-rc-c-fv
[akoeeriiηgania]
'he is (always) folding himself'

|η-ko-ee-riiηg-an-i-a a-re|
f-15-rf-fold-rc-c-fv 1-be
[ηkoeeriiηgania are]
'he is folding himself'

|rii-βaati rii-ko-riiηg-or-w-a|
5-corrugated iron 5-t-fold-rt-p-fv
[riiβaati riikoriiηgorwa]
'the corrugated iron is being folded' (v.t.)

|rii-βaati e-ri rii-ko-riiηg-or-w-a|
5-corrugated iron 5-that 5-t-fold-rt-p-fv
[riiβaati eri riikoriiηgorwa]
'this corrugated iron is being folded' (v.t.)

Another possibility of semantic specialisation may be due not so much to the loss of some affix's original meaning, but to a specific combination of two or more extension affixes. In this case, the basic meaning of the root is not changed because each affix contributes its individual semantic element to it, but because their combination makes a semantic contribution that is more than the sum of its parts. In Gusii there is at least one such case, viz. the combination of the applicative, reciprocal, and causative suffixes[134], as in (248),

(248) -er-an-i

Though in some derived verbs these suffixes may simply retain their original meaning it seems that they may also express close conjunction or connection of activity, especially when all three of them are combined in one verb, as in (249),

(249) /ko-riNγ-er-an-i-a/
15-fold-ap-rc-c-fv
[koriiŋgerania]
'to fold in some way with respect to each other'

/ko-rɔɔs-er-an-i-a/
15-fix-ap-rc-c-fv
[kɔrɔɔsɛrania]
'to fix (sth) together with (someone else)'

/ko-βutor-er-an-i-a/
15-cut-ap-rc-c-fv
[koβutorerania]
'to cut together, to cut one after the other'

/ko-iyek-er-an-i-a/
15-cook-ap-rc-c-fv
[koiyekerania]
'to cook (by boiling) together, to cook one after the other (by boiling)'

These examples suggest that close conjunction or connection of activity may involve simultaneity or immediate succesion.

To conclude this section, it may be observed that semantic specialisation in Gusii is an interesting area that calls for further research. Specifically, the meanings of a broader range of semantically different types of verb need to be examined, in order to refine or to elaborate the definition of the meanings of some of the extension affixes and also the study of their possible combinations. This may arguably be achieved by studying their interaction with the basic meanings of these verbs. On this basis, the interaction of the

134 Possibly, /-er-an/ are essential, while /-i/ is not, as in [kɔγɛɛndɛrana] 'to go simultaneously, to go with each other', from [kɔγɛɛnda] 'to go', but this needs to be checked.

meanings of the affixes themselves may be understood more clearly and fully. An extensive, detailed study would have to take into account the linguistic judgments of many speakers, if only because this is a complex aspect of the language that often causes a good deal of pondering on their part, and sometimes produces differing judgments.

It is possible to change the order of some suffixes, but this regularly involves a change in meaning, as in (250),

(250) a. [γɔtεma] 'to cut'
[γɔtεmεra] 'to cut for'
[γɔtεmana] 'to cut each other'

[γɔtεmεrana] 'to cut for each other'
[γɔtεmanera] 'to cut with each other'

[βaaγɔtεmanera] 'they are cutting with each other'
(i.e. they are assist e.o. in cutting, using one tool which is regularly exchanged)

[βaaγɔtεmεrana] 'they are cutting for each other (alternately, possibly a third party)'

reduplication of one suffix, separated by another:

[βaaγɔtεmanerana] 'they cut together/simultaneously for each other' (i.e. so that everyone uses his own tool; here the agents are the beneficiaries)

b. [γɔkɔrεra] 'to do for'
[γɔkɔrεrεra] 'to do for with'
[γɔkɔrεrania] 'to do simultaneously'
[γɔkɔraneria] 'to do for each other'

Such change in suffix order also requires further examination. I will now turn to other aspects of verbal structure.

3.3.3. Tensed verbal structure and verbal markers.

Verbal tenses may be characterised loosely in a number of related ways. They are those verb forms that may relate the activity expressed by a verb (activity taken in the broadest sense of the term) in some way to time. Or they may relate one event to another, with or without reference to time. Or they may relate a speaker's attitude toward the activity expressed by the verb, whether or not in relation to time, other events, or both.

Whiteley (1960: 12) differentiates four distinct classes of tenses in terms of their endings, as in (251),

(251) tenses

type:	A	B	C	D
ending:	-a	-e	-ire	-ete

However, from a semantic point of view, these distinctions seem too broad. His A-tenses, for example, include a variety of distinct meanings. This approach thus serves primarily as a somewhat arbitrary means of listing the tenses. More research is needed, before we are in a position to give an arrangement of the Gusii tenses that is sufficiently refined and systematic from a semantic point of view. However, this will not be attempted here.

Generally, the categories of tense, mood, and aspect are not expressed strictly or even consistently by means of distinct sets of morphemes for each category. For example, though perfective suffix /-ir/ may be an exception in this respect, since it may express perfective aspect, it seems to have become grammaticalised in at least some tenses, and there is no exhaustive system of paradigms contrasting non-perfective tenses with their corresponding perfective counterpart. For reasons such these, the term 'tense' will be used here as a broad cover-term for any of the three categories tense, mood, and aspect individually, or for any possible combination of them.

The verbal elements introduced in section 3.3.1 were also said to function in tensed forms, except the augment. The category slots that make up the structure of verbal tenses may thus be summarised as in (252),

(252) verbal structure and markers

Slot: f n1 sm n2 t t t t t t om root x t fv
rm

Fillers: n ti βa ta a ko1 raa V na ko2 mo ruγ an et/ir {e/i} a u
ka

The question whether the referential prefix may function as an actual verbal prefix, is left open, and the prefix is not included in this summary. Various elements that may express the verbal categories have been added for exemplification. It must be borne in mind that (252) is merely a general summary. As such, it disregards actual combinations of markers in specific tenses. Nor does it express which slots may, and which may not, co-occur. Items occurring in one column are to be interpreted as mutually exclusive, as previously explained. Strictly, the categories of object marker (om) and extension suffixes (x) are irrelevant for tenses, but have been added for the sake of completeness.

Though the number of tense morphemes is relatively small, the number of Gusii tenses is nonetheless considerable. Many of them are distinguished by different combinations of tense morphemes. In the following subsections, the slots and markers introduced so far will be elaborated a little further.

3.3.3.1. Focus marker.

The verbal marker of what is here conveniently termed focus is homomorphous with existential or identificatory /na-/ or /n-/ and may well derive etymologically from this element. Its allomorphy may be accounted for by (253),

(253) allomorphy: focus marker ==>

a. na- / --- [-cons]
b. n- / --- [+cons]

The /a/ of /na-/ is regularly delinked through /a/-Delinking (see section 2.3.16), followed by compensatory lengthening of the following vowel. Allomorph /n-/ is subject to applicable nasal rules (see sections 2.3.2-6). For example, it regularly prenasalises to the following consonant and, depending on the context and the style of speech, may surface as [m], [n], [ñ], [η], or [im], [in], [iñ], [iη]. Whenever /na-/ immediately precedes an allomorph of the first person singular subject marker, homomorphous /na-/ or /n-/, the latter is always turned into allomorph |iN|, so that the sequence of focus and first person singular subject marker, |na-iN-|, is always turned into |niiN-| (where N represents any of the four Gusii nasals).

/nV-/ might be postulated as an alternative for /na-/. A following vowel then arguably spreads leftward, e.g. the |i| of allomorph 1s |iN|, whereas the /V/ remains silent before a following consonant. However, because /na/ may occur next to /n-/ in some tenses, e.g. (307), because conjunction of preposition /na/ 'and, with' may plausibly be considered to be the etymon of the focus, and because /a/-Delinking is regularly applicable, /na/ is postulated in the present study.

Whiteley calls the focus "pre-initial n-" (1960: 9) or "initial n-" (1960: 12), but does not discuss it, nor in (1956). It expresses the concept of theme. Possible other semantic details require further examination and, if any, more exact definition. Closer examination of the tense system, with special reference to the contrast between non-focussed and focussed tenses, and possibly also to different sentence-types, may be necessary as well.

The focus is provisionally analysed as a verbal element, rather than as a pre-clitic.

3.3.3.2. Negative markers and Morpholexical /i/-Deletion.

The negative marker slots 'n' in (252) involve the concept of negation. There are two negative markers in Gusii. Of these, n1 /ti-/ means 'not (yet)', n2 /ta-/ means 'not'. They never co-occur in one verb form.

At this point, it may be observed that allomorph /-i/ is used instead of the usual final vowel /-e/ in negative perfective or past tenses that contain /ti-/ or /ta-/, but no tense prefixes, so that these end in [-iri] instead of [-ire], and [-eti] instead of [-ete] (see Whiteley 1960: 14, 16, 43-45, 51-52, 57-58). For example, compare (254),

(254) infinitive

/ko-tiNrek-a|
15-bury-fv
[γotiindeka][135]
'to bury'

a. /ti-na-a-tiindek-ir-e/
N1-1s-t-bury-st-pv-fv
[tinaatiindekire]
'I was not buried (long ago)'
(note the passive meaning, and the contrast with [tinaatiindeka] 'I have not buried (long ago))

similarly,

2s |ti-ko-a-tiind-ek-ir-e| --> [tiγwaatiindekire]
3s |ti-a-a-tiind-ek-ir-e| --> [taatiindekire][136]
1p |ti-to-a-tiind-ek-ir-e| --> [titwaatiindekire]
2p |ti-mo-a-tiind-ek-ir-e| --> [timwaatiindekire]
3p |ti-βa-a-tiind-ek-ir-e| --> [tiβaatiindekire]

b. |ti-n-tiind-ek-ir-i|
N1-1s-bury-st-pv-fv
[tiintiindekiri]
'I have not been buried'

similarly,

2s |ti-o-tiind-ek-ir-i| --> [totiindekiri]
3s |ti-a-tiind-ek-ir-i| --> [tatiindekiri]
1p |ti-to-tiind-ek-ir-i| --> [titotiindekiri]
2p |ti-mo-tiind-ek-ir-i| --> [timotiindekiri]
3p |ti-βa-tiind-ek-ir-i| --> [tiβatiindekiri]

Another observation concerns negative marker /ti-/. Whiteley (1960: 3) correctly notes that "Sequences of the negative preprefix 'ti-' and a following verbal prefix 'o' or 'a' are realised as 'to, ta'." In short, ti + o > to, and ti + a > ta. This observation is correct as far as it goes, but several points may be added or further refined.

---

135 This root does not seem to be related to [γotiinda] 'to be drunk' and its derivative [γotiindeka] 'to become sober', unless 'to be buried' is a metaphor for being drunk. In the latter case, the underlying representation must be /...tind-ek.../ or /...tiNr-ek.../, depending on which analysis one takes of prenasals.

136 Apparently mistranscribed as [tatiindekire] by Whiteley (1960: 45).

First, since the vowel following /ti-/ is never lengthened compensatorily, the /i/ is not merely delinked, but deleted. Second, since the rule affects neither /i/ in general, nor other morphemes in particular, it is correctly implied that only the /i/ of /ti-/ is deleted; hence the rule is strictly morpholexical. Third, deletion before vowels other than /o/ or /a/ is not considered, but does in fact occur, as in (255)

(255) 'sm did not [verb] (recently)'

a. /ti-i/: no evidence

b. /ti-e-rem-et-i/
not-sm9-dig-t-fv
¦tieremeti¦
[teremeti]
'9-it did not dig (recently)'

c. /ti-e-tɛm-et-i/
not-sm9-beat-t-fv
¦tiɛtɛmɛti¦ (through MVHS, see section 2.3.14)
[tɛtɛmɛti]
'9-it did not beat (recently)'

d. /ti-a-rem-et-i/
not-3s-dig-t-fv
[taremeti]
'he/she did not dig (recently)'

e. /ti-o-tɛm-et-i/
not-sm2s-beat-t-fv
¦tiɔtɛmɛti¦ (through MVHS)
[tɔtɛmɛti]
'2s-you did not beat (recently)'

f. /ti-o-rem-et-i/
not-2s-dig-t-fv
[toremeti]
'2s-you did not dig (recently)'

g. /ti-u/: no evidence[137]

---

[137] That the underlying representations postulated for the examples presented here, are correct, becomes clear from a comparison with, for example,

/ti-βa-rem-et-i/
not-3p-dig-t-fv
[tiβaremeti]
'they did not dig (recently)'

No evidence was found for the sequences in (255a,g). Since no verbal marker or affix that might possibly follow the /i/ of negative marker /ti-/ begins with /i/ or /u/, such evidence is not likely to be found. These gaps in the data may therefore be considered as structural.

Pending further research into its nature and extent, the rule handling this change may be formulated as in (256),

(256) Morpholexical /i/-Deletion (MiD)

$$\begin{array}{l} \quad\quad\; \emptyset \\ \quad\;\; \nearrow \\ \text{ti} \;] \quad [\text{-cons}] \end{array}$$

negative
marker

It deletes the /i/ of negative marker /ti-/ before any vowel and regularly applies in any tense, whenever its structural description is met. Whenever /ti-/ is followed by two or more identical vowels, the resulting long surface vowel is thus not triggered by a mere delinking of the /i/ and concomitant spreading of the following vowel, but to the fact that a sequence of identical vowels is already present underlyingly. For example, /ti-a-a-rom-a/ --> [tááromá] '(so/but) he did not bite (earlier today or recently)' and /ti-o-V-rom-ɛ/ --> [tooroma], from '2s-you did not bite (habitually).

To conclude this section, another apparently negative tense, which I have not been able to account for systematically, is exemplified in (257),

(257) a. [βaatɛɛβié mbáaŋááká] (ɛɛ, m = H)
'tell them not to beat me'

contrast with

[βaatɛɛβié βááŋaaké] (ɛɛ = H)
'tell them to beat me')

b. [ntɛɛβie mmorome]
'tell them not to bite him'

compare with the more regular

[ntɛɛβie timoroma]
'tell them not to bite him'

3.3.3.3. Relative marker.

The relative marker (rm), mentioned here in the general order of verbal markers merely for completeness' sake, is considered to have been sufficiently discussed in section 3.2.3.2, where its usage as a pronominal prefix was also indicated.

3.3.3.4. Subject marker.

The verbal subject prefix or marker (sm) is the morpheme that encodes the subject category onto the verb. Its forms for the various morphosyntactic classes have already been discussed in section 3.2.3.1.

3.3.3.5. Tense markers.

The abbreviatory symbol t in (252) is a label used to designate the category of tense, in the broad sense of the term already explained (i.e. including tense proper, mood, and aspect), or some specific tense marker. The part of (252) relevant to tense marking is repeated in (258),

(258)											
	Slot:	t	t	t	t	t	t	(om)	root	t	FV
	Filler:	a	ko1	raa ka	V	na	ko2	(om)	ruγ	et ir	{e i} a u

As indicated, there are at least six distinct tense slots in the pre-root domain. Since the final vowel is not only used to mark the infinitive, but also imperatives and tenses, it may properly be included among the tense markers. Hence at least two tense slots may be said to occur in the post-root domain. Thus we have a total of at least eight tense slots. At least six of these (if we include the final vowel) may be combined in one tense form, as in (259) below.

These eight slots may be filled by at least thirteen tense markers. However, not all of these may co-occur in one verb form. As the maximum number of tense slots that may co-occur appears to be six, so no more than six tense markers may thus co-occur. Moreover, some tense markers (those placed in the same column) are mutually exclusive.

The relative order of tense affixes is fixed. At least five tense prefixes may co-occur in a single tense form, as in (259),

(259) /βa-ta-a-ko-raa-na-ko-saNγ-er-er-ek-an-a/
3p-N2-t-t-t-t-meet-sx-ap?-st-rc-fv
[βataakoraañaγosaaŋgererekana]
'they should keep on meeting together', or

'let them keep on meeting together' (adhortation)[138]

If underspecified vowel /V-/ is correctly included as a distinct tense marker, at least seven distinct tense prefixes may fill the various tense-slots. Of these, /ka-/ and /ko1-/ are mutually exclusive, and /ko1-/ is distinct from /ko2-/ (see section 3.3.3.7).

Though the final vowel is often distinguished as such in Bantu linguistics on suprasegmental grounds, at least in Gusii it also marks tense in combination with other tense affixes. For this reason we can say that, in addition to the tense slots in the pre-root domain, there are two more tense slots in the post-root domain. These involve at least six distinct markers.

Tense suffixes /-et/ and /-ir/ are mutually exclusive and only co-occur with /-e/ or its allomorph /-i/. The final vowels also exclude each other. As already noted in section 3.3.3.2, final /-i/ only occurs in a few negative tenses that take no tense prefix. However, [titóráarometi] 'we did not bite (recently)', etc., involving tense prefix /raa-/, may be an exception (though there is some doubt on this; see the note on tense (335)).

The occurrence of /u/ as a final vowel, as in (260), appears to be rare,

(260) [koβua] 'to conquer'
/βa-a-βu-ir-e/ --> [βaaβuire] 'they have conquered'

/ko-βu-u/ --> [koβuu] 'to be conquered' (exceptional passive infinitive)
/βa-a-βu-ir-u/ --> [βaaβuiru] 'they have been conquered'

3.3.3.6. Object marker.

3.3.3.6.1. Morphology and usage.

The morphology and allomorphy of the object markers for the various morphosyntactic classes, and their function in marking morphosyntactic agreement, have been discussed and exemplified in section 3.2.3.3. These points need not be elaborated here. But a few additional aspects will be considered in the next three subsections.

On the usage of the object marker, Whiteley (1956: 25) observes that "it is necessary to insert an object infix, wherever the object is not named, and [it is] often stylistically desirable to [insert an infix], even where [the object is named]". However, these observations are inadequate at least on two counts.

As to the first part of this statement, in situations where no object-noun is explicitly mentioned in the sentence, but where the object is nonetheless pragmatically clear or understood, an object marker need not necessarily be inserted.

---

138 Called 'indefinite future' by Whiteley 1960: 14, 37.

As to the second part of the quote, it is not exactly clear what is meant by "stylistically desirable". This criterion is not explained. Details such as these may well be relevant and thus require further research, but since they come under the headings of syntax, pragmatics, and semantics, this will not be done here.

3.3.3.6.2. Relative position in verbal structure.

As already shown in (252), the position taken by the object marker in verbal structure is the one immediately preceding the verbal root. The root may or may not be extended, as long as the result is logically and semantically consistent. For example, if reciprocal suffix /-an-/, which expresses the idea of reciprocity and is usually translated '(to, for) each other', is present and retains its full semantic force, a third party may not be referred to by some object marker.

As the term suggests, the object marker obviously marks an object, often a direct object, but in the Gusii verb it may also designate indirect objects and other types of object (see sections 3.3.6.3-4). Whiteley's remark that this object marker (which he calls "verbal infix") "occurs immediately before the root" (1956: 25) is correct, if we take object in the broadest sense of the term. The object marker domain does indeed precede the root in the structure of the verb. But it will be obvious that, whenever several object marker co-occur in a single verb form, not all of them may occur immediately before the verbal root. They occur in a specific order. Moreover, whenever several of them do so co-occur, no other type of verbal element may intervene. Hence they always occur in immediate succession in the object domain.

It was observed in section 3.3.2.1 that reflexive prefix /ee-/ might be considered as a type of object marker, since it typically marks a reflexive object and occurs immediately before the root. Though this is true, the reflexive marker and the other object markers are mutually exclusive, arguably for logical and semantic reasons. They never co-occur, except when either one or the other has entirely lost its original sense. Even so, this is also true of other types of object. Thus, as long as these semantic restrictions are borne in mind, the reflexive marker may well be called a type of object marker.

The position of the object marker in verbal structure may be characterised most generally, then, as in (261),

(261) verbal object marker position (general)

```
... om          - root (x) ...
   {rfl   }
   {other }
```

Here (x) designates any possible number of optional extension suffixes, 'rfl' the reflexive marker, and 'other' any other type of object marker. Placement in a braced column expresses mutual exclusiveness of the latter two.

In non-tensed forms (the infinitive and some imperatives), the object marker is usually preceded by the infinitive marker. In tensed forms, it is regularly preceded by a tense prefix (possibly underspecified vowel V), by negative marker /ta-/ in negative forms, and by the subject marker in some positive tense forms. Generally, the optional and obligatory co-occurrence of these elements may thus be summarised as in (262),

(262) verbal object marker position in tensed forms

slot:	(f)	(n1)	sm	(n2)	(t_n)	om { rfl / other }	root	(t)	fv
e.g.	(n)	(ti)	βa	(ta)	(a)	ee- mo-	ruγ	(et)	e/i a u

In this figure, t_n designates any possible number of tense markers. As explained in section 3.3.3.2, /ti-/ and /ta-/ may not co-occur.

3.3.3.6.3. Distinct types of object marker.

A number of distinct types of object may be differentiated, according to the distinct semantic roles they express. All of these may be encoded on the verb. Hence their markers may be distinguished and termed accordingly. It would seem that at least those in (263) may be differentiated,

(263) patient (P) (or, perhaps, direct object DO)
recipient (R) (or, perhaps, indirect object IO)
beneficiary (B)
causee (C)
instrumental (I)

The question whether, and if so, to what extent, patient objects may or must be identified as direct objects (DO), and recipient and beneficiary objects as indirect objects (IO), is left to future research.

3.3.3.6.4. Relative order of object markers.

It was previously suggested that extension prefix /ee-/ might be considered as a type of object marker, especially when it retains its original meaning, since semantically it does mark a reflexive object and syntactically it does take the same pre-root position as other object markers do. Nonetheless, it may lose at least some of its reflexive force and so become lexicalised, and its co-occurrence is more restricted than that of other object markers. In fact, with reflexive meaning it cannot co-occur with any of the other object markers, whereas these may so co-occur.

Apart from this, at least four distinct object markers may co-occur in a single verb form. When two or more of them do so co-occur, their relative order tends to be fixed. However, in some cases this may possibly vary somewhat. The object marker domain in verbal structure (252, 258, 262) may be elaborated as in (264),

(264) Slot: om-domain root (T) FV

Filler: {om1 om2 om3 om4 / ee-} ruγ a

This figure expresses not only the fact that reflexive /ee-/ and any of the other object markers are mutually exclusive, but also that four object markers may co-occur in any one verb form. It does not specify which type of object marker must precede which other type. The relative order of the various types of object marker will be tentatively postulated in a moment, but more extensive research on this particular aspect of the language is needed to verify this postulate.

However, first consider the examples in (265),

(265) two object markers

causee - patient

/n-βa-a-to-mo-sɔɔm-et-i-e e-ke-taaβu ime/
f-3p-t-1p-3s-read-past-c-fv a-7-book in
sm C P
[mbaatɔmɔsɔɔmɛtie eγetaaβu ime]
'they taught us about him in the book'

causee - recipient

/n-βa-a-to-mo-sɔɔm-er-et-i-e e-ke-taaβu/
f-3p-t-1p-3s-read-ap-past-c-fv a-7-book
sm C R
?[mbaatɔmɔsɔɔmɛrɛtie eγetaaβu]
'they made us read a book to him'
[twaaβamɔsɔɔmɛrɛtɛ eγetaaβu]

/n-βa-a-to-mo-sɔɔm-er-et-i-e/
f-3p-t-1p-3s-read-ap-past-c-fv
sm C R
?[mbaatɔmɔsɔɔmɛrɛtie]
'they made us read to him'
[twaaβamɔsɔɔmɛrɛtie]

beneficiary - recipient (causee implicit)

/n-βa-a-to-mo-sɔɔm-er-et-i-e e-ke-taaβu/
f-3p-t-1p-3s-read-ap-past-c-fv a-7-book
sm B R
[mbaatɔmɔsɔɔmɛrɛtie eγetaaβu]
'they made (someone) read a book to him on our behalf'

/n-βa-a-to-mo-sɔɔm-er-et-i-e/
f-3p-t-1p-3s-read-ap-past-c-fv
sm B R
[mbaatɔmɔsɔɔmɛrɛtie]
'they made (someone) read to him on our behalf'

/n-βa-a-to-mo-sɔɔm-er-et-e/
f-3p-t-1p-3s-read-ap-past-fv
sm B R
[mbaatɔmɔsɔɔmɛrɛtɛ]
'they read to him on our behalf'

beneficiary - causee

/n-βa-a-ko-mo-sɔɔm-er-et-i-e/
f-3p-t-2s-3s-read-ap-past-c-fv
sm B C
[mbaakɔmɔsɔɔmɛrɛtie]
'they made him read on your-2s behalf'

[ηkwaamɔsɔɔmɛrɛtie]
'you caused (someone) to read to him'

These data exhibit some of the variation that is possible, when two object markers are involved. Next, consider (266),

(266) causee - recipient - patient

/n-βa-a-ko-mo-ke-sɔɔm-er-et-i-e/
f-3p-t-t-3s-7-read-ap-past-c-fv
sm C R P
[mbaakɔmɔγɛsɔɔmɛrɛtie]
'they made you read 7-it to him'

causee - patient - recipient

/n-βa-a-ko-ke-mo-sɔɔm-er-et-i-e/
f-3p-t-2s-7-3s-read-ap-past-c-fv
sm C P R
?[mbaaγɔkɛmɔsɔɔmɛrɛtie]
'they made you read it to him'

causee - beneficiary - recipient

/n-βa-a-ko-to-mo-sɔɔm-er-et-i-e/
f-3p-t-2s-1p-3s-read-ap-past-fv
sm C B R
[mbaaγɔtɔmɔsɔɔmεrεtie]
'they made you-2s read to him on our behalf'

causee - beneficiary - patient

/n-βa-a-to-mo-ke-sɔɔm-et-i-e e-ke-taaβu/
f-3p-t-1p-3s-7-read-past-c-fv a-7-book
sm C B P
[mbaatɔmɔγεsɔɔmεtie eγetaaβu]
'they made us read the book to him' (definite)

(same as previous example, but with applicative suffix:)

beneficiary - causee - patient

/n-βa-a-to-mo-ke-sɔɔm-er-et-i-e e-ke-taaβu/
f-3p-t-1p-3s-7-read-ap-past-c-fv a-7-book
sm B C P
[mbaatɔmɔγεsɔɔmεrεtie eγetaaβu]
'on our behalf they made him read the book' (definite)

/n-βa-a-to-mo-ke-sɔɔm-er-et-i-e/
f-3p-t-1p-3s-7-read-ap-past-c-fv
sm C B P
[mbaatɔmɔγεsɔɔmεrεtie]
'they made us read 7-it for/to him'

/n-to-a-βa-mo-ke-sɔɔm-er-et-i-e/
f-1p-t-3p-3s-7-read-ap-past-c-fv
sm C B P
[ntwaβamɔγεsɔɔmεrεtie]
'we made them read 7-it to him'.

These data exemplify co-occurrence of three object markers. Finally, four object markers may also co-occur, as in (267), though apparently this is rare,

(267) causee - patient - beneficiary - recipient

/n-βa-V-ko-ke-to-mo-sɔɔm-er-et-i-e/
f-3p-t-2s-7-1p-3s-read-ap-past-c-fv
sm C P B R
[mbaakɔγεtɔmɔsɔɔmεrεtie]
'on our behalf they made you read 7-it to him'

causee - recipient - beneficiary - patient

/n-to-V-βa-mo-ko-ke-sɔɔm-er-et-i-e/
f-1p-t-3p-3s-2s-7-read-ap-past-c-fv
  sm C R B P
[ntooβamɔkɔγεsɔɔmεrεtie]
'we made them read 7-it to him on your behalf'

Various object markers may also co-occur in the infinitive, as in (268),

(268) /ko-rem-a/
15-dig-fv
[korema]
'to dig, to hoe, to plough'

/ko-rem-i-a/
15-plough-c-fv
[koremia]
'to make (e.g. animals) plough'

/ko-rem-er-i-a/
15-plough-ap-c-fv
[koremeria]
'to make plough on behalf of'

beneficiary:

/ko-mo-rem-er-i-a/
15-3s-plough-ap-c-fv
  B
[komoremeria]
'to make plough on his behalf'

beneficiary - causee:

/ko-mo-ci-rem-er-i-a/
15-3s-10-plough-ap-c-fv
  B C
[komociremeria]
'to make 10-them plough on his behalf'

beneficiary - recipient - causee:

/ko-mo-to-ci-rem-er-i-a/
15-3s-1p-10-plough-ap-c-fv
  B R C
[komotociremeria]
'to make 10-them plough for him on our behalf'

What is presumably a double causee is found in the following example (269),

(269) a. causee - beneficiary - causee:

/ko-to-mo-ci-rem-er-i-a/
15-1p-3s-10-plough-ap-c-fv
C_1 B C_2
[γotomociremeria]
'to make us make 10-them plough for him'

causee - causee - beneficiary

/ko-to-ci-mo-rem-er-i-a/
15-1p-10-3s-plough-ap-c-fv
C_1 C_2 B
[γotocimoremeria]
'to make us make 10-them plough for him'

b. causee - beneficiary - causee

/n-βa-a-ko-to-mo-sɔɔm-er-et-i-e/
f-3p-t-2s-1p-3s-read-ap-past-c-fv a-7-book
sm C_1 B C_2
[mbaaγɔtɔmɔsɔɔmɛrɛtie eγetaaβu]
'they made 2s-you make him read on our behalf'

A double-check of the previous data with the help of Lilian Nyanchama, about half a year after they were first recorded, indicated that her use of object markers in tensed forms seemed more consistent. This usage evinced the tendency exemplified in (270),

(270) a. |m-ba-a-ko-mo-rem-er-et-i-e|
f-3p-t-t-2s-3s-dig-ap-t-c-fv
sm C B
[mbaakomoremeretie]
'3p-they made 2s-you dig for 3s-him'

|m-ba-a-kɔ-mɔ-γɛ-kɔr-ɛt-i-e|
f-3p-t-t-2s-3s-7-dig-t-c-fv
sm C B P
[mbaakɔmɔγɛkɔrɛtie]
'they made 2s-you do 7-it for 3s-him'

b. |m-ba-a-kɔ-mɔ-kɔr-ɛt-i-e|
f-3p-t-t-2s-3s-dig-t-c-fv
sm C B
[mbaakɔmɔkɔrɛtie]
'3p-they made 2s-you work for 3s-him'

c. |m-ba-a-mɔ-kɔ-kɔr-ɛt-i-e|
f-3p-t-t-3s-2s-dig-t-c-fv
sm C B
[mbaamɔkɔkɔrɛtie]
'3p-they made 3s-him work for 2s-you'

d. |m-ba-a-kɔ-mɔ-ɔrɔk-ɛr-ɛt-i-e|
f-3p-t-t-2s-3s-show-ap-t-c-fv
sm B R
[mbaakɔmɔɔrɔkɛrɛtie]
'3p-they showed (to) 3s-him (for) 2s-you'
'they showed to him on your behalf'

e. |m-ba-a-kɔ-mɔ-γɛ-sɔɔm-ɛr-ɛt-ɛ|
f-3p-t-t-2s-3s-7-read-t-fv
sm B R P
[mbaakɔmɔγɛsɔɔmɛrɛtɛ]
'they PASt-read 7-it to 3s-him on 2s-your behalf'
'they read it to him on your behalf'

However, examples as in (271) were also found,

(271) a. |m-ba-a-γɔ-γɛ-tɔ-mɔ-sɔɔm-ɛr-ɛt-i-e|
f-3p-t-t-2s-7-1p-3s-read-t-c-fv
sm C P B R
[mbaakɔγɛtɔmɔsɔɔmɛrɛtie]
'they made you read 7-it to him for us'

b. |m-ba-a-γɔ-tɔ-γɛ-mɔ-sɔɔm-ɛr-ɛt-i-e|
f-3p-t-t-2s-1p-7-3s-read-t-c-fv
sm C B P R
[mbaaγɔtɔγɛmɔsɔɔmɛrɛtie]
'they made 2s-you teach 7-it to 3s-him on 1p-our behalf'
'they made you read it to him on our behalf'

c. |m-ba-a-γɔ-tɔ-mɔ-γɛ-sɔɔm-ɛr-ɛt-i-e|
f-3p-t-t-2s-1p-3s-7-read-t-c-fv
sm C B R I
[mbaaγɔtɔmɔγɛsɔɔmɛrɛtie]
'they made 2s-you read it to him for 1p-us'

The preceding examples evince a tendency toward the following order of object markers (272), where labels printed in bold-face on the same row represent object markers that supposedly occur in marked order,

(272) order tendencies of object markers

a. two om's

C	<	P		
		R		
B	<	R		
B	<	**C**		

b. 3 om's

C	<	B	<	P		
C	<	B	<	R		
C	<	C	<	B		
C	<	**B**	<	**C**		
		B	<	I	<	R
		B	<	R	<	**C**
		B	<	R	<	P
		B	<	**C**	<	P
		B	<	R	<	**C**

c. 4 om's

C	<	**R**	<	**B**	<	P
C	<	**P**	<	**B**	<	R
C	<	B	<	P	<	R
C	<	B	<	R	<	I

It must be added, however, that occurrences of more than two object markers in one verb form are relatively rare, and that co-occurrence of four object markers seems to be exceptional. It was often doubted by most informants. At least some of the data on which (272c) was based, were judged to be somewhat artificial and caused much pondering and hesitation on their part. Whiteley, who records a maximum of two object markers (1956: 55), does not consider possible co-occurrence of more than two, nor disconfirm it.

Nonetheless, all things considered, it would seem that the following postulate (273) may be put forward on the order of object markers, at least as a generally observable tendency,

(273) tentative order of object markers

a. unmarked

causee < beneficiary < recipient < patient/instrumental

b. marked

beneficiary < causee
recipient < beneficiary
patient < beneficiary

It may be added, first, that some degree of variation in the relative order of R and P/I seems to be permitted, since both R < P and P < R occur, but the determinants of this variation are as yet unclear. Second, P and I may be mutually exclusive, but this too requires verification by checking whether I < P and P < I may occur. Third, determinants of the change from unmarked to marked order still need to be made explicit. Difference in pragmatic emphasis may be one such determinant, but in the given state of research one can only speculate.

In a more comprehensive examination of the various functions and orders of object markers, at least the following factors will have to be taken into account: (1) presence or absence of a distinct object following the verb in the sentence; (2) the precise number of and distinctions between the semantic roles involved; (3) the question whether or not there is a need to differentiate direct and indirect object; and (4) a possible correlation between difference in pragmatic or some other type of emphasis of objects and a change in the order of their markers.

Factors such as these, which may determine variation in order, have not yet been investigated sufficiently, so that the presentation given here must be considered as a tentative sketch in these respects. Admittedly, the data cited are scarce and inconclusive, and a considerable amount of research is still needed to clarify our understanding of this area of Gusii lexical morphology and syntax. Yet their inclusion is at least a beginning. It is hoped that the present analysis, however brief and tentative, may stimulate more comprehensive research of this interesting sub-system of the language.

3.3.3.7. Infinitive marker.

It was already noted in section 3.3.1 that class prefix 15 /ko-/ may function as the marker of the infinitive.

It may be added here that this element has probably become grammaticalised in certain tenses. By and large, these seem to be tenses that may have been composite originally, but now seem to have become synthesized. In this usage, the element thus functions as a tense prefix. As such, it is designated as ko2 (see section 3.3.3.5), in order to distinguish it from the homomorphous tense suffix ko1, which, however, occurs in a preceding tense slot.

3.3.3.8. Root.

As pointed out in section 3.3.1, the root may be considered to constitute the morphological and semantic core of the verb. As such, it may be extended (see section 3.3.2). It may also be reduplicated (see section 3.4.3). No further discussion is needed at this point.

3.3.3.9. Final vowel.

Since the distinction of the final vowel as a separate unit is based not only on suprasegmental, but also on morphosyntactic grounds, because it combines with other relevant affixes to mark tense, it was briefly discussed in section 3.3.3.5. Nothing need be added here.

3.3.3.10. Locative.

At least with certain verbs, meaning 'to be', the locative meaning 'there' may be expressed through suffix /-ɔ/, as in (274),

(274) /n-β-e-ɔ/
1s-be-fv-there
[imbɛɔ]
'I be there'

e.g. [niiγɔ βaantɛɛβia imbɛɔ βaaγoocia βaañɔɔrɛ]
'they told me to be there, so that when they come they will find me'

/n-n-β-e-ɔ/
f-1s-be-fv-there
[niimbɛɔ]
'I will be there'

/ke-β-e-ɔ/
7-be-fv-there
[kɛβɛɔ]
'it-7 will be there'

/n-ke-β-e-ɔ/
f-7-be-fv-there
[ŋkɛβɛɔ]
'will it-7 be there?'

/n-ke-re-ɔ/
f-7-be-there
[ŋkɛrɛɔ]
'it-7 is there'

/n-na-a-reNγe-ɔ/
f-1s-t-be-loc
[nnaarengeɔ]
'I was there (recently)'

similarly,

2s	[ŋkwaarengeɔ]
3s	[naarengeɔ]
1p	[ntwaarengeɔ]
2p	[mmwaarengeɔ]
3p	[mbaarengeɔ]

Also note the following allomorphy,

(275) 'sm is/are there'

1s	[niindɛɔ]	[niindɔɔ]	[nɔɔ nde]
2s	[nɔɔrɛɔ]	[nɔɔrɔɔ]	[nɔɔ ore]
3s	[naarɛɔ]	[naarɔɔ]	[nɔɔ are]
1p	[ntɔrɛɔ]	[ntɔrɔɔ]	[nɔɔ tore]
2p	[mmɔrɛɔ]	[mmɔrɔɔ]	[nɔɔ more]
3p	[mbarɛɔ]	[mbarɔɔ]	[nɔɔ βare]

Whether the suffix may be postulated as /-o/ underlyingly, may be a matter for further examination. Whiteley postulates /-o/ (1960:11). In tenses derived from /kɔβa/ (see appendix 1), Mid Vowel Height Spreading may be argued to apply regularly. Forms such as [nnaarengeɔ][139], where the rule does not apply, because there is no lower mid root vowel to trigger it, and the suffix yet surfaces as [-ɔ], provide strong evidence for postulating /-ɔ/. It is [ŋkɛrɛɔ] and similar surface representations that appear to be exceptional, in contrast with, for example, [ŋkorema ore] '2s-you are digging', not *[ɔre]. Even if it be argued that the locative element is not a suffix, but an independent morpheme that may, however, cliticise to the preceding word, as in (276),

(276) /n-βa-re ɔ/
f-3p-be loc
[mbarɛɔ]
'3p-they are there'

e.g. |aβaanto mbarɛɔ βaisaine|
'there are enough people'
(literally, 'people are there who are enough')

Mid Vowel Height Spreading applies exceptionally, since it is not due to a trigger in the

[139] Some informants claimed that [nnaarengeɔ] is "short for" [nnaarenge arɔrɔ] 'I was there' ([arɔrɔ] 'that place, there').

root /-re/, but to one outside of it. This may be a case of lexicalisation.[140]

Location or direction may also be expressed in another way. If considered morphologically, it may be said to be expressed pronominally; or, if considered syntactically, it may said to be expressed adverbially, as in (277),

(277)	/ko-sɔɔm-a a-rɔ-rɔ/ 15-read-fv 16-there [γosɔɔma a-rɔ-rɔ] 'to read there'	/ko-sɔɔm-a aiγa/ 15-read-fv 16-there [γosɔɔma aiγa] 'to read here'
	/ko-sɔɔm-a aa/ 15-read-fv 16-here [γosɔɔma aa] 'to read here'	/ko-sɔɔm-a ime/ 15-read-fv 16-here [γosɔɔma ime] 'to read inside'

However, it may be added that a form such as *[γosɔɔmaɔ] is not acceptable. For some other data also see section 3.3.6.4.

3.3.4. Morphological fusion.

3.3.4.1. Perfective /r/-Deletion

Since extended verbs may be conjugated like any non-extended or basic verb, and extension suffixes and tense suffixes /-et/ and /-ir/ (followed by /-e/ or its allomorph /-i/) occur in the same post-root domain, juxtaposition of these affixes may occasion a type of surface variation known as morphological fusion, in Bantu studies sometimes also called imbrication.

Before some of the specific changes involved are considered, it is necessary to review the relevant data. The passive and causative extension suffixes follow the perfective and past tense suffixes, whereas the other extension suffixes precede them, as in (278),

(278) order of extension and tense suffixes

	2	3 4	5	6	7	t	8	9	FV
root	-ak	-ok -or	-ek	-er	-an	-et -ir	-i	-γu	-e

This figure represents the basic relative order of verbal extension and tense suffixes.

[140] Should my transcriptions be in error, and [mbareɔ] would be the actual surface, all difficulties disappear and the analysis, as given, stands without a need for any further qualifications.

Reduplication of extension suffixes /-ek/ and /-er/ is not taken into account here, since it does not affect the nature of morphological fusion.

The contrast between infinitival and tense endings of extended verbs in the following presentation (279) exemplifies the morphological fusion to be accounted for,

(279) infinitival ending — perfective ending

infinitival ending	perfective ending
-u-a	-ir-u-e
pass-fv	pv-p-fv
[-wa]	[-irwe]

e.g. [γɔsɔɔma] 'to read'
[γɔsɔɔmwa] 'to be read'
[γiasɔɔmirwe] '7-it has just been read'

infinitival ending	perfective ending
-i-a	-ir-i-e
c-fv	pv-c-fv
[-ia]	[-irie]

e.g. /-kɔr-/ 'do'
[γɔkɔria] 'to cause to do'
[twaakɔririe] 'we have caused to do'

infinitival ending	perfective ending
-i-γu-a	-ir-i-γu-e
c-p-fv	pv-c-p-fv
[-iγwa]	[-iiγwe]

e.g. [γɔkɔriγwa] 'to be done'
[γiakɔriiγwe] '7-it has been done'

infinitival ending	perfective ending
-ok-a	-ok-ir-e
st-fv	st-pv-fv
[-oka]	[-okire]

e.g. /-βuat-/ 'hold', |-βuat-ok-| 'stop holding'
[twaaβwaatokire] 'we have stopped holding'

infinitival ending	perfective ending
-er-a	-er-ir-e
ap-fv	ap-pv-fv
[-era]	[-eire]

e.g. /-ɛr-/ 'finish (v.i.)'
|-ɛrɛr-| 'be finished for (v.i.)'
[kiaɛrɛire] '7-it has just got finished for (v.i.)'

-er-u-a	-er-ir-u-e
ap-p-fv	ap-pv-p-fv
[-erwa]	[-eirwe]

e.g. [γɔkɔrɛrwa] 'to be done for'
[γiaakɔrɛirwe] '7-it has just been done for'[141]

-er-i-a	-er-ir-i-e
ap-c-fv	ap-pv-c-fv
[-eria]	[-eirie]

e.g. [γɔsɔɔmɛria] 'to teach by means of/with'
[twaasɔɔmɛirie] 'we have just taught with'

-er-i-γu-a	-er-ir-i-γu-e
ap-c-p-fv	ap-pv-c-p-fv
[-eriγwa]	[-eriiγwe]

e.g. [γɔsɔɔmɛriγwa] 'to be taught by means of'
[γiasɔɔmɛriiγwe] '7-it has just been taught with'

-er-an-a	-er-an-ir-e
ap-rc-fv	ap-rc-pv-fv
[-erana]	[-eranire]

e.g. [γɔsɔɔmɛrana] 'to read to/for each other'
[βaasɔɔmɛranire] 'they have just read to each other'

-er-an-i-a	-er-an-ir-i-e
ap-rc-c-fv	ap-rc-pv-c-fv
[-erania]	[-eranirie]

e.g. [γɔsɔɔmɛrania] 'to continue reading (i.e. something else)'
[βaasɔɔmɛranirie] 'they have just continued reading'

[141] From /ke-a-kɔr-er-ir-u-e/
sm7-t-do-ap-pv-p-fv

The /r/ of the applicative extension suffix is dropped. Compare this with the same tense of the basic verb [γiaakɔrirwe] '7-it has just been done', which is derived from /ke-a-kɔr-ir-u-e/.

-er-an-i-γu-a
ap-rc-c-p-fv
[-eraniγwa]

-er-an-ir-i-γu-e
ap-rc-pv-c-p-fv
[-eraniiγwe]

e.g. [γɔsɔɔmεraniγwa] 'to be taught simultaneously'
[βaasɔɔmεriiγwe] 'they have just been taught simultaneously'

and

-er-an-et-i-γu-e
ap-rc-past-c-p-fv
[-eranetiγwe]

e.g. [mbaasɔɔmεranetiγwe] 'they were taught simultaneously (recently/long ago[142])'

-an-a
rc-fv
[-ana]

-an-ir-e
rc-pv-fv
[-anire]

e.g. [komañana] 'to know each other'
[βamañanire] 'they have just known each other'
(i.e. they have just become acquainted)

-an-i-a[143]
rc-c-fv
[-ania]

-an-ir-i-e
rc-pv-c-fv
[-anirie]

e.g. [γɔsɔɔmania] 'to teach each other'
[βaasɔɔmanirie] 'they have just taught each other'

-an-i-γu-a
rc-c-p-fv
[-aniγwa]

-an-ir-i-γu-e
rc-pv-c-p-fv
[-aniiγwe]

e.g. [γɔsɔɔmaniγwa] 'to be caused to teach each other'
[βaasɔɔmaniiγwe] 'they have just been made to teach each other'

---

142 These distinct meanings have a different tone pattern.

143 The ending in

-an-u-a
rc-p-fv
[-anwa]

is semantically impossible, since it incongruously combines the idea of transitive reciprocity with that of passivity.

and -an-et-i-γu-e
rc-past-c-p-fv
[-anetiγwe]

e.g. [βaasɔɔmanetiγwe] 'they were made to teach each other (recently/long ago)'

The surface variation in the stems in (279) is co-accounted for partly by the allomorphy of the passive marker, /-u/ or /-γu/.

First, one case of morphological fusion may merely be apparent, because it consistently involves a change in meaning. Compare the words in (280),

(280) a. /βa-a-sɔɔm-an-ir-e/
3p-t-learn-rc-pv-fv
[βaasɔɔmanire]
'they have just come to know each other'

?/βa-sɔɔm-an-ir-e/
3p-learn-rc-pv-fv
[βasɔɔmaine]
'they (have come to) know each other (recently)'

b. /βa-a-tεεm-an-ir-e/
3p-t-try-rc-pv-fv
[βaatεεmanire]
'they have just tried each other'

?/βa-a-ko-tεεm-aine/
3p-t-t-try-suffixes
[βaaγɔtεεmaine]
'they are (in the process of) trying each other'
(same meaning: [βátεεmaíné], εε = H)

?/βa-a-tεεm-ir-an-e/
3p-t-try-pv-rc-fv
[βáatεεmáíné]
'they are (in the process of) trying each other'

c. ?/to-aNγ-an-e/
[twááŋgáíné] 'we hate e.o.'

?/to-aNγ-an-ir-e/
[twaaŋganire]
'we have (just) hated e.o.'

/to-aNγ-an-ir-i-e/
[twaaŋganirie]
'we have (just) caused to hate e.o.'

d. [βááñcainé] 'they like each other' (untimed fact or general 'present')
[βáañcáíné] 'they like each other (recently)'
[βaañcanire] 'they have come to like each other' (just now)[144]

e. [βacɔɔraine] 'they have chosen each other' (untimed fact)
[βaacɔɔranire] 'they have chosen each other (just now)'

The question-marks indicate that I do not quite know how to analyse these examples or to account for them. Barring minor details, Whiteley says that this type of variation involves "a small group of reciprocal forms (...) which have a general present in -aine as well as a normal perfect in -anire" (1956: 52). This may be correct, but he does not define the group by enumerating its members or the distinctive characteristics that they share. A tense ending in -aine may occur in at least some verbs, as in (280), but a definitive account of the full extent of its occurrence requires more research.

Clear cases of morphological fusion are two changes that may delete /r/ in root- or post-root domain; specifically, root- or suffix-final /r/. The more specific one of the two involves the flapped liquid of perfective suffix /-ir/. Consider the examples in (281), which exhibit increasing morphological complexity, both in terms of this rule, and, as we shall see in section 3.3.4.2, in terms of the other, more general rule of /r/-Deletion,

(281) a. /βa-a-sɔɔm-ir-i-γu-i/[145]
3p-t-read-pv-c-p-fv
[βaasɔɔmiiγwi]
'they have just been taught'

---

[144] Compare

[βááñcaneté] 'they liked each other (recently)'
[βáañcánété] 'they liked each other (long ago)'

[βaañcíre] 'they have liked (just now)'
[βááñceté] 'they liked (recently)'
[βáañcété] 'they liked (long ago)'

[145] The alternation between final vowel [i] and [ə] (see the same tense under (281b), unless one of them is a transcriptional error, or a distinction between class 1 and 2 on the one hand and non-personal classes on the other is involved, appears to be free in at least some tenses containing both the causative and the passive suffix.

b. /ke-a-kɔr-ir-i-γu-e]
sm7-t-do-pv-c-p-fv
[γiakɔriiγwe]
'7-it has been done'

c. /βa-a-sɔɔm-an-ir-i-γu-e/
3p-t-read-rc-pv-c-p-fv
[βaasɔɔmaniiγwe]
'they have just been made to teach each other'

/βa-a-sɔɔm-er-an-ir-i-γu-e/
3p-t-read-ap-rc-pv-c-p-fv
[βaasɔɔmεriiγwe]
'they have just been taught simultaneously'

d. /ke-a-sɔɔm-er-ir-i-γu-e/
sm7-t-read-ap-pv-c-p-fv
[γiasɔɔmεriiγwe]
'7-it has just been taught with'

/βa-a-sɔɔm-er-ir-i-γu-i/
3p-t-read-ap-pv-c-p-fv
[βaasɔɔmεriiγwi]
'they have just been taught for/with'

/ke-a-tiγar-ir-i-γu-e/
sm7-t-remain-pv-c-p-fv
[γiatiγariiγwe]
'7-it was caused to remain (earlier today)'

/ke-a-tiγar-er-ir-i-γu-e/
sm7-t-remain-ap-pv-c-p-fv
[γiatiγareriiγwa]
'7-it has just been caused to remain for'

In all these examples, where both the causative and the passive suffix, in that order, follow the perfective suffix, the /r/ of the latter is deleted, regardless of what precedes it. To anticipate the discussion of the other rule of /r/-Deletion, also note that no preceding /r/, whether root- or suffix-final, is deleted in this context. Since this change occurs exclusively in passive causative perfectives, it may be accounted for as in (282),

(282) Perfective /r/-Deletion

Ø
↑
[ir [i [γu
pv c p

This rule simply deletes the flapped /r/ of the perfective tense suffix obligatorily, whenever the latter is followed by both the causative and the passive suffix.

Though it may appear to be somewhat ad hoc, it is nonetheless necessary, for at least two reasons. First, the /r/ of other morphemes is not deleted in the same context, as is evidenced by representative data such as (283),

(283) /ko-sɔɔm-er-i-γu-a/
15-read-ap-c-p-fv
[γɔsɔɔmεriγwa], *[γɔsɔɔmεiγwa]
'to be taught by means of'

Second, the /r/ of the perfective suffix is not deleted in other contexts, as is shown by representative examples such as those in (284),

(284) /to-a-βuat-ok-ir-e/
1p-t-hold-ri-pv-fv
[twaaβwaatokire], *[twaaβwaatokie]
'we have stopped holding'

/ci-a-βusur-ir-u-e/
sm10-t-sow-pv-p-fv
[ciaβusuirwe], *[ciaβusuriγwe]
'10-they have just been sown'

/to-a-kɔr-ir-i-e/
1p-t-do-pv-c-fv
[twaakɔririe], *[twaakɔriie]
'we have caused to do'[146]

These data (283, 284) corroborate the fact that the perfective suffix must be followed by both the causative and the passive marker, in order for the rule to apply.

3.3.4.2. /r/-Deletion.

The rule discussed in this section concerns the optional deletion of /r/, whenever it is followed by perfective tense suffix /-ir/.

---

[146] The fact that [ciaβusuririγwe] 'they have just been caused to be sown' was given as the surface representation of /ci-a-βusur-ir-i-γu-e/, that is, the fact that the rule does not apply in this case, unless it indicates an error of transcription on my part or an error of judgment of the informant concerned, or perhaps an idiolectal peculiarity, suggests that the rule is not applied, in order to preserve morphological identity. However, in view of the regularity with which the rule is applied, and by analogy to all the other relevant examples, I suspect that [ciaβusuririγwe] is perfectly possible and correct, at least in some idiolects.

Whiteley notes the process under the following general observation. "The realization of the radical + ire varies according to the shape of the radical" (1960: 10). This characterisation includes the following aspects of verbal morphology: the process under discussion, the fact that the causative and passive suffixes follow both the perfective suffix /-ir/ and the past tense suffix /-et/, allomorphy involving /-ire/ after roots ending in /u/, and finally, the fact that, when the causative and the passive suffix co-occur, they occur in that order and the latter's allomorph is /-ɣu/, thus /-i-ɣu-/. However, these points are not formally stated and the quoted general observation is insufficient as a treatment of the rule at hand, even though the six examples cited (1960: 11), though partial, are appropriate enough.

The contextual details of the process appear to be somewhat involved and will therefore be considered first. Several points may be noted. First, the status or identity of the morphological material of which the target /r/ is a part, is irrelevant for the operation of the rule. In (285), for example, it constitutes the final segment of the root,

(285) /βa-a-βusur-ir-e/
sm3p-t-sow-pv-fv
[βaaβusurire], [βaaβusuire]
'they have (just) sown'

/βa-a-kɔrɔr-ir-e/
sm3p-t-cough-pv-fv
[βaakɔrɔrire], [βaakɔrɔire]
'they have (just) coughed'

/e-a-tiɣar-ir-e/
sm9-t-wait-pv-fv
[yaatiɣarire], [yaatiɣaire]
'9-it has (just) remained behind'

/βa-a-βutor-ir-e/
sm3p-t-chop-pv-fv
[βaaβutorire], [βaaβutoire]
'they have (just) chopped'

/βa-a-iɣor-ir-e/
3p-t-open-pv-fv
[βaiɣorire], [βaiɣoire]
'they have (just) opened (v.t.)'

The fact that the surface representations are alternatives, underlines the optionality of the rule. However, if the root is monosyllabic, the application of the rule tends to be blocked in the same context, as in (286),

(286) /βa-a-sir-ir-e/
sm3p-t-get lost-pv-fv
[βaasirire]
but not *[βaasiire]
'they have (just) got lost'

/βa-a-tiir-ir-e/
sm3p-t-climb-pv-fv
[βaatiirire]
but not *[βaatii(i)re]
'they have (just) climbed'

/βa-a-tɛɛr-ir-e/
sm3p-t-sing-pv-fv
[βaatɛɛrire]
but not *[βaatɛɛire]
'they have (just) sung'

/βa-a-mer-ir-e/
sm3p-t-get lost-pv-fv
[βaamerire]
but not *[βaameire]
'they have (just) swallowed'

The motivation for this prohibition arguably lies in the tendency toward preservation of morphological identity, which is generally applicable, especially to roots. However, in the following example (287), root-final /r/ may probably be deleted,

(287) /βa-a-taar-ir-e/
sm3p-t-walk-pv-fv
[βaataarire], ?[βaataaire][147]
'they have (just) walked'

and in (288) it may certainly be deleted,

(288) a. /βa-a-raar-ir-e/
sm3p-t-sleep-pv-fv
[βaaraarire], [βaaraaire]
'they have (just) slept'

b. /βa-a-rer-ir-e/
sm3p-t-cry/wail-pv-fv
[βaarerire], [βaareire]
'they have (just) cried'

Both examples in (288) are adapted from Whiteley (1960: 11), but only the latter has been checked. The possibility that the rule may be applicable in the one segmental type (-cvvc-), but not in the other (-cvc-), remains to be checked.

Given data such as the preceding ones, I assume that, unless and until pervasive evidence to the contrary is discovered, root-final /r/ is not generally deleted when it immediately precedes perfective suffix /-ir/, if the root is monosyllabic, due to preservation of root-integrity. I further assume that exceptions are few, and therefore propose that they be marked in the lexicon as exempt from the type of /r/-deletion under discussion.

In (289), it belongs to some extension suffix,

(289) /βa-a-raar-er-ir-e/	/ke-a-ɛr-er-ir-e/
sm3p-t-sleep-ap-pv-fv	sm7-t-finish-ap-pv-fv
[βaaraareire]	[kiaɛrɛire]
'they have (just) slept on'	'7-it has just got finished for (v.i.)'

[147] Not to be confused with

/βa-a-ta-ir-e/
sm3p-t-pour-pv-fv
[βaataire]
'they have (just) poured'

/to-a-sɔɔm-er-ir-i-e/	/ke-a-kɔr-er-ir-u-e/
1p-t-read-ap-pv-c-fv	sm7-t-do-ap-pv-p-fv
[twaasɔɔmɛirie]	[γiaakɔrɛirwe]
'we have just taught with'	'7-it has just been done for'[148]
/βa-a-βusur-er-ir-e/	/βa-a-iγor-er-ir-e/
sm3p-t-sow-ap-pv-fv	sm3p-t-open-ap-pv-fv
[βaaβusureire]	[βaiγoreire],
'they have (just) sown for'	?[βaiγorerire] 'they have (just) opened for (v.t.)'
/βa-a-tiir-er-ir-e/	/βa-a-tɛɛr-er-ir-e/
sm3p-t-climb-ap-pv-fv	sm3p-t-sing-ap-pv-fv
[βaatiireire]	[βaatɛɛreire]
but not *[βaatiirerire]	'they have (just) sung for'
'they have (just) climbed with'	
/to-a-βutor-er-ir-e/	/to-a-βutor-er-er-ir-e/
1p-t-cut-ap-pv-fv	1p-t-cut-ap-ap-pv-fv
[twaaβutorerire]	[twaaβutorererire]
or [twaaβutoreire]	or [toaβutorereire]
'we have just cut for'	'we have just cut for by means of'
/βa-a-mer-er-ir-e/	
sm3p-t-swallow-ap-pv-fv	
[βaamereire]	
but not *[βaameeire]	
'they have (just) swallowed with'	

Given data such as these, it may be inferred that the domain of the target is the stem, not merely the root.

Furthermore, the fact that, for example, *[βaaraaeire] is not an acceptable alternative for the first item in (289), makes it clear that the rule involved is not an iterative one. The same observation, mutatis mutandis, applies to all the other examples in (289) and similar ones. The optionality of the rule is exemplified for the two pre-final items, which further emphasise that it is only the /r/ immediately preceding the perfective suffix that may be deleted. These properties are generally applicable.

It may be added that /r/ may not be deleted, whenever it occurs before a suffix other than /-ir/. This is exemplified in (290),

---

[148] From /ke-a-kɔr-er-ir-u-e/
sm7-t-do-ap-pv-p-fv

The /r/ of the applicative extension suffix is dropped. Compare this with the same tense of the basic verb [γiaakɔrirwe] '7-it has just been done', derived from /ke-a-kɔr-ir-u-e/.

(290) /ko-βer-er-a/
15-boil-ap-fv
[koβerera]
but not *[koβeera]
'to boil for'

/kɔ-sɛr-er-a/
15-push-ap-fv
[γɔsɛrɛra]
but not *[γɔsɛɛra]
'to push for/with'[149]

/kɔ-ɛr-er-a/
15-finish-ap-fv
[kɔɛrɛra]
but not *[kɔɛɛra]
'to finish for/with'

/ko-βusur-er-a/
15-sow-ap-fv
[koβusurera]
but not *[koβusuera]
'to sow for'

/ko-iγor-er-a/
15-open-ap-fv
[koiγorera]
but not *[koiγoera][150]
'to open for (v.t.)'

/ko-kɔr-er-u-a/
15-do-ap-p-fv
[γɔkɔrɛrwa]
but not *[γɔkɔɛrwa]
'to be done for'

/ko-tiir-er-a/
15-climb-ap-fv
[γotiirera]
but not *[γotiiera]
'to climb with'

/ko-mer-er-a/
15-swallow-ap-fv
[γomerera]
but not *[γomeera]
'to swallow with'

/ko-βutor-er-a/
15-chop-ap-fv
[koβutorera]
but not *[koβutoera]
'to chop for'

/ko-βutor-er-er-a/
15-chop-ap-ap-fv
[koβutorerera]
but not *[koβutoreera]
'to chop for by means of'

However, there appears to be one counter-example to this general tendency, viz. (291),

(291) /ko-rer-er-a/
15-cry-ap-fv
[korerera] or [koreera]
'to cry for'

To the best of my knowledge, it is the only one. Hence I propose to mark it in the lexicon as an exception to the rule at hand.

If the analysis of the data discussed is correct, the rule accounting for them may be formulated as in (292),

[149] The basic meaning is uncertain.

[150] Compare [koiγuera] or [kwiiγweera] 'to hear, to obey'.

(292) /r/-Deletion (optional)

Ø
↑
r [-ir
perfective

Condition: may not apply, if the trigger belongs to a monosyllabic root

It states that /r/ may be deleted optionally, whenever it is immediately followed by perfective tense suffix /-ir/.[151] Given the uniqueness of /-ir/, the rule (292) automatically applies only once. For example, /to-a-βutor-er-ir-e/ will not surface as *[toaβutoeire]. Characterised as optional, (292) may optionally not apply as well. The few words to which it may not apply at all, may be marked as exceptions. The rule may be strictly characteristic of informal or casual speech, and thus be style-dependent, but this point will not be pursued here.

Finally, the structural descriptions of Perfective /r/-Deletion (282) and /r/-Deletion (292) clearly overlap. That is, the application of the one ipso facto destroys the structural description of the other. Given the fact that a sequence like /-er-ir-i-γu-e/ never surfaces as *[-eiriγwe], but always as [-eriiγwe], it may be concluded that Perfective /r/-Deletion precedes /r/-Deletion, and if applicable, bleeds the latter. Whenever it is not applicable, the latter, being optional, may or may not apply.

However, the rules need not be ordered explicitly with respect to each other. Perfective /r/-Deletion (282) is the more specific of the two and may be assumed to apply before /r/-Deletion (292), in virtue of the Elsewhere Condition proposed by Kiparsky (1982: 136). Put informally, in a somewhat simplified manner, it states that, when two rules in the same component of the language may apply to the same string of segments, but have a different output, the more specific rule applies first.

So much for the two rules of /r/-deletion, involving the perfective suffix /-ir/ and its context, and the morphological fusion they may cause. Yet another type of fusion, involving the vowel of this suffix, is discussed in the next section.

3.3.4.3. Perfective Suffix Vowel Delinking

In some roots ending in /-u/, the following type of fusion occurs,

[151] Since this is the only suffix of this shape in the language, the term 'perfective' might well be omitted from the formulation of the rule.

(293) irregular perfective endings

/ko-ru-a/	/βa-a-ru-ir-e/
15-give-fv	3p-t-give-pv-fv
[korwa]	[βaaruure], *[βaaruire]
'to give'	'they have (just) given'
/ko-tu-a/	/βa-a-tu-ir-e/
15-fall/pick-fv	3p-t-fall/pick-pv-fv
[γotwa]	[βaatuure], *[βaatuire]
(1) 'to fall (v.i.)'	'they have (just) fallen'
(2) 'to pick (v.t)'[152]	'they have (just) picked'
/ko-ñu-a/	/βa-a-ñu-ir-e/
15-drink-fv	3p-t-drink-pv-fv
[koñwa]	[βaañuure], *[βaañuire]
'to drink'	'they have (just) drunk'

These examples may be accounted for by arguing that /i/ of the perfective suffix is delinked and that the preceding root-final /u/ is lengthened compensatorily, i.e. spread rightward. But in at least one verb, similar to those in (293), this change does not take place. Compare (294),

(294)	/ko-βu-a/	/βa-a-βu-ir-e/
	15-win-fv	3p-t-win-pv-fv
	[koβwa]	[βaaβuire], *[βaaβuure]
	'to win'	'they have (just) won'

When confronted with data such as these, one must ask, which represent the rule and which the exception to it. A mere count of the individual items is insufficient to settle the matter. The system of the language, at least the relevant part of it, must be taken into account. In this case, since Gusii roots of the shape /-CV-/ are relatively few (see appendix 1), the data in (293) may plausibly be argued to be basic in the respect under consideration.

The next question is how similar verbs behave. The answer is that the rule does not apply with them, as exemplified in (295),

(295)	/ko-βɔ-a/	/βa-a-βɔ-ir-e/
	15-tie-fv	3p-t-tie-pv-fv
	[kɔβɔa]	[βaaβɔire], *[βaaβɔɔre]
	'to tie'	'they have (just) tied'

---

[152] See Appendix One. This and the previous example is based on Whiteley (1956: 71).

/ko-sɔ-a/	/βa-a-sɔ-ir-e/
15-enter-fv	3p-t-enter-pv-fv
[γɔsɔa]	[βaasɔire], *[βaasɔɔre]
'to enter'	'they have (just) entered'
/ko-rɛ-a/	/βa-a-rɛ-ir-e/
15-thin-fv	3p-t-thin-pv-fv
[kɔrɛa]	[βaarɛire], *[βaarɛɛre]
'to be thin'	'they have (just) been/become thin'
/ko-a-a/	/βa-a-a-ir-e/
15-pluck-fv	3p-t-pluck-pv-fv
[kwaa]	[βaaire], *[βaare]
'to pluck'	'they have (just) plucked'
/ko-βV-a/	/βa-a-β-e-ir-e/
15-be-fv	3p-t-be-pv-fv
[kɔβa]	[βaaβɛire], *[βaaβɛɛre]
'to be'	'they have (just) been'

However, /-CV-/ roots ending in /i/ are indeterminate in this respect, since they may arguably be interpreted either way. Consider the data in (296),

(296)	/ko-ri-a/	/βa-a-ri-ir-e/
	15-eat-fv	3p-t-eat-pv-fv
	[koria]	[βaariire]
	'to eat'	'they have (just) eaten'
	/ko-ni-a/	/βa-a-ni-ir-e/
	15-defecate-fv	3p-t-defecate-pv-fv
	[koria]	[βaariire]
	'to defecate'	'they have (just) defecated'

One possible interpretation of these perfective tenses, is to argue that the /i/ of /-ir/ is not delinked; in other words, that the rule does not apply. The other interpretation is to argue that it does. That is, the /i/ of perfective suffix is delinked and the root vowel is lengthened compensatorily through rightward spreading. Because the latter is also /i/, the output simply turns out to be identical to the input. Because it is the second interpretation that allows for the most general formulation of the rule at hand, it is the one adopted here.

Accordingly, the data in (293, 296) may be accounted for as in (297),

(297) Perfective Suffix Vowel Delinking

```
          x                     x
          |                     ‡
          o [-cons]             o [-cons]
          |                     |
     [ +high ]            [ +high  ]
     [ -mid  ]            [ -mid   ]
                        [ [ -back  ]
                        [
                        perfective
                        suffix
```

This rule states that the /i/ of the perfective suffix is delinked, whenever it is immediately preceded by a high vowel, whether front or back. No further changes need be indicated, since subsequently the preceding high vowel will be spread to x vacated by (297), in virtue of the Linking Rule (see section 2.3.8). The root /-ßu-/, which is irregular also in other respects, may be marked [-(297)] in the lexicon, i.e as an exception to the rule.

3.3.5. The tense system.

It has not been possible to study the tenses so as to be able to present a definitive arrangement that takes their meanings fully into account, but an outline of the system will be given in a moment. A few other points connected with the system will be considered first, together with occasional suggestions for further research toward a full analysis of it.

The following adverbs of time (298) are commonly used in combination with tenses,

(298) [rɛɛrɔ] 'today'
[iɣɔrɔ] 'yesterday'
[moisoonde] 'the day before yesterday'
[moisoonde nde] 'the day before the day before yesterday'
[ewiiki] 'week', plural [ciwiiki]
[ewiiki eria] 'last week' (literally, 'that week')
[ewiiki eɣooca] 'next week' (literally, 'coming week')
[ewiiki ende] 'next week'
[omotieni] 'month', plural [emetieni]
[omotieni oria] 'last month' (literally, 'that month')
[omotieni oɣooca] 'next month' (literally, 'coming month')
[omwaaka] 'year', plural [emiaaka]
[omwaaka oeta] 'last year' (literally, 'the year that has passed')
[omwaaka oɣooca] 'next year' (literally, 'coming year')
[maambia] (a) 'morning', (b) 'tomorrow'
[maambia ende] 'the day after tomorrow'
[maambia ende ende] 'the day after the day after tomorrow', also pronounced [maambieendeende]

Some of these are also discussed elsewhere.

A definitive tonal analysis of the tense system must include a thorough check of what different tone patterns may result (a) in tenses and non-finite forms of segmentally different types of verb (i.e. verbs that differ from each other in terms of their CV-structure), (b) when the tenses of these verbs take one, two, or more object markers, (c) when they have different types of subject or object marker, (d) when they take one or more extension affixes, (e) when several or all of these variables are combined.

In the following account of the Gusii tenses, those consisting of one finite form are termed simple tenses. Tenses containing a finite form plus another finite form or an infinitive, are called complex tenses. The treatment given here is synchronic. A brief, but interesting account of the expansion of the Gusii tense system considered against the background of Proto-Bantu, is given in Kingston (1983).

With respect to the presentation of the Gusii tense system given here, it may well be asked whether this has not already been done sufficiently by Whiteley (1960). In some respects the answer to this question is indeed an affirmative one. His publication on the Gusii tenses arguably belongs to his best descriptive work, when considered in terms of thoroughness and attempted systematicness of approach.

Still, several observations are in order. First, there is a high proportion of transcriptional error in his work (1956, 1960), which mostly affects his examples, but sometimes also his analysis. Second, his highly analytic and somewhat ad hoc formal labelling and distributive classification occasionally detracts from the perspicuity of the system as a whole and diminishes the insight into semantic relations between various tenses. Third, because underlying and surface representations are not differentiated, and no morphological analysis and interlinear translation are given, many examples are hard to interpret for readers who have no prior knowledge of the language, the more so since tense analyses are not exemplified throughout for all morphosyntactic classes. Finally, a few tenses appear to be postulated erroneously.

However, despite these criticisms, the present treatment acknowledges and builds on Whiteley's work. It must be added that the present study has not been been able to correct or supplement all, or even most, of the points criticised. Its breadth of scope combined with the available resources did not allow for this. The presentation given here uses the paradigm of 1-3s/p for example, differentiates underlying and surface representations, and records tone for two tonally distinct verbs throughout.

Since Whiteley's arrangement of the Gusii tenses is primarily formal and secondarily distributional (1960: 11-13), simple tenses (called "one-word" tenses) are analysed somewhat arbitrarily, first, according to the four distinct endings that occur, and labelled accordingly, as in (299),

(299) arrangement and labels of simple tenses (Whiteley 1960)

labels of positive tenses	ending	labels of corresponding negative (ti-) tenses
A	-a	P
B	-e	Q
C	-ire	R
D	-ete	S

Whenever some negative tense corresponds to a positive one either in form or in meaning, P, Q, R, or S is used as a label for it. But if it corresponds to the positive tense both in form and in meaning, two letters are used, thus AP, BQ, CR, DS. It must be added, however, that in this respect Whiteley's usage is not always consistent. Negative tenses containing /ta-/ are labelled 'x', whereas negative tenses containing /ti-/ are not labelled 'x'; for example, Px, as opposed to P.

Second, Whiteley further subdivides tenses according to the number and type of tense affixes they contain. These are numbered, as in (300),

(300)

tense label	tense affix
1	Z
2	-a-
4	-ka-
7	-na-
9	-raa-

Z stands for 'zero', i.e. segmentally zero. But given the data, it must be interpreted as designating an underspecified vowel. Combination of the lettering in (299) with the numbering in (300) yields A1, A2, etc. For example, A29 designates a tense that contains two tense affixes, viz. -a-raa- (2 and 9), and that ends in -a, since it is called an A-tense.

Third, a further subdivision is made according to tonal pattern, whenever this is distinctive. More precisely, the addition to some tense label of /1 is said to indicate a high tone, /2 a low tone, and /3 a high-low contour, on tense affix 2 /-a-/, which occurs in tenses thus differentiated. Tenses with a tone pattern analysed as invariant are labelled IP, short for invariant pattern.

In actual fact, however, this convention may involve the tone of tense markers other than /-a-/. Also, because in at least some of these tenses the tone of other elements may also vary, all other things are not equal. Further, though it labels what is tonally distinct at the surface, it does so without revealing the underlying tonal system and without taking into account or at least exemplifying all the distinct verbal tone patterns for each tense which may be found in distinct segmental verb types. Therefore, though this system of tonal subdivision may be useful descriptively as a means of labelling differences on the surface, from a systematic point of view it must be considered ad hoc and somewhat obscurantist.

For additional remarks on tone, especially on the sometimes exceptional tonal behaviour of subject prefixes 1, 4, and 9, see Whiteley (1960: 8-10).

Fourth, whenever a focus element occurs in some tense, the letter 'a' is attached at the end of its label, for example A1a, as distinct from A1. Concerning this focus, Whiteley makes the following correct observations. First, some focussed tenses have no corresponding non-focussed tense. Second, where both exist, focussed tenses introduce a new theme, by starting a conversation or by introducing a new topic in an ongoing one. Here, these are called thematic tenses. In contrast, their non-focussed counterparts are used to continue an ongoing theme and conversation (1956: 33, 92). These are called rhematic tenses. Third, apparently except for APx1a, only positive tenses may be focussed (1960: 12, 22). Fourth, instead of, and equivalent to, some focussed tense, [iγɔ] or [niiγɔ] may also be used, together with a non-focussed tense, in order to introduce a new theme or to begin an entire conversation. (1956: 92). Here, these are also called thematic tenses. Some exceptions are noted by Whiteley.

Fifth, and finally, R is Whiteley's symbol for any low-toned, Ŕ for any high-toned root. However, as pointed out, the tonal pattern may vary per tense in roots of verbs belonging to distinct segmental patterns. Since this is taken into account sometimes, but not always, one cannot be certain that his postulated tonal patterns are correct, though of course they do reflect his postulates.

Such, then, is Whiteley's system of analytic formal labelling (1960: 13-15, and passim). It has provided the starting-point for the present outline. His analysis has been checked in all respects and, wherever necessary and possible, corrected and supplemented. Even so, as already pointed out, a considerable amount of work remains to be done.

I have used the following method. First, the structure and the surface representations of the paradigm for each tense, using the forms for 1-3 singular and plural, were ascertained with the help of Shem Orioki, who pronounced all finite forms in isolation, using the verb /-rúγ-/ 'cook' [korúγá], or, where the meaning demanded it, some other verb. Half a year later, all of this material was double-checked with the help of Lilian Nyanchama, this time using the verbs /-róm-/ [korómá] 'to bite' and /-rut-/ [koruta] 'to throw'. Since the tonal patterns of /-rúγ-/ were found to correspond sometimes with those of /-róm-/, but sometimes with those of /-rut-/, only Lilian's pronunciations have been reproduced hereafter, in order to maintain consistency. These have been thoroughly rechecked with Judith Moraa and Janet Mokaye (see Appendix Two).

Tone is lexically distinctive only to a small extent in Gusii, and therefore involves only few actual minimal pairs. Even its grammatical distinctiveness seems to be rather restricted. Whiteley's treatment of the subject is justly cautious, not always sufficiently explicit, but sometimes seems to suggest more than is warranted (1956: 6, 33, 68, 80-81; 1960: 6-7, 9-10, 12, 15, and some particular tenses). Nonetheless, whatever a comprehensive treatment of the tonal system may reveal, given the recorded surface representations, it may be safely assumed that most, if not all, words bear tone underlyingly, as in the case of [korómá] and [koruta]. Whether low tone may be derived from no tone underlyingly, remains to be examined.

Whenever Whiteley's transcriptions or analyses are different from mine, this has been indicated by including his postulate, using the first person plural. In comparing these, it must be borne in mind that pronunciations of some of my informants sometimes differed from those recorded by Whiteley, even when I used his test-verb [korúγá] 'to cook' in checking Orioki's speech. Nor did Nyanchama's pronunciation of [korómá] always tally with Orioki's pronunciation of [korúγá] for all tenses. Comparison is further encumbered by the fact that Whiteley does not elucidate possible interaction between the lexical tone of verbs and tense tone. Nor do I. Whiteley's tense labels and page-numbers are nonetheless added in parenthesis, in order to facilitate quick cross-referencing. Since his analysis is insufficiently systematic from a tonal point of view, and mine too, a few tonal variations noted by him for certain tenses are not repeated here.

All of Whiteley's analyses have been checked several times over, and all of his examples have been re-recorded. Also, the tenses have been recorded paradigmatically, which is also the way in which they are presented here. It may not have been possible to exclude the kind of interference that may result from such paradigmatic recording, but possible interference with phrasal or sentence intonation definitely has been excluded thereby. Due to limitations of time and resources, it has been impossible to collect sufficient data on postlexical phonology, for such interaction to be taken into account systematically in this connection.

Specifically, tenses will be spelled out in the following presentation, using the paradigm for the first, second, and third person singular and plural of the animate class. Tonal surface patterns are recorded, such that the tones of lower mid vowels are mentioned separately, due to representational limitations of the computer programme used. Supposedly corresponding positive, negative, focussed, and non-focussed tenses are placed together. No comprehensive systematic analysis of their tone has been attempted.

In order to make the tonal factors of the Gusii tense system explicit, future research must answer systematically at least the following questions. First, what are **all** of the distinct underlying verbal tone patterns? Second, which tense tones or tonal patterns **precisely** are distinctive? Third, how do these factors interact? If the suprasegmental and segmental tiers interact, how and to what extent do they do so? Such answers will enable us to formulate a system of tonal rules that is both necessary and sufficient, in order to account for all the surface variety. The variation between [korómá] and [koruta] exemplifies at least some of this variety, and some of the added comments may resolve at least some points, but only a comprehensive approach can do so definitively.

The arrangement of the tenses given below follows that of Whiteley's (1960: 13-14, 21-37). Despite its recognised shortcomings, it indicates what must necessarily be included in a definitive arrangement. I will refer to his publication in the presentation only by giving its date. Each tense is conjoined with its negative and relative counterparts, if any. Simple tenses are presented first, complex tenses afterwards.

It should also be remembered that the nasal parts of word-initial prenasalised consonants are usually syllabic. This is left unmarked, thus [mb, nd, mm, nn], etc. When the consonant that is prenasalised is itself a nasal, three surface renderings are possible in word-initial position. First, the first nasal part may be syllabic, viz. [mm], [nn], [ññ], or [ŋŋ]. Second, especially in more rapid speech, the first nasal part may be almost imperceptible. Thus, for example, 1s [nnaa] may virtually sound as [naa], and 2s [mmwaa] as [mwaa]. Third, the first nasal part may be realised word-initially as [iN]; for example, [imo] instead of [mmo]. This may be accounted for relatively informally as in (301),

(301)	input	n-mo
	prenasalisation	mmo
	nasal allomorphy	immo
	degemination	imo

Compensatory lengthening does not occur word-initially, so that we do not find *[iimo.

Furthermore, word-initial syllabic nasals always bear H or L tone. In line with common representational practice, L is here left unmarked, while H is marked by an accute accent, e.g. [ń]. For computer reasons, a high-toned velar nasal is represented by [ŋ̇]. Syllabic [m] and alveolo-palatal [ñ] cannot be marked by an accute accent, so whenever these bear H, this will be mentioned separately, thus: [m] = H, [ñ] = H. Similarly, H-toned lower mid back vowel [ɔ]: [ɔ] = H. In Whiteley's analyses, some vowel or root occasionally bears mid tone, here indicated by M, as in: R = M (mid-toned root).

Gusii differentiates at least three types of past and future tense in terms of temporal proximity to, or distance from, the speech act. Grading them from lesser to greater distance from the present, the following terminology may be used. With respect to the past, they may be called hodiernal, recent, and far past, respectively indicated in their glosses by '(today)', '(recently)', and '(long ago)'. Hodiernal past refers to an activity occurring, or a state obtaining, earlier today; recent past to something happening during or within the past few days, possibly back to the last few weeks; and far past to something any, or some specific, time before that. The Gusii tense system does not include a separate hesternal past, i.e. a tense that specifically refers to something that happened yesterday, and yesterday only. Given these observations, the following classification (302) of past tenses may be tentatively proposed,

(302) a. hodiernal (earlier today)

e.g. [ńtwáárómá] 'we bit (earlier today)'

sometimes differentiated into
1. immediate (back to about half a day ago)
2. non-immediate (before about half a day ago)

b. recent (before today, back to about one or two weeks ago)

e.g. [ntwaarómete] 'we bit (recently)'

c. long ago (before recently, as defined under b)

e.g. [ńtwáarómete] 'we bit (long ago)'

Some tenses may have both hodiernal and recent time reference, such that the difference depends on the context. Indeed, the finer distinctions of the system in (302) may apparently be conceived differently sometimes by different speakers. More semantic research on the tenses is needed, in order for a comprehensively argued semantic arrangement to be produced.

The future tenses may be differentiated as hodiernal, near, and far future, respectively indicated in their glosses by '(today)', '(soon)', and '(far)'. An immediate future may also be distinguished, but it is implicitly hodiernal and refers to something that will, or is supposed to, happen in the moments or hours immediately following the speech act. Hodiernal future refers to something that will happen later today. Near future refers to something that will happen during the next few days, possibly up to the next few weeks. Far future refers to something that will happen any or some time after that.

What are generally called present tenses may actually express a variety of temporal concepts. Indeed, one distinction seems to involve reference versus no reference to real time, though, indirectly, time may be understood in the latter. Tenses without any overt reference to a specific point or period of time are dubbed 'untimed'. The distinguishing characteristic of such tenses is not necessarily a lack of time reference. Rather, the term indicates that tenses so designated express a proposition. Time reference may or may not be implied; in some cases it may be added through an adverbial expression. Greater or lesser proximity to the speech act, also, may possibly be expressed in some present tenses. Or perhaps the distinction is between definiteness and indefiniteness, as in some past and future tenses.

In conditional sentences expressing putative, hypothetical, or otherwise attitudinal statements, rather than statements of supposed fact in real time, the conditional sub-clause may be introduced by [ɔñɛ] 'if', while the consequential main clause is introduced by [aŋga] 'then' (compare Whiteley 1956: 72-73).

Tenses beginning with focus element /n-/ or /na-/ are labelled 'focussed'. Those without it are left unmarked in this respect as to their labels. Similarly, tenses expressing negation are dubbed 'negative', while positive tenses are not labelled as such. Again, tenses used as a relative are labelled as such, non-relative tenses are not.

Aspectual distinctions, such as the expression of habit or some sort of continuity or frequency of action, may also be expressed. The same is true of various types and degrees of volition. Similarly, intellectual or mental judgments, such as possibility, probability, certainty, which in many languages are associated with a subjunctive mood, may also be expressed. Several types of volition may be distinguished on the basis of increasing degrees of urgency or imperativeness, such as a suggestion, a wish, a request (or, conversely, a permission), an adhortation, an obligation, or a command.[153]

Aspect may also be involved in consecutive tenses, which regularly express activity

---

[153] Some such distinctions have been made in the following presentation, but these may well be made more precise.

following and continuing the activity expressed by another, preceding tense. Similarly, antecedent tenses regularly express an activity preceding the activity expressed by another, following tense. Semantic distinctions such as these and the ones mentioned in the previous paragraph, are expressed by particular combinations of tense affixes. These require closer examination than they have received here.

Parenthesised terms in tense labels indicate optional meaning. For example, 'negative (relative) present perfect continuous' signifies that the tense concerned may be used either in a relative, or in a non-relative sense. Parenthesis in glosses indicates implied meaning.

Finally[154], the following point may be noted with regard to the meaning of the tenses. Despite the impressive descriptive study on the tense system in (1960) and the work embodied in the present more modest section, the **system** of the meanings of Gusii tenses remains a matter for more refined research. Even so, all of Whiteley's definitions of meaning ("connotation") have been checked several times over. The results of this work are reflected in the tense labels and the glosses given here.

With these preliminaries, we may now consider the tenses themselves, beginning with paradigms ending in -a (303-360).

(303) untimed habit or fact

to-róm-á 'we bite'
to-rut-á 'we throw'

[ndómá]	[ndutá]
[orómá]	[orutá]
[arómá]	[arutá]
[torómá]	[torutá]
[morómá]	[morutá]
[βarómá]	[βarutá]

Compare with A1, to-Z-R-a (1960: 21-22; "expresses continuity over a long period of time without specific time reference".) Corresponding negative: P1/Ai1, see (305). Hereafter, the translation of only one of the two verbs, viz. [koroma], will be given by way of example.

---

[154] Considerably more may be said about the tenses and the system into which they enter, much may be said on many of Whiteley's examples, and examples collected by myself might be added. However, the pressure of other work, in combination with the broad scope of the present study and the nature of available resources, limited time in particular, rendered it impossible to incorporate all this additional information.

(304) negative indefinite habitual past: 'we did not bite'

/ti-n-V-ko-rom-a/	-->	[tííŋkorómá]
/ti-o-V-ko-rom-a/	-->	[tóókorómá]
/ti-a-V-ko-rom-a/	-->	[táákorómá]
/ti-to-V-ko-rom-a/	-->	[titóókorómá]
/ti-mo-V-ko-rom-a/	-->	[timóókorómá]
/ti-βa-V-ko-rom-a/	-->	[tiβáákorómá][155]
/ti-n-V-ko-rut-a/	-->	[tííŋkoruta]
/ti-o-V-ko-rut-a/	-->	[tóókoruta]
/ti-a-V-ko-rut-a/	-->	[táákoruta]
/ti-to-V-ko-rut-a/	-->	[titóókoruta]
/ti-mo-V-ko-rut-a/	-->	[timóókoruta]
/ti-βa-V-ko-rut-a/	-->	[tiβáákoruta]

This, in contrast with Whiteley, is the negative of the previous tense. Compare P5/2 (1960: 29), see (320, 321). Underlyingly, /-V-/ is postulated to account for the long surface vowels of the negative marker and the subject markers. The assumption that /-V-/ is deleted between two consonants, prenasalisation of n + k, and compensatory lengthening of the preceding [i], might co-account for the surface representation of the first person singular.

(305) a. negative hodiernal present continuous

'we are not biting'

b. negative untimed fact or habit

'we do not bite (anytime or usually)'

/ti-n-r-i ko-rom-a/	-->	[tííndi korómá]
/ti-o-r-i ko-rom-a/	-->	[tóri korómá]
/ti-a-r-i ko-rom-a/	-->	[tári korómá]
/n-to-r-i ko-rom-a/	-->	[ntóri korómá]
/n-mo-r-i ko-rom-a/	-->	[mmóri korómá] or [imóri ..]
/n-βa-r-i ko-rom-a/	-->	[mbári korómá]
/ti-n-r-i ko-rut-a/	-->	[tííndi koruta]
/ti-o-r-i ko-rut-a/	-->	[tóri koruta]
/ti-a-r-i ko-rut-a/	-->	[tári koruta]
/n-to-r-i ko-rut-a/	-->	[ntóri koruta]
/n-mo-r-i ko-rut-a/	-->	[mmóri koruta] or [imóri ..]
/n-βa-r-i ko-rut-a/	-->	[mbári koruta]

[155] Final [HH] in this paradigm may possibly be [HL].

Compare P1/Ai1. ti-tó-rí kó-R-a (1960: 57). Compare (429, 450). Negative of (428) [ŋkoroma nde], Ai2/A1 (1960: 57). In 2-3s of this tense, the /i/ of /ti-/ is deleted through Morpholexical /i/-Deletion. Similarly elsewhere, when it is followed by a vowel (see 3.3.3.2). In connection with the alllomorph for 2p, see the introductory remark on surface variation involving word-initial prenasals.

(306) negative untimed obligation: 'you should not bite'

[tíindómá]	[tííndutá]
[tóorómá]	[tóórutá]
[táarómá]	[táárutá]
[titóorómá]	[titóórutá]
[timóorómá]	[timóórutá]
[tiβáarómá]	[tiβáárutá]

This tense may be used as a complement to another (past, present, or future) tense: 'that we should not bite'. Its underlying representation, exemplified for the first person singular, is /ti-to-V-R-a/. Hereafter, this person will be used mostly for illustration, except when the form for some other person may be considered more clear. Compare P1, IP, ti-tó-Z-R-a (1960: 13, 38). See (362).

(307) a. untimed conditional, focussed
b. present conditional, focussed

'even if/even though we bite, ...'

/na-n-rom-a/	-->	[niindómá]
/na-o-rom-a/	-->	[noorómá]
/na-a-rom-a/	-->	[naarómá]
/na-to-rom-a/	-->	[natorómá] or [ntorómá]
/na-mo-rom-a/	-->	[namorómá] or [mmorómá]
/na-βa-rom-a/	-->	[naβarómá] or [mbarómá]

/na-n-rut-a/	-->	[niindutá]
/na-o-rut-a/	-->	[noorutá]
/na-a-rut-a/	-->	[naarutá]
/na-to-rut-a/	-->	[natorutá] or [ntorutá]
/na-mo-rut-a/	-->	[namorutá] or [mmorutá]
/na-βa-rut-a/	-->	[naβarutá] or [mbarutá]

Underlying representation /na-to-R-a/, in contrast with A1a, n-to-Z-R-a (1960: 22; "Always associated with 'although..'. Time reference present or general"). Presumably, the focussed form for this tense may alternate with its non-focussed form preceded by /na/ 'and', used as a conjunction, which suggests that the focus may have derived from /na/. See (448).

Its corresponding negative is (308),

(308) a. negative untimed conditional, focussed
b. negative present conditional, focussed

'even if/even though we do not throw, ...'

/na-n-ta-rom-a/ --> [niintárómá]
/na-o-ta-rom-a/ --> [nootárómá]
/na-a-ta-rom-a/ --> [naatárómá]
[ntotárómá] or [natotárómá]
[mmotárómá] or [namotárómá]
[mbatárómá] or [naβatárómá]

/na-n-ta-rut-a/ --> [niintárútá]
/na-o-ta-rut-a/ --> [nootárútá]
/na-a-ta-rut-a/ --> [naatárútá]
[ntotárútá] or [natotárútá]
[mmotárútá] or [namotárútá]
[mbatárútá] or [naβatárútá]

Compare APx1a n-to-tá-R-a (1960: 22). For the alternations, see the remark on the preceding tense.

(309) hodiernal past: 'we bit (earlier today)'

/iγɔ na-a-rom-a/	--> [íγɔ naaroma]
/iγɔ ko-a-rom-a/	--> [íγɔ kwaaroma]
/iγɔ a-a-rom-a/	--> [íγaaroma]
/iγɔ to-a-rom-a/	--> [íγɔ twaaroma]
/iγɔ mo-a-rom-a/	--> [íγɔ mwaaroma]
/iγɔ βa-a-rom-a/	--> [íγɔ βaaroma]
/iγɔ na-a-rut-a/	--> [íγɔ naaruta]
/iγɔ ko-a-rut-a/	--> [íγɔ kwaaruta]
/iγɔ a-a-rut-a/	--> [íγaaruta]
/iγɔ to-a-rut-a/	--> [íγɔ twaaruta]
/iγɔ mo-a-rut-a/	--> [íγɔ mwaaruta]
/iγɔ βa-a-rut-a/	--> [íγɔ βaaruta]

This tense may have non-immediate or immediate meaning. More general than the hodiernal or recent untimed habitual or obligatory past activity. Compare A2/1, tó-á-R-a. For verbs of the type /-róm-/: tó-á-R-a (where R = M; 1960: 22-24; "Time reference 'past', generally within the past hour or so". The addition, "but there is some looseness particularly in the younger generation" is not explained). See (310, 313, 432, 433, 445, 446).

(310) recent past: 'we bit (recently)'

/iγɔ na-a-rom-a/ --> [íγɔ náarómá]
/iγɔ ko-a-rom-a/ --> [íγɔ kwáarómá]
/iγɔ a-a-rom-a/ --> [íγáarómá]
/iγɔ to-a-rom-a/ --> [íγɔ twáarómá]
/iγɔ mo-a-rom-a/ --> [íγɔ mwáarómá]
/iγɔ βa-a-rom-a/ --> [íγɔ βáarómá]

/iγɔ na-a-rut-a/ --> [íγɔ náarutá]
/iγɔ ko-a-rut-a/ --> [íγɔ kwáarutá]
/iγɔ a-a-rut-a/ --> [íγáarutá]
/iγɔ to-a-rut-a/ --> [íγɔ twáarutá]
/iγɔ mo-a-rut-a/ --> [íγɔ mwáarutá]
/iγɔ βa-a-rut-a/ --> [íγɔ βáarutá]

[ɔ] = H. This tense may be used untypically to refer to the far past, if this seems only recent in the speaker's mind, though to use -ete would be more grammatical in that case. For example [omwaaka oeta] 'last year' (literally, 'the year that has passed'. Compare A2/1 (ii) (1960: 23). See (309, 313, 432, 433, 445, 446).

(311) obligation: '(that) we should/must bite'

/na-a-rom-a/ --> [nááromá]
/ko-a-rom-a/ --> [kwááromá]
/o-a-rom-a/ --> [óromá]
/to-a-rom-a/ --> [twááromá]
/mo-a-rom-a/ --> [mwááromá]
/βa-a-rom-a/ --> [βááromá]

/na-a-rut-a/ --> [náárutá]
/ko-a-rut-a/ --> [kwáárutá]
/o-a-rut-a/ --> [órutá]
/to-a-rut-a/ --> [twáárutá]
/mo-a-rut-a/ --> [mwáárutá]
/βa-a-rut-a/ --> [βáárutá]

This tense occurs without [iγɔ] and is specifiable by the context. For example, [γiiŋgɔkɔ oβosi, kwaaroma] 'whenever I give you sugar-cane, you must bite.'

(312) hodiernal past, focussed: 'we bit (earlier today)'

/n-na-a-rom-a/ --> [ńnáárómá]
/n-ko-a-rom-a/ --> [ŋ́kwáárómá]
/n-a-a-rom-a/ --> [náárómá]
/n-to-a-rom-a/ --> [ńtwáárómá]
/n-mo-a-rom-a/ --> [mmwáárómá]
/n-βa-a-rom-a/ --> [mbáárómá]

/n-na-a-rut-a/ --> [ńnáárútá]
/n-ko-a-rut-a/ --> [ŋ̍kwáárútá]
/n-a-a-rut-a/ --> [ńáárútá]
/n-to-a-rut-a/ --> [ńtwáárútá]
/n-mo-a-rut-a/ --> [mmwáárútá]
/n-βa-a-rut-a/ --> [mbáárútá]

Word-initial [m] = H (2-3p). Compare with A2a/1, n-tɔ́-á-R-a (1960: 24; the additional remark that "some looseness is observable in the speech of the younger generation" is not further explained). See (312, 313, 315).

(313) a. negative hodiernal past
b. negative recent past

'(so/but) we did not bite (earlier today/recently)'

/ti-na-a-rom-a/ --> [tinááromá]
/ti-ko-a-rom-a/ --> [tikwááromá]
/ti-a-a-rom-a/ --> [tááromá]
/ti-to-a-rom-a/ --> [titwááromá]
/ti-mo-a-rom-a/ --> [timwááromá]
/ti-βa-a-rom-a/ --> [tiβááromá]

(or [..áár!ómá])

/ti-na-a-rut-a/ --> [tinááruta]
/ti-ko-a-rut-a/ --> [tikwááruta]
/ti-a-a-rut-a/ --> [tááruta]
/ti-to-a-rut-a/ --> [titwááruta]
/ti-mo-a-rut-a/ --> [timwááruta]
/ti-βa-a-rut-a/ --> [tiβááruta]

Underlying representation /ti-to-a-R-a/. Given the surface representations and applicable rules, this seems to be a more plausible segmental postulate than Whiteley's. If this tense is turned into a question, the tonal pattern is identical, but raised. Compare the negative hodiernal past P2/1, ti-tó-áá-R-a (1960: 13), and ti-tó-á(á)-R-a (1960: 25). Its positive counterparts are A2/1 (1960: 22-24), see (309, 310, 313, 432, 433, 445, 446); and A2a/1, (1960: 24), see (312, 313, 315). A contrast with the negative recent past P2/2, IP ti-tó-áa-Ŕ-a is postulated (1960: 25-26), but as a contrast between inherently different tonal patterns this is disconfirmed by the present research.

(314) recent past: 'we bit'

[náarómá]	[náarutá]
[kwáarómá]	[kwáarutá]
[áarómá]	[áarutá]
[twáarómá]	[twáarutá]
[mwáarómá]	[mwáarutá]
[βáarómá]	[βáarutá]

A remark on tonal representation is in order here. To take 2s for example, [kwáarutá] probably derives from /kó-a-rut-á/. Due to complex segment formation (ko > kw) and compensatory lengthening of the following vowel (koa > kwx'a > kwaa, where x' represents a floating x), the H of the subject prefix (2s ko-) tends to be realised on the first timing-unit of the long vowel, thus kó + a > [kwáa]. But it must be borne in mind that phonetically the glide [w] of the complex segment [kw] is also realised as H, however briefly. In identical contexts, the same holds for front-glide [y]. Such interaction between the tonal and the segmental tiers, though common, is noted here once for all. Elsewhere, both it and its somewhat inadequate manner of phonetic representation exemplified here will be understood. Compare A2/2, tó-a-R-a (1960: 24). See (315, 434, 435, 446).

(315) recent past, focussed: 'we bit'

[ńnáarómá]	[ńnáarutá]
[ŋ́kwáarómá]	[ŋ́kwáarutá]
[náarómá]	[náarutá]
[ńtwáarómá]	[ńtwáarutá]
[mmwáarómá]	[mmwáarutá]
[mbáarómá]	[mbáarutá]

Word-initial [m] = H. Compare with A2a/2, n-tó-a-R-a (1960: 13, 24-25, where R is said to be M in low-toned verbs of the segmental types -cvvc-, -cvv-, and -vvc-. Compare past A2a/1 and also recent past A2/2. See (314, 315, 434, 435, 446).

(316) a. negative hodiernal/recent past: 'we did not bite (today or recently)'
b. negative present continuous: 'we are not biting'
c. negative untimed fact or habit: 'we do not bite'

[ntááromá]	[ntáárutá]
[otááromá]	[otáárutá]
[atááromá]	[atáárutá]
[totááromá]	[totáárutá]
[motááromá]	[motáárutá]
[βatááromá]	[βatáárutá]

This tense is regularly used in a conditional or explanatory clause or sentence. In an antecedent clause, it can often be translated by 'if', even if [ɔñɛ] 'if' is absent. In a consequent clause, this tense may be used to express a request or a suggestion, which may be translated 'why don't we/you..?. Compare with Px2/1, to-tá-á-R-a (1960: 13, 26-27). See (316, 319, 441, 442, 444).

(317) relative negative hodiernal or recent past: 'we (are the ones who) did not bite'

[nííñce ńtáarómá]	[nííñce ńtáarutá]
[nááye ótáarómá]	[nááye ótáarutá]
[nεεrε ótáarómá]	[nεεrε ótáarutá]
[nííntwe tótáarómá]	[nííntwe tótáarutá]
[níínwe mótáarómá]	[níínwe mótáarutá]
[naβúó βátáarómá]	[naβúó βátáarutá]
or [mbaraβúó βátáarómá]	or [mbaraβúó βátáarutá]

[εε] of [nεεrε] = H. The tonal pattern may be different at least among the younger generation. Contrast with non-relative [nεεrε ataaroma] (tone unrecorded) 'he is the one (whom) she did not bite'. Compare Px2/2 to-tá-a-R-a (1960: 13, 27; tone of R said to vary per segmental verb type). See (343).

(318) a. consecutive recent past
b. consecutive far past

'we bit (recently/long ago, consecutively)'

[ŋkarómá]	[ŋkaruta]
[okarómá]	[okaruta]
[akarómá]	[akaruta]
[tokarómá]	[tokaruta]
[mokarómá]	[mokaruta]
[βakarómá]	[βakaruta]

Compare with A4, to-ka-R-a (1960: 13, 27-28, final vowel [â] in segmental verb types -cvc-, -vc-, -cv-). See (347). Negative: P2/2. See (313, 440).

(319) a. completive continuous: '(us) biting'
b. present continuous: 'we are biting'
c. untimed fact or habit: 'we bite'

[ŋ́kóromá]	[ŋ́kóruta]
[ókóromá]	[ókóruta]
[ákóromá]	[ákóruta]
[tóókóromá]	[tóókóruta]
[móókóromá]	[móókóruta]
[βáákóromá]	[βáákóruta]

Underlying representation: singular /sm-ko-root-a/, plural /sm-V-ko-root-a/. As a completive continuous, it is regularly used as a verbal part of the predicate (such as, in English, would be expressed by, for example, 'I saw him working'). Depending on the context, it may refer to present, recent, or far past time. Compare A5, to-ko-R-a, distinguished from tó-kó-R-a (1960: 13, 28-29). Its corresponding negative is (Px2/1-Ai1), see (441, 442, 444).

(320) negative immediate future:: 'we are not going to bite (right now)'

/ti-n-V-ko-rom-a/ --> [tíiηkóromá]
/ti-o-V-ko-rom-a/ --> [tóokóromá]
/ti-a-V-ko-rom-a/ --> [táakóromá]
/ti-to-V-ko-rom-a/ --> [titóokóromá]
/ti-mo-V-ko-rom-a/ --> [timóokóromá]
/ti-βa-V-ko-rom-a/ --> [tiβáakóromá]

/ti-n-V-ko-rut-a/ --> [tíiηkorutá]
/ti-o-V-ko-rut-a/ --> [tóokórutá]
/ti-a-V-ko-rut-a/ --> [táakorutá]
/ti-to-V-ko-rut-a/ --> [titóokorutá]
/ti-mo-V-ko-rut-a/ --> [timóokorutá]
/ti-βa-V-ko-rut-a/ --> [tiβáakorutá][156]

The underlying representation postulated here seems more plausible than Whiteley's, given the surface representations. Compare P5/1, ti-tó-kó-R-a (1960: 13, 40), see (321), and P5/2, IP, ti-tó-ko-Ŕ-a (1960: 13, 29; where R = M in high-toned verbs of the types -cvc-, -cv-, and -vc-), see (304, 321).

(321) negative recent/far past continuous/habitual

'while we were not biting/did not bite'
'we would not bite, we used not to bite'

/ti-n-V-ko-rom-a/ --> [tíiηkorómá]
/ti-o-V-ko-rom-a/ --> [tóokorómá]
/ti-a-V-ko-rom-a/ --> [táakorómá]
/ti-to-V-ko-rom-a/ --> [titóokorómá]
/ti-mo-V-ko-rom-a/ --> [timóokorómá]
/ti-βa-V-ko-rom-a/ --> [tiβáakorómá]

/ti-n-V-ko-rut-a/ --> [tíiηkoruta]
/ti-o-V-ko-rut-a/ --> [tóokoruta]
/ti-a-V-ko-rut-a/ --> [táakoruta]
/ti-to-V-ko-rut-a/ --> [titóokoruta]
/ti-mo-V-ko-rut-a/ --> [timóokoruta]
/ti-βa-V-ko-rut-a/ --> [tiβáakoruta]

Compare P5/1 ti-tó-kó-R-a (1960: 13, 40), see (320), and P5/2 ti-tó-ko-Ŕ-a (1960: 13,

156 The long vowels before /ko/ in this paradigm may be H, rather than HL, in the case of [koruta].

29), see (304, 320). The underlying representation postulated here is different. The tonal pattern recorded here is based on P5/1 (1960: 29, sentence 1); my record of the tone of the citations forms is not unambiguous.

(322) polite request or imperative: 'let us bite', 'allow us to bite'

/n-raa-rom-a/	/n-raa-rut-a/
[ńdáarómá]	[ńdáarutá]
[óráarómá]	[óráarutá]
[áráarómá]	[áráarutá]
[tóráarómá]	[tóráarutá]
[móráarómá]	[móráarutá]
[βáráarómá]	[βáráarutá]

When used as a polite imperative or mild adhortation, e.g. 'you will bite', it regularly precedes another future activity. When used as a request, i.e. interrogatively, the tonal pattern for the first person plural is [tóráaróma] and [tóraarutá] (RAISED) 'may we bite?' Compare A9, tó-raa-R-a (1960: 13, 29-30), see (324, 325).

(323) untimed incompletive

'we have not yet bitten'

/ti-n-raa-rom-a/	--> [tííndáarómá]
/ti-o-raa-rom-a/	--> [tóráarómá]
/ti-a-raa-rom-a/	--> [táráarómá]
[titóráarómá]	
[timóráarómá]	
[tiβáráarómá]	

/ti-n-raa-rut-a/	--> [tííndáaruta]
/ti-o-raa-rut-a/	--> [tóráaruta]
/ti-a-raa-rut-a/	--> [táráaruta]
[titóráaruta]	
[timóráaruta]	
[tiβáráaruta]	

Compare P9, ti-tó-raa-R-a (1960: 13, 30).

(324) antecedent future obligation (immediate)

'we had better bite (before doing something else)'

/na-n-raa-rom-a/	--> [niindáarómá]
/na-o-raa-rom-a/	--> [nooráarómá]
/na-a-raa-rom-a/	--> [naaráarómá]
/na-to-raa-rom-a/	--> [natoráarómá]
/na-mo-raa-rom-a/	--> [namoráarómá]

/na-βa-raa-rom-a/ --> [naβaráarómá]

/na-n-raa-rut-a/ --> [niindáarutá]
/na-o-raa-rut-a/ --> [nooráarutá]
/na-a-raa-rut-a/ --> [naaráarutá]
/na-to-raa-rut-a/ --> [natoráarutá]
/na-mo-raa-rut-a/ --> [namoráarutá]
/na-βa-raa-rut-a/ --> [naβaráarutá]

This tense expresses a future activity that regularly precedes another future activity. As in [namoráarutá, mómáñá kɔγεεnda] ([ɔ] = H) 'you had better throw (i.e. now), and then leave'. Compare A9a, n-tó-raa-R-a (1960: 13, 30), see (322, 325).

(325) continuative untimed future habit

'we will keep on biting (as we have been doing)'

/na-n-raa-rom-a/ --> [níındáarómá]
/na-o-raa-rom-a/ --> [nóóráarómá]
/na-a-raa-rom-a/ --> [nááráarómá]
/n-to-raa-rom-a/ --> [ńtóráarómá]
/n-mo-raa-rom-a/ --> [mmóráarómá]
/n-βa-raa-rom-a/ --> [mbáráarómá]

/na-n-raa-rut-a/ --> [níındáarutá]
/na-o-raa-rut-a/ --> [nóóráarutá]
/na-a-raa-rut-a/ --> [nááráarutá]
/n-to-raa-rut-a/ --> [ńtóráarutá]
/n-mo-raa-rut-a/ --> [mmóráarutá]
/n-βa-raa-rut-a/ --> [mbáráarutá]

This tense expresses intention of continuing an activity in the (unspecified) future, whether a habit or an event. All nasal elements of initial prenasals in 1-3p are H. Compare A9a, n-tó-raa-R-a (1960: 13, 30), see (322, 324).

(326) antecedent untimed incompletive

'we have not yet bitten'
'before we had bitten'

[ńtáráarómá]	[ńtáráaruta]
[ótáráarómá]	[ótáráaruta]
[átáráarómá]	[átáráaruta]
[tótáráarómá]	[tótáráaruta]
[mótáráarómá]	[mótáráaruta]
[βátáráarómá]	[βátáráaruta]

This tense can be used with any past or future tense. Compare relative Px9 (i, ii), tó-táraa-R-a (1960: 13, 30-31, subject marker vowel L for classes 1, 4, 9).

(327) polite request or adhortation: 'should we bite?'

[ńtáakóromá]	[ńtáakóruta]	(RAISED)
[ótáakóromá]	[ótáakóruta]	
[átáakóromá]	[átáakóruta]	
[tótáakóromá]	[tótáakóruta]	
[mótáakóromá]	[mótáakóruta]	
[βátáakóromá]	[βátáakóruta]	

The positive meaning of this tense is stated in the form of a rhetorical question. Its tonal surface pattern as a whole is raised (/kó/ = extra H).[157] This is indicated by the term RAISED in parenthesis, a practice to be continued hereafter. Compare Px25/1, to-tá-á-kó-R-a (1960: 13, 31).

The tense postulated by Whiteley as Px25/2, to-tá-á-ko-R-a (1960: 13, 31-32), which is segmentally identical to, but tonally different from, (327), seems to be non-existent. It is said to have 'past time reference, with continuity over a period', and it is noted that very limited contexts are available for concomitant tenses (his A5 and P5/2). But only one example is given, a proverb, containing moreover several mistakes. My informants doubted its correctness and were unable to exemplify this tense otherwise.

(328) antecedent hodiernal/recent past (continuous)

'we have bitten, we bit, we were biting (earlier today/recently, before doing something else)'

[náárááarómá]	[náárááarutá]
[kwáárááarómá]	[kwáárááarutá]
[árááarómá]	[árááarutá]
[twáárááarómá]	[twáárááarutá]
[mwáárááarómá]	[mwáárááarutá]
[βáárááarómá]	[βáárááarutá]

Word-initial [m] = H (2p). Compare A29/1, tó-á-raa-R-a (1960: 13, 32; negative: AP29/1, ti-tó-á-raa-R-a). See (329, 330, 334).

[157] The tonal pattern for [koroma] is based on Judith's speech. The final /a/ was low in Lilian's speech.

(329) antecedent hodiernal/recent past, focussed (continuous)

'we have bitten, we bit, we were biting (earlier today/recently, before doing something else)'

[ńnááráaróma ́]	[ńnááráarutá]
[ŋ́kwááráaróma ́]	[ŋ́kwááráarutá]
[nááráaróma ́]	[nááráarutá]
[ńtwááráaróma ́]	[ńtwááráarutá]
[mmwááráaróma ́]	[mmwááráarutá]
[mbááráaróma ́]	[mbááráarutá]

Word-initial [m] = H (2-3p). Example: [mmwááráarutá mmwáamaña kɔγεεnda][158] 'you threw, before you left'. Compare with A29a/1, ń-tó-á-raa-R-a (1960: 13, 32; negative, AP29/1, ti-tó-á-raa-R-a).[159] See (328, 329, 330, 331, 334).

(330) negative antecedent hodiernal or recent past

'we did not ... (before doing something else)'

/ti-na-a-raa-rom-a/ --> [tináaráaróma ́]
/ti-ko-a-raa-rom-a/ --> [tikwáaráaróma ́]
/ti-a-a-raa-rom-a/ --> [táaráaróma ́]
[titwáaráaróma ́]
[timwáaráaróma ́]
[tiβáaráaróma ́]

[tináaráarutá]
[tikwáaráarutá]
[táaráarutá]
[titwáaráarutá]
[timwáaráarutá]
[tiβáaráarutá]

As in [timwááráaróma ́, mwáamaña kɔγεεnda] '2p-you did not bite, before 2p-you left'.

---

158 The use of [komaña] 'to know' in this and some other tenses requires further investigation.

159 Apparently, an alternative equivalent tense (tone unrecorded) is

[ndaaraaroma]
[oraaraaroma]
[araaraaroma]
[toraaraaroma]
[moraaraaroma]
[βaraaraaroma]

Compare AP29/1 (1960: 13, 32). See (328, 329, 330, 334). The present research has disconfirmed Whiteley's AP29/2, which supposedly has the same meaning as AP29/1, but with 'remoter past time reference', adding that 'the occurrence of this tense is not accepted by all informants' (1960: 32).

(331) recent or far past habit: 'we used to bite (recently/long ago)'

/n-na-a-raa-rom-a/	-->	[ńnáaráarómá]	(RAISED)
/n-ko-a-raa-rom-a/	-->	[ŋ́kwáaráarómá]	
/n-a-a-raa-rom-a/	-->	[náaráarómá]	
/n-to-a-raa-rom-a/	-->	[ńtwáaráarómá]	
/n-mo-a-raa-rom-a/	-->	[mmwáaráarómá]	
/n-βa-a-raa-rom-a/	-->	[mbáaráarómá]	
/n-na-a-raa-rut-a/	-->	[ńnáaráarutá]	
/n-ko-a-raa-rut-a/	-->	[ŋ́kwáaráarutá]	
/n-a-a-raa-rut-a/	-->	[náaráarutá]	
/n-to-a-raa-rut-a/	-->	[ńtwáaráarutá]	
/n-mo-a-raa-rut-a/	-->	[mmwáaráarutá]	
/n-βa-a-raa-rut-a/	-->	[mbáaráarutá]	

Word-initial [m] = H (2-3p). The implication is that the activity expressed by the verb has stopped. In Whiteley's terminology this tense should have been A29a/2, but it is not recorded as such. Compare with A29a/1 (1960: 13, 32). See (329).

Equivalent to the previous tense is (332),

(332) recent or far past habit: 'we used to bite (recently/long ago)'

[níiγɔ náaráarómá]	[níiγɔ náaráarutá]
[níiγɔ kwáaráarómá]	[níiγɔ kwáaráarutá]
[níiγɔ áráarómá]	[níiγɔ áráarutá]
[níiγɔ twáaráarómá]	[níiγɔ twáaráarutá]
[níiγɔ mwáaráarómá]	[níiγɔ mwáaráarutá]
[níiγɔ βáaráarómá]	[níiγɔ βáaráarutá]

[ɔ] = H. Compare A29/2, tó-a-raa-R-a (1960: 13, 32; negative: AP29/2 ti-tó-a-raa-R-a). See (328, 329, 330, 331, 334).

(333) negative recent or far past (fact or habit)

'we did not used to bite (recently/long ago)'

[níiγɔ ntáaráaróómá]	[níiγɔ ntáaráarutá]
[níiγɔ ótáaráaróómá]	[níiγɔ ótáaráarutá]
[níiγɔ átáaráaróómá]	[níiγɔ átáaráarutá]
[níiγɔ tótáaráaróómá]	[níiγɔ tótáaráarutá]
[níiγɔ mótáaráaróómá]	[níiγɔ mótáaráarutá]
[níiγɔ ßátáaráaróómá]	[níiγɔ ßátáaráarutá]

In these paradigms, [ɔ] = H.

(334) consecutive antecedent recent past: 'you bit/threw'

[ŋkaráaróómá]	[ŋkaráarutá]
[okaráaróómá]	[okaráarutá]
[akaráaróómá]	[akaráarutá]
[tokaráaróómá]	[tokaráarutá]
[mokaráaróómá]	[mokaráarutá]
[ßakaráaróómá]	[ßakaráarutá]

This tense is used in expressing a series of recent past activities. Compare A49, IP, to-ka-ráá-R-a (where R = M; 1960: 13, 32).

The negative postulated for this tense by Whiteley (1960: 13, 32), i.e. the doubtful AP29/2, has been disconfirmed as such by the present research. Negative antecedent hodiernal or recent past (330) may be used instead. Compare AP29/1 (1960: 13, 32).[160] See (328, 329, 330)

[160] The following alternative negative, given by Lilian Nyanchama, may be incorrect,

'we did not bite (recently)'

[tííndáarometi]	[tííndáaruteti]
[tóráarometi]	[tóráaruteti]
[táráarometi]	[táráaruteti]
[titóráarometi]	[titóráaruteti]
[timóráarometi]	[timóráaruteti]
[tißáráarometi]	[tißáráaruteti]

(335) untimed occasional activity: 'we occasionally bite'

[íγɔ ŋ́kóráarómá]	[íγɔ ŋ́kóráarutá]
[íγɔ ókóráarómá]	[íγɔ ókóráarutá]
[íγɔ ákóráarómá]	[íγɔ ákóráarutá]
[íγɔ tóókóráarómá]	[íγɔ tóókóráarutá]
[íγɔ móókóráarómá]	[íγɔ móókóráarutá]
[íγɔ βáákóráarómá]	[íγɔ βáákóráarutá]

[ɔ] = H. The activity expressed may, but need not[161], be followed by another activity. Compare A59, tó-kó-raa-R-a (1960: 13, 33; tone of R varies per segmental verb type; negative: complex tense A1/Ai3).

(336) untimed fact or habit: 'we (always) bite'

/n-na-ko-rom-a/	/n-na-ko-rut-a/
[iñákóromá]	[iñákóruta]
[oñákóromá]	[oñákóruta]
[añákóromá]	[añákóruta]
[toñákóromá]	[toñákóruta]
[moñákóromá]	[moñákóruta]
[βañákóromá]	[βañákóruta]

Note: [-ña-], but not [-na-]. Compare A75, tó-ná-kó-R-a (1960: 13, 33; tone of R is said to vary per segmental verb type; the suggestion that "in some positive and all negative contexts there is also an implication of obligation" is disconfirmed). See (339).

(337) untimed future continuous: 'we will keep on biting'

/n-na-ko-rom-a/	/n-na-ko-rut-a/
[íñákóromá]	[íñákóruta]
[óñákóromá]	[óñákóruta]
[áñákóromá]	[áñákóruta]
[tóñákóromá]	[tóñákóruta]
[móñákóromá]	[móñákóruta]
[βáñákóromá]	[βáñákóruta]

[161] As claimed by Whiteley, 'with the implcation of doing something subsequent to the action in question' (1960: 33).

(338) a. negative near future continuous
b. negative indefinite future continuous

'we will not bite/be biting (soon/anytime)'

/ti-n-V-na-ko-rom-a/ --> [tíiñákóromá][162]
/ti-o-V-na-ko-rom-a/ --> [tóoñákóromá]
/ti-a-V-na-ko-rom-a/ --> [táañákóromá]
[titóoñákóromá]
[timóoñákóromá]
[tiβáañákóromá]

/ti-n-V-na-ko-rut-a/ --> [tíiñákóruta]
/ti-o-V-na-ko-rut-a/ --> [tóoñákóruta]
/ti-a-V-na-ko-rut-a/ --> [táañákóruta]
[titóoñákóruta]
[timóoñákóruta]
[tiβáañákóruta]

The time referred to by this tense usually begins with the present and continues into the future. Compare P75, IP, ti-tó-ná-kó-R-a (1960: 13, 33; tone of R is said to vary per segmental verb type; morphological and other tonal variation is also recorded).

---

162 The following derivational sketch may suffice to account for part of this surface representation,

input and affixation	/ti-n-V-na-ko-rom-a/
V-Deletion	∅
Prenasalisation	nna
/i/-Insertion	inna
Degemination	ina
Nasal Palatalisation	iña
other rules	
output	[tíiñákóromá]

(339) indefinite future continuous: 'you will be biting (anytime in the future)'

/na-na-na-ko-rom-a/ --> [niiñákóromá][163]
/na-o-na-ko-rom-a/ --> [nooñákóromá]
/na-a-na-ko-rom-a/ --> [naañákóromá]
[natoñákóromá] or [ntoñákóromá]
[namoñákóromá] or [mmoñákóromá]
[naβañákóromá] or [mbañákóromá]

/na-n-na-ko-rut-a/ --> [niiñákóruta]
/na-o-na-ko-rut-a/ --> [nooñákóruta]
/na-a-na-ko-rut-a/ --> [naañákóruta]
[natoñákóruta] or [ntoñákóruta]
[namoñákóruta] or [mmoñákóruta]
[naβañákóruta] or [mbañákóruta]

Compare A75a, n-to-n(y)á-kó-R-a (1960: 14, 33-34; tone of R varies per verb type).[164] See (336).

---

[163] The derivation of this surface representation first person singular is exemplified partially as follows,

partial input	/nanVna...	
Nasal Palatalisation	ñ	(intervocalically)
Internasal V-deletion	Ø	
Prenasalisation	ñña	
Nasal Allomorphy	iñña	
Degemination	ixña	
Compensatory Lengthening	iiña	
/a/-Delinking	Ø	
Compensatory Lengthening	iiiña	
x-Trimming	Ø	
partial output	[niiña..	

[164] Instead of [ña], [na] was judged less common by Lilian and less correct by Judith, who said however that some people do pronounce [na].

(340) antecedent polite adhortation (hodiernal or near future)

'we had better bite'
(later today/soon, i.e. before something else)'

[ńtáakóráaróma]	[ńtáakóráarutá]	(RAISED)
[ótáakóráaróma]	[ótáakóráarutá]	
[átáakóráaróma]	[átáakóráarutá]	
[tótáakóráaróma]	[tótáakóráarutá]	
[mótáakóráaróma]	[mótáakóráarutá]	
[βátáakóráaróma]	[βátáakóráarutá][165]	

Raised tone pattern. Compare Px259, to-tá-á-kó-raa-R-a (1960: 14, 34). Its negative is (341),

(341) negative antecedent polite adhortation (hodiernal or near future)

'we had better not bite, perhaps we should not bite (later today or soon, before doing something else)'

[tííηkóráarómá]	[tííηkóráarutá]
[tóókóráarómá]	[tóókóráarutá]
[táákóráarómá]	[táákóráarutá]
[titóókóráarómá]	[titóókóráarutá]
[timóókóráarómá]	[timóókóráarutá]
[tiβáákóráaróma]	[tiβáákóráarutá]

Underlying representation /ti-to-V-ko-raa-rom-a/. Compare P59, ti-tó-kó-raa-R-a (1960: 14 and, unlabelled, 34; tone of R is said to vary in some verb types). Corresponding positive is (340).

(342) untimed future continuous intended habit: 'we will keep on biting'

[ññákóromá]	[ññákóruta]	(RAISED)
[óñákóromá]	[óñákóruta]	
[áñákóromá]	[áñákóruta]	
[tóñákóromá]	[tóñákóruta]	
[móñákóromá]	[móñákóruta]	
[βáñákóromá]	[βáñákóruta]	

Initial [ñ] = H. Underlying representation /to-na-ko-R-a/. The implication is that the subject has started the activity expressed by the verb now and will continue it in the future. Compare tonally and semantically with indefinite future continuous (343).

---

165 These surface representations are based on Judith's speech. Lilian's speech was identical, except that final /a/ was low in the paradigm for [koruta].

(343) untimed far present perfect continuous

'we have been biting (for a long time up to now)'

/na-a-na-ko-rom-a/ --> [náañákóromá]
/ko-a-na-ko-rom-a/ --> [kwáañákóromá]
/a-a-na-ko-rom-a/ --> [âñákóromá]
/to-a-na-ko-rom-a/ --> [twáañákóromá]
/mo-a-na-ko-rom-a/ --> [mwáañákóromá]
/βa-a-na-ko-rom-a/ --> [βáañákóromá]

/na-a-na-ko-rut-a/ --> [náañákóruta]
/ko-a-na-ko-rut-a/ --> [kwáañákóruta]
/a-a-na-ko-rut-a/ --> [âñákóruta]
/to-a-na-ko-rut-a/ --> [twáañákóruta]
/mo-a-na-ko-rut-a/ --> [mwáañákóruta]
/βa-a-na-ko-rut-a/ --> [βáañákóruta]

Compare A275, to-á-ná-ko-R-a (1960: 14, 34). See (345). Negative said to be P275, ti-tó-áa-ná-ko-R-a. See (346). Compare (349).

(344) untimed far present perfect continuous

'we have been biting (up to and including now)'

[níiγɔ náañákóromá] [níiγɔ náañákóruta]
[níiγɔ kwáañákóromá] [níiγɔ kwáañákóruta]
[níiγɔ áañákóromá] [níiγɔ áañákóruta]
[níiγɔ twáañákóromá] [níiγɔ twáañákóruta]
[níiγɔ mwáañákóromá] [níiγɔ mwáañákóruta]
[níiγɔ βáañákóromá] [níiγɔ βáañákóruta]

[ɔ] = H. Through liaison, 3s also [níγáañá..].

(345) relative far present perfect continuous

'(it is) we who have been biting (for a long time up to now)'

[níiñcé naañákóromá] [níiñcé naañákóruta]
[náayɛ kwaañákóromá] [náayɛ kwaañákóruta]
[nɛɛrɛ oñákóromá] [nɛɛrɛ oñákóruta]
[níintwé twaañákóromá] [níintwé twaañákóruta]
[níinwé mwaañákóromá] [níinwé mwaañákóruta]
[naβúó βaañákóromá] [naβúó βaañákóruta]

First and last ɛ of nɛɛrɛ = H. Compare A275, to-á-ná-ko-R-a (1960: 14, 34). See (343).

(346) negative relative untimed present perfect continuous

'we (who) have not been biting (for a long time)'

[tináaañákorómá]	[tináaañákóruta]
[tikwáaañákorómá]	[tikwáaañákóruta]
[táañákorómá]	[táañákóruta]
[titwáaañákorómá]	[titwáaañákóruta]
[timwáaañákorómá]	[timwáaañákóruta]
[tiβáañákorómá]	[tiβáañákóruta]

Compare P275, ti-to-áa-ná-ko-R-a (1960: 14, 34). See (343). Compare (247, 353, 349).

(347) negative far future continous: 'we will not be biting (for a long time)'

/ti-n-V-ko-na-ko-rom-a/ --> [tííŋkóñakorómá]
/ti-o-V-ko-na-ko-rom-a/ --> [tóókóñakorómá]
/ti-a-V-ko-na-ko-rom-a/ --> [táákóñakorómá]
[titóókóñakorómá]
[timóókóñakorómá]
[tiβáákóñakorómá]

/ti-n-V-ko-na-ko-rut-a/ --> [tííŋkóñakoruta]
/ti-o-V-ko-na-ko-rut-a/ --> [tóókóñakoruta]
/ti-a-V-ko-na-ko-rut-a/ --> [táákóñakoruta]
[titóókóñakoruta]
[timóókóñakoruta]
[tiβáákóñakoruta]

Underlying representation /ti-to-V-ko-na-ko-rut-a/. Compare P575/1, ti-tó-kó-ná-ko-R-a (1960: 14, 36, which is said to have future meaning). See (353).

(348) negative recent past continuous: 'we have not been biting (recently)'

[ńtáañákóromá]	[ńtáañákóruta]
[ótáañákóromá]	[ótáañákóruta]
[átáañákóromá]	[átáañákóruta]
[tótáañákóromá]	[tótáañákóruta]
[mótáañákóromá]	[mótáañákóruta]
[βátáañákóromá]	[βátáañákóruta]

Compare Px275/1, to-tá-á-ná-ko-R-a (1960: 14, 34-35). Compare (343, 346).

(349) negative untimed far present perfect: 'we have not bitten (ever, up to now)'

[ntáañákorómá]	[ntááñakoruta]
[otáañákorómá]	[otááñakoruta]
[atáañákorómá]	[atááñakoruta]
[totáañákorómá]	[totááñakoruta]
[motáañákorómá]	[motááñakoruta]
[βatáañákorómá]	[βatááñakoruta][166]

Compare Px275/2, to-tá-a-ná-kó-R-a (1960: 14, 35; tone of R said to vary per verb type; the meaning 'less recent past' seems insufficient). Compare (343, 346, 347).

(350) untimed past continuous

'we kept on biting (earlier today/recently/long ago)'

[ŋkañakorómá]	[ŋkañakoruta]
[okañakorómá]	[okañakoruta]
[akañakorómá]	[akañakoruta]
[tokañakorómá]	[tokañakoruta]
[mokañakorómá]	[mokañakoruta]
[βakañakorómá]	[βakañakoruta][167]

This tense may be used as a hodiernal, recent, or far past, depending on the context. Compare A475, to-ka-ná-ko-R-a (1960: 14, 35).

---

[166] Based on Judith's speech. Lilian's speech agreed, except for the following paradigm for [koruta],

[ntáañákórutá]
[otáañákórutá]
[atáañákórutá]
[totáañákórutá]
[motáañákórutá]
[βatáañákórutá]

[167] Based on Judith's speech. An earlier recording of Lilian's speech showed the following tonal pattern for the paradigm of [koruta],

[ŋkáñákóruta]
[ókáñákóruta]
[ákáñákóruta]
[tókáñákóruta]
[mókáñákóruta]
[βákáñákóruta]

(351) a. negative recent past continuous
b. negative far past continuous

'we have not been biting (recently or long ago)'
'we have not kept on biting (recently or long ago)'

[tinááñakorómá]	[tinááñakoruta]
[tikwááñakorómá]	[tikwááñakoruta]
[tááñakorómá]	[tááñakoruta]
[titwááñakorómá]	[titwááñakoruta]
[timwááñakorómá]	[timwááñakoruta]
[tiβááñakorómá]	[tiβááñakoruta]

(352) untimed present continuous

'we are biting (currently)'
'we keep on biting (regularly)'

[ŋ́kóñakorómá]	[ŋ́kóñakoruta]
[ókóñakorómá]	[ókóñakoruta]
[ákóñakorómá]	[ákóñakoruta]
[tóókóñakorómá]	[tóókóñakoruta]
[móókóñakorómá]	[móókóñakoruta]
[βáákóñakorómá]	[βáákóñakoruta]

Expresses continuity over a period of time, including the present. Compare A575, tó-kó-ná-ko-R-a (1960: 14, 35-36; negative: complex tense P1/Ai4).

(353) negative indefinite future continuous

'we will not be biting'
'we will not go on biting'

/ti-n-ko-na-ko-rom-a/ -->	[tííŋkóñakorómá]
/ti-o-ko-na-ko-rom-a/ -->	[tóókóñakorómá]
/ti-a-ko-na-ko-rom-a/ -->	[táákóñakorómá]
[titóókóñakorómá]	
[timóókóñakorómá]	
[tiβáákóñakorómá]	

/ti-n-ko-na-ko-rut-a/ -->	[tííŋkóñakoruta]
/ti-o-ko-na-ko-rut-a/ -->	[tóókóñakoruta]
/ti-a-ko-na-ko-rut-a/ -->	[táákóñakoruta]
[titóókóñakoruta]	
[timóókóñakoruta]	
[tiβáákóñakoruta]	

When unqualified, the meaning of this tense is indefinite, but it may be made definite by specifying a particular point or period of time in the context. Compare tonally and segmentally with P575/1, ti-tó-kó-ná-ko-R-a (1960: 14, 36). See (347).

(354) negative untimed adhortation: 'we are not supposed to be biting'

/ti-n-V-ko-na-ko-rom-a/ -->	[tííŋkoñakorómá]
/ti-o-V-ko-na-ko-rom-a/ -->	[tóókoñakorómá]
/ti-a-V-ko-na-ko-rom-a/ -->	[táákoñakorómá]
[titóókoñakorómá]	
[timóókoñakorómá]	
[tiβáákoñakorómá]	
/ti-n-V-ko-na-ko-rut-a/ -->	[tííŋkoñakoruta]
/ti-o-V-ko-na-ko-rut-a/ -->	[tóókoñakoruta]
/ti-a-V-ko-na-ko-rut-a/ -->	[táákoñakoruta]
[titóókoñakoruta]	
[timóókoñakoruta]	
[tiβáákoñakoruta]	

Compare P575/2 ti-tó-kó-na-ko-R-a (1960: 14, 36). See (347, 352, 353).

(355) antecedent untimed future continuous (intentive)

'we will be biting (before something else)'

[ńdáañákóromá]	[ńdáañákóruta]
[óráañákóromá]	[óráañákóruta]
[áráañákóromá]	[áráañákóruta]
[tóráañákóromá]	[tóráañákóruta]
[móráañákóromá]	[móráañákóruta]
[βáráañákóromá]	[níγɔ βáráañákóruta]

Thematic, when preceded by [níiγɔ] (ɔ = H). The meaning of this tense is basically indefinite, but definite time may be specified in the context or implied by the co-text, whether hodiernal, near, or far future. Compare A975, tó-raa-ná-kó-R-a (1960: 14, 36-37). See (356, 357).

Here and hereafter, the term co-text is used to designate the past and present or expected future conceptual and/or external non-linguistic state of affairs. The term context is used to designate the preceding or current express linguistic text connected with the expression(s) under consideration, from the smallest or lowest units, such as phonological features, through words, phrases, clauses, and sentences, to the highest or greatest unit, the entire discourse.

(356) antecedent future continuous, focussed: 'we will be biting (before something else)'

/n-n-raa-na-ko-rom-a/ --> [níindáañákóromá]
/na-o-raa-na-ko-rom-a/ --> [nóóráañákóromá]
/na-a-raa-na-ko-rom-a/ --> [nááráañákóromá]
[ńtóráañákóromá]
[mmóráañákóromá]
[mbáráañákóromá]

/n-n-raa-na-ko-rut-a/ --> [níindáañákóruta]
/na-o-raa-na-ko-rut-a/ --> [nóóráañákóruta]
/na-a-raa-na-ko-rut-a/ --> [nááráañákóruta]
[ńtóráañákóruta]
[mmóráañákóruta]
[mbáráañákóruta]

The meaning of this tense is essentially the same as that of the previous tense. It is basically indefinite, but definite time may be specified in the context or implied by the co-text, whether hodiernal, near, or far future. Word-initial [m] = H (2-3p). Compare A975a, n-tó-raa-ná-kó-R-a (1960: 14, 37). See (355, 357).

(357) relative future continuous: '(it is) we who will be biting'

[níiñcé ńdáañákóromá] [níiñcé ńdáañákóruta]
[náayɛ óráañákóromá] [náayɛ óráañákóruta]
[nɛɛrɛ áráañákóromá] [nɛɛrɛ áráañákóruta]
[níintwé tóráañákóromá] [níintwé tóráañákóruta]
[níinwé móráañákóromá] [níinwé móráañákóruta]
[naβúó βáráañákóromá] [naβúó βáráañákóruta]

Final [ɛ] of [náayɛ] and first and last [ɛ] of [nɛɛrɛ] = H. Compare A975, to-raa-ná-ko-R-a (1960: 14, 36-37). See (355, 356). Though this tense is inherently indefinite, the time referred to may be definitely hodiernal, near, or far future, whether expressed adverbially in the context or implied by the co-text.

(358) immediate antecedent polite adhortation (continuous)

'should we not bite (right now, before something else)?'
'should we not be biting (right now, before something else)?'
'should we not go ahead and bite (right now, before something else)?'

[ńtáakóñakoróma] [ńtáakóñakoruta] (RAISED)
[ótáakóñakoróma] [ótáakóñakoruta]
[átáakóñakoróma] [átáakóñakoruta]
[tótáakóñakoróma] [tótáakóñakoruta]
[mótáakóñakoróma] [mótáakóñakoruta]
[βátáakóñakoróma] [βátáakóñakoruta]

This positive adhortation is put in the form of a negative rhetorical question. Compare Px2575, to-tá-á-kó-ná-ko-R-a (1960: 14, 37).

(359) antecedent polite adhortation continuous

'should we not keep on biting (before something else)?'
'should we not be biting (before something else)?'

[ńtáákóráañákóromá]	[ńtáákóráañákóruta]	(RAISED)
[ótáákóráañákóromá]	[ótáákóráañákóruta]	
[átáákóráañákóromá]	[átáákóráañákóruta]	
[tótáákóráañákóromá]	[tótáákóráañákóruta]	
[mótáákóráañákóromá]	[mótáákóráañákóruta]	
[βátáákóráañákóromá]	[βátáákóráañákóruta]	

Or [...kór!ómá]. This positive adhortation is put in the form of a negative rhetorical question. Compare Px25975, to-tá-á-kó-raa-ná-kó-R-a (1960: 14, 37).

(360) negative near or far adhortation continuous

'should we not be biting (after today)?'

[tíiŋgóócǎ koñakorómá]	[tíiŋgóócǎ koñakoruta]
[tóoγóócǎ koñakorómá]	[tóoγóócǎ koñakoruta]
[táaγóócǎ koñakorómá]	[táaγóócǎ koñakoruta]
[titóoγóócǎ koñakorómá]	[titóoγóócǎ koñakoruta]
[timóoγóócǎ koñakorómá]	[timóoγóócǎ koñakoruta]
[tiβáaγóócǎ koñakorómá]	[tiβáaγóócǎ koñakoruta]

So much for simple tenses ending in /-a/.

Next, simple tenses ending in /-e/ are presented in (361-370), called 'B-tenses' by Whiteley (1960: 14, where not all final vowels are given, and 37-43). The exception is (362), which is placed here on account of its meaning.

(361) untimed subjunctive

a. adhoration/obligation: 'let us bite, we must bite'
b. intentive/purposive/volitional: '(in order) that we bite, in order to bite'
c. explanatory consecutive

[ńdóme]	[ńdúte]
[óróme]	[órúte]
[áróme]	[árúte]
[tóróme]	[tórúte]
[móróme]	[mórúte]
[βáróme]	[βárúte]

Considering its wide range of usage, the term 'present' subjunctive may be insufficient and somewhat misleading. In sense (361c), this tense always follows another tense, which it explains or completes. Whiteley (1960: 39) has it: 'associated with the second (and subsequent) action(s) in a sequence, but not necessarily a sequence in time'. Compare B1, IP, tó-Z-R-e (1960: 14, 37-40, where tone of R is said to vary per segmental verb-type). See (363, 370). The corresponding negative is (362),

(362) negative untimed subjunctive

a. negative obligatory: 'we are not to bite, we must not bite'
b. negative adhortative: 'let us not bite, you should not bite'
c. negative intentive/purposive: '(in order) that we do not bite'

[tíindóma]	[tíindutá]
[tóoróma]	[tóorutá]
[táaróma]	[táarutá]
[titóoróma]	[titóorutá]
[timóoróma]	[timóorutá]
[tiβáaróma][168]	[tiβáarutá]

Compare P1, IP ti-tó-Z-R-a (1960: 13, 38). See (303, 305, 306, 352, 362, 429, 450). Corresponding positive is (361).

[168] Based on Judith's speech. Lilian's is identical, except for the tone of the final vowel of the paradigm for [koroma], as in,

[tíindómá]
[tóorómá]
[táarómá]
[titóorómá]
[timóorómá]
[tiβáarómá]

(363) (indefinite) simple future: 'we will bite'

/n-n-rom-e/	--> [níındómé]
/na-o-rom-e/	--> [nóórómé]
/na-a-rom-e/	--> [náárómé]
/n-to-rom-e/	--> [ńtórómé]
/n-mo-rom-e/	--> [mmórómé]
/n-βa-rom-e/	--> [mbárómé]
/n-n-rut-e/	--> [níındúté]
/na-o-rut-e/	--> [nóórúté]
/na-a-rut-e/	--> [náárúté]
/n-to-rut-e/	--> [ńtórúté]
/n-mo-rut-e/	--> [mmórúté]
/n-βa-rut-e/	--> [mbárúté]

The meaning of this tense is basically indefinite, but the time may also be definite (whether hodiernal, near, or far future), depending on what is specified in the context or implied by the co-text. Word-initial [m] = H (2-3p). Compare B1a, IP, n(a)-tó-Z-R-e (1960: 14, 40-41, R = M). See (361, 370).

(364) (indefinite) simple future: 'we will bite'

[níiγɔ ńdáarómé]	[níiγɔ ńdáaruté]
[níiγɔ óráarómé]	[níiγɔ óráaruté]
[níiγɔ áráarómé]	[níiγɔ áráaruté]
[níiγɔ tóráarómé]	[níiγɔ tóráaruté]
[níiγɔ móráarómé]	[níiγɔ móráaruté]
[níiγɔ βáráarómé]	[níiγɔ βáráaruté]

[ɔ] = H. The meaning of this tense is basically indefinite, but the time may also be definite (whether hodiernal, near, or far future), depending on what is specified in the context or implied by the co-text. Compare B9, IP, tó-ráá-R-e (1960: 14, 41, R = M). Its relative counterpart has the same tonal pattern, e.g. [níintwé tóráarómé] '(it is) we (who) will bite'. See (365, 366, 451).

(365) tentative near future continuous: 'we may be biting'

[níındáarómé]	[níındáaruté]
[nóóráarómé]	[nóóráaruté]
[nááráarómé]	[nááráaruté]
[ńtóráárómé]	[ńtóráaruté]
[mmóráarómé]	[mmóráaruté]
[mbáráarómé]	[mbáráaruté]

Word-initial [m] = H. Underlying represention account for the long subject marker vowels, e.g. /na-o-raa-rut-e/. Compare B9a, IP, n-tó-ráá-R-e (1960: 14), which is said to occur in 'restricted s[outhern] dialects' (presumably intending South Mugirango), but not exemplified. However, it probably occurs also in other dialects.[169] See (364, 366, 451).

(366) future continuous interrogative: 'will we be biting (soon)?'

[nííndáaróme]	[nííndáaruté]	(RAISED)
[nóóráaróme]	[nóóráaruté]	
[nááráaróme]	[nááráaruté]	
[ńtóráároóme]	[ńtóráaruté]	
[mmóráaróme]	[mmóráaruté]	
[mbáráaróme]	[mbáráaruté][170]	

Word-initial [m] = H. Compare B9a, IP, n-tó-ráá-R-e (1960: 14). See (364, 365, 451).

(367) indefinite future: 'we will not bite'

[ntáaróme]	[ntáaruté]
[otáaróme]	[otáaruté]
[atáaróme]	[atáaruté]
[totáaróme]	[totáaruté]
[motáaróme]	[motáaruté]
[βatáaróme]	[βatáaruté]

Though basically indefinite, the meaning may be definite (whether hodiernal, near, or far future), if the time is so specified in the context or implied by the co-text. Compare Qx2/1, IP, to-tá-á-R-ē (1960: 14, 42; R = M). See (368).

---

[169] Thus Lilian Nyanchama.

[170] Based on Judith's speech. In Lilian's speech, the final vowel in the paradigm for [koruta] was low, as in,

[nííndáarute]	(RAISED)
[nóóráarute]	
[nááráarute]	
[ńtóráarute]	
[mmóráarute]	
[mbáráarute]	

(368) polite future

'are we not going to bite (today/soon/far ahead)?'
'will we not bite (today/soon/far ahead)?'

[ńtáarómé]	[ńtáaruté]
[ótáarómé]	[ótáaruté]
[átáarómé]	[átáaruté]
[tótáarómé]	[tótáaruté]
[mótáarómé]	[mótáaruté]
[βátáarómé]	[βátáaruté]

This tense expresses a polite statement or suggestion in the form of a negative rhetorical question. Apart from its tonal pattern, it is otherwise identical to (367). Compare Qx2/2, IP, tó-tá-a-R̂-ē (1960: 14,42-43, where its meaning is said to be emphatic). Whiteley also differentiates Qx2/3, IP, to-tá-á-R-e (1960: 14, 43), but this relative was found to be tonally identical with his Qx2/1, i.e. non-relative (369).

(369) negative indefinite future, focussed

'we will not bite'

[nííntáaróme]	[nííntáaruté]
[nóótáaróme]	[nóótáaruté]
[náátáaróme]	[náátáaruté]
[ńtótáároḿe]	[ńtótáaruté]
[mmótáaróme]	[mmótáaruté]
[mbátáaróme]	[mbátáaruté]

Word-initial [m] = H (2-3p). The basic meaning is indefinite, but definite time may be specified in the context or implied by the co-text, whether hodiernal, near, or far future. From /n(V)-sm-ta-a-root-e/.

(370) a. negative hodiernal future interrogative
b. negative near future interrogative

'will we not bite (today/soon)?'

[nííntáaróme]	[nííntáarute]	(RAISED)
[nóótáaróme]	[nóótáarute]	
[náátáaróme]	[náátáarute]	
[ńtótáároḿe]	[ńtótáarute]	
[mmótáaróme]	[mmótáarute]	
[mbátáaróme]	[mbátáarute]	

Both naB1, IP, nâ-tó-Z-R-e, an indefinite future with optative implication (exemplified by two examples judged inadequate by my informants), and its corresponding negative, γaaP5, IP, γáá-ti-tó-kó-R-a (not exemplified), are listed by Whiteley (1960: 14, 43). Both are disconfirmed by the present research. See (361, 363).

Of the following tenses (371-401), (371-400) end in -ire and correspond to Whiteley's C-tenses' (1960: 14, 43-50). Here, (401) is added on account of its meaning.

(371) resultative present perfect

'we have been bitten, (hence:) we are bitten'

[ńdómíré]	[ńdútiré]
[órómíré]	[órútiré]
[árómíré]	[árútiré]
[tórómíré]	[tórútiré]
[mórómíré]	[mórútiré]
[βárómíré]	[βárútiré]

This tense expresses a resulting or untimed present state. It is in the active voice, but regularly has a patient subject. Forms of this tense may be preceded by [níiγɔ] (ɔ = H). Here, as elsewhere in this study, any word-final sequence of L*H (where L* stands for any sequence of low tones) may surface as !H over the tone bearers involved. The surface representations suggest that /to-R-ir-e/ is a more plausible underlying representation than C1/1, to-Z-R-íre (1960: 14, 43; negative: CR1, ti-tó-Z-R-ire; also compare C1/2, IP, tō-Z-R-ire, where R = M; 1960: 14, 44-45). See (372).

(372) negative indefinite past

'we have not yet been bitten (contrary to expectation)'

/ti-n-rom-ir-i/ -->	[tííndómirí]
/ti-o-rom-ir-i/ -->	[tórómirí]
/ti-a-rom-ir-i/ -->	[tárómirí]
[titórómirí]	
[timórómirí]	
[tiβárómirí]	

/ti-n-rut-ir-i/ -->	[tííndútirí]
/ti-o-rut-ir-i/ -->	[tórútirí]
/ti-a-rut-ir-i/ -->	[tárútirí]
[titórútirí]	
[timórútirí]	
[tiβárútirí][171]	

The meaning of this tense is basically indefinite, but may be definite by specification in the context or implication in the co-text. Compare CR1, ti-tó-R-iri (1960: 14, 43-44, but

[171] Based on Judith's speech. In Lilian's speech, the last two tones, unless they were !H, appeared to be L.

not exemplified and should be CR1/1) and CR1/2, IP?, ti-tó-R-irí (1960: 14, 44-45; said to be rare, with IP question-marked). See (371).

(373) recent past negative: 'we were not bitten (recently)

[tináárómíre]	[tináárutire]
[tikwáárómíre]	[tikwáárutire]
[táárómíre]	[táárutire]
[titwáárómíre]	[titwáárutire]
[timwáárómíre]	[timwáárutire]
[tiβáárómíre]	[tiβáárutire]

Underlying representation /ti-to-a-rom-ir-e/. No corresponding tense is given in (1960).

(374) far past negative: 'we were not bitten (long ago)'

[tináarómíre]	[tináarútire]
[tikwáarómíre]	[tikwáarútire]
[táarómíre]	[táarútire]
[titwáarómíre]	[titwáarútire]
[timwáarómíre]	[timwáarútire]
[tiβáarómíre]	[tiβáarútire]

Underlying representation /ti-to-a-rom-ir-e/. Contrast R1, ti-tó-R-ire (1960: 14, 45). See (386). Said to have the same meaning as C1/1 = C1/2, i.e. no time reference, but expressing a state current with the time of utterance). See (382). This is exemplified only by [tatindekire], which should however be [taatindekiri].

(375) present perfect, focussed: 'we have been (hence: we are) bitten'

/n-n-rom-ir-e/ -->	[nííndómíré]
/na-o-rom-ir-e/ -->	[nóórómíré]
/na-a-rom-ir-e/ -->	[náárómíré]
[ńtórómíré]	
[mmórómíré]	
[mbárómíré]	

/n-n-rut-ir-e/ -->	[nííndútiré]
/na-o-rut-ir-e/ -->	[nóórútiré]
/na-a-rut-ir-e/ -->	[náárútiré]
[ńtórútiré]	
[mmórútiré]	
[mbárútiré]	

Word-initial [m] = H (2-3p). Expresses an untimed state of affairs relevant to the present. Compare C1a, n-tó-Z-R-ire (1960: 14, 45; tone of the last two vowels is said to vary per verb type).

(376) hodiernal present perfect immediate: 'we have bitten (just now)'

[naarómíre]	[naarútire]
[kwaarómíre]	[kwaarútire]
[orómíre]	[orútire]
[twaarómíre]	[twaarútire]
[mwaarómíre]	[mwaarútire]
[βaarómíre]	[βaarútire]

Compare C2/1, IP, to-a-Ŕ-ire (1960: 14, 45-46; where the root tone is said to vary per verb type). Corresponding relative is (377). Corresponding negative is (387) (also in 1960).

(377) hodiernal present perfect immediate thematic: 'we have just bitten'

[níiγɔ náarómíré]	[níiγɔ náarutíré]
[níiγɔ kwáarómíré]	[níiγɔ kwáarutíré]
[níiγɔ arómíré]	[níiγɔ arutíré]
[níiγɔ twáarómíré]	[níiγɔ twáarutíré]
[níiγɔ mwáarómíré]	[níiγɔ mwáarutíré]
[níiγɔ βáarómíré]	[níiγɔ βáarutíré]

[ɔ] = H. Another informant had 3s /o-/. Surface of 3s, through liaison, also [níγáar...]. Compare C2/2, tó-á-R-ire (1960: 14, 46; -ír in verbs of the type -rut-, -vc-, and -cv-; negative: CRx2/1, to-tá-á-R-ír-e). Corresponding positive is (376). See (381, 384, 389, 390).

(378) relative hodiernal present perfect: '(it is) we (who) have been (hence: are) bitten'

[níiñcé naarómíré]	[níiñcé naarutíré]
[náayε kwaarómíré]	[nááyε kwaarutíré]
[nεεrε orómíré]	[nεεrε orutíré]
[níintwé twáarómíré]	[níintwé twáarutíré]
[níinwé mwáarómíré]	[níinwé mwáarutíré]
[naβúó βáarómíré]	[naβúó βáarutíré]

Word-final [ε], and the first [ε] in [nεεrε] = H.

(379) negative hodiernal past: 'we have not been bitten (earlier today)'

[tináárómíre]	[tináárutire]
[tikwáárómíre]	[tikwáárutire]
[táárómíre]	[táárutire]
[titwáárómíre]	[titwáárutire]
[timwáárómíre]	[timwáárutire]
[tiβáárómíre]	[tiβáárutire]

(380) negative hodiernal past: 'we have not been/were not bitten (earlier today)'

[ńtáaarómíré]	[ńtáárútiré]
[ótáarómíré]	[ótáárútiré]
[átáarómíré]	[átáárútiré]
[tótáarómíré]	[tótáárútiré]
[mótáarómíré]	[mótáárútiré]
[βátáarómíré][172]	[βátáárútiré]

(381) relative negative hodiernal past: '(it is) we (who) were not bitten (earlier today)'

[níiñcé ntáárómíre]	[ntáárútire]
[náayɛ otáárómíre]	[otáárútire]
[nɛɛrɛ otáárómíre]	[otáárútire]
[níintwé totáárómíre]	[totáárútire]
[níinwé motáárómíre]	[motáárútire]
[naβúó βatáárómíre]	[βatáárútire][173]

Compare the (C)Rx2/ tenses in (1960: 14, 46-48). See (377, 381, 384, 389, 390) and (386, 387).

(382) recent past: 'we were bitten (recently)'

[náárómiré]	[náárútiré]
[kwáárómiré]	[kwáárútiré]
[árómiré]	[árútiré]
[twáárómiré]	[twáárútiré]
[mwáárómiré]	[mwáárútiré]
[βáárómiré]	[βáárútiré]

May be preceded, with the same tone pattern but with thematic meaning, by [níiγɔ] (ɔ = H), in which case also 3s [níiγáár..]. Compare C1/1 and C1/2 (1960: 43-45).

[172] The tonal surface pattern of this paradigm as recorded is not certain.

[173] Also recorded as follows,

[ntárómirí]	[ntárútirí]
[otárómirí]	[otárútirí]
[atárómirí]	[atárútirí]
[totárómirí]	[totárútirí]
[motárómirí]	[motárútirí]
[βatárómirí]	[βatárútirí]

again preceded by [níiñce] etc.

(383) negative recent past: 'we were not bitten (recently)'

[tináaromíre]	[tináarutire]
[tikwáaromíre]	[tikwáarutire]
[táaromíre]	[táarutire]
[titwáaromíre]	[titwáarutire]
[timwáaromíre]	[timwáarutire]
[tiβáaromíre]	[tiβáarutire]

(384) negative recent past: 'we were not bitten (recently)'

[ńtáarómíré]	[ńtáarutíré]
[ótáarómíré]	[ótáarutíré]
[átáarómíré]	[átáarutíré]
[tótáarómíré]	[tótáarutíré]
[mótáarómíré]	[mótáarutíré]
[βátáarómíré]	[βátáarutíré]

Underlying representation: /to-ta-a-R-ir-e/. Compare CRx2/1, to-tá-á-R-íre, or CRx2/2, IP, to-tá-a-Ŕ-íre (1960: 14, 47; root tone is said to vary per verb type). See (377, 381, 384, 389, 390) and (386, 387, 390).

(385) relative negative recent past

[níiñcé ntáárómíre]	[níiñcé ntáárutire]
[náayɛ otáárómíre]	[náayɛ otáárutire]
[nɛɛrɛ otáárómíre]	[nɛɛrɛ otáárutire]
[níintwé tótáárómiré]	[níintwé tótáárútiré]
[níinwé mótáárómiré]	[níinwé mótáárútiré]
[naβúó βátáárómiré]	[naβúó βátáárútiré]

Each word-final ɛ and the first ɛ of [nɛɛrɛ] = H. The tonal pattern is different for singular and plural in each paradigm.

(386) far past: 'we were bitten'

[níiγɔ náarómíré]	[níiγɔ náarutíré]
[níiγɔ kwáarómíré]	[níiγɔ kwáarutíré]
[níiγɔ áromíré][174]	[níiγɔ árutíré]
[níiγɔ twáarómíré]	[níiγɔ twáarutíré]
[níiγɔ mwáarómíré]	[níiγɔ mwáarutíré]
[níiγɔ βáarómíré]	[níiγɔ βáarutíré]

Compare C2/3, IP, to-â-R-íre (1960: 14, 47). Its corresponding negative is (374) above

174 Possibly from |áaróm..|, with deletion of tense marker /a/ and rightward tone shift.

(compare R1, ti-tó-R-ire, 1960: 14, 45), but given as CRx2/2, IP, to-tá-a-Ŕ-íre in (1960: 14, 47). See (387, 390).

(387) far past thematic: 'we did not bite (long ago)'

[níiɣɔ ńtáarómíré]	[níiɣɔ ńtáarutíré]
[níiɣɔ ótáarómíré]	[níiɣɔ ótáarutíré]
[níiɣɔ átáarómíré]	[níiɣɔ átáarutíré]
[níiɣɔ tótáarómíré]	[níiɣɔ tótáarutíré]
[níiɣɔ mótáarómíré]	[níiɣɔ mótáarutíré]
[níiɣɔ ßátáarómíré]	[níiɣɔ ßátáarutíré]

[ɔ] = H. Underlying representation: /to-ta-a-R-ir-e/. Liaison is applicable in 2-3s. Compare CRx2/2, IP, to-tá-a-Ŕ-íre (1960: 14, 47; root tone is said to vary per verb type). See (386, 390).

(388) negative far past: 'we were not bitten'

[tináarómíre]	[tináarútire]
[tikwáarómíre]	[tikwáarútire]
[táarómíre]	[táarútire]
[titwáarómíre]	[titwáarútire]
[timwáarómíre]	[timwáarútire]
[tißáarómíre]	[tißáarútire]

Underlying representation: /ti-to-a-rom-ir-e/. Compare (383) above. No corresponding tense is given in (1960).

(389) negative far past: 'we were not bitten'

[ntáarómíre]	[ntáarútire]
[otáarómíre]	[otáarútire]
[atáarómíre]	[atáarútire]
[totáarómíre]	[totáarútire]
[motáarómíre]	[motáarútire]
[ßatáarómíre]	[ßatáarútire]

Compare CRx2/1, to-tá-á-R-íre (1960: 14, 46) and Rx2/1, IP to-tá-á-Ŕ-íre (1960: 14, 47). See (377, 381, 384, 390).

(390) relative negative far past: '(it is) we (who) were bitten (long ago)'

[nííñcé ntáarómíré]	[nííñcé ntáarutíré]
[náayɛ otáarómíré]	[náayɛ otáarutíré]
[nɛɛrɛ otáarómíré]	[nɛɛrɛ otáarutíré]
[nííntwé totáarómíré]	[nííntwé totáarutíré]
[nííinwé motáarómíré]	[nííinwé motáarutíré]
[naßúó ßatáarómíré]	[naßúó ßatáarutíré]

Compare Rx2/1, IP, to-tá-á-Ŕ-íre (1960: 14, 47-48). See (377, 381, 384, 386, 387, 389, 390).

(391) hodiernal present perfect continuous: 'we have been biting (today)'

[náákárómiré]	[náákárutíré]
[γwáákárómiré]	[γwáákárutíré]
[ákárómiré]	[ákárutíré]
[twáákárómiré]	[twáákárutíré]
[mwáákárómiré]	[mwáákárutíré]
[βáákárómiré]	[βáákárutíré]

May be preceded by [níiγɔ] (ɔ = H) with thematic meaning, in which case 3s, through liaison, may be pronounced [níγááká..]. Compare C24/1, to-a-ka-R-íre (1960: 14, 48). Corresponding negative is (392). See (393).

(392) negative hodiernal present perfect continuous

'we have not been biting (earlier today)'

/ti-na-a-ka-rom-ir-e/ -->	[tináákarómíre]
/ti-ko-a-ka-rom-ir-e/ -->	[tiγwáákarómíre]
/ti-a-a-ka-rom-ir-e/ -->	[táákarómíre]
[titwáákarómíre]	
[timwáákarómíre]	
[tiβáákarómíre]	

/ti-na-a-ka-rut-ir-e/ -->	[tináákarutire]
/ti-ko-a-ka-rut-ir-e/ -->	[tiγwáákarutire]
/ti-a-a-ka-rut-ir-e/ -->	[táákarutire]
[titwáákarutire]	
[timwáákarutire]	
[tiβáákarutire]	

One informant said this tense may have recent meaning, limited to the last few days. Corresponding positive is (391). Compare CR24/1, ti-tó-á-ka-R-ire (1960: 14, 48).

(393) recent or far past continuous: 'we bit, we were biting (recently/long ago)'

[náákarómíré]	[náákarutíré]
[γwáákarómíré]	[γwáákarutíré]
[ákarómíré]	[ákarutíré]
[twáákarómíré]	[twáákarutíré]
[mwáákarómíré]	[mwáákarutíré]
[βáákarómíré]	[βáákarutíré]

Compare C24/2, to-a-ka-R-íre (1960: 14, 48). See (391) and (394).

(394) negative far past continuous: 'we were not biting (long ago)'

/ti-na-a-ka-rom-ir-e/ --> [tináakárómíre]
/ti-ko-a-ka-rom-ir-e/ --> [tiɣwáakárómíre]
/ti-a-a-ka-rom-ir-e/ --> [táakárómíre]
[titwáakárómíre]
[timwáakárómíre]
[tiβáakárómíre]

/ti-na-a-ka-rut-ir-e/ --> [tináakárútire]
/ti-ko-a-ka-rut-ir-e/ --> [tiɣwáakárútire]
/ti-a-a-ka-rut-ir-e/ --> [táakárútire]
[titwáakárútire]
[timwáakárútire]
[tiβáakárútire]

Compare CR24/2 ti-tó-áa-ká-R-ire (1960: 14, and, presumably misprinted, ti-tó-áa-R-ire, 48). See (393).

(395) negative hodiernal present perfect continuous: 'we have not been biting (today)'

[ńtáákárómiré]	[ńtáákárutiré]
[ótáákárómiré]	[ótáákárutiré]
[átáákárómiré]	[átáákárutiré]
[tótáákárómiré]	[tótáákárutiré]
[mótáákárómiré]	[mótáákárutiré]
[βátáákárómiré]	[βátáákárutiré]

May be preceded, with thematic meaning, by [níiɣɔ] (ɔ = H). Word-final L*H may be realised as !H, as is generally possible.[175] Compare CRx24/2, to-tá-a-ka-R-ire (1960: 14) and Rx24/2 (1960: 14, 49). See (396).

[175] A somewhat informal statement of such word-final downstep would be

Word-final downstep

L*H --> !H / ---]word

Generally, downdrift is regular. For example, in HLH*LH, the H following each L is downstepped automatically, as in [níintwé tótáákárómiré] (see following relative of this tense). An alternative pronounciation of this example is H*!HL!H, as in [níintw!é tótáákárómiré].

(396) relative negative hodiernal/recent present perfect continuous

'(it is) we (who) have not been biting (today/recently)'

[níiñcé ńtáákarómíre] [níiñcé ntáákarutire]
[náayɛ ótáákarómíre] [náayɛ ótáákarutire]
[nɛɛrɛ ótáákarómíre] [nɛɛrɛ ótáákarutire]
[níintwé tótáákárómiré] [níintwé tótáákárutire]
[níinwé mótáákárómiré] [níinwé mótáákárutire]
[naβúó βátáákárómiré] [naβúó βátáákárutire]

Word-final ɛ and the first ɛ of [nɛɛrɛ] = H. The singular and plural tonal patterns are distinct in each paradigm. Compare CRx24/1, to-tá-á-ká-R-ire (1960: 14) and Rx24/1 to-tá-ká-R-ire (1960: 49, where tense marker -á- is omitted). See (395).

(397) relative negative far past continuous: 'we (are the ones who) used not to bite'

[níiñcé ńtáákarómíré] [níiñcé ńtáákarutíré]
[nááyɛ ótáákarómíré] [nááyɛ ótáákarutíré]
[nɛɛrɛ ótáákarómíré] [nɛɛrɛ ótáákarutíré]
[níintwé tótáákarómíré] [níintwé tótáákarutíré]
[níinwé mótáákarómíré] [níinwé mótáákarutíré]
[naβúó βátáákarómíré] [naβúó βátáákarutíré]

Word-final ɛ and the first ɛ of [nɛɛrɛ] = H. Usually habitual.

(398) negative hodiernal/recent present perfect continuous thematic

[ńtáákarómíré] [ńtáákarutíré]
[ótáákarómíré] [ótáákarutíré]
[átáákarómíré] [átáákarutíré]
[tótáákarómíré] [tótáákarutíré]
[mótáákarómíré] [mótáákarutíré]
[βátáákarómíré] [βátáákarutíré]

May be preceded, instead, by [níiγɔ] (ɔ = H) with thematic meaning, in which case, through liaison, 2s may be pronounced [níγóóká..] and 3s [níγááká..].

(399) hodiernal present perfect continuous: 'you have been biting'

[naaráarómíré] [naaráarutíré]
[kwaaráarómíré] [kwaaráarutíré]
[oráarómíré] [oráarutíré]
[twaaráarómíré] [twaaráarutíré]
[mwaaráarómíré] [mwaaráarutíré]
[βaaráarómíré] [βaaráarutíré]

Underlying representation: /to-a-raa-rom-ir-e/. Compare C29, to-a-ráá-R-íre (where R =

M; 1960: 14, 49).

(400) hodiernal present perfect continuous thematic: 'you have been biting (today)'

[níiγɔ náaráarómíré]	[níiγɔ náaráarutíré]
[níiγɔ kwáaráarómíré]	[níiγɔ kwáaráarutíré]
[níiγɔ áráarómíré]	[níiγɔ áráarutíré]
[níiγɔ twáaráarómíré]	[níiγɔ twáaráarutíré]
[níiγɔ mwáaráarómíré]	[níiγɔ mwáaráarutíré]
[níiγɔ βáaráarómíré]	[níiγɔ βáaráarutíré]

[ɔ] = H.

(401) negative hodiernal present perfect continuous: 'you have not been biting (today)'

[tíindáaráaróma]	[tíindáaráarúta]
[tóráaráaróma]	[tóráaráarúta]
[táráaráaróma]	[táráaráarúta]
[titóráaráaróma]	[titóráaráarúta]
[timóráaráaróma]	[timóráaráarúta]
[tiβáráaráaróma]	[tiβáráaráarúta]

The following tenses (402-426) correspond to Whiteley's 'D-tenses' (1960: 14-15, 50-57). To begin with, consider (402),

(402) untimed truth or fact: 'we bite'

[ńdóméte]	[ńdúteté]
[óróméte]	[órúteté]
[áróméte]	[árúteté]
[tóróméte]	[tórúteté]
[móróméte]	[mórúteté]
[βáróméte]	[βárúteté]

From /to-R-et-e/. Compare D1, tó-Z-R-ete (1960: 14, 50 root tone said to be H in low-toned verbs of the types -cvc-, -vc-, and -cv-). See (404).

(403) relative untimed truth or fact: '(it is) we (who) bite'

[níiñcé ndóméte]	[níiñcé ndutéte]
[náayε oróméte]	[náayε orutéte]
[nεεrε oróméte]	[nεεrε arutéte]
[níintwé tóróméte]	[níintwé tórúteté]
[níinwé móróméte]	[níinwé mórúteté]
[naβúó βáróméte]	[naβúó βárúteté]

Word-final ε and the first ε of [nεεrε] = H. [níiñcé ndóméte] may be rendered [níiñc!é ńdóméte]. The singular and plural tonal patterns are distinct in these paradigms.

(404) untimed fact, focussed: 'we bite'

/n-n-rom-et-e/ --> [nííndómété]
/na-o-rom-et-e/ --> [nóórómété]
/na-a-rom-et-e/ --> [náárómété]
[ńtórómété]
[mmórómété]
[mbárómété]

/n-n-rut-et-e/ --> [nííndúteté]
/na-o-rut-et-e/ --> [nóórúteté]
/na-a-rut-et-e/ --> [náárúteté]
[ńtórúteté]
[mmórúteté]
[mbárúteté]

Word-initial [m] = H (2-3p). Compare D1a, n-tó-Z-R-ete (1960: 14, 50-51, claimed to be 'restricted to certain radicals'). See (402).

(405) a. negative untimed truth or fact: 'we do not bite'
b. negative hodiernal past: 'we have not bitten/did not bite (today)'

/ti-n-rom-et-i/ --> [tííndómetí]
/ti-o-rom-et-i/ --> [tórómetí]
/ti-a-rom-et-i/ --> [tárómetí]
[titórómetí]
[timórómetí]
[tiβárómetí]

/ti-n-rut-et-i/ --> [tííndútetí]
/ti-o-rut-et-i/ --> [tórútetí]
/ti-a-rut-et-i/ --> [tárútetí]
[titórútetí]
[timórútetí]
[tiβárútetí]

[i] of negative marker /ti-/ is deleted together with its tone in 2-3s. Compare S1, ti-tó-Z-R-eti (1960: 14, 51), but, given the surfaces recorded here, /ti-to-R-et-i/ is a more plausible underlying representation.

(406) negative untimed conditional: '(if) we do not bite'

[ńtárómetí] [ńtárútetí]
[ótárómetí] [ótárútetí]
[átárómetí] [átárútetí]
[tótárómetí] [tótárútetí]
[mótárómetí] [mótárútetí]
[βátárómetí] [βátárútetí]

Underlying representation /to-ta-R-et-i/. When used in an antecedent clause, this tense must be translated into English by a clause beginning with 'if' (negative 'if...not, unless'). The consequent clause in Gusii may contain a hodiernal, near, or far future. Without time being specified in the context or implied in the co-text, the reference will be understood as hodiernal. Contrast Sx1, to-tá-Z-R-eti (1960: 14, mislabelled Sx1/1, 51-52, which should have been Sx1 or DSx1). See (407).

(407) negative untimed past: 'we did not bite'

[ńtáarómété]	[ńtáarutété]
[ótáarómété]	[ótáarutété]
[átáarómété]	[átáarutété]
[tótáarómété]	[tótáarutété]
[mótáarómété]	[mótáarutété]
[βátáarómété]	[βátáarutété]

Compare Sx1/ and Sx2/ tenses (1960: 14-15, 52-55), especially Sx2/2, to-tá-a-R-éte (1960: 15, 55). Also compare Sx1/2, to-tá-a-R-eti (1960: 14, 51; mislabelled, should have been Sx2/2. See (406, 410, 415).

(408) hodiernal or recent past: 'we bit (earlier today/recently)'

[náárómeté]	[náárúteté]
[kwáárómeté]	[kwáárúteté]
[árómeté]	[árúteté]
[twáárómeté]	[twáárúteté]
[mwáárómeté]	[mwáárúteté]
[βáárómeté]	[βáárúteté]

Compare D2/1, tó-á-R-ete (1960: 14, 52). See (414). Corresponding negative is (409).

(409) negative hodiernal or recent past: 'we did not bite (today/recently)'

[tináárómete]	[tináárutete]
[tikwáárómete]	[tikwáárutete]
[táárómete]	[táárutete]
[titwáárómete]	[titwáárutete]
[timwáárómete]	[timwáárutete]
[tiβáárómete]	[tiβáárutete]

Underlying representation: /ti-to-a-R-et-e/, etc. Compare DS2/1 ti-tó-á-R-éte (1960: 14, 52). Corresponding positive is (408). Contrast with (411).

(410) negative far past: 'we did not bite (long ago)'

[ńtáarómété] [ńtáarutété]
[ótáarómété] [ótáarutété]
[átáarómété] [átáarutété]
[tótáarómété] [tótáarutété]
[mótáarómété] [mótáarutété]
[βátáarómété] [βátáarutété]

Compare Sx2/2, IP, to-tá-a-R-éte (1960: 15, 55). See (407, 415).

(411) negative far past: 'we did not bite (long ago)'

[tináaróméte] [tináarútete]
[tikwáaróméte] [tikwáarútete]
[táaróméte] [táarútete]
[titwáaróméte] [titwáarútete]
[timwáaróméte] [timwáarútete]
[tiβáaróméte] [tiβáarútete]

Underlying representation: /ti-to-a-R-et-e/, etc. Compare DS2/2, IP, ti-tó-á-Ŕ-ēte (1960: 14, 54; not exemplified).

(412) hodiernal or recent past thematic: 'we bit (today/recently)'

[níiγɔ náárómeté] [níiγɔ náárúteté]
[níiγɔ kwáárómeté] [níiγɔ kwáárúteté]
[níiγɔ árómeté] [níiγɔ árúteté]
[níiγɔ twáárómeté] [níiγɔ twáárúteté]
[níiγɔ mwáárómeté] [níiγɔ mwáárúteté]
[níiγɔ βáárómeté] [níiγɔ βáárúteté]

[ɔ] = H.

(413) relative hodiernal or recent past: '(it is) we (who) bit (today/recently)'

[níiñcé nááróméte] [níiñcé náárutete]
[náayɛ kwááróméte] [náayɛ kwáárutete]
[nɛɛrɛ órómété] [nɛɛrɛ órutete]
[níintwé twáárómeté] [níintwé twáárúteté]
[níinwé mwáárómeté] [níinwé mwáárúteté]
[naβúó βáárómeté] [naβúó βáárúteté]

Word-final ɛ and the first ɛ of [nɛɛrɛ] = H. Downstep is possible. The singular and plural tone patterns are distinct in these paradigms.

(414) hodiernal or recent past, focussed: 'we bit (today/recently)'

[ńnáárómeté]	[ńnáárúteté]
[ŋ̍kwáárómeté]	[ŋ̍kwáárúteté]
[náárómeté]	[náárúteté]
[ńtwáárómeté]	[ńtwáárúteté]
[mmwáárómeté]	[mmwáárúteté]
[mbáárómeté]	[mbáárúteté]

Word-initial [m] = H (2-3p). Compare D2a/1, n-tó-á-R-ete (1960: 14, 53); and also D2a/2, n-tó-a-R-ete (1960: 15, 54-55, root tone is said to vary). See (408).

(415) negative hodiernal or recent past: 'we did not bite (today/recently)'

[ntáárómète]	[ntáárutete]
[otáárómète]	[otáárutete]
[atáárómète]	[atáárutete]
[totáárómète]	[totáárutete]
[motáárómète]	[motáárutete]
[βatáárómète]	[βatáárutete]

The final -e in the left paradigm may possibly be M. Compare Sx2/1, to-ta-a-R-éte (1960: 15, 53-54, but ending in -ete in low-toned verbs of the type -cvc-, -cv-, and -vc-). See (407, 410).

(416) far past: 'we bit (long ago)'

[náarómété]	[náarutété]
[kwáarómété]	[kwáarutété]
[ârómété]	[ârutété]
[twáarómété]	[twáarutété]
[mwáarómété]	[mwáarutété]
[βáarómété]	[βáarutété]

Compare D2/2, tó-a-R-ete (1960: 14), also given as tó-a-R-éte (1960: 54; where it is said that root tone may also be H). 3s [â] derives from /á-a..'; at least one informant had 3s [ô..]. See (418). Contrast with (408, 414).

(417) relative far past: '(it is) we (who) bit (long ago)'

[níiñcé naarómété]	[níiñcé naarutété]
[náayɛ kwaarómété]	[náayɛ kwaarutété]
[nɛɛrɛ orómété]	[nɛɛrɛ orutété]
[níintwé twáarómété]	[níintwé twáarutété]
[níinwé mwáarómété]	[níinwé mwáarutété]
[naβúó βáarómété]	[naβúó βáarutété]

First and final /ɛ/ of [nɛɛrɛ] = H. Its negative is (411): [tináárómète] and [tináárútete].

(418) far past, focussed: 'we bit (long ago)'

[ńnáarómété]	[ńnáarutété]
[ŋ̍kwáarómété]	[ŋ̍kwáarutété]
[náarómété]	[náarutété]
[ńtwáarómété]	[ńtwáarutété]
[mmwáarómété]	[mmwáarutété]
[mbáarómété]	[mbáarutété]

Word-initial [m] = H (2-3p). Compare D2a/2, n-tó-a-R-ete (1960: 15, 54-55, where root tone is said to vary) and D2a/1, n-tó-á-R-ete (1960: 14, 53). See (416). Contrast (408, 414).

(419) untimed (hodiernal/recent) past: 'we have bitten (today/recently)'

[ŋ̍kárómété]	[ŋ̍kárutété]
[ókárómété]	[ókárutété]
[ákárómété]	[ákárutété]
[tókárómété]	[tókárutété]
[mókárómété]	[mókárutété]
[βákárómété]	[βákárutété]

Basically untimed, hodiernal or recent past time may be specified in the context or implied by the co-text. The place of activity is usually far away from the speaker.[176] Compare D4, tó-ká-R-éte (1960: 15, 55). See (421).

(420) negative hodiernal or recent past: 'we did not bite/have not bitten (today/recently)'

[tíŋkárómetí]	[tíŋkárutétí]
[tókárómetí]	[tókárutétí]
[tákárómetí]	[tákárutétí]
[titókárómetí]	[titókárutétí]
[timókárómetí]	[timókárutétí]
[tiβákárómetí]	[tiβákárutétí]

Downstep may apply. This tense is unusual, in that it contains a tense prefix and yet ends in -i. The place of the activity is usually distant from the speaker.[177] Compare DS4, IP, ti-tó-ká-R-ete (1960: 15, 55; labelled DS/4, IP on page 15).

[176] Thus Lilian.

[177] Thus Lilian.

(421) untimed present perfect, focussed

'we have bitten (anytime before, today, recently)'

[níí𝜂kárómété]	[níí𝜂kárutété]
[nóókárómété]	[nóókárutété]
[náákárómété]	[náákárutété]
[ńtókárómété]	[ńtókárutété]
[mmókárómété]	[mmókárutété]
[mbákárómété]	[mbákárutété]

Initial [m] = H. Downstep may apply. Compare D4a, n-tó-ká-R-éte (1960: 15, 56). Basically untimed, hodiernal or recent past time may be specified in the context or implied by the co-text. See (419).

(422) interrogative untimed present perfect, focussed

'have we bitten (anytime before, today, recently)'?'

[níí𝜂kárómúte]	[níí𝜂kárutéte]	(RAISED)
[nóókárómúte]	[nóókárutéte]	
[náákárómúte]	[náákárutéte]	
[ńtókárómúte]	[ńtókárutéte]	
[mmókárómúte]	[mmókárutéte]	
[mbákárómúte]	[mbákárutéte]	

Word-initial [m] = H (2-3p).

(423) recent present perfect: 'we have bitten (recently)'

[náákárómeté]	[náákárutété]
[γwáákárómeté]	[γwáákárutété]
[ákárómeté]	[ákárutété]
[twáákárómeté]	[twáákárutété]
[mwáákárómeté]	[mwáákárutété]
[βáákárómeté]	[βáákárutété]

Compare D24/1, tó-á-ká-R-éte (1960: 15, 56, with the comment, on page 15, that the 'first e of -ete [is] in tonal contrast with the radical [i.e. root]'). Contrast (424).

(424) far past: 'we bit (long ago)'

[náákarómété]	[náákarutété]
[γwáákarómété]	[γwáákarutété]
[ákarómété]	[ákarutété]
[twáákarómété]	[twáákarutété]
[mwáákarómété]	[mwáákarutété]
[βáákarómété]	[βáákarutété]

[ká] sounded slightly lower than the following H's in the left-hand paradigm, probably due to the L that immediately precedes it. Compare D24/2, tó-a-ka-R-éte (1960: 15, 56). Contrast (423).

(425) antecedent recent past: 'we bit (recently, before something else)'

/n-na-a-raa-rom-et-e/ -->	[ńnáárááarómété]
/n-ko-a-raa-rom-et-e/ -->	[ŋ̇kwáárááarómété]
/na-a-a-raa-rom-et-e/ -->	[náárááarómété]
[ńtwaárááarómété]	
[mmwáárááarómété]	
[mbáárááarómété]	

/n-na-a-raa-rut-et-e/ -->	[ńnáárááarutété]
/n-ko-a-raa-rut-et-e/ -->	[ŋ̇kwáárááarutété]
/na-a-a-raa-rut-et-e/ -->	[náárááarutété]
[ńtwáárááarutété]	
[mmwáárááarutété]	
[mbáárááarutété]	

Initial [m] = H (2-3p). Compare D29a/1, IP, n-tó-á-raa-R-éte (1960: 56); root also given as H: n-tó-á-raa-Ŕ-éte (1960: 15). Contrast (426).

(426) far past perfective: 'we had bitten (long ago, before something else')

[ńnáarááarómété]	[ńnáarááarutété]
[ŋ̇kwáarááarómété]	[ŋ̇kwáarááarutété]
[náarááarómété]	[náarááarutété]
[ńtwáarááarómété]	[ńtwáarááarutété]
[mmwáarááarómété]	[mmwáarááarutété]
[mbáarááarómété]	[mbáarááarutété]

Initial [m] = H (2-3p). Compare D29a/2, IP, n-tó-á-ráa-R-éte (1960: 15, 57). Contrast (425).

Though recent and far past, and similarly near and far future, are indeed differentiated by their tonal pattern, the surface patterns themselves, underlying lexical patterns, the latter's interaction with clause- or sentence-intonation, and the possible relevance of cv-structure for the tonal pattern all require further investigation.

So much for the simple tenses of Gusii. In addition to these, several simple tenses, or, more usually, a simple tense plus an infinitive, may be combined to form complex tenses, called 'two-word' tenses by Whiteley (1960). These are presented in (427-452),

(427) untimed fact/occasional habit: 'we bite (occasionally)

[ŋ̇kóráaromá ńdé]	[ŋ̇kóráárutá ńdé]
[ŋ̇kóráaromá óré]	[ŋ̇kóráárutá óré]
[ŋ̇kóráaromá áré]	[ŋ̇kóráárutá áré]
[ŋ̇kóráaromá tóré]	[ŋ̇kóráárutá tóré]
[ŋ̇kóráaromá móré]	[ŋ̇kóráárutá móré]
[ŋ̇kóráaromá βáré]	[ŋ̇kóráárutá βáré][178]

(428) a. present continuous: 'we are biting'
b. untimed fact/habit 'we (always/usually) bite'

[ŋ̇kóroma ńdé]	[ŋ̇kóruta ńdé]
[ŋ̇kóroma óré]	[ŋ̇kóruta óré]
[ŋ̇kóroma áré]	[ŋ̇kóruta áré]
[ŋ̇kóroma tóré]	[ŋ̇kóruta tóré]
[ŋ̇kóroma móré]	[ŋ̇kóruta móré]
[ŋ̇kóroma βáré]	[ŋ̇kóruta βáré]

Compare Ai2/A1, n-ko-R-a to-ré (1960: 16, 57-58).[179] See (305, 445, 446).

(429) a. negative present continuous: 'we are not biting'
b. negative untimed fact/habit: 'we do not bite (ever, usually)'

[tííndi kóromá]	[tííndi kóruta]
[tóri kóromá]	[tóri kóruta]
[tári kóromá]	[tári kóruta]
[titóri kóromá]	[titóri kóruta]
[timóri kóromá]	[timóri kóruta]
[tiβári kóromá]	[tiβári kóruta]

Compare P1/Ai1, ti-tó-rí kó-R-a (1960: 16, 57-58). See (303, 305, 306, 352, 362, 450).

178 The tone patterns of these paradigms as recorded are not entirely certain. This tense is not recorded in (1960).

179 Postlexical leftward tone spreading occurs in contexts such as these, as in [ŋ̇kóromááándé].

(430) a. negative present continuous (explanation): 'we are not biting'
b. negative untimed fact/habit: 'we do not bite (ever/usually)'

[ńtári kóromá]	[ńtári kóruta]
[ótári kóromá]	[ótári kóruta]
[átári kóromá]	[átári kóruta]
[tótári kóromá]	[tótári kóruta]
[mótári kóromá]	[mótári kóruta]
[βátári kóromá]	[βátári kóruta]

Compare Px1/Ai1, to-tá-rí kó-R-a (1960: 16; and 58, where the root tone is said to be mid in high-toned verbs of type -cvc-, -cv-, and -vc-). See (319, 431, 441, 442, 444).

(431) a. negative hodiernal present continuous thematic: 'we are not biting'
b. negative untimed fact/habit thematic: 'we do not bite (ever/usually)'

[níiγɔ ńtári kóromá]	[níiγɔ ńtári kóruta]
[níiγɔ ótári kóromá]	[níiγɔ ótári kóruta]
[níiγɔ átári kóromá]	[níiγɔ átári kóruta]
[níiγɔ tótári kóromá]	[níiγɔ tótári kóruta]
[níiγɔ mótári kóromá]	[níiγɔ mótári kóruta]
[níiγɔ βátári kóromá]	[níiγɔ βátári kóruta][180]

[ɔ] = H. Compare Px1/Ai1, to-tá-rí kó-R-a (1960: 16, 58). See (319, 430, 441, 442, 444).

(432) hodiernal past continuous: 'we were biting (today)'

[nááré kóromá]	[nááré kóruta]
[kwááré kóromá]	[kwááré kóruta]
[áré kóromá]	[áré kóruta]
[twááré kóromá]	[twááré kóruta]
[mwááré kóromá]	[mwááré kóruta]
[βááré kóromá]	[βááré kóruta]

Compare A2/1-Ai1, tó-á-re ko-R-a (1960: 16, 58-59; root tone said to be H in monosyllabic roots). See (309, 310, 313, 446).

[180] The final vowel of the auxiliary verb may possibly be H, thus [ńtárí], etc.

(433) recent past continuous: 'we were biting (recently)'

[nááre kóromá]	[nááre kóruta]
[kwááre kóromá]	[kwááre kóruta]
[áre kóromá]	[áre kóruta]
[twááre kóromá]	[twááre kóruta]
[mwááre kóromá]	[mwááre kóruta]
[βááre kóromá]	[βááre kóruta]

Compare A2/1-Ai1, tó-á-re ko-R-a (1960: 16, 58-59 root tone said to be H in monosyllabic roots). See (309, 310, 313, 432, 445, 446).

(434) hodiernal future unreal condition: 'if we are to bite (today)'

[nááré kóromá]	[nááré kóruta]
[kwááré kóromá]	[kwááré kóruta]
[áré kóromá]	[áré kóruta]
[twááré kóromá]	[twááré kóruta]
[mwááré kóromá]	[mwááré kóruta]
[βááré kóromá]	[βááré kóruta]

Compare A2/2-Ai1, to-a-ré kó-R-a (1960: 16, 59). See (314, 315, 435, 446).

(435) near future unreal condition: 'if we are to bite (soon)'

[náаré kóromá]	[náаré kóruta]
[kwáaré kóromá]	[kwáaré kóruta]
[âré kóromá]	[âré kóruta]
[twáaré kóromá]	[twáré kóruta]
[mwáaré kóromá]	[mwáré kóruta]
[βáaré kóromá]	[βáré kóruta]

Or 3s [áa..]. Compare A2/2-Ai1, to-a-ré kó-R-a (1960: 16, 59). See (314, 315, 434, 446).

(436) negative hodiernal past continuous: 'we were not biting (today)'

/ti-na-a-re ko-rom-a/ --> [tinááre korómá]
/ti-ko-a-re ko-rom-a/ --> [tikwááre korómá]
/ti-a-a-re ko-rom-a/ --> [tááre korómá]
[titwááre korómá]
[timwááre korómá]
[tiβááre korómá]

/ti-na-a-re ko-rut-a/ --> [tinááre koruta]
/ti-ko-a-re ko-rut-a/ --> [tikwááre koruta]
/ti-a-a-re ko-rut-a/ --> [tááre koruta]
[titwááre koruta]
[timwááre koruta]
[tiβááre koruta]

Compare AP2/1-Ai1, IP, ti-tó-á(a)-re ko-R-a (1960: 16, 59-60, ti-tó-á(**á**)-re ko-R-a on pp. 59-60). See (440).

(437) hodiernal past continuous thematic

'we were biting (today)'

[níiγɔ nááré kóromá]	[níiγɔ nááré kóruta]
[níiγɔ kwááré kóromá]	[níiγɔ kwááré kóruta]
[níiγɔ âré kóromá]	[níiγɔ âré kóruta]
[níiγɔ twááré kóromá]	[níiγɔ twááré kóruta]
[níiγɔ mwááré kóromá]	[níiγɔ mwááré kóruta]
[níiγɔ βááré kóromá]	[níiγɔ βááré kóruta]

Final ɔ = H. 3s may be [níiγɔ áare] or [níiγáaré], etc. Downstep possible.

(438) recent past continuous thematic: 'we were biting (recently)'

[níiγɔ náaré kóromá]	[níiγɔ náaré kóruta]
[níiγɔ kwáaré kóromá]	[níiγɔ kwáaré kóruta]
[níiγɔ âré kóromá]	[níiγɔ âré kóruta]
[níiγɔ twáaré kóromá]	[níiγɔ twáaré kóruta]
[níiγɔ mwáaré kóromá]	[níiγɔ mwáaré kóruta]
[níiγɔ βáaré kóromá]	[níiγɔ βáaré kóruta]

Final ɔ = H. 3s may be [níiγɔ áare] or [níiγáaré], etc. Downstep possible.

(439) immediate present continuous interrogative: 'are we biting (right now)?'

[níiγɔ nááré kóroma] [níiγɔ nááré kóruta] (RAISED)
[níiγɔ kwááré kóroma] [níiγɔ kwááré kóruta]
[níiγɔ âré kóroma] [níiγɔ âré kóruta]
[níiγɔ twááré kóroma] [níiγɔ twááré kóruta]
[níiγɔ mwááré kóroma] [níiγɔ mwááré kóruta]
[níiγɔ βááré kóroma] [níiγɔ βááré kóruta]

Final ɔ = H. The tone rises slowly up to kó, which is extra H. 3s may be [níiγɔ áare] or [níiγáaré], etc. Downstep possible.

(440) negative recent past continuous: 'we were not biting (recently)'

/ti-na-a-re ko-rom-a/ --> [tináaré korómá]
/ti-ko-a-re ko-rom-a/ --> [tikwáaré korómá]
/ti-a-a-re ko-rom-a/ --> [táaré korómá]
[titwáaré korómá]
[timwáaré korómá]
[tiβáaré korómá]

/ti-na-a-re ko-rut-a/ --> [tináaré kóruta]
/ti-ko-a-re ko-rut-a/ --> [tikwáaré kóruta]
/ti-a-a-re ko-rut-a/ --> [táaré kóruta]
[titwáaré kóruta]
[timwáaré kóruta]
[tiβáaré kóruta]

Compare AP2/2-Ai1, IP, ti-tó-á(a)-ré ko-R-a (1960: 16, 60). See (436).

(441) negative recent past continuous thematic: 'we were not biting (recently)'

[níiγɔ ńtááré kóromá] [níiγɔ ńtááré kóruta]
[níiγɔ ótááré kóromá] [níiγɔ ótááré kóruta]
[níiγɔ átááré kóromá] [níiγɔ átááré kóruta]
[níiγɔ tótááré kóromá] [níiγɔ tótááré kóruta]
[níiγɔ mótááré kóromá] [níiγɔ mótááré kóruta]
[níiγɔ βátááré kóromá] [níiγɔ βátááré kóruta]

Final ɔ = H. Regular liaison in 2-3s. Compare Px2/1-Ai1, to-tá-á-ré kó-R-a (1960: 16, 60), where root tone is said to be mid in high-toned verbs of the types -cvc-, -cv-, -vc. See (316, 319, 442, 444).

(442) relative negative recent past continuous: '(it is) we (who) were not biting (recently)'

[níiñcé ńtááre korómá]	[níiñce ńtááre koruta]
[náayɛ ótááre korómá]	[náayɛ ótááre koruta]
[nɛɛrɛ ótááre korómá]	[nɛɛrɛ ótááre koruta]
[níintwé tótááré kóromá]	[níintwé tótááré kóruta]
[níinwé mótááré kóromá]	[níinwé mótááré kóruta]
[naβúó βátááré kóromá]	[naβúó βátááré kóruta]

First and final ɛ of [nɛɛrɛ] = H. Liaison and downstep are possible. The singular and plural tone patterns are distinct in these paradigm (the singular relative subject markers may possibly be L). Compare Px2/1-Ai1, to-tá-á-ré kó-R-a (1960: 16, 60). See (316, 319, 441, 444).

(443) negative far past continuous thematic: 'we were not biting (long ago)'

[níiɣɔ ńtáaré kóromá]	[níiɣɔ ńtáaré kóruta]
[níiɣɔ ótáaré kóromá]	[níiɣɔ ótáaré kóruta]
[níiɣɔ átáaré kóromá]	[níiɣɔ átáaré kóruta]
[níiɣɔ tótáaré kóromá]	[níiɣɔ tótáaré kóruta]
[níiɣɔ mótáaré kóromá]	[níiɣɔ mótáaré kóruta]
[níiɣɔ βátáaré kóromá]	[níiɣɔ βátáaré kóruta]

Final ɔ = H. Regular liaison in 2-3s. Compare Px2/2-Ai1, to-tá-a-ré kó-R-a (1960: 16, 61). See (317).

(444) relative negative far past continuous: '(it is) we (who) were not biting (long ago)'

[níiñcé ńtáaré kóromá]	[níiñcé ńtáaré kóruta]
[náayɛ ótáaré kóromá]	[náayɛ ótáaré kóruta]
[nɛɛrɛ ótáaré kóromá]	[nɛɛrɛ ótáaré kóruta]
[níintwé tótáaré kóromá]	[níintwé tótáaré kóruta]
[níinwé mótáaré kóromá]	[níinwé mótáaré kóruta]
[naβúó βátáaré kóromá]	[naβúó βátáaré kóruta]

Final ɛ and the first ɛ of [nɛɛrɛ] = H. Liaison and downstep possible. The singular relative subject markers may possibly be L. Compare Px2/2-Ai1, to-tá-a-ré kó-R-a (1960: 16, 61).

(445) hodiernal past continuous: 'we were biting (today)'

[ή̀kóromá nááré]	[ή̀kóruta nááré]
[ή̀kóromá kwááré]	[ή̀kóruta kwááré]
[ή̀kóromá áré]	[ή̀kóruta áré]
[ή̀kóromá twááré]	[ή̀kóruta twááré]
[ή̀kóromá mwááré]	[ή̀kóruta mwááré]
[ή̀kóromá βááré]	[ή̀kóruta βááré]

Downstep possible. Compare Ai2-A2/1, n-kó-R-a tó-á-re (1960: 16, 61; but defined as recent past). See (305, 428, 446).

(446) recent or far past continuous: 'we are biting (recently/long ago)'

[ŋ̍kóromá náaré]	[ŋ̍kóruta náaré]
[ŋ̍kóromá kwáaré]	[ŋ̍kóruta kwáaré]
[ŋ̍kóromá âré]	[ŋ̍kóruta âré]
[ŋ̍kóromá twáaré]	[ŋ̍kóruta twáaré]
[ŋ̍kóromá mwáaré]	[ŋ̍kóruta mwáaré]
[ŋ̍kóromá βáaré]	[ŋ̍kóruta βáaré]

Compare Ai2-A2/1, n-kó-R-a tó-á-re, and Ai2-A2/2, n-kó-R-á tó-a-re (1960: 16, 61). See (305, 428, 445).

(447) a. present continuous: 'we are biting'
b. untimed unreal uncertain conditional future: 'if we were to bite'

[ŋ̍káré kóromá]	[ŋ̍káré kóruta]
[ókáré kóromá]	[ókáré kóruta]
[ákáré kóromá]	[ákáré kóruta]
[tókáré kóromá]	[tókáré kóruta]
[mókáré kóromá]	[mókáré kóruta]
[βákáré kóromá]	[βákáré kóruta]

Compare A4/Ai1, to-ká-ré ko-R-a (1960: 62). See (318).

The following tenses (448-452) involve the root /-is-/,

(448) untimed real condition thematic: '(even) if we (should) bite'

[niinsá kóromá]	[niinsá kóruta]
[noisá kóromá]	[noisá kóruta]
[naisá kóromá]	[naisá kóruta]
[natoisá kóromá]	[natoisá kóruta]
[namoisá kóromá]	[namoisá kóruta]
[naβaisá kóromá]	[naβaisá kóruta]

Though basically untimed, present or future time may be specified in the context or implied by the co-text. Underlying representation /na-to-is-a ko-R-a/.[181] Compare

[181] [koisa] means 'to be about to'. Its singulars may be postulated underlyingly as follows:

1 /na-n-is-a/ --> [niinsa]
2 /na-o-is-a/ --> [noisa]
3 /na-a-is-a/ --> [naisa]

A1a/Ai1, n-to-sá ko-R-a (1960: 16, 62). See (307).

(449) untimed real condition: 'if we should bite'

[íŋísé kóromá]	[íŋísé kóruta]
[óísé kóromá]	[óísé kóruta]
[áísé kóromá]	[áísé kóruta]
[tóísé kóromá]	[tóísé kóruta]
[móísé kóromá]	[móísé kóruta]
[βáísé kóromá]	[βáísé kóruta]

Firs person singular [íínsé] is a possible alternative for [íŋísé]. Though basically untimed, present or future time may be specified in the context or implied by the co-text.

Whiteley also mentions the following three tenses. First, "present or [near, J.C.] future (..) conditional" B1/Ai1, tó-ís-é kó-R-a (1960: 16, 62; also tó-sé kó-R-a on page 62). Second, "purposive" B1/Ai1, tó-βáís-e kó-R-a (1960: 62-63; not mentioned on page 16; said to have no time reference). This tense was disconfirmed by Lilian. Third, B1a/Ai1, n-tó-ís-e kó-R-a (1960: 16, but not given or exemplified, 62-63).[182]

In 2-3s, the /a/ of /na/ is delinked, the following subject marker vowel spread leftward, and then shortened again before the following /i/, or not spread in the first place. The derivation of 1s seems to be idiosyncratic.

[182] Unfortunately, my own data are also inconclusive at this point. Though somewhat at random, the following items may be recorded (without tone),

|ti-o-V-βa-is-e koroma|
not-2s-t-?-be about to-fv bite (them?)
[tɔɔβaise koroma]
'2s-do not bite (them?) (right now)'

|ti-mo-V-βa-is-e koroma|
not-2p-t-?-be about to-fv bite (them?)
[tɔɔβaise koroma]
'2p-do not bite (them?) (right now)'

The postulated underlying representations are tentative. The lower mid vowels in the surface representations may be due to the plstulate that the underspecified vowel is lower mid, or possibly caused by the /a/ of /βa/.

Another imperfectly recorded tense is the following one:

(450) negative immediate intention: 'we are not about to bite (right now)'

[tináísa korómá]	[tináísa koruta]
[tiγwáísa korómá]	[tiγwáísa koruta]
[táísa korómá]	[táísa koruta]
[titwáísa korómá]	[titwáísa koruta]
[timwáísa korómá]	[timwáísa koruta]
[tiβáísa korómá]	[tiβáísa koruta]

Underlying representation /ti-to-a-is-a/. Compare P1/Ai1 ti-tó-áísa ko-R-a (1960: 16, but ti-to-aisa ko-R-a, 62-63; not exemplified). See (303, 305, 306, 352, 362).

(451) uncertain present/future possibility: 'we may bite'

[ńdáaβáísé kóromá]	[ńdáaβáísé kóruta]
[óráaβáísé kóromá]	[óráaβáísé kóruta]
[áráaβáísé kóromá]	[áráaβáísé kóruta]
[tóráaβáísé kóromá]	[tóráaβáísé kóruta]
[móráaβáísé kóromá]	[móráaβáísé kóruta]
[βáráaβáísé kóromá]	[βáráaβáísé kóruta]

Compare B9/Ai1, to-raa-ís-e ko-R-a (1960: 16). Also given as tó-ráá-ís-e or tó-ráá-βáís-e, without ko-R-a (1960: 63, only one example recorded). See (364, 365, 366).

(452) immediate future: 'we are about to bite'

[náisíré kóromá]	[náisíré kóruta]
[γwáisíré kóromá]	[γwáisíré kóruta]
[áisíré kóromá]	[áisíré kóruta]
[twáisíré kóromá]	[twáisíré kóruta]
[mwáisíré kóromá]	[mwáisíré kóruta]
[βáisíré kóromá]	[βáisíré kóruta]

Underlying representation /to-a-is-ir-e ko-R-a/. Possibly, the tonal pattern is [..áís!íré..] or [..á!ísíré..] in all persons. Compare C2/1-Ai1, to-a-ís-ire ko-R-a (1960: 16, 63). See (376, 377).

?negative imperative thematic: 'we should not bite'

[tíinsá kóromé]
[tóisá kóromé]
[táisá kóromé]
[titóisá kóromé]
[timóisá kóromé]
[tiβáisá kóromé]

It is not recorded in (1960).

Some complex tenses contain a form of [komaña] 'to know', used as an auxiliary. They express activity consequent on some previous activity. This idea may be translated by "and then". The construction is [antecedent sm] [sm-a-mañ-a infinitive] (where the subject markers agree morphosyntatically). Compare (1960: 63). Alternatively, the following construction may be used: |erio sm-a-root-a|, where [erio] means '(and) then'.

Finally, the morpheme /ko-/ or its allomorph [γo-] may be prefixed to some finite form, in order to express the concept of simultaneity, expressed in English by the conjunctives 'when' or 'while'. For some examples, see (1960: 64).

3.3.6. To be and not to be.

3.3.6.1. Linking usage: na, -re.

In this section, an element is discussed that may arguably be morphologically and semantically related to the focus element that occurs in many tenses. Even so, this focus seems to have become grammaticalised by now, at least in a number of tenses, and there are semantic differences between the two elements as well. Synchronically, therefore, the homomorph discussed here may plausibly be considered as an independent lexical item that is distinct from the focus element proper, though there it may be linked to the following word through liasion.

Its meaning is declarative or positive, and may be used to emphasize or identify, and may be translated 'it is' or 'they are'. It is here called the linking usage of 'to be'. Its negation is expressed through a negative tense of the (different) root /-re/. The forms will be discussed in this order.

This type of linking element commonly occurs in many Bantu languages. For example, compare Swahili **ne** 'it is, they are'. For Gusii, Whiteley postulates /n-/ underlyingly (1956: 36-37), but this seems to be insufficient. For reasons to be explained in a moment, its underlying representation is postulated here as /na/, with /n/ for its allomorph.

Since this element is used to state or confirm the identity or some attribute of something or someone, its basic usage is that of a linking verb and its basic meaning identificatory. Hence it may be called identificatory /na/. Whiteley compares it to the use of 'is' in English in phrases of the type 'X is Y', but correctly notes that it differs from the English verb 'to be' in a number of respects. From a syntactic point of view, this element is exceptional in that it does not participate in the morphosyntactic class system of agreement. Hence, Whiteley's statements that "it has neither root nor suffix nor prefix", and that "it is simply a 'Connector' linking two items", are substantially correct (1956: 36).

It may well be asked whether, and how closely, identificatory /na/ and the homomorphous focus element are related, and it might plausibly be argued that the focus etymologically derives from independent /na/. Their morphological surface details are similar too, as we will see in a moment. Again, it may be asked whether /na/ must be considered as an independent word regularly undergoing certain postlexical rules that have the combined effect of liaison. Whiteley's postulate /n-/ and his orthography suggest that he considers it as a clitic or a dependent morpheme. Here too, it is considered as a clitic, or as an element that is in the process of becoming one.

Allomorphy involving this element may be formulated as in (453),

(453) allomorphy: identificatory element ==>

a. na- / --- [-cons]
b. n- / --- [+cons]

This is briefly, but typically, exemplified in (454),

(454) a. |...na omotaambe| --> [noomotaambe] '...is 1/3-big'

b. /n taata/
is father
[ntaata]
'(he/this) is (my) father, it is father'

c. /n βaaβa/
is mother
[mbaaβa]
'(she/this) is (my) mother, it is mother'

After cliticisation, lexical /a/-Delinking may be adduced to account for the regular delinking of /a/ in /na-/ before a vowel. Together with subsequent spreading of the following vowel, this accounts for all the surface variation involving this element. This also holds for the focus, especially in 1-3 singular of many tenses (see section 3.3.5). Whenever allomorph /n-/ cliticises to words beginning with a consonant (which occur less frequently than vowel-initial words), nasal rules apply. If /nV-/ would be postulated underlyingly, /V/ would not sound inter-consonantally.

The surface allomorphy of identificatory /na/ may be exemplified in combination with the nominal class prefixes, as in (455),

(455) 'is, are'

	underlying representation		example of possible surface representation (normal rapid speech)
1	/na omo-/	-->	[noomoremi] 'farmer'
1a	/n mo-/	-->	[mmoγaaka] 'old man'
1b	/n-/	-->	[ntaata] 'father'
2	/na aβa-/	-->	[naaβaremi] 'farmers'
3	/na omo-/	-->	[noomote] 'tree'
4	/na eme-/	-->	[neemete] 'trees'
5	/na eri-/	-->	[neeriitɔɔkɛ] 'banana'
6	/na ama-/	-->	[naamatɔɔkɛ] 'bananas'
7	/na eke-/	-->	[neekeroγo] 'chair'
8	/na eβi-/	-->	[neeβiroγo] 'chairs'
9	/na e-/	-->	[nɛɛηɔɔmbɛ] 'cow'
10	/na eci-/	-->	[neeciɔɔmbɛ] 'cows'
	/n ci-(n-)/	-->	[ñciɔɔmbɛ] 'cows'[183]
11	/na oro-/	-->	[nooroko] '(piece of) firewood'
12	/na aka-/	-->	[naaγaanto] 'smaal thing'
14	/na oβo-/	-->	[nooβokima] 'ugali'
15	/na oko-/	-->	[nɔɔkɔβɔkɔ] 'arm'
16	/na a-/	-->	[naase] 'place'
21	/n ña-/	-->	[ññaγɛɛηkɛ] 'Nyageenke village'

The distinction between 10 and 10a may be connected with data such as (456a), as distinct from (456b),

(456) a. |rii-nani eri na eriinɛnɛ|
5-forest 5-this is 5-big
[riinani eri neeriinɛnɛ]
'this forest is big'

b. |riinani eri riinɛnɛ| 'this big forest'

However, such a difference in augmentation is not found in (457),

(457) a. |aβaa-nto aβa na aβa-ya|
2-person 2-these are 2-good
[aβaanto aβa naaβaya]
'these people are good'

b. |aβaanto aβa aβaya| 'these good people'

In any case, (456a, 457a) disconfirm Whiteley's suggestion (1956: 36) that identificatory

183 There is an accidental gap in the data here, since 9a-10a is not exemplified.

/n(a)/ may be omitted after a demonstrative.

So much for the declarative, predicative use of identificatory /na/. As Whiteley (1956: 36) correctly notes, its negation may also be expressed, through a negative form of /-re/ 'to be', which is here used as a linking verb (for its use as an auxiliary, see section 3.3.7). This form contains negative marker /ti-/, and any such tense, one possibly excepted, which does not contain any tense prefixes ends in /-i/ (see section 3.3.3.2). The underlying representation of this particular negative may thus be postulated as in (458),

(458) generalised underlying representation: 'is not, are not'

/ti-sm-r-i/
not-sm-be-fv

Further, it will be recalled that, whenever negative marker /ti-/ is followed by a vowel, its /i/ is lexically deleted, without compensatory lengthening of the following vowel. The paradigm may be worked out systematically, as in (459),

(459) 'is not, are not'

	underlying representation		surface representation
1	/ti-a-r-i/	-->	[tari]
2	/ti-βa-r-i/	-->	[tiβari]
3	/ti-o-r-i/	-->	[tori]
4	/ti-e-r-i/	-->	[teri]
5	/ti-ri-r-i/	-->	[tiriri]
6	/ti-a-r-i/	-->	[tari]
7	/ti-ke-r-i/	-->	[tikeri]
8	/ti-βi-r-i/	-->	[tiβiri]
9	/ti-e-r-i/	-->	[teri]
10	/ti-ci-r-i/	-->	[ticiri]
11	/ti-ro-r-i/	-->	[tirori]
12	/ti-ka-r-i/	-->	[tikari]
14	/ti-βo-r-i/	-->	[tiβori]
15	/ti-ko-r-i/	-->	[tikori]
16	/ti-a-r-i/	-->	[tari][184]
21	= 9 or 16		

It may be added that the present research does not corroborate Whiteley's observations, first, that the form for classes 1 and 6, [tari], may be used invariably with all classes; and second, that [tai] may be used, instead of it, in the same general way.

Finally, in connection with the general relative tense, Whiteley (1956: 59) observes that

[184] Whiteley's [taari] appears to be a mistranscription (1956: 36).

"the connector n- [i.e. na or n] frequently occurs as a matter of good style". The examples he gives, without translation, are repeated, more explicitly, in (460),

(460) a. |ama-γena a-ko-ri-a|
6-stone sm3s-t-eat-fv
[amaγena akoria]
'he is eating eggs'

b. |na ama-γena a-ko-ri-a|
is 6-stone sm3s-t-eat-fv
[naamaγena akoria]
'(it is) eggs he is eating'

of which (460b) is judged "better", but, as the translations suggest, the difference seems to be one of rhema (460a) and theme (460b).

3.3.6.2. Auxiliary usage: -re, -β-.

The expression of the concept of 'being' and its various semantic and syntactic uses in Gusii are reasonably well discussed by Whiteley (1956: 36-37, 39, 56-58).

The use of /-re/ 'to be' as a linking verb, forming the negative counterpart of identificatory clitic /na/ 'is/are' was discussed in section 3.3.6.1.

Its use as an auxiliary verb is exemplified in section 3.3.5. Generally, a finite form of /-re/ preceded by a subject marker, thus /sm-re/, is used with a focussed or non-focussed infinitive, in order to form a complex tense. Depending on the particular tense, it may precede or follow the infinitive. The paradigm may be worked out more fully, as in (461),

(461) a. animate class (including 1 and 2)

singular

1	/n-re/ --> [nde]
2	/o-re/
3	/a-re/

plural

1	/to-re/
2	/mo-re/
3	/βa-re/

b. other classes (not exemplified in section 3.3.5)

3	/o-re/
4	/e-re/
5	/ri-re/
6	/a-re/
7	/ke-re/
8	/βi-re/
9	/e-re/
10	/ci-re/
11	/ro-re/
12	/ka-re/
14	/βo-re/
15	/ko-re/
16	/a-re/
21	= 9 or 16

Except in the case of the animate class first person singular, all surface representations in (461) are identical to the underlying ones from which they are derived.

As such, /-re/ may also be used in certain past tense forms (1956: 56) with the suffix /-Nγe/, as in (462),

(462) a. generalised underlying representation

/sm-a-re-Nγe/
sm-t-be-sx(past)
'sm was/were'

b. animate class (including 1 and 2)

singular

1	/na-a-re-Nγe/ -->	[naareeŋge]
2	/ko-a-re-Nγe/ -->	[kwaareeŋge]
3	/a-a-re-Nγe/ -->	[(a)areeŋge]

plural

1	/to-a-re-Nγe/ -->	[twaareeŋge]
2	/mo-a-re-Nγe/ -->	[mwaareeŋge]
3	/βa-a-re-Nγe/ -->	[βaareeŋge]

c. other classes

3	/ko-a-re-Nγe/ -->	[kwaareeŋge]
4	/e-a-re-Nγe/ -->	[yaareeŋge]
5	/ri-a-re-Nγe/ -->	[ryaareeŋge]
6	/a-a-re-Nγe/ -->	[aareeŋge]
7	/ke-a-re-Nγe/ -->	[kyaareeŋge]
8	/βi-a-re-Nγe/ -->	[βyaareeŋge]
9	/e-a-re-Nγe/ -->	[yaareeŋge]
10	/ci-a-re-Nγe/ -->	[cyaareeŋge]
11	/ro-a-re-Nγe/ -->	[rwaareeŋge]
12	/ka-a-re-Nγe/ -->	[kaareeŋge]
14	/βo-a-re-Nγe/ -->	[βwaareeŋge]
15	/ko-a-re-Nγe/ -->	[kwaareeŋge]
16	/a-a-re-Nγe/ -->	[aareeŋge]
21	= 9 or 16	

The negatives of the forms in (462) are formed by prefixation of /ti-/, as in (463),

(463) a. generalised underlying representation

/ti-sm-a-re-Nγe/
neg-sm-t-be-sx(past)
'sm was/were not'

b. animate class (including 1 and 2)

singular

1	[tinaareeηge]
2	[tikwaareeηge]
3	[taareeηge]

plural

1	[titwaareeηge]
2	[timwaareeηge]
3	[tiβaareeηge]

c. other classes

3	[tikwaareeηge]
4	[tiyaareeηge]
5	[tiryaareeηge]
6	[taareeηge]
7	[tikyaareeηge]
8	[tiβyaareeηge]
9	[tiyaareeηge]
10	[ticyaareeηge]
11	[tirwaareeηge]
12	[tikaareeηge]
14	[tiβwaareeηge]
15	[tikwaareeηge]
16	[taareeηge]
21	= 9 or 16

There is also another root which means 'to be', viz. /-β-/. It occurs in positive and negative tenses, and is normally used with a verbal complement, as in (464),

(464) a. present perfect

/na-a-β-e-ir-e/ -->	[naaβɛire] 'I have been ...'
/ko-a-β-e-ir-e/ -->	[kwaaβɛire] 'you have been ...'
/a-a-β-e-ir-e/ -->	[aaβɛire] 'he has been ...'
etc.	

b. future

/na-n-β-e/ -->	[niimbɛ] 'I will be ...'
/na-o-β-e/ -->	[nɔɔβɛ] 'you will be ...'
/na-a-β-e/ -->	[naaβɛ] 'he will be ...'
etc.	

c. past

/n-na-a-β-e-et-e/[185] -->	[nnaaβɛɛtɛ] 'I was ...'
/n-ko-a-β-e-et-e/ -->	[ηkwaaβɛɛtɛ] 'you were ...'
/na-a-β-e-et-e/ -->	[naaβɛɛtɛ] 'he was ...'

d. negative present perfect incompletive ('not yet')

/ti-n-raa-β-a/ -->	[tiindaaβa] 'I have not yet been ...'
/ti-o-raa-β-a/ -->	[toraaβa] 'you have not yet been...'
/ti-a-raa-β-a/ -->	[taraaβa] 'he has not yet been...'
etc.	

(after Whiteley 1956: 56)

3.3.6.3. Relative usage: -re, -yi-.

Relative forms of 'to be' are again expressed through /-re/, and are identical to those in (461). However, the relative form for the second person singular of the animate class, is /ko-a-re/ --> [kwaare] (Whiteley 1956: 56). The general meaning of these forms is 'who/which is/are?'.

Related, but semantically slightly different, is the meaning 'who/which (specifically) is/are?'. With some morphosyntactic classes, the stem /-re/ is preceded by a referential prefix, i.e. /rpx-re/, with others it is preceded by a referential prefix plus a relative marker, i.e. /rpx-rm-re/, as in (465),

---

[185] By analogy to the future forms under (464b), I have postulated /n-na-a-β-e-et-e/, rather than /n-na-a-β-a-et-e/.

(465) 'who/which (specifically) is/are'

1	/oyo-o-re/	-->	[oyoore]	(= singular 1-3)
2	/aβa-re/	-->	[aβare]	(= plural 1-3)
3	/oyo-o-re/	-->	[oyoore]	
4	/eye-e-re/	-->	[eyeere]	
5	/eri-re/	-->	[erire]	
6	/aya-a-re/	-->	[ayaare]	
7	/eke-re/	-->	[ekere]	
8	/eβi-re/	-->	[eβire]	
9	/eye-e-re/	-->	[eyeere]	
10	/eci-re/	-->	[ecire]	
11	/oro-re/	-->	[orore]	
12	/aka-re/	-->	[akare]	
14	/oβo-re/	-->	[oβore]	
15	/oko-re/	-->	[okore]	
16	/aya-a-re/	-->	[ayaare]	
21	= 9 or 16			

These surface representations may be acounted for by the following rule,

(466) allomorphy: relative -re

a. rpx-rm-/ --- re [1, 3, 6, 9, 16

b. rpx-/ --- re [elsewhere

The corresponding negative relative counterparts, meaning 'who/which is/are not', are formed differently, by using the root /-yi-/, followed by the suffix /-o/, and preceded by negative marker /ta-/, which in turn is preceded by the subject marker, as in (467),

(467) 'who/which is/are not'

pattern: sm-ta-yi-o
n2

1	/o-ta-yi-o/	-->	[otayio]	(= singular 1-3)
2	/βa-ta-yi-o/	-->	[βatayio]	(= plural 1-3)
3	/o-ta-yi-o/	-->	[otayio]	
4	/e-ta-yi-o/	-->	[atayio]	
5	/ri-ta-yi-o/	-->	[ritayio]	
6	/a-ta-yi-o/	-->	[atayio]	
7	/ke-ta-yi-o/	-->	[γetayio]	
8	/βi-ta-yi-o/	-->	[βitayio]	
9	/e-ta-yi-o/	-->	[etayio]	
10	/ci-ta-yi-o/	-->	[citayio]	
11	/ro-ta-yi-o/	-->	[rotayio]	
12	/ka-ta-yi-o/	-->	[γatayio]	
14	/βo-ta-yi-o/	-->	[βotayio]	
15	/ko-ta-yi-o/	-->	[γotayio]	
16	/a-ta-yi-o/	-->	[atayio]	
21	= 9 or 16			

Whiteley (1956: 57) gives /-y-/ instead of /-yi-/, thus [otayo], [βatayo], etc, but this appears to be mistaken.

3.3.6.4. Locative usage: -re.

Auxiliary or linking verb /-re/ may be used independently as well. The locative English phrases 'It is there' and 'It is in ... (or: at, on)', and the latter's interrogative counterpart 'Where is ..?' are briefly discussed by Whiteley (1956: 39). His account may be summarised, a little more explicitly, as in (468),

(468) locative interrogative phrase: 'where is/are...?'

a. noun {kai / ηai} sm-ka-re / sm-t-be

b. sm-re

To this question, a number of responses are possible. First consider (469),

(469) locative declarative phrase: 'it is (t)here'

thematic

a. na aiγa sm-ka-re 'it is/they are here'
b. na aria sm-ka-re 'it is/they are there'
c. na arɔrɔ sm-ka-re 'it is/they are there'

rhematic

/aiγa sm-re/ e.g. [aiγa βare] 'they are here'
/aria sm-re/ e.g. [aria βare] 'they are (over) there'
/arɔrɔ sm-re/ e.g. [arɔrɔ βare] 'they are there'

Also consider (470),

(470) 'sm is/are there'

1s	[niindɛɔ]	[niindɔɔ]	[nɔɔ nde]
2s	[nɔɔrɛɔ]	[nɔɔrɔɔ]	[nɔɔ ore]
3s	[naarɛɔ]	[naarɔɔ]	[nɔɔ are]
1p	[ntɔrɛɔ]	[ntɔrɔɔ]	[nɔɔ tore]
2p	[mmɔrɛɔ]	[mmɔrɔɔ]	[nɔɔ more]
3p	[mbarɛɔ]	[mbarɔɔ]	[nɔɔ βare]

	'sm is there' or	'sm is there'[186]	'sm is not there'
1	[naareɔ]	[nɔɔ are]	[tariɔɔ]
2	[mbareɔ]	[nɔɔ βare]	[mbariɔɔ]
3	[nooreɔ]	[nɔɔ ore]	[toriɔɔ]
4	[neereɔ]	[nɔɔ ere]	[teriɔɔ]
5	[ndiireɔ]	[nɔɔ rire]	[tiririɔɔ]
6	[naareɔ]	[nɔɔ are]	[tariɔɔ]
7	[ηkereɔ]	[nɔɔ kere]	[ηkeriɔɔ]
8	[mbireɔ]	[nɔɔ βire]	[mbiriɔɔ]
9	[neereɔ]	[nɔɔ ere]	[teriɔɔ]
10	[ñcireɔ]	[nɔɔ cire]	[ñciriɔɔ]
11	[ndoreɔ]	[nɔɔ rore]	[ndoriɔɔ]
12	[ηkareɔ]	[nɔɔ kare]	[ηkariɔɔ]
14	[mboreɔ]	[nɔɔ βore]	[mboriɔɔ]
15	[ηkoreɔ]	[nɔɔko re]	[ηkoriɔɔ]
16	[naareɔ]	[nɔɔ are]	[tariɔɔ]
21	= 9 or 16	9 or 16	9 or 16

---

[186] Compare the future

'he will be there'

1	[naaβɛɔ]
2	[mbaβɛɔ]
3	[nɔɔβɛɔ]
4	[nɛɛβɛɔ]
5	[ndiβɛɔ]
6	[naaβɛɔ]
7	[ηkɛβɛɔ]
8	[mbiβɛɔ]
9	[nɛɛβɛɔ]
10	[ñciβɛɔ]
11	[ndɔβɛɔ]
12	[ηkaβɛɔ]
14	[mbɔβɛɔ]
15	[ηkɔβɛɔ]
16	[naaβɛɔ]
21	= 9 or 16

A negative response may be expressed through /ti-sm-r-i/ 'it is/they are not' in combination with [aiγa] 'it is/they are here', [aria] 'it is/they are there', or [arɔrɔ] 'it is/they are there', as in (471),

(471) a. [tikeri aiγa] '7-it is not here'
b. [tikeri aria] '7-it is not (over) there'
c. [tikeri arɔrɔ] '7-it is not there'

An alternative negative response is (472),

(472)	1	/ti-a-iyo/	-->	[taiyo]
	2	/ti-βa-iyo/	-->	[tiβaiyo]
	3	/ti-o-iyo/	-->	[toiyo]
	4	/ti-e-iyo/	-->	[teiyo]
	5	/ti-ri-iyo/	-->	[tiriiyo]
	6	/ti-a-iyo/	-->	[taiyo]
	7	/ti-ke-iyo/	-->	[tikeiyo]
	8	/ti-βi-iyo/	-->	[tiβiiyo]
	9	/ti-e-iyo/	-->	[teiyo]
	10	/ti-ci-iyo/	-->	[ticiiyo]
	11	/ti-ro-iyo/	-->	[tiroiyo]
	12	/ti-ka-iyo/	-->	[tikaiyo]
	14	/ti-βo-iyo/	-->	[tiβoiyo]
	15	/ti-ko-iyo/	-->	[tikoiyo]
	16	/ti-a-iyo/	-->	[taiyo]
	21	= 9 or 16		

Whiteley (1956: 39) suggests that "The 'ka' occurs where the object referred to is distant from the speaker". In constrast, one informant[187] suggested that forms containing /ka/ are more specific. This requires further examination.

3.3.6.5. To be with: -re, -βuat-.

The concept of possesion is usually expressed by using a form of /-re/ or /-βuat-/ together with linking element /na/. Thus 'to be with' means 'to have'. Positive, negative, relative, and interrogative forms, using /-re na/ may all occur, and the reader is referred to the places where the forms of this verb are discussed. The following examples (after Whiteley 1956: 58) may be given here,

[187] Judith Moraa.

(473) a. |(iñce) n-n-re na εγεtɔɔŋga|
1s-I f-1s-be with basket
[(iñce) niinde nεεγεtɔɔŋga]
'I have a basket' (literally, 'I am with a basket')

compare [..ntore..] 'we have ..'

b. |(iñce) ti-n-r-i na εγεtɔɔŋga|
1s-I neg-1s-be with basket
[(iñce) tiindi nεεγεtɔɔŋga]
'I do not have a basket' (literally, 'I am not with a basket')

compare [..titore..] 'we do not have ..'

The alternatives that contain the parenthesised forms are emphatic, the ones that do not are non-emphatic.

The root /-ßuat-/ may be used in a similar construction expressing possession. Whiteley calls it a "defective verb", but without explaining what he means by this, and adds that it is "not to be confused with ßwaata 'grasp, have', though possibly related to it" (1956: 58). His examples, worked out more explicitly here, are repeated in (474),

(474) a. |(iñce) n-ßwaat-e εγεtɔɔŋga|
1s-I 1s-be-fv basket
[(iñce) mbwaate εγεtɔɔŋga]
'I have a basket'

compare [(intwe) toßwaate..] 'we have ..'

b. |(iñce) ti-n-ßwaat-i εγεtɔɔŋga|
1s-I neg-1s-be-fv basket
[(iñce) tiimbwaati εγεtɔɔŋga]
'I do not have a basket'

compare [(intwe) titoßwaati..] 'we do not have ..'

Finally, attention may be drawn to a general relative construction used to express possession, involving /-re/. Thus the English phrase 'the noun whom/which I have' may be expressed in Gusii through the formula 'the noun I am with it', as in (475),

(475) |riiγena n-re na ri-ɔ|
5-stone I-am with 5-it
[riiγenaande na riɔ]
'the stone (that) I have'

compare 1p [riiγena tore na riɔ]

Its negative counterpart is expressed along the same lines, so that English 'the noun (that)

I do not have' in Gusii becomes 'the noun I am not with it', as in (476),

(476) |riiγena ti-n-ri na ri-ɔ|
5-stone I-am-not with 5-it
[riiγena tiindi na riɔ]
'the stone I do not have'
compare 1p [riiγena ntori na riɔ][188]

This concludes the discussion of several common Gusii forms expressing the concepts of 'to be' and 'not to be' in their various uses.

3.4. Lexical derivation.

3.4.1. Primary and secondary derivation.

Interesting questions may be raised with respect to lexical derivation in Bantu languages generally, especially relative to their characteristic morphosyntactic word-class systems and the agreement of these classes in the sentence, but also relative to the agglutinative verbal morphology characteristic of most Bantu languages. In these respects, Gusii is no exception. Most words are regularly derived by affixation of their root in a manner related to the properties just mentioned.

More specifically, first, Gusii roots are regularly prefixed by at least one of the morphosyntactic class prefixes previously discussed and exemplified. Second, all words end in a vowel. Some stems may be unanalysable, but other ones may be analysed into a root and at least one derivational suffix. Third, many (mostly, but not exclusively verbal) roots receive additional extension suffixes (see section 3.3.2), so that extension may be included under affixation as a means of lexical derivation

One question concerns the exact manner in which words are derived. Are all of them derived immediately from underling roots through affixation, i.e. is Gusii characterised by what might be called primary derivation only? Or are at least some words, such as deverbal nouns and denominal verbs, derived from or via other lexical categories, i.e. does secondary derivation also play a role in the language?

The following sections will not address these and related questions exhaustively, whether from a theoretical or from a descriptive point of view. In order to provide answers that

---

[188] The full paradigms for class 1 are

[tiindi]	and	[ntari]
[tori]		[otari]
[tari]		[atari]
[ntori]		[totari]
[mmori]		[motari]
[mbari]		[βatari]

are both necessary and sufficient, more research would be needed than it has been possible to do for the present study. However, some problems will be sketched and, related to these, some lines of approach will be suggested towards answering at least some of the questions raised. Future research may wish to take up these points more systematically.

In this context, reduplication may be mentioned as a special form of derivation through affixation. A word or part of it is reduplicated and then attached to that very word or part, whether to its right or to its left. Because of these special characteristics, reduplication is discussed separately in section 3.4.3.

3.4.2. Derivation through affixation.

Since, as pointed out in the preceding section and elsewhere, affixation is the most important means of lexical derivation Gusii uses, it deserves some additional attention by itself.

Gusii arguably has no circumfixes and infixes. Two apparent cases of the latter may be explained otherwise. Prefixes 9a /e-n-/ and 10a /ci-n-/, of which the nasal element reappears in derived diminutives and augmentatives, may thus plausibly be considered as cases of prefix-stacking. As such, they are distinct from prefixes 9 /e-/ and 10 /ci-/, and appear to be lexically governed allomorphs. Second, /-et-e/ and /-ir-e/ are plausibly considered as discontinuous morphemes, since not only may causative suffix /-i/ and passive marker /-u/ occur between the respective elements of which they are made up, but final vowel /-e/ may also be replaced by allomorph /-i/ in some tenses, which is presumably the causative suffix or a copy of it. Straightforward prefixation and suffixation are common and pervasive and will be reconsidered briefly in the next two subsections.

3.4.2.1. Prefixation: augmentation and non-augmentation.

In various places, it was pointed out that, though nominals (i.e. nouns and adjectives) and pronominals are usually both augmented and prefixed, non-augmentation and even non-prefixation may also occur. Here augmentation and non-augmentation are briefly reconsidered in summary fashion.

It would seem that, in most cases, the absence of the augment is probably best considered simply as prefixation without augmentation. In some cases, however, its absence may arguably be considered as a matter of augment deletion. Lexically, mere non-augmentation accounts for most surface representations, except those of words clearly derived from other lexical categories. Such derivation may arguably account for the actual shape of the prefixes involved. Postlexically, augment deletion accounts for most surface representations. In either case, semantics cannot be ruled out completely. This point will be taken up in a moment.

This aspect of Gusii requires more detailed investigation, but, on the basis of Whiteley

(1959) and the research underlying the present study, at least the following cases of lexically determined non-augmentation (477) may arguably be distinguised,

(477) lexical non-augmentation

a. kinship terms
b. proper names (including personal names, placenames, and cattle terms)
c. adverbs
d. conjunctions
e. infinitives

Of these, case (477a) corresponds to Whiteley's case 10 (1959: 254).

For the following outline of postlexical non-augmentation, I rely chiefly, though not exclusively, on Whiteley's work. If his analysis is correct, at least the following cases (478) may be differentiated,

(478) postlexical non-augmentation

a. noun used as a verbal complement
    1. functioning as an adverb or adverbial phrase
    2. functioning as a verbal complement or a verbal part of the predicate
b. in certain interrogative sentences
c. in certain 'general' sentences
d. in certain negative, especially non-verbal sentences
e. vocative

Of these cases, first, (478a1) presumably includes Whiteley's sub-case 1, designated as expressing 'motion-towards, withinness, or time' (1959: 253). It also includes his case 9 of 'class 15 nouns (those associated with a verbal radical) following a verbal' (1959: 254). However, the latter characterisation seems to be inappropriate, for his example [akaγεεnda kɔmɔrɔra] 'he went to see him', must be analysed as in (479),

(479) |a-ka-γεεnd-a ko-mo-rɔr-a|
he-t-go-fv 15-him-see-fv
[akaγεεnda kɔmɔrɔra]
'he/she went to see him/her'

and thus exemplifies a complex tense or verbal construction containing an infinitival complement. Infinitives are typically non-augmented in any position in the sentence, whereas verbal nouns are typically augmented, except when postlexical non-augmentation applies. From this it follows that Whiteley's case 9 is non-existent as a distinct sub-case.

Second, (478a2) seems to include Whiteley's case 4 (1959: 254), which is defined somewhat non-specifically as 'certain specific contexts' and may perhaps more properly be considered as expressing the definiteness of a verbal complement. It is exemplified by /tuuñ-a mo-nto/ --> [tuuña moonto] 'call for the man (a particular individual)!'

Third, (478b) is Whiteley's case 3, exemplified by [maγena ki] 'what stones' and /βi-nto βi-a βi-a-ηo/ --> [βiinto βia βiaηo] 'whose things?' (1959: 254). Which sub-type of interrogative question is intended here, is not explained by him, but the examples seem to indicate that definite subjects are involved. However, it would seem that [βiinto βiaaηo] 'whose things?' occurs more commonly.

By comparison, fourth, Whiteley's example for (478c) seems to indicate that indefiniteness, as opposed to definiteness, is intended here: /βa-ana βa-nre/ --> [βaana βaande] '(any) other children', versus /a-βa-ana a-βa-nre/ --> [aβaana aβaande] '(some, the) other children'. However, these phrases require more context, in order to determine which type or types of sentence are involved here.

Fifth, Whiteley's examples illustrating (478d) are not quite clear. Thus in /ma-ηana a-ya ta-ri ma-ya/ --> [maηana aya tari maya] 'these words are not good'[189] it is not clear whether subject or object is intended (1959: 254). By analogy to his corresponding Kuria example, it may be deduced that an object function is intended here, but this seems to make (478d) a sub-case of (478a2), since [maya] 'good' may be taken as a nominal predicate of the auxiliary [tari] 'are not'.

Sixth, and finally, Whiteley (1959: 254) adds three more cases which he characterises as mainly or only occurring in Kuria. They are repeated in (480),

(480) a. in certain positive non-verbal sentences (mainly Kuria)
b. in address: as a general phenomenon mainly in Kuria
c. in the formation of proper names; Kuria only

Naturally, therefore, none of these cases is exemplified for Gusii. However, the characterisation of and the examples for (480a) are unclear. Moreover, contrary to what he says, (480b) and (480c) also occur in Gusii.

Negatively, it may be commented that Whiteley's definitions or characterisations tend to be too general, in order for them to be sufficiently distinctive. Moreover, partly as a result of this, some of his examples are insufficiently clear, especially where no context and not much more than general characterisations are given. It may be concluded, therefore, that at least postlexical non-augmentation calls for further and more definite research.

Positively, it may be concluded that in such research at least the following factors and

---

189 This expression was said by one informant to have general (possibly referential) meaning, as opposed to the supposedly specific [amaηana aya tari amaya] 'these words ..'. I have not been able to check this systematically, but suspect that the following analysis will prove to be more correct,

non-specific: [maηana tari maya], possibly also [amaηana tari amaya], 'words are not good'
specific: [amaηana aya tari amaya] 'the(se) words are not good'

distinctions are likely to be relevant: sentence-type (declarative, interrogative, negative, or imperative), grammatical function or position (subject versus object), and perhaps also definiteness versus indefiniteness. Gusii seems to resemble Kuria in this respect (compare Cammenga 1994: 163-166).

3.4.2.2. Suffixation.

Suffixation being another sub-type of Gusii derivation through affixation, three brief general observations may be made on it separately here, by way of anticipating the discussion in sections 3.4.4-9.

First, the morphological make-up of lexical items is not equally clear in all cases. Some items are clearly parsible into a root and one or more suffixes. Some are not, in which cases all that follows the prefix will be considered, unless and until evidence to the contrary turns up, as unanalysable stems. More extensive lexical and semantic research on the language may clarify some of these cases.

Second, the suffixes that may be established with certainty as underlyingly derivational suffixes, are /-i, -e, -o, -a, -u/. The status of lower mid vowels /-ɛ/ and /-ɔ/ as such, is arguably somewhat less certain.

Third, there appears to be a certain amount of free variation word-finally, at least in some words involving [e] or [ɛ], and [o] or [ɔ]. Especially in some lexical take-overs, there may be variation between final [u] or [o] as well. Such variation occurs and occurred in many languages that exist in spoken form only or mostly. For example, when printing and reading were not yet widespread, European languages exhibited a considerable amount of variation in spelling, if not in pronunciation. But whenever printing and reading become more common, standardisation tends to be the result.

3.4.3. Derivation through reduplication.

Reduplication of extension suffixes was discussed in section 3.3.2. Reduplication of stems also occurs. The following derivations (481) even exemplify reduplication of words,

(481) a. input /-ηɔra/ 'slow'[190]
reduplication ==> ηɔraηɔra
output [ηɔraηɔra] 'slowly by slowly'

b. input /-taNβ-/
suffixation -taNβe
nasal rules -tambe
compensatory
lengthening --> -taambe 'long, tall' (compare 1956: 119)
prefixation ==> βotaambe 'always'[191]

reduplication ==> [βotaambeβotaambe] 'always' (compare 1960: 36)

c. input /mo-nɔ/
various rules mɔnɔ 'very'
reduplication ==> [mɔnɔmɔnɔ] 'very much' (compare 1960: 63)

It could be argued, however, that in the case of these adverbs repetition, rather than reduplication, is involved, in order to intensify the basic idea. Anyhow, intensity is one of the basic meanings expressed by reduplication or repetition. Be that as it may, the explanation given for [βotaambeβotaambe] was in fact that it has the same meaning as [βotaambe] 'always', but expresses greater intensity. Derivation from the nominal root /-taNβ-/ via the class 14 noun [oβotaambe] 'length' would account for the shape of its prefix. Alternatively, prefix 14 may be interpreted as one that typically derives adverbs, which results in the more immediate derivation in (481b).

A few verbal sample derivations are given in (482),

(482) reduplicated verbs

a. input /-sɔɔm-/ 'read'
suffixation sɔɔm-a
reduplication sɔɔma-sɔɔma
prefixation ko-sɔɔmasɔɔma
other rules
output [γɔsɔɔmasɔɔma] 'to read in a desultory fashion'

---

190 Compare [aβaanto βare ηɔra] 'people who are slow', 'slow people' with ?[aβaanto aβaηɔra] 'slow people'. The presence of the question-mark indicates that it remains to be verified whether the underlying representation of this word may be postulated as /ηɔra/ or as /-ηɔra/.

191 Note the semantic specialisation (compare 1960: 23).

similarly:

b. /ko-it-a-it-a/
15-beat-fv-beat-fv
[γoitaita]
'to beat regularly (every now and then)'

c. /n-n-raa-na-ko-tooη-a-tooη-a/
f-1s-t-t-t-be left out-fv-remain-fv
[niindaañaγotooηatooηa]
'I will be left out repeatedly/always'
(after Whiteley 1960: 37)

d. [γotaarataara] 'to keep on walking leisurely, to walk aimlessly or leisurely (i.e. with brief stops in between)'

e. [kɔγεεndaγεεnda] 'to go intermittently, to go and stop'

Reduplication is a regular and productive process in Gusii. Pending more detailed research, the rule may be formulated tentatively as in (483),

(483) reduplication: copy the stem to the left of input

A few comments may be made. First, the present state of our knowledge of the process is such that there does not seem to be any compelling reason, as yet, for determining whether the copying is to the left or to the right of the input.

Second, if strings of segments shorter than the stem may be copied, 'string' or a more definite term may replace 'the stem' in the formulation of the rule. This would include some extension suffixes.

Third, and finally, it is not yet possible to define the full range of meaning that may be expressed by reduplication. Tentatively, I would suggest that it may express at least either of the following meanings: (1) intensity of activity; (2) intermittent activity, expressing alternation between the progress of some activity and its cessation, repetitition, or frequency of occurrence. A connotation of desultoriness or randomness may possibly be included in the latter sometimes.

I conclude this section with the observation that the meaning of reduplication is an area for further investigation, which must arguably include a more thorough study of a wider range of reduplicated verbs belonging to semantically distinct sub-types.

3.4.4. Derivation of nouns.

Primary derivation.

Most Gusii nouns are structured morphosyntactically as in (484),

(484) noun structure: augment-prefix-root-suffix(es)

Lexically, some may lack the augment, some may lack both the augment and the segmental prefix, and some appear to be unanalysable altogether, but all nouns end in a vowel, whether or not this may be parsed as a distinct suffix.

In some lexical sub-categories, such as proper names and cattle-terms, the augment is regulary absent. But most nouns that have the structure in (484) are the result of primary derivation, and as such they normally have at least one suffix, viz. a final vowel (fv) attached to the root.

All seven vowels may occur as a word-final vowel in the surface representation of nouns. However, to establish their status as a derivational suffix, may require further study, at least for phonological reasons. Because, for example, Mid Vowel Height Spreading (see 2.3.14) is regularly applicable, it is difficult to establish whether some word-final lower mid vowel derives from an underlying upper mid one, or whether it may or must be postulated as lower mid underlyingly. This problem is enhanced by the apparent indeterminacy, in at least some words, of /a/ as a trigger for Mid Vowe Height Spreading. Nor is it possible, in the present state of our knowledge of Gusii, to obtain a sufficient understanding of the productivity of certain derivational suffixes. To determine questions such as these definitively, would require more resources than were available, and more lexical research than was possible, for the present study.

To begin with, consider the nouns ending in /-i/, in (485),

(485) /o-βo-aNc-an-i/
a-14-love-rc-fv
[oβwaañcani]
'love'

(compare /ko-aNc-an-a/ [γwaañcana] 'to love each other')

/o-mo-rem-i/
a-1-dig-fv
[omoremi]
'farmer'

(compare /ko-rem-a/ [korema] 'to dig')

/o-βo-taar-i/
a-14-walk-fv
[oβotaari]
'stroll, leisurely walk'

(compare /ko-taar-a/ [γotaara] 'to walk leisurely, to stroll')

/o-βo-γanβ-i/
a-14-rule-fv
[oβoγaambi]
'art of ruling, kingdom, chiefdom'

(compare /ko-γanβ-a/ [koγaamba] 'to rule, to converse, to talk')

/e-ke-ranr-i/
a-7-crawl-fv
[ekeraandi]
'gourd'

(the meaning of this word reflects the manner of growth of the shrub from which the gourd is taken; compare /ko-ranr-a/ [koraanda] 'to grow (in meandering crawling, climbing, or sprawling fashion)'

In all of these nouns, final /-i/ may be clearly identified as a derivational suffix, on the basis of their contrast with verbs to which they are morphologically and semantically related. By contrast, in a word such as (486) the final vowel of the noun must be considered as part of the stem,

(486) /o-βo-riri/
a-14-foolish
[oβoriri]
'foolishness, stupidity'

compare

/ko-rir-i-a/ --> [koriria] 'to be/become foolish'
/ko-riri-i-a/ --> [koririia] 'to make foolish', but *[korira]

Second, the following nouns (487), ending in /-e/, suggest that it is slightly more difficult to substantiate the case for final /-e/ as a derivational suffix,

(487) a. /e-ke-te/
a-7-tree
[eγete]
'stick'[192]

/o-mo-iseke/	/o-mo-βere/
a-1-girl	a-3-body
[omoiseke]	[omoβere]
'(uncircumcised) girl'	'body'

[192] This word is related to [omote] 'tree': prefix 7 seems to express specialised diminutive meaning here.

/o-mo-amate/, plural [aβaamate]
[omwaamate] or [omoamate]
'neighbour'
(also compare a-14-neighbour [oβoamate] 'neighbourliness, (human) relationship', [eamate] 'neighbourhood')

b. /o-mo-sik-e/ — /o-β o-sik-e/
a-1-honour-fv — a-14-honour-fv
[omosike] — [oβosike]
'honourable person' — 'honour, respect'

compare:

/ko-sik-a/
15-honour-fv
[γosika]
'to honour, to respect'

c. |o-mo-taamb-e| — |o-βo-taamb-e|
a-1-long-fv — a-14-long-fv
[omotaambe] — [oβotaambe]
'tall person' — 'length'

compare:

|ko-taamb-a|
15-long-fv
[γotaamba]
'to spread, to stretch'[193]

The stems in (487a) appear to be unanalysable and therefore merely indicate that /e/ may occur word-finally. However, those in (487b,c) may be analysed into a root plus a derivational suffix, in virtue of their contrast with verbs to which they are morphologically and semantically related. Therefore, /-e/ is indeed established as a derivational suffix. Some such nouns appear to be more immediately deverbal, as in (488),

[193] This word may be archaic, since nowadays this meaning is more commonly expressed through [koraambora].

(488) /-ruar-/ 'become ill'

a. /o-ruar-ir-e/
3s-be ill-pv-fv
[oruaire][194]
'you are ill'
(compare Whiteley 1960: 19)

b. /o-mo-ruar-ir-e/
a-1-be ill-pv-fv
[omorwaire]
'sick person'
(literally, 'one who has become, or is, ill')
(compare Whiteley 1960: 64)

c. /o-βo-ruar-ir-e/
a-14-be ill-pv-fv
[oβorwaire]
'sickness, illness'
(literally, 'condition of having become, or being, ill')
(compare Whiteley 1956: 132)

Third, some nouns ending in /ɛ/ are exemplified in (489),

---

[194] Contrast

[nduaire] 'I am ill'
[oruaire] 'you are ill'
[aruaire] 'he is ill'

with

[naaruarire] 'I have (just) become ill'
[kwaaruarire] 'you have (just) become ill'
[oruarire] 'he has (just) become ill'

It is remarkable that deletion of root-final /r/, which seems a purely phonological process, may apparently occur in the first, but not in the second, paradigm. This is as yet the only example, where this contrast was found to involve a corresponding distinction in meaning. It may require further investigation.

(489) /e-ke-ɛ/
a-7-basket
[ɛkɛɛ]
'basket, container (made of finely woven sisal and leather, used to carry ugali)'

/rii-cɔr-e/
5-weave-fv
[riicɔrɛ]
'(type of) weaver-bird'
compare [γɔcɔra] 'to weave'

/o-mo-tɛɛr-er-er-e/
a-1-sing-ap-ap-fv
[ɔmɔtɛɛrɛɛrɛ][195]
'(species of) tree'
(literally, 'singing tree', plural [ɛmɛ-])

compare

/ko-tɛɛr-a/ --> [γɔtɛɛra] 'to sing'
/ko-tɛɛr-er-er-a/ --> [γɔtɛɛrɛrɛra] 'to sing for continuously'

|e-tɛɛŋg-o| --> [ɛtɛɛŋgɔ] 'dance'
compare [γɔtɛɛŋga] 'to dance'

In the first item in (489), the final vowel may be postulated as /-ɛ/. However, it is not a suffix, but the root. Hence it affords no evidence for establishing /-ɛ/ as a derivational suffix. In the other examples, either /-e/ or /-ɛ/ may be postulated, but in view of the pervasiveness of Mid Vowel Height Spreading (see 2.3.14), /-e/ seems more plausible. It may be concluded, then, that though there seems to be a fair number of words ending in [ɛ], no unambiguous examples have been found on the basis of which this vowel could be postulated underlyingly as a regular derivational suffix.

Fourth, besides verbs, which in their infinitives, some imperatives, and a number of tense

---

[195] In view of the comparable related verb, the postulated underlying representation of this item is presumably as given, and its derivation, partially considered, as follows,

input	|tɛɛr-er-er|
r-deletion	|tɛɛr-e-er|
mid vowel height spreading	|tɛɛrɛɛr|
etc.	

This is one of two examples suggesting that, in addition to the types of /r/-Deletion discussed in sections 3.3.4.1 and 3.3.4.2, the flapped liquid may occasionally be deleted in other contexts as well. But the data are as yet too scanty to warrant general conclusions.

forms, all end in /-a/, there are words belonging to other lexical categories that also end in this vowel. Some examples are given in (490),

(490) a.
/e-ke-ina/[196]
a-7-legal case
[ekiina]
'legal (court-) case'
(plural /e-βi-ina/
--> [eβiina])

/e-ke-ara/
a-7-finger
[ekiara]
'finger'
(plural /e-βi-ara/
--> [eβiara])

/o-βo-kima/
a-14-ugali
[oβokima]
'ugali'

/rii-tina/
5-stem
[riitina]
'(tree-) stem'
(plural /a-ma-tina/
--> [amatina])

b.
/e-ke-siic-a/
a-7-flower-fv
[eγesiica]
'flower'
(plural [eβisiica])

compare

/ko-siic-a/, [γosiica] 'to flower, to blossom'
/ko-siic-i-a/, [γosiicia] 'to cause to flower'

---

[196] The underlying representation of this word is somewhat problematic. Given the data and applicable phonological rules, two analyses are possible. One is to postulate /e-ke-ina/, plural /e-βi-ina/. On this postulate, the word would have to be entered exceptionally as [+UMVR], so that the prefix vowel of the singular will be raised, from |ke-ina| to |kiina|, even though Upper Mid Vowel Raising is conditioned not to apply, whenever target /e/ precedes /i/. On this analysis, the surface representation of the singular is accounted for, while that of the plural, [eβiina], is unproblematic. Its diminutive, [aγakiina] 'small case', must then be interpreted as an instance of prefix-stacking, derived from /a-ka-ke-ina/.

A possible alternative analysis would be to postulate /-kiina/ underlyingly. This would straightforwardly account for the diminutive surface representation [aγakiina], but not for the basic singular and plural. The singular could then only be accounted for as class 9, viz. /e-kiina/, while the plural, *[eβikiina] being unacceptable, would still require either prefix-stacking, as above, or deletion of /ki/, which would be ad hoc. To postulate /-ina/, and to adduce prefix-stacking, already independently established for other contexts, seems to be the more plausible synchronic analysis, in order to account for the singular, plural, and diminutive.

Many, if not most, nominals ending in [a], such as (490b), appear to be morphologically and semantically related to verbs. This raises the question, whether such words are mediately derived from the stem of the verbal infinitive, which includes final /-a/, or immediately from the root through /-a/ functioning as a nominal derivational suffix. If from the latter, it would be a suffix deriving verbs and nominals. If nominals ending in [a] may be derived from a verbal stem only, and if no clear cases of immediate nominal derivation containing this suffix /-a/ would be available, then it would be possible to establish final [a] only as a verbal derivational suffix. In any case, its status as a derivational suffix is thus well established.

Fifth, consider the examples of nouns ending [ɔ], in (491),

(491) a. /o-βo-ritɔ/
a-14-heavy
[oβoritɔ]
'weight, heaviness, (human) pregnancy'

compare

/ko-ritɔ-a/ --> [koritɔa] 'to be/become heavy'

b. /o-mo-γɔɔk-o/
a-1-happy-fv
[ɔmɔγɔɔkɔ]
'happiness'
(plural [ɛmɛγɔɔkɔ] 'hapinesses (i.e. in the sense of 'types of happines');

compare

/ko-γɔɔk-a/ --> [kɔγɔɔka] to be happy'
/ko-γɔɔk-i-a/ --> [kɔγɔɔkia] 'to make happy'

c. /e-n-sɔɔk-o/
9a-spring-fv
[ɛnsɔɔkɔ]
'spring, well'

compare

/ko-sɔɔk-a/ --> [γɔsɔɔka] '(of water) to well up, to come out of'

d. /e-ñuɔm-o/
9-marry-fv
[eñwɔɔmɔ]
'marriage'
(plural [ciñwɔɔmɔ])

compare /ko-ñuɔm-a/ --> [koñwɔɔma] 'to marry'

e. ¦o-mo-ɔndɔk-a¦
a-3-fear-fv
[ɔmɔɔndɔka]
'fear'

compare ¦ko-ɔndɔk-a¦ --> [kɔɔndɔka] or [kwɔɔndɔka] 'to fear'

f. ¦o-mo-caaŋg-ɔ¦ compare ¦ko-caaŋg-a¦
a-3-contribute-fv 15-contribute-fv
[omocaaŋgɔ] [γocaaŋga]
'contribution' 'to contribute'

g. ¦o-mo-caand-ɔ¦ compare ¦ko-caand-a¦
a-3-(make) difficult-fv 15-make difficult-fv
[omocaandɔ] [γocaanda]
'difficulty, hardship' 'to cause difficulty or hardship to'

h. /o-mo-cεγ-o/ compare [γɔcεγa] 'to annoy, to vex'
a-3-annoy-fv
[ɔmɔcεγɔ]
'annoyance'

In (491a), where the nominal stem or root must be postulated as /-ritɔ/, on the basis of its comparison with the verb to which it is morphologocically and semantically related, the final vowel cannot be established as a nominal derivational suffix. Given the applicability of Mid Vowel Height Spreading, final [ɔ] may be argued to be derived from underlying /-o/ in all the other examples, so that these do not furnish hard and fast cases establishing /-ɔ/ underlyingly.

It is only in examples such as those in (492) that it may arguably be postulated underlyingly as a derivational suffix,

(492) a. /o-mo-εr-i-ɔ/
a-3-finish-c-fv
[ɔmɔεriɔ]
'finish'

compare /ko-εr-a/ --> [kɔεra] 'to finish (v.i.)'
/ko-εr-i-a/ --> [kɔεria] 'to finish (v.t.)'

b. ¦o-mo-ikaraans-ɔ¦
a-3-sit-fv
[omwiikaraansɔ]
'sitting, session'

compare [eγekaraansero] 'seat'
¦ko-ikaraans-a¦, [γwiikaraansa] 'to sit down'

In (492a), Mid Vowel Height Spreading (see 2.3.14) regularly applies to the left, but, being blocked by opaque causative vowel /i/, cannot affect the final vowel to the right. Yet the surface representation, [ɔmɔɛriɔ], contains a lower mid final back vowel. This can only be accounted for by postulating /-ɔ/ underlyingly. Moreover, if /a/ may not trigger the rule, (492b) confirms /-ɔ/ as a derivational suffix. But if /a/ may trigger Mid Vowel Height Spreading, (492b) cannot be adduced as corroborative evidence. This point remains to be examined more closely. I tentatively conclude that /-ɔ/ does seem to function as a derivational suffix, but that further supportive evidence would be welcome.[197]

Sixth, consider the examples in (493),

(493) a. /o-mo-ɣoko/
a-3-furrow
[omoɣoko]
'gutter, wadi, furrow (caused by running water or ploughing), running water'
(plural [emeɣoko])

b. /o-ɣo-to/
a-15-ear
[oɣoto]
'ear'
plural [amato]

c. /o-mo-rem-o/
a-3-dig-fv
[omoremo]
'work' (i.e. on the land, or generically)

compare /o-βo-rem-o/
a-14-dig-fv
[oβoremo]
'plot, land (owned by someone)'

and contrast /ko-rem-a/
15-dig-fv/sx
[korema]
'to dig, to cultivate')

[197] As in the case of /ɛ/, either of the following contexts is needed to establish /-ɔ/ more firmly as a derivational suffix underlyingly: /root-ɔ/ or /ɔ-root/, where the root (or stem) contains /u/, /i/, or perhaps also /a/, only.

d. /o-mo-irur-o/
a-3-winnow-fv
[omoiruro] or [omwiruro]
'chaff' (literally, 'something winnowed')

contrast with

/ko-irur-a/
15-winnow-fv/sx
[koirura]
'to winnow'

e. [omoriiko] 'handwriting'
[omoriiki] 'writer'
[koriika] 'to write'

f. [aβiso] 'hiding-place'
[koβisa] 'to hide'

g. [omocaakano] 'beginning'
[γocaakana] 'to begin'

In (493a-b), where no related verb or other type of lexical item seems to be available for contrast, the final vowel is arguably a part of the root or stem. But in the other examples a contrast with a related word, mostly verbs, does exist. In these cases, the final vowel is thus definitely established as a nominal derivational suffix.

Seventh, and finally, consider (494),

(494) a. /rii-tɛɛm-u/ or /a-ma-tɛɛm-u-a/
5-try-fv a-6-try-p-fv
[amatɛɛmu] [amatɛɛmwa]
'test, trial, temptation' 'test, trial, temptation'

(both alternatives are plural only)

compare

/ko-tɛɛm-a/, [γɔtɛɛma] 'to test, to try, to tempt'
/ko-tɛɛm-u-a/, [γɔtɛɛmwa] 'to be tested, etc.'
/ko-tɛɛm-i-a/, [γɔtɛɛmia] 'to make (someone) try, to put (something or someone) to the test'

b. /o-βo-sook-u/
a-14-shy-fv
[oβosooku]
'shyness, shamefulness'

compare

/ko-sook-a/ --> [γosooka]
'to become shy, to be become ashamed'[198]

c. /o-βo-kɔη-u/
a-14-hard-fv
[ɔβɔkɔηu]
'hardship, difficulty'

(compare /ko-kɔη-a/ [γɔkɔηa] 'to become hard', and
/ko-kɔη-i-a/ [γɔkɔηia] 'to make hard')

These examples provide necessary and sufficient grounds for establishing /-u/ as a nominal derivatinal suffix.

This discussion of primary nominal derivation may be concluded by saying that, if the data adduced here are representative, then vowels /-i/, /-e/, /-a/, /-o/, and /-u/ are definitely established as derivational suffixes underlyingly. Similarly, though perhaps less firmly, /-ɔ/. Lower mid /-ɛ/ is not yet so established, though it certainly occurs word-finally, whether derived from underlying /-e/, or simply as a word-final vowel of an otherwise unanalysable root or stem. If /a/ may not trigger Mid Vowel Height Spreading, it may be possible, after all, to establish at least /-ɔ/ underlyingly as a derivational suffix.

Secondary derivation.

As suggested in section 3.4.1, superficially some nouns may arguably be derived from verbs through augmentation, as in the partial derivations in (495),

[198] Inchoative verbs like this tend to take on a resultative meaning in perfective tenses, e.g. '(to) have become shy', hence '(to) be shy'.

(495) input /-am-/ 'grow (intransitive)'

a. verbal derivation

affixation ko-am-a
phonological rules
output [kwaama] 'to grow (v.i.)'[199]

b. deverbal nominal derivation

input |koama| (verb)
augmentation |o-koama| (verbal noun)
phonological rules
output [okwaama] 'growth'

On this interpretation, the following representations (496) would be derived along the same lines,

(496) a. /ko-γanβ-a/
15-talk-fv
[koγaamba]
'to rule, to converse, to talk'

compare

/o-ko-γanβ-a/
a-15-talk-fv
[okoγaamba]
'kingdom, conversation'
(compare synonym [oβoγaambi])

b. /ko-tεt-a/
15-have intercourse-fv
[γɔtεta]
'to have sexual intercourse'

compare

/o-ko-tεt-a/
a-15-have intercourse-fv
[ɔγɔtεta]
'(the act of) sexual intercourse'
(compare synonym [ɔβɔtεti])

---

[199] This verb takes an inanimate subject-referent. Contrast with [γokiina] 'to grow (s-ref: animate)'.

These derivations are relatively straightforward.

However, if other surface facts are taken into account, the interpretation of some nouns as deverbal would require more complex derivations, involving deletion of one suffix and addition of another instead of it, i.e. suffix replacement, as well as prefix replacement, and augmentation. This is exemplified in (497),

(497) input /-rem-/ 'dig'

a. primary derivation

suffixation	|rem-a|
prefixation	|ko-rema|
output	[korema] 'to dig'

b. secondary derivation

input	|korema| 'to dig'
suffix-deletion	|korem|
resuffixation	|koremi|
prefix-deletion	|remi|
reprefixation	|mo-remi|
augmentation	|o-moremi|
output	[omoremi] 'digger, farmer'

The nominal derivation in (497b) could be simplified, if it is also assumed to be primary, as in (498),

(498)	input	/-rem-/ 'dig'
	suffixation	|remi|
	prefixation	|mo-remi|
	augmentation	|o-moremi|
	output	[omoremi] 'digger, farmer'

This postulate would allow us, first, to dispense with the deletion of the prefix and the suffix in (497b), and second, with re-suffixation and re-prefixation.

This approach raises a question with respect to nouns that could be argued more strongly than the previous examples to be deverbal. Consider the partial derivation in (499),

(499)	input	/-anc-/ 'like, love'
	various rules	|aañc|
	extension through	
	suffixation	|aañc-an| 'love each other'
	suffixation	|aañcana|
	prefixation	|ko-aañcana|
	other rules	
	output	[γwaañcana] 'to love each other'

As explained, the term 'extension' designates a type of affixation, operative in Bantu languages, that extends a root morphologically by adding one or more prefixes and/or suffixes to it, thereby also extending or modifying its core meaning. It is generally considered that this process typically applies to verbal roots. Presumably for this reason, nominals that contain extension suffixes typically occurring in verbs, are usually interpreted as deverbal. Analogous to (499), this would necessitate the following derivation (500),

(500) input | ¦koaañcana¦ 'to love each other'
suffix-deletion | ¦koaañcan¦
resuffixation | ¦koaañcan-i¦
prefix-deletion | ¦aañcani¦
reprefixation | ¦βo-añcani¦
augmentation | ¦o-βoañcani¦
other rules
output | [oβwaañcani] 'love'

However, if such extension, even more typical of verbs, may be assumed to apply also in nominals, this derivation could be simplified, because deletion of the prefix and the suffix could be dispensed with again. Alternatively, if certain roots may or must be characterised in the lexicon as underlyingly verbal, and extension would be assumed to be applicable to such roots only, then nominals could be assumed to be derivable from these in the following manner (501),

(501) a. input | /-anc-/ 'like, love'
phonological rules | ¦aañc¦
extension | ¦aañc-an¦ 'love each other'

from this point onward, the verbal and nominal derivations might be assumed to diverge as follows:

b. first primary derivation

input | ¦aañc-an¦ 'love each other'
suffixation | ¦aañcana¦
prefixation | ¦ko-aañcana¦
other rules
output | [γwaañcana] 'to love each other'

c. second primary derivation

input | ¦aañc-an¦ 'love each other'
suffixation | ¦aañcan-i¦
prefixation | ¦βo-aañcani¦
augmentation | ¦oβoaañcani¦
other rules
output | [oβwaañcani] 'love'

Unless compelling evidence to the contrary turns up, the approach exemplified here will be assumed to be basic to Gusii word derivation. Still, this approach allows for cases of secondary derivation. For example, it remains possible to analyse [okorema] 'digging' as a verbal noun derived simply by augmentation from the verb [korema] 'to dig'.

By the same token, finally, the reverse account would be possible in the case of denominal verbs. Thus, if /-ritɔ/ 'heavy' may be postulated underlyingly, the related noun and verb derived from this possibly nominal root may be accounted for as in (502),

(502) a. underlying representation: /-ritɔ/ 'heavy'

b. nominal derivation

input	/-ritɔ/ 'heavy'
prefixation	¦βo-ritɔ¦
augmentation	¦o-βoritɔ¦
output	[oβoritɔ] 'weight, heaviness' (i.e. the property or quality of being heavy)

c. verbal derivation

input	/-ritɔ/ 'heavy'
suffixation	¦okoritɔ-a¦
prefixation	¦ko-ritɔ¦
output	[koritɔa] 'to be/become heavy'[200]

d.

input	¦koritɔa¦
augmentation	¦o-koritɔ¦
output	[okoritɔa] 'being heavy'

(verbal noun emphasizing activity or state; its synonym [oβoritɔ] 'heaviness' refers to a property conceived more abstractly)

---

[200] Compare Kuria,

/o-ko-ritɔ-h-a/
a-15-heavy-inc-fv
[okoritɔha]
'to be/become heavy'

where the verb is derived through inchoative derivational suffix /-h/ from a nominal root. Kuria [oβoritɔ] 'heaviness' also occurs.

3.4.5. Derivation of adjectives.

3.4.5.1. Non-derived adjectives.

Non-derived adjectives may be defined as those that do not participate in the system of morphosyntactic classes and agreement; in short, invariant adjectives. These appear to be very few. Possibly, only [kera] 'all, every' and [γete] 'some (particular)' may belong to this group.

Alternatively, non-derived adjectives may be defined as those that are not obviously derived from, or related to, another word belonging to some other lexical category. To the best of my knowledge, however, there are no items in Gusii that may function as an adjective only. Whether some root or stem may be more plausibly interpreted as a basic noun or adjective, most, if not all of these, may nonetheless function as either. I will not speculate on this, but would rather suggest that more detailed lexical and semantic research on this and related questions is needed to give us a better insight in this aspect of the lexicon and lexical derivation.

3.4.5.2. Derived adjectives.

Derived adjectives, in contrast to non-derived ones, appear to be most common, though some adjectival roots may exist. But since these even these may be used also as nouns, there are probably no adjective-only roots. Generally, their derivation is quite unproblematic and proceeds regularly through affixation. If we take class 7 for an example, this may be exemplified as in (503),

(503) a. underlying representation: /-yia/ 'new'

derivation:

input /-yia/ 'new'
prefixation |ke-yia|
augmentation |e-keyia|
output [ekeyia] '7-new'

e.g. [eγeento ekeyia] 'a new thing'

b. /o-βo-kima o-βo-ɔrɔɔrɔ/
a-14-ugali a-14-soft
[oβokima oβwɔɔrɔɔrɔ]
'soft ugali'

compare [kwɔɔrɔɔrɔβa] 'to be soft', [oβwɔɔrɔɔrɔ] 'softness', *[ɔβɔɔrɔɔrɔ]

c. [omoonto omoγusu] 'light (of weight) person'
compare /ko-γusu-a/ [koγusua] 'to be light (of weight)'

Second, however, the adjectival concept may also be expressed in Gusii by means of a relative verb-form. This is common in other Bantu languages too. Some examples are given in (504),

(504) /o-βo-kima βo-isan-ir-e/
a-14-ugali 14-suffice-pv-fv
|oβo-kima βo-isaine| (relative perfective)
[oβokima βoisaine]
'enough ugali' (literally, 'ugali which has sufficed')

or [oβokima βwaisaine] 'ugali which is enough', 'enough ugali'

/rii-mo-Nto ri-a-c-ir-e/
5-1-person 5-t-come-pv-fv
[riimoonto riacire]
'a very big person (who) has come'

or [riimoonto riria riacire]
'a very big person (who) has come'

Third, the adjectival concept may also be expressed by means of the associative construction discussed in section 3.2.11, as in (505),

(505) /e-βi-Nto βi-a o-ko-aNc-i-a/
a-8-thing 8-of a-15-like-c-fv
|eβiinto βia oγoaañcia|
things of causing-to-like
[eβiinto βiooγwaañcia]
'pleasant things'

/rii-ηana ri-a o-ko-caNr-ek-i-a/
5-word 5-of a-5-trouble-St-c-fv
|riiηana ria oγocaandekia|
word of causing-to-be-troubled
[riiηana riooγocaandekia]
'a disturbing matter'

(after Whiteley 1956: 30)

From the examples given so far, it will be clear that some adjectives may be considered as deverbal, or at least verb-related, while other adjectives may not. Some more examples are given in (506),

(506) types of adjective

a. not derived from other categories

/-βariiri/ 'red'

e.g. |ekeroγo na ekeβariiri|
7-chair is 7-red
[ekeroγo neekeβariiri]
'the chair is red'

b. verb-related

/-βuc-u/ 'plenty, sufficient (number of)'

e.g. |eβiinto eβiβucu| 'plenty things'

compare /ko-βuc-a/ --> [koβuca] 'to be plenty'

c. deverbal

/ko-isan-a/ --> [γoisana] 'to be enough'

e.g. [cɔɔmbɛ ñcisaine] 'the cows are enough'
[cɔɔmbɛ cire βweeri ciisaine] 'the cows that are in the enclosure are enough' (βweeri is the enclosure or stable in a homestead)

Sometimes an adjectival idea, or what in many languages would be expressed by a verb or an adjective, may be expressible by a verb only. This seems to be the case at least in the expression of the comparative idea in (507a) and the adjectival idea in (507b),

(507) a. [aβaana aβa niiγɔ βarɛɛŋaine]
children these function-word they-are-of-the-same-size
'these children are of the same size (or height)'

from /ko-rɛɛŋain-a/
[kɔrɛɛŋaina] 'to be of the same height'

b. [eciaraine] '9-they are flat'

from /ko-ar-an-a/ 'to be flat'
/ko-ar-a/ 'to spread out (v.t.)'

Though these ideas are expressed synthetically in the Gusii words, rather than analytically (as in the English phrases used to translate them), one might speak of adjectivally used verbs in cases such as these.

In contrast, the morphological derivation of at least some of the following verbs (508) seems to have operated in the opposite direction,

(508) a. /-rɛ/ 'thin'

==>	/ko-rɛ-a/ 15-thin-fv [kɔrɛa] 'to be thin'	==>	/ko-rɛ-i-a/ 15-thin-c-fv [kɔrɛia] 'to make thin'

compare

[kɔñɛrɛrɛa] 'to be slim/slender'
[kɔñɛrɛrɛia] 'to make slim/slender'
[ɔmɔñɛrɛrɛ] '1-slim/slender'
[ɛñɛrɛrɛ] '9-slim/slender'

b. /-ritɔ/ 'heavy'

==>	/ko-ritɔ-a/ 15-heavy-fv [koritɔa] 'to be heavy'	==>	/ko-ritɔ-i-a/ 15-heavy-c-fv [koritɔia] 'to make heavy'

c. /-γote-/ 'narrow'

==> |ko-γote-a| --> [koγotea] 'to be narrow'
==> |ko-γote-i-a| --> [koγoteia] 'to make narrow'

d. /-γare-/ 'wide'

==> |ko-γare-a| --> [koγarea] 'to be wide'
==> |ko-γare-i-a| --> [koγareia] 'to make wide'

e. /-nor-/ 'fat

verbal derivation ==> |konora| 'to be fat'
nominal derivation ==> |-noru| 'fat'
nominal derivation ==> [omonoru] 'fat person' (negative connotation)

f. /-nɛt-/ 'fat

verbal derivation ==> [kɔnɛta] 'to be fat'
verbal derivation ==> [kɔnɛtia] 'to make fat'
nominal derivation ==> |-nɛtu| 'fat'
nominal derivation ==> [ɔmɔnɛtu] 'fat person' (neutral or positive connotation)

g. /-taambe/ 'long, tall'

==> [γotaambea] 'to be long/tall'
==> [γotaambeia] 'to make long/tall'

Whether adjectives are used attributively or predicatively, they always agree morphosyntactically with the class of the noun they modify. The same agreement rules hold for their nominal usage. Whenever they are used as a noun, they enter the morphosyntactic class that is appropriate. It is here that the partly semantic origin of the Gusii morphosyntactic class system comes into play. For example, consider (509),

(509) a. attributive usage

[omosaaca omotaambe] 'the tall man'

b. predicative usage

[omosaaca niiγɔ are omotaambe] 'the man is tall'
[omosaaca niiγɔ areeŋge omotaambe] 'the man was tall'

The paradigm of a relative verb form used as an adjective is exemplified in (510),

(510) /-aNc-ir-e/
love-pv-fv
|-aañcire| '(is) beloved'

1 |βo-aañcire| --> [βwaañcire] 'who is beloved'
2 |βa-aañcire| --> [βaañcire] 'who are beloved'
3 |βo-aañcire| --> [βwaañcire] 'which is beloved'
4 |e-aañcire| --> [yaañcire] 'which are beloved'
5 |ri-aañcire| --> [riaañcire] etc.
6 |a-aañcire| --> [añcire]
7 |ke-aañcire| --> [γiaañcire]
8 |βi-aañcire| --> [βiaañcire]
9 |e-aañcire| --> [yaañcire]
10 |ci-aañcire| --> [c(y)aañcire]
11 |ro-aañcire| --> [rwaañcire]
12 |ka-aañcire| --> [γaañcire]
14 |βo-aañcire| --> [βwaañcire]
15 |ko-aañcire| --> [γwaañcire]
16 |a-aañcire| --> [añcire]
21 = 9 |e-aañcire| --> [yaañcire]
16 |a-aañcire| --> [añcire]

A final, apparently somewhat idiomatic expression is given in (511),

(511) |o-mo-iseke ña-ke-eni ke-ya|
a-1-girl 21-7-beauty 7-good
[omoiseke ñakieni kiya]
'a good-looking (pretty, beautiful) girl'
(literally, 'a girl with a good appearance': [ekieni], plural [eβieni], means 'beauty')

compare

[omoonto ore ekieni] 'a person who is good-looking'

contrast with

[akɔrɔrɛkana βuya] 'he is looking good'
[omoonto omuya] 'a good person' (in character or looks)

So much for adjectives.

3.4.5.3. Comparatives and superlatives.

Whiteley's brief observation on comparison (1956: 37) is to the point and may well be reiterated here. In English terms, if we take the adjective 'big', for example, it may be stated as follows. Rather than 'x is bigger than y', Gusii expresses the same meaning by saying 'x is big, to surpass y'. To do this, it uses the infinitive of the verb /-βu-/, viz. /ko-βu-a/ --> [koβua] 'to overcome, to surpass, to conquer (e.g. in a contest)', as in (512),

(512) |oyo na ɔmɔ-nɛnɛ koβua o-ri-a|
1/3-this is 1-big to-surpass 1/3-that
[oyo nɔɔmɔnɛnɛ koβua oria]
'1/3-this one is bigger than 1/3-that one'

|iñce na omotaambe koβua aβaana βaande βoonsi|
I am 1-big to-surpass 2-children 2-other 2-all
|iñce noomotaambe koβua aβaana βaande βoonsi|
'I am bigger than all the other children'

(after Whiteley 1956: 37)

This manner of expressing comparison is also found in other Bantu languages. For example, Swahili uses the infinitive kushinda 'to overcome'.

Superlatives may be expressed in several, related ways. One is simply to express a high degree of some quality or property. This may be done lexically, as in (513a), or by what may for the nonce be called 'expressive vowel lengthening', as in (513b),

(513) a. |iñce na omotaambe mɔnɔ|
I am 1-big very
[iñce noomotaambe mɔnɔ]
'I am very tall'

b. |iñce na omotaaambe|
I am 1-big
[iñce noomotaaambe][201]
'I am very very tall'

Either of these means may be combined with the expression for comparision exemplified in (512), as in (514),

(514) [iñce noomotaambe mɔnɔ koβua βaria]
I am tall very to-surpass those'
'I am the tallest'

[iñce noomotaaambe koβua βaria]
I am very-tall to-surpass those'
'I am the tallest'

Finally, when something or someone is compared with several entities, a complex expression such as (515) may be the result,

(515) [iñce noomotaambe koβua aβa na (i)nde noomotaambe nde mɔnɔ koβua βaria]
I am tall to-surpass them and I-am focus-tall I-am very to-surpass those'
'I am tall compared to them and I am even taller compared to those'

3.4.5.4. Some adjectives: 'alone, good, many, like, -self'.

The adjective (possibly quantifier, see section 3.2.12) meaning 'alone, only' exhibits allomorphy that may be accounted for by the following rule (516),

(516) allomorphy: 'alone, only, by itself/themselves' ==>

a. class 1 (i.e. 1-3s): /-e-ka/
b. elsewhere: /-o-ka/

(after Whiteley 1956: 88)

The prefixation of this adjective in its attibutive usage and some of its surface variation are exemplified in (517),

---

[201] Also compare, for example, [koγaaña] 'to wait and wait', as in 'I have waited and waited' with [koγaña] 'to wait'.

(517) 'alone, only, by itself/themselves'

1	/βo-eka/	-->	¦βueka¦	-->	[βweeka]
2	/βa-oka/	-->	¦βooka¦	-->	[βooka]
3	/βo-oka/	-->	¦βuoka¦	-->	[βwooka]
4	/e-oka/	-->	¦ioka¦	-->	[yooka]
5	/ri-oka/	-->	¦rioka¦	-->	[riooka], [ryooka]
6	/a-oka/	-->	¦ooka¦	-->	[ooka]
7	/ke-oka/	-->	¦kioka¦	-->	[γyooka]
8	/βi-oka/	-->	¦βioka¦	-->	[βioka], [βiooka]
9	/e-oka/	-->	¦ioka¦	-->	[yooka]
10	/ci-oka/	-->	¦cioka¦	-->	[cyooka], [ciooka]
11	/ro-oka/	-->	¦ruoka¦	-->	[ruoka], [ruooka], [rwooka]
12	/ka-oka/	-->	¦kooka¦	-->	[γooka]
14	/βo-oka/	-->	¦βuoka¦	-->	[βwooka]
15	/ko-oka/	-->	¦kuoka¦	-->	[γwooka]
16	/a-oka/	-->	¦ooka¦	-->	[ooka]
21	= 9 or 16[202]				

Forms of the adjective meaning 'good' (compare Whiteley 1956: 8) are exemplified in (518) for the various morphosyntactic classes,

(518) 1	/omo-ya/	-->	[omuya]
2	/aβa-ya/	-->	[aβaya]
3	/omo-ya/	-->	[omuya]
4	/eme-ya/	-->	[emiya]
5	/rii-γi-ya/	-->	[riiγiya]
6	/ama-ya/	-->	[amaya]
7	/eke-ya/	-->	[ekiya]
8	/eβi-ya/	-->	[eβiya]
9a	/e-n-γi-ya/	-->	[eηgiya]
10a	/ci-n-γi-ya/	-->	[ciiηgiya]
11	/oro-ya/	-->	[oruya]
12	/aka-ya/	-->	[akaya]
14	/oβo-ya/	-->	[oβuya]
15	/oko-ya/	-->	[okuya]
16	/a-γi-ya/	-->	[aγiya]
21	= 9a or 16		

Its underlying representation may be postulated as /-ya/. The upper mid vowels of the relevant prefixes 1, 3, 4, 7, 11, 14, and 15 are raised exceptionally before its stem-initial front glide, presumably by Upper Mid Vowel Raising. Even if /-ia/ were postulated underlyingly, which would result in ¦-ya¦ through Glide Formation, this application of Upper Mid Vowel Raising would still be exceptional, since it does not regularly apply

---

202 2, 6, 12, and 16 undergo /a/-Delinking and compensatory spreading of the next vowel.

before high vowels (*e+i > ii, *o+u > uu). Hence this item must be marked [+(UMVR)] in the lexicon.

A second point relating to possible allomorphy of prefix 5 involves the adjective /-ya/ 'good'. In combination with prefix 5, it surfaces as [riiγiya] '5-good', as contrasted with, for example, [umuya] '1-good'. However, this allomorpy is treated as being connected with the stem, rather than with the prefix. My main reason for this is that this particular adjectival stem exhibits exceptional morphological behaviour also in connection with other prefixes. However, once given the allomorphic consonant-initial stem /-γi-ya/, correct prefixation follows automatically.

Next, the paradigm of the adjective /-Nγe/ 'many' is partial, as it may not always combine with a singular, as in (519),

(519)	1	
	2	[aβaaŋge]
	3	[omooŋge], e.g. [omooño omooŋge] 'much salt'
	4	[emeeŋge]
	5	
	6	[amaaŋge]
	7	
	8	[eβiiŋge]
	9a	[eñiiŋge], [e.g. ecuumbi eñiiŋge] 'much salt'
	10a	¦ci-n-ii-Nγe¦ --> [ciñiiŋge][203]
	11	
	12	[akaaŋge], e.g. [aγaanto akaaŋge] 'much of a small thing'
	14	[oβooŋge][204]
	15	
	16	
	21	

Another stem, /-Nγe/ 'be like' (compare Whiteley 1956: 88), takes the pronominal prefix, and may be worked out as in (520),

[203] [ciŋiiŋge] was produced by Lilian, but disconfirmed by Judith.

[204] As in [oβomwaana oβooŋge] 'a lot of childishness'.

(520) 'like'

animate class

singular

1	/n-Nγe/	-->	[iηge]
2	/o-Nγe/	-->	[oηge]
3	/a-Nγe/	-->	[aηge] (= class 1)

plural

1	/to-Nγe/	-->	[tooηge]
2	/mo-Nγe/	-->	[mooηge]
3	/βa-Nγe/	-->	[βaaηge] (= class 2)

other classes

3	/o-Nγe/	-->	[oηge]
4	/e-Nγe/	-->	[eηge]
5	/ri-Nγe/	-->	[riiηge]
6	/a-Nγe/	-->	[aηge]
7	/ke-Nγe/	-->	[keeηge]
8	/βi-Nγe/	-->	[βiiηge]
9	/e-Nγe/	-->	[eηge]
10	/ci-Nγe/	-->	[ciiηge]
11	/ro-Nγe/	-->	[rooηge]
12	/ka-Nγe/	-->	[kaaηge]
14	/βo-Nγe/	-->	[βooηge]
15	/ko-Nγe/	-->	[kooηge]
16	/a-Nγe/	-->	[aηge]
21	= 9 or 16		

Compare the examples in (521),

(521) [iñce niiγɔ iηge maama] 'I am like my mother'
[ayε niiγɔ aηge oria] '2s-you are like that one'
[oyo niiγɔ aηge iñce] 'he/this one is like me'
[intwe niiγɔ tooηge εrε] 'we are like him'
[inwe niiγɔ ηge βaraβuɔ] '2p-you are like them'
[βaraβuɔ niiγɔ ηge intwe] 'they are like us'

The paradigm for the Gusii word for '-self' (compare Whiteley 1956: 88), finally, is given in (522),

(522) animate

1	[ɔmɔñɛnɛ] 'owner'
2	[aβañɛnɛ] 'owners'

other classes:

/V-rɔ/ 'the one'
/CV-rɔ-CV-i-ɔ/ 'the ones'

3	/o-rɔ/	-->	[ɔrɔ]
4	/e-rɔ/	-->	[ɛrɔ]
5	/ri-rɔ-ri-ɔ/	-->	[rirɔriɔ]
6	/a-r-ɔ/	-->	[arɔ]
7	/ke-rɔ-ke-ɔ/	-->	[kɛrɔkiɔ]
8	/βi-rɔ-βi-ɔ/	-->	[βirɔβiɔ]
9	/e-rɔ/	-->	[ɛrɔ]
10	/ci-rɔ-ci-ɔ/	-->	[cirɔciɔ]
11	/ro-rɔ-ro-ɔ/	-->	[rɔrɔrwɔ]
12	/ka-ra-ka-ɔ/	-->	[karakwɔ]
14	/βo-rɔ-βo-ɔ/	-->	[βɔrɔβwɔ]
15	/ko-rɔ-ko-ɔ/	-->	[kɔrɔkwɔ]
16	/a-rɔrɔ/	-->	[arɔrɔ]
21	= 9 or 16		

3.4.6. Derivation of verbs.

Verbs are regularly derived through affixation. Infinitives are derived by prefixing 15 /ko-/ (hence also called the infinitive marker) and suffixing /-a/ to the root. Tenses and other morphological details of verbal morphology have been discussed at some length in section 3.3.

Obviously, some verbs are morphologically and semantically related to nouns or words belonging to other lexical categories. Some examples were given in section 3.4.4. It has been argued, however, that in the Gusii morphosyntactic class system most, but not all, related words belonging to different lexical categories may arguably and advantageously be viewed as derived from the same root through primary affixation, rather than secondarily from each other.

There are a few exceptions to this strong general tendency, as in the case of some nouns that contain typically verbal extension suffixes and that are obviously related to some verb also in other respects. To the best of my knowledge, however, no verbs appear to exist that may be argued to derive from nouns in a one-way fashion. But some verbs are derived from roots that seem to have adjectival meaning. These might be viewed, therefore, as deadjectival verbs, both from a morphological and a semantic point of view. Some examples are given in (523),

(523) /-ritɔ/ 'heavy', [koritɔa] 'to be/become heavy'
/-nɛnɛ/ 'big', [kɔnɛnɛa] 'to be/become big'
/-kɛ/ 'small', [γɔkɛa] 'to be/become small'

These roots may also be used nominally. There are other, similar verbs.

However, the propriety of the adjective as a universal category has been debated. Moreover, in many Bantu languages there are relatively few adjectives, and many 'adjectives' are deverbal in the sense that a relative verb form is used to perform the adjectival function. So, by and large, also in Gusii. A number of verbs derive from arguably 'typical' adjectival roots, at least semantically considered. This point is not further pursued here.

3.4.7. Derivation of adverbs.

As pointed out in section 3.1.5, adverbs typically have no augment. Depending on what interpretation is ultimately adopted, this may be viewed either as zero-augmentation or as augment-deletion. In addition to this, it should be noted that some adverbs do not take a prefix either. Therefore, though Whiteley provides interesting examples, his generalisation that "adverbs have neither suffixes nor prefixes, [but] are invariable' is insufficient (1956: 43-44).

To consider the latter first, adverbs that take neither augment nor prefix may be accounted for by assuming that they are immediately derived from an underlying representation through zero-prefixation, as in (524),

(524) input: /-ηɔra/ 'slow'

derivation:

==> |0-ηɔra| (zero-derivation)
--> [ηɔra] 'slowly'

Alternatively, they may be entered in the lexicon as invariant items, as in (525),

(525) input: /ηɔra/ 'slowly'

--> [ηɔra] 'slowly'

However, in this particular case, the occurrence of (526),

(526) input	/o-mo-ηɔra/
	a-1-slow
Pre-nasal Vowel Insertion	omoVηɔra
other rules	[ɔmɔɔηɔra] 'slow person'

suggests that /-ηɔra/ may be postulated underlyingly, rather than /ηɔra/ (similarly, plural [aβaaŋɔra] 'slow person', and [ɔβɔɔŋɔra] 'slowness')[205]. The following adverbs are also invariant or zero-prefixed,

(527) a. /rɛɛrɔ/ --> [rɛɛrɔ] 'today, recently'

b. /-ñuma/ ==> |0-ñuma| --> [ñuma] 'back'

e.g. /ko-cia 0-ñuma/ --> [γocia ñuma] 'backwards, toward the back' (literally, 'going back')

also used prepositionally in the phrase:

/0-ñuma e-a/, [ñuma ya] 'at the back of'

e.g. |ñuma ya eñoomba|
[ñuma yeeñoomba]
'at the back of/behind the house'

c. /iγɔrɔ/ --> [iγɔrɔ] 'yesterday'

d. /iγoro/ --> [iγoro] 'up'

e. /na ɔñɛ/
and if
[nɔɔñɛ]
'even'

f. /ŋarɛ/ 'far away'

e.g. /rii-γena ŋarɛ ri-re/
5-egg far 5-be
'the egg is far away'

compare /n ŋarɛ/ --> [ŋŋarɛ] 'it is far'

The underlying representations of some of these adverbs require further checking.

Second, at least two accounts are possible of adverbs that take no augment, but only a prefix. One approach would be to argue that such adverbs are derived immediately from an underlying representation through prefixation only, i.e. without augmentation. This is analogous to the account already argued in other cases, and in this view their derivation

[205] Forms such as these may be adduced as evidence for pre-velar nasal vowel lengthening. There are not many such words, but most of those that occur do exhibit this process. On the other hand, [omoonto ore ŋɔra] 'a slow person' (literally, 'a person who is slow') was judged more acceptable by Lilian Nyanchama, and the phrase [kɔβa ŋɔra] 'to be slow' also occurs.

would be primary only. Another approach is to consider them as derived from other lexical categories by augment-deletion. In this view, they would be cases of secondary derivation. Both views are theoretically possible, and no compelling evidence seems to be available in favour of either one.

Perhaps one argument in favour of secondary derivation is that this approach accounts for the actual shape of the prefix of such adverbs. For example, (528b) is clearly derived from (528a), while (528d) clearly combines (528b) and (528c).

(528) a. /o-mo-γaso/ --> [omoγaso] 'sunshine'
b. /mo-γaso/ --> [moγaso] 'day-time' (literally, 'at the time of sunshine')
c. /γati/ --> [γati] 'in the middle'
d. /mo-γaso γati/ --> [moγaso γati] 'at noon'
(literally, 'in the middle of the sunshine')

The fact that we have [moγaso] in (528b, d), rather than, say, the equally possible, but unacceptable *[βoγaso], seems to argue in favour of deriving this form specifically from (528a).

There is in fact quite a variety of prefixes involved in the formation of adverbs and each of these may bear a number of meanings. If we assume a strictly primary derivation of adverbs, these facts remain unexplained, but if we allow for secondary derivation, they may be readily accounted for. So, pending possibly different results of future research that might necessitate another view, the latter is the approach provisionally taken here with respect to adverbs.

Some more examples of adverbial derivation, presented somewhat informally, are given in (529),

(529) a. /o-mo-tue/ --> [omotwe] 'head'

augment-deletion ==> [motwe] 'ahead'

e.g. |ko-ci-a mo-twe| --> [γocia motwe] 'ahead, to the front' (literally, 'going ahead')

b. /-rɔɔβ-/ 'set (of the sun)'

==> /ko-γɔrɔɔβ-a/ --> [kɔγɔrɔɔβa] 'to set'

e.g. /rii-rɛ ri-a-ko-γɔrɔɔβ-ir-e/
5-sun 5-t-15-set-pv-fv
[riirɛ riaγɔrɔɔβire]
'the sun is setting'[206]

deverbal noun derivation:

==> /mo-γɔrɔɔβ-a/
3-set-fv
[mɔγɔrɔɔβa]
'in the evening'
([ɔmɔγɔrɔɔβa] 'evening, plural [ɛmɛγɔrɔɔβa])

denominal adverb derivation:

augment-deletion ==> [mɔγɔrɔɔβa] 'in the evening'
(literally, 'at (the time of) sunset')
plural [ɛmɛγɔrɔɔβa]

c. /e-n-se/
9a-ground
[ense]
'ground, earth'

augment-deletion ==> |nse|
pre-nasal /i/-insertion --> [inse] 'down'

[206] [riirɛ], used for 'sun' when setting, may also mean 'cloud', in which case the plural is [amarɛ]. Compare [riisase] 'sun', used when it is shining. Also compare [omoγaso orimire] 'the sun is off' (i.e. beclouded), [korima] 'to be off or gone'.

d. /-anγo/ --> |-aanγo| 'quick'

==> |oβo-aaηgo| --> [oβwaaηgo] 'quickness'

augment-deletion ==> |βo-aaηgo|
--> [βwaaηgo] 'quickly'

(literally, 'in the manner of quickness')

e.g. |iγɔ a-ko-γɛɛnd-a βo-aaηgo|
so 3s-t-walk-fv 14-quick
[iγaakɔγɛɛnda βwaaηgo]
'he walks quickly'

e. /-ya/ [+(UMVR)] 'good'

prefixation ==> /o-βo-ya/
UMVR --> |oβuya| 'goodness'
Augment Deletion ==> [βuya] 'well'

similarly:

f. /ko-βis-a/ --> [koβisa] 'to hide'
/o-βo-βis-i/ --> [oβoβisi] 'secret'
/βo-βis-i/ --> [βoβisi] 'secretly'

g. /e-ke-γima/ --> [ekeγima] 'whole thing'
/ke-γima/ --> [keγima] 'wholly, fully'
/ke-n-γima/ --> [keηgima] 'immediately, instantly'
(compare /e-n-γima/ --> [eηgima] 'a whole')

h. /o-βo-tanβ-e/ --> [oβotaambe] 'length'
==> |βo-taambe| --> [βotaambe] 'usually, always'
(compare /ko-tanβ-a/ --> [γotaamba] 'to be long'

i. /ka-rɛ/ --> [karɛ] 'remote (i.e. in time), long ago'

j. /a-rɛ/ --> [arɛ] 'far ahead' (i.e. remote in future time); this may also mean 'remote place', i.e. far from the speaker)

The adverbs in (530) are clearly verb-related,

(530) a. /ma-sooγoot-a/ --> [masooγoota] '(while lying) supinely'

compare /ko-sooγoot-a/ --> [γosooγoota] 'to lie supine, to lie on one's back (face up)'

b. [maraamama] '(while lying) on one's belly (face down)'

compare /ko-raamam-a/ --> [koraamama] 'to lie on one's belly, or with one's face down'

Several adverbs are formed by means of prefix 16 /a-/ or the word for place, [ase], as in,

(531) a. /a-ηe na/
16-near with
[aηe na]
'near'

[aηe] 'nearby'

e.g. /rii-γena a-ηe ri-re/
5-egg 16-near 5-be
[riiγena aηe rire]
'the egg is nearby'

used prepositionally in |a-ηe na e-ñoomba| --> [aηe neeñoomba]
'near the house'

b. /a-nre/
16-other
[ande]
'nowhere' ?maybe (literally, '16-other, another place')

[γose] 'what do you think' (asks for someone's suggestion or reaction)

c. /a-nre a-ɔ-nsi/
16-other 16-alone
[ande ɔnsi] or [aandɔɔnsi]
'anywhere' (literally, 'any place whatever')

d. /a-mɔ/ --> [amɔ] 'together', '16-one (place)'
/a-mɔ na/ --> [amɔ na] 'together with', 'including'
(literally, '16-one (place) with')

[γaca eβitaaβu eβi amɔ na ecikaraamu]
keep 8-books 8-these together with 10-pens
'keep these books together with the pens'

e. /ri-mɔ/ 'once'
/o-yo-a-mɔ a-se o-yo-a-mɔ/
--> [ɔyɔɔmɔ ase ɔyɔɔmɔ]
or [ɔyɔɔmaasɔɔyɔɔmɔ]
'1-one by 1-one', or '3-one by 3-one'

f. /e-ke-mɔ a-se e-ke-mɔ/
--> [ɛkɛmɔ ase ɛkɛmɔ]
or [ɛkɛmaasɛɛkɛmɔ]
'7-one by 7-one'

Adverbs involving [ase] are also briefly discussed by Whiteley (1956: 38).

A specific type of place adverb is derived from the form for class 16 of the semi-proximate demonstrative, referring to an object that is remote from both speaker and hearer, discussed in section 3.2.5.3. Consider (532),

(532) /n-a-a-renγe a-ri-a/
f-he-t-be 16-that-over-there
[naareeηge aria]
'he was (in that particular place) over there'

/n-a-a-renγe a-ro-rɔ/
f-he-t-be 16-that-there
[naareeηge arɔrɔ]
'he was (in that place) there'

|ko-γɛɛnd-a to-re-ɔ|
15-go-fv we-be-there
[kɔγɛɛnda toreɔ]
'we are going there' (i.e. any particular place)

/na-a-Vc-ir-e aiγa/
I-t-come-pv-fv here
[naacire aiγa] or [naaciraiγa]
'I have come here'

/oor-a aγuo/ or /a-yo-o/
thresh-fv there
[oora aγuo] or [ayuo]
'thresh there' (particular place near the addressee)

[koora], or [kwoora] means 'to thresh by rolling' (especially as applied to millet)

*/oor-a-ɔ/
thresh-there
[ooraɔ]
'thresh there' (the place referred to is not visible)

/tiɣ-a a-or-e a-rɔ-rɔ/
leave-fv he-thresh-fv 16-that
[tiɣa oore arɔrɔ]
'let him thresh (in that place) there'

/tiɣ-a a-oor-e-ɔ/
leave-fv he-thresh-fv 16-that
[tiɣa aooreɔ]
'let him thresh (in that wisible place) there'

Three observations may be made. One, [naareeŋgeɔ] was given as an acceptable alternative for [naareeŋge arɔrɔ]. It was explained by at least one informant as an abbreviation of the latter. Though possible, an alternative, more plausible account for this variation might be to say that there are two distinct ways of referring to place in Gusii: one expressed through a separate adverb, viz. [arɔrɔ], the other by encoding postclitic /-ɔ/ onto the verb.

Two, an alternative given by at least one informant for [naacire aiɣa] was [naaciraa], presumably from /naacire a-a/.

Three, Mid Vowel Height Spreading does not seem to apply in [toreɔ], because the trigger of this rule is lower mid root-vowel: as the lower mid back vowel in this expression is a suffix, the structural description of the rule is not met.

Third, some examples of the distinct semantic types of adverb differentiated in section 3.1.5 may now be given. Some adverbs of time, which may refer to a specific point or period of time, are (533),

(533) adverbs of time

[ßoira] 'always' ('all day' in Whiteley 1960: 22)
[ßokaira] 'all day' (compare [koira] 'to become dark (in the evening)'
[ßotaambe] 'always' (from Whiteley 1960: 23)
[ßotuko] 'during the night' (from Whiteley 1960: 27)
[ßɔɔnɔ] 'now' (from Whiteley 1960: 39)

Adverbs of place or direction usually take the form of a non-augmented noun, and often function as a verbal complement. Some are given or repeated in (534),

(534) [ñoomba] 'in/into the house' (from Whiteley 1960: 20)
[moɣoondo] 'to the shamba' (from Whiteley 1960: 21, 25)
[inse] 'down, downward (i.e. to the ground), below' (from Whiteley 1960: 23)
[maate] 'downwards' (general indication of direction, not necessarily to the actual ground; e.g. downhill)
[ɣesuumu] 'Kisumu (town), in Kisumu, to Kisumu'

Some adverbs of manner are (535),

(535) [βwaaŋgo] 'quickly' (from Whiteley 1960: 21)
[βuya] 'well' (from Whiteley 1960: 23)
[keγima] 'immediately' (from Whiteley 1960: 63)

Perhaps [βoori] 'really, actually' may be classed as an attitudinal or sentence adverb ([βɔɔiri] in Whiteley 1960: 23).

The adverb /βo-sa/ --> [βosa] has a wide range of meanings, viz. 'free, for nothing, empty, naked, for no (good) reason, without cause, useless, worthless'. In addition to this, syntactically it may also be used as an adjective, as in (536),

(536) ¦o-mo-nto o-r-e βo-sa¦
a-1-person rpx1-is 14-naked etc.
[omoonto ore βosa]
'a person who is naked etc.'

¦o-mo-nto βo-sa¦
a-1-person 14-naked
[omoonto βosa]
'a useless etc. person' (but *naked)

(compare [omoonto ore γesoβono] 'a person who is naked', or 'a naked person')

¦e-ke-nto βo-sa¦
a-7-person 14-naked
[eγeento βosa]
'a useless etc. thing'

Though /βo-/ also occurs in tensed verb forms as an allomorph for pronominal prefix 1 /o-/, in examples such as (533, 536) the shape of the prefix may be regularly interpreted as 14 /βo-/.[207]

---

[207] I have not been able to check fully the following apparently irregular usage,

/o-βo-yia/, [oβoyia] newness'
/e-ke-yia/, [ekeyia] newness'
/βo-yia/ 'anew, afresh'

but

/o-mo-nto o-cak-ir-e o-βo-yia/ -->
a-1-person 3s-start-pv-fv a-14-new
[omoonto ocakire oβoyia] 'the person has started afresh'

3.4.8. Derivation of adpositions.

Semantically, Gusii prepositions and postpositions perform the same kinds of function and express the same kinds of relation as they commonly perform and express in other languages. For example, they may express relations of space, spatial order, or motion. Some may be both prepositive and postpositive.

The word /a-se/ --> [ase] or [aase] 'place' may be used prepositionally in the (local or temporal) sense of 'at, in', but also 'from', 'for', 'among, before, in the presence of', 'by' (see also Whiteley 1956: 82-83), as in (537),

(537) /a-se ci-n-γaki ci-a/
16-place 10a-time 10-of
[ase ciηgaki cia]
'at the time of'

from [ciηgaki] 'times, seasons', as in

/a-se ci-n-γaki ci-a rii-γεsa n-βa-a-n-taar-er-et-e/
16-place 10a-time 10-of 5-harvest f-2-t-me-visit-ap-t-fv
[ase ciηgaki cia riiγεsa mbaantaarerete]
'at the time of the harvest they visited me'

e.g. /n-βa-a-n-taar-er-et-e ci-n-γaki ci-a rii-γεsa/
f-3p-t-me-visit-ap-t-fv 10a-time 10-of 5-harvest
[mbaantaarerete ciηgaki cia riiγεsa]
'they visited me during the harvest'

/a-se e-n-sεεm-ɔ/
16-place 9a-?-fv
[ase εnsεεmɔ] or [asεεnsεεmɔ]
'at/to the side of, next to, beside'

[ase Ekeγusii] 'in the Gusii language'

|ase omonoa βwa ekeγusii|
in 3-mouth 3-of 7-Gusii
[ase omonoa βweekeγusii]
'in the Gusii language'

[mbuya mɔnɔ ase endaaγera]
'thank you for the food'

and interrogatively,

[na ase ki γwaacera]
'for what reason did you come?'

Prepositional phrases may also be formed from a noun and associative /-a/, as in (538),

(538) a. /ci-n-γaki ci-a/
10a-time 10-of
[ciŋgaki cia]
'at the time of, during'
(compare the first sentence in (537) for example)

b. /βo-sio βo-a/
14-forehead 14-of
[βosio βwa]
'at the front of, in front of'

c. /o-ko-ri-o ko-a/
a-15-eat-fv 15-a
[okorio kwa]
'at/to the right of'

from /o-ko-ri-o/ 'the right, right'[208]

compare |ɔkɔβɔkɔ koa okorio| --> [ɔkɔβɔkɔ γwookorio] 'the right hand' (literally, the hand of the right')

[γocia okorio] 'to(wards) the right'

d. /o-ko-βεε/ 'left, the left hand' (may refer to position only, not to the physical)
==> /o-ko-βεε ko-a/
a-15-left hand 15-of
--> [ɔkɔβεε kwa]
'at/to9 the left of'

also: [γocia ɔkɔβεε] 'to(ward) the left'

Prepositional phrases may also be formed from an adverb plus associative /-a/, as in (539),

(539) [isiko y(a) eñoomba] 'outside the house'
[isiko y(a) eñoomba εnεnε] 'outside the big house'
[ime y(a) eñoomba] 'inside the house'
[ime y(a) eñoomba εnεnε] 'inside the big house'
[iγoro ya] 'on top of'

Postpositive usage is exemplified in (540),

---

[208] Since, traditionally, one eats with one's right hand in Gusii culture, this word may possibly be related to /ko-ri-a/ --> [koria] 'to eat'.

(540) [eñoomba isiko] or [ñoomba isiko] 'outside the house'
[eñoomba ime] or [ñoomba ime] 'inside the house'
[eñoomba iγoro] 'on top of the house'

Some prepositions are deverbal, as in (541),

(541) /ko-ci-a/ --> [γocia] 'to go to'

[γocia ñoomba] 'into the house'

[γooñcora γocia ekeγusii]
'to translate into Gusii'
(literally, |ko-oncor-a| --> [γooñcora] means to change' 'to turn' (e.g. one's head, a car)

Postlexical augment-deletion may also be used as a means of expressing prepositional meaning, as in (542),

(542) [kɔγεεnda βosooηgo] 'to go to Kisii town'
[kɔγεεnda γocia βosooηgo]
'to go towards Kisii town' (i.e. in the direction of, not necessarily all the way to, Kisii town)

|ime ya omo-cie βosooηgo|
inside of 3-town 14-Kisii
[ime yoomocie βosooηgo]
'in(side) the town of Kisii'

[kɔγεεnda βosooηgo ime]
'to go into Kisii town'

[ime ya βosooηgo] 'in Kisii town'
[γocia βosooηgo ime] 'into Kisii town'

[korwa βosooηgo] 'from Kisii town'

[riiγena ime] 'inside the egg'
[γocia riiγena ime] 'into the egg'
[korwa riiγena ime] 'from inside the egg'
[korwa ime ya riiγena ime] 'from inside of the inner egg'
[korwa ase riiγena] 'from the egg, out of the egg'

/ko-et-er-a/ --> [γoetera] 'to pass through'
15-pass-ap-fv
zero derivation ==> [γoetera] '(passing) through, via'

e.g. /n-βa-a-ci-et-e Mombasa ko-et-er-a nairobi/
[mbaaciete Mombasa γoetera Nairobi]
'they went to Mombasa through/via Nairobi'

Thus placenames, which are regularly non-augmented, are arguably used as adverbs.

3.4.9. Derivation of conjunctions.

The class of conjunctions is relatively small, and since their derivation does not involve any processes other than those previously discussed, a few examples may suffice. Some conjunctions appear to be unanalysable, such as (543),

(543) a. /iγɔ/, [iγɔ] 'therefore, thus, so' (also used as a grammatical function word)

e.g. [iγɔ ambooria εkεεrɔ iηgooca] 'he asked me, when I would come'

b. [βuna] 'like'

e.g. /o-a-ñoor-ir-u-e[209] βuna n-ce/
3s-t-be late-pv-p-fv like f-me
[oñoorirwe βuna iñce] or [...βunaañce]
'he is late like me'

c. /γose/ --> [γose] (a) 'or', (b) whether, if

e.g. [riiγena γose eγekaaβu][210]
'(either) the egg or the basket'

|n-tεεβi-e γose n-ko-Vc-a a-re|
om1s-tell-fv whether f-15-come-fv 3s-be
[ntεεβie γose ηgooca are]
'tell me, whether he will come'

---

209 Compare [mwaañoorirue] '2p-you ..'.

210 Compare Swahili **kikapu** 'basket'.

d. /na/ --> [na] 'and'[211]

e.g. [riiγena na eγekaaβu] or [riiγena neeγekaaβu]
'the egg and the basket'

e. /ko/ --> [ko] 'but'

f. /rakini/ --> [rakini] 'but' (from Swahili: lakini)

g. /ɔñɛ/ 'if, unless'

e.g. [ɔñɛ tooγooca, tɔɔkɔɔñɔɔra][212]
'if you will not come, you will not get me (soon)'
'unless you come', etc.

The following conjunctions (544) may presumably be considered as derived,

(544) a. /n-ri/
[indi]
'when?'[213]

e.g. [indi oγooca] 'when are you coming?'

---

[211] Altogether, four homomorphs of the shape /na/ have been differentiated in this chapter, viz.,

a. /na/ 'and' (conjunction)
b. /na/ 'with' (preposition)
c. /na/ 'be' (linking verb)
d. /na/ thematic focus element

Of these, (a-b) may plausibly be interpreted as reflects of Proto-Bantu /na/, and (c-d) as reflects of Proto-Bantu /ni/. It might be argued that in the context of focus plus sm1, it is this historical form that appears, thus /ni + n/. However, synchronically /na/ is well supported, though it is possible to postulate /nV-/ alternatively. In the case of (c-d), /na/ occurs before vowels, its allomorph /n/ before consonants. In a few tenses, /na/ may appear exceptionally as an alternative for /n/ before consonants, but it is just possible that in these cases we have to do with (a). This point must await further research.

[212] Presumably from /ti-o-V-ko-ñɔɔr-a/.

[213] Used in main-clause questions; compare Swahili **lini**

b. [γotatiγa] or [otatiγa]

e.g. [kera omoonto oraaγeire γotatiγa iñce]
'everybody has eaten, except I'

/ko-ta-tiγ-a/ --> [γotatiγa] 'except'
15-not-leave-fv
(literally, 'not to leave')
(from /ko-tiγ-a/ --> [γotiγa] 'to leave')

c. /ko-ik-a/ --> [γoika] 'to arrive at'
15-arrive-fv

zero derivation ==> [γoika] 'until'
(literally, 'to arrive')

Finally, a few complex or compound conjunctions are (545),

(545) /a-se/ --> [ase] 'for'
(its usage is similar to that of Swahili **kwa**)

/a-se iγɔ/ --> [ase iγɔ]
'therefore, thus, so, hence, for that reason'

/e-ηenco/ --> [eηeeñco] 'style'

==> [ase eηeeñco] 'because'
==> |a-se e-ηeeñco e-ye-o| --> [ase eηeeñco eyio]
'because of that'

3.5. Other lexical processes.

3.5.1. Compounding and phrasal lexicalisation.

A few examples of compounding or phrasal lexicalisation may be given here. Consider (546),

(546) a. /ko-kɔηɔɔnt-a/ --> [γɔkɔηɔɔnta] 'to knock (on)'

==> /e-ke-kɔηɔɔnt-a mo-te/
a-7-knock-fv 3-tree

--> [εγεkɔηɔɔnta mote] 'woodpecker' (literally, 'tree-knocker, (bird) that knocks on a tree'; orthographically, this phrase is usualy written as a single word)

b. /e-ke-tar-i ma-ŋana/
a-7-spread-fv 6-word
'someone (pejorative) spreading words'
--> [eγetari maŋana] 'slanderer, tale-bearer'

compare /ko-tar-i-a/ --> [γotaria] 'to spread'[214]

c. /o-mo-et-i n-cera/
a-1-pass-fv 9a-road
'someone who passes the road'
[omweeti ñcera]
'pedestrian, road-user, unfaithful woman'[215]

d. /mo-sanβ-a mo-a-yɛ/
1-burn-fv 1-of-3s
'one-who-burns her-home'
[mosaambamwaayɛ]
'first wife'[216]

e. /mo-sɛr-a i-βu/
1-scrape-fv 5-ashes
one-scraping the-ashes
[mɔsɛra iβu]
'lazy person'[217]

---

[214] Possibly, the root in these related words is /-tar-/ or /-tari-/. This was imperfectly checked.

[215] That a faithful woman is one who takes care of the home, is the thought that is understood. Perhaps there may be a suggestion of walking the road with intent. Traditionally, there was no Gusii equivalent for 'unfaithful husband', presumably because polygamy was customary. Of course, this does not mean that the language could not or cannot express this concept by other means; for example, through paraphrase.

[216] According to one explanation, given by an old man living in the neighbourhood of informant Shem Mogaka, this apparently lexicalised phrase originally referred to a first wife whose co-wife was paid for with the brideprice originally intended for her (the first wife's) daughter. The original reference may have been literal, if her burning her house was the actual custom, or it may have been merely symbolical. In any case, the import of the phrase was that her daughter was now unable to set up house for lack of a brideprice and thus to carry on the family-line of the mother. The word has generic meaning now and may designate any first wife.

[217] [riiβu] 'ash, ashes' refers to ashes already taken out of the fire. The import of this lexicalised phrase seems to be that someone who does not work outside, as everybody else normally does or is supposed to, will sit near the fireplace inside the hut and spend his time scraping the ashes, that is, doing nothing useful, or, in other words, lazing

f. /ke-mincor-i imi/
6-escape-fv morning-dew
someone-who-has-escaped the-morning-dew
[kemiñcoria imi]
'hard-working person'[218]

This is an area for further research.

3.5.2. Lexical take-over and adaptation.

The traditional terms used to designate the process discussed in this section, or the lexical items that it involves, are 'loan', 'borrowing', and 'to adopt'. However, none of these appear to be sufficiently adequate. Words thus 'borrowed' are never given back to the donor language. The term 'lexical take-over', or simply 'take-over', will therefore be used instead, because it is considered to express the process concerned more adequately. For whenever some word or phrase is transferred from one (the 'donor') language to another (the 'receptor' language), the word or phrase remains in the donor language.

An example of lexical take-over is provided by two lexical sets used in Gusii to refer to the days of the week. One of these is (547),

(547) [cuuma] 'Friday'
[cumamoosi] 'Saturday
[cumapiiri] 'Sunday'
[cumataato] 'Monday'
[cumainɛ] 'Tuesday'
[cumataanɔ] 'Wednesday'
[aramiisi] 'Thursday'

Originally, this set derives from Islamic usage and has been taken over from the Swahili names for the weekdays (548),

(548) Ijumaa 'Friday'
Jumamosi 'Saturday' (the first day after)
Jumapili 'Sunday' (the second day after)
Jumatatu 'Monday' (the third day after)
Jumanne 'Tuesday' (the fourth day after)
Jumatano 'Wednesday' (the fifth day after)
Alhamisi 'Thursday' (literally, 'day of preparation', i.e. for the holy day)

The corresponding Gusii set in (547) is structured the same way. Friday, being the Islamic holy day, provides the point of reference for the naming of the other days of the

about.

[218] The underlying idea is that the person referred to rises at dawn.

week.

The other set derives from Christian, particularly Seventh Day Adventist, usage, and is given in (549),

(549) [omokuβio] 'Sunday'
[tiici rimɔ] 'Monday' ('first day')
[tiici kaβere] 'Tuesday' ('second day')
[tiici γatato] 'Wednesday' ('third day')
[tiici kanε] 'Thursday' ('fourth day')
[tiici γataanɔ] 'Friday' ('fifth day')
[εñɔɔηgεεsa][219] or [esaβato][220] 'Saturday'

This set reflects the Seventh Day Adventist belief that the Christian day of rest is as in the Old Testament, on the seventh day of the week, rather than on the day on which Jesus Christ rose from the dead.

Lexical take-overs tend to be adapted phonologically and in terms of syllable-structure. Thus in /rii-saβu/ --> [riisaβu] 'reserve', for example, taken over from the English, with the same meaning[221], the following phonological adaptations have taken place. The word-initial English retroflexed liquid has become a flap, the short unrounded high central vowel of 're' has become a long high front vowel [ii], the English voiced alveolar [z] has become voiceless alveolar [s], the long schwa of 'er' has become a short central low vowel [a], and the final labio-dental voiced fricative [v] (written 've', though the final -e is silent) has become bilabial fricative [β]. Moreover, where the English word ends in a fricative, Gusii adds a word-final [u], so that the word now conforms to the regular derived syllabic CV-pattern of the language. This amounts to seven changes and the word-final addition.

These changes exemplify adaptation of lexical take-overs to the Gusii phonological and syllabic sub-systems. At first sight or hearing, at least to someone who is unfamilar with the language, the surface form [riisaβu] may not look or sound recognizably similar to its English source 'reserve'. But once its phonology and syllabification are sufficiently understood, the adaptations turn out to be quite regular.

---

[219] Possibly from [kɔγεεsa] 'to add', possibly related to Swahili **kuongeza** 'to add'. Another meaning is 'to stay awake all night, to hold a wake', possibly related to Swahili **kukesha** 'to pray all night'.

[220] From 'Sabbath'.

[221] It is sometimes supposed that the original meaning of this word, which stems from colonial times, necessarily had a pejorative meaning. Its primary sense, however, was an administrative one, viz. 'reserve, area reserved for native Kenyans'. Of course, some may well have used the word with pejorative connotations. Nowadays it tends to be used for any remote area away from town or 'civilisation'.

From this example, it may be noted that processes generally operative in adaptation are at least the following ones. One regular tendency is to replace sounds in the source-word by those Gusii sounds that correspond to them most closely. However, when some word has been adapted to the Gusii system only in part, the sounds of the source language are sometimes retained, at least for some time. Apparently this tends to happen especially, when a word is used frequently in some sub-section of society. An example is [paapa] 'Pope'.[222] In this respect, though Whiteley's early note of the occurrence of [p] was keen enough, his account of it as being "increasingly noticeable in the speech of the younger generation" (1960: 4) seems at once too vague and too restrictive.

Another regular tendency in adaptation is the insertion of sounds, usually in order to make the word conform to Gusii (especially derived) syllable patterns. In the case of [riisaβu], this is exemplified by word-final [u]. But in some words, which are well-adaptated in other respects, addition of such a final vowel may be omitted. For example, the English word catechism has become [ekaatikisim] (Catholic usage). Disregarding other changes, we may note that, though [i] has been inserted between s and m (see the next paragraph), no final vowel has been added here, nor have the two k's been changed into γ through Consonantal Voicing Dissimilation, which is nonetheless applicable to both. But [eγaatiγisimu] also occurs.

A second type of insertion, which is quite common, is Vowel Epenthesis. This may be defined as the insertion of a vowel between any two consecutive consonants. In the case of Gusii, this process involves at least sequences of two obstruents, a liquid and an obstruent, and, perhaps less frequently, sequences of an obstruent and a liquid, or a fricative and another consonant. However, the phrase '**any** two consonants' in this definition implies that in a more complex sequence such as 'str' (fricative-obstruent-liquid), a vowel will tend to be inserted both between the s and t, and between the t and r. Though I have not collected any such examples, I assume that they exist. Should they turn out to be impossible in principle, the definition just given may be adapted to 'two consonants only'.

Though Gusii has sequences of a nasal and a consonant underlyingly, these always end up as complex segments, viz. as prenasalised consonants, in the course of the derivation. It is only exceptionally, at the beginning of a word, that the nasal element of such complex segments may become syllabic. But in all cases the nasal is homorganic with the consonant with which it forms a complex segment. The language has no other types of consonant sequences underlyingly. Presumably for this reason, it tends to insert a vowel between any two successive consonants, whenever it adopts a word from another language that has such a sequence. The change from English **altar** to [aritaaria] (Catholic usage), where, besides other changes, an [i] is inserted between the [l] and [t] of the source word, is a case in point. Also note the addition of word-final [ia] here.

Whenever some adopted word contains a sequence of an obstruent and a liquid, in that order, or a fricative and an obstruent, Vowel Epenthesis may possibly apply slightly less frequently. An example of a retained sequence of an obstruent and a liquid may be found

---

[222] Though some said that [βaaβa] may also occur with this meaning, others denied this. The regular meaning of this word is 'mother'.

in [ekrismas] 'Christmas' (S.D.A. usage), where the [t] is elided, though it is not pronounced in English, either. Surface representations such as [ekirisimaasi] and [ekerisimaasi] also occur.

Retention of sequences of a fricative and another consonant seems to be even more common, as in [eβraasta] 'plaster', plural [ciβraasta], [estaambu] 'stamp', plural [cistaambu], and [isram] 'Islam'. Examples such as [βoru] or [βoru] 'blue', where [o] or [u] is inserted between [β] and [r], are also found. Again, however, more adapted forms of the words just mentioned also occur, such as [eβuraasta] and [isiraamu].

In view of examples such as the aforementioned, I conclude that lexical take-over to a lesser or greater degree, but quite regularly, involves adaptation of the words concerned. Supposedly, such adaptation tends to correlate both to time-depth and to sociolinguistic factors. There is much scope for comparative, historical, etymological, and sociolinguistic research on this aspect of the language. A few more examples are (550),

(550) [esiindaγooγi] or [esi(i)naγooγi] 'altar' (S.D.A. usage, from English: synagogue)
/e-nɔεεri/ --> [εnɔεεri] 'Christmas' (Catholic usage)
[βεεndεεnsia] 'penitence' (Cath. usage)
[εεβa] 'Eve' (possibly from the English, or more directly from Arabic **Hewa**)
[awa] 'Eve' (from Arabic Hawa)

Sometimes, however, foreign concepts have been introduced for which Gusii words or phrases have been come to be employed, by new application or amplification of the meaning, as in (551),

(551) a. /maria o-mo-ee-kunγ-i/
Mary a-1-rf-protect-fv
[maria omweekuuηgi] (Cath. usage)
'the Virgin Mary'

compare:

|ko-kuuηg-a| --> [γokuuηga] 'to protect'
|ko-ee-kuuηg-a|, [γoeekuuηga] 'to protect oneself', 'to be a virgin' (arguably from the extended sense of protecting one's virtue)

b. /o-ko-ee-it-i-a/
a-15-rf-beat-c-fv
causing to beat oneself
'penitence'

compare:

/ko-it-a/ --> [γoita] 'to beat, kil, hurt',
/ko-it-i-a/ --> [γoitia] 'to cause to beat, etc.'

c. /o-ko-anγam-a/

a-15-confess-fv
asking for forgiveness
'confession'
(compare Swahili kuangama)

More examples may be found in Whiteley (1956: 41-42).

Generally, then, the kinds of adaptation in lexical take-over discussed in this section regularly tend to effect at least three things. First, foreign segments tend to be adapted to the nature of the segments in the receptor language. Second, foreign syllable patterns tend to be adapted to the syllable structure and syllabification rules of the receptor language, e.g. English CC to Gusii CVC. Third, as the usage of some lexical take-over becomes more frequent and longstanding, morphological and phonological rules tend to apply increasingly to its segments.

To sum up, at least the following changes (552) frequently play a role in such adaptation in Gusii,

(552) a. segmental adaptation

[b] > [β]
[g] > [γ]
[k] > [γ]
[l] > [r]
[p] > [β]

b. syllabic adaptation

Vowel Epenthesis

$\emptyset$ --> [-cons] / [+cons] --- [+cons]

Final Vowel Addition

$\emptyset$ --> [-cons] / [+cons] ---]$_{word}$

c. morphological adaptation

morphosyntactic interpretation and assignment to morphosyntactic class

d. phonological adaptation: according to applicable rules

Finally, as some of the examples indicate, adaptation may, at least for some time, fail to apply. Or it may apply partially. This sometimes causes unusual segments and sequences to occur in lexical take-overs.

3.5.3. Idiomatic expressions.

Like other languages, Gusii also has its share of idiomatic expressions and lexical innovation. Some of these are interesting from the point of view of morphological derivation, others are interesting from a semantic point of view. However, only some examples have been collected. First, some adverbial phrases are given in (553),

(553) a. /rɛɛrɔ/ 'today, /iγa/ 'thus, like this'
[mɔγɔrɔɔβa] 'in the evening'

==> /rɛɛrɔ iγa/ --> [rɛɛrɔ iγa] 'recently (i.e. usually before today)'
==> [mɔγɔrɔɔβa rɛɛrɔ] 'tonight' (literally, 'at sunset today)

b. /a-ma-isɔ/ 'eyes', /-rɔr-/ 'see'

augment-deletion
or non-augmentation ==> [maisɔ] 'in eyes'

adverbial phrase derivation

==> |ma-isɔ ma-rɔr-ɛ|
6-eye 6-see-fv
[maisɔ marɔrɛ] 'openly'
(literally, 'in eyes that see')

c. /ko-riγ-er-er-i-a/
1-look-ap-ap-t-c-fv
[koriγereria] 'to face, to look'

[ense] 'ground'

adverbial phrase formation ==>

/ke-riγ-er-er-et-i-e n-se/
7-look-ap-ap-t-c-fv 9a-ground
[keriγereretie inse] or [keriγereretiinse]
'facing down' (literally, 'in the manner of something facing down')

compare [keriγereretie iγoro] 'facing up'

Second, some common general geographical expressions are given in (554),

(554) a. /mo-Vca/ --> [mooca] 'east'

(Possibly from /Vc-a/ 'come', it may refer to the direction where the sun comes up, but this etymology is uncertain)

b. /βo-sonγo/ --> [βosooŋgo] 'west'

(As explained elsewhere, this word also means 'Kisii town', and literally,' place of white people' (Swahili: mzungu))

c. /suγusu/ --> [suγusu] 'north'

d. [iriañi] 'south'

Third, possessive pronouns used independently may be used as expressions to designate the home or the home area of the speaker(s), when they are near or around the home, as in (555),

(555) /mo-a-nε/ --> [mwaanε] 'at (my) home'
/mo-a-o/ --> [mwaao] 'at (your-2s) home'
/mo-a-yε/ --> [mwaayε] 'at (his) home'

[miinto] 'our'
[miino] your
[mwaaβɔ] 'their'

With positional or directional meaning, the forms in (556) are used, when the speaker is far from home,

(556) a. singular

1	/βo-o-nε/ -->	[βwɔɔnε]	'(at) (my) home'
2	/βo-o-o/ -->	[βwoo]	'(at) (your) home'
3	/βo-o-yε/ -->	[βwɔɔyε]	'(at) (his/her) home'

b. plural

1	/βo-a-ito/ -->	[βwaito]	'(at) (our) home'
2	/βo-a-ino/ -->	[βwaino]	'(at) (your) home'
3	/βo-a-βɔ/ -->	[βwaaβɔ]	'(at) (their) home'

The plurals (556b), again with either positional or directional meaning, may also take the following alternative forms (557),

(557) 1p /a-se ito/ --> [seito] '(at) (our) home'
2p /a-se ino/ --> [seino] '(at) (your) home'
3p /a-se o-βɔ/ --> [sɔɔβɔ] '(at) (their) home'

These forms are accounted for by the deletion of word-initial /a/ of [ase], and in the case of 3p, by regularly applicable postlexical rules. These form are said by some to be more common in fact than the ones in (556). The forms in (557) may have become lexicalised.

The forms in (556), where the phrase [--- ŋgocia] 'I am going to ---' has been used as a test-frame, may be focussed, as in (558),

(558) a. singular

1 [mbwɔɔnɛ ŋgocia] 'I am going home'
2 [mbwoo ŋgocia] 'I am going to yours (i.e. to your place or home'
3 [mbwɔɔyɛ ŋgocia] 'I am going to his/her home'

b. plural

1 [(n)seito ŋgocia] 'I am going to our home'
(uncommonly, [mbwaito ...])
2 [(n)seino ŋgocia] 'I am going to your home'
(uncommonly, [mbwaino ...])
3 [(n)sɔɔβɔ ŋgocia] 'I am going to their home'
(uncommonly, [mbwaaβɔ ...])

Fourth, some monetary expressions that are probably no longer common among the younger generation were recorded by Whiteley (1956: 18), and are repeated in (559),

(559) /e-ɛɛra/ --> [ɛɛɛra] 'unit of two cents' (old coin, from German 'Heller' and Swahili 'hela', plural [cieera])
[ɛβɛɛsa], plural [ciβɛɛsa]
(a) '(unit of) two cents' (old coin; the expression may still be used by older generations)
(b) 'money' (generic; current usage)
[enturuuru] '(unit of) five cents' (former usage), plural [cinturuuru]
[ñaiŋasa] '(unit of) five cents' (Machoge dialect)
[etooŋgoro] '(unit of) ten cents' (probably from Luo)
[esomoni] '(unit of) five cents' (compare Swahili 'sumni' or 'sumuni')
[eroβia] (a) former usage: '(unit of) two shillings', plural [ciroβia] (from 'rupee');
(b) modern usage: a big amount of money
[enusu] '(unit of) one shilling', plural [cinusu] (former usage)
[enuusi] '(unit of) one shilling', plural [cinuusi] (modern usage)
[esiriiŋgi] 'shilling', plural [cisiriiŋgi] (current usage)
[riinooti ria esaanɔ] 'a (bank-)note of five, a fiver'[223]

Fifth, for fractions, at least the following words are used (560),

---

[223] Physical examples of some of the old coins and notes may be found in the National Museum of Kenya, Nairobi.

(560) [ekeŋese], plural [eβiŋese] 'half'[224]
[ɛkɛɛra], [eβiɛɛra] 'quarter'
[eβiɛɛra isato] 'three quarters'

Sixth, common expressions referring to points or periods of time during the day are given in (561),

(561) temporal expressions

[maambia] 'morning, at sunrise (i.e. very early in the morning)'
[maambia etuko] 'very early in the morning'
[ɛkɛrɔ βwaakiire] 'when 3-it has risen', i.e. '(at) dawn'[225]
[omoβaso okoβara] 'sunrise'
(literally, 'the sun is rising')
[omoβaso oβarete] 'the sun is rising'
[omoβaso oβarire] 'the sun has risen'
[ɛkɛrɔ omoβaso ore koβara] '(at) the time (when) the sun was rising' (usage of the young generation)
[ɛkɛrɔ kia maambia] 'morning hours'
[moβaso] 'afternoon' (literally, 'in the sun'); also 'after sunrise'
[moβaso γati] 'noon' (literally, 'in the sun between, in the midday sun')
[mɔγɔrɔɔβa] 'evening' (i.e. from about 15.00 till sunset)
[βotuko] '(at) night'

From a social or cultural point of view, reference to specific hours, half hours, etc., is a relatively recent phenomenon. In the old reckoning, six o'clock in the morning was, as it were, zero hour. Thus Whiteley correctly observes that "any hour can be calculated by subtracting 6 before 12 o'clock [at noon] and adding 6 after 12 o'clock" (1956: 19). Alternatively, one may add up 'one, 'two', 'three', etc., starting from 6 o'clock in the morning, in order to designate the hours during the daytime, or starting from 6 o'clock in the evening, in order to designate the hours in the evening. Thus, for example, English 'eleven o'clock' becomes 'five hours' (11 - 6 = **5**, or 6 + **5** = 11). Accordingly, to repeat Whiteley's examples, in current parlance the following expressions may be used for 'eleven o'clock',

(562) [ciinsa isaanɔ] (five hours)
[ciinsa isaanɔ maambia] 11 a.m. (five hours after sunrise)
[ciinsa isaanɔ βotuko] 11 p.m. (five hours after sundown)

Seventh, the old names of the months appear to be no longer current. In the 1950s, Whiteley did not record them either, but merely comments that "(...) the Gusii year

224 This word may be used figuratively and abusively for any short person, especially a hottentot or a midget, and must therefore be used cautiously.

225 This expression refers to [omoβaso] 'the sun' and refers to the time in the morning, during which it may or may not be up, but when there is light already.

started in our November (...) the English names are in common use" (1956: 19). It is not clear from this account whether the Gusii names had actually gone out of use by then. In any case, none of my (relatively young) informants knew them anymore, so that the trend of using the English names instead seems to have persisted. Thanks to some research by Lilian Nyanchama, it has been possible at least to record the names in (563),

(563) names of the month

English	Gusii
January	omonuηguno o βaarema
February	eγetamo
March	riwata
April	eβwaγi
May	amaumuunti
June	eηkoromoni
July	riete
August	?
September	tureti ya keβaki
October	?
November	eγesuunte γetaηgani ('first darkness')
December	eγesuunte γia kaβere ('second darkness')

The precise form of some of these is uncertain, however, and the precise meaning of most are not recorded here. Presumably, the meanings are connected with the natural, seasonal, or cultural cycle of life (associated with sowing, plowing, harvest, summer, winter, etc.). A literal translation of some has been added in parenthesis.

Eighth, the names for the week-days have already given in (547) and (549).

Finally, an interesting example of modern lexical development in the language comes from sports. Football is a popular game in many African countries, including Kenya. Some of the terms in (564)[226] are lexical take-overs, some are existing Gusii words whose meaning has been remotivated to suit the game,

[226] Kindly supplied by Webber Ombiro Orenge, an avowed football enthusiast, who was born in 1975 and comes from the Bosansa sub-location in Bobaasi.

(564) a game of soccer

[βeγi] 'back' (from the English word)
[γɔsɛra] 'to kick off' (literally 'to push away')
[eγetii], plural [eβitii], 'field' (generically; and specifically, 'football-field')
[eriiβari] 'referee' (taken over from English), plural [ciriiβari]
[reisimans] 'linesmen' (from the English word)
[esiriimbi] 'whistle', plural [cisiriimbi]
[koβuγia] 'to whistle'
[eγetaamba] 'flag'
[eγoori] 'goal', plural [ciγoori] (from the English)
[γotoma] 'to (give a) pass' (literally, 'to send')
[oβwaatire] 'hands' (literally, 'he has grasped it', i.e. the ball, with his hands)
[eraaβu] 'foul (play)'
[γɔtɛɛka] 'to put (the ball) in a certain spot (for a free kick or a penalty)'
[oγwaita βwaito] 'our advantage'
[maγoro kumi na naanɛ] 'free kick' (literally, 'legs eighteen', i.e. a free kick outside the penalty, or 18 metres, area; note that 'kumi' is Swahili)
[maγoro kumi] 'penalty' (literally, 'legs ten', i.e. a free kick ten metres from the goal; 'kumi' is Swahili)
[ɛγɛsɛrɛrɔ] 'the kick-off dot' (literally, the 'place to push away on', from /e-ke-sɛr-er-o/; [γɔsɛra] means 'to push away with the feet')
[cirisaaβu] 'reserves, reserve players' (from the English)
[eγoori yaañuure] 'it's a goal' (literally, 'the goal has drunk', from /e-a-ñu-ir-e/, perfective of [koñua] 'to drink')
[oγotuγuta] literally 'throw-away', used when the ball is kicked out, in order to gain time or to disrupt the game; compare the different use of this verb in [ntwaatuγuta] 'we have thrown away' (said when a penalty or some other opportunity is missed, or when the game is lost)
[ntwaasiria] 'we have lost'
[okoruta] 'throw-in'
[eseeγi] 'fight, scuffle', plural [ciseeγi]
[γoseeγa] 'to challenge'
[koγua] 'to win', [βaaβuire] 'they have won'
[koγuu] 'to lose', [βaaβuiru] 'they have lost'

[omopiira oiγoro oβweetu na Posta]
the-match 3-yesterday rm3-was-passed by Posta
'the match of yesterday was won by Posta'
(this passive construction probably derives from Swahili; Posta is one of the Kenyan League teams; [omopiira] also means 'ball' and is probably a take-over from Swahili **mpira**)
[omopiira ɔɛɛrire] 'the match has ended' (/ko-ɛr-a/ 'to finish')

3.6. Summary of rules.

A number of important rules presented and discussed in this chapter are enumerated in (565) for quick reference, regular affixation rules being largely left out,

(565) summary of rules

a. allomorphy

nominal prefix-augmentation (13)
nominal prefix 5 (26, 30, 33)
subject marker 1s (52)
non-relative subject marker 2s (53)
non-relative subject marker 3s (57)
prefix 4, 9 (69)
relative agent subject marker 2s (75)
relative patient subject marker 2s (79)
relative agent subject marker 3s (83)
relative patient subject marker 3s (88)
free morphological variation (optional) (101)
semi-proximate demonstrative (118)
independent pronoun (129)
interrogative pronoun (141, 142)
possessive personal pronominal stem (153)
/-V-Nsi/ (181)
passive voice marker (242)
focus marker (253)
identificatory element (453)

b. morphological rules

Tense /a/-Deletion (86)
Morpholexical /a/-Raising (117)
Morpholexical /i/-Deletion (MiD) (256)
Perfective /r/-Deletion (282)
/r/-Deletion (optional) (292)
Perfective Suffix Vowel Delinking (297)

c. morphological adaptation rules

Vowel Epenthesis (552)
Final Vowel Addition (552)

CHAPTER FOUR

GUSII ORTHOGRAPHY

4.0. Introduction.

This chapter does not contain an exhaustive discussion of Gusii orthography. It is added, in order to note certain problems and to make some suggestions towards solving these. Perhaps the spelling as a whole may be somewhat improved thereby.

4.1. Different types of representation.

Conversion table (25) in section 2.1.2 shows how linguistic representations of Gusii words employed in this study may be converted to their orthographical representations or spelling commonly used by Gusii people when they write their own language. For the sake of convenience, this table is repeated here in (1), with a few additional suggestions, in column 4, to be made in the present chapter,

(1) conversion table

1	2	3	4
international phonetic alphabet (I.P.A.)	traditional phonological and phonetic representation in this study	suggested orthographical representation	possible improvements
a. consonants and glides:			
/t/	/t/	<t>	
/k/	/k/	<k>	
/β/	/β/	<b>	
/γ/	/γ/	<g>	
/cç/	/c/	<ch>	<c>
/s/	/s/	<s>	
/ /	/r/	<r>	
/m/	/m/	<m>	
/n/	/n/	<n>	
/n/	/ñ/	<ny>	<ñ>
/η/	/η/	<ng'>	<n'>
[w]	[w]	<w>	
/y/	/y/	<y>	
b. vowels:			
/i/	/i/	<i>	
/e̲/	/e/	<e>	
/ɛ̲/	/ɛ/	<e>	<e̲>
/a/	/a/	<a>	
/ɔ̲/	/ɔ/	<o>	<o̲>
/o̲/	/o/	<o>	
/u/	/u/	<u>	

A few comments on these orthographical symbols and on the spelling of words will be added in the following sections.

4.2. The spelling of consonants and glides.

In the spelling that has become common in Gusiiland, presented in column 3 of figure (1), the consonants, including nasals and glides, have not posed any serious problems socially. Of course, it would be possible to write some of them differently from, and more economically than, the way in which they have been written so far. For example, <kɔgɛɛca> could be written instead of <kɔgɛɛcha> 'to hate, to cut, to fell', <komaña> instead of <komanya> 'to (get) to know', and <ɛgɛkɔn'u> or <ɛgɛkɔηu> instead of <ɛgɛkɔng'u> '7-difficult'.

In words that contain two or more occurrences of any of the composite letters <ny>, <ch>, and <ng'>, such simplification would be even more noticeable. Compare <eng'eencho> 'custom, habit' with <en'eenco>, for example, and bear in mind that that in this context the term 'symbol' may designate an entire letter or a diacritic (a diacritic is a mark that may be added to some letter, in order to distinguish it from otherwise identical letters). Now, because <en'eenco> has two symbols less than <eng'eencho>, some text containing thirty occurrences of this word would require sixty symbols less in writing. The spelling <eηeenco> has three symbols less than <eng'eencho>, so that the same text would require even ninety symbols less, and it would contain thirty symbols less than an orthography using the spelling <en'eenco>.

At first glance, this example may not seem to mean much. In fact, however, it represents a considerable gain in terms of time, space, effort, and money. For when we realise that it illustrates the possible simplification of the spelling of only a single word, it may become clear how great the gain would be in an entire orthography in which the spelling of all the words containing any of the three composite letters <ch>, <ny>, and <'ng> would be simplified in the way suggested here.

One reason for such spelling simplification would be brevity. The relevant underlying principle is plain. The fewer letters have to be written, the sooner one will finish writing. This makes writing easier and less of a strain. The most telling case in point may be <ng'>, since it has no less than three orthographic symbols for a single sound: n, g, and '.

Another reason lies in reduced costs. When fewer letters have to be printed, the cost of printing is reduced. This saves money. When thousands of words are printed, cost-reduction is likely to be substantial. Eventually, when books printed in Gusii become common, they may contain tens of thousands of words (one fully written A4 page contains about 300 words). In texts of such size the gain may be great. This will save much money.

The examples previously given in this section illustrate how phonetic symbols, such as the ones used in this study, may also be used as letters in the everyday spelling of words. Once people have become accustomed to writing words in some new spelling, this will be just as easy as the old or current spelling. In fact, when changes are improvements -after all, that is, or at least should be, the intention of any proposed change- a new spelling will tend to be more consistent, and hence easier to learn and write.

It might however be objected, as some have argued in fact, that a change in spelling would involve too many problems. If a proposed change does not simplify and improve matters, of course this objection would be valid. But if the change does simplify and improve, the objection disappears. It may be well to point out therefore that in a number respects the suggested improvements would not be problematic.

From a printing and publishing point of view, there would be few problems involved in the changes proposed, because, for one, very few publications in Gusii have actually appeared. The number of publications requiring adjustments would be few. Moreover, if available letter types would be adopted, the changes could easily be incorporated in new editions. New publications would present no problem at all, since available new letters may simply be used. No revised type-setting would be necessary. In these cases, the objection that a change of spelling would be insurmountable does not hold. Rather, an improved spelling would only bring advantages.

In this connection, computers present no problem either. The present study, which was written with the help of one, illustrates this point. Nor will typewriters present any problem, if the simplified letters are chosen carefully.

It is possible, and in some cases probable, that at least some persons who are used to the current spelling of Gusii consonants may have certain problems in adjusting to a new spelling. However, in most cases such problems are likely to be temporary. Practice usually makes perfect soon enough, especially when good instruction is offered.

For the younger generation, learning how to write its language for the first time, problems of adjustment would not exist. They would simply learn the new spelling straight off. Thus it would soon become customary, as well.

Meanwhile, those used to the (by then) old spelling could simply continue using that, should problems of adjustment prove to be insurmountable for them, after all. Thus the old and new spelling could co-exist for a while. The introduction of a new spelling could then proceed smoothly and silently, and its advantages could be implemented in due course. The new spelling would thus gain currency and come to be used with ease and accuracy, within one or two generations.

It may be observed that, because the symbol <η> is easy to write, and because it occurs in the special character set for Greek that is included in most computer software programmes nowadays, it would present no problem for either handwriting or computerwriting. However, it is not usually found on typewriters. Thus two solutions may be proposed. One is to use <η> in hand- and computerwriting, but <n'> in typewriting. Both letters would simplify the currently used <ng'>.

The other solution would be to use either <η> or <n'>, instead of <ng'>, throughout in hand-, type-, and computerwriting. To use <n'> seems preferable, for two reasons. First, since it closely resembles the currently used <ng'>, it is probably easier to learn than <η>. Second, it is easy to write by hand, on computer, and on typewriters, whereas <η> tends not to occur on typewriters.

It may be added, that in Gusii the orthographic use of the apostrophe (') in <n'> does not clash with its frequent use, in other languages, to indicate the genitive (e.g. "John's house") or to mark quotes (e.g. 'John', 'house'), for, first, genitival relations are expressed differently in Gusii, by expressions of the type 'x of y', and secondly, <n'> never occurs word-finally, so that sequences of <n''> or <n'"> would not occur. Thus conceivable uses of the apostrophe, other than this orthographic use in <n'>, present no case against it.

To conclude this section, the improved orthography of Gusii consonants suggested here, including nasals and glides, may be summed up in alphabetical order and exemplified, as in (2),

(2) spelling of consonants, nasals, and glides

proposed spelling	example	old spelling (if different)
<b>	<ko**b**ata> 'to press'[1]	
<g>	<**g**osika> 'to respect'	
<c>	<koeeba**ca**> 'to evade'	<koeeba**cha**>
<k>	<**k**obata> 'to press'	
<m>	<kore**ma**> 'to dig'	
<n>	<koga**na**> 'to tell (a story)'	
<ñ>	<koga**ña**> 'to wait'	<koga**nya**>
<n'>	<ko**n'**aata> 'to starve'	<ko**ng'**aata>
<r>	<ko**r**ema> 'to dig'	
<s>	<go**s**ika> 'to respect'	
<t>	<koba**ta**> 'to press'	
<w>	<koñ**wa**> 'to drink'	
<y>	<koi**ya**> 'to uproot, to pull up'	

4.3. The spelling of prenasals.

Prenasalised consonants, also called prenasals, constitute complex phonological units in the language, at least at the surface. In any case, they have to be written. The question asked here is, How?

The prenasals and postglided nasals involded here (discussed in sections 2.1.3, 2.3.2-4 and 2.3.11, respectively) are repeated in (3),

(3)	Bilabial	Alveolar	(Alveolo-) Palatal	Velar
Obstruent		[nt]		[ηk]
	[mb]	[nd]		[ηg]
Continuant		[ns]	[ñc]	
			[ndž]	
Nasal	[mm]	[nn]	[ññ]	[ηη]
Glide	[mw]	[nw]	[ñw]	[ηw]
	[my]	[ny]	[ñy]	[ηy]

---

[1] That is, 'to press with one's hand or finger'.

Given the simplified spelling of Gusii consonants proposed in section 4.2, most of the segments in (3) may be written simply by combining the symbols in (2). However, some simplifications may be proposed in addition.

First, though [ηk] could be written <ng'k> or <n'k>, it may be written more simply as <nk> by leaving out the apostrophe in these composite letters. It seems preferable to use <n'>. One reason is that both <n> and <'> are immediately available not only on typewriters, but also on computer, and are thus easier to type than <η>, which occurs as a special character in the set for Greek. Another reason is, <n'> is shorter than <ng'>.

Similarly, second, [ηg] is more simply written <ng>, than <ng'g> or even <n'g>, and third, [ηη] is more simply written <nn'>, than <ng'ng'>, <nng'>, or even <n'n'>.

Fourth, [ñc] may be written more simply <nc>, than <nyc> or even <ñc>, and fifth, [ññ] more simply <nñ>, than <nyny>, <nny>, or even <ññ>, by leaving out the tilde on top of the first item of each of these composite letters.

Sixth, the nasal parts of postglided nasals must be kept distinct. Thus <ñw>, <n'w>, <ñy>, and <n'y> must be proposed for the less common types. The remaining four may be written as in (3).

Finally, though [ndž] is largely a South Mugirango variant of [ñc], sometimes it also occurs in other dialects as a unique allomorph of the combination of focus element /n-/ with subject marker 4, 9 /e-/ or object marker 4, 9 /ye-/, whenever the marker is followed by a vowel. If the difference in pronunciation must be expressed in writing, the spelling might be <nj>. Contrasted with [ndž], <nj> saves two symbols, viz. <z> and the diacritic <ˇ> on top of it, and <j> replaces <d>.

The improved or supplemented orthography of prenasalised consonants and postglided nasals, as suggested here, is exemplified, in alphabetical order, in (4),

(4) a. prenasals

composite letter	example
<mb>	<mbaasoomete> 'they read (recently)'
<nc>	<ncaβe> or <incaβe> 'beat me'
<nd>	<ndooserie> 'make for me'
<ng>	<gotwaanga> 'to beat, to hit'
<nk>	<enkoro> 'heart'
<mm>	<mmoruga> 'even though/if 2p-you cook'[2]
	<mmomaña> 'I know him'[3]
<nn>	<nnaaruga> 'I cooked (earlier today)'
<nñ>	<nñoorere> 'get me'
<nn'>	<nn'aine> 'cheat me'
<ns>	<ense> 'earth'
<nt>	<komeenta> 'to add'

---

[2] Though [mmoruga] is acceptable, [namoruga], with this meaning, as in

[namoruga, tiinkoraagera]
'even if you cook, I will not eat'

was judged more acceptable by my informants. This form presumably derives from

/na-mo-rug-a/
f-you-cook-fv
sm2p

where morpheme /na-/ may possibly originate from the word /na/ 'and'. Alternatively, it may have been misheard, or it may have been a 'reduced' pronunciation for

/na n-mo-rug-a/
and f-you-cook-fv
sm2p
'and if/even if you cook'

[mmoruga] derives from

/n-mo-rug-a/
f-you-cook-fv
sm2p

[3] From /n-mo-mañ-a/
sm1s-om3s-know-fv

b. postglided nasals

composite letter	example
<mw>	<koremwa> 'to be dug'
<my>	<emyoomo> '4-dry (ones)'[4]
<nj>	<njaeta>[5] '4-they/9-it passed (recently or long ago)'
<nw>	<komiinwa> 'to be plaited'[6]
<ny>	?<komeenya> 'to cause to lick'[7]
<ñw>	<koñwa> 'to drink'
<ñy>	<komañya> 'to cause to know'[8]
<n'w>	no examples found
<n'y>	no examples found

The phonetic representation of some of these examples may be found in sections 2.1.3, 2.3.2-4, and 2.3.11.

Finally, note that the phonetic significance of <ny> in the spelling proposed here is [ny], and that this is different from its significance in the old, or current, spelling, where its phonetic significance is [ñ]. So much for prenasals.

4.4. The spelling of vowels.

4.4.0. Preliminaries.

The quality of vowels is due to the nature of the articulation and air-production necessary to produce them. These determine or at least co-determine their phonetic characteristics. Phonologically, their qualitative differences involve at least minimally necessary distinctive features.

The differences between functionally distinct vowel segments may be defined, exhaustively or distinctively, in terms of a plus or minus value in respect of these features. Exhaustive definition aims to include all the phonological features and their

---

[4] From /e-me-omo/
a-npx4-dry

[5] From /n-e-a-et-a/.

[6] From /ko-miin-u-a/
15-plait-p-fv

[7] Apparently, [kɔmɛɛnia] <komeenia> is more acceptable.

[8] From /ko-mañ-i-a/
15-know-c-fv

specifications, whereas distinctive definition includes those specified features that are necessary and sufficient to differentiate any segment from all other segments. At least functionally different segments are usually reflected in an orthography. Thus, from a phonological point of view, seven functional qualitative distinctions must be made among Gusii vowels, viz. /i, e, ɛ, a, ɔ, o, u/.

The spelling of these vowels presents a different case from that of the consonants, nasals, and glides. Specifically, it raises two questions. One concerns the way in which some of the qualitatively different vowels may or should be written, i.e. what actual letters may or should be used for them. The other question concerns vowel length and equally involves all the qualitatively distinct vowels. These questions, in this order, will be addressed briefly in the next two sections.

4.4.1. Vowel quality.

In the current spelling, five letters are used to write all the vowels, viz. <i, e, a, o, u>, as in column 3 of figure (1b). But there is a difficulty here. Gusii actually has seven different vowel sounds. This means that four out of the seven vowel sounds are not properly differentiated in the current orthography.

For example, we cannot know either the meaning or the pronunciation of the word <komera>, unless its context be given. In fact, it can have at least two different meanings and pronunciations. But its spelling does not tell us straight off, which of these we are confronted with.

In contrast, anyone who understands the significance of the kind of phonetic symbols used in most dictionaries nowadays can know immediately how the words are to be pronounced, if their phonetic representation is added to their spelling. The phonetic representation signifies their pronunciation. When the pronunciation of a word is clear, it is usually clear what meanings it may have. No further information is needed. This is so, regardless of which language is involved, whether English, French, Spanish, Arabic, or an Afican language.

The same is true of any orthography. If the significance of its letters is clear and consistent, and the words are written clearly and consistently, a reader may know immediately how to pronounce any word, and hence what it means, even when no further context is given. This is the great advantage of any clear-cut phonetic or orthographic writing system.

If, now, Gusii orthography would include sufficient letters for differentiating all its vowels, the two distinct words hidden in the spelling of the word cited a moment ago, viz. <komera>, may be distinguished, for example, by writing them <komera> and <kɔmɛra>. Even without any meaning or context, we may now know immediately how these words are to be pronounced from the way they are written, i.e. written differently, as long as we know the phonetic significance of the letters used in writing them. And thus, still without any context, we may know immediately what their meanings are, viz. <komera> 'to swallow' and <kɔmɛra> 'to come up (of seeds)'.

The trouble with a five-letter spelling is that such words cannot be written differently, even though they have both a different pronunciation and a different meaning. A major characteristic of a good spelling, however, is that it can express **all** the differences in sound and meaning that a language requires. In fact, if a spelling is to be immediately and unambiguously clear, it must be capable of this.

Since Gusii is a fine language in its own right, it is not really necessary to use another language, whether European or African, as a model for its spelling; the more so, when the other language is too different from it to be able to serve as such. On reflection, most Gusii people would probably realise that because theirs is a language that is alright in and of itself, it is only necessary to understand sufficiently how it is made up, in order to devise an orthography best suited to it without having to resort to another language as a spelling model.

It is important to realise that practically there are no problems at all with regard to the spelling of the Gusii vowels proposed here. It is easy to make all the distinctions that the language requires, provided that the diacritics chosen may be found on all, or at least on most, good typewriters and computer software programmes. Any spelling that can make such distinctions by using commonly available diacritics will be simple and therefore easy and cheap to use.

To take [ɔ] for example, some of the diacritics used in African languages to write this lower mid back vowel, are <ò, ö, ɔ, o, or o̲>. All of these (combinations of) symbols are included in the sets of regular and special characters incorporated in recent computer software programmes. All of them, except ɔ, occur on any good typewriter. And all of them are easy to write by hand. The question is: which letter would best serve the needs of Gusii?

In this connection, it may pointed out that diacritics on top of some letter have the drawback that they leave little room, if at all, for additional diacritics, such as tonal marks. Yet this is relevant for African languages. Many of these are tone languages, wholly or partly, so that space above vowel letters may be usefully reserved for marking tone in their spellings.

This point may be relevant for the spelling of Gusii too, since tone is distinctive at least in some of its tenses. Should future writers of the language wish to use the space above vowels for marking tone, any spelling allowing for this possibility would therefore have to bar its use for other purposes, such as marking vowel quality. Of the possible letters for [ɔ] just mentioned, this would rule out the use of <ò> and <ö> merely to mark the quality of the vowel.

For example, upper mid back vowel [o] may be written <o> or <ò>, if low-toned, and <ó>, if high-toned. Now if, instead, lower mid back vowel [ɔ], as such, would be written <ò>, the following questions may be raised. First, how should high- or low-toned [ɔ] be written, and second, how should the tones of upper mid back vowel <o> be written? The grave accent would not be available for marking low tone on [o], since <ò> would already designate [ɔ] as such, though <o> could designate low [o], low tone being left unmarked. Then <ó> could designate high toned [o]. However, with these possibilities already used, and <ò> designating [ɔ], how now to mark tone on this lower mid back vowel? The only option available to write low tone seems to be a double grave accent, but such separate accents are not available in computer software programmes or on typewriters, and are cumbersome to write by hand. And how to write high tone on the lower mid back vowel? The only options seem to be to write ˇ or ˆ on top of <o>, but normally these diacritics are used to mark rising and falling tone, respectively. But in that case, how to write rising and falling tone on this vowel? For that matter, how to write rising and falling tone on upper mid <o>?

Problems such as these suggest that any solution in which the space above the Gusii vowels is left free for tonal purposes may be advisable. It may be achieved in either of two ways. The vowels, particularly the upper and lower mid vowels, may be written by using different shapes altogether. Or they may be differentiated by means of diacritics which are not placed above the vowel letters, but elsewhere.

Since, of the possible candidates previously mentioned, <ò> and <ö> have just been argued against, and <o> is already reserved for [o], this leaves us with <ɔ> or <o̲>. Since, further, <ɔ> does not normally occur on typewriters, nor in all computer software (though it is included in the latest "Windows" programmes and bound to be included in most future softwares), and since <ɔ> would also constitute a greater departure from the current spelling than <o̲>, adopting the latter would seem to be the more advisable and practicable solution. Alternatively, this might be used in typewriter and computer typescript, while <ɔ> could be used in hand-writing.

The command 'control-F4 block F8' in the Word Perfect 5.1 programme underlines any item thus selected, a key for underling a letter is included on all good typewriters, and underlining is easy to do by hand. So if underlining be adopted as a means of differentiating the Gusii upper and lower mid vowels, and tone is provisonally left unmarked, only the two symbols in (5),

(5) Gusii lower mid vowels

front <e̲>
back <o̲>

need be added to the current spelling, in column 3 of (1b), in order to make it not only more adequate, but complete. All the necessary vowels of the language would thus be differentiated sufficiently in writing, as in (6),

(6)

	front		back
high	<i>		<u>
upper mid	<e>		<o>
lower mid	<e̲>		<o̲>
back		<a>	

This is also Whiteley's orthographical practice in (1956), though in (1960) he also uses ɛ and ɔ, taken from the International Phonetic Alphabet, to indicate the front and back lower mid vowels respectively, while reserving various diacritics for marking tone.

To conclude this section, if the spelling in (6) be adopted, anyone who wishes to mark tone, can easily do so, as shown for the Gusii mid vowels, in (7),

(7) orthography of low- and high-toned mid vowels

a. <e, é> <o, ó>

<e̲, é̲> <o̲, ó̲>

b. <o> low-toned upper mid back vowel

<ó> high-toned upper mid back vowel
(control-V ' o)

<o̲> low-toned lower mid back vowel
(o, control F4 block F8)

<ó̲> high-toned upper mid back vowel
(control-V ' o, control F4 block F8)

<e> upper mid front vowel

<é> high-toned upper mid front vowel
(control-V ' e)

<e̲> lower mid front vowel
(e, control F4 block F8)

<é̲> high-toned lower mid front vowel
(control-V ' e, control F4 block F8)

where under (7b) the relevant Word Perfect 5.1 commands have been added in parenthesis. Of course, low and high toned <i> and <í>, <u> and <ú>, <a> and <á> would also be part of this spelling, so that the full vowel spelling would be as in (8),

(8)

	front		mid		back	
	L	H	L	H	L	H
high	<i>	<í>			<u>	<ú>
upper mid	<e>	<é>			<o>	<ó>
lower mid	<e̱>	<é̱>			<o̱>	<ó̱>
back			<a>	<á>		

This is exemplified, partly, in (9),

(9) <korina> 'to refuse (a request)'
<koríína> 'to climb'

<goteba> 'to be barren'
<gotéébá> 'not to forget'

<go̱té̱má> 'to hit'
<go̱te̱e̱ma> 'to try'

<gosabia> 'to make pray'
<gosáábia> 'to assist in washing (someone's) hands'

where, however, pair members are contrasted not merely through tone, but also through vowel length, so that, strictly, they are not minimally contrastive in terms of tone. Though tone does differentiate some tenses, these appear to be few, and since the context generally seems to be sufficient to disambiguate these, it may be argued that tone need not be written at all. If so, the previously discarded <ö> and <ò> might prove viable alternatives to <o̱>, after all, but this would have to be examined more systematically.

At any rate, for those who wish to leave Gusii tone unmarked the spelling in (6) is sufficient.

4.4.2. Vowel length.

As to the other question mentioned in section 4.4.0, on vowel length and its representation in writing, it may be noted at once that there is no real problem here as far as the language itself is concerned. It has seven short vowels and seven corresponding long ones. These are distinctive. That is, words otherwise segmentally identical, but semantically distinct, may be distinguished from each other by vowel length alone. Many pairs of words are in fact so differentiated. There may be additional differences in tone between them, but a spelling leaving tone unmarked would not indicate this.

It is important, in such cases, that differences in vowel length be clearly marked. But for the sake of accuracy it is important to express such differences anyway, even when distinctive word pairs are not found. Vowel length can easily be indicated by writing double letters, as in (10),

(10)	front		back
high	<i>, <ii>		<u>, <uu>
upper mid	<e>, <ee>		<o>, <oo>
lower mid	<e̲>, <e̲e̲>		<o̲>, <o̲o̲>
low		<a>, <aa>	

In the following examples (11) these distinctions are relevant underlyingly as well as on the surface,

(11) <gosika> 'to respect'
<gosiika> 'to prepare beer'

<korema> 'to dig'
<koreema> 'to lack, to be without, not to have'

<go̲te̲ma> 'to hit'
<go̲te̲e̲ma> 'to try'

<kobasa> 'to elope (s-ref: girl)'
<koβaasa> 'to skin'

<go̲ko̲na> 'to bewitch'
<go̲ko̲o̲na> 'to show dislike to'

<kobora> 'to miss, not to find'
<koboora> 'to say'

<kobuca> 'to be plenty'
<kobuuca> 'to take (a large quantity of) water (from a well or river)'

There are also cases of derived vowel length. This is vowel length that appears merely on the surface, not underlyingly. There are several phonological rules that account for such lengthening. For example, Prenasalisation, Complex Segment Formation, and Glide Formation, all discussed in Chapter Two. Ultimately, it may be accounted for as compensatory, but here the question is whether or not such derived lengthening should be reflected in the spelling of the words concerned.

The answer is that it is possible, but not necessary, to write such automatically derived surface length. If the arguments of space, time, effort, and economy used for reducing certain consonant letters in section 4.2 may be applied here, they would argue against expressing such vowel length in writing. A phonological argument would be that, since the length of these vowels is not distinctive, but derived automatically, their length need not be indicated in writing.

Thus, for example, it may well be argued that the alternative spellings in (12), though possible, are not necessary,

(12) a. /ko-γɛNra/ --> [kɔγɛɛnda] 'to go'

possible sufficient spelling: <kogenda>
possible elaborate spelling: <kogeenda>

b. /ko-βuat-a/ --> [koβwaata] 'to grasp'

possible sufficient spelling: <kobwata>
possible elaborate spelling: <kobwaata>

Since the lengthening of [ɛ] and [a] in (12) is automatic, the resulting outputs are never distinctive. There are no semantic contrasts in the language between, for example, <kogenda> and <kogeenda> or <kobwata> and <kobwaata>. This provides a strong argument for saying that derived long vowels need not be written as long. And not writing them saves time, space, effort, and money.

From a different point of view, viz. consistency or simplicity of spelling based on the surface representations of words containing such automatically lengthened vowels, some might maintain that any vowel that is pronounced long must, after all, be written long. Strictly, however, this is unnecessary. But whichever of these two spellings is chosen, <kobwata> or <kobwaata>, etc, it is of paramount importance that the one adopted, once it is chosen, be applied consistently, not only because consistency is necessary in its own right, but also because this will promote standardisation and hence ease of writing.

This last point is socially all the more relevant, because distinctions in vowel length still cause spelling problems for many Gusii people. This may be due to inadequate instruction. But, whatever the cause, if such distinctions are adequately taught, consistent spelling of the vowels, including their length, is bound to become more common. It is hoped that this discussion may contribute toward such a result.

In teaching people how to write Gusii, teachers and literacy workers will have to be alert with respect to the kinds of problematic or potentially problematic aspects of the spelling discussed. Everyone engaged in this socially and educationally important work is therefore encouraged to promote the best possible Gusii orthography. This would not only represent the language to its best possible advantage, but, in turn, could well promote an interest in further education through the use of it, and thus a greater interest in the language itself.

The orthography of Gusii vowels, consonants, nasals, glides, prenasals, and postglided nasals discussed here may be summarised, in alphabetical order, as in (13),

(13) proposed Gusii orthography

vowels		consonants nasals glides	prenasals	postglided nasals
i, ii	b		mb	
e, ee	c		nc	
e̱, e̱e̱	g		ng	
a, aa	k		nk	
o̱, o̱o̱	m		mm	
o, oo	n		nn	
u, uu	ñ		nñ	
		n'	nn'	
		r	nd	
		s	ns	
		t	nt	
		w		mw, nw, ñw, (n'w),
		y		my, ny, ñy, nj, (n'y)

In contrast with the traditional or current spelling, it may be noted that <c> is proposed instead of <ch>, <ñ> instead of <ny>, and /n'/ instead of <ng'>, while <e̱>, <e̱e̱>, <o̱>, and <o̱o̱> have been added, for reasons discussed. Thus there are seven vowel letters, of which <e̱> and <o̱> consist of a letter and a diacritic; seven composite letters for long vowels; eleven letters for the consonants and nasals, of which <ñ> and <n'> are composite; two letters for glides; eleven composite letters for prenasals, such that all consonants may be prenasalised, and prenasalised <r> written as <d>; and nine composite letters for postglided nasals, which may be reduced to seven, should <n'w> and <n'y> turn out to be unnecessary, and if so, to six, if <nj> would be replaced by <nc>.

If prenasals may be interpreted as complex segments composed of a nasal and a consonantal element, and postglided nasals as complex segments composed of a nasal and a glide element, so that their combinations need not be listed separately, and if the distinction between short and long vowels may be left understood, then the orthography in (13) may reduced to the basic alphabet in (14),

(14) basic Gusii alphabet

a, b, c, d, e, e̱, g, i, j, k, m, n, ñ, n', o, o̱, r, s, t, u, w, y

It consists of twenty-two letters, but it must be borne in mind that any vowel may also be long. Making the long vowels explicit in the orthography, would give us the twenty-eight items in (15),

(15) Gusii alphabet (in full)

a, aa, b, c, d, e, ee, e̲, e̲e̲, g, i, j, ii, k, m, n, ñ, n', o, oo, o̲, o̲o̲, r, s, t, u, uu, w, y

It must be remembered however that in both summaries (14-15) all consonants, including nasals, may be prenasalised or postglided, with the possible exception of <n'w> and <n'y>. Furthermore, as pointed out in section 4.3, some complex segments may be written in a way other than by merely putting their constituent elements together. It was proposed, for example, to write <nñ> instead of <ññ>, and <nd> instead of <nr>. Making these orthographically explicit, would give us the alphabet of 47, or, without <n'w> and <n'y>, 45, simple and composite letters in (16),

(16) a, aa, b, mb, c, nc, nd, e, ee, e̲, e̲e̲, g, ng, i, ii, k, nk, m, mm, n, nn, ñ, nñ, n', nn', o, oo, o̲, o̲o̲, r, s, ns, t, nt, u, uu, w, mw, my, nj, nw, ny, ñw, y, ñy, (n'w, n'y).

So much for the Gusii alphabet and some suggested improvements on it.

4.5. The spelling of words.

4.5.1. Postlexical considerations.

It now remains to consider some aspects of the spelling of words considered as a whole. Some of the phonological and morphological rules discussed in this study make it clear that this is necessary at least for the following reasons.

First, the pronunciation of Gusii words may, and often does, vary according to the attention, the deliberation, and, often connected with these factors, the speed with which they are pronounced. Thus it is possible to distinguish roughly between the following styles or rates of speech,

(17) a. monitored: thoughtful and deliberate, hence usually fairly slow and distinct;

b. normal: less thoughtful and deliberate than (17a), but more so than (17c), hence usually pronounced at a normal rapid rate; that is, neither slow nor very rapid, and usually distinctly, but sometimes indistinctly;

c. unmonitored: pronounced without much thinking and deliberation, hence usually very rapidly and indistinctly.

These distinctions are relative. Thus, as a mean in between (17a) and (17c), normal style of speech might alternatively be called "less monitored" or "less unmonitored" speech. More importantly, these speech styles allow for the possibility of a certain amount of variation across languages and idiolects. Yet, their conception allows for their basic distinction to be maintained, even though their realisation may turn out to be somewhat variable comparatively.

Second, even at a normal rate of utterance, Gusii words tend to be linked together in concatenated speech. This process also occurs in other languages -French, for example, where it is called liaison. It is a process whereby initial and final vowels are frequently and commonly dropped, whereby words are linked together. Whenever the pronunciation of words varies in ways such as these in some language, a major question is how they should be spelled.

To get a more specific idea of what is meant here, consider the examples in (18),

(18) a. context: a) (o

underlying representation:

/o-mo-ana βo-a o-mo-kuNγu/
a-1-child 1-of a-1-(married) woman

intermediate representation; in this case, monitored speech:

¦omwana βwa omokuŋgu¦

surface representation; in this case, less monitored speech:

[omwaana βwoomokuuŋgu]

'the child of the woman'

b. context: e) (a

underlying representation:

/o-tom-e a-βa-Nto/
sm2s-send-fv a-2-person

intermediate representation (h.l. monitored speech):

¦otome aβaanto¦

surface representation; in this case, less monitored speech:

[otom(a)aβaanto] '(may) you send people'

c. context: ε) (e

underlying representation:

/e-ηɔNbε e-ye/
9-cow 9-this

intermediate representation; in this case, monitored speech:

¦εηɔɔmbε eye¦

surface representation; in this case, less monitored speech:

[εηɔɔmbeeye] 'this cow'

Here, as elsewhere in this study, the input for the derivation of these utterances is the underlying representation of the words (in slashes); it comprises the basic morphemes of which words are composed and to which no rules have applied as yet. The intermediate representation of words (in perpendicular slashes) exhibit the form to which some, but not all relevant rules have applied. The systematic phonetic representation of words (in square brackets) gives the form to which all phonological, morphological, and systematic (not necessarily all possible) phonetic rules have applied.

Now, stated generally, the question is: should the underlying, the intermediate, or the surface representation of words be selected as the model for the spelling of a language? Since devising a spelling must usually take more into account than merely linguistic arguments, and thus also consider possible social and practical problems, this question cannot be answered universally; nor even generally with respect to some particular language.

The underlying representation of words in a language rarely, if at all, serves as a model for its orthography. Certainly, it may not do so consistently. More often, it is the surface representation that performs this function, but usually even this cannot do so throughout. Mostly, it is some intermediate representation of the words that functions as a model for its orthography. This is of course another way of saying that the spelling model of some language usually is, and perhaps in the nature of the case must be, a mixture of considerations.

Applied to the examples in (18), the general question may be applied as follows. First, should (18a) be written, according to its underlying representation, <omoana βoa omokuNγu> or perhaps <omoana βoa omokunγu>; according to its intermediate representation, <omwana bwa omokungu>; or, according to its surface representation, <omwana bwoomokungu>, or perhaps, as suggested by Whiteley (1956: 20-21 and passim), <omwana bw' omokungu>?

Second, should (18b) be written, according to its underlying representation, <otome aβaNto>; according to its intermediate representation, <otome abanto> or perhaps <otome abaanto>; or, according to its surface representation, <otoma abaanto>, or perhaps <otom' abaanto>?

And third, should (18c) be written according to its underlying representation, <eηɔNbɛ eye> or perhaps <eηɔmbɛ eye>; according to its intermediate representation, <e̲n'o̲mbe̲ eye> or perhaps <e̲n'o̲o̲mbe̲ eye>; or, according to its surface representation, <e̲n'o̲o̲mbe̲ eye> or perhaps <e̲n'o̲o̲mb' eye>?

To try and answer these questions from a relatively consistent point of view, the following consideration seems important. In many languages, words tend to be pronounced differently in different phrases or sentences. This is also true of Gusii. Thus a change of context may cause a change in pronunciation. Since, in the nature of the case, context is variable, it cannot provide a stable criterion for determining the standard pronunciation of a word. Nor, therefore, for determining its spelling. However, when words are pronounced in isolation, i.e. between pauses, and at a normal, but especially at a monitored, rate of speech, their pronunciation tends to remain relatively constant. Therefore, it is argued, a monitored pronunciation (18a) provides a more viable spelling standard than the other two styles of speech distinguished in (18).

Accordingly, I would like to suggest that the spelling rule in (19), will furnish a good practicable guideline for finding out the standard pronunciation of most, if not all, Gusii words,

(19) write a word as it is pronounced by itself, thoughtfully, deliberately, and slowly

Here 'by itself' refers to the use of a word between pauses, often called its citation form. It might also be designated as its use in isolation. Hence (19) may also serve as a heuristic guideline for devising the spelling of words.

Applied to the words in (18), for example, this spelling rule arguably yields the following results,

(20) a. <omwana bwa omokungu>
b. <otome abanto>
c. <e̲n'o̲mbe̲ eye>

For reasons explained earlier, vowels automatically lengthened at the lexical level have been written short. Thus <omwana> instead of <omwaana>, <omokungu> instead of <omokuungu>, <abanto> instead of <abaanto>, and <e̲n'o̲mbe̲> instead of <e̲n'o̲o̲mbe̲>. They could be written long. For more examples to which the basic spelling rule in (19) may be applied to advantage, the reader is referred to some of the paradigms in Chapter Three.

4.5.2. Lexical considerations.

Not only may a different context of phrase or sentence cause Gusii words to be pronounced differently, especially at their margins, but certain vowels or consonants may also vary due to the operation of lexical rules, i.e. the influence of the word-internal context. Such variation depends on whether or not, and which, lexical phonological and morphological rules are applicable in some context (see Chapters Two and Three).

A few examples illustrating the operation of some of these rules may perhaps be cited again here, in order to see what sort of spelling problems may be involved. Consider (21),

(21)	a.	/a-ko-aak-ete/	b.	/ko-aak-a/
		he-you-hit-t		15-hit-fv
		[akoaaγete]		[γoaaka]
		'he hit you (recently/long ago)'[9]		'to hit'

Depending on the word-internal context, Consonantal Voicing Dissimilation (see section 2.3.1) may affect different targets in two different forms involving the same root, viz. /-aak-/ 'hit'. Triggered by /t/ in the post-root domain, the rule affects root-final /k/ in (21a), whereas it is this very /k/ that triggers off the rule in (21b), thereby causing voicing, and by default concomitant fricativisation, of the preceding /k/ of infinitive marker /ko-/.

The question is: should the spelling of the words in (21) and comparable ones be based on their underlying -, surface -, or an intermediate representation? The underlying representation as a model might be argued on the ground that, since on the present analysis Consonantal Voicing Dissimilation applies regularly, everybody will apply it automatically and pronounce the words in (21) correctly anyway. On this argument, they could be spelled <akoaakete> and <koaaka>. However, if the surface representation is taken as a model, in these cases the spellings would be <akoaagete> and <goaaka>.

It was mentioned earlier that, in resolving most problems of word spelling, some intermediate representation is usually taken as a model. It may be added here that generally the one nearest to the surface is preferable, because it will be most easily recognised by the speakers of the language. Hence it is suggested that in this case, and in similar cases involving Consonantal Voicing Dissimilation, the surface representation be used as a model. Thus I propose to write the words in (21) as <akoaagete> and <goaaka>. While this presents no problem for a native speaker, someone who wishes to learn the language will have to learn the rule, in order to realise that <g>, pronounced as [γ], may be derived from underlying /k/ through Consonantal Voicing Dissimilation in some contexts.

Mutatis mutandis, the same type of reasoning holds for determining the spelling of words in which other rules are applicable. Thus it is suggested that all nasals and prenasals (see sections 2.3.2-7) be written as they are pronounced in accordance with spelling rule (19). This will result in the orthography summarised in (13-16).

It is suggested further that, by and large, the same guideline be used for the spelling of

[9] Note that [ákóáágete] 'he hit you (recently)' is tonally distinct from [ákoaágété] 'he hit you (long ago)'.

glides (see sections 2.3.10-13) and vowels, except where compensatory lengthening is involved (see sections 2.3.9-10,14-19). To take one rule for example, consider the effects of Mid Vowel Height Spreading, discussed section 2.3.14, in (22),

(22)	a.	/e-ke-tɔNγa/	b.	/to-γεNr-e/
		a-7-basket		we-go-fv
		[εγεtɔ ɔηga][10]		[tɔγεεndε][11]
		'basket'		'let us go'

In (22a), this rule operates in the pre-root domain, while in (22b) it operates in both the pre- and the post-root domain. If some intermediate representation of these words is taken for a model, such that Consonantal Voicing Dissimilation is taken into account, they would be written <egetonga> and <togende>. Spellings based on their surface representation, through (19), would be <egetoonga> and <togeende>, which reflect Mid Vowel Height Spreading, Consonantal Voicing Dissimilation, and compensatory vowel lengthening through the Linking Rule.

As to the latter, however, it has already been suggested to write derived long vowels as short, since compensatory lengthening is a fairly regular and automatic process (it may be triggered by Prenasalisation, Complex Segment Formation, or Glide Formation). Thus the examples may be written <egetonga> and <togende>, rather than as in the preceding paragraph. The main advantage is saving of time, space, energy, and money. But otherwise, these and similar spellings, being close to the surface, accurately reflect the pronunciation of the words in writing, illustrate the simplicity and consistency of applying spelling rule (19), and so generally promote ease in learning how to write and recognise Gusii words on a page.

Finally, the argumentation of the present and the preceding section may be summed up in two points. First, most words tend to be pronounced differently in different contexts, due to influences within and across words, so that spelling problems involved may be resolved fairly easily and consistently through application of spelling rule (19). Second, once a particular spelling has been adopted, it must be applied and promoted consistently. In the long run, adherence to these two principles is bound to facilitate the writing of, and thus to promote communication in, the Gusii language.

---

[10] Surface tone (L unmarked),

```
H      H
|     /
[εγεtɔ ɔηga]
```

[11] Surface tone (L unmarked),

```
H H  H
| |  /
[tɔγεεndε]
```

4.6. Punctuation.

In any comprehensive orthography, questions of punctuation also must be answered. However, the present discussion is not comprehensive. Moreover, current orthographical practice largely follows that of English and Swahili, in this respect, and presents no major problems. Therefore, it need not be discussed here.

Perhaps one remark may be made, nonetheless. Some examples in Whiteley (1960) involving multi-tense sentences suggest that the punctuation currently used, especially the use of commas, may be further refined. For example, subclauses in conditional sentences may be marked more clearly and consistently.

4.7. Capitalisation.

A few words may be said concerning capitalisation. Assuming that writing capital letters is useful, the most important question that remains is, where should one write capitals in Gusii words and sentences? It may be answered briefly by suggesting the following general rule (23),

(23) capitalisation rule: write a capital letter

a. to begin any sentence and
b. to begin any name.

Presumably, criterion (23a) presents no problem at all. It is plain and simple: begin any sentences with a capital letter.

Criterion (23b) concerns any name. This term is here defined so as to include all and any official titles and proper names. Again, the principle is plain and simple enough. However, in different Bantu languages names are sometimes capitalised in different ways.

If we take the name of the language itself for example, i.e. <ekegusii>, and disregard the option of non-capitalisation, the three remaining logically possible ways to apply (23b), are those in (24),

(24) '(the) Gusii (language)'

a. <ekeGusii>
b. <EkeGusii>
c. <Ekegusii>

An argument sometimes given in favour of spelling (24a) is that it ensures that the root or stem of a name will always be written consistently with a capital in all related words containing it. For example, compare <ekeGusii>, <omoGusii> 'a Gusii person' and <abaGusii> '(the) Gusii people'. However, on this option, orthographic variation in terms of capitalisation still remains. Whenever words thus capitalised in accordance with (23a) occur at the beginning of a sentence, the initial letter would be capitalised too in accordance with (23b). Sentence-initially, (24a) would thus be spelled <EkeGusii>, but elsewhere in the sentence it would be written <ekeGusii>.

Should such variation be considered an insurmountable problem, the second spelling, <EkeGusii> (24b), may be chosen instead. An advantage over spelling (24a) is that this would be written the same way throughout, regardless of its position in the sentence. However, some might still object to writing a capital letter within a word, such as the <G> in (24a,b), and others might object to consistently having to write two capitals in one word, as in (24b).

Therefore, <Ekegusii> (24c) is here proposed as the preferred spelling of the three. Though on this option the root or stem is <gusii>, any word in which it occurs will always begin with a capital letter, regardless of whether the word occurs at the beginning of a sentence or elsewhere. For example, compare <Ekegusii>, <Omogusii>, and <Abagusii>. These names will always be written with an initial capital letter, even when they occur alone.

This spelling seems preferable for at least three reasons. First, the objections that may be levelled against the spellings in (24a,b) do not obtain in the case of (24c). Second, the latter follows naturally and logically from the capitalisation rule proposed in (23). Third, a result of this proposal, if adopted, is that capitalisation of any words of which the spelling would be variable in either of the other two alternatives (24a,b), will always be uniform.

Since (23) is arguably the simplest guideline possible, it is easy to learn, to remember, and to apply. Hence the advantages of adopting it are considerable, not only with respect to the example in (24) and similar ones, but in education generally, specifically in the teaching and promotion of literacy.

Accordingly, if proposal (23) be adopted, any writer of Gusii need not worry about when, and when not, to write a capital in a name: any name always takes one capital, and one only. Nor need he worry about where to write this capital: it must always be written at the beginning of a name, and there only. Thus (23b) boils down to this: any name always **begins** with a capital.

4.8. Summary.

The present brief discussion of Gusii orthography may perhaps be concluded with a few additional observations and a brief summary of the main points.

A Gusii friend, who kindly offered to read through the present chapter, suggested that more exercises illustrating some of the problems mentioned here might be usefully included, and also that more problems should be included. More difficulties that many people still have in spelling their language would thus be pointed out. At the same time, more solutions might be given. Accordingly, I have included more examples than the original version of this chapter contained.

However, given the linguistic emphasis of this study, it seemed appropriate not to add any more. Nonetheless, the suggested exercises would no doubt serve a useful purpose. Hopefully, some future discussion of Gusii orthography will treat these more exhaustively.

So the resolution of possible other spelling problems is left to a later date. It is hoped, however, that the explanations and suggestions offered here, and the rules formulated in Chapters Two and Three, will prove to be of some help to those who, having learnt how to write the language with proficiency, would wish to resolve any remaining problems they might have, or otherwise to improve the existing orthography.

The considerations on the basis of which the present spelling has been suggested, have primarily taken the phonology and the morphology of the language into account, both at the lexical and the postlexical level. However, several social aspects of Gusii orthography, though not extensively discussed, have also been noted. First and foremost, the aim has been to contribute towards producing the best possible spelling for Gusii.

The main suggested improvements have been the following ones. One concerns the simplification of the three consonants in (25),

(25)	<c>	for current <ch>
	<ñ>	for current <ny>
	<n'>	for current <ng'>

Second, in order to be able to differentiate orthographically between the Gusii upper and lower mid vowels, introduction of the letters <e̲> and <o̲> has been argued, as in (26),

(26)	[e]:	<e>
	[ɛ]:	<e̲> for current <e>
	[o]:	<o>
	[ɔ]:	<o̲> for current <o>

Third, clear and consistent spelling of vowels has been argued for, not only with regard to their quality, but also with regard to their quantity, or length, at least whenever such length crucially marks a difference in meaning. It has been suggested therefore that the distinctions in length in (27), whenever they have this function, be consistently maintained,

(27)	<i> versus <ii>
	<e> versus <ee>
	<e̲> versus <e̲e̲>
	<a> versus <aa>
	<o̲> versus <o̲o̲>
	<o> versus <oo>
	<u> versus <uu>

A fourth suggestion is to simplify some of the prenasalised consonants and nasals, as in

(28),

(28) [ñc]: <nc> for current <nch>
[ññ]: <nñ> for current <nyny>
[ηη]: <nn'> for current <ng'ng'>[12]

The spelling of any postglided nasal is supposed to be made up simply of a combination of the letter for the nasal with the letter for the postglide in question, as in (4b).

A fifth suggestion is to begin every name (title, proper name) and every sentence with a capital letter.

Sixth, the monitored pronunciation (17a) of the citation form of words (19) has been proposed as a general basis and a useful experimental guideline for deciding on their spelling. Such pronunciation usually conforms to some intermediate representation of the words, usually one that is relatively close to the surface. From a lexical point of view, this combined guideline covers the spelling of most words.

Seventh, this same suggestion provides a useful guideline for deciding the spelling of words that involve a good deal of phonetic variation postlexically.

4.9. Conclusion.

In conclusion, the aim of the present study has been to produce a phonology and morphology of Gusii. In order to achieve this, Whiteley's pioneering work (1956, 1959, 1960) was carefully examined and fresh data were collected. Wherever this proved necessary and possible, I have attempted to supplement and correct his work, and to make the description of the language more explicit and systematic. Admittals of the need for further research are as many evident recognitions that I have not always succeeded in doing so within the limits of the research on which this study is based. In a number of areas the depth of the undertaking had to be sacrificed to its attempted breadth. For reasons such as these, I feel that not all of the details of Gusii have received the attention they might have deserved or that I would have liked to have given them, but I hope that the improvements will nonetheless turn out to be sufficient, in order to promote more definitive research of areas and details that require closer scrutiny.

J. Cammenga
Kampen, June 2000

Deo Soli Gloria

[12] Though <nyny> and <ng'ng'> are not usually written out consistently according to the rules of current spelling, they are what should be written, according to those rules, if current writing were accurate and consistent.

APPENDICES

APPENDIX ONE

TEST WORDS

This appendix contains a list of roots and a few stems used for testing phonological and morphological processes involving Gusii vowels. Most roots begin with a vowel, some verbal roots end in one, and some arguably consist of one. A few verbal roots postulated as /-VC-/ may turn out to be /-VVC-/, but this requires further research.

The words are arranged according to the following order. Vowels: i, e, ε, a, ɔ, o, u, V (underspecified vowel). Consonants: β, c, γ, k, m, n, ñ, η, r, s, t, w, y. In the case of prenasalised consonants, the arrangement follows the order of the consonantal segment.

1. Verbal roots: initial vowel		Verbal roots: final vowel	
		-ci-	'go'
-iγor-	'open'		
-ik-	'arrive'	-ni-	'defecate'
-ir-	'take'	-ri-	'eat'
-irok-	'fear'		
-it-	'beat'		
-eβ-	'forget'		
-eγ-	'practice'		
-er-	'murmur (s-ref: river)		
-et-	'pass'		
-εγ-	'seduce'		
-εγεk- 'lean on'			
-εr-	(a) 'be finished (v.i.)' (ε=H)		
	(b) 'winnow' (ε=L)		
-anc-	'love		
-ak-	'beat'		
-am-	'grow'		
-ar-	'spread'		
		-βɔ-	'tie'
-ɔk-	'give light'		
-ɔm-	'smear'		
-ɔni-	'sell'		
-ɔrɔk-	'show'	-sɔ-	'enter'
-om-	'dry'		
-orok-	'appear'		
		-βu-	'win'
		-ñu-	'drink'
-ur-	'take (by force)'	-ru-	'give'
-ut-	'blow'		
		-βV-	'be' [kɔβa]
-Vc-	'come' [γooca]		

Verbal roots: vocalic

-a-	'pluck (vegetable)', /ko-a-a/ --> [kwaa] or [koaa]
-á-	'to carry (a child on one's hip or side)', [ko-á-a] --> [kóáá]
-V-	'give', /ko-V-a/ --> [kɔa]

The underspecified vowel V of /-βV-/ 'be' and /-V-/ 'give' is supposed to be [-high, +mid], i.e. lower mid, to account for Mid Vowel Height Spreading of vowels contiguous on the vowel projection and for lengthening of the following vowel. The V in /-Vc-/ 'come' is not postulated as lower mid: in forms containing this root the preceding vowel is lengthened only.

The possible alternative postulates, /-βa-/ and /-a-/, might account for lengthening of the next vowel, triggered by /a/-Delinking, but /a/ would then have to be allowed as a trigger for Mid Vowel Height Spreading. The /a/ is not lengthened word-finally: [kɔβa], [kɔa], subject to the constraint on marginal long vowels. However, /-a-/ 'pluck' and /-á-/ 'carry' do not trigger such Spreading, but their final vowel is, exceptionally, long, so that they must be exempted from the constraint on marginal long vowels: [koaa] and [kóáá]. To allow /a/ as a trigger for Mid Vowel Height Spreading may be ad hoc. To account for such data, the present analysis employs underspecification to a limited extent, rule-exemption, and preservation of morphological identity.

2. Nominal roots and stems

initial vowel		final vowel	
-eŋe	'short'		
-et-i	'passer by'		
-ɛ	'basket'		
		-kɛ-	'small'
-ɛnɛ	'true'		
		-rɛ-	'thin'
-aŋgo	'quick'		
-ara	'finger'		
-ɔγɔ	'cassava'		
-ɔrɔ	'lazy'		
-oγe	'sharp'		
-usi	'thread'		
-ut-i	'blower'		

The borderline between verbal and adjectical roots may be fuzzy. Some adjectives may be derived from what are arguably verbal roots and some verbs may be derived from what are arguably nominal (i.e. noun and adjective) roots. The nominal stems /-et-i/ and /-ut-i/ are arguably deverbal.

APPENDIX TWO

INFORMANT FILES

To facilitate adequate identification of the speech on which this study is based, some linguistically relevant background information is given here on the informants who supplied it.

Ernest Mauti Maoto

1. Born: 7-2-1958

2. Tribe: Gusii; Clan: Mwaraki; Sub-clan: Mwaombooga (of grandfather)

3. First language: Gusii; Second language: English; Third language: Swahili

4. Residences: Nyagɛɛnkɛ Village (place of birth and childhood, i.e. home)

5. Education and career:

   1976-77 Gakeero Secondary School
   1978-79 Kisii Town
   1980-1982 Utalii College (Nairobi)
   1985-1990 work as Restaurant Staff at Egerton University (Njoro)
   1990-1996 ibid. at Maseno University

6. Father's language: Gusii (Nyagɛɛnkɛ); dialect: Majoge

7. Mother's language: Gusii; dialect: South Mugirango

8. Additional remarks: the informant says he understands Kuria for about forty to fifty percent.

Janet Nyamoita Mokaaya <Mokaya>

1. Born: 1-5-1974

2. Tribe: Gusii
   Extended family:
   Mwaamokaaya (father)
   Mwɔɔγɛɛra (grandfather)
   Mwoomooro <Mwomollo> (grandfather)

3. First language: Swahili
   Second language: Gusii
   Third language: English
   Fourth language: Kikuyu (fluent)
   understands Luyia for about 50 percent
   understands Kuria for 20-40 percent

4. Residences: home village is Ikɔɔηgɛ <Ikonge> (Sub-location: Kemera, Location: Manga, District: Nyamira), but born, bred, and lifelong residence in Nairobi.

5. Education and career.

   Schooling: Nairobi
   1991 finished Secondary School
   1994-1996 Catering
   1996-1997 work in beauty parlour, hairdressing
   1997 Secretarial College
   Hobbies: hiking, singing (choir)

6. Father: John Mokaaya Ogeera [ɔγɛɛra]

   Born: 1940s
   First language: Gusii
      Second language: Swahili
      Third language: English
      Fourth language: Kikuyu (good, passive and active)
   Residences: home village Ikonge; to Nairobi in 1970s
   Education: Primary School. Further: not recorded
   Occupation: Civil servant

7. Mother: Jane Moraa Mokaaya (sister of Lilian's father)
   First language: Gusii
   Second language: Swahili
   Third language: Kikuyu
   Fourth language: English (good understanding)

Richard Omae Oira

1. Born: 23-8-1970

2. Tribe: Gusii, Nyaribaari Chaache Constituency

3. First language: Gusii
   Second language: English
   Third language: Swahili

4. Residences and education:

   1970-1988 Nyosia (place of birth and childhood)
   1988-1990 Nairobi
   1990-1994 Kericho (secondary school)
   1994-1995 Nyosia
   1995-1996 Maseno University, Maseno (near Kisumu)
   Subject: English Language and Literature

5. Previous occupations: work at homestead

6. Father's language: Gusii (from Nyosia Village)

7. Mother's language: Gusii (from Botondo, nearby in Nyaribaari Chaache Constituency)

8. Additional remarks: the informant says he understands Kuria for about fifty percent

Lilian Nyanchama Onsare

1. Born: 31-3-1974

2. Tribe: Gusii
   Clan: Bobaasi
   Sub-clan: Bosaansa
   Extended Family: Mwabeeri

3. First language: Gusii. Second language: Swahili. Third language: English.
   Also: some Maasai greetings and expressions

4. Residences: born and bred in Mocheengo Village, Baasi Borabu Location, Kisii District (home)

5. Education and career:

   1981-1988 Boarding School at Kilgoris (holidays spent at home; English and Swahili spoken in class; Swahili, English, and the vernacular out of class)
   1989-1993 Kilgoris Secondary School
   1994-1995: teaching at a Primary School in Riakemooni Academy

6. Father: Gilbert Onsare Aenda (brother of Janet's mother)
   1. Born: 1940s (d. 1995)
   2. Tribe: Gusii
      Clan: Bobaasi
      Sub-clan: Bosaansa
      Family: Mwaberi (pronounced [mwaaβeeri])
   3. First language: Gusii (Kiabonyoro). Second language: English. Third language: Swahili
   4. Residences
      Place of birth: Nyabioosi (near Mocheengo)
      Home: Mocheengo (moved there shortly after marriage)
   5. Education
      Primary School at Nyabioosi
      Secondary School at Nyamagwa
   6. Career: Manager at Kenya Tea Development Authority

7. Mother: Rebeccah Nyabiya Aenda

   1. Born: 1950s
   2. Tribe: Gusii. Clan: Bobaasi. Family: Mwasindiga.
   3. First language: Gusii (Baasi). Second language: Swahili. Third language: English

8. Additional remarks: the informant says she understands Kuria for about forty percent

Judith Moraa Onsomu

1. Born: 28-12-1971

2. Tribe: Gusii
   Clan/Sub-location: Bokiamburi
   Extended family: Mwanyokaae (closely related to Mwaondeki and Mwaachuma)

3. First language: Gusii
   Second language: Swahili
   Third language: English
   Fourth language: Kikamba (passive and active)

4. Residences:

   Born in Mwongori Village, 1971-1993, Nyamira District (North Mugirango).
   Home village: Nyaimaiya, Masosa Location, Bokiamburi Sub-location.

5. Education and career:

   School in Menyenya, 1982-1986, Nyamira District, about 15 km from Mwongori (same dialect)
   1988-1990 stay in Mombasa
   1990-1994 Machakos (Secretarial College, 1993-1994)
   1994-present Nairobi
   work as a copy-typist in Machakos and Nairobi

6. Father: Nelson Maenda Onsomu Ondieki

   Born: 1930s
   Extended family: same as informant's
   First language: Gusii
   Second language: Swahili
   Third language: English
   Home village: Nyamaiya
   Profession: Teacher and Headmaster, Amasago Secondary School, Kisii District, Keumbo)

7. Mother: Biria Mwango Kebagɛndi

   Born: 1938
   Extended family: Mwaabogoonko (Getutu)
   First language: Gusii
   Second language: a little Swahili
   Work: traditional

8. Additional remarks: the informant says she understands Kuria for about fifty percent

Shem Mogaka Orioki

1. Born: 19-4-1972

2. Tribe: Gusii
    Clan: Bogesumi
    Sub-clan: Mwanyamoki

3. First language: Gusii
    Second language: English
    Third language: Swahili

4. Residences: born and bred in Kiabonyoro Village, Getara Location, Ekerenyo Division, Nyamira District (home)

5. Education:

    1987-1991 Boarding School Cardinal Otunga, Kisii District
    1993-1996 Maseno University (subject: English Language and Literature)

6. Father's first language: Gusii (Kiabonyoro)

7. Mother's first language: Gusii (Bogichoori, West Mugirango, Nyamira District, speech similar to that of the informant)

8. Additional remarks: the informant says he understands Kuria for about fifty percent.

CITED REFERENCES

CITED REFERENCES

Aksenova, I.S. 1977. Imennye klassy jazyka Kurija. Ochotina, N.V., ed. Mladopis'mennye jazyki Afriki, Voprosy Filologii i Grammatiki. Moskva. Nauta.

Anderson, S.R. 1980. Problems and prespectives in the description of vowel harmony. R.M. Vago, ed. Issues in Vowel Harmony. Amsterdam. Benjamins. 1-48.

Bendor Samuel, J.T. 1983. Introduction to Practical Phonetics. Summer Institute of Linguistics. Horsleys Green, High Wycombe. [foreword by Bendor Samuel, otherwise no name of autor(s) on title-page or frontispiece]

Booij, G.E. and J. Rubach. 1987. Postcyclic versus postlexical rules in lexical phonology. **Linguistic Inquiry**. 18: 1-44.

Cammenga, J. 1990. Kuria Dictionary. [computer ms.]

Cammenga, J. 1994. Kuria Phonology and Morphology. Ph.D. Dissertation. Amsterdam. Free University.

Cammenga, J. (forthcoming). Gusii vowel height change.

Clements, G.N. 1977. The autosegmental treatment of vowel harmony. W.U. Dressler and O.E. Pfeiffer, eds. Phonologica 1976. Institut für Sprachwissenschaft, Innsbruck. 111–119.

Clements, G.N. 1986. Compensatory lengthening and consonant gemination in LuGanda. W.L. Wetzels and E. Sezer, eds. Studies in Compensatory Lengthening. Dordrecht. Foris.

Clements, G.N. 1991. Vowel height assimilation in Bantu languages. K. Hubbard, ed. Proceedings of the Seventeenth Annual Meeting of the Berkeley Linguistic Society. Berkeley. UCLA.

Gould, L.J. 1987. Evidence for ambiguous targets in Kuria advancement strategies. D. Odden, ed. Current Approaches to African Linguistics, 4. Dordrecht. Foris.

Guthrie, M. 1971. Comparative Bantu. Farnborough, Hants. Gregg. Vols 1-4.

Heine, B. 1976. Knowledge and use of second language in Musoma region, a quantitative survey. Kiswahili. 46: 49-59.

Heine, B., and W.J.G. Möhlig 1980. Language and Dialect Atlas of Kenya. Berlin. Reimer Verlag.

Hinnebusch, Th.H., D. Nurse, and M. Mould 1981. Studies in the Classification of the Eastern Bantu Languages. Hamburg. Helmut Buske Verlag.

IPA. The Principles of the International Association. 1949. 1974 (repr). London. University College (abbreviated as IPA).

Johnston, H. 1919, 1922. A comparative Study of the Bantu and Semi-Bantu languages. Vols. 1 and 2. Oxford. Clarendon Press.

Kingston, J. 1983. The expansion of the Gusii tense system. J. Kaye, et al. eds. Current Approaches to African Linguistics. Dordrecht. Dordrecht. Foris. 31-56.

Kiparksy, P. 1982. Lexical morphology and phonology. H. van der Hulst and N. Smith, eds. The Structure of Phonological Representations. Dordrecht. Foris. Vols. 1-2.

Kiparsky, P. 1985. Some consequences of lexical phonology. C. Ewen and J. Anderson, eds. Phonology Yearbook 2. Cambridge. Cambridge University Press.

McCarthy, J.J. 1986. OCP effects: gemination and antigemination. **Linguistic Inquiry**. 17: 207-263.

McCarthy, J.J. 1988. Feature geometry and dependency: a review. **Phonetica**. 43: 84-108.

Meeussen, A.E. 1967. Bantu Grammatical Reconstructions. Musée Royal de l'Afrique Centrale, Koninklijk Museum voor Midden-Afrika. Tervuren. Belgique/België.

Meeussen, A.E. 1980. Bantu Lexical Reconstructions. Musée Royal de l'Afrique Centrale, Koninklijk Museum voor Midden-Afrika. Tervuren. Belgique/België. Archief voor Antropologie, Archives d'Anthroplogie, No. 27.

Mekacha, R.D.K. 1985. Phonological Processes Affecting Ki-Nata Vowels. University of Dar-es-Salaam. M.A. Dissertation.

Muniko, S.M., B. Muita oMagige, M.J. Ruel. 1996. Kuria-English Dictionary. E.J. Brill. Leiden.

Ochieng', W.R. 1974. A Pre-Colonial History of the Gusii of Western Kenya: from c. A.D. 1500 to 1914. Kampala. East African Literature Bureau.

Reh, M. 1994. Suba und Luo in Tansania. Bayreuth. Universität Bayreuth.

Reinhart, J. 1965. Wordlist Kuria-English, English-Kuria. [unpublished typed ms.]

Rottland, F. 1993. "Suba": searching for linguistic correlates to an ethnic notion. **Afrikanistische Arbeitspapiere (AAP)** 33. 7-36. Institut für Afrikanistik. Universität zu Köln, Germany.

Rottland, F. Tape collection (Nata data).

Schoenbrun, D.L. 1990. Early History in Eastern Africa's Great Lakes Region: Linguistic, Ecological, and Archeological Approaches, ca 500 BC to ca AD 1000. Ph.D. Thesis. University of California, Los Angeles.

Stewart, J.M. 1967. Tongue root position in Akan vowel harmony. **Phonetica** 16. 185-204.

Welmers, W.E. 1974. African Language Structures. Berkeley. University of California Press.

Whiteley, W.H. 1955. The Kuria Verbal and its Position in the Sentence. London. University of London. Ph.D. Dissertation.

Whiteley, W.H. 1956 (1960). The Gusii Tense System. Kampala. East African Institute of Social Research.

Whiteley, W.H. 1959. Kinship terminology and the initial vowel. **Africa** 29. 253-262.

Whiteley, W.H. 1965. A Practical Introduction to Gusii. Kampala. East African Literature Bureau.

Wilson, P.M. 1979. Simplified Swahili. Nairobi. Kenya Literature Bureau.

Rüdiger Köppe Verlag

Languages and Cultures (Selected Publications)

East African Languages and Dialects

ed. by Bernd Heine and Wilhelm J.G. Möhlig

1. C. Maganga / Th. C. Schadeberg: *Kinyamwezi. Grammar, Texts, Vocabulary*, 1992, 325 pp. ISBN 3-927620-40-8
2. R. Klein-Arendt: *Gesprächsstrategien im Swahili. Linguistisch-pragmatische Analysen von Dialogtexten einer Stegreiftheatergruppe*, 1992, 400 pp. ISBN 3-927620-41-6
3. R. Botne: *A Lega and English Dictionary. With an index to Proto-Bantu roots* 1994, XVIII, 138 pp., 2 maps ISBN 3-927620-39-4
4. F. Mpiranya: *Swahili Phonology Reconsidered in a Diachronical Perspective*, 1995, VIII, 87 pp. ISBN 3-927620-38-6
5. M. H. Abdulaziz: *Transitivity in Swahili,* 1996, 292 pp., 21 diagrams, 2 tables, index ISBN 3-927620-37-8
6. L. Walusimbi: *Relative Clauses in Luganda*, 1996, 100 pp., 4 diagrams ISBN 3-89645-020-4
7. H. Neumüller: *Zwei Elefanten. Untersuchung zu den Beziehungen zwischen Sprache und Kultur anhand ausgewählter Wortfelder des Kikuyu*, 1996, 303 pp., 1 map, 18 tables, 25 graphs ISBN 3-89645-021-2
8. A. Amidu: *Classes in Kiswahili. A Study of their Forms and Implications*, 1997, XVIII, 440 pp., 11 tables, 5 diagrams ISBN 3-89645-022-0
9. L.T. Rubongoya: *A Modern Runyoro-Rutooro Grammar*, 1999, XX, 326 pp., 14 tables, subject index ISBN 3-89645-023-9
10. J. Blommaert: *State Ideology and Language in Tanzania*, 1999, 204 pp. ISBN 3-89645-024-7
11. Th.C. Schadeberg / F.U. Mucanheia: *Ekoti. The Maka or Swahili Language of Angoche*, 2000, XIV, 272 pp., 2 maps, 2 ill., 43 tables ISBN 3-89645-025-5

Grammatical Analyses of African Languages

ed. by W.J.G. Möhlig and Bernd Heine

1. Th. C. Schadeberg: *A Sketch of Umbundu*, 1990, 61 pp. ISBN 3-927620-15-7
2. Th. C. Schadeberg: *A Sketch of Swahili Morphology*, 3rd revised edition, 1992, 39 pp. ISBN 3-927620-16-5
3. J.-Cl. Naba: *Le Gulmancema: essai de systématisation*, 1994, XIV, 398 pp. ISBN 3-927620-17-3
4. S. Brauner: *A Grammatical Sketch of Shona. Including historical notes*, 1995, 66 pp., 2 tables ISBN 3-927620-18-1
5. H. Pasch: *Kurzgrammatik des Ewe*, 1995, 93 pp., 1 map ISBN 3-927620-19-X

6. F. Ahoua: *Prosodic Aspects of Baule. With special reference to the German of Baule speakers,* 1996, 221 pp., 1 map, 65 tables, 13 diagr. ISBN 3-927620-14-9
7. G. Atindogbé: *Bankon (A40). Eléments de phonologie, morphologie et tonologie,* 1996, XXII, 273 pp., 3 maps, 2 diagrams, numerous tables ISBN 3-89645-030-1
8. F. Gbéto: *Le Maxi du Centre-Bénin et du Centre-Togo: Une approche autosegmentale et dialectologique d'un parler Gbe de la section Fon,* 1997, 220 pp., 2 maps, numerous tables and diagrams ISBN 3-89645-031-X
9. N. Cyffer: *A Sketch of Kanuri*, 1998, 80 pp., 4 graphs, 2 maps, numerous tables ISBN 3-89645-032-8
10. J.A. Blanchon / D. Creissels (ed.): *Issues in Bantu Tonology*, 1999, VIII, 198 pp., numerous tables ISBN 3-89645-033-6
11. K.K. Lébikaza: *Grammaire kabiyè: une analyse systématique*, 1999, 559 pp., 1 map, 23 tables, numerous graphs ISBN 3-89645-034-4
12. M. Kossmann: *Essai sur la phonologie du proto-berbère*, 1999, 316 pp., index ISBN 3-89645-035-2
13. F. Gbéto: *Les emprunts linguistiques d'origine européenne en Fon (Nouveau Kwa, Gbe: Bénin). Une étude de leur intégration au plan phonético-phonologique,* 2000, 90 pp., numerous tables and diagrams ISBN 3-89645-036-0
14. B. Ngila: *Expérience végétale bolia (République Démocratique du Congo). Catégorisation, utilisation et dénomination des plantes*, 2000, 149 pp., 1 map, 9 tables, 6 diagrams ISBN 3-89645-037-9
15. A. Fleisch: *Lucazi Grammar. A Morphosemantic Analysis*, 2000, 363 pp., 42 tables, appendix: a Lucazi tale with an interlinear translation, author, subject and source index ISBN 3-89645-038-7
16. C. Griefenow-Mewis: *A Grammatical Sketch of Written Oromo*, 2001, 117 pp., 44 tables ISBN 3-89645-039-5
17. N.M. Mutaka / S.B. Chumbow (eds.): *Research Mate in African Linguistics: Focus on Cameroon. A Fieldworker's Tool for Deciphering the Stories Cameroonian Languages Have to Tell. In Honor of Professor Larry M. Hyman*, 2001, XII, 359 pp., 1 map, 1 b/w photo, 8 illustrations, 49 tables, index of languages ISBN 3-89645-041-7
18. A.A. Amidu: *Argument and Predicate Relations in Kiswahili. A New Analysis of Transitiveness in Bantu*, 2001, XX, 505 pp., num. tables ISBN 3-89645-042-5

Kuschitische Sprachstudien · Cushitic Language Studies · KuS

ed. by Hans-Jürgen Sasse

H. Stroomer: *A Grammar of Boraana Oromo (Kenya)* (KuS 11), 1995, XIV, 315 pp. ISBN 3-927620-27-0

T. Hirpo: *Goldgrube. Oromo-Sprichwörter und -Redewendungen* (KuS 12), 1996, 215 pp., 2 maps, appendix: vocabulary, num. tables ISBN 3-927620-29-7

M. Tosco: *Af Tunni. Grammar, Texts, and Glossary of a Southern Somali Dialect* (KuS 13), 1997, X, 304 pp., 30 tables, app. ISBN 3-89645-060-3

S. Pillinger / L. Galboran: *A Rendille Dictionary. Including a Grammatical Outline and an English-Rendille Index* (KuS 14), 1999, IV, 416 pp., 122 drawings, 1 graph, numerous tables ISBN 3-89645-061-1

Tamene Bitima: *A Dictionary of Oromo Technical Terms, Oromo–English* (KuS 15), 2000, 286 pp., numerous tables, appendices ISBN 3-89645-062-X

H. Stroomer: *A Concise Vocabulary of Orma Oromo (Kenya). Orma–English, English–Orma* (KuS 16), 2001, XII, 157 pp., 1 map ISBN 3-89645-063-8

M. Tosco: *The Dhaasanac Language. Grammar, Texts and Vocabulary of a Cushitic Language of Ethiopia* (KuS 17), 2001, XIV, 614 pp., 1 map, 20 coloured photographs, 1 colour chart ISBN 3-89645-064-6

M. Mous / M. Qorro / R. Kießling: *Iraqw-English Dictionary. With an English and a Thesaurus Index* (KuS 18), 2002, VIII, 203 pp., 1 table ISBN 3-89645-065-4

Mande Languages and Linguistics · Langues et Linguistique Mandé

ed. by Raimund Kastenholz

Th. Blecke: *Lexikalische Kategorien und grammatische Strukturen im Tigemaxo (Bozo, Mande)* (Vol. 1), 1996, XIV, 283 pp., 2 maps, numerous tables ISBN 3-89645-070-0

R. Kastenholz: *Sprachgeschichte im West-Mande. Methoden und Rekonstruktionen* (Vol. 2), 1996, 281 pp., 1 map, num. tables. ISBN 3-89645-071-9

H. Tröbs: *Funktionale Sprachbeschreibung des Jeli (West-Mande)* (Vol. 3), 1998, XIV, 241 pp., 1 map, appendix, num. tables ISBN 3-89645-072-7

V. Vydrine: *Esquisse contrastive du kagoro (Manding)* (Vol. 4), 2001, 280 pp., 1 colour folding map, 34 graphs, 66 tables, appendix: three Kagoro tales, vocabulary Kagoro/French ISBN 3-89645-073-5

NISA · NILO SAHARAN · Linguistic Analyses and Documentation

ed. by M. Lionel Bender, Franz Rottland and Norbert Cyffer

C. Kutsch Lojenga: *Ngiti. A Central-Sudanic Language of Zaire* (NISA 9), 1994, XIV, 517 pp. ISBN 3-927620-71-8

R. Nicolaï / F. Rottland (eds.): *Actes du Cinquième Colloque de Linguistique Nilo-Saharienne / Proceedings of the Fifth Nilo-Saharan Linguistics Colloquium, Nice, 24–29 August 1992* (NISA 10), 1995, 430 pp., ISBN 3-927620-72-5

M. Reh: *Anywa Language. Description and Internal Reconstructions* (NISA 11), 1996, XIX, 575 pp., 1 map, numerous tables, app. ISBN 3-927620-73-4

D. Okoth Okombo: *A Functional Grammar of Dholuo* (NISA 12), 1997, VIII, 177 pp., 1 graph, numerous tables ISBN 3-89645-130-8

G. J. Dimmendaal / M. Last (eds.): *Surmic Languages and Cultures* (NISA 13), 1998, VIII, 458 pp., 2 b/w photos, 2 maps ISBN 3-89645-131-6

M. Reh: *Anywa-English and English-Anywa Dictionary*, with the ass. of Sam A. Akwey/Cham U. Uriat (NISA 14), 1999, XVI, 134 pp. ISBN 3-89645-132-4

B. Heine: *Ik Dictionary* (NISA 15), 1999, 187 pp., 1 map ISBN 3-89645-133-2

J.T. Creider / C.A. Creider: *A Dictionary of the Nandi Language* (NISA 16), 2001, 398 pp. ISBN 3-89645-134-0

Research in Khoisan Studies · Quellen zur Khoisan-Forschung · QKF
ed. by Rainer Vossen

H.-J. Heinz: *Social Organization of the !Ko Bushmen*, ed. by K. Keuthmann (QKF 10), 1994, 232 pp., 8 b/w photos ISBN 3-927620-57-2

M. Szalay: *The San and the Colonization of the Cape 1770–1879* (QKF 11), 1995, 151 pp., 33 b/w photos, 1 map ISBN 3-927620-58-0

R. Vossen: *Die Khoe-Sprachen. Ein Beitrag zur Erforschung der Sprachgeschichte Afrikas* (QKF 12), 1997, 536 pp., 5 maps, num. tables ISBN 3-927620-59-9

E. N. Wilmsen (ed.): *The Kalahari Ethnographies (1896–1898) of Siegfried Passarge. Nineteenth Century Khoisan- and Bantu-speaking Peoples* (QKF 13), 1997, 332 pp., 1 b/w photo ISBN 3-89645-141-3

B. Sands: *Eastern and Southern African Khoisan. Evaluating Claims of Distant Linguistic Relationships* (QKF 14), 1998, 251 pp., 1 map, 5 graphs, 56 tables, appendices ISBN 3-89645-142-1

M. Schladt (ed.): *Language, Identity, and Conceptualization among the Khoisan* (QKF 15), 1998, 503 pp., numerous graphs and tables ISBN 3-89645-143-X

W.H.G. Haacke: *The Tonology of Khoekhoe (Nama/Damara)* (QKF 16), 1999, XVI, 233 pp., 45 illustrations, 23 tables ISBN 3-89645-144-8

Westafrikanische Studien
ed. by Herrmann Jungraithmayr, Norbert Cyffer and Rainer Vossen

18. A. Abu-Manga: *Hausa in the Sudan. Process of Adaptation of Arabic*, 1999, XVIII, 215 pp., 1 map, numerous tables, appendix with 9 speech samples ISBN 3-89645-105-7
19. J. Heath: *A Grammar of Koyraboro (Koroboro) Senni. The Songhay of Gao, Mali*, 1999, XVI, 402 pp., 1 map, morpheme and subject index, numerous tables ISBN 3-89645-106-5
20. A. Storch: *Das Hone und seine Stellung im Zentral-Jukunoid*, 1999, XXII, 412 pp., 2 maps, 5 graphs, 50 tables, appendix ISBN 3-89645-107-3
21. S. Dinslage / A. Storch: *Magic and Gender. A Thesaurus of the Jibe of Kona (Northeastern Nigeria)*, 2000, XVI, 266 pp., 13 b/w photos, 2 maps, 5 tables, 3 graphs, 18 figures, 29 wordlists, index Englisch-Jibe ISBN 3-89645-108-1
22. G. Tucker Childs: *A Dictionary of the Kisi Language, with an English-Kisi Index*, 2000, XXIV, 524 pp., 1 map, 2 graphs, 16 tables ISBN 3-89645-109-X
23. H. Jungraithmayr: *Sindi. Tangale Folktales*, 2002, XL, 455 pp., 1 transcription table, 2 b/w photos ISBN 3-89645-110-3
24. R. Kawka (ed.): *From Bulamari to Yerwa to Metropolitan Maiduguri. Interdisciplinary Studies on the Capital of Borno*, 2002, 187 pp., 4 maps, 30 graphs, 46 tables ISBN 3-89645-460-9